# *Cookies*
## brownies
## & more

Publications International, Ltd.

Favorite Brand Name Recipes at www.fbnr.com

**Microwave Cooking:** Microwave ovens vary in wattage. Use the cooking times as guidelines and check for doneness before adding more time.

**Preparation/Cooking Times:** Preparation times are based on the approximate amount of time required to assemble the recipe before cooking, baking, chilling or serving. These times include preparation steps such as measuring, chopping and mixing. The fact that some preparations and cooking can be done simultaneously is taken into account. Preparation of optional ingredients and serving suggestions is not included.

# Contents

## 5
### Cookie Jar Favorites
CHAPTER ONE

## 63
### Classic Cookie Cutouts
CHAPTER TWO

## 95
### Righteous Refrigerator Cookies
CHAPTER THREE

## 123
### Scrumptious Shape & Bake Cookies
CHAPTER FOUR

## 171
### Special Occasion Cookies
CHAPTER FIVE

## 205
### Festive Holiday Cookies
CHAPTER SIX

## 253
### Especially for Kids
CHAPTER SEVEN

## 299
### Quick & Easy No-Bakes
CHAPTER EIGHT

## 325
### Bar Cookie Bonanza
CHAPTER NINE

## 383
### Brownies & Blondies Galore
CHAPTER TEN

## 431
### Fabulous Cakes & Cheesecakes
CHAPTER ELEVEN

## 485
### Perfect Pies & Tarts
CHAPTER TWELVE

## 535
### Delightfully Cool Creations
CHAPTER THIRTEEN

## 583
### Delectable Desserts
CHAPTER FOURTEEN

## 637
### The Confection Connection
CHAPTER FIFTEEN

Acknowledgments . . . .682

Index . . . . . . . . . . . . . . . . .683

# Cookie Jar
# Favorites

CHAPTER ONE

# Chunky Milk Chocolate Chip Cookies

**Makes 2½ dozen cookies**

**Note:**

Check cookies halfway through the baking time to make sure they're browning evenly. If necessary, rotate the cookie sheets from front to back and top to bottom.

2 cups all-purpose flour
1 teaspoon baking soda
¼ teaspoon salt
1¼ cups packed brown sugar
1 cup (2 sticks) butter or margarine, softened
1 teaspoon vanilla extract

1 large egg
1¾ cups (11.5-ounce package) NESTLÉ® TOLL HOUSE® Milk Chocolate Morsels
1 cup chopped nuts
1 cup raisins

**PREHEAT** oven to 375°F.

**COMBINE** flour, baking soda and salt in small bowl. Beat sugar, butter and vanilla extract in large mixer bowl until creamy. Beat in egg. Gradually beat in flour mixture. Stir in morsels, nuts and raisins. Drop by heaping tablespoon onto ungreased baking sheets; flatten slightly.

**BAKE** for 9 to 11 minutes or until edges are lightly browned. Cool on baking sheets for 2 minutes; remove to wire racks to cool completely.

# Double Lemon Delights

2¼ cups all-purpose flour
½ teaspoon baking powder
½ teaspoon salt
1 cup (2 sticks) butter, softened
¾ cup granulated sugar
1 egg

2 tablespoons grated lemon
  peel, divided
1 teaspoon vanilla
  Additional sugar
1 cup powdered sugar
4 to 5 teaspoons lemon juice

Makes about 1 dozen
(4-inch) cookies

*1.* Preheat oven to 375°F.

*2.* Combine flour, baking powder and salt in small bowl;
set aside. Beat butter and granulated sugar in large bowl of
electric mixer at medium speed until light and fluffy. Beat in
egg, 1 tablespoon lemon peel and vanilla until well blended.
Gradually beat in flour mixture on low speed until blended.

*3.* Drop dough by level ¼ cupfuls onto ungreased cookie sheets,
spacing 3 inches apart. Flatten dough until 3 inches in diameter
with bottom of glass that has been dipped in additional sugar.

*4.* Bake 12 to 14 minutes or until cookies are just set and edges
are golden brown. Cool on cookie sheets 2 minutes; transfer to
wire racks. Cool completely.

*5.* Combine powdered sugar, lemon juice and remaining
1 tablespoon lemon peel in small bowl; drizzle mixture over
cookies. Let stand until icing is set.

# Banana Jumbles

**Makes 18 cookies**

2 extra-ripe, medium DOLE®
   Bananas
¾ cup packed brown sugar
½ cup creamy peanut butter
¼ cup margarine, softened
1 egg

1½ cups old-fashioned oats
1 cup all-purpose flour
1½ teaspoons baking powder
½ teaspoon salt
¾ cup DOLE® Seedless Raisins

*Note:*

Deep yellow skin and brown speckles are signs that bananas are ripe. When the skins develop black patches, they are overripe—no longer as good for eating, but still excellent for use in baked goods.

• Mash bananas with fork. Measure 1 cup.

• Beat brown sugar, peanut butter and margarine in large bowl. Beat in egg and mashed bananas.

• Combine oats, flour, baking powder and salt. Stir into banana mixture until well combined. Stir in raisins.

• Drop by heaping tablespoonfuls onto cookie sheets coated with nonstick cooking spray. Shape cookies with back of spoon. Bake at 375°F 12 to 14 minutes until lightly browned. Cool on wire racks.

# Hershey's Classic Chocolate Chip Cookies

2¼ cups all-purpose flour
1 teaspoon baking soda
½ teaspoon salt
1 cup (2 sticks) butter, softened
¾ cup granulated sugar
¾ cup packed light brown sugar

1 teaspoon vanilla extract
2 eggs
2 cups (12-ounce package) HERSHEY'S Semi-Sweet Chocolate Chips
1 cup chopped nuts (optional)

Makes 5 dozen cookies

*1.* Heat oven to 375°F.

*2.* Stir together flour, baking soda and salt. Beat butter, granulated sugar, brown sugar and vanilla in large bowl with mixer until creamy. Add eggs; beat well. Gradually add flour mixture, beating well. Stir in chocolate chips and nuts, if desired. Drop by rounded teaspoons onto ungreased cookie sheet.

*3.* Bake 8 to 10 minutes or until lightly browned. Cool slightly; remove from cookie sheet to wire rack. Cool completely.

**"Perfectly Chocolate" Chocolate Chip Cookies:** *Add ⅓ cup HERSHEY'S Cocoa to flour mixture.*

**Pan Recipe:** *Spread batter into greased 15½×10½×1-inch jelly-roll pan. Bake at 375°F 20 minutes or until lightly browned. Cool completely. Cut into bars. Makes about 48 bars.*

**Ice Cream Sandwiches:** *Press one small scoop of vanilla ice cream between two cookies.*

**High Altitude Directions:** *Increase flour to 2⅔ cups. Decrease baking soda to ¾ teaspoon. Decrease granulated sugar to ⅔ cup. Decrease packed light brown sugar to ⅔ cup. Add ½ teaspoon water with flour. Bake at 375°F 5 to 7 minutes or until top is light golden with golden brown edges.*

# Maple Walnut Cookies

**Makes about 3 dozen cookies**

1¼ cups firmly packed light
    brown sugar
¾ Butter Flavor CRISCO® Stick
    or ¾ cup Butter Flavor
    CRISCO® all-vegetable
    shortening
2 tablespoons maple syrup
1 teaspoon vanilla

1 teaspoon maple extract
1 egg
1¾ cups all-purpose flour
1 teaspoon salt
¾ teaspoon baking soda
½ teaspoon ground cinnamon
1½ cups chopped walnuts
30 to 40 walnut halves

*1.* Heat oven to 375°F. Place sheets of foil on countertop for cooling cookies.

*2.* Place brown sugar, ¾ cup shortening, maple syrup, vanilla and maple extract in large bowl. Beat at medium speed of electric mixer until well blended. Add egg; beat well.

*3.* Combine flour, salt, baking soda and cinnamon. Add to shortening mixture; beat at low speed just until blended. Stir in chopped walnuts.

*4.* Drop dough by rounded measuring tablespoonfuls 3 inches apart onto ungreased baking sheets. Press walnut half into center of each cookie.

*5.* Bake one baking sheet at a time at 375°F for 8 to 10 minutes for chewy cookies, or 11 to 13 for crisp cookies. *Do not overbake.* Cool 2 minutes on baking sheet. Remove cookies to foil to cool completely.

# Orange Marmalade Cookies

**Cookies**
- 2 cups sugar
- ½ cup shortening
- 2 eggs
- 1 cup sour cream
- ½ cup SMUCKER'S® Sweet Orange Marmalade
- 4 cups all-purpose flour
- 2 teaspoons baking powder
- 1 teaspoon baking soda
- ½ teaspoon salt

**Icing**
- 3 cups powdered sugar
- ½ cup butter or margarine
- ¼ cup SMUCKER'S® Sweet Orange Marmalade
- Orange juice

Makes 5 dozen cookies

Combine sugar, shortening and eggs; beat until well mixed. Add sour cream and ½ cup marmalade; mix well. Add remaining cookie ingredients; mix well. Chill dough.

Drop by rounded teaspoonfuls onto greased cookie sheets. Bake at 400°F for 8 to 10 minutes. Cool.

Combine all icing ingredients, adding enough orange juice for desired spreading consistency (none may be needed). Ice cooled cookies.

# White Chocolate Chunk Brownie Drops

**Makes 3 dozen cookies**

1 cup semisweet chocolate chips
½ Butter Flavor CRISCO® Stick or ½ cup Butter Flavor CRISCO® all-vegetable shortening
½ cup sugar

2 eggs
1 teaspoon vanilla
1 cup uncooked oats
¾ cup all-purpose flour
1 teaspoon baking powder
½ cup cubed white baking bar

*1.* Heat oven to 350°F. Place sheets of foil on countertop for cooling cookies.

*2.* Place chocolate chips in microwavable measuring cup or bowl. Microwave at MEDIUM (50% power). Stir after 1 minute. Repeat until smooth (or melt on rangetop in small saucepan on very low heat). Cool slightly.

*3.* Combine ½ cup shortening, sugar, eggs and vanilla in large bowl. Beat at medium speed with electric mixer until well blended. Add melted chocolate. Mix well.

*4.* Combine oats, flour and baking powder. Stir into chocolate mixture. Stir in white baking bar cubes. Drop by rounded measuring tablespoonfuls 2 inches apart onto ungreased baking sheet.

*5.* Bake for 7 to 8 minutes. Cookies will look moist. *Do not overbake.* Cool 2 minutes on baking sheet. Remove cookies to foil to cool completely.

# Drop Sugar Cookies

**2½ cups sifted all-purpose flour**
**½ teaspoon ARM & HAMMER®**
   **Baking Soda**
**¼ teaspoon salt**
**½ cup butter, softened**
**½ cup butter-flavored**
   **shortening**

**1 cup sugar**
**1 egg** *or* **¼ cup egg substitute**
**1 teaspoon vanilla extract**
**2 teaspoons skim milk**

**Makes about
5½ dozen cookies**

Preheat oven to 400°F. Sift together flour, Baking Soda and salt; set aside. Beat butter and shortening in large bowl with electric mixer on medium speed until blended; add sugar gradually and continue beating until light and fluffy. Beat in egg and vanilla. Add flour mixture and beat until smooth; blend in milk. Drop dough by teaspoonfuls about 3 inches apart onto greased cookie sheets. Flatten with bottom of greased glass that has been dipped in sugar.

Bake 12 minutes or until edges are lightly browned. Cool on wire racks.

## *Note:*

**When creaming mixtures of butter or shortening and sugar, start the electric mixer at a low setting to blend the ingredients, then gradually increase the speed to high to get more volume into the batter.**

# Chocolate Toffee Chip Popcorn Cookies

**Makes about 2½ dozen cookies**

6 tablespoons margarine or butter, softened
½ cup packed light brown sugar
⅓ cup granulated sugar
2 large egg whites
1 teaspoon vanilla extract
1⅓ cups all-purpose flour
1 teaspoon baking soda
2 cups popped NEWMAN'S OWN® Butter Flavored Microwave Popcorn, chopped in food processor

1 cup semisweet chocolate chips
1 (3½-ounce) jar macadamia nuts, chopped (optional)
½ cup uncooked quick-cooking oats
½ cup toffee bits

Preheat oven to 375°F. In large bowl, with mixer at high speed, beat margarine and sugars until light and creamy. Add egg whites and vanilla; beat until smooth. Add flour and baking soda; beat on low speed just until blended. Stir in remaining ingredients. Drop by rounded tablespoonfuls onto *ungreased* cookie sheet. Bake 12 to 15 minutes or until lightly browned. Transfer to wire rack to cool.

# Cowboy Cookies

**Makes about 4 dozen cookies**

½ cup (1 stick) butter, softened
½ cup packed light brown sugar
¼ cup granulated sugar
1 egg
1 teaspoon vanilla
1 cup all-purpose flour
2 tablespoons unsweetened cocoa powder
½ teaspoon baking powder

¼ teaspoon baking soda
1 cup uncooked old-fashioned oats
1 cup (6 ounces) semisweet chocolate chips
½ cup seedless and/or golden raisins
½ cup chopped nuts

Preheat oven to 375°F. Lightly grease cookie sheets or line with parchment paper.

Beat butter and sugars in large bowl until blended. Add egg and vanilla; beat until fluffy. Combine flour, cocoa, baking powder and baking soda in small bowl; stir into butter mixture. Add oats, chocolate chips, raisins and nuts. Drop by rounded teaspoonfuls 2 inches apart onto prepared cookie sheets.

Bake 10 to 12 minutes or until lightly browned around edges. Remove to wire racks to cool.

*Note:*

It's very important to preheat the oven for 10 to 15 minutes—cookies placed in a cold oven won't bake properly.

# Chewy Lemon-Honey Cookies

| | |
|---|---|
| 2 cups all-purpose flour | 1 tablespoon grated lemon peel |
| 1½ teaspoons baking soda | ¼ cup EGG BEATERS® Healthy |
| ½ cup honey | Real Egg Product |
| ⅓ cup FLEISCHMANN'S® | Lemon Glaze, optional |
| Original Margarine | (recipe follows) |
| ¼ cup granulated sugar | |

**Makes 3½ dozen cookies**

**Prep Time:**
*20 minutes*

**Cook Time:**
*8 minutes*

In small bowl, combine flour and baking soda; set aside.

In large bowl, with electric mixer at medium speed, beat honey, margarine, granulated sugar and lemon peel until creamy. Add Egg Beaters®; beat until smooth. Gradually stir in flour mixture until blended.

Drop dough by rounded teaspoonfuls, 2 inches apart, onto lightly greased baking sheets. Bake at 350°F for 7 to 8 minutes or until lightly browned. Remove from sheets; cool completely on wire racks. Drizzle with Lemon Glaze, if desired.

**Lemon Glaze:** *In small bowl, combine 1 cup powdered sugar and 2 tablespoons lemon juice until smooth.*

# Almond Cream Cookies

**Makes about 4 dozen cookies**

¾ cup (1½ sticks) margarine, softened
¾ cup granulated sugar
½ cup plus 2 tablespoons soft-style cream cheese, divided
1 egg
1 teaspoon almond extract
1¼ cups all-purpose flour

¾ cup QUAKER® Corn Meal
½ teaspoon baking powder
½ cup coarsely chopped almonds
1 cup powdered sugar
1 tablespoon milk or water
Red or green candied cherries (optional)

*Note:*

Nuts have a high fat content and thus can go rancid quickly. Purchase nuts in small quantities and store them in a cool, dry place. Always taste nuts before using them, as a few bad nuts can ruin an entire recipe.

Preheat oven to 350°F. Beat margarine, granulated sugar and ½ cup cream cheese at medium speed of electric mixer until fluffy. Add egg and almond extract; mix until well blended. Gradually add combined flour, corn meal and baking powder; mix well. Stir in almonds. Drop by rounded teaspoonfuls onto ungreased cookie sheet. Bake 12 to 14 minutes or until edges are golden brown. Cool on cookie sheet for 2 minutes; remove to wire rack. Cool completely.

Mix remaining 2 tablespoons cream cheese and powdered sugar until blended. Add milk; mix until smooth. Spread over cookies. Garnish with halved red or green candied cherries, if desired. Store tightly covered.

# Oatmeal Macaroons

1¼ cups all-purpose flour
1 teaspoon baking soda
1 cup (2 sticks) margarine, softened
1 cup packed brown sugar
2 eggs

½ teaspoon almond extract
3 cups QUAKER® Oats (quick or old fashioned uncooked)
1 package (4 ounces) flaked or shredded coconut

Makes 4½ dozen cookies

In medium bowl, combine flour and baking soda. In large bowl, cream margarine and sugar until light and fluffy. Blend in eggs and almond extract. Add flour mixture; mix well. Stir in oats and coconut. Drop dough by rounded teaspoonfuls onto greased cookie sheets. Bake in preheated 350°F oven 10 minutes or until light golden brown. Let cookies cool 1 minute before removing from cookie sheets to wire racks.

# Banana Peanut Jumbles

2 ripe, medium DOLE® Bananas
½ cup packed brown sugar
½ cup peanut butter

½ cup roasted peanuts
1⅓ cups buttermilk baking mix
1 tablespoon water

Makes 18 cookies

Prep Time:
*15 minutes*

Bake Time:
*25 minutes*

• **Mash** bananas; measure 1 cup.

• **Combine** bananas, brown sugar, peanut butter and peanuts. Add baking mix and water. Stir until well blended.

• **Drop** batter by heaping tablespoonfuls onto cookie sheets coated with cooking spray.

• **Bake** at 350°F 20 to 25 minutes or until golden. Cool on rack.

# Soft Apple Cider Cookies

| Makes 4 dozen cookies | | |
|---|---|---|

**Prep Time:**
*30 minutes*

**Cook Time:**
*12 minutes*

1 cup firmly packed light brown sugar
½ cup FLEISCHMANN'S® Original Margarine, softened
½ cup apple cider
½ cup EGG BEATERS® Healthy Real Egg Product

2¼ cups all-purpose flour
1½ teaspoons ground cinnamon
1 teaspoon baking soda
¼ teaspoon salt
2 medium apples, peeled and diced (about 1½ cups)
¾ cup almonds, chopped
Cider Glaze (recipe follows)

In large bowl, with electric mixer at medium speed, beat sugar and margarine until creamy. Add cider and Egg Beaters®; beat until smooth. With electric mixer at low speed, gradually blend in flour, cinnamon, baking soda and salt. Stir in apples and almonds.

Drop dough by tablespoonfuls, 2 inches apart, onto greased baking sheets. Bake at 375°F for 10 to 12 minutes or until golden brown. Remove from sheets; cool on wire racks. Drizzle with Cider Glaze.

**Cider Glaze:** *In small bowl, combine 1 cup powdered sugar and 2 tablespoons apple cider until smooth.*

# Walnut-Orange Chocolate Chippers

1½ cups all-purpose flour
½ cup packed brown sugar
½ cup granulated sugar
1½ teaspoons baking powder
½ teaspoon salt
⅓ cup butter, softened
2 eggs, slightly beaten

2 cups (12 ounces) semisweet chocolate chips
1 cup coarsely chopped California walnuts
2 tablespoons grated orange rind

Makes about 3½ dozen cookies

Combine flour, brown sugar, granulated sugar, baking powder and salt in large bowl; mix in butter and eggs. Add remaining ingredients and mix thoroughly (batter will be stiff). Drop tablespoonfuls of dough 2 inches apart onto ungreased cookies sheets. Bake in preheated 350°F oven 9 to 11 minutes or until lightly browned. Cool 1 minute on cookie sheets; transfer to wire racks to cool completely.

**Variation:** *Prepare dough as directed above. Spread evenly into greased and floured 9-inch square pan (use wet hands to smooth). Bake at 350°F 25 minutes or until golden brown. Cool; cut into 36 squares.*

Favorite recipe from **Walnut Marketing Board**

*Baked these!*

# Peanut Butter Oatmeal Treats

**Makes 3½ dozen cookies**

1¾ cups all-purpose flour
1 teaspoon baking soda
½ teaspoon salt
½ cup butter or margarine, softened
½ cup SMUCKER'S® Creamy Natural Peanut Butter
1 cup sugar
1 cup firmly-packed light brown sugar
2 eggs
¼ cup milk
1 teaspoon vanilla
2½ cups uncooked oats
1 cup semi-sweet chocolate chips

Combine flour, baking soda and salt; set aside. In large mixing bowl, combine butter, peanut butter, sugar and brown sugar. Beat until light and creamy. Beat in eggs, milk and vanilla. Stir in flour mixture, oats and chocolate chips. Drop dough by rounded teaspoonfuls about 3 inches apart onto ungreased cookie sheets.

Bake at 350°F for 15 minutes or until lightly browned.

# Baker's® Premium Chocolate Chunk Cookies

1¾ cups flour
¾ teaspoon baking soda
¼ teaspoon salt
¾ cup (1½ sticks) butter or
   margarine, softened
½ cup granulated sugar
½ cup firmly packed brown
   sugar

1 egg
1 teaspoon vanilla
1 package (12 ounces)
   BAKER'S® Semi-Sweet
   Chocolate Chunks
1 cup chopped nuts (optional)

**Makes about 3 dozen cookies**

Prep Time:
*15 minutes*

Bake Time:
*11 to 13 minutes*

**HEAT** oven to 375°F.

**MIX** flour, baking soda and salt in medium bowl; set aside.

**BEAT** butter and sugars in large bowl with electric mixer on medium speed until light and fluffy. Add egg and vanilla; beat well. Gradually beat in flour mixture. Stir in chocolate chunks and nuts. Drop by heaping tablespoonfuls onto ungreased cookie sheets.

**BAKE** 11 to 13 minutes or just until golden brown. Cool on cookie sheets 1 minute. Remove to wire racks and cool completely.

**Bar Cookies:** *Spread dough in greased foil-lined 15×10×1-inch baking pan. Bake at 375°F for 18 to 20 minutes or until golden brown. (Or, bake in 13×9-inch pan for 20 to 22 minutes.) Cool completely in pan on wire rack. Makes 3 dozen.*

**Chocolate Chunkoholic Cookies:** *Omit nuts. Stir in 2 packages (12 ounces each) BAKER'S® Semi-Sweet Chocolate Chunks. Drop by scant ¼ cupfuls onto cookie sheets. Bake at 375°F for 12 to 14 minutes. Makes about 22 large cookies.*

**Freezing Cookie Dough:** *Freeze heaping tablespoonfuls of cookie dough on cookie sheet 1 hour. Transfer to airtight plastic container or freezer zipper-style plastic bag. Freeze dough up to 1 month. Bake frozen cookie dough at 375°F for 15 to 16 minutes or just until golden brown.*

*Note:*
For an extra-special after-school treat, create an irresistible ice cream sandwich: layer a scoop of vanilla ice cream between two just-baked cookies.

# Pineapple Carrot Cookies

| | |
|---|---|
| **Makes about 3 dozen cookies** | |

**Prep Time:**
*30 minutes*

**Bake Time:**
*20 minutes per batch*

2 cans (8 ounces each) DOLE® Crushed Pineapple
¾ cup margarine, softened
½ cup granulated sugar
½ cup packed brown sugar
1 egg
1 teaspoon vanilla extract
1 cup shredded DOLE® Carrots

1 cup chopped walnuts
1 cup DOLE® Seedless Raisins
1½ cups all-purpose flour
1 teaspoon ground cinnamon
½ teaspoon ground ginger
½ teaspoon baking powder
¼ teaspoon salt

• Preheat oven to 375°F.

• Drain crushed pineapple well; reserve juice for beverage.

• Beat margarine and sugars until light and fluffy. Beat in egg and vanilla. Beat in crushed pineapple, carrots, walnuts and raisins.

• Combine remaining ingredients; beat into pineapple mixture until well blended.

• Drop batter by heaping tablespoonfuls onto greased cookie sheets. Flatten tops with spoon. Bake 15 to 20 minutes.

# Hershey's Mint Chocolate Cookies

¾ cup (1½ sticks) butter or
    margarine, softened
1 cup sugar
1 egg
1 teaspoon vanilla extract
1½ cups all-purpose flour

½ teaspoon baking soda
¼ teaspoon salt
1⅔ cups (10-ounce package)
    HERSHEY'S Mint Chocolate
    Chips

**Makes about
2½ dozen cookies**

*1.* Heat oven to 350°F.

*2.* Beat butter and sugar in large bowl until fluffy. Add egg
and vanilla; beat well. Stir together flour, baking soda and salt;
gradually blend into butter mixture. Stir in mint chocolate chips.
Drop by rounded teaspoons onto ungreased cookie sheet.

*3.* Bake 8 to 9 minutes or just until lightly browned. Cool slightly;
remove from cookie sheet to wire rack. Cool completely.

*Note:*

Let cookie sheets cool
to room temperature
before putting more
dough on them. If
placed on a warm
surface, cookie dough
can begin to melt and
spread, which will
affect the shape and
texture of the cookies.

# Fresh Orange Cookies

**Makes about 4 dozen cookies**

1½ cups all-purpose flour
½ teaspoon baking soda
¼ teaspoon salt
½ cup butter or margarine, softened
½ cup granulated sugar
½ cup packed light brown sugar
1 egg

1 unpeeled SUNKIST® orange, finely chopped*
½ cup chopped walnuts
Orange Glaze (recipe follows)

*Chop SUNKIST® orange in blender or food processor, or by hand, to equal ¾ cup chopped fruit.

Sift together flour, baking soda and salt. In large bowl, beat butter and sugars until light and fluffy. Add egg and chopped orange; beat well. Gradually blend in dry ingredients. Stir in walnuts. Cover and chill at least 1 hour. Drop dough by teaspoons onto lightly greased cookie sheets. Bake at 375°F for 10 to 12 minutes. Cool on wire racks. Spread cookies with Orange Glaze.

## Orange Glaze

1 cup confectioners' sugar
1 to 2 tablespoons fresh SUNKIST® orange juice

1 tablespoon butter or margarine, softened
1 teaspoon grated SUNKIST® orange peel

In small bowl, combine all ingredients until smooth.

*Makes about ½ cup*

# Triple Chocolate Cookies

1 package DUNCAN HINES®
   Moist Deluxe® Swiss
   Chocolate Cake Mix
½ cup butter or margarine,
   melted
1 egg

½ cup semisweet chocolate
   chips
½ cup milk chocolate chips
½ cup coarsely chopped white
   chocolate
½ cup chopped pecans

**Makes 3½ to 4 dozen cookies**

*1.* Preheat oven to 375°F.

*2.* Combine cake mix, melted butter and egg in large bowl. Beat at low speed with electric mixer until blended. Stir in all 3 chocolates and pecans.

*3.* Drop by rounded tablespoonfuls onto ungreased baking sheets. Bake at 375°F for 9 to 11 minutes. Cool 1 minute on baking sheet. Remove to cooling racks.

<u>Tip:</u> *Cookies may be stored in an airtight container in freezer for up to 6 months.*

# Southern Belle White Chocolate Cookies

**Makes 1½ dozen cookies**

½ cup PETER PAN® Creamy Peanut Butter
¼ cup WESSON® Vegetable Oil
¼ cup (½ stick) butter
½ cup granulated sugar
½ cup firmly packed brown sugar
1 egg, at room temperature, slightly beaten
2 teaspoons vanilla

½ teaspoon baking soda
½ teaspoon baking powder
1¼ cups all-purpose flour
2 (4-ounce) bars white confection candy bar for baking and eating, broken into small chunks
1⅓ cups coarsely chopped macadamia nuts

Preheat oven to 350°F. In a large mixing bowl, using an electric mixer, beat Peter Pan® Peanut Butter, Wesson® Oil and butter together until creamy. Add *next 6* ingredients, ending with baking powder; beat on medium speed until well blended. Add flour and continue mixing until well blended. Fold candy chunks and nuts into cookie dough. Place heaping tablespoons of dough onto an ungreased cookie sheet 1½ inches apart, pressing dough down slightly with the back of spoon. Bake 10 to 12 minutes or until lightly brown around edges. Remove from cookie sheet; cool on wire rack.

# Banana Oatmeal Cookies with Banana Frosting

**Cookies**

¾ **Butter Flavor CRISCO® Stick or ¾ cup Butter Flavor CRISCO® all-vegetable shortening plus additional for greasing**
1 **cup firmly packed brown sugar**
1 **egg**
1 **cup mashed ripe bananas (2 to 3 medium)**
1½ **cups all-purpose flour**
1 **teaspoon salt**
1 **teaspoon ground cinnamon**
½ **teaspoon baking soda**
¼ **teaspoon ground nutmeg**
1¾ **cups quick oats (not instant or old-fashioned)**
½ **cup coarsely chopped walnuts**

**Banana Frosting**

2 **tablespoons Butter Flavor CRISCO® all-vegetable shortening**
¼ **cup mashed ripe banana**
1 **teaspoon lemon juice**
2 **cups confectioners' sugar Finely chopped walnuts (optional)**

Makes about 5 dozen cookies

*1.* Heat oven to 350°F. Grease baking sheets with shortening. For cookies, combine ¾ cup shortening and sugar in large bowl. Beat at medium speed of electric mixer until well blended. Beat in egg. Add 1 cup mashed banana. Beat until blended.

*2.* Combine flour, salt, cinnamon, baking soda and nutmeg in medium bowl. Mix into creamed mixture at low speed until blended. Stir in oats and nuts with spoon.

*3.* Drop 2 level measuring tablespoonfuls of dough into a mound on prepared baking sheet. Repeat for each cookie, placing mounds 2 inches apart.

*4.* Bake at 350°F for 15 to 17 minutes or until set. Cool 1 minute on baking sheet. Remove to cooling rack. Cool completely.

*5.* For frosting, combine 2 tablespoons shortening, ¼ cup mashed banana and lemon juice in medium bowl. Beat at medium speed of electric mixer until well blended. Add confectioners' sugar, 1 cup at a time. Beat at low speed after each addition until blended. Frost cooled cookies. Sprinkle with nuts, if desired.

# Double Chocolate Chunk Cookies

**Makes about 2 dozen cookies**

**Prep Time:**
*15 minutes*

**Bake Time:**
*10 minutes*

1 package (12 ounces) BAKER'S® Semi-Sweet Chocolate Chunks, divided
1 cup flour
½ teaspoon CALUMET® Baking Powder
¼ teaspoon salt

½ cup (1 stick) butter *or* margarine, softened
½ cup firmly packed brown sugar
1 egg
1 teaspoon vanilla
1 cup chopped nuts (optional)

**HEAT** oven to 375°F.

**MICROWAVE** 1 cup of the chocolate chunks in microwavable bowl on HIGH 2 minutes until almost melted. Stir until chocolate is completely melted; set aside. Mix flour, baking powder and salt in medium bowl; set aside.

**BEAT** butter and sugar in large bowl with electric mixer on medium speed until light and fluffy. Add egg and vanilla; beat well. Stir in melted chocolate. Gradually beat in flour mixture. Stir in chocolate chunks and nuts. Drop by heaping tablespoonfuls onto ungreased cookie sheets.

**BAKE** 10 minutes or until cookies are puffed and feel set to the touch. Cool on cookie sheets 1 minute. Remove to wire racks and cool completely.

**Black and White Chocolate Chunk Cookies:** *Melt 1 package (6 squares) BAKER'S® Premium White Baking Chocolate as directed on package. Dip half of each cookie in melted white chocolate. Let stand at room temperature or refrigerate on wax paper-lined tray 30 minutes or until chocolate is firm.*

# Lemon Pecan Cookies

1 Butter Flavor CRISCO® Stick
   or 1 cup Butter Flavor
   CRISCO® all-vegetable
   shortening
1½ cups granulated sugar
2 large eggs

3 tablespoons fresh lemon juice
3 cups all-purpose flour
2 teaspoons baking powder
¼ teaspoon salt
1 cup chopped pecans

**Makes about 6 dozen cookies**

*1.* Heat oven to 350°F.

*2.* Combine 1 cup shortening and sugar in large bowl. Beat at medium speed with electric mixer until well blended. Beat in eggs and lemon juice until well blended.

*3.* Combine flour, baking powder and salt in medium bowl. Add to creamed mixture; mix well. Stir in pecans. Spray cookie sheets lightly with CRISCO® No-Stick Cooking Spray. Drop dough by teaspoonfuls about 2 inches apart onto prepared cookie sheets. Bake at 350°F for 10 fo 12 minutes or until lightly browned. Cool on cookie sheets 4 minutes; transfer to cooling rack.

## *Note:*

Room temperature lemons yield more juice than cold ones. To get the most juice from your lemons, press down as you roll them on the countertop with the palm of your hand before squeezing.

# Powdered Sugar Cookies

| Makes 7 dozen cookies |
|---|

1½ cups (3 sticks) I CAN'T
    BELIEVE IT'S NOT
    BUTTER!® Spread, softened
1⅓ cups confectioners' sugar
1 teaspoon vanilla extract

3½ cups all-purpose flour
1⅓ cups chopped walnuts
    Additional confectioners'
    sugar

Preheat oven to 350°F.

In large bowl, with electric mixer, beat I Can't Believe It's Not Butter!® Spread and sugar until light and fluffy, about 5 minutes. Beat in vanilla, then flour, scraping sides occasionally, until blended. Stir in walnuts.

On *ungreased* baking sheets, drop dough by heaping teaspoonfuls, 2 inches apart. With palm of hand or spoon, gently flatten each cookie.

Bake 10 minutes or until light golden around edges. On wire rack, let stand 2 minutes; remove from sheets and cool completely. Sprinkle with additional sugar.

# Double Chocolate Dream Cookies

| Makes about 4½ dozen cookies |
|---|

2¼ cups all-purpose flour
½ cup NESTLÉ® TOLL HOUSE®
    Baking Cocoa
1 teaspoon baking soda
½ teaspoon salt
1 cup (2 sticks) butter or
    margarine, softened
1 cup packed brown sugar

¾ cup granulated sugar
1 teaspoon vanilla extract
2 large eggs
2 cups (12-ounce package)
    NESTLÉ® TOLL HOUSE®
    Semi-Sweet Chocolate
    Morsels

**PREHEAT** oven to 375°F.

**COMBINE** flour, cocoa, baking soda and salt in small bowl. Beat butter, brown sugar, granulated sugar and vanilla extract in large mixer bowl until creamy. Beat in eggs for about 2 minutes or until light and fluffy. Gradually beat in flour mixture. Stir in morsels. Drop by rounded tablespoon onto ungreased baking sheets.

**BAKE** for 8 to 10 minutes or until cookies are puffed. Cool on baking sheets for 2 minutes; remove to wire racks to cool completely.

# Pineapple Oatmeal Crunchies

| | | |
|---|---|---|
| 2 cans (8 ounces each) DOLE® Crushed Pineapple<br>1½ cups margarine<br>1½ cups packed brown sugar<br>2 eggs<br>3 cups all-purpose flour<br>3 cups old-fashioned rolled oats | 1 teaspoon baking powder<br>1 teaspoon ground cinnamon<br>½ teaspoon salt<br>5 bags (1.4 ounces each) chocolate covered toffee nuggets | **Makes 24 large cookies**<br><br>Prep Time:<br>*20 minutes*<br><br>Bake Time:<br>*30 minutes per batch* |

• Drain crushed pineapple well, reserving ½ cup juice.

• Beat margarine and sugar until light and fluffy. Beat in eggs. Stir in pineapple and reserved juice.

• Combine flour, oats, baking powder, cinnamon and salt. Add to pineapple mixture and mix well. Stir in candy.

• Drop by ¼ cup scoopfuls 1 inch apart onto cookie sheets coated with cooking spray. Flatten slightly. Bake at 375°F 30 minutes.

# Chewy Brownie Cookies

**Makes about 3 dozen cookies**

1½ cups firmly packed light brown sugar
⅔ CRISCO® Stick or ⅔ cup CRISCO® all-vegetable shortening
1 tablespoon water
1 teaspoon vanilla
2 eggs

1½ cups all-purpose flour
⅓ cup unsweetened baking cocoa
½ teaspoon salt
¼ teaspoon baking soda
2 cups semisweet chocolate chips (12-ounce package)

*1.* Heat oven to 375°F. Place sheets of foil on countertop for cooling cookies.

*2.* Combine brown sugar, ⅔ cup shortening, water and vanilla in large bowl. Beat at medium speed of electric mixer until well blended. Beat eggs into creamed mixture.

*3.* Combine flour, cocoa, salt and baking soda. Mix into creamed mixture at low speed just until blended. Stir in chocolate chips.

*4.* Drop rounded measuring tablespoonfuls of dough 2 inches apart onto ungreased baking sheet.

*5.* Bake one baking sheet at a time at 375°F for 7 to 9 minutes, or until cookies are set. *Do not overbake.* Cool 2 minutes on baking sheet. Remove cookies to foil to cool completely.

# Applesauce Raisin Chews

1 cup (2 sticks) margarine or
   butter, softened
1 cup firmly packed brown
   sugar
1 cup applesauce
1 egg
1 teaspoon vanilla

2 cups all-purpose flour
1 teaspoon baking soda
1 teaspoon ground cinnamon
½ teaspoon salt (optional)
2½ cups QUAKER® Oats (quick or
   old fashioned, uncooked)
1 cup raisins

**Makes about 4 dozen cookies**

Heat oven to 350°F. Beat together margarine and sugar until creamy. Add applesauce, egg and vanilla; beat well. Add combined flour, baking soda, cinnamon and salt; mix well. Stir in oats and raisins. Drop by rounded tablespoonfuls onto ungreased cookie sheets. Bake 11 to 13 minutes or until light golden brown. Cool 1 minute on cookie sheets; remove to wire rack. Cool completely. Store in tightly covered container.

## Are They Done Yet?

How can you tell when a cookie is done? It depends on what kind of cookie it is. Whatever the type, always check the cookies for doneness at the minimum time given in the recipe.

Here are some simple tests to help figure out if your cookies are done:

**DROP COOKIES:** Done when their tops and edges are lightly browned, and a slight imprint remains after touching the surface

**CUTOUT COOKIES:** Done when the edges are firm and the bottoms are lightly browned

**REFRIGERATOR COOKIES:** Done when the edges are firm and the bottoms are lightly browned

**CAKEY BAR COOKIES:** Done when a toothpick inserted in the center comes out clean and dry

**SHAPED COOKIES:** Done when the edges are lightly browned

**FUDGY BAR COOKIES:** Done when the surface appears dull and a slight imprint remains after touching the surface

# Spicy Ginger Molasses Cookies

**Makes about 1 dozen (4-inch) cookies**

2 cups all-purpose flour
1½ teaspoons ground ginger
1 teaspoon baking soda
½ teaspoon ground cloves
¼ teaspoon salt
¾ cup (1½ sticks) butter, softened

1 cup sugar
¼ cup molasses
1 egg
Additional sugar
½ cup yogurt-covered raisins

*1.* Preheat oven to 375°F.

*2.* Combine flour, ginger, baking soda, cloves and salt in small bowl; set aside.

*3.* Beat butter and 1 cup sugar in large bowl of electric mixer at medium speed until light and fluffy. Add molasses and egg; beat until well blended. Gradually beat in flour mixture on low speed just until blended.

*4.* Drop dough by level ¼-cupfuls onto parchment-lined cookie sheets, spacing 3 inches apart. Flatten each ball of dough until 2 inches in diameter with bottom of glass that has been dipped in additional sugar. Press 7 to 8 yogurt-covered raisins into dough of each cookie.

*5.* Bake 11 to 12 minutes or until cookies are set. Cool cookies 2 minutes on cookie sheets; slide parchment paper and cookies onto countertop. Cool completely.

# Chewy Oatmeal Trail Mix Cookies

¾ Butter Flavor CRISCO® Stick or ¾ cup Butter Flavor CRISCO® all-vegetable shortening plus additional for greasing
1¼ cups firmly packed light brown sugar
1 egg
⅓ cup milk
1½ teaspoons vanilla
2½ cups quick oats, uncooked

1 cup all-purpose flour
½ teaspoon baking soda
½ teaspoon salt
¼ teaspoon ground cinnamon
1 cup (6 ounces) semisweet or milk chocolate chips
¾ cup raisins
¾ cup coarsely chopped walnuts, pecans or peanuts
½ cup sunflower seeds

**Makes about 3 dozen cookies**

*1.* Heat oven to 375°F. Grease baking sheets. Place sheets of foil on countertop for cooling cookies.

*2.* Combine ¾ cup shortening, brown sugar, egg, milk and vanilla in large bowl. Beat at medium speed of electric mixer until well blended.

*3.* Combine oats, flour, baking soda, salt and cinnamon. Mix into shortening mixture at low speed just until blended. Stir in chocolate chips, raisins, nuts and sunflower seeds.

*4.* Drop rounded tablespoonfuls of dough 2 inches apart onto prepared baking sheets.

*5.* Bake one baking sheet at a time at 375°F for 10 to 12 minutes or until lightly browned. *Do not overbake.* Cool 2 minutes on baking sheets. Remove cookies to foil to cool completely.

**Tip:** *You may substitute 3 cups of prepared trail mix (available in grocery or health food stores) for the chips, raisins, nuts and sunflower seeds.*

*Note:*

Always measure brown sugar by packing it firmly into a measuring cup. (The brown sugar should hold the shape of the measuring cup when released.)

# Banana Spice Lemon Drops

Makes 3 dozen cookies

2 cups all-purpose flour
1 teaspoon baking soda
¼ teaspoon ground cinnamon
⅛ teaspoon ground cloves
6 tablespoons margarine, divided
1 cup packed brown sugar

1 egg
1 large, ripe DOLE® Banana, mashed (about ⅔ cup)
Vegetable cooking spray
2 cups powdered sugar
2 to 3 tablespoons lemon juice

• **Combine** flour, baking soda, cinnamon and cloves in small bowl; set aside.

• **Beat** 4 tablespoons margarine, brown sugar and egg in large bowl until blended. Stir in banana. Add flour mixture; stir until well blended.

• **Drop** dough by rounded teaspoonfuls onto baking sheets sprayed with vegetable cooking spray, 1 inch apart.

• **Bake** at 375°F 10 to 12 minutes or until edges are light brown. Remove to wire rack; let cool completely.

• **Beat** remaining margarine, powdered sugar and 2 tablespoons lemon juice in small bowl until smooth, adding additional lemon juice, if needed. Spread frosting over cooled cookies.

# Giant Peanut Butter Cup Cookies

**Makes 9 cookies**

½ cup (1 stick) butter or
    margarine, softened
¾ cup sugar
⅓ cup REESE'S® Creamy or
    Crunchy Peanut Butter
1 egg

½ teaspoon vanilla extract
1¼ cups all-purpose flour
½ teaspoon baking soda
¼ teaspoon salt
16 REESE'S® Peanut Butter Cup
    Miniatures, cut into fourths

*1.* Heat oven to 350°F.

*2.* Beat butter, sugar and peanut butter in medium bowl until creamy. Add egg and vanilla; beat well. Stir together flour, baking soda and salt. Add to butter mixture; blend well. Drop dough by level ¼ cup measurements onto ungreased cookie sheets, three cookies per sheet. (Cookies will spread while baking.) Push about seven pieces of peanut butter cup into each cookie, flattening cookie slightly.

*3.* Bake 15 to 17 minutes or until light golden brown around the edges. Centers will be pale and slightly soft. Cool 1 minute on cookie sheet. Remove to wire rack; cool completely.

# Mocha Melt Cookies

**Makes about 3 dozen cookies**

**Prep Time:**
*15 minutes*

**Bake Time:**
*9 minutes*

*Note:*

Heavy-gauge, shiny aluminum cookie sheets are best for producing evenly baked and browned cookies. Darker cookie sheets absorb more heat and can cause overbrowning or burning.

4 squares BAKER'S® Unsweetened Baking Chocolate
½ cup (1 stick) butter *or* margarine, softened
1¼ cups sugar
1 egg
1 teaspoon vanilla

⅓ cup milk
1¼ cups flour
½ cup GENERAL FOODS INTERNATIONAL COFFEES®, any flavor
2 teaspoons CALUMET® Baking Powder

**HEAT** oven to 350°F.

**MICROWAVE** chocolate in large microwavable bowl on HIGH 1½ minutes or until almost melted. Stir until chocolate is completely melted.

**BEAT** in butter and sugar with electric mixer on medium speed until well blended. Add egg and vanilla; beat well. Blend in milk. Beat in flour, flavored instant coffee and baking powder on low speed. Drop by tablespoonfuls, 2 inches apart, onto ungreased cookie sheets.

**BAKE** 9 minutes or until cookies are puffed and a slight indentation remains when touched lightly. Cool on cookie sheets 2 minutes. Remove to wire racks and cool completely.

**Storage Know-How:** *Store in tightly covered container up to 1 week.*

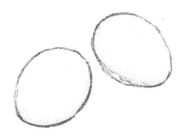

# Fudgy Oatmeal Butterscotch Cookies

1 package (18.25 ounces)
   devil's food cake mix
1½ cups quick-cooking or
   old-fashioned oats,
   uncooked
¾ cup (1½ sticks) butter, melted

2 large eggs
1 tablespoon vegetable oil
1 teaspoon vanilla extract
1¼ cups "M&M's"® Chocolate
   Mini Baking Bits
1 cup butterscotch chips

**Makes about 3 dozen cookies**

Preheat oven to 350°F. In large bowl combine cake mix, oats, butter, eggs, oil and vanilla until well blended. Stir in "M&M's"® Chocolate Mini Baking Bits and butterscotch chips. Drop by heaping tablespoonfuls about 2 inches apart onto ungreased cookie sheets. Bake 10 to 12 minutes. Cool 1 minute on cookie sheets; cool completely on wire racks. Store in tightly covered container.

# Pistachio Chip Cookies

½ cup (1 stick) butter
⅓ cup light corn syrup
2 tablespoons frozen orange
   juice concentrate, thawed
1 tablespoon grated orange
   peel

⅔ cup packed dark brown sugar
1 cup all-purpose flour
½ cup chopped pistachio nuts
1 cup (6 ounces) semisweet
   chocolate chips

**Makes about 4 dozen cookies**

Preheat oven to 375°F. Line cookie sheets with foil; lightly grease foil. Combine butter, corn syrup, orange concentrate, orange peel and sugar in saucepan. Bring to a boil over medium heat, stirring constantly. Remove from heat; gradually stir in flour and nuts. Cool completely. Stir in chips. Drop batter by teaspoonfuls 3 inches apart onto prepared cookie sheets. Bake 8 to 10 minutes or until golden and lacy. (Cookies are soft when hot, but crisp up as they cool.) Cool completely on foil, then peel foil from cookies.

# Chocolate Chip Almond Oatmeal Cookies

**Makes about 4 dozen cookies**

1 Butter Flavor CRISCO® Stick or 1 cup Butter Flavor CRISCO® all-vegetable shortening
1 cup granulated sugar
1 cup firmly packed dark brown sugar
2 large eggs
1 teaspoon vanilla
½ teaspoon almond extract
2 cups all-purpose flour
1 teaspoon baking soda
½ teaspoon salt
2 cups rolled oats
9 ounces semisweet chocolate chips
1 cup slivered almonds

*1.* Heat oven to 350°F.

*2.* Combine 1 cup shortening and sugars in large bowl. Beat at medium speed with electric mixer until well blended. Beat in eggs, vanilla and almond extract until well blended.

*3.* Combine flour, baking soda and salt in medium bowl. Add to creamed mixture; mix well. Add oats; mix well. Add chocolate chips and almonds.

*4.* Spray cookie sheets with CRISCO® No-Stick Cooking Spray. Drop dough by tablespoonfuls 2 inches apart onto prepared cookie sheets. Bake at 350°F for 10 to 12 minutes or until lightly browned. Cool on cookie sheets 4 minutes; transfer to cooling racks.

# Mini Morsel Meringue Cookies

| | | |
|---|---|---|
| 4 large egg whites<br>½ teaspoon salt<br>½ teaspoon cream of tartar<br>1 cup granulated sugar | 2 cups (12-ounce package)<br>NESTLÉ® TOLL HOUSE®<br>Semi-Sweet Chocolate Mini<br>Morsels | **Makes about 5 dozen cookies** |

**Prep Time:**
*15 minutes*

**Cook Time:**
*20 minutes*

PREHEAT oven to 300°F. Grease baking sheets.

BEAT egg whites, salt and cream of tartar in small mixer bowl until soft peaks form. Gradually add sugar; beat until stiff peaks form. Gently fold in morsels ⅓ cup at a time. Drop by level tablespoon onto prepared baking sheets.

BAKE for 20 to 25 minutes or until meringues are dry and crisp. Cool on baking sheets for 2 minutes; remove to wire racks to cool completely. Store in airtight containers.

# Chunky Peanut Butter Cookies

| | | |
|---|---|---|
| ½ cup chunky peanut butter<br>2 tablespoons reduced-calorie<br>margarine<br>1⅓ cups packed brown sugar | 2 egg whites<br>½ teaspoon vanilla<br>1⅛ cups all-purpose flour<br>¼ teaspoon baking soda | **Makes about 34 cookies** |

Preheat oven to 375°F. Spray cookie sheet with nonstick cooking spray. Beat peanut butter and margarine with electric mixer on medium speed. Beat in sugar, egg whites and vanilla. Blend in flour and baking soda. Drop by teaspoonfuls about 2 inches apart onto cookie sheet; press flat with fork. Bake 8 to 10 minutes.

Favorite recipe from **The Sugar Association, Inc.**

# Kentucky Oatmeal-Jam Cookies

**Makes about 2 dozen cookies**

½ Butter Flavor CRISCO® Stick or ½ cup Butter Flavor CRISCO all-vegetable shortening plus additional for greasing
¾ cup sugar
1 egg
¼ cup buttermilk*
½ cup SMUCKER'S® Strawberry Jam
1 teaspoon vanilla
1 cup all-purpose flour
½ cup unsweetened cocoa powder

1 teaspoon ground cinnamon
½ teaspoon baking soda
¼ teaspoon nutmeg
¼ teaspoon ground cloves
1½ cups quick oats (not instant or old-fashioned), uncooked
½ cup raisins
½ cup chopped pecans (optional)
About 24 pecan halves (optional)

*You may substitute ¾ teaspoon lemon juice or vinegar plus enough milk to make ¼ cup for buttermilk. Stir. Wait 5 minutes before using.*

*1.* Heat oven to 350°F. Grease baking sheet. Place foil on countertop for cooling cookies.

*2.* Combine ½ cup shortening, sugar, egg, buttermilk, jam and vanilla in large bowl. Beat at medium speed of electric mixer until well blended.

*3.* Combine flour, cocoa, cinnamon, baking soda, nutmeg and cloves. Mix into creamed mixture at low speed until blended. Stir in oats, raisins and chopped nuts with spoon.

*4.* Drop 2 tablespoonfuls of dough in a mound on baking sheet. Repeat for each cookie, spacing mounds 3 inches apart. Top each with pecan half.

*5.* Bake 10 to 12 minutes or until set. *Do not overbake.* Cool 2 minutes on baking sheet. Remove cookies to foil to cool completely.

# Oatmeal Hermits

3 cups QUAKER® Oats (quick or old fashioned, uncooked)
1 cup all-purpose flour
1 cup (2 sticks) butter or margarine, melted
1 cup firmly packed brown sugar
1 cup raisins
½ cup chopped nuts
1 egg
¼ cup milk
1 teaspoon ground cinnamon
1 teaspoon vanilla
½ teaspoon baking soda
½ teaspoon salt (optional)
¼ teaspoon ground nutmeg

**Makes about 3 dozen**

*Note:*

Old-fashioned chewy hermits are said to have been so named because they're better when hidden away for several days.

Heat oven to 375°F. In large bowl, combine all ingredients; mix well. Drop by rounded tablespoonfuls onto ungreased cookie sheets. Bake 8 to 10 minutes. Cool 1 minute on cookie sheets; remove to wire cooling rack.

# "Orange and Spice Make Everything Nice" Cookies

½ cup (1 stick) butter, softened
⅔ cup granulated sugar
1 large egg
3 tablespoons orange juice
1 teaspoon grated orange zest
2 cups all-purpose flour
1 teaspoon baking soda
1 teaspoon ground cinnamon
¼ teaspoon salt
¼ teaspoon ground nutmeg
⅛ teaspoon ground cloves
1¼ cups "M&M's"® Chocolate Mini Baking Bits
½ cup raisins

**Makes 3 dozen cookies**

Preheat oven to 350°F. In large bowl cream butter and sugar until light and fluffy; beat in egg, orange juice and orange zest. In medium bowl combine flour, baking soda, cinnamon, salt, nutmeg and cloves; add to creamed mixture. Stir in "M&M's"® Chocolate Mini Baking Bits and raisins. Drop by heaping tablespoonfuls about 2 inches apart onto ungreased cookie sheets. Bake 9 to 10 minutes. Cool 1 minute on cookie sheets; cool completely on wire racks. Store in tightly covered container.

# Easy Lemon Cookies

**Makes 4 dozen cookies**

1 package DUNCAN HINES®
   Moist Deluxe® Lemon Cake
   Mix
2 eggs

½ cup vegetable oil
1 teaspoon grated lemon peel
Pecan halves for garnish

*Note:*

**Before removing the peel from a lemon, thoroughly scrub the lemon to remove wax and any traces of insecticide. Remove only the peel (the colored portion) with a grater or zester, not the bitter white pith underneath.**

*1.* Preheat oven to 350°F.

*2.* Combine cake mix, eggs, oil and lemon peel in large bowl. Stir until thoroughly blended. Drop by rounded teaspoonfuls 2 inches apart onto ungreased baking sheets. Press pecan half into center of each cookie. Bake at 350°F for 9 to 11 minutes or until edges are light golden brown. Cool 1 minute on baking sheets. Remove to wire racks. Cool completely. Store in airtight container.

**Tip:** *You can substitute whole almonds or walnut halves for the pecan halves.*

# Scrumptious Chocolate Fruit and Nut Cookies

1¼ cups (2½ sticks) butter or
    margarine, softened
2 cups sugar
2 eggs
2 teaspoons vanilla extract
2 cups all-purpose flour
¾ cup HERSHEY'S Cocoa
1 teaspoon baking soda

½ teaspoon salt
2 cups (12-ounce package)
    HERSHEY'S Semi-Sweet
    Chocolate Chips
1 cup chopped dried apricots
1 cup coarsely chopped
    macadamia nuts

**Makes about 2 dozen
(3½-inch) cookies**

*1.* Heat oven to 350°F.

*2.* Beat butter and sugar in large bowl until fluffy. Add eggs and vanilla; beat well. Stir together flour, cocoa, baking soda and salt; blend into butter mixture. Stir in chocolate chips, apricots and nuts. Using ice cream scoop or ¼-cup measuring cup, drop dough 3 to 4 inches apart onto ungreased cookie sheet.

*3.* Bake 14 to 16 minutes or until set. Cool slightly; remove from cookie sheet to wire rack. Cool completely.

# Old-Fashioned Harvest Cookies

**Makes about 4 dozen cookies**

¾ Butter Flavor CRISCO® Stick or ¾ cup Butter Flavor CRISCO® all-vegetable shortening
1 cup firmly packed dark brown sugar
¾ cup canned solid-pack pumpkin
1 egg
2 tablespoons molasses

1½ cups all-purpose flour
1 teaspoon ground nutmeg
½ teaspoon baking powder
½ teaspoon baking soda
¼ teaspoon salt
¼ teaspoon ground cinnamon
2½ cups quick oats (not instant or old-fashioned), uncooked
1½ cups finely chopped dates
½ cup chopped walnuts

*1.* Heat oven to 350°F. Grease baking sheet. Place sheets of foil on countertop for cooling cookies.

*2.* Combine ¾ cup shortening and sugar in large bowl. Beat at medium speed of electric mixer until well blended. Beat in pumpkin, egg and molasses.

*3.* Combine flour, nutmeg, baking powder, baking soda, salt and cinnamon. Mix into creamed mixture at low speed until just blended. Stir in, one a time, oats, dates and nuts with spoon.

*4.* Drop rounded tablespoonfuls of dough 2 inches apart onto baking sheet.

*5.* Bake at 350°F for 10 to 12 minutes or until bottoms are lightly browned. *Do not overbake.* Cool 2 minutes on baking sheet. Remove cookies to foil to cool completely.

# Oatmeal Scotchies

1¼ cups all-purpose flour
1 teaspoon baking soda
½ teaspoon ground cinnamon
½ teaspoon salt
1 cup (2 sticks) butter or
    margarine, softened
¾ cup granulated sugar
¾ cup packed brown sugar
2 large eggs

1 teaspoon vanilla extract *or*
    grated peel of 1 orange
3 cups quick or old-fashioned
    oats
1⅔ cups (11-ounce package)
    NESTLÉ® TOLL HOUSE®
    Butterscotch Flavored
    Morsels

**Makes about 4 dozen cookies**

**PREHEAT** oven to 375°F.

**COMBINE** flour, baking soda, cinnamon and salt in small bowl. Beat butter, granulated sugar, brown sugar, eggs and vanilla extract in large mixer bowl. Gradually beat in flour mixture. Stir in oats and morsels. Drop by rounded tablespoon onto ungreased baking sheets.

**BAKE** for 7 to 8 minutes for chewy cookies or 9 to 10 minutes for crispy cookies. Cool on baking sheets for 2 minutes; remove to wire racks to cool completely.

<u>**Pan Cookie Variation:**</u> *GREASE 15×10-inch jelly-roll pan. Spread dough into prepared pan. Bake for 18 to 22 minutes or until light brown. Cool completely in pan on wire rack. Makes 4 dozen bars.*

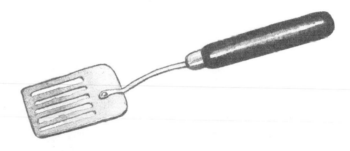

# Death By Chocolate Cookies

**Makes about 18 large cookies**

**Prep Time:**
*15 minutes*

**Bake Time:**
*13 to 14 minutes*

2 packages (8 squares each) BAKER'S® Semi-Sweet Baking Chocolate, divided
¾ cup firmly packed brown sugar
¼ cup (½ stick) butter *or* margarine

2 eggs
1 teaspoon vanilla
½ cup flour
¼ teaspoon CALUMET® Baking Powder
2 cups chopped nuts (optional)

**HEAT** oven to 350°F. Coarsely chop 8 squares (1 package) of the chocolate; set aside.

**MICROWAVE** remaining 8 squares chocolate in large microwavable bowl on HIGH 2 minutes. Stir until chocolate is melted and smooth. Stir in sugar, butter, eggs and vanilla with wooden spoon until well blended. Stir in flour and baking powder. Stir in reserved chopped chocolate and nuts. Drop by scant ¼ cupfuls onto ungreased cookie sheets.

**BAKE** 13 to 14 minutes or until cookies are puffed and feel set to the touch. Cool on cookie sheet 1 minute. Remove to wire racks and cool completely.

<u>**Note:**</u> *If omitting nuts, increase flour to ¾ cup to prevent spreading. Makes about 15 large cookies.*

**Everything-But-The-Kitchen-Sink Cookies:** *Prepare as directed, substituting 2 cups total of any of the following for the nuts: raisins, toasted BAKER'S® ANGEL FLAKE® Coconut, dried cherries, chopped macadamia nuts, dried cranberries, toasted slivered almonds, dried chopped apricots, or dried mixed fruit bits.*

**Bar Cookies:** *Spread dough in greased, foil-lined 13×9-inch baking pan. Bake at 350°F for 22 to 24 minutes. Cool completely in pan on wire rack. Makes 2 dozen.*

**Smaller Cookies:** *Drop by heaping tablespoonfuls onto ungreased cookie sheets. Bake at 350°F for 12 to 13 minutes. Makes about 2½ dozen smaller cookies.*

**Make Ahead:** *After cookies are completely cooled, wrap in plastic wrap and place in an airtight plastic container or freezer zipper-style plastic bag. Freeze cookies up to 1 month. Bring cookies to room temperature before serving.*

**Freezing Cookie Dough:** *Freeze ¼ cupfuls of cookie dough on cookie sheet 1 hour. Transfer to airtight plastic container or freezer zipper-style plastic bag. Freeze dough up to 1 month. Bake frozen cookie dough on ungreased cookie sheet at 350°F for 20 to 23 minutes.*

*Note:*

Since both heat and moisture adversely affect chocolate, it should be stored in a cool, dry place wrapped in foil or waxed paper, but not plastic wrap.

# Chocolate Bursts

**Makes about 3 dozen cookies**

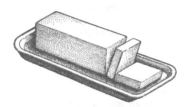

6 squares (1 ounce each) semisweet chocolate
½ cup (1 stick) I CAN'T BELIEVE IT'S NOT BUTTER!® Spread
¾ cup sugar
2 eggs
⅓ cup all-purpose flour
¼ cup unsweetened cocoa powder

1½ teaspoons vanilla extract
1 teaspoon baking powder
¼ teaspoon salt
2 cups coarsely chopped pecans or walnuts
1 cup semisweet chocolate chips

Preheat oven to 325°F. Grease baking sheets; set aside.

In medium microwave-safe bowl, heat chocolate squares and I Can't Believe It's Not Butter! Spread on HIGH (Full Power) 1 to 2 minutes or until chocolate is almost melted. Stir until completely melted.

In large bowl, with electric mixer, beat sugar and eggs until light and ribbony, about 2 minutes. Beat in chocolate mixture, flour, cocoa, vanilla, baking powder and salt, scraping side occasionally, until well blended. Stir in nuts and chocolate chips. Drop dough by rounded tablespoonfuls onto prepared sheets, about 2 inches apart.

Bake 15 minutes or until cookies are just set. On wire rack, let stand 2 minutes; remove from sheets and cool completely.

# Oatmeal Raisin Cookies

**Makes about 3 dozen**

¼ cup (4 tablespoons)
   margarine, softened
1¼ teaspoons EQUAL®
   Measure (5 packets) *or*
   2 tablespoons fructose *or*
   3 tablespoons granulated
   sugar
¼ cup egg substitute *or* 2 egg
   whites
¾ cup unsweetened applesauce
¼ cup frozen unsweetened
   apple juice concentrate,
   thawed

1 teaspoon vanilla
1 cup all-purpose flour
1 teaspoon baking soda
½ teaspoon ground cinnamon
¼ teaspoon salt (optional)
1½ cups QUAKER® Oats (quick or
   old fashioned, uncooked)
⅓ cup raisins, chopped

Heat oven to 350°F. Lightly spray cookie sheets with vegetable oil cooking spray. Beat together margarine and Equal® Measure until creamy. Beat in egg substitute. Add applesauce, apple juice concentrate and vanilla; beat well. Blend in combined flour, baking soda, cinnamon and salt. Stir in oats and chopped raisins. Drop by rounded teaspoonfuls onto prepared cookie sheets. Bake 15 to 17 minutes or until cookies are firm to the touch and lightly browned. Cool 1 minute on cookie sheets; remove to wire rack. Cool completely. Store in airtight container.

# Heath Bits Peanut Butter Cookies

**Makes 3 dozen cookies**

½ cup shortening
¾ cup REESE'S® Creamy Peanut Butter
1¼ cups packed light brown sugar
3 tablespoons milk
1 tablespoon vanilla extract

1 egg
1½ cups all-purpose flour
¾ teaspoon baking soda
¾ teaspoon salt
1⅓ cups (8-ounce package) HEATH® BITS, divided

*Note:*

If cookies start to fall apart when removing them from the cookie sheet, allow them to stand another minute or two—they should firm up slightly before being transferred to a wire rack.

*1.* Heat oven to 375°F.

*2.* Beat shortening, peanut butter, brown sugar, milk and vanilla in large bowl until well blended. Add egg; beat just until blended. Combine flour, baking soda and salt; gradually beat into peanut butter mixture. Stir in 1 cup Heath Bits; reserve remainder for topping.

*3.* Drop by heaping teaspoons about 2 inches apart onto ungreased cookie sheet; top each with reserved Heath Bits.

*4.* Bake 7 to 8 minutes or until set. *Do not overbake.* Cool 2 minutes. Remove to wire rack. Cool completely.

# Pistachio and White Chocolate Cookies

1 cup shelled pistachio nuts
1¼ cups firmly packed light
   brown sugar
¾ Butter Flavor CRISCO® Stick
   or ¾ cup Butter Flavor
   CRISCO® all-vegetable
   shortening
2 tablespoons milk

1 tablespoon vanilla
1 egg
1¾ cups all-purpose flour
1 teaspoon salt
¾ teaspoon baking soda
1 cup white chocolate chips or
   chunks

Makes about 3 dozen cookies

*1.* Heat oven to 350°F. Spread pistachio nuts on baking sheet. Bake at 350°F for 7 to 10 minutes or until toasted, stirring several times. Place nuts in kitchen towel; rub with towel to remove most of skin. Cool nuts. Chop coarsely; reserve.

*2.* Increase oven temperature to 375°F. Place sheets of foil on countertop for cooling cookies.

*3.* Place brown sugar, ¾ cup shortening, milk and vanilla in large bowl. Beat at medium speed with electric mixer until well blended. Add egg; beat well.

*4.* Combine flour, salt and baking soda in medium bowl. Add to shortening mixture; beat at low speed just until blended. Stir in white chocolate chips and reserved pistachios.

*5.* Drop by rounded tablespoonfuls of dough 3 inches apart onto ungreased baking sheets.

*6.* Bake one baking sheet at a time at 375°F for 8 to 10 minutes for chewy cookies, or 11 to 13 minutes for crisp cookies. *Do not overbake.* Cool 2 minutes on baking sheet. Remove to foil to cool completely.

# Raisin Spice Drops

**Makes about 4½ dozen cookies**

¾ cup (1½ sticks) margarine, softened
⅔ cup granulated sugar
⅔ cup firmly packed brown sugar
2 eggs
1 teaspoon vanilla
2½ cups QUAKER® Oats (quick or old fashioned, uncooked)
1¼ cups all-purpose flour
1 teaspoon ground cinnamon
½ teaspoon baking soda
½ teaspoon salt (optional)
¼ teaspoon ground nutmeg
⅔ cup raisins
½ cup chopped nuts

Preheat oven to 350°F. In large bowl, beat margarine and sugars until fluffy. Blend in eggs and vanilla. Add remaining ingredients; mix well. Drop dough by rounded teaspoonfuls onto ungreased cookie sheets. Bake 8 to 10 minutes or until light golden brown. Cool on wire rack. Store tightly covered.

# Reese's® Chewy Chocolate Cookies

**Makes about 4½ dozen cookies**

2 cups all-purpose flour
¾ cup HERSHEY'S Cocoa
1 teaspoon baking soda
½ teaspoon salt
1¼ cups (2½ sticks) butter or margarine, softened
2 cups sugar
2 eggs
2 teaspoons vanilla extract
1⅔ cups (10-ounce package) REESE'S® Peanut Butter Chips

*1.* Heat oven to 350°F. Stir together flour, cocoa, baking soda and salt; set aside.

*2.* Beat butter and sugar in large bowl with mixer until fluffy. Add eggs and vanilla; beat well. Gradually add flour mixture, beating well. Stir in peanut butter chips. Drop by rounded teaspoons onto ungreased cookie sheet.

*3.* Bake 8 to 9 minutes. (Do not overbake; cookies will be soft. They will puff while baking and flatten while cooling.) Cool slightly; remove from cookie sheet to wire rack. Cool completely.

# Crunchy Chocolate Chip Cookies

| | | |
|---|---|---|
| 2¼ cups unsifted all-purpose flour<br>1 teaspoon ARM & HAMMER® Baking Soda<br>1 teaspoon salt<br>1 cup softened margarine or butter<br>¾ cup granulated sugar | ¾ cup packed brown sugar<br>1 teaspoon vanilla extract<br>2 eggs<br>2 cups (12 ounces) semi-sweet chocolate chips<br>1 cup chopped nuts (peanuts, walnuts or pecans) | **Makes about 8 dozen 2-inch cookies** |

Preheat oven to 375°F. Sift together flour, Baking Soda and salt in small bowl. Beat margarine, sugars and vanilla in large bowl with electric mixer until creamy. Beat in eggs. Gradually add flour mixture; mix well. Stir in chocolate chips and nuts. Drop by rounded teaspoons onto ungreased cookie sheets. Bake 8 minutes or until lightly browned.

*Note:*

When baking cookies, space the mounds of dough about 2 inches apart on cookie sheets to allow for spreading unless the recipe directs otherwise.

# Cherry Cashew Cookies

**Makes 4½ dozen cookies**

1 cup butter or margarine, softened
¾ cup granulated sugar
¾ cup packed brown sugar
2 eggs
1 teaspoon vanilla extract

2¼ cups all-purpose flour
1 teaspoon baking soda
1 (10-ounce) package vanilla milk chips (about 1⅔ cups)
1½ cups dried tart cherries
1 cup broken salted cashews

In large mixer bowl, combine butter, granulated sugar, brown sugar, eggs and vanilla. Mix with electric mixer on medium speed until thoroughly combined. Combine flour and baking soda; gradually add flour mixture to butter mixture. Stir in vanilla milk chips, dried cherries and cashews. Drop by rounded tablespoonfuls onto ungreased baking sheets.

*Note:*

Granulated sugar will keep indefinitely stored in a container in a cool, dry place. Brown sugar has a shorter shelf life; it will dry out and harden if exposed to air. Adding an apple slice to the container will return moisture to the sugar.

Bake in preheated oven 375°F 12 to 15 minutes or until light golden brown. Cool on wire racks and store in airtight container.

Favorite recipe from **Cherry Marketing Institute**

# Ginger Snap Oats

¾ Butter Flavor CRISCO® Stick
   or ¾ cup Butter Flavor
   CRISCO® all-vegetable
   shortening plus additional
   for greasing
1 cup packed brown sugar
½ cup granulated sugar
½ cup molasses
2 teaspoons vinegar

2 eggs
1¼ cups all-purpose flour
1 tablespoon ground ginger
1½ teaspoons baking soda
½ teaspoon ground cinnamon
¼ teaspoon ground cloves
2¾ cups quick oats (not instant
   or old-fashioned), uncooked
1½ cups raisins

**Makes about 5 dozen cookies**

*1.* Heat oven to 350°F. Grease baking sheets with shortening. Place sheets of foil on countertop for cooling cookies.

*2.* Combine ¾ cup shortening, brown sugar, granulated sugar, molasses, vinegar and eggs in large mixer bowl. Beat at medium speed of electric mixer until well blended.

*3.* Combine flour, ginger, baking soda, cinnamon and cloves. Mix into shortening mixture at low speed until blended. Stir in oats and raisins.

*4.* Drop dough by rounded teaspoonfuls 2 inches apart onto prepared baking sheets.

*5.* Bake one baking sheet at a time 350°F for 11 to 14 minutes. *Do not overbake.* Cool 2 minutes on cookie sheets. Remove cookies to foil to cool completely.

*Note:*

Before measuring molasses or other sticky liquids, lightly coat a measuring cup with nonstick cooking spray so the molasses will slide out easily instead of clinging to the cup.

# Fudge Cookies

**Makes about 5 dozen cookies**

1 cup (6 ounces) semisweet chocolate chips
½ cup (1 stick) butter, softened
1 cup granulated sugar
2 eggs
1½ cups all-purpose flour

Dash salt
1½ cups coarsely chopped pecans or walnuts
Fudge Frosting (recipe follows)

*1.* Preheat oven to 375°F. Lightly grease cookie sheets or line with parchment paper. Melt chocolate chips in top of double boiler over hot, not boiling, water. Remove from heat; cool. Beat butter, granulated sugar and eggs in large bowl until smooth. Beat in melted chocolate. Gradually add flour and salt, mixing until smooth. Stir in nuts.

*2.* Drop dough by rounded teaspoonfuls 2 inches apart onto prepared cookie sheets. Bake 10 to 12 minutes or until slightly firm. Cool 5 minutes on cookie sheet, then remove to wire racks. While cookies bake, prepare Fudge Frosting. Frost cookies while still warm. Cool until frosting is set.

## Fudge Frosting

1 square (1 ounce) semisweet chocolate
3 tablespoons heavy cream

1 cup powdered sugar
1 teaspoon vanilla

Melt chocolate with cream in small heavy saucepan over medium heat, stirring until chocolate melts completely. Remove from heat; beat in powdered sugar and vanilla. Spread over cookies while frosting is still warm.

# Ranger Cookies

1 cup (2 sticks) margarine or
   butter, softened
1 cup granulated sugar
1 cup firmly packed brown
   sugar
2 eggs
1 teaspoon vanilla
2 cups all-purpose flour
1 teaspoon baking soda

½ teaspoon baking powder
½ teaspoon salt (optional)
2 cups QUAKER® Oats (quick or
   old fashioned, uncooked)
2 cups cornflakes
½ cup flaked or shredded
   coconut
½ cup chopped nuts

**Makes 2 dozen large cookies**

Heat oven to 350°F. Beat margarine and sugars until creamy. Add eggs and vanilla; beat well. Add combined flour, baking soda, baking powder and salt; mix well. Stir in oats, cornflakes, coconut and nuts; mix well. Drop dough by heaping tablespoonfuls onto ungreased cookie sheets. Bake 10 to 12 minutes or until light golden brown. Cool 1 minute on cookie sheets; remove to wire rack. Cool completely. Store tightly covered.

# Peanut Chip Cookies

**Makes 4 dozen cookies**

1½ cups packed dark brown sugar
1 cup PETER PAN® Crunchy Peanut Butter
¾ cup butter
¾ cup granulated sugar
¼ cup water
1 egg

1¼ teaspoons vanilla extract
2 cups rolled oats
1½ cups all-purpose flour
1½ teaspoons baking powder
¼ teaspoon salt
1 cup semi-sweet chocolate chips

In large mixer bowl, beat *first* 4 ingredients until creamy and well blended. Beat in water, egg and vanilla. In medium bowl, mix *remaining* ingredients. Stir into peanut butter mixture until well blended. Drop by heaping teaspoonfuls onto greased baking sheets. Bake at 350°F 12 to 15 minutes or until lightly browned around edges. Cool on wire racks and store in an airtight container.

# Red's Ultimate "M&M's"® Cookies

**Makes about 3 dozen cookies**

1 cup (2 sticks) butter, softened
½ cup granulated sugar
½ cup firmly packed light brown sugar
1 large egg
1 teaspoon vanilla extract

2 cups all-purpose flour
½ teaspoon baking soda
⅛ teaspoon salt
2 cups "M&M's"® Milk Chocolate Mini Baking Bits
¾ cup chopped nuts, optional

Preheat oven to 350°F. In large bowl cream butter and sugars until light and fluffy; beat in egg and vanilla. In medium bowl combine flour, baking soda and salt; blend into creamed mixture.

Stir in "M&M's"® Milk Chocolate Mini Baking Bits and nuts, if desired. Drop by heaping tablespoonfuls about 2 inches apart onto ungreased cookie sheets. Bake 10 to 13 minutes or until edges are lightly browned and centers are still soft. Do not overbake. Cool 1 minute on cookie sheets; cool completely on wire racks. Store in tightly covered container.

# Spicy Oatmeal Raisin Cookies

1 package DUNCAN HINES®
   Moist Deluxe® Spice Cake
   Mix
4 egg whites
1 cup uncooked quick-cooking
   oats (not instant or
   old-fashioned)

½ cup vegetable oil
½ cup raisins

**Makes about 4 dozen cookies**

*1.* Preheat oven to 350°F. Grease baking sheets.

*2.* Combine cake mix, egg whites, oats and oil in large mixing bowl. Beat at low speed with electric mixer until blended. Stir in raisins. Drop by rounded teaspoonfuls onto prepared baking sheets.

*3.* Bake at 350°F for 7 to 9 minutes or until lightly browned. Cool 1 minute on baking sheets. Remove to cooling racks; cool completely.

## *Note:*

Quick-cooking and old-fashioned rolled oats are very similar; the quick-cooking oats simply cook faster because they have been rolled into thinner flakes. Instant oats have been cut into very small pieces, cut and dried—they cannot be used in baking.

# Chocolate-Nut Cookies

**Makes 3½ dozen cookies**

1⅓ cups all-purpose flour
⅓ cup unsweetened cocoa powder
½ teaspoon baking soda
¼ teaspoon salt
1 cup (2 sticks) IMPERIAL® Spread, softened
¾ cup granulated sugar
¾ cup firmly packed light brown sugar
2 large eggs

2 squares (1 ounce each) unsweetened chocolate, melted and cooled slightly
½ teaspoon vanilla extract
1 cup chopped pecans, toasted
1 cup semi-sweet chocolate chips
½ cup skinned hazelnuts, coarsely chopped and toasted

In medium bowl, combine flour, cocoa, baking soda and salt; set aside.

In large bowl, with electric mixer, beat Imperial Spread, granulated sugar and brown sugar until light and fluffy, about 5 minutes. Beat in eggs, one at a time, beating well after each addition. Beat in melted chocolate and vanilla. With mixer on low, beat in flour mixture until combined. Stir in pecans, chocolate chips and hazelnuts. Cover and freeze dough until firm, about 1 hour.

Preheat oven to 375°F. On *ungreased* baking sheets, drop dough by level tablespoonfuls, 2 inches apart.

Bake 10 minutes or just until set on top. On wire rack, let stand 1 minute; remove from sheets and cool completely.

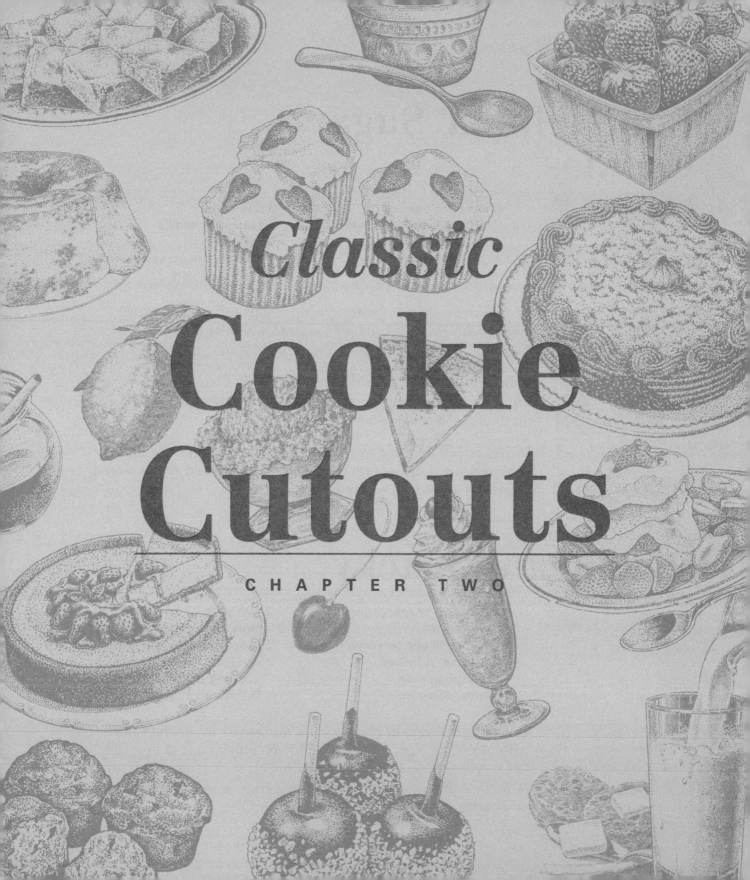

# Classic
# Cookie
# Cutouts

## CHAPTER TWO

# Philadelphia® Sugar Cookies

**Makes 3½ dozen**

**Prep Time:**
*10 minutes plus refrigerating*

**Bake Time:**
*15 minutes*

1 package (8 ounces) PHILADELPHIA® Cream Cheese, softened
1 cup (2 sticks) butter *or* margarine, softened

⅔ cup sugar
¼ teaspoon vanilla
2 cups flour
Colored sugar, sprinkles and colored gels

BEAT cream cheese, butter, ⅔ cup sugar and vanilla with electric mixer on medium speed until well blended. Mix in flour. Refrigerate several hours or overnight.

ROLL dough to ¼-inch thickness on lightly floured surface. Cut into desired shapes; sprinkle with colored sugar. Place on ungreased cookie sheets.

BAKE at 350°F for 12 to 15 minutes or until edges are lightly browned. Cool on wire racks. Decorate as desired with colored sugar, sprinkles and colored gels.

# European Kolacky

**Makes about 3 dozen cookies**

1 cup butter or margarine, softened
1 package (8 ounces) cream cheese, softened
1 tablespoon milk
1 tablespoon sugar

1 egg yolk
1½ cups all-purpose flour
½ teaspoon baking powder
1 can SOLO® or 1 jar BAKER® Filling (any flavor)
Powdered sugar

Cream butter, cream cheese, milk and sugar in medium bowl with electric mixer until thoroughly blended. Beat in egg yolk. Sift together flour and baking powder; stir into butter mixture to make stiff dough. Cover and refrigerate several hours or overnight.

Preheat oven to 400°F. Roll out dough on lightly floured surface to ¼-inch thickness. Cut dough with floured 2-inch cookie cutter. Place cookies on ungreased cookie sheets about 1 inch apart. Make depression in centers of cookies with thumb or back of spoon. Spoon ½ teaspoon filling into centers of cookies.

Bake 10 to 12 minutes or until lightly browned. Remove from baking sheets and cool completely on wire racks. Sprinkle with powdered sugar just before serving.

# Old-Fashioned Molasses Cookies

| | | |
|---|---|---|
| 4 cups sifted all-purpose flour<br>2 teaspoons ARM & HAMMER® Baking Soda<br>2 teaspoons ground ginger<br>1 teaspoon ground cinnamon<br>⅛ teaspoon salt<br>1½ cups molasses | ½ cup butter-flavored shortening<br>¼ cup butter or margarine, melted<br>⅓ cup boiling water<br>Sugar | **Makes about 3 dozen cookies** |

In medium bowl, combine flour, Baking Soda, spices and salt. In large bowl, mix molasses, shortening, butter and water. Add dry ingredients to molasses mixture; blend well. Cover; refrigerate until firm, about 2 hours. Roll out dough ¼ inch thick on well-floured surface. Cut out with 3½-inch cookie cutters; sprinkle with sugar. Place 2 inches apart on ungreased cookie sheets. Bake in preheated 375°F oven about 12 minutes. Remove to wire racks to cool.

*Note:*

If a recipe doesn't specify the type of molasses, either dark or light may be used. Dark molasses has a more robust, slightly less sweet flavor than light molasses. Do not use blackstrap molasses, which is somewhat bitter.

# Berry Treasures

**Makes about 2 dozen sandwich cookies**

| | |
|---|---|
| 2½ cups all-purpose flour | ¼ teaspoon baking soda |
| ½ cup sugar | 2 tablespoons milk |
| ⅔ cup butter | 1½ teaspoons vanilla |
| 1 egg | ¾ cup mixed berry preserves |
| ½ teaspoon salt | Additional sugar |

*1.* Preheat oven to 350°F. Combine flour, ½ cup sugar, butter, egg, salt, baking soda, milk and vanilla in large bowl. Beat 3 to 4 minutes, scraping bowl often, until well mixed.

*2.* Roll out dough, ½ at a time, to ⅛-inch thickness on well-floured surface. Cut out cookies with 2½-inch round cookie cutter. Place ½ of cookies 2 inches apart on ungreased cookie sheets; place level teaspoonful preserves in center of each cookie.

*3.* Make small "X" or cutout with very small cookie cutter in top of each remaining cutout. Place second cookie over preserves; press edges together with fork. Sprinkle with sugar.

*4.* Bake 11 to 13 minutes or until edges are very lightly browned. Remove cookies immediately to wire racks to cool completely.

# Cinnamon-Chocolate Cutouts

2 squares (1 ounce each) unsweetened chocolate
½ cup (1 stick) butter, softened
1 cup granulated sugar
1 egg
1 teaspoon vanilla
3 cups all-purpose flour

2 teaspoons ground cinnamon
½ teaspoon baking soda
¼ teaspoon salt
½ cup sour cream
Decorator Icing (page 68)

Makes about 6 dozen cookies

Melt chocolate in top of double boiler over hot, not boiling, water. Remove from heat; cool. Cream butter, melted chocolate, granulated sugar, egg and vanilla in large bowl until light. Combine flour, cinnamon, baking soda and salt in small bowl. Stir into creamed mixture with sour cream until smooth. Cover; refrigerate at least 30 minutes.

Preheat oven to 400°F. Lightly grease cookie sheets or line with parchment paper. Roll out dough, one fourth at a time, ¼ inch thick on lightly floured surface. Cut out with cookie cutters. Place 2 inches apart on prepared cookie sheets. Bake 10 minutes or until lightly browned, but not dark. Remove to wire racks to cool.

Prepare Decorator Icing. Spoon into pastry bag fitted with small tip, or small heavy-duty plastic bag. (If using plastic bag, close securely. With scissors, snip off small corner from one side of bag.) Decorate cookies with icing.

# Cocoa Gingerbread Cookies

**Makes about 6 dozen cookies**

¼ cup butter, softened
2 tablespoons shortening
⅓ cup packed brown sugar
¼ cup dark molasses
1 egg
1½ cups all-purpose flour
¼ cup unsweetened cocoa
   powder

½ teaspoon baking soda
½ teaspoon ground ginger
½ teaspoon ground cinnamon
¼ teaspoon salt
¼ teaspoon ground nutmeg
⅛ teaspoon ground cloves
   Decorator Icing (recipe
   follows)

Preheat oven to 400°F. Lightly grease cookie sheets or line with parchment paper. Cream butter, shortening, brown sugar and molasses in large bowl. Add egg; beat until light. Combine flour, cocoa, baking soda, ginger, cinnamon, salt, nutmeg and cloves in small bowl. Blend into creamed mixture until smooth. (If dough is too soft to handle, cover and refrigerate until firm.) Roll out dough ¼ inch thick on lightly floured surface. Cut out with cookie cutters. Place 2 inches apart on prepared cookie sheets. Bake 8 to 10 minutes or until firm. Remove to wire racks to cool. Prepare Decorator Icing. Spoon into pastry bag fitted with small tip. Decorate cookies with icing.

## Decorator Icing

1 egg white*
3½ cups powdered sugar
1 teaspoon almond or lemon
   extract

2 to 3 tablespoons water

*Use clean, uncracked egg.

Beat egg white in large bowl until frothy. Gradually beat in powdered sugar until blended. Add almond extract and enough water to moisten. Beat until smooth and glossy.

# Butterfly Cookies

2¼ cups all-purpose flour
¼ teaspoon salt
1 cup sugar
¾ cup (1½ sticks) butter, softened
1 egg
1 teaspoon vanilla

1 teaspoon almond extract
White frosting, assorted food colors, colored sugars, assorted small decors, gummy fruit and hard candies for decoration

**Makes about 20 to 22 cookies**

*Note:*

**When cutting out cookies, be sure to press down firmly on the cookie cutter so it cuts all the way through the dough. Use a small offset spatula to transfer the cutouts to a cookie sheet.**

*1.* Combine flour and salt in medium bowl; set aside.

*2.* Beat sugar and butter in large bowl at medium speed of electric mixer until fluffy. Beat in egg, vanilla and almond extract. Gradually add flour mixture. Beat at low speed until well blended. Divide dough in half. Cover; refrigerate 30 minutes or until firm.

*3.* Preheat oven to 350°F. Grease cookie sheets. Roll half of dough on lightly floured surface to ¼-inch thickness. Cut out cookies using butterfly cookie cutters. Repeat with remaining dough.

*4.* Bake 12 to 15 minutes or until edges are lightly browned. Remove to wire racks; cool completely.

*5.* Tint portions of white frosting with assorted food colors. Spread desired colors of frosting over cookies. Decorate as desired.

# Cut-Out Sugar Cookies

**Makes about 3 to 4 dozen cookies**

1¼ cups granulated sugar
1 Butter Flavor CRISCO® Stick or 1 cup Butter Flavor CRISCO® all-vegetable shortening
2 eggs
¼ cup light corn syrup or regular pancake syrup

1 tablespoon vanilla
3 cups all-purpose flour plus 4 tablespoons, divided
¾ teaspoon baking powder
½ teaspoon baking soda
½ teaspoon salt
Granulated sugar or colored sugar crystals

*1.* Combine sugar and 1 cup shortening in large bowl. Beat at medium speed of electric mixer until well blended. Add eggs, syrup and vanilla. Beat until well blended and fluffy.

*2.* Combine 3 cups flour, baking powder, baking soda and salt. Add gradually to shortening mixture at low speed. Mix until well blended.

*3.* Divide dough into 4 quarters. Wrap each quarter of dough with plastic wrap. Refrigerate at least 1 hour. Keep refrigerated until ready to use.

*4.* Heat oven to 375°F. Place sheets of foil on countertop for cooling cookies.

*5.* Spread 1 tablespoon flour on large sheet of waxed paper. Place one quarter of dough on floured paper. Flatten slightly with hands. Turn dough over and cover with another large sheet of waxed paper. Roll dough to ¼-inch thickness. Remove top sheet of waxed paper. Cut out with floured cutters. Place 2 inches apart on ungreased baking sheets. Repeat with remaining dough.

*6.* Sprinkle with granulated sugar or colored sugar crystals, or leave plain to frost or decorate when cooled.

*7.* Bake one baking sheet at a time at 375°F for 5 to 9 minutes, depending on size of cookies (bake smaller, thinner cookies closer to 5 minutes; larger cookies closer to 9 minutes). *Do not overbake.* Cool 2 minutes on baking sheets. Remove cookies to foil to cool completely, then frost and decorate, if desired.

# Cookie Pops

| 1 package (20 ounces) refrigerated sugar cookie dough<br>All-purpose flour (optional) | 20 (4-inch) lollipop sticks<br>Assorted frostings, glazes and decors | Makes 20 cookies |

*1.* Preheat oven to 350°F. Grease cookie sheets.

*2.* Remove dough from wrapper according to package directions. Sprinkle with flour to minimize sticking, if necessary.

*3.* Cut dough in half. Reserve 1 half; refrigerate remaining dough. Roll reserved dough to ⅛-inch thickness. Cut out cookies using 3½-inch cookie cutters.

*4.* Place lollipop sticks on cookies so that tips of sticks are imbedded in cookies. Carefully turn cookies so sticks are in back; place on prepared cookie sheets. Repeat with remaining dough.

*5.* Bake 7 to 11 minutes or until edges are lightly browned. Cool cookies on cookie sheets 2 minutes. Remove cookies to wire racks; cool completely.

*6.* Decorate with frostings, glazes and decors as desired.

*Note:*

To give Cookie Pops as gifts or party favors, wrap them individually in plain or colored cellophane and tie them with ribbon or raffia. Cookie Pops can also be used as place cards; use frosting to personalize each pop with a guest's name.

# Peanut Butter & Jelly Kolacky

**Makes 2½ dozen cookies**

¼ cup (½ stick) butter, softened
1 package (3 ounces) cream cheese, softened
3 tablespoons creamy peanut butter, divided
¾ cup all-purpose flour

2 tablespoons plus 1½ teaspoons any flavor seedless jam
½ cup "M&M's"® Chocolate Mini Baking Bits
Powdered sugar

*Note:*

**Make sure that the cookies have cooled completely before dusting with powdered sugar. If sprinkled on warm cookies, the sugar will simply dissolve and disappear.**

In medium bowl beat butter, cream cheese and 2 tablespoons peanut butter until well blended; stir in flour. Wrap and refrigerate dough 2 hours. Preheat oven to 350°F. Lightly grease cookie sheets; set aside. In small bowl combine remaining 1 tablespoon peanut butter with jam. On lightly floured surface roll dough to ⅛-inch thickness. Cut into 2-inch squares. Place rounded ¼ teaspoon jam mixture and 4 to 5 "M&M's"® Chocolate Mini Baking Bits on each square. Pinch together 2 opposite corners; fold down. Place 1 inch apart on prepared cookie sheets. Press 1 "M&M's"® Chocolate Mini Baking Bit onto fold of each cookie. Bake 10 to 12 minutes. Cool on cookie sheets 1 minute; cool completely on wire racks. Sprinkle with powdered sugar. Store in tightly covered container.

# Gingerbread Cookies

½ cup shortening
⅓ cup packed light brown sugar
¼ cup dark molasses
1 egg white
½ teaspoon vanilla
1½ cups all-purpose flour

½ teaspoon baking soda
¼ teaspoon baking powder
½ teaspoon salt
1 teaspoon ground cinnamon
½ teaspoon ground ginger

Makes about
2½ dozen cookies

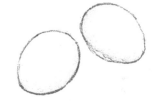

*1.* Beat shortening, brown sugar, molasses, egg white and vanilla in large bowl at high speed of electric mixer until smooth. Combine flour, baking soda, baking powder, salt and spices in small bowl. Add to shortening mixture; mix well. Cover; refrigerate until firm, about 8 hours or overnight.

*2.* Preheat oven to 350°F. Grease cookie sheets.

*3.* Roll dough on lightly floured surface to ⅛-inch thickness. Cut into desired shapes with cookie cutters. Place on prepared cookie sheets.

*4.* Bake 6 to 8 minutes or until edges begin to brown. Remove to wire racks; cool completely.

# Lone Star Peanut Butter Cutouts

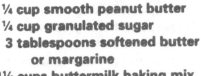

| Makes about 2 dozen cookies | |
|---|---|

¼ cup smooth peanut butter
¼ cup granulated sugar
3 tablespoons softened butter or margarine
1¼ cups buttermilk baking mix
2 tablespoons water

½ teaspoon ground cinnamon
⅔ cup dry-roasted peanut halves
½ cup semisweet chocolate chips

In large bowl, stir together peanut butter, sugar and butter until smooth. Stir in baking mix, water and cinnamon until well-blended. Shape mixture into ball. Wrap dough with plastic wrap and chill about 1 hour or until firm. Cut dough in half. Roll each piece ⅛ inch thick on lightly floured board. Cut dough into shapes with cookie cutter; transfer cutouts to *ungreased* cookie sheets. Press several roasted peanut halves into top of each cookie. Bake in preheated 375°F oven 8 to 10 minutes or until golden brown around edges. With spatula, transfer cookies to cooling rack.

Melt chocolate chips in microwave on HIGH 2 minutes; stir until smooth. Drizzle chocolate glaze over each cookie. Refrigerate until glaze is set. Store cookies in airtight container.

Favorite recipe from **Texas Peanut Producers Board**

# Jam-Up Oatmeal Cookies

1 Butter Flavor CRISCO® Stick or 1 cup Butter Flavor CRISCO® all-vegetable shortening plus additional for greasing
1½ cups firmly packed brown sugar
2 eggs
2 teaspoons almond extract
2 cups all-purpose flour

1 teaspoon baking powder
1 teaspoon salt
½ teaspoon baking soda
2½ cups quick oats (not instant or old-fashioned), uncooked
1 cup finely chopped pecans
1 jar (12 ounces) strawberry jam
Sugar for sprinkling

**Makes about 2 dozen cookies**

*1.* Combine 1 cup shortening and brown sugar in large bowl. Beat at medium speed of electric mixer until well blended. Beat in eggs and almond extract.

*2.* Combine flour, baking powder, salt and baking soda. Mix into shortening mixture at low speed until just blended. Stir in oats and chopped nuts with spoon. Cover and refrigerate at least 1 hour.

*3.* Heat oven to 350°F. Grease baking sheets with shortening. Place sheets of foil on countertop for cooling cookies.

*4.* Roll out dough, half at a time, to about ¼-inch thickness on floured surface. Cut out with 2½-inch round cookie cutter. Place 1 teaspoonful of jam in center of half of the rounds. Top with remaining rounds. Press edges to seal. Prick centers; sprinkle with sugar. Place 1 inch apart on baking sheets.

*5.* Bake one baking sheet at a time at 350°F for 12 to 15 minutes or until lightly browned. *Do not overbake*. Cool 2 minutes on baking sheets. Remove cookies to foil to cool completely.

# Double-Dipped Hazelnut Crisps

**Makes about 4 dozen cookies**

¾ cup semisweet chocolate chips
1¼ cups all-purpose flour
¾ cup powdered sugar
⅔ cup whole hazelnuts, toasted, hulled and finely ground*
¼ teaspoon instant espresso powder
Dash salt
½ cup butter, softened

2 teaspoons vanilla
4 squares (1 ounce each) bittersweet or semisweet chocolate
2 teaspoons shortening, divided
4 ounces white chocolate

*To grind hazelnuts, place in food processor or blender. Process until thoroughly ground with a dry, not pasty, texture.

*1.* Preheat oven to 350°F. Lightly grease cookie sheets or line with parchment paper. Melt chocolate chips in top of double boiler over hot, not boiling, water. Remove from heat; cool. Blend flour, powdered sugar, hazelnuts, espresso powder and salt in large bowl. Blend in butter, melted chocolate and vanilla until dough is stiff but smooth. (If dough is too soft to handle, cover and refrigerate until firm.)

*2.* Roll out dough, ¼ at a time, to ⅛-inch thickness on lightly floured surface. Cut out with 2-inch scalloped round cutters. Place 2 inches apart on prepared cookie sheets. Bake 8 minutes or until not quite firm. (Cookies should not brown. They will puff up during baking and then flatten again.) Remove to wire racks to cool.

*3.* Place bittersweet chocolate and 1 teaspoon shortening in small bowl. Place bowl over hot water; stir until chocolate is melted and smooth. Dip cookies, 1 at a time, halfway into bittersweet chocolate. Place on waxed paper; refrigerate until chocolate is set. Repeat melting process with white chocolate. Dip plain halves of cookies into white chocolate; refrigerate until set. Store cookies in airtight container in cool place. (If cookies are frozen, chocolate might discolor.)

# Peek-A-Boo Apricot Cookies

4 ounces bittersweet chocolate
    candy bar, broken into
    pieces
3 cups all-purpose flour
½ teaspoon baking soda
½ teaspoon salt

⅔ cup butter, softened
¾ cup sugar
2 eggs
2 teaspoons vanilla
    Apricot preserves

Makes about
1½ dozen sandwich
cookies

*1.* Melt chocolate in small bowl set in larger bowl of very hot water, stirring twice. Combine flour, baking soda and salt in medium bowl.

*2.* Beat butter and sugar in large bowl with electric mixer at medium speed until light and fluffy. Beat in eggs, 1 at a time, beating well after each addition. Beat in vanilla and melted chocolate. Beat in flour mixture at low speed until well blended.

*3.* Divide dough into 2 rounds; flatten into discs. Wrap in plastic wrap; refrigerate 2 hours or until firm.

*4.* Preheat oven to 350°F. Roll out dough on lightly floured surface to ¼- to ⅛-inch thickness. Cut out rounds with 2½-inch cutter. Cut 1-inch centers out of half the rounds. Reserve scraps. Place rounds and rings on ungreased cookie sheets. Repeat rolling and cutting with remaining scraps of dough.

*5.* Bake cookies 9 to 10 minutes or until set. Let cookies stand on cookie sheets 2 minutes. Remove to wire racks; cool completely.

*6.* To assemble cookies, spread about 1½ teaspoons preserves over flat side of cookie rounds; top with cookie rings to form sandwiches. Store tightly covered at room temperature.

Note: *These cookies do not freeze well.*

*Note:*

When melting
chocolate in a double
boiler, be careful that
no steam or water
gets into the chocolate.
Moisture, whether
from utensils or a drop
of water, may cause
chocolate to seize
(become stiff and
grainy).

# Cinnamon Stars

| Makes 3 to 3½ dozen cookies |
|---|

2 tablespoons sugar
¾ teaspoon ground cinnamon
¾ cup butter or margarine, softened
2 egg yolks

1 teaspoon vanilla extract
1 package DUNCAN HINES®
   Moist Deluxe® French
   Vanilla Cake Mix

*1.* Preheat oven to 375°F. Combine sugar and cinnamon in small bowl. Set aside.

*2.* Combine butter, egg yolks and vanilla extract in large bowl. Blend in cake mix gradually. Roll dough to ⅛-inch thickness on lightly floured surface. Cut with 2½-inch star cookie cutter. Place 2 inches apart on ungreased baking sheet.

*3.* Sprinkle cookies with cinnamon-sugar mixture. Bake at 375°F for 6 to 8 minutes or until edges are light golden brown. Cool 1 minute on baking sheet. Remove to cooling rack. Cool completely. Store in airtight container.

<u>Tip:</u> *You can use your favorite cookie cutter in place of the star cookie cutter.*

# Black and White Cutouts

| Makes 3 to 4 dozen cookies |
|---|

1 cup butter, softened
¾ cup granulated sugar
¾ cup packed light brown sugar
2 eggs
1 teaspoon vanilla
2¾ cups plus 2 tablespoons
   all-purpose flour, divided
1 teaspoon baking soda

¾ teaspoon salt
¼ cup unsweetened cocoa
   powder
1 (4-ounce) white baking bar,
   broken into ½-inch pieces
1 (4-ounce) package semisweet
   chocolate chips

Beat butter, granulated sugar and brown sugar in large bowl until light and fluffy. Beat in eggs, one at a time; add vanilla. Combine 2¾ cups flour, baking soda and salt in medium bowl; add to butter mixture. Beat well; reserve half of dough.

To make chocolate dough, beat cocoa into remaining dough until well blended. To make butter cookie dough, beat remaining 2 tablespoons flour into reserved dough. Flatten each dough into disc; wrap in plastic wrap and refrigerate 1½ hours or until firm. (Dough may be refrigerated up to 3 days before baking.)

Preheat oven to 375°F. Working with one type of dough at a time, place dough on lightly floured surface. Roll out to ¼-inch thickness. Cut into desired shapes with cookie cutters. Place cut-outs 1 inch apart on ungreased cookie sheets. Bake 9 to 11 minutes or until set. Let cookies stand on cookie sheets 2 minutes. Remove to wire racks; cool completely.

For white chocolate drizzle, place baking bar pieces in small resealable plastic bag; seal bag. Heat in microwave oven at MEDIUM (50% power) 1 minute. Turn bag over; heat at MEDIUM 1 to 2 minutes or until melted. Knead bag until white chocolate is smooth. Cut off very tiny corner of bag; pipe or drizzle white chocolate onto chocolate cookies. Let stand until white chocolate is set, about 30 minutes.

For chocolate drizzle, place chocolate chips in small resealable plastic bag; seal bag. Heat in microwave oven at HIGH 1 minute. Turn bag over; heat at HIGH 1 to 2 minutes or until chocolate is melted. Knead bag until chocolate is smooth. Cut off tiny corner of bag; pipe or drizzle chocolate onto butter cookies. Let stand until chocolate is set, about 40 minutes.

**Black and White Sandwiches:** *Prepare dough and roll out as directed. Cut out both doughs with same cookie cutter. Bake as directed. Spread thin layer of prepared frosting on bottom side of chocolate cookie. Place bottom side of butter cookie over frosting. Drizzle either side of cookie with melted chocolate or white chocolate.*

*Note:*

Cookies that are frosted or decorated should be stored in an airtight container with waxed paper between each layer of cookies. This will prevent them from sticking together.

# "M&M's"® Jam Sandwiches

**Makes 1 dozen sandwich cookies**

½ cup (1 stick) butter, softened
¾ cup granulated sugar
1 large egg
1 teaspoon almond extract
½ teaspoon vanilla extract
1⅓ cups all-purpose flour

¼ teaspoon baking powder
¼ teaspoon salt
Powdered sugar
½ cup seedless raspberry jam
½ cup "M&M's"® Chocolate Mini Baking Bits

In large bowl cream butter and sugar until light and fluffy; beat in egg, almond extract and vanilla. In small bowl combine flour, baking powder and salt; blend into creamed mixture. Wrap and refrigerate dough 2 to 3 hours. Preheat oven to 375°F. Working with half the dough at a time on lightly floured surface, roll to ⅛-inch thickness. Cut into desired shapes using 3-inch cookie cutters. Cut out equal numbers of each shape. (If dough becomes too soft, refrigerate several minutes before continuing.) Cut 1½- to 2-inch centers out of half the cookies of each shape. Reroll trimmings and cut out more cookies. Using rigid spatula, carefully transfer shapes to ungreased cookie sheets. Bake 7 to 9 minutes. Cool on cookie sheets 1 to 2 minutes; cool completely on wire racks. Sprinkle powdered sugar on cookies with holes. Spread about 1 teaspoon jam on flat side of whole cookies, spreading almost to edges. Place cookies with holes, flat side down, over jam. Place "M&M's"® Chocolate Mini Baking Bits over jam in holes. Store between layers of waxed paper in tightly covered container.

# Buttery Almond Cutouts

1½ cups granulated sugar
1 cup (2 sticks) butter, softened
¾ cup sour cream
2 eggs
3 teaspoons almond extract, divided
1 teaspoon vanilla
4⅓ cups all-purpose flour

1 teaspoon baking powder
1 teaspoon baking soda
½ teaspoon salt
2 cups powdered sugar
2 tablespoons milk
1 tablespoon light corn syrup
Assorted food colorings

**Makes about 3 dozen cookies**

**Make-Ahead Time:**
*up to 3 days in refrigerator or up to 3 months in freezer*

**Final Prep Time:**
*30 minutes*

*1.* Beat granulated sugar and butter in large bowl until light and fluffy. Add sour cream, eggs, 2 teaspoons almond extract and vanilla; beat until smooth. Add flour, baking powder, baking soda and salt; beat just until well blended.

*2.* Divide dough into 4 pieces; flatten each piece into a disc. Wrap each disc tightly with plastic wrap. Refrigerate at least 3 hours or up to 3 days.

*3.* Combine powdered sugar, milk, corn syrup and remaining 1 teaspoon almond extract in small bowl; stir until smooth. Cover and refrigerate up to 3 days.

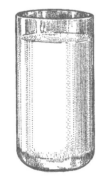

*4.* Preheat oven to 375°F. Working with 1 disc of dough at a time, roll out on floured surface to ¼-inch thickness. Cut dough into desired shapes using 2½-inch cookie cutters. Place about 2 inches apart on ungreased baking sheets. Bake 7 to 8 minutes or until edges are firm and bottoms are brown. Remove from baking sheets to wire racks to cool.

*5.* Separate powdered sugar mixture into 3 or 4 batches in small bowls; tint each batch with desired food coloring. Frost cookies.

**Note:** *To freeze dough, place wrapped discs in resealable plastic food storage bags. Thaw at room temperature before using. Or, cut out dough, bake and cool cookies completely. Freeze unglazed cookies for up to 2 months. Thaw and glaze as desired.*

# Cocoa Almond Cut-Out Cookies

**Makes about 6 dozen 3-inch cookies**

¾ cup (1½ sticks) butter or margarine, softened
1 (14-ounce) can sweetened condensed milk (NOT evaporated milk)
2 eggs
1 teaspoon vanilla extract
½ teaspoon almond extract

2¾ cups all-purpose flour
⅔ cup HERSHEY₀S Cocoa
2 teaspoons baking powder
½ teaspoon baking soda
½ cup finely chopped almonds
Chocolate Glaze
    (recipe follows)

*1.* Beat butter, sweetened condensed milk, eggs and extracts in large bowl until well blended. In another large bowl combine flour, cocoa, baking powder and baking soda; add to butter mixture. Beat until well blended. Stir in almonds. Divide dough into 4 equal portions. Wrap each portion in plastic wrap; flatten. Chill until firm enough to roll, about 2 hours.

*2.* Heat oven to 350°F. Lightly grease cookie sheet.

*3.* Working with 1 portion at a time (keep remaining dough in refrigerator), on floured surface, roll to about ⅛-inch thickness. Cut into desired shapes. Place on prepared cookie sheets. Bake 6 to 8 minutes or until set. Remove from cookie sheet to wire racks; cool completely. Drizzle with Chocolate Glaze. Store tightly covered at room temperature.

<u>Chocolate Glaze:</u> *Melt 1 cup HERSHEY₀S Semi-Sweet Chocolate Chips with 2 tablespoons shortening (do not use butter, margarine, spread or oil.) Makes about ⅔ cup.*

# Lemony Butter Cookies

½ cup (1 stick) butter, softened
½ cup sugar
1 egg
1½ cups all-purpose flour
2 tablespoons fresh lemon juice

1 teaspoon grated lemon peel
½ teaspoon baking powder
⅛ teaspoon salt
Additional sugar

Makes about
2½ dozen cookies

Beat butter and sugar in large bowl with electric mixer at medium speed until creamy. Beat in egg until light and fluffy. Mix in flour, lemon juice and peel, baking powder and salt. Cover; refrigerate about 2 hours or until firm.

Preheat oven to 350°F. Roll out dough, a small portion at a time, on well-floured surface to ¼-inch thickness. (Keep remaining dough in refrigerator.) Cut with 3-inch round or fluted cookie cutter. Transfer to ungreased cookie sheets. Sprinkle with sugar.

Bake 8 to 10 minutes or until edges are lightly browned. Cool 1 minute on cookie sheets. Remove to wire racks; cool completely. Store in airtight container.

## Cutout Cookie Troubleshooting

| Problems: | Solutions: |
|---|---|
| • Dough is too soft or sticky when rolled | • Chill the dough until it is firm |
| | • Add a small amount of flour to the dough, then chill until firm |
| • Dough crumbles and cracks when rolled | • Add a small amount of liquid (milk, cream or water) to the dough and mix well |
| | • If the dough is too cold, let it stand at room temperature 10 to 15 minutes until pliable |
| • Cookies spread too much during baking | • Let cookie sheets cool to room temperature before adding more dough |
| | • Keep the dough in the refrigerator between batches so it does not get too warm |

# Festive Lebkuchen

**Makes 1 dozen cookies**

3 tablespoons butter
1 cup packed brown sugar
¼ cup honey
1 egg
   Grated peel and juice of
    1 lemon

3 cups all-purpose flour
2 teaspoons ground allspice
½ teaspoon baking soda
½ teaspoon salt
   White decorator's frosting

Melt butter with brown sugar and honey in medium saucepan over low heat, stirring constantly. Pour into large bowl. Cool 30 minutes. Add egg, lemon peel and juice; beat 2 minutes with electric mixer at high speed. Stir in flour, allspice, baking soda and salt until well blended. Cover; refrigerate overnight or up to 3 days.

Preheat oven to 350°F. Grease cookie sheets. Roll out dough to ½-inch thickness on lightly floured surface with lightly floured rolling pin. Cut out with 3-inch cookie cutters. Transfer to prepared cookie sheets. Bake 15 to 18 minutes until edges are light brown. Cool 1 minute. Remove to wire racks; cool completely. Decorate with white frosting. Store in airtight container.

# Frosted Sugar Cookies

**Makes 7 dozen cookies**

10 tablespoons margarine,
   softened
1 cup sugar
2 egg whites
1 teaspoon vanilla
2 cups all-purpose flour

1 teaspoon baking powder
½ teaspoon salt
   Vanilla Frosting
    (recipe follows)
   Ground nutmeg or cinnamon

*1.* Preheat oven to 375°F. Spray cookie sheets with nonstick cooking spray.

*2.* Beat margarine and sugar in large bowl with electric mixer at medium speed until fluffy. Beat in egg whites and vanilla.

*3.* Combine flour, baking powder and salt in medium bowl. Add flour mixture to margarine mixture; mix well. Refrigerate 3 to 4 hours.

*4.* Roll out dough on generously floured surface to ¼-inch thickness (dough will be soft). Cut decorative shapes out of dough with 2-inch cookie cutters and place on prepared cookie sheets.

*5.* Bake 8 to 10 minutes or until cookies turn golden brown. Remove from cookie sheets to wire racks; cool completely. Meanwhile, prepare Vanilla Frosting.

*6.* Frost cookies; sprinkle with nutmeg or cinnamon.

## Vanilla Frosting

| | |
|---|---|
| 2 cups powdered sugar<br>2 to 3 tablespoons fat-free<br>   (skim) milk, divided | 1 teaspoon vanilla |

Mix powdered sugar, 2 tablespoons milk and vanilla in medium bowl with fork. Add additional 1 tablespoon milk until desired spreading consistency is reached. *Makes about ½ cup frosting*

**Tip:** *To get the most cookies out of the dough, cut cookies as close together as possible. Press the dough scraps together, being careful not to overhandle them. Then, re-roll the dough on a floured surface and continue to cut more cookies.*

*Note:*

**To avoid having the cookie dough stick to the cookie cutter, dip the cutter in flour before each use. (Make sure you shake off the excess flour before cutting.)**

# Peanut Butter Cut-Out Cookies

**Makes about 3 dozen cookies**

½ cup (1 stick) butter or margarine
1 cup REESE'S® Peanut Butter Chips
⅔ cup packed light brown sugar
1 egg

¾ teaspoon vanilla extract
1⅓ cups all-purpose flour
¾ teaspoon baking soda
½ cup finely chopped pecans
Chocolate Chip Glaze (recipe follows)

*1.* Place butter and peanut butter chips in medium saucepan; cook over low heat, stirring constantly, until melted. Pour into large bowl; add brown sugar, egg and vanilla, beating until well blended. Stir in flour, baking soda and pecans, blending well. Refrigerate 15 to 20 minutes or until firm enough to roll.

*2.* Heat oven to 350°F.

*3.* Roll a small portion of dough at a time on lightly floured board, or between 2 pieces of wax paper to ¼-inch thickness. (Keep remaining dough in refrigerator.) With cookie cutters, cut dough into desired shapes; place on ungreased cookie sheets.

*4.* Bake 7 to 8 minutes or until almost set (do not overbake). Cool 1 minute; remove from cookie sheets to wire racks. Cool completely. Drizzle Chocolate Chip Glaze onto each cookie; allow to set.

**Chocolate Chip Glaze:** *Place 1 cup HERSHEY'S Semi-Sweet Chocolate Chips and 1 tablespoon shortening (do not use butter, margarine spread or oil) in small microwave-safe bowl. Microwave at HIGH (100%) 1 minute; stir. If necessary, microwave at HIGH an additional 15 seconds at a time, stirring after each heating, just until chips are melted and mixture is smooth.*

# Autumn Leaves

1½ cups unsalted butter,
    softened
⅔ cup packed light brown sugar
1 egg
½ teaspoon vanilla
3 cups all-purpose flour
1 teaspoon ground cinnamon
½ teaspoon salt

⅛ teaspoon ground ginger
⅛ teaspoon ground cloves
2 tablespoons unsweetened
    cocoa powder
Yellow, orange and red food
    colors
¼ cup semisweet chocolate
    chips

**Makes about
1½ dozen cookies**

*1.* Beat butter and brown sugar in large bowl with electric mixer at medium speed until light and fluffy. Beat in egg and vanilla. Add flour, cinnamon, salt, ginger and cloves; beat at low speed until well blended.

*2.* Divide dough into 5 equal sections; reserve 1 section. Stir cocoa into 1 section until well blended. Stir yellow food color into 1 section until well blended. Repeat with remaining 2 sections and orange and red food colors.

*3.* Preheat oven to 350°F. Lightly grease cookie sheets. Working with half of each dough color, press colors together lightly. Roll out dough on lightly floured surface to ¼-inch thickness. Cut out dough with leaf-shaped cookie cutters of various shapes and sizes. Place 2 inches apart on prepared cookie sheets. Repeat with remaining dough sections and scraps.

*4.* Bake 10 to 15 minutes or until edges are lightly browned. Remove to wire racks; cool completely.

*5.* Place chocolate chips in small resealable plastic food storage bag; seal. Microwave at HIGH 1 minute; knead bag lightly. Microwave at HIGH for additional 30-second intervals until chips are completely melted, kneading bag after each 30-second interval. Cut off very tiny corner of bag. Pipe chocolate onto cookies in vein patterns.

*Note:*

The most popular type of food color is the liquid form commonly available at many supermarkets. It imparts intense color and should initially be used sparingly, a drop or two at a time.

# Toffee Spattered Sugar Stars

**Makes about 3½ dozen cookies**

1¼ cups granulated sugar
1 Butter Flavor CRISCO® Stick
   or 1 cup Butter Flavor
   CRISCO® all-vegetable
   shortening
2 eggs
¼ cup light corn syrup or
   regular pancake syrup
1 tablespoon vanilla

3 cups all-purpose flour (plus
   4 tablespoons), divided
¾ teaspoon baking powder
½ teaspoon baking soda
½ teaspoon salt
1 package (6 ounces) milk
   chocolate English toffee
   chips, divided

*1.* Place sugar and 1 cup shortening in large bowl. Beat at medium speed of electric mixer until well blended. Add eggs, syrup and vanilla; beat until well blended and fluffy.

*2.* Combine 3 cups flour, baking powder, soda and salt. Add gradually to shortening mixture; beat at low speed until blended.

*3.* Divided dough into 4 equal pieces; shape each into disk. Wrap with plastic wrap. Refrigerate 1 hour or until firm.

*4.* Heat oven to 375°F. Place sheets of foil on countertop for cooling cookies.

*5.* Sprinkle about 1 tablespoon flour on large sheet of waxed paper. Place disk of dough on floured paper; flatten slightly with hands. Turn dough over; cover with another large sheet of waxed paper. Roll dough to ¼-inch thickness. Remove top sheet of waxed paper. Sprinkle about ¼ of toffee chips over dough. Roll lightly into dough. Cut out with floured star or round cookie cutter. Place 2 inches apart on ungreased baking sheet. Repeat with remaining dough and toffee chips.

*6.* Bake one baking sheet at a time at 375°F for 5 to 7 minutes or until cookies are lightly browned around edges. *Do not overbake.* Cool 2 minutes on baking sheet. Remove cookies to foil to cool completely.

# Chocolate Mint Ravioli Cookies

1 package (15 ounces)
    refrigerated pie crusts
1 bar (7 ounces) cookies 'n'
    mint chocolate candy

1 egg
1 tablespoon water
Powdered sugar

**Makes 2 dozen cookies**

**Prep and Cook Time:**
*30 minutes*

*1.* Preheat oven to 400°F. Unfold 1 pie crust on lightly floured surface. Roll into 13-inch circle. Using 2½-inch cutters, cut pastry into 24 circles, rerolling scraps if necessary. Repeat with remaining pie crust.

*2.* Separate candy bar into pieces marked on bar. Cut each chocolate piece in half. Beat egg and water together in small bowl with fork. Brush half of pastry circles lightly with egg mixture. Place 1 piece of chocolate in center of each circle (there will be some candy bar left over). Top with remaining pastry circles. Seal edges with tines of fork.

*3.* Place on *ungreased* baking sheets. Brush tops of cookies with egg mixture.

*4.* Bake 8 to 10 minutes or until golden brown. Remove from cookie sheets; cool completely on wire racks. Dust with powdered sugar.

*Note:*

Mix it up! Substitute your favorite candy bar for the cookies 'n' mint chocolate candy. The cookies will have a completely different— but delicious—taste.

# Ukrainian Rolled Cookies

**Makes about 8 dozen cookies**

1 cup packed light brown sugar
¾ cup shortening or margarine
⅓ cup dark molasses
2 large eggs
2 tablespoons finely grated
    lemon peel

3¼ to 3½ cups all-purpose flour
1 teaspoon baking powder
1 teaspoon baking soda

*1.* Beat brown sugar and shortening in large bowl with electric mixer at medium speed until light and fluffy. Beat in molasses, eggs and lemon peel until well blended.

*2.* Gradually add 3 cups flour, baking powder and baking soda. Beat at low speed until well blended. Stir in enough remaining flour with spoon to form stiff dough. Form dough into 2 discs; wrap in plastic wrap and refrigerate until firm, 1 hour or overnight.

*3.* Preheat oven to 375°F. Grease 3 cookie sheets; set aside.

*4.* Working with 1 disc at a time, unwrap dough and place on lightly floured surface. Roll out dough with lightly floured rolling pin to ⅛-inch-thick rectangle. Cut dough with floured 2¾-inch star or scalloped cookie cutter. Place cutouts ½ inch apart on prepared cookie sheets.

*5.* Gently press dough trimmings together; reroll and cut out more cookies.

*6.* Bake 7 to 8 minutes or until lightly browned around edges. Remove cookies with spatula to wire racks; cool completely.

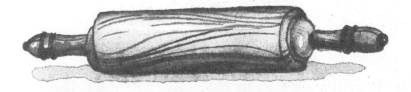

# Mini Lemon Sandwich Cookies

**Cookies**
- 2 cups all-purpose flour
- 1 cup (2 sticks) butter, softened
- ⅓ cup whipping cream
- ¼ cup granulated sugar
- 1 teaspoon lemon peel
- ⅛ teaspoon lemon extract
- Granulated sugar for dipping

**Filling**
- ¾ cup powdered sugar
- ¼ cup (½ stick) butter, softened
- 1 to 3 teaspoons lemon juice
- 1 teaspoon vanilla
- Food coloring (optional)

Makes 4½ dozen sandwich cookies

*1.* For cookies, combine flour, 1 cup butter, whipping cream, ¼ cup granulated sugar, lemon peel and lemon extract in small bowl. Beat 2 to 3 minutes, scraping bowl often, until well blended. Divide dough into thirds. Wrap each portion in waxed paper; refrigerate until firm.

*2.* Preheat oven to 375°F. Roll out each portion of dough to ⅛-inch thickness on well-floured surface. Cut out with 1½-inch round cookie cutter. Dip both sides of each cookie in granulated sugar. Place 1 inch apart on ungreased cookie sheets. Pierce with fork. Bake 6 to 9 minutes or until slightly puffy but not brown. Cool 1 minute on cookie sheets; remove to wire racks to cool completely.

*3.* For filling, combine powdered sugar, ¼ cup butter, lemon juice and vanilla in small bowl. Beat 1 to 2 minutes, scraping bowl often, until smooth. Tint with food coloring, if desired. Spread ½ teaspoon filling each on bottoms of half the cookies. Top with remaining cookies.

# Ultimate Sugar Cookies

**Makes about 3 to 4 dozen cookies**

**Cookies**

1¼ cups granulated sugar
1 Butter Flavor CRISCO® Stick
   or 1 cup Butter Flavor
   CRISCO® all-vegetable
   shortening
2 eggs
¼ cup light corn syrup or
   regular pancake syrup
1 tablespoon vanilla

3 cups all-purpose flour plus
   4 tablespoons, divided
¾ teaspoon baking powder
½ teaspoon baking soda
½ teaspoon salt
Decorations of your choice:
   granulated sugar, colored
   sugar crystals, frosting,
   decors, candies, chips, nuts,
   raisins, decorating gel

*1.* Combine sugar and 1 cup shortening in large bowl. Beat at medium speed of electric mixer until well blended. Add eggs, syrup and vanilla. Beat until well blended and fluffy.

*2.* Combine 3 cups flour, baking powder, baking soda and salt. Add gradually to creamed mixture at low speed. Mix until well blended. Divide dough into 4 quarters. Wrap each quarter of dough with plastic wrap. Refrigerate 1 hour. Keep dough refrigerated until ready to roll.

*3.* Heat oven to 375°F. Place sheets of foil on countertop for cooling cookies.

*4.* Spread 1 tablespoon flour on large sheet of waxed paper. Place one fourth of dough on floured paper. Flatten slightly with hands. Turn dough over and cover with another large sheet of waxed paper. Roll dough to ¼-inch thickness. Remove top sheet of waxed paper.

**5.** Cut out cookies with floured cutter. Transfer to ungreased baking sheet with large pancake turner. Place 2 inches apart. Roll out remaining dough. Sprinkle with granulated sugar, colored sugar crystals, decors or leave plain to frost or decorate when cooled.

**6.** Bake one baking sheet at a time at 375°F for 5 to 9 minutes, depending on the size of your cookies (bake smaller, thinner cookies closer to 5 minutes: larger cookies closer to 9 minutes). *Do not overbake.* Cool 2 minutes on baking sheet. Remove cookies to foil to cool completely, then frost if desired.

# Biscochitos

| | |
|---|---|
| 3 cups all-purpose flour | ¾ cup sugar, divided |
| 2 teaspoons anise seeds | 1 egg |
| 1½ teaspoons baking powder | ¼ cup orange juice |
| ½ teaspoon salt | 2 teaspoons ground cinnamon |
| 1 cup (2 sticks) butter | |

**Makes 4 to 5 dozen cookies**

Preheat oven to 350°F. Combine flour, anise seeds, baking powder and salt in medium bowl; set aside. Beat butter in large bowl with electric mixer at medium speed until creamy. Add ½ cup sugar; beat until fluffy. Blend in egg. Gradually add flour mixture alternately with orange juice, mixing well after each addition.

Divide dough in half. Roll out one portion at a time on lightly floured surface to ¼-inch thickness; cover remaining dough to prevent drying. Cut out cookies with fancy cookie cutters 2 to 2½ inches in diameter, adding scraps to remaining dough. If dough becomes too soft to handle, refrigerate briefly. Place cookies 1 inch apart on ungreased baking sheets.

Combine remaining ¼ cup sugar and cinnamon; lightly sprinkle over cookies. Bake 8 to 10 minutes or until edges are lightly browned. Let cool on wire racks; store in airtight container.

# Frosted Butter Cookies

**Makes about 3 dozen cookies**

### Cookies

1½ cups (3 sticks) butter, softened
¾ cup granulated sugar
3 egg yolks
3 cups all-purpose flour
1 teaspoon baking powder
2 tablespoons orange juice
1 teaspoon vanilla

### Frosting

4 cups powdered sugar
½ cup butter, softened
3 to 4 tablespoons milk
2 teaspoons vanilla
Food coloring (optional)
Colored sugars, flaked coconut and cinnamon candies for decoration

*Note:*

To prevent cookies from losing their shape, use a metal spatula to transfer them to the cookie sheet. Metal spatulas ar e thinner than plastic, with sharper edges that lift cookies more easily without mangling them.

For cookies, beat 1½ cups butter and granulated sugar in large bowl until creamy. Add egg yolks; beat until light and fluffy. Add flour, baking powder, orange juice and 1 teaspoon vanilla; beat until well mixed. Cover; refrigerate 2 to 3 hours or until firm.

Preheat oven to 350°F. Roll out dough, half at a time, to ¼-inch thickness on well-floured surface. Cut out shapes with cookie cutters. Place 1 inch apart on ungreased cookie sheets. Bake 6 to 10 minutes or until edges are golden brown. Remove to wire racks to cool completely.

For frosting, beat powdered sugar, butter, milk and vanilla in bowl until fluffy. If desired, divide frosting into small bowls and tint with food coloring. Frost cookies; decorate as desired.

# Righteous
# Refrigerator
# Cookies

## CHAPTER THREE

# Chocolate-Peanut Butter Checkerboards

**Makes about 4½ dozen cookies**

½ cup (1 stick) butter or margarine, softened
1 cup sugar
1 egg
1 teaspoon vanilla extract
1 cup plus 3 tablespoons all-purpose flour, divided

½ teaspoon baking soda
¼ cup HERSHEY₆S Cocoa
½ cup REESE'S® Peanut Butter Chips, melted

*Note:*

All refrigerator cookie dough needs to be chilled until it's very firm. If it hasn't been chilled long enough, slicing the dough evenly will be too difficult.

*1.* Beat butter, sugar, egg and vanilla in large bowl until fluffy. Add 1 cup flour and baking soda; beat until blended. Remove ¾ cup batter to small bowl; set aside. Add cocoa and remaining 3 tablespoons flour to remaining batter in large bowl; blend well.

*2.* Place peanut butter chips in small microwave-safe bowl. Microwave at HIGH (100%) 30 seconds or until melted and smooth when stirred. Immediately add to batter in small bowl, stirring until smooth. Divide chocolate dough into four equal parts. Roll each part between plastic wrap or wax paper into a log 7 inches long and about 1 inch in diameter. Repeat with peanut butter dough. Wrap each roll individually in waxed paper or plastic wrap. Refrigerate several hours until very firm.

*3.* Heat oven to 350°F. Remove rolls from waxed paper. Place 1 chocolate roll and 1 peanut butter roll side by side on cutting board. Top each roll with another roll of opposite flavor to make checkerboard pattern. Lightly press rolls together; repeat with remaining four rolls. Working with one checkerboard at a time (keep remaining checkerboard covered and refrigerated), cut into ¼-inch slices. Place on ungreased cookie sheet.

*4.* Bake 8 to 9 minutes or until peanut butter portion is lightly browned. Cool 1 minute; remove from cookie sheet to wire rack. Cool completely.

# Cappuccino Cookies

1 cup (2 sticks) butter, softened
2 cups packed brown sugar
2 tablespoons milk
2 tablespoons instant coffee
    granules
2 eggs
1 teaspoon rum extract
½ teaspoon vanilla

4 cups all-purpose flour
1 teaspoon baking powder
½ teaspoon ground nutmeg
¼ teaspoon salt
    Chocolate sprinkles or melted
        semisweet and/or white
        chocolate chips (optional)

**Makes about 5 dozen cookies**

Beat butter in large bowl with electric mixer at medium speed until smooth. Add brown sugar; beat until well blended.

Heat milk in small saucepan over low heat; add coffee granules, stirring to dissolve. Add milk mixture, eggs, rum extract and vanilla to butter mixture. Beat at medium speed until well blended.

Combine flour, baking powder, nutmeg and salt in large bowl. Gradually add flour mixture to butter mixture, beating at low speed after each addition until blended.

Shape dough into 2 logs, about 2 inches in diameter and 8 inches long. (Dough will be soft; sprinkle lightly with flour if too sticky to handle.) Roll logs in chocolate sprinkles, if desired, coating evenly (⅓ cup sprinkles per roll). Or, leave rolls plain and dip cookies in melted chocolate after baking. Wrap each log in plastic wrap; refrigerate overnight.

Preheat oven to 350°F. Grease cookie sheets. Cut rolls into ¼-inch-thick slices; place 1 inch apart on cookie sheets. (Keep unbaked rolls and sliced cookies chilled until ready to bake.)

Bake 10 to 12 minutes or until edges are lightly browned. Transfer to wire racks to cool. Dip plain cookies in melted chocolate, if desired. Store in airtight container.

# Orange-Cardamom Thins

**Makes about 8 dozen cookies**

1¼ cups granulated sugar
1 Butter Flavor CRISCO® Stick or 1 cup Butter Flavor CRISCO® all-vegetable shortening plus additional for greasing
1 egg
¼ cup light corn syrup or regular pancake syrup
1 teaspoon vanilla

1 tablespoon grated orange peel
½ teaspoon orange extract
3 cups all-purpose flour
1¼ teaspoons cardamom
¾ teaspoon baking powder
½ teaspoon baking soda
½ teaspoon salt
½ teaspoon cinnamon

*1.* Place sugar and 1 cup shortening in large bowl. Beat at medium speed of electric mixer until well blended. Add egg, syrup, vanilla, orange peel and orange extract; beat until well blended and fluffy.

*2.* Combine flour, cardamom, baking powder, baking soda, salt and cinnamon. Add gradually to shortening mixture, beating at low speed until well blended.

*3.* Divide dough in half. Roll each half into 12-inch-long log. Wrap with plastic wrap. Refrigerate for 4 hours or until firm.

*4.* Heat oven to 375°F. Grease baking sheets with shortening. Place sheets of foil on countertop for cooling cookies.

*5.* Cut rolls into ¼-inch-thick slices. Place 1 inch apart on prepared baking sheets.

*6.* Bake one baking sheet at a time at 375°F for 7 to 9 minutes or until bottoms of cookies are lightly browned. *Do not overbake.* Cool 2 minutes on baking sheet. Remove cookies to foil to cool completely.

# Peanut Butter and Chocolate Spirals

| | | |
|---|---|---|
| 1 package (20 ounces) refrigerated sugar cookie dough<br>1 package (20 ounces) refrigerated peanut butter cookie dough | ¼ cup unsweetened cocoa powder<br>⅓ cup peanut butter-flavored chips, chopped<br>¼ cup all-purpose flour<br>⅓ cup miniature chocolate chips | **Makes 4 dozen cookies** |

*1.* Remove each dough from wrapper according to package directions.

*2.* Place sugar cookie dough and cocoa in large bowl; mix with fork to blend. Stir in peanut butter chips.

*3.* Place peanut butter cookie dough and flour in another large bowl; mix with fork to blend. Stir in chocolate chips. Divide each dough in half; cover and refrigerate 1 hour.

*4.* Roll each dough on floured surface to 12×6-inch rectangle. Layer each half of peanut butter dough onto each half of chocolate dough. Roll up doughs, starting at long end to form 2 (12-inch) rolls. Wrap in plastic wrap; refrigerate 1 hour.

*5.* Preheat oven to 375°F. Cut dough into ½-inch-thick slices. Place cookies 2 inches apart on ungreased cookie sheets.

*6.* Bake 10 to 12 minutes or until lightly browned. Remove to wire racks; cool completely.

*Note:*

To keep the shape of the roll of dough round when slicing, rotate the roll about a quarter turn every few slices. This will prevent any one side of the dough from becoming too flat and producing oddly shaped cookies.

# Mint Chocolate Pinwheels

**Makes about 3 dozen cookies**

1¼ cups all-purpose flour
1 teaspoon baking powder
½ teaspoon salt
⅔ cup butter, softened
1 cup sugar

1 egg
1 teaspoon vanilla
1 cup uncooked quick oats
1 cup mint chocolate chips

*Note:*

Protect rolls of dough from picking up other flavors and odors in the refrigerator by double wrapping them. This is especially important if the dough will be refrigerated overnight.

*1.* Combine flour, baking powder and salt in small bowl; set aside. Beat butter and sugar in large bowl with electric mixer at medium speed until light and fluffy. Add egg and vanilla; beat well. Gradually add flour mixture. Beat at low speed. Stir in oats.

*2.* Place chocolate chips in 1-cup glass measure. Microwave at HIGH about 2 minutes or until melted, stirring after 1½ minutes. Divide cookie dough in half. Add melted chocolate to one half; mix well.

*3.* Roll out each half of dough between 2 sheets of waxed paper into 15×10-inch rectangle. Remove waxed paper from top of each rectangle.

*4.* Place chocolate dough over plain dough; remove bottom sheet of waxed paper from bottom of chocolate dough. Starting at long side, tightly roll up dough jelly-roll fashion, removing waxed paper as you roll. Wrap dough in plastic wrap; refrigerate at least 2 hours or up to 24 hours.

*5.* Preheat oven to 350°F. Lightly grease cookie sheets; set aside.

*6.* Unwrap log. Cut dough into ¼-inch slices. Place 3 inches apart on prepared cookie sheets. Bake 10 to 12 minutes or until set. Remove cookies to wire racks; cool completely. Store tightly covered at room temperature or freeze up to 3 months.

# Chocolate-Dipped Cinnamon Thins

1¼ cups all-purpose flour
1½ teaspoons ground cinnamon
¼ teaspoon salt
1 cup (2 sticks) unsalted butter, softened

1 cup powdered sugar
1 egg
1 teaspoon vanilla
4 ounces broken bittersweet chocolate candy bar, melted

**Makes about 2 dozen cookies**

*1.* Combine flour, cinnamon and salt in small bowl; set aside. Beat butter in large bowl with electric mixer at medium speed until light and fluffy. Add powdered sugar; beat well. Add egg and vanilla. Gradually add flour mixture. Beat at low speed just until blended.

*2.* Place dough on sheet of waxed paper. Using waxed paper to hold dough, roll it back and forth to form a log, about 12 inches long and 2½ inches in diameter. Securely wrap log in plastic wrap. Refrigerate at least 2 hours or until firm. (Log may be frozen up to 3 months; thaw in refrigerator before baking.)

*3.* Preheat oven to 350°F. Cut dough into ¼-inch-thick slices. Place 2 inches apart on ungreased cookie sheets. Bake 10 minutes or until set. Let cookies stand on cookie sheets 2 minutes. Remove cookies with spatula to wire racks; cool completely.

*4.* Dip each cookie into chocolate, coating 1 inch up sides. Transfer to wire racks or waxed paper; let stand at cool room temperature about 40 minutes or until chocolate is set.

*5.* Store cookies between sheets of waxed paper at cool room temperature or in refrigerator. These cookies do not freeze well.

# Domino® Sugar Cookies

**Makes about 3 dozen cookies**

1 cup DOMINO® Granulated
    Sugar
1 cup (2 sticks) butter or
    margarine, softened
1 egg

1 tablespoon vanilla
2¼ cups all-purpose flour
1 teaspoon baking soda
Additional DOMINO®
    Granulated Sugar

In large bowl, blend sugar and butter. Beat in egg and vanilla until light and fluffy. Mix in flour and baking soda. Divide dough in half. Shape each half into roll about 1½ inches in diameter. Wrap and refrigerate 1 hour until chilled.* Cut rolls into ¼-inch slices. Place on ungreased baking sheet and sprinkle generously with additional sugar. Bake in 375°F oven for 10 to 12 minutes or until lightly browned around edges. Cool on wire rack.

*Tip: To chill dough quickly, place in freezer for 30 minutes.*

# Party Peanut Butter Cookies

**Makes about 2 dozen cookies**

1½ cups all-purpose flour
½ cup sugar
½ teaspoon baking soda
¾ cup JIF® Creamy Peanut
    Butter, divided

½ Butter Flavor CRISCO® Stick
    or ½ cup Butter Flavor
    CRISCO® all-vegetable
    shortening
¼ cup light corn syrup
1 teaspoon vanilla

*1.* Combine flour, sugar and baking soda in medium bowl. Cut in ½ cup peanut butter and ½ cup shortening until mixture resembles coarse meal. Stir in syrup and vanilla until blended.

*2.* Form dough into 2-inch-thick roll. Wrap in waxed paper. Refrigerate 1 hour.

**3.** Heat oven to 350°F. Place sheets of foil on countertop for cooling cookies.

**4.** Cut dough into ¼-inch slices. Place ½ of slices 2 inches apart on ungreased baking sheet. Spread ½ teaspoon peanut butter on each slice. Top with remaining slices. Seal edges with fork.

**5.** Bake at 350°F for 10 minutes, or until lightly browned. *Do not overbake.* Cool 2 minutes on baking sheet. Remove to foil to cool completely.

# Confetti Cookies

| | | Makes 3 dozen cookies |
|---|---|---|
| 2⅓ cups all purpose flour | ¾ cup sugar | |
| 1½ teaspoons baking soda | ¼ cup cholesterol-free egg | |
| ¼ teaspoon salt | substitute | |
| ¼ cup margarine or butter, softened | ½ teaspoon almond extract | |
| 3 ounces reduced-fat cream cheese | 1 cup dried fruit bits | |
| | Sliced almonds (optional) | |

**1.** Combine flour, baking soda and salt in medium bowl; set aside.

**2.** Beat margarine and cream cheese in large bowl with electric mixer at medium speed until blended. Add sugar, egg substitute and almond extract; beat until well blended. Stir in dry ingredients; add fruit bits.

**3.** Shape dough into 2 logs, each about 9 inches long. Wrap each log in waxed paper or plastic wrap. Refrigerate 1 hour or overnight.

**4.** Preheat oven to 350°F. Lightly coat cookie sheet with nonstick cooking spray. Cut logs into ½-inch-thick slices. Place on prepared cookie sheet. Arrange three almond slices on top of each cookie in decorative pattern. Bake 10 minutes or until firm to touch. Remove to wire rack and cool completely.

# Almond Cream Cheese Cookies

| Makes about 4 dozen cookies | | |
|---|---|---|

1 (3-ounce) package cream cheese, softened
1 cup butter, softened
1 cup sugar
1 egg yolk

1 tablespoon milk
⅛ teaspoon almond extract
2½ cups sifted cake flour
1 cup BLUE DIAMOND® Sliced Natural Almonds, toasted

Beat cream cheese with butter and sugar until fluffy. Blend in egg yolk, milk and almond extract. Gradually mix in flour. Gently stir in almonds. (Dough will be sticky.) Divide dough in half; place each half on large sheet of waxed paper. Working through waxed paper, shape each half into 12×1½-inch roll. Chill until very firm.

Preheat oven to 325°F. Cut rolls into ¼-inch slices. Bake on ungreased cookie sheets 10 to 15 minutes or until edges are golden. (Cookies will not brown.) Cool on wire racks.

# Lip-Smacking Lemon Cookies

| Makes about 4 dozen cookies | | |
|---|---|---|

*Note:*

**Most recipes are developed using large eggs, so use large unless otherwise specified.**

½ cup (1 stick) butter, softened
1 cup sugar
1 egg
2 tablespoons lemon juice
2 teaspoons grated lemon peel

2 cups all-purpose flour
1 teaspoon baking powder
⅛ teaspoon salt
Dash ground nutmeg

Beat butter in large bowl with electric mixer at medium speed until smooth. Add sugar; beat until well blended. Beat in egg, lemon juice and peel; mix well. Combine flour, baking powder, salt and nutmeg in large bowl. Gradually add flour mixture to butter mixture at low speed, blending well after each addition.

Shape dough into 2 logs, each about 1½ inches in diameter and 6½ inches long. Wrap each log in plastic wrap. Refrigerate 2 to 3 hours or up to 3 days.

Preheat oven to 350°F. Grease cookie sheets. Cut logs into ¼-inch-thick slices; place 1 inch apart on cookie sheets.

Bake about 15 minutes or until edges are light brown. Transfer to wire rack to cool. Store in airtight container.

# Spiced Wafers

½ cup (1 stick) butter, softened
1 cup sugar
1 egg
2 tablespoons milk
1 teaspoon vanilla
1¾ cups all-purpose flour
2 teaspoons baking powder

1 teaspoon ground cinnamon
½ teaspoon ground nutmeg
¼ teaspoon ground cloves
Red hot candies or red colored sugar for garnish (optional)

**Makes about 4 dozen cookies**

Beat butter in large bowl with electric mixer at medium speed until smooth. Add sugar; beat until well blended. Add egg, milk and vanilla; beat until well blended.

Combine flour, baking powder, cinnamon, nutmeg and cloves in large bowl. Gradually add flour mixture to butter mixture at low speed, blending well after each addition.

Shape dough into 2 logs, each about 2 inches in diameter and 6 inches long. Wrap each log in plastic wrap. Refrigerate 2 to 3 hours or overnight.

Preheat oven to 350°F. Grease cookie sheets. Cut logs into ¼-inch-thick slices; decorate with candies or colored sugar, if desired. Place at least 2 inches apart on cookie sheets. Bake 11 to 13 minutes or until edges are light brown. Transfer to wire racks to cool. Store in airtight container.

# Peppersass Cookies

**Makes about 5 dozen cookies**

2¼ cups flour
½ teaspoon baking soda
½ teaspoon salt
1½ cups sugar, divided
⅔ cup butter *or* margarine, at room temperature

1 egg
2 teaspoons TABASCO® brand Pepper Sauce
1 teaspoon vanilla extract

Combine flour, baking soda and salt in small bowl. Beat 1 cup sugar and butter in large bowl with electric mixer at low speed until well blended. Add egg, TABASCO® Sauce, vanilla and flour mixture; beat until smooth.

Divide dough in half; place halves on plastic wrap. Shape each half into log about 1½ inches in diameter. Cover and refrigerate until firm, 2 to 3 hours or overnight.

Preheat oven to 350°F. Place remaining ½ cup sugar in shallow dish. Cut dough logs into ¼-inch-thick slices; dip each slice in sugar. Place slices 1 inch apart on ungreased cookie sheets. Bake 10 to 12 minutes or until cookies are golden around edges. Cool on wire racks.

# Mocha Pecan Pinwheels

**Makes about 5 dozen cookies**

1 square (1 ounce) unsweetened chocolate
½ cup (1 stick) butter, softened
¾ cup packed brown sugar
1 egg
1 teaspoon vanilla

¼ teaspoon baking soda
1¾ cups all-purpose flour
½ cup chopped pecans
1 teaspoon instant espresso coffee powder

Melt chocolate in small bowl over hot, not boiling, water. Stir until smooth. Beat butter, brown sugar, egg, vanilla and baking soda in large bowl; mix well. Stir in flour to make stiff dough. Remove half of dough; place in another bowl. Blend pecans and coffee powder into half of dough. Stir melted chocolate into remaining half of dough. Cover doughs; refrigerate 30 minutes.

Roll out coffee dough into 15×8-inch rectangle between 2 sheets of plastic wrap. Repeat process with chocolate dough. Remove top sheets of plastic wrap. Place coffee dough over chocolate dough. Remove remaining sheets of plastic wrap. Roll up tightly, jelly-roll fashion, starting with long side. Wrap in plastic wrap; freeze until firm enough to handle. (Dough can be frozen up to 6 weeks.)

Preheat oven to 350°F. Line cookie sheets with parchment paper or leave ungreased. Cut frozen dough into ¼-inch-thick slices; place 2 inches apart on prepared cookie sheets. Bake 9 to 12 minutes or until set. Remove to wire racks to cool.

*Note:*

Instant espresso powder is available in Italian grocery stores and some supermarkets. If you can't find it, instant coffee powder can be substituted (but the coffee flavor will not be as strong).

# P.B. Swirls

| | | Makes 2 dozen cookies |
|---|---|---|
| ½ cup shortening | 1¼ cups sifted flour | |
| 1 cup sugar | ½ teaspoon salt | |
| ½ cup crunchy peanut butter | ½ teaspoon baking soda | |
| 1 egg | 1 (6-ounce) package chocolate chips | |
| 2 teaspoons milk | | |

Preheat oven to 375°F. Cream shortening and sugar. Beat in peanut butter, egg and milk. In separate bowl, mix flour, salt and baking soda; blend into peanut butter mixture. Place dough on lightly greased waxed paper; pat dough into rectangle. Melt chocolate chips and spread over dough. Starting at long edge, roll up dough jelly-roll style. Chill ½ hour. Slice into ¼-inch slices. Place on ungreased cookie sheet. Bake at 375°F for 8 to 10 minutes.

Favorite recipe from **Peanut Advisory Board**

# Pinwheel Cookies

**Makes about 3½ dozen cookies**

½ cup shortening plus additional for greasing
⅓ cup plus 1 tablespoon butter, softened and divided
2 egg yolks

½ teaspoon vanilla extract
1 package DUNCAN HINES® Moist Deluxe® Fudge Marble Cake Mix

*Note:*

If your refrigerator shelves have lines or ridges, place the wrapped rolls of dough on a cookie sheet or a flexible cutting board so they won't end up with indentations in the dough.

**1.** Combine ½ cup shortening, ⅓ cup butter, egg yolks and vanilla extract in large bowl. Mix at low speed of electric mixer until blended. Set aside cocoa packet from cake mix. Gradually add cake mix. Blend well.

**2.** Divide dough in half. Add cocoa packet and remaining 1 tablespoon butter to one half of dough. Knead until well blended and chocolate colored.

**3.** Roll out yellow dough between two pieces of waxed paper into 18×12×⅛-inch rectangle. Repeat for chocolate dough. Remove top pieces of waxed paper from chocolate and yellow doughs. Place yellow dough directly on top of chocolate dough. Remove remaining layers of waxed paper. Roll up jelly-roll fashion, beginning at wide side. Refrigerate 2 hours.

**4.** Preheat oven to 350°F. Grease baking sheets.

**5.** Cut dough into ⅛-inch slices. Place sliced dough 1 inch apart on prepared baking sheets. Bake at 350°F for 9 to 11 minutes or until lightly browned. Cool 5 minutes on baking sheets. Remove to cooling racks.

# Almond Kissed Cookies

1 cup sliced almonds, divided
1¾ cups all-purpose flour
1 teaspoon baking soda
1 cup (2 sticks) butter or
    margarine, softened
1½ cups powdered sugar
1 egg

1 to 2 teaspoons freshly grated
    orange peel
½ teaspoon almond extract
1 cup HERSHEY₀S MINI
    KISSES™ Semi-Sweet
    or Milk Chocolates

**Makes about
3½ dozen cookies**

*1.* Grind ½ cup almonds in food processor or blender. Stir together flour, ground almonds and baking soda; set aside.

*2.* Beat butter and powdered sugar in large bowl until fluffy. Add egg, orange peel and almond extract; beat on low speed until blended. Add flour mixture; beat on low speed until blended.

*3.* Shape dough into two logs, about 1½ inches in diameter. (Refrigerate dough about 15 minutes, if necessary, before shaping). Wrap each roll separately in wax paper or plastic wrap; refrigerate until well chilled, at least two hours.

*4.* Heat oven to 375°F. Lightly grease cookie sheets. Slice dough into ½-inch-thick slices. Place on cookie sheet about 2 inches apart.

*5.* Bake 6 to 8 minutes or until edges are lightly browned. Immediately place 3 Mini Kisses™ and 3 almond slices on top of each cookie, pressing down lightly. Remove from cookie sheet to wire rack. Cool completely.

# Chocolate Mint Sandwiches

**Makes about 3 dozen sandwich cookies**

2 squares (1 ounce each) unsweetened chocolate
½ cup (1 stick) butter, softened
1 cup packed light brown sugar
1 egg
1 teaspoon vanilla
⅛ teaspoon baking soda
2 cups all-purpose flour
Creamy Mint Filling (recipe follows)

*1.* Melt chocolate in top of double boiler over hot, not boiling, water. Remove from heat; cool. Cream butter and brown sugar in large bowl. Beat in egg, vanilla, melted chocolate and baking soda until light and fluffy. Stir in flour to make stiff dough. Divide dough into four parts. Shape each part into roll about 1½ inches in diameter. Wrap in plastic wrap; refrigerate at least 1 hour or up to 2 weeks. (For longer storage, freeze up to 6 weeks.)

*2.* Preheat oven to 375°F. Cut rolls into ⅛-inch-thick slices; place 2 inches apart on ungreased cookie sheets. Bake 6 to 7 minutes or until firm. Remove to wire racks to cool. Prepare Creamy Mint Filling. Spread filling on bottoms of half the cookies. Top with remaining cookies, bottom sides down.

<u>**Creamy Mint Filling:**</u> *Beat 2 tablespoons softened butter or margarine, 1½ cups powdered sugar and 3 to 4 tablespoons half-and-half in small bowl until smooth and creamy. Stir in ¼ teaspoon peppermint extract and several drops green food coloring; mix well.*

# Butterscotch Thins

2⅔ cups all-purpose flour
1½ teaspoons baking soda
1⅔ cups (11-ounce package)
    NESTLÉ® TOLL HOUSE®
    Butterscotch Flavored
    Morsels

1 cup (2 sticks) butter or
    margarine, cut into pieces
1⅓ cups packed brown sugar
2 large eggs
1½ teaspoons vanilla extract
⅔ cup finely chopped nuts

**Makes about 6 dozen cookies**

**COMBINE** flour and baking soda in medium bowl.

**MICROWAVE** morsels and butter in large, microwave-safe mixer bowl on MEDIUM-HIGH (70%) power for 1 minute; stir. Microwave at additional 10- to 20-second intervals, stirring until smooth. Beat in sugar, eggs and vanilla extract. Gradually beat in flour mixture; stir in nuts. Cover; refrigerate for about 1 hour or until firm. Shape into two 14×1½-inch logs; wrap in plastic wrap. Refrigerate for 2 hours or until firm.

**PREHEAT** oven to 375°F.

**UNWRAP** logs; slice into ¼-inch-thick slices. Place slices on ungreased baking sheets.

**BAKE** for 5 to 6 minutes or until edges are set. Cool on baking sheets for 2 minutes; remove to wire racks to cool completely.

*Note:*
The best baking sheets to use are those with little or no sides, as they allow the oven's heat to circulate evenly for even browning. Placing only one baking sheet at a time in the center of the oven will also help promote even baking.

# Jammy Pinwheels

**Makes about 4 dozen cookies**

1¼ cups granulated sugar
1 Butter Flavor CRISCO® Stick
   or 1 cup Butter Flavor
   CRISCO® all-vegetable
   shortening or plus
   additional for greasing
2 eggs
¼ cup light corn syrup or
   regular pancake syrup

1 tablespoon vanilla
3 cups all-purpose flour (plus
   2 tablespoons), divided
¾ teaspoon baking powder
½ teaspoon baking soda
½ teaspoon salt
1 cup SMUCKER'S® Apricot,
   Strawberry or Seedless
   Raspberry Jam

*Note:*

It's helpful to rub your rolling pin with flour before rolling out the dough so it doesn't get too sticky. After rolling, brush off any excess flour left on the cookie dough—this will bake into the dough and make the cookies tough.

*1.* Place sugar and 1 cup shortening in large bowl. Beat at medium speed of electric mixer until well blended. Add eggs, syrup and vanilla; beat until well blended and fluffy.

*2.* Combine 3 cups flour, baking powder, baking soda and salt. Add gradually to shortening mixture, beating at low speed until well blended.

*3.* Divide dough in half. Pat each half into thick rectangle. Sprinkle about 1 tablespoon flour on large sheet of waxed paper. Place rectangle of dough on floured paper. Turn dough over; cover with another large sheet of waxed paper. Roll dough into 12×8-inch rectangle about ⅛ inch thick. Trim edges. Slide dough and waxed paper onto ungreased baking sheets. Refrigerate 20 minutes or until firm. Repeat with remaining dough.

*4.* Heat oven to 375°F. Grease baking sheets. Place sheets of foil on counter for cooling cookies.

**5.** Place chilled dough rectangle on work surface. Remove top sheet of waxed paper. Cut dough into 2-inch squares. Place squares 2 inches apart on prepared baking sheets. Make a 1-inch diagonal cut from each corner of square almost to center. Place 1 teaspoon jam in center. Lift every other corner and bring together in center of cookie. Repeat with remaining dough.

**6.** Bake at 375°F for 7 to 10 minutes or until edges of cookies are golden brown. *Do not overbake.* Cool 2 minutes on baking sheet. Remove cookies to foil to cool completely.

# Choco-Coco Pecan Crisps

½ cup (1 stick) butter, softened
1 cup packed light brown sugar
1 egg
1 teaspoon vanilla
1½ cups all-purpose flour

1 cup chopped pecans
⅓ cup unsweetened cocoa powder
½ teaspoon baking soda
1 cup flaked coconut

Makes about 6 dozen cookies

Cream butter and brown sugar in large bowl until light and fluffy. Beat in egg and vanilla. Combine flour, pecans, cocoa and baking soda in small bowl until well blended. Add to creamed mixture, blending until stiff dough is formed. Sprinkle coconut on work surface. Divide dough into 4 parts. Shape each part into roll about 1½ inches in diameter; roll in coconut until thickly coated. Wrap in plastic wrap; refrigerate until firm, at least 1 hour or up to 2 weeks. (For longer storage, freeze up to 6 weeks.)

Preheat oven to 350°F. Cut rolls into ⅛-inch-thick slices. Place 2 inches apart on ungreased cookie sheets. Bake 10 to 13 minutes or until firm, but not overly browned. Remove to wire racks to cool.

# Cream Cheese Chocolate Chip Pastry Cookies

**Makes about 2 dozen cookies**

1 package (17.25 ounces) frozen puff pastry sheets, thawed
1 package (8 ounces) cream cheese, softened
3 tablespoons granulated sugar

1¾ cups (11.5-ounce package) NESTLÉ® TOLL HOUSE® Milk Chocolate Morsels, *divided*

**UNFOLD** *1* puff pastry sheet on lightly floured surface. Roll out to make 14×10-inch rectangle. Combine cream cheese and sugar in small bowl until smooth. Spread *half* of cream cheese mixture over pastry, leaving 1-inch border on one long side. Sprinkle with *half* of morsels. Roll up puff pastry starting at long side covered with cream cheese. Seal end by moistening with water. Repeat steps with *remaining* ingredients. Refrigerate for 1 hour.

**PREHEAT** oven to 375°F. Lightly grease baking sheets or line with parchment paper.

**CUT** rolls crosswise into 1-inch-thick slices. Place cut side down on prepared baking sheets.

**BAKE** for 20 to 25 minutes or until golden brown. Cool on baking sheets for 2 minutes; remove to wire racks to cool completely.

# Date Pinwheel Cookies

1¼ cups dates, pitted and finely chopped
¾ cup orange juice
½ cup granulated sugar
1 tablespoon butter
3 cups plus 1 tablespoon all-purpose flour, divided

2 teaspoons vanilla, divided
4 ounces cream cheese
¼ cup shortening
1 cup packed brown sugar
2 eggs
1 teaspoon baking soda
½ teaspoon salt

Makes 6 dozen cookies

*1.* Heat dates, orange juice, granulated sugar, butter and 1 tablespoon flour in medium saucepan over medium heat. Cook 10 minutes or until thick, stirring frequently; remove from heat. Stir in 1 teaspoon vanilla; set aside to cool.

*2.* Beat cream cheese, shortening and brown sugar about 3 minutes in large bowl until light and fluffy. Add eggs and remaining 1 teaspoon vanilla; beat 2 minutes longer.

*3.* Combine remaining 3 cups flour, baking soda and salt in medium bowl. Add to shortening mixture; stir just until blended. Divide dough in half. Roll one half of dough on lightly floured surface into 12×9-inch rectangle. Spread half of date mixture over dough. Spread evenly, leaving ¼-inch border at top short edge. Starting at short side, tightly roll up dough jelly-roll style. Wrap in plastic wrap; freeze for at least 1 hour. Repeat with remaining dough.

*4.* Preheat oven to 350°F. Grease cookie sheets. Unwrap dough. Using heavy thread or dental floss, cut dough into ¼-inch slices. Place slices 1 inch apart on prepared cookie sheets.

*5.* Bake 12 minutes or until lightly browned. Let cookies stand on cookie sheets 2 minutes. Remove cookies to wire racks; cool completely.

*Note:*

If you purchase whole dates, they can be chopped with a knife, kitchen scissors or the food processor. Whichever tool you use, spray it first with nonstick cooking spray to prevent the dates from sticking to it.

# Viennese Hazelnut Butter Thins

**Makes about 3 dozen cookies**

1 cup hazelnuts
1¼ cups all-purpose flour
¼ teaspoon salt
1¼ cups powdered sugar
1 cup (2 sticks) butter, softened

1 egg
1 teaspoon vanilla
1 cup semisweet chocolate
   chips

*1.* Preheat oven to 350°F. To remove skins from hazelnuts, spread in single layer on baking sheet. Bake 10 to 12 minutes or until toasted and skins begin to flake off; let cool slightly. Wrap hazelnuts in heavy kitchen towel; rub against towel to remove as much of the skins as possible.

*2.* Place hazelnuts in food processor. Process using on/off pulses until hazelnuts are ground but not pasty.

*3.* Combine flour and salt in small bowl. Beat powdered sugar and butter in medium bowl with electric mixer at medium speed until light and fluffy. Beat in egg and vanilla. Gradually add flour mixture. Beat in ground hazelnuts at low speed until well blended.

*4.* Place dough on sheet of waxed paper. Using waxed paper to hold dough, roll back and forth to form log 12 inches long and 2½ inches wide. Wrap log in plastic wrap; refrigerate until firm, at least 2 hours or up to 48 hours.

*5.* Preheat oven to 350°F. Cut dough into ¼-inch-thick slices; place on ungreased cookie sheets.

*6.* Bake 10 to 12 minutes or until edges are very lightly browned. Let cookies stand on cookie sheets 1 minute. Remove cookies to wire racks; cool completely.

*7.* Place chocolate chips in 2-cup glass measure. Microwave at HIGH 1 to 1½ minutes or until melted, stirring after 1 minute and at 30-second intervals after first minute.

*Note:*

Regular (salted) butter can be stored in the refrigerator for up to one month. It should be wrapped airtight, as it absorbs other flavors readily. Unsalted butter is more perishable and should be refrigerated for no more than two weeks.

*8.* Dip cookies into chocolate, coating about half of each cookie, letting excess drip back into cup. Or, spread chocolate on cookies with narrow spatula. Transfer cookies to waxed paper; let stand at room temperature 1 hour or until set.

**Tip:** *To store cookies, place in airtight container between layers of waxed paper. Cookies can be frozen for up to 3 months.*

# Chocolate & Peanut Butter Tweed Cookies

| | |
|---|---|
| 1 cup (2 sticks) butter, softened | ½ cup peanut butter chips, chopped* |
| ½ cup packed light brown sugar | |
| ¼ cup granulated sugar | ½ cup semisweet chocolate chips, chopped* |
| 1 egg | |
| ¼ teaspoon baking soda | |
| 2½ cups all-purpose flour | *Chips can be chopped in a food processor. |

**Makes about 6 dozen cookies**

Beat butter and sugars in large bowl with electric mixer at medium speed until smooth. Add egg and baking soda; beat until light and fluffy. Stir in flour until dough is smooth. Blend in chopped chips. Divide dough into 4 parts. Shape each part into roll, about 1½ inches in diameter. Wrap in plastic wrap; refrigerate until firm, at least 1 hour or up to 2 weeks. (For longer storage, freeze up to 6 weeks.)

Preheat oven to 375°F. Lightly grease cookie sheets or line with parchment paper. Cut rolls into ⅛-inch-thick slices; place 2 inches apart on prepared cookie sheets. Bake 10 to 12 minutes or until lightly browned. Remove to wire racks to cool.

# P.B. and Jelly Peanut Log

**Makes about 3 dozen cookies**

*Note:*

Flour should be stored in an airtight container in a cool, dry place at room temperature. Always use up the remaining flour in the container before adding new flour (don't mix the two) and clean the container before adding new flour.

1 Butter Flavor CRISCO® Stick or 1 cup Butter Flavor CRISCO® all-vegetable shortening
1 cup JIF® Creamy Peanut Butter
¾ cup granulated sugar
¾ cup firmly packed light brown sugar
2 eggs
1 teaspoon vanilla
2½ cups all-purpose flour
1 teaspoon salt
1 teaspoon baking soda
½ cup SMUCKER'S® Seedless Red Raspberry Jam*
⅔ cup very finely chopped peanuts

*If desired, top cookies with additional jam before serving.*

*1.* Combine 1 cup shortening, peanut butter, granulated sugar and brown sugar in large bowl. Beat at medium speed of electric mixer until well blended. Beat in eggs and vanilla.

*2.* Combine flour, salt and baking soda. Add gradually to creamed mixture at low speed. Beat until well blended.

*3.* Cut parchment paper to line 17×11-inch pan. Press dough out to edges of paper. Spread with preserves to within ½ inch of edges.

*4.* Lift up long side of paper. Loosen dough with spatula. Roll dough up jelly-roll fashion. Seal seam. Sprinkle nuts on paper. Roll dough over on nuts. Press on any extra nuts. Wrap in paper. Place in plastic bag. Refrigerate overnight.

*5.* Heat oven to 375°F. Line baking sheet with foil or parchment paper. Unwrap dough. Cut into ½-inch slices. Place 2 inches apart on prepared baking sheet.

*6.* Bake at 375°F for 10 to 12 minutes or until set. Cool about 5 minutes on baking sheet before removing to new foil.

# Cinnamon Nut Chocolate Spirals

1½ cups all-purpose flour
¼ teaspoon salt
⅓ cup butter, softened
¾ cup sugar, divided
1 egg
1 cup mini semisweet
    chocolate chips

1 cup very finely chopped
    walnuts
2 teaspoons ground cinnamon
3 tablespoons butter

**Makes about 2 dozen cookies**

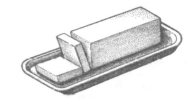

Combine flour and salt in small bowl; set aside. Beat softened butter and ½ cup sugar in large bowl with electric mixer at medium speed until light and fluffy. Beat in egg. Gradually add flour mixture. Dough will be stiff. (If necessary, knead dough by hand until it holds together.)

Roll out dough between 2 sheets of waxed paper into 12×10-inch rectangle. Remove waxed paper from top of rectangle.

Combine chips, walnuts, remaining ¼ cup sugar and cinnamon in medium bowl. Melt 3 tablespoons butter; pour hot melted butter over chocolate chip mixture; mix well. (Chips will partially melt.) Spoon mixture over dough. Spread evenly, leaving ½-inch border on long edges.

Using bottom sheet of waxed paper as guide and starting at long side, tightly roll up dough jelly-roll style, removing waxed paper as you roll. Wrap in plastic wrap; refrigerate 30 minutes to 1 hour.*

Preheat oven to 350°F. Lightly grease cookie sheets. Unwrap dough. Using heavy thread or dental floss, cut dough into ½-inch slices. Place slices 2 inches apart on prepared cookie sheets.

Bake 14 minutes or until edges are light golden brown. Cool completely on wire racks.

*If dough is chilled longer than 1 hour, slice with sharp, thin knife.*

*Note:*

To roll dough to an even thickness, roll the dough from the center, pushing the rolling pin away from you. Give the dough a quarter turn and continue rolling out from center. Don't roll back and forth—this can make the dough tough.

# Mini Chip Slice and Bake Cookies

**Makes about 6 dozen cookies**

⅓ cup butter or margarine, softened
¾ cup granulated sugar
½ cup packed light brown sugar
1 egg
1 teaspoon vanilla extract
2½ cups all-purpose flour

1 teaspoon baking soda
½ teaspoon baking powder
½ teaspoon salt
2 to 3 tablespoons milk
1 cup HERSHEY₅S MINI CHIPS™ Semi-Sweet Chocolate Chips

*1.* Beat butter, granulated sugar and brown sugar in large bowl on medium speed of mixer until creamy. Add egg and vanilla; beat well. Stir together flour, baking soda, baking powder and salt; gradually add to butter mixture, beating until well blended. Add milk, 1 tablespoon at a time, until dough holds together. Stir in small chocolate chips.

*2.* Divide dough in half. Shape each half into 1½-inch-thick roll. Wrap tightly in wax paper; refrigerate 5 to 24 hours.

*3.* Heat oven to 350°F. Lightly grease cookie sheet.

*4.* Using sharp knife and sawing motion, cut rolls into ¼-inch slices. Place on prepared cookie sheet.

*5.* Bake 8 to 10 minutes or until set. Remove from cookie sheet to wire rack. Cool completely.

*Note:*

When purchasing cookie sheets, keep in mind that dark ones are generally not the best choice. They absorb more heat and bake cookies too quickly, often resulting in overly dark and/or dry cookies.

# Cardamom-Chocolate Sandwiches

| | | |
|---|---|---|
| 1½ cups all-purpose flour<br>1 teaspoon ground cardamom<br>½ teaspoon baking soda<br>½ teaspoon salt<br>¾ cup plus 2 tablespoons butter,<br>    softened, divided | ¾ cup packed light brown sugar<br>¼ cup half-and-half<br>½ cup milk chocolate chips<br>2 tablespoons milk<br>1 cup sifted powdered sugar | **Makes about 1 dozen<br>sandwich cookies** |

Combine flour, cardamom, baking soda and salt in small bowl. Beat ¾ cup butter and brown sugar with electric mixer at medium speed until light and fluffy. Beat in half-and-half. Gradually add flour mixture; blend well.

Spoon dough down center of sheet of waxed paper. Using waxed paper to hold dough, roll back and forth to form tight, smooth 10-inch log. If dough is too soft, refrigerate 1 hour and reroll log until smooth. Wrap securely. Refrigerate about 4 hours or until firm. (Dough may be kept refrigerated up to 3 days.)

Preheat oven to 375°F. Cut dough into ¼-inch slices with long, sharp knife. Place 2 inches apart on ungreased cookie sheets. Bake 10 to 12 minutes or until edges are golden brown and cookies are set. Cool on cookie sheets 2 minutes. Cool completely on wire racks.

For filling, place chocolate chips and remaining 2 tablespoons butter in small microwavable bowl. Microwave at HIGH 1½ minutes or until melted, stirring after 1 minute. Stir in milk until smooth. Beat in powdered sugar. Spread filling over bottom side of half the cookies; top with remaining cookies.

# Cinnamon Roll Cookies

**Makes about 5 dozen cookies**

Cinnamon Mixture
  4 tablespoons granulated sugar
  1 tablespoon ground cinnamon

Cookie Dough
  1 Butter Flavor CRISCO® Stick
    or 1 cup Butter Flavor
    CRISCO® all-vegetable
    shortening

1 cup firmly packed light brown
    sugar
2 large eggs
1 teaspoon vanilla
3 cups all-purpose flour
2 teaspoons baking powder
½ teaspoon salt
1 teaspoon ground cinnamon

*1.* For cinnamon mixture, combine granulated sugar and 1 tablespoon cinnamon in small bowl; mix well. Set aside.

*2.* For cookie dough, combine 1 cup shortening and brown sugar in large bowl. Beat at medium speed with electric mixer until well blended. Beat in eggs and vanilla until well blended.

*Note:*

Be careful when working with this dough. It is a stiff dough and can crack easily when rolling. Roll the dough slowly and smooth any cracks with your finger as you go.

*3.* Combine flour, baking powder, salt and 1 teaspoon cinnamon in small bowl. Add to creamed mixture; mix well.

*4.* Turn dough onto sheet of waxed paper. Spread dough into 9×6-inch rectangle using rubber spatula. Sprinkle with 4 tablespoons cinnamon mixture to within 1 inch of edge. Roll up jelly-roll style into log. Dust log with remaining cinnamon mixture. Wrap tightly in plastic wrap; refrigerate 4 hours or overnight.

*5.* Heat oven to 375°F. Spray cookie sheets with CRISCO® No-Stick Cooking Spray.

*6.* Slice dough ¼ inch thick. Place on prepared cookie sheets. Bake at 350°F for 8 minutes or until lightly browned on top. Cool on cookie sheets 4 minutes; transfer to cooling racks.

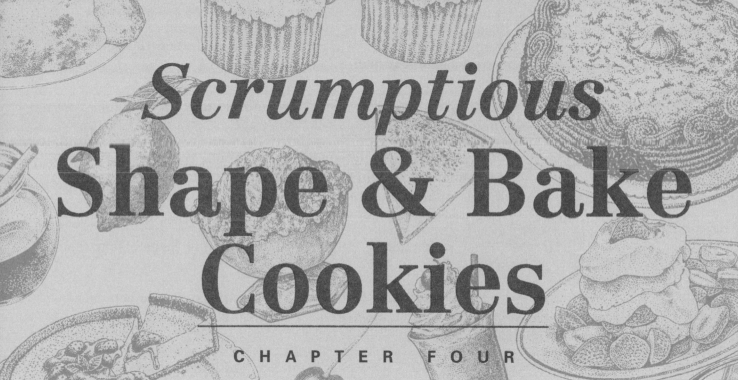

# Scrumptious
# Shape & Bake
# Cookies

CHAPTER FOUR

# Chocolate Crackles

**Makes 4 dozen cookies**

⅓ cup CRISCO® Oil*
1½ cups granulated sugar
1½ teaspoons vanilla
1 egg
2 egg whites
1⅔ cups all-purpose flour

½ cup unsweetened cocoa powder
1½ teaspoons baking powder
½ teaspoon salt
½ cup confectioners' sugar

*Use your favorite Crisco Oil product.

*1.* Heat oven to 350°F. Place sheets of foil on countertop for cooling cookies.

*2.* Combine oil, granulated sugar and vanilla in large bowl. Beat at medium speed of electric mixer until blended. Add egg and egg whites. Beat until well blended. Stir in flour, cocoa, baking powder and salt with spoon.

*3.* Place confectioners' sugar in shallow dish or large plastic food storage bag.

*4.* Shape dough into 1-inch balls. Roll or shake in confectioners' sugar until coated. Place about 2 inches apart on ungreased baking sheet.

*5.* Bake at 350°F for 7 to 8 minutes or until almost no indentation remains when touched lightly. (Do not overbake.) Cool on baking sheet 2 minutes. Remove cookies to foil to cool completely.

# Greek Lemon-Herb Cookies

2½ cups all-purpose flour
1 teaspoon baking soda
¼ teaspoon salt
1 cup (2 sticks) butter, softened
1¼ cups sugar, divided

2 large egg yolks
4 teaspoons grated lemon peel, divided
½ teaspoon dried rosemary leaves, crushed

**Makes about 4 dozen cookies**

*1.* Preheat oven to 375°F. Combine flour, baking soda and salt in large bowl.

*2.* Beat butter and 1 cup sugar in large bowl with electric mixer at medium speed until light and fluffy. Beat in egg yolks, 3 teaspoons lemon peel and rosemary. Gradually add flour mixture. Beat at low speed until well blended.

*3.* Combine remaining ¼ cup sugar and 1 teaspoon lemon peel in shallow bowl.

*4.* Roll tablespoonfuls of dough into 1-inch balls; roll in sugar mixture to coat.

*5.* Place balls 2 inches apart on *ungreased* cookie sheets. Press balls to ¼-inch thickness using flat bottom of drinking glass.

*6.* Bake 10 to 12 minutes or until edges are golden brown. Remove cookies to wire racks; cool completely.

*7.* Store tightly covered at room temperature or freeze up to 3 months.

*Note:*

Recipes using dried herbs often call for them to be crushed—this makes the particles finer, helps release the aromatic oils and adds more flavor. Simply rub dried herbs between your thumb and fingers as you add them to the dish.

# Vanilla Butter Crescents

**Makes 4 dozen cookies**

1 package DUNCAN HINES®
Moist Deluxe® French
Vanilla Cake Mix
¾ cup butter, softened
1 vanilla bean, very finely
chopped (see Tip)

1 cup finely chopped pecans or
walnuts
Confectioners' sugar

*1.* Preheat oven to 350°F.

*2.* Place cake mix and butter in large bowl. Cut in butter with pastry blender or 2 knives. Stir in vanilla bean and pecans. Since mixture is crumbly, it may be helpful to work dough with hands to blend until mixture holds together. Shape dough into balls. Roll 1 ball between palms until 4 inches long. Shape into crescent. Repeat with remaining balls. Place 2 inches apart on ungreased baking sheets. Bake at 350°F for 10 to 12 minutes or until light golden brown around edges. Cool 2 minutes on baking sheets. Remove to cooling racks. Dust with confectioners' sugar. Cool completely. Dust with additional confectioners' sugar, if desired. Store in airtight container.

**Tip:** *To quickly chop vanilla bean, place in work bowl of food processor fitted with knife blade. Process until fine.*

# Chocolate Chunk Cookies

**Makes about 4½ dozen cookies**

3 eggs
1 cup vegetable oil
¾ cup packed brown sugar
1 teaspoon baking powder
1 teaspoon vanilla
¼ teaspoon baking soda

¼ teaspoon salt
2½ cups all-purpose flour
1 package (12 ounces)
semisweet chocolate
chunks

Preheat oven to 350°F. Lightly grease cookie sheets or line with parchment paper. Beat eggs in large bowl until foamy. Add oil and brown sugar; beat until light and frothy. Blend in baking powder, vanilla, baking soda and salt. Mix in flour until dough is smooth. Stir in chocolate chunks. Shape dough into 1-inch balls. Place 2 inches apart on prepared cookie sheets. Bake 10 to 12 minutes or until lightly browned. Remove to wire racks to cool.

# Chocolate Almond Buttons

1⅓ cups flour
⅓ cup unsweetened cocoa
    powder
¼ teaspoon salt
1 cup BLUE DIAMOND®
    Blanched Almond Paste
½ cup plus 1½ tablespoons
    softened butter, divided

¼ cup corn syrup
1 teaspoon vanilla extract
3 squares (1 ounce each)
    semisweet chocolate
⅔ cup BLUE DIAMOND®
    Blanched Whole Almonds,
    toasted

**Makes 6 dozen cookies**

Sift flour, cocoa powder and salt; reserve. Cream almond paste and ½ cup butter until smooth. Beat in corn syrup and vanilla. Beat in flour mixture, scraping sides of bowl occasionally, until well blended. Shape into ¾-inch balls. Place on lightly greased cookie sheet; indent centers of cookies with finger. Bake at 350°F for 8 to 10 minutes or until done. (Cookies will be soft but will become firm when cooled.) In top of double boiler, stir chocolate and remaining 1½ tablespoons butter over simmering water until melted and smooth. With spoon, drizzle small amount of chocolate into center of each cookie. Press an almond into chocolate on each cookie.

*Note:*

To toast nuts, spread them in a single layer on a baking sheet and bake in a preheated 350°F oven for 8 to 10 minutes or until very lightly browned.

# Walnut Minichips Biscotti

**Makes about 4 dozen biscotti**

1 cup walnut pieces, toasted*
½ cup (1 stick) butter or
   margarine, softened
1 cup sugar
2 eggs
1 teaspoon vanilla extract
2½ cups all-purpose flour
1 teaspoon baking powder
¼ teaspoon salt

2 cups (12-ounce package)
   HERSHEY₅S MINI CHIPS™
   Semi-Sweet Chocolate
   Chips, divided
2 teaspoons shortening
   (do not use butter,
   margarine, spread or oil)

*To toast walnuts: Heat oven to 350°F. Spread walnuts in thin layer in shallow baking pan. Bake 6 to 8 minutes, stirring occasionally, until golden brown. Cool completely.*

*Note:*

**Toasting nuts intensifies their flavor, gives them a crisp texture, and, in the case of lighter-colored nuts, also gives them an appealing golden color.**

*1.* Heat oven to 350°F. Grind cooled toasted walnuts in food processor; set aside.

*2.* Beat butter and sugar in large bowl until well blended. Add eggs and vanilla; beat until smooth. Stir together flour, baking powder and salt; gradually add to butter mixture, beating until smooth. (Dough will be thick.) Using wooden spoon, work 1 cup small chocolate chips and walnuts into dough. Divide dough into four equal parts. Shape each part into a log about 9 inches long. Place on ungreased cookie sheet, at least 2 inches apart.

*3.* Bake 25 minutes or until logs are set. Remove from oven; let cool on cookie sheet 15 minutes. Using serrated knife and sawing motion, cut logs diagonally into ½-inch slices. Discard end pieces. Arrange slices, cut sides down and close together on cookie sheet.

*4.* Bake 5 to 6 minutes. Turn each slice over; bake an additional 5 to 6 minutes. Remove from oven; cool on cookie sheet.

*5.* Combine remaining 1 cup small chocolate chips and shortening in small microwave-safe bowl. Microwave at HIGH (100%) 30 seconds; stir. Microwave an additional 15 seconds at a time, stirring after each heating, until chips are melted. Drizzle tops of cookies.

# Mexican Sugar Cookies (Polvorones)

1 cup (2 sticks) butter, softened
½ cup powdered sugar
2 tablespoons milk
1 teaspoon vanilla
1 teaspoon ground cinnamon, divided

1½ to 1¾ cups all-purpose flour
1 teaspoon baking powder
1 cup granulated sugar
1 square (1 ounce) semisweet chocolate, finely grated

**Makes about 2 dozen cookies**

*1.* Preheat oven to 325°F. Grease cookie sheets; set aside.

*2.* Beat butter, powdered sugar, milk, vanilla and ½ teaspoon cinnamon in large bowl with electric mixer at medium speed until light and fluffy, scraping down side of bowl once. Gradually add 1½ cups flour and baking powder. Beat at low speed until well blended, scraping down side of bowl once. Stir in additional flour with spoon if dough is too soft to shape.

*3.* Roll tablespoonfuls of dough into 1¼-inch balls. Place balls 3 inches apart on prepared cookie sheets. Flatten each ball into 2-inch round with bottom of glass dipped in granulated sugar.

*4.* Bake 20 to 25 minutes or until edges are golden brown. Let stand on cookie sheets 3 to 4 minutes.

*5.* Meanwhile, combine granulated sugar, grated chocolate and remaining ½ teaspoon cinnamon in small bowl; stir to combine. Transfer cookies, one at a time, with spatula to sugar mixture; coat both sides. Remove with spatula to wire racks; cool completely.

*6.* Store tightly covered at room temperature or freeze up to 3 months.

*Note:*

The easiest way to grate chocolate by hand is with a rotary grater. Otherwise, you can use a box grater placed over a piece of waxed paper. Hold the chocolate with paper towel to prevent your hands from melting it.

# Molasses Oatmeal Cookies

**Makes about 4 dozen cookies**

1 Butter Flavor CRISCO® Stick or 1 cup Butter Flavor CRISCO® all-vegetable shortening plus additional for greasing
1 cup firmly packed brown sugar
1 cup granulated sugar
2 eggs
1 tablespoon milk
1 tablespoon light molasses

2 teaspoons vanilla
2 cups all-purpose flour
1½ teaspoons cinnamon
1 teaspoon baking soda
½ teaspoon baking powder
½ teaspoon ground cloves
¼ teaspoon salt
2 cups quick oats (not instant or old-fashioned)
1 cup coarsely chopped pecans
½ cup raisins

*Note:*

If you discover that your raisins are a little hard and dried out, don't throw them away yet! They can be revived—just soak them in hot water for 20 minutes to plump them. Drain well before using in a recipe.

*1.* Heat oven to 350°F. Grease baking sheet with shortening. Place sheets of foil on countertop for cooling cookies.

*2.* Combine 1 cup shortening, brown sugar, granulated sugar, eggs, milk, molasses and vanilla in large bowl. Beat at medium speed of electric mixer until well blended.

*3.* Combine flour, cinnamon, baking soda, baking powder, cloves and salt. Stir into creamed mixture with spoon until well blended. Stir in oats, nuts and raisins.

*4.* Form dough into 1-inch balls. Place 2 inches apart on baking sheet.

*5.* Bake at 350°F for 11 to 12 minutes, or until edges are lightly browned. *Do not overbake.* Cool 2 minutes on baking sheet. Remove cookies to foil to cool completely.

# Flourless Peanut Butter Cookies

| | | |
|---|---|---|
| 1 cup peanut butter<br>1 cup packed light brown sugar<br>1 egg | 24 milk chocolate candy stars or other solid milk chocolate candy | **Makes about 2 dozen cookies** |

Preheat oven to 350°F. Combine peanut butter, sugar and egg in medium bowl; beat until blended and smooth.

Shape dough into 24 balls about 1½ inches in diameter. Place 2 inches apart on ungreased cookie sheets. Press one chocolate star on top of each cookie. Bake 10 to 12 minutes or until set. Transfer to wire racks to cool completely.

# Honey Carrot Cookies

| | | |
|---|---|---|
| 1 cup sugar<br>½ cup (1 stick) butter, softened<br>2 eggs<br>3 tablespoons honey<br>1 teaspoon vanilla | 2¼ cups all-purpose flour<br>2 teaspoons baking soda<br>½ teaspoon ground nutmeg<br>¼ teaspoon salt<br>½ cup shredded carrot | **Makes about 3 dozen cookies** |

Preheat oven to 325°F. Combine sugar and butter in large bowl. Beat well. Add eggs, honey and vanilla; beat until well mixed. Combine flour, baking soda, nutmeg and salt in medium bowl. Stir dry ingredients into butter mixture; mix well. Stir in carrot. Using well-floured hands, shape rounded teaspoonfuls of dough into 1-inch balls. Place 2 inches apart on ungreased cookie sheets.

Bake 13 to 18 minutes or until edges are lightly browned. Remove immediately to wire racks to cool.

# Chocolate Sugar Cookies

**Makes about 3½ dozen cookies**

**Prep Time:**
*20 minutes plus refrigerating*

**Bake Time:**
*10 minutes*

*Note:*

**If the dough starts to stick to your hands when shaping it into balls, lightly moisten your hands with cool water.**

2 cups flour
1 teaspoon baking soda
¼ teaspoon salt
3 squares BAKER'S® Unsweetened Baking Chocolate

1 cup (2 sticks) butter or margarine
1 cup sugar
1 egg
1 teaspoon vanilla
Additional sugar

**HEAT** oven to 375°F. Mix flour, baking soda and salt in medium bowl.

**MICROWAVE** chocolate and butter in large microwavable bowl on HIGH 2 minutes or until butter is melted. Stir until chocolate is completely melted.

**STIR** 1 cup sugar into melted chocolate mixture until well blended. Mix in egg and vanilla until completely blended. Stir in flour mixture until well blended. Refrigerate dough about 15 minutes or until easy to handle.

**SHAPE** dough into 1-inch balls; roll in additional sugar. Place on ungreased cookie sheets.

**BAKE** 8 to 10 minutes or until set. (If flatter, crisper cookies are desired, flatten with bottom of glass before baking.) Remove from cookie sheets. Cool on wire racks. Store in tightly covered container.

**Jam-Filled Chocolate Sugar Cookies:** *Prepare Baker's® Chocolate Sugar Cookie dough as directed. Roll in finely chopped nuts in place of sugar. Make indentation in each ball; fill center with your favorite jam. Bake as directed.*

**Chocolate-Caramel Sugar Cookies:** *Prepare Baker's® Chocolate Sugar Cookie dough as directed. Roll in finely chopped nuts in place of sugar. Make indentation in each ball; bake as directed. Microwave 1 package (14 ounces) KRAFT® Caramels with 2 tablespoons milk in microwavable bowl on HIGH 3 minutes or until melted, stirring after 2 minutes. Fill centers of cookies with caramel mixture. Drizzle with melted Baker's® Semi-Sweet Chocolate.*

# Double Nut Chocolate Chip Cookies

| | | |
|---|---|---|
| 1 package DUNCAN HINES®<br>    Moist Deluxe® Classic<br>    Yellow Cake Mix<br>½ cup butter or margarine,<br>    melted | 1 egg<br>1 cup semisweet chocolate<br>    chips<br>½ cup finely chopped pecans<br>1 cup sliced almonds, divided | **Makes 3 to 3½ dozen cookies** |

*1.* Preheat oven to 375°F. Grease baking sheets.

*2.* Combine cake mix, butter and egg in large bowl. Mix at low speed with electric mixer until just blended. Stir in chocolate chips, pecans and ¼ cup almonds. Shape rounded tablespoonfuls of dough into balls. Place remaining ¾ cup almonds in shallow bowl. Press tops of cookies into almonds. Place 1 inch apart on prepared baking sheets.

*3.* Bake at 375°F for 9 to 11 minutes or until lightly browned. Cool 2 minutes on baking sheets. Remove to cooling racks.

# Easy Lemon Pudding Cookies

| Makes about 20 cookies | 1 cup BISQUICK® Original Baking Mix<br>1 package (4-serving size) JELL-O® Lemon Flavor Instant Pudding & Pie Filling<br>½ teaspoon ground ginger (optional) | 1 egg, lightly beaten<br>¼ cup vegetable oil<br>Sugar<br>3 squares BAKER'S® Premium White Baking Chocolate, melted |
|---|---|---|

**Prep Time:**
*10 minutes*

**Bake Time:**
*10 minutes*

**HEAT** oven to 350°F.

**STIR** baking mix, pudding mix and ginger in medium bowl. Mix in egg and oil until well blended. (Mixture will be stiff.) With hands, roll cookie dough into 1-inch diameter balls. Place balls 2 inches apart on lightly greased cookie sheets. Dip flat-bottom glass into sugar. Press glass onto each dough ball and flatten into ¼-inch-thick cookie.

**BAKE** 10 minutes or until edges are golden brown. Immediately remove from cookie sheets. Cool on wire racks. Drizzle cookies with melted white chocolate.

<u>**How To Melt Chocolate:**</u> *Microwave 3 squares BAKER'S® Premium White Baking Chocolate in heavy zipper-style plastic sandwich bag on HIGH 1 to 1½ minutes or until chocolate is almost melted. Gently knead bag until chocolate is completely melted. Fold down top of bag; snip tiny piece off 1 corner from bottom. Holding top of bag tightly, drizzle chocolate through opening across tops of cookies.*

# English Thumbprint Cookies

1 cup pecan pieces
1¼ cups all-purpose flour
¼ teaspoon salt
½ cup (1 stick) butter, softened
½ cup packed light brown sugar

1 teaspoon vanilla
1 large egg, separated
2 to 3 tablespoons seedless
   raspberry or strawberry jam

**Makes about
2½ dozen cookies**

*1.* Preheat oven to 350°F. To toast pecans, spread on ungreased baking sheet. Bake 8 to 10 minutes or until golden brown, stirring frequently. Remove pecans from baking sheet and cool. Process cooled pecans in food processor until finely chopped; transfer to shallow bowl.

*2.* Place flour and salt in medium bowl; stir to combine. Beat butter and brown sugar in large bowl with electric mixer at medium speed until light and fluffy. Beat in vanilla and egg yolk. Gradually beat in flour mixture. Beat egg white with fork until frothy.

*3.* Shape dough into 1-inch balls. Roll balls in egg white; roll in nuts to coat. Place balls on ungreased cookie sheets. Press deep indentation in center of each ball with thumb.

*4.* Bake 8 minutes or until set. Remove cookies from oven; fill each indentation with about ¼ teaspoon jam. Return filled cookies to oven; continue to bake 4 to 6 minutes or until lightly brown. Immediately remove cookies to wire racks; cool completely.

*5.* Store cookies tightly covered at room temperature or freeze up to 3 months.

*Note:*

Filled cookies like thumbprints are best stored in a single layer to avoid cookies sticking to each other. If that's not possible, store them in layers with waxed paper between each layer of cookies.

# Oatmeal Toffee Lizzies

**Makes about
2½ dozen cookies**

¾ Butter Flavor CRISCO® Stick
or ¾ cup Butter Flavor
CRISCO® all-vegetable
shortening plus additional
for greasing
1¼ cups firmly packed light
brown sugar
1 egg
⅓ cup milk

1½ teaspoons vanilla
3 cups quick oats, uncooked
1 cup all-purpose flour
½ teaspoon baking soda
½ teaspoon salt
1½ cups semisweet chocolate
chips
½ cup almond brickle chips
½ cup finely chopped pecans

*1.* Heat oven to 375°F. Grease baking sheets with shortening.
Place sheets of foil on countertop for cooling cookies.

*2.* Combine ¾ cup shortening, brown sugar, egg, milk and vanilla
in large bowl. Beat at medium speed of electric mixer until well
blended.

*3.* Combine oats, flour, baking soda and salt. Mix into creamed
mixture at low speed just until blended. Stir in chocolate chips,
almond chips and pecans.

*4.* Shape dough into 1¼- to 1½-inch balls with lightly floured
hands. Place 2 inches apart onto prepared baking sheet. Flatten
slightly.

*5.* Bake one baking sheet at a time at 375°F for 10 to
12 minutes, or until lightly browned. *Do not overbake.* Cool
2 minutes on baking sheet. Remove cookies to foil to cool
completely.

# Molasses Spice Cookies

1¾ cups all-purpose flour
1 teaspoon baking soda
1 teaspoon ground ginger
1 teaspoon ground cinnamon
¼ teaspoon ground cloves
¼ teaspoon salt
1 cup granulated sugar
¾ cup (1½ sticks) butter or
     margarine, softened

1 large egg
¼ cup unsulphured molasses
2 cups (12-ounce package)
   NESTLÉ® TOLL HOUSE®
   Premier White Morsels
1 cup finely chopped walnuts

**Makes about
2½ dozen cookies**

**COMBINE** flour, baking soda, ginger, cinnamon, cloves and salt in small bowl. Beat sugar and butter in large mixer bowl until creamy. Beat in egg and molasses. Gradually beat in flour mixture. Stir in morsels. Refrigerate for 20 minutes or until slightly firm.

**PREHEAT** oven to 375°F.

**ROLL** dough into 1-inch balls; roll in walnuts. Place on ungreased baking sheets.

**BAKE** for 9 to 11 minutes or until golden brown. Cool on baking sheets for 2 minutes; remove to wire racks to cool completely.

*Note:*

Try to purchase ground spices in the smallest amounts possible, as they lose flavor over time. Store them in a cool, dark place—exposure to heat, light and moisture will make them deteriorate more quickly.

# Lemon Cookies

**Makes about 3 dozen cookies**

1 package DUNCAN HINES®
   Moist Deluxe® Lemon
   Supreme Cake Mix
2 eggs
⅓ cup vegetable oil

1 tablespoon lemon juice
¾ cup chopped nuts or flaked
   coconut
Confectioners' sugar

*1.* Preheat oven to 375°F. Grease baking sheets.

*2.* Combine cake mix, eggs, oil and lemon juice in large bowl. Beat at low speed with electric mixer until well blended. Add nuts. Shape dough into 1-inch balls. Place 1 inch apart on prepared baking sheets.

*3.* Bake at 375°F for 6 to 7 minutes or until lightly browned. Cool 1 minute on baking sheets. Remove to cooling racks. Sprinkle with confectioners' sugar.

**Tip:** *You can frost cookies with 1 cup confectioners' sugar mixed with 1 tablespoon lemon juice instead of sprinkling cookies with confectioners' sugar.*

# Banana Sandies

**Makes about 2 dozen sandwich cookies**

2⅓ cups all-purpose flour
1 cup (2 sticks) butter, softened
¾ cup granulated sugar
¼ cup brown sugar
½ cup ¼-inch slices banana
   (about 1 medium)
1 teaspoon vanilla

¼ teaspoon salt
⅔ cup chopped pecans
Prepared cream cheese
   frosting
Yellow food coloring
   (optional)

*1.* Preheat oven to 350°F. Grease cookie sheets. Combine flour, butter, sugars, banana slices, vanilla and salt in large bowl. Beat 2 to 3 minutes, scraping bowl often, until well blended. Stir in pecans. Shape rounded teaspoonfuls of dough into 1-inch balls. Place 2 inches apart on prepared cookie sheets. Flatten cookies to ¼-inch thickness with bottom of glass dipped in sugar. Bake 12 to 15 minutes or until edges are lightly browned. Remove immediately to wire racks; cool completely.

*2.* Tint frosting with food coloring, if desired. Spread 1 tablespoon frosting over bottoms of half the cookies. Top with remaining cookies.

# Peanut Blossom Cookies

| | | |
|---|---|---|
| 1 (14-ounce) can EAGLE® BRAND Sweetened Condensed Milk (NOT evaporated milk)<br>¾ cup peanut butter | 2 cups biscuit mix<br>1 teaspoon vanilla extract<br>⅓ cup sugar<br>60 solid milk chocolate candy kisses, unwrapped | Makes about 5 dozen cookies |

*1.* Preheat oven to 375°F. In large mixing bowl, beat Eagle Brand and peanut butter until smooth. Add biscuit mix and vanilla; mix well. Shape into 1-inch balls. Roll in sugar. Place 2 inches apart on ungreased baking sheets.

*2.* Bake 6 to 8 minutes or until lightly browned (do not overbake). Immediately remove from oven; press candy kiss in center of each cookie. Cool. Store tightly covered at room temperature.

*Note:*

Sweetened condensed milk is a canned product that is the result of evaporating about half of the water from whole milk and adding cane sugar or corn syrup to sweeten and preserve the milk.

# Shortbread Cookies

**Makes about 6 dozen cookies**

**Prep Time:**
*15 minutes*

**Bake Time:**
*13 minutes*

1½ cups (3 sticks) butter or margarine, softened
1 package (8 ounces) PHILADELPHIA® Cream Cheese, softened

½ cup granulated sugar
3 cups flour
Powdered sugar

**MIX** butter, cream cheese and granulated sugar until well blended. Mix in flour.

**SHAPE** dough into 1-inch balls; place on ungreased cookie sheets.

**BAKE** at 400°F for 10 to 13 minutes or until light golden brown and set; cool on wire racks. Sprinkle with powdered sugar.

<u>Holiday Cookies:</u> *Tint dough with a few drops of food coloring before shaping to add a festive touch.*

# Chocolate Cherry Cookies

**Makes about 4 dozen cookies**

½ cup (1 stick) butter, softened
½ cup sugar
1 egg
2 squares (1 ounce each) unsweetened chocolate, melted and cooled
2 cups cake flour

1 teaspoon vanilla
¼ teaspoon salt
Maraschino cherries, well drained (about 48)
1 cup semisweet or milk chocolate chips

Beat butter and sugar in large bowl until light. Add egg and melted chocolate; beat until fluffy. Stir in cake flour, vanilla and salt until well blended. Cover; refrigerate until firm, about 1 hour.

Preheat oven to 400°F. Lightly grease cookie sheets or line with parchment paper. Shape dough into 1-inch balls. Place 2 inches apart on prepared cookie sheets. With knuckle of finger, make deep indentation in center of each ball. Place cherry into each indentation. Bake 8 minutes or just until set. Meanwhile, melt chocolate chips in small bowl over hot water. Stir until melted. Remove cookies to wire racks. Drizzle melted chocolate over tops of cookies while still warm. Refrigerate cookies until chocolate is set.

# Simpler Than Sin Peanut Chocolate Cookies

| | | |
|---|---|---|
| 1 cup PETER PAN® Extra Crunchy Peanut Butter<br>1 cup sugar<br>1 egg, at room temperature and beaten | 2 teaspoons vanilla<br>1 (6-ounce) dark or milk chocolate candy bar, broken into squares | **Makes 21 to 24 cookies**<br><br>**Prep Time:**<br>*10 minutes*<br><br>**Bake Time:**<br>*19 minutes* |

Preheat oven to 350°F. In medium bowl, combine Peter Pan® Peanut Butter, sugar, egg and vanilla; mix well. Roll dough into 1-inch balls. Place 2 inches apart on ungreased cookie sheet. Bake 12 minutes. Remove from oven and place chocolate square in center of each cookie. Bake an additional 5 to 7 minutes or until cookies are lightly golden around edges. Cool 5 minutes. Remove to wire rack. Cool.

**Note:** *This simple recipe is unusual because it doesn't contain any flour—but it still makes great cookies!*

# Jeremy's Famous Turtles

**Makes about 7½ dozen cookies**

**Cookies**
- 3 egg whites
- 1 egg yolk
- 1¼ Butter Flavor CRISCO® Sticks or 1¼ cups Butter Flavor CRISCO® all-vegetable shortening plus additional for greasing
- ¾ cup firmly packed brown sugar
- ½ cup granulated sugar
- 1 teaspoon vanilla
- 1¾ cups all-purpose flour
- 1 teaspoon baking soda
- ¾ teaspoon salt
- ½ cup butterscotch chips
- ½ cup semisweet chocolate chips
- ½ cup chopped dates
- ½ cup chopped pecans
- ½ cup diced dried fruit bits
- ⅓ cup cinnamon applesauce
- ¼ cup toasted wheat germ
- ¼ cup ground shelled sunflower seeds
- 2 tablespoons honey
- 3 cups oats (quick or old-fashioned), uncooked
- 8 ounces pecan halves (2 cups)

**Coating**
- 1 to 2 egg whites, lightly beaten
- ½ cup granulated sugar

*Note:*

If you're baking big batches of cookies, you'll need good storage containers. Choose cookie jars or tins with tight-fitting lids, so air cannot seep in and turn the cookies stale in a hurry.

**1.** For cookies, place 3 egg whites in medium bowl. Beat at medium speed of electric mixer until frothy. Beat in egg yolk until well blended.

**2.** Combine 1¼ cups shortening, brown sugar and granulated sugar in large bowl. Beat at medium speed until well blended. Add egg mixture and vanilla. Beat until well blended.

**3.** Combine flour, baking soda and salt. Add gradually to shortening mixture at low speed. Stir in, 1 at a time, butterscotch chips, chocolate chips, dates, chopped nuts, fruit bits, applesauce, wheat germ, sunflower seeds, honey and oats. Cover. Refrigerate dough 1 hour.

**4.** Heat oven to 350°F. Grease baking sheets with shortening. Place sheets of foil on countertop for cooling cookies.

*5.* Shape dough into 1½-inch balls. Cut pecan halves into 4 lengthwise pieces for legs. Save broken pieces for heads and tails.

*6.* For coating, dip top of cookie ball in beaten egg white, then dip in sugar. Place cookies, sugar side up, 2½ inches apart on prepared baking sheets. Insert lengthwise nut pieces for legs. Flatten slightly. Place nut sliver for tail and rounded nut piece for head.

*7.* Bake one baking sheet at a time at 350°F for 9 to 11 minutes or until lightly browned. *Do not overbake.* Reposition nuts, if necessary. Cool 30 seconds on baking sheets. Remove cookies to foil to cool completely.

# Super-Duper Chocolate Pecan Cookies

| | |
|---|---|
| ½ cup (1 stick) butter, softened | 1 package (12 ounces) semisweet chocolate chunks *or* 4 semisweet chocolate bars (3 ounces each), cut into squares |
| ⅓ cup peanut butter | |
| ⅓ cup granulated sugar | |
| ⅓ cup packed light brown sugar | |
| 1 egg | |
| 1 teaspoon vanilla | 1 cup pecan halves, cut into pieces |
| 1¼ cups all-purpose flour | |
| ½ teaspoon baking soda | |

**Makes 1 dozen cookies**

Preheat oven to 350°F. Lightly grease two cookie sheets or line with parchment paper. Beat butter, peanut butter, sugars, egg and vanilla in large bowl until light and fluffy. Blend in combined flour and baking soda. Scoop out ⅓ cupfuls of dough, forming into 12 balls. Place on prepared cookie sheets, spacing about 4 inches apart. Press each cookie to flatten slightly. Press chocolate chunks and pecan pieces into cookies, dividing equally. Bake 15 to 17 minutes or until firm in center. Remove to wire racks to cool.

# Double Peanut Butter Cookies

**Makes about 4 dozen cookies**

¼ cup (½ stick) butter or margarine, softened
¼ cup shortening
½ cup REESE'S® Creamy Peanut Butter
½ cup granulated sugar
½ cup packed light brown sugar
1 egg

1¼ cups all-purpose flour
¾ teaspoon baking soda
½ teaspoon baking powder
¼ teaspoon salt
1⅔ cups (10-ounce package) REESE'S® Peanut Butter Chips

*1.* Heat oven to 375°F.

*2.* Combine butter, shortening, peanut butter, granulated sugar, brown sugar and egg in large bowl; beat on medium speed of mixer until well blended. Stir together flour, baking soda, baking powder and salt; gradually add to butter mixture, beating until blended. Stir in peanut butter chips.

*3.* Shape dough into 1-inch balls. Place 2 inches apart onto ungreased cookie sheet. Using fork dipped in additional granulated sugar, flatten balls to about ¼-inch thickness by pressing fork in two directions to form crisscross pattern.

*4.* Bake 8 to 10 minutes or until set. Cool slightly; remove from cookie sheet to wire rack. Cool completely.

# Spicy Lemon Crescents

**Makes about 2 dozen cookies**

1 cup (2 sticks) butter or margarine, softened
1½ cups powdered sugar, divided
½ teaspoon lemon extract
½ teaspoon grated lemon zest
2 cups cake flour
½ cup finely chopped almonds, walnuts or pecans

1 teaspoon ground cinnamon
½ teaspoon ground cardamom
½ teaspoon ground nutmeg
1¾ cups "M&M's"® Chocolate Mini Baking Bits

Preheat oven to 375°F. Lightly grease cookie sheets; set aside. In large bowl cream butter and ½ cup sugar; add lemon extract and zest until well blended. In medium bowl combine flour, nuts, cinnamon, cardamom and nutmeg; add to creamed mixture until well blended. Stir in "M&M's"® Chocolate Mini Baking Bits. Using 1 tablespoon of dough at a time, form into crescent shapes; place about 2 inches apart onto prepared cookie sheets. Bake 12 to 14 minutes or until edges are golden. Cool 2 minutes on cookie sheets. Gently roll warm crescents in remaining 1 cup sugar. Cool completely on wire racks. Store in tightly covered container.

# Butter Almond Classic Cookies

| 1 cup (2 sticks) I CAN'T BELIEVE IT'S NOT BUTTER!® Spread<br>½ cup confectioners' sugar | ¾ teaspoon almond extract<br>1¾ cups all-purpose flour<br>½ cup finely chopped almonds |
|---|---|

**Makes 40 cookies**

In large bowl, with electric mixer beat I Can't Believe It's Not Butter! Spread and ½ cup sugar until light and fluffy, about 5 minutes. Beat in almond extract, then flour until blended. Beat in almonds. Turn dough onto plastic wrap and shape into flat circle. Cover and refrigerate at least 1 hour.

Preheat oven to 350°F. Divide dough into 8 pie-shaped wedges. On lightly floured surface, with lightly floured hands, roll each wedge into 1-inch-thick log. Cut each log into 2- to 3-inch slices. Shape each slice into crescent; arrange on ungreased baking sheets.

Bake 15 minutes or until edges are lightly golden. On wire rack, let stand 2 minutes; remove from sheets and cool completely. Before serving, sprinkle cookies with additional sugar.

*Note:*
If the dough sticks to your hands as you are shaping the crescents, keep your hands very lightly dusted with flour.

# Chocolate Malted Cookies

**Makes about 4 dozen cookies**

½ cup (1 stick) butter, softened
½ cup shortening
1¾ cups powdered sugar, divided
1 teaspoon vanilla
2 cups all-purpose flour

1 cup malted milk powder, divided
¼ cup unsweetened cocoa powder

*Note:*

Malt comes from soaked barley grains that are allowed to germinate before being dried, roasted and then ground into a powder. Malted milk powder is a mixture of malt sugar and powdered milk.

*1.* Beat butter, shortening, ¾ cup powdered sugar and vanilla in large bowl. Add flour, ½ cup malted milk powder and cocoa until well blended. Refrigerate several hours or overnight.

*2.* Preheat oven to 350°F. Shape slightly mounded teaspoonfuls of dough into balls. Place dough balls about 2 inches apart on ungreased cookie sheets. Bake 14 to 16 minutes or until lightly browned.

*3.* Meanwhile, combine remaining 1 cup powdered sugar and ½ cup malted milk powder in medium bowl. Remove cookies to wire racks; cool 5 minutes. Roll cookies in powdered sugar mixture.

**Tip:** *Substitute 6 ounces melted semisweet chocolate for the 1 cup powdered sugar and ½ cup malted milk powder used to roll the cookies. Instead, dip cookies in melted chocolate and let dry on wire racks until coating is set.*

# Chocolate Oat Chewies

1 package DUNCAN HINES®
    Moist Deluxe® Devil's Food
    Cake Mix
1⅓ cups old-fashioned oats,
    uncooked
1 cup flaked coconut, toasted
    and divided

¾ cup butter or margarine,
    melted
2 eggs, beaten
1 teaspoon vanilla extract
5 bars (1.55 ounces each) milk
    chocolate, cut into
    rectangles

**Makes about
4½ dozen cookies**

*1.* Preheat oven to 350°F.

*2.* Combine cake mix, oats, ½ cup coconut, butter, eggs and vanilla extract in large bowl. Cover and chill 15 minutes.

*3.* Shape dough into 1-inch balls. Place balls 2 inches apart on ungreased baking sheets. Bake at 350°F for 12 minutes or until tops are slightly cracked. Remove from oven. Press one milk chocolate rectangle into center of each cookie. Sprinkle with remaining ½ cup coconut. Remove to cooling racks.

## Chocolate 101

**Chocolate liquor:** This is the dark, rich liquid that is pressed from roasted cocoa beans during the manufacturing process. It is the basis of all types of chocolate.

**Unsweetened chocolate:** Also known as baking or bitter chocolate, this is pure chocolate—no sugar or flavorings have been added. It is used only for baking and is never eaten plain.

**Bittersweet chocolate:** This is pure chocolate with some sugar added. If unavailable, substitute half unsweetened chocolate and half semisweet chocolate.

**Semisweet chocolate:** This is pure chocolate combined with sugar and extra cocoa butter. It is interchangeable with bittersweet chocolate in most recipes.

**Milk chocolate:** This is pure chocolate with sugar, extra cocoa butter and milk solids added. It can't be used interchangeably with other chocolates because the milk solids change its melting and cooking properties.

**White chocolate:** This is not considered real chocolate since it contains no chocolate liquor. It is a combination of cocoa butter, sugar, milk solids, vanilla and emulsifiers.

# Devil's Food Fudge Cookies

**Makes 3 dozen cookies**

1 package DUNCAN HINES®
   Moist Deluxe® Devil's Food
   Cake Mix
2 eggs

½ cup vegetable oil
1 cup semisweet chocolate
   chips
½ cup chopped walnuts

*1.* Preheat oven to 350°F. Grease baking sheets.

*2.* Combine cake mix, eggs and oil in large bowl. Stir until thoroughly blended. Stir in chocolate chips and walnuts. (Mixture will be stiff.) Shape dough into 36 (1¼-inch) balls. Place 2 inches apart on prepared baking sheets.

*3.* Bake at 350°F for 10 to 11 minutes. (Cookies will look moist.) *Do not overbake.* Cool 2 minutes on baking sheets. Remove to cooling racks. Cool completely. Store in airtight container.

**Tip:** *For a delicious flavor treat, substitute peanut butter chips for the chocolate chips and chopped peanuts for the chopped walnuts.*

# Peanut Butter Thumbprints

1¼ cups firmly packed light
    brown sugar
¾ cup JIF® Creamy Peanut
    Butter
½ CRISCO® Stick or ½ cup
    CRISCO® all-vegetable
    shortening
3 tablespoons milk

1 tablespoon vanilla
1 egg
1¾ cups all-purpose flour
¾ teaspoon baking soda
¾ teaspoon salt
    Granulated sugar
¼ cup SMUCKER'S® Strawberry
    Jam, stirred

**Makes about 4 dozen cookies**

*1.* Heat oven to 375°F. Place sheets of foil on countertop for cooling cookies.

*2.* Place brown sugar, peanut butter, ½ cup shortening, milk and vanilla in large bowl. Beat at medium speed of electric mixer until well blended. Add egg; beat just until blended.

*3.* Combine flour, baking soda and salt. Add to shortening mixture; beat at low speed just until blended.

*4.* Shape dough into 1-inch balls. Roll in granulated sugar. Place 2 inches apart on ungreased baking sheets.

*5.* Bake one baking sheet at a time at 350°F for 6 minutes. Press centers of cookies immediately with back of measuring teaspoon. Bake 3 minutes longer or until cookies are set and just beginning to brown. *Do not overbake*. Cool 2 minutes on baking sheet. Spoon jam into center of each cookie. Remove cookies to foil to cool completely.

*Note:*

Make sure your cookies have cooled completely before storing them. If cookies are put away while still warm, the steam they produce will cause all the cookies in the container to become soggy and soft.

# Tropical Gardens Cookies

**Makes about 7 dozen cookies**

½ cup (1 stick) butter or margarine, softened
½ cup shortening
1 cup granulated sugar
¼ cup packed light brown sugar
1 teaspoon vanilla extract
1 egg
1 tablespoon freshly grated orange peel

2¾ cups all-purpose flour
1½ teaspoons baking soda
1 teaspoon salt
¼ cup orange juice
2 cups (12-ounce package) HERSHEY₅S MINI CHIPS™ Semi-Sweet Chocolate Chips
Additional granulated sugar

***Note:***

**When grating orange peel, remove only the outer orange layer of the skin, which is very sweet and flavorful. Avoid grating into the white pith, as it has a bitter taste.**

***1.*** Beat butter, shortening, 1 cup granulated sugar, brown sugar and vanilla in large bowl until fluffy. Add egg and orange peel; blend well. Stir together flour, baking soda and salt; add alternately with orange juice to butter mixture. Stir in small chocolate chips. Cover; refrigerate dough about 1 hour or until firm enough to handle.

***2.*** Heat oven to 350°F.

***3.*** Shape dough into 1-inch balls; roll in granulated sugar. Place on ungreased cookie sheet; flatten by crisscrossing with tines of fork.

***4.*** Bake 8 to 10 minutes or until lightly browned. Cool slightly; remove from cookie sheet to wire rack. Cool completely.

# Fudgy Raisin Pixies

**Makes about 4 dozen cookies**

½ cup (1 stick) butter, softened
2 cups granulated sugar
4 eggs
2 cups all-purpose flour, divided
¾ cup unsweetened cocoa powder

2 teaspoons baking powder
½ teaspoon salt
½ cup chocolate-covered raisins
Powdered sugar

Beat butter and granulated sugar in large bowl until light and fluffy. Add eggs; mix until well blended. Combine 1 cup flour, cocoa, baking powder and salt in small bowl; add to butter mixture. Mix until well blended. Stir in remaining 1 cup flour and chocolate-covered raisins. Cover; refrigerate until firm, 2 hours or overnight.

Preheat oven to 350°F. Grease cookie sheets. Coat hands with powdered sugar. Shape rounded teaspoonfuls of dough into 1-inch balls; roll in powdered sugar. Place 2 inches apart on prepared cookie sheets. Bake 14 to 17 minutes or until firm to the touch. Immediately remove cookies to wire racks; cool completely.

# Cashew-Lemon Shortbread Cookies

| | | |
|---|---|---|
| ½ cup roasted cashews | 1 teaspoon vanilla | **Makes 2 to 2½ dozen cookies** |
| 1 cup (2 sticks) butter, softened | 2 cups all-purpose flour | |
| ½ cup sugar | Additional sugar | **Prep and Bake Time:** |
| 2 teaspoons lemon extract | | *30 minutes* |

*1.* Preheat oven to 325°F. Place cashews in food processor; process until finely ground. Add butter, sugar, lemon extract and vanilla; process until well blended. Add flour; process using on/off pulses until dough is well blended and begins to form a ball.

*2.* Shape dough into 1½-inch balls; roll in additional sugar. Place about 2 inches apart on ungreased baking sheets; flatten.

*3.* Bake cookies 17 to 19 minutes or just until set and edges are lightly browned. Remove cookies from baking sheets to wire rack to cool.

# Swiss Chocolate Crispies

**Makes about 4 dozen cookies**

*Note:*

If you use insulated baking sheets—the ones with an air pocket —your cookies won't get quite as crisp. They may also take slightly longer to bake.

1 package DUNCAN HINES®
    Moist Deluxe® Swiss
    Chocolate Cake Mix
½ cup shortening plus
    additional for greasing
½ cup butter or margarine,
    softened

2 eggs
2 tablespoons water
3 cups crispy rice cereal,
    divided

*1.* Combine cake mix, ½ cup shortening, butter, eggs and water in large bowl. Beat at low speed with electric mixer for 2 minutes. Fold in 1 cup cereal. Refrigerate 1 hour.

*2.* Crush remaining 2 cups cereal into coarse crumbs.

*3.* Preheat oven to 350°F. Grease baking sheets. Shape dough into 1-inch balls. Roll in crushed cereal. Place on baking sheets about 1 inch apart.

*4.* Bake at 350°F for 11 to 13 minutes. Cool 1 minute on baking sheets. Remove to wire racks.

# Lemon Yogurt Cookies

**Makes about 4 dozen cookies**

½ cup (1 stick) margarine,
    softened
1¼ cups granulated sugar
½ cup plain fat-free yogurt or
    lemon lowfat yogurt
2 egg whites *or* 1 egg
1 tablespoon grated lemon peel

½ teaspoon vanilla
2 cups QUAKER® Oats (quick or
    old fashioned, uncooked)
1½ cups all-purpose flour
1 teaspoon baking powder
½ teaspoon baking soda
¼ cup powdered sugar

Lightly spray cookie sheets with no-stick cooking spray or oil lightly. Beat margarine and 1¼ cups granulated sugar until fluffy. Add yogurt, egg whites, lemon peel and vanilla; mix until well blended. Gradually add combined remaining ingredients except powdered sugar; mix well. Cover and refrigerate 1 to 3 hours.

Heat oven to 375°F. With lightly floured hands, shape dough into 1-inch balls; place on prepared cookie sheets. Using bottom of glass dipped in granulated sugar, press into ⅛-inch-thick circles. Bake 10 to 12 minutes or until edges are lightly browned. Cool 2 minutes on cookie sheets; remove to wire rack. Sift powdered sugar over warm cookies. Cool completely. Store tightly covered.

# Snow-Covered Almond Crescents

| | | |
|---|---|---|
| 1 cup (2 sticks) margarine or butter, softened<br>¾ cup powdered sugar<br>½ teaspoon almond extract *or*<br>    2 teaspoons vanilla extract<br>2 cups all-purpose flour | ¼ teaspoon salt (optional)<br>1 cup QUAKER® Oats (quick or old fashioned, uncooked)<br>½ cup finely chopped almonds<br>Additional powdered sugar | **Makes about 4 dozen cookies** |

Preheat oven to 325°F. Beat margarine, ¾ cup powdered sugar and almond extract until fluffy. Add flour and salt; mix until well blended. Stir in oats and almonds. Shape level measuring tablespoonfuls of dough into crescents. Place on ungreased cookie sheets about 2 inches apart.

Bake 14 to 17 minutes or until bottoms are light golden brown. Remove to wire rack. Sift additional powdered sugar generously over warm cookies. Cool completely. Store tightly covered.

# Mini Chip Snowball Cookies

**Makes about 5 dozen cookies**

1½ cups (3 sticks) butter or margarine, softened
¾ cup powdered sugar
1 tablespoon vanilla extract
½ teaspoon salt
3 cups all-purpose flour

2 cups (12-ounce package) NESTLÉ® TOLL HOUSE® Semi-Sweet Chocolate Mini Morsels
½ cup finely chopped nuts
Powdered sugar

*Note:*

Never store two kinds of cookies in the same container, because their flavors and textures can change.

**PREHEAT** oven to 375°F.

**BEAT** butter, sugar, vanilla extract and salt in large mixer bowl until creamy. Gradually beat in flour; stir in morsels and nuts. Shape level tablespoons of dough into 1¼-inch balls. Place on ungreased baking sheets.

**BAKE** for 10 to 12 minutes or until cookies are set and lightly browned. Remove from oven. Sift powdered sugar over hot cookies on baking sheets. Cool on baking sheets for 10 minutes; remove to wire racks to cool completely. Sprinkle with additional powdered sugar, if desired. Store in airtight containers.

# Marshmallow Sandwich Cookies

1¼ cups sugar
⅔ cup butter
¼ cup light corn syrup
1 egg
1 teaspoon vanilla
2 cups all-purpose flour

½ cup unsweetened cocoa powder
2 teaspoons baking soda
¼ teaspoon salt
Additional sugar for rolling
24 large marshmallows

**Makes about 2 dozen sandwich cookies**

Preheat oven to 350°F. Beat 1¼ cups sugar and butter in large bowl until light and fluffy. Beat in corn syrup, egg and vanilla. Combine flour, cocoa, baking soda and salt in medium bowl; add to butter mixture. Beat until well blended. Cover and refrigerate dough 15 minutes or until firm enough to roll into balls.

Place sugar in shallow dish. Roll tablespoonfuls of dough into 1-inch balls; roll in sugar to coat. Place cookies 3 inches apart on ungreased cookie sheets. Bake 10 to 11 minutes or until set. Remove cookies to wire racks; cool completely.

To assemble sandwiches, place one marshmallow on flat side of one cookie on paper plate. Microwave at HIGH 12 seconds or until marshmallow is softened. Immediately place another cookie, flat side down, on top of hot marshmallow; press together slightly. Repeat with remaining cookies and marshmallows.

*Note:*

Sandwich cookies should not be assembled more than two days in advance or they'll become soggy. It's best to fill them on the same day that they will be eaten.

# Honey Ginger Snaps

**Makes 3½ dozen cookies**

2 cups all-purpose flour
1 tablespoon ground ginger
2 teaspoons baking soda
⅛ teaspoon salt
⅛ teaspoon ground cloves
½ cup shortening

¼ cup (½ stick) butter, softened
1½ cups sugar, divided
¼ cup honey
1 egg
1 teaspoon vanilla

Preheat oven to 350°F. Grease cookie sheets. Combine flour, ginger, baking soda, salt and cloves in medium bowl.

Beat shortening and butter in large bowl with electric mixer at medium speed until smooth. Gradually beat in 1 cup sugar until blended; increase speed to high and beat until light and fluffy. Beat in honey, egg and vanilla until fluffy. Gradually stir in flour mixture until blended.

Shape mixture into 1-inch balls. Place remaining ½ cup sugar in shallow bowl; roll balls in sugar to coat. Place 2 inches apart on prepared cookie sheets.

Bake 10 minutes or until golden brown. Let cookies stand on cookie sheets 5 minutes; transfer to wire racks to cool completely. Store in airtight container up to 1 week.

# Fudgey German Chocolate Sandwich Cookies

1¾ cups all-purpose flour
1½ cups sugar
¾ cup (1½ sticks) butter or
    margarine, softened
⅔ cup HERSHEY⅔S Cocoa or
    HERSHEY⅔S Dutch
    Processed Cocoa
¾ teaspoon baking soda

¼ teaspoon salt
2 eggs
2 tablespoons milk
1 teaspoon vanilla extract
½ cup finely chopped pecans
    Coconut and Pecan Filling
    (recipe follows)

**Makes about
17 sandwich cookies**

**Prep Time:**
*25 minutes*

**Bake Time:**
*9 minutes*

**Cool Time:**
*35 minutes*

*1.* Heat oven to 350°F. Combine flour, sugar, butter, cocoa, baking soda, salt, eggs, milk and vanilla in large bowl. Beat at medium speed of mixer until blended (batter will be stiff). Stir in pecans.

*2.* Form dough into 1¼-inch balls. Place on ungreased cookie sheet; flatten slightly.

*3.* Bake 9 to 11 minutes or until almost set. Cool slightly; remove from cookie sheet to wire rack. Cool completely. Spread about 1 heaping tablespoon Coconut and Pecan Filling onto bottom of one cookie. Top with second cookie to make sandwich. Serve warm or at room temperature.

## Coconut and Pecan Filling

½ cup (1 stick) butter or
    margarine
½ cup packed light brown sugar
¼ cup light corn syrup
1 cup MOUNDS® Sweetened
    Coconut Flakes, toasted*

1 cup finely chopped pecans
1 teaspoon vanilla extract

*\*To toast coconut: Heat oven to 350°F. Spread
coconut in even layer on baking sheet. Bake
6 to 8 minutes, stirring occasionally, until
golden.*

Melt butter in medium saucepan over medium heat; add brown sugar and corn syrup. Stir constantly, until thick and bubbly. Remove from heat; stir in coconut, pecans and vanilla. Use warm.

*Makes about 2 cups filling*

# Double Chocolate Peanut Butter Thumbprint Cookies

**Makes 3½ dozen cookies**

1½ cups all-purpose flour
⅓ cup NESTLÉ® TOLL HOUSE® Baking Cocoa
1½ teaspoons baking powder
¼ teaspoon salt
2 cups (12-ounce package) NESTLÉ® TOLL HOUSE® Semi-Sweet Chocolate Morsels, *divided*

1 cup granulated sugar
About 1 cup chunky or smooth peanut butter (not all-natural), *divided*
⅓ cup butter or margarine, softened
1½ teaspoons vanilla extract
2 large eggs

**PREHEAT** oven to 350°F.

**COMBINE** flour, cocoa, baking powder and salt in small bowl. Melt *1 cup* morsels in small, *heavy-duty* saucepan over low heat; stir until smooth. Beat granulated sugar, *⅓ cup* peanut butter, butter and vanilla extract in large mixer bowl until creamy. Beat in melted chocolate. Add eggs, one at a time, beating well after each addition. Gradually beat in cocoa mixture. Stir in *remaining* morsels. Cover; refrigerate just until firm.

**SHAPE** into 1½-inch balls. Place 2 inches apart on ungreased baking sheets. Press thumb into tops to make about ½-inch-deep depressions. Fill each depression with about ½ teaspoon peanut butter.

**BAKE** for 10 to 15 minutes or until sides are set but centers are still slightly soft. Cool on baking sheets for 2 minutes; remove to wire racks to cool completely.

# Gingerbread Teddies

1 cup butter or margarine
⅔ cup DOMINO® Light Brown
    Sugar, packed
⅓ cup DOMINO® Granulated
    Sugar
½ cup molasses
1 egg, beaten

2 teaspoons vanilla
4 cups all-purpose flour
1½ teaspoons ground cinnamon
1 teaspoon ground ginger
¾ teaspoon baking soda
½ teaspoon ground cloves
    Chocolate chips

**Makes 4 large cookies**

In medium saucepan, combine butter, sugars and molasses. Heat and stir over medium heat until butter is melted and sugars are dissolved. Pour into large mixing bowl; cool 10 minutes. Add egg and vanilla; mix well. Stir together flour, cinnamon, ginger, baking soda and cloves. Add to butter mixture; beat until well mixed. Divide dough in half. Wrap in plastic wrap; chill at least 2 hours.

For each bear, shape dough into one 3-inch ball, one 2-inch ball, six ¾-inch balls and five ½-inch balls.

On ungreased cookie sheet, flatten 3-inch ball to ½-inch thickness for body. Attach 2-inch ball for head; flatten. Attach ¾-inch balls for arms, legs and ears. Place ½-inch balls at ends of arms and legs to make paws. Add last ball to face to make nose. Use chocolate chips for eyes and navel. Melt 1 to 2 tablespoons chocolate chips. Using decorator's tip, pipe on mouth.

Bake in 350°F oven for 10 minutes or until lightly browned. Remove and cool on wire rack. Decorate with red satin ribbon.

*Note:*

To soften brown sugar that has hardened, place a cut piece of apple in the bag or container and close it tightly for one or two days.

# Cherry Coconut Cookies

**Makes 3½ dozen cookies**

¾ cup sugar
⅔ Butter Flavor CRISCO® Stick
    or ⅔ cup Butter Flavor
    CRISCO® all-vegetable
    shortening
1 egg
1 teaspoon grated lemon peel
¾ teaspoon almond extract

½ teaspoon salt
1¾ cups all-purpose flour
1 teaspoon baking powder
½ teaspoon baking soda
¾ cup flaked coconut
½ cup coarsely chopped pecans
⅓ cup quartered maraschino
    cherries, well drained

*1.* Heat oven to 350°F. Place sheets of foil on countertop for cooling cookies.

*2.* Combine sugar, ⅔ cup shortening, egg, lemon peel, almond extract and salt in large bowl. Beat at medium speed with electric mixer until well blended.

*3.* Combine flour, baking powder and baking soda. Add gradually to creamed mixture at low speed. Mix until blended. Stir in coconut, pecans and cherries. Shape dough into 1-inch balls. Place 2 inches apart on ungreased baking sheet.

*4.* Bake for 11 to 12 minutes. *Do not overbake.* Cool 2 minutes on baking sheet. Remove cookies to foil to cool completely.

# Classic Peanut Butter Cookies

**Makes 4 dozen cookies**

1 cup unsalted butter, softened
1 cup crunchy peanut butter
1 cup granulated sugar
1 cup light brown sugar, firmly
    packed

2 eggs
2½ cups all-purpose flour
1½ teaspoons baking soda
1 teaspoon baking powder
½ teaspoon salt

Beat butter, peanut butter and sugars until creamy. Beat in eggs. In separate bowl, sift flour, baking soda, baking powder and salt. Stir into batter until blended. Refrigerate 1 hour. Roll dough into 1-inch balls and place on baking sheets. Flatten each ball with fork, making criss-cross pattern. Bake in preheated 375°F oven about 10 minutes or until cookies begin to brown. Do not overbake.

Favorite recipe from **Peanut Advisory Board**

*Note:*

**Both baking soda and baking powder should both be stored in a cool, dry place. Replace them after 6 months to ensure that your baked goods rise properly.**

# Cinnamon Crinkles

| | |
|---|---|
| 2 tablespoons sugar | 1 teaspoon vanilla extract |
| ½ teaspoon ground cinnamon | 1 package DUNCAN HINES® |
| 2 eggs, separated | Moist Deluxe® French |
| 1 teaspoon water | Vanilla Cake Mix |
| ¾ cup butter or margarine, softened | 48 whole almonds or pecan halves for garnish |

**Makes 4 dozen cookies**

*1.* Preheat oven to 375°F. Combine sugar and cinnamon in small bowl. Set aside. Combine egg whites and water in another small bowl; beat lightly with fork. Set aside.

*2.* Combine butter, egg yolks and vanilla extract in large bowl. Blend in cake mix gradually. Beat at low speed with electric mixer until blended. Roll 1 rounded teaspoon of dough into ball. Dip half the ball into egg white mixture then into cinnamon-sugar mixture. Place ball sugar side up on ungreased baking sheet. Press almond on top. Repeat with remaining dough, placing balls 2 inches apart.

*3.* Bake at 375°F for 9 to 12 minutes or until edges are light golden brown. Cool 2 minutes on baking sheets. Remove to cooling racks. Store in airtight container.

<u>Note:</u> *Cookies will be slightly puffed when removed from the oven and will settle during cooling.*

# Peanut Butter Brickle Cookies

**Makes about 4 dozen cookies**

1½ cups all-purpose flour
1 cup granulated sugar
1 cup (2 sticks) butter, softened
½ cup peanut butter
1 egg
2 tablespoons packed light
    brown sugar

1 teaspoon vanilla
½ teaspoon baking soda
1 package (6 ounces) almond
    brickle bits

Preheat oven to 350°F. Grease cookie sheets. Combine flour, granulated sugar, butter, peanut butter, egg, brown sugar, vanilla and baking soda in large bowl. Beat at medium speed of electric mixer 2 to 3 minutes until well blended, scraping bowl often. Stir in almond brickle bits.

Shape rounded teaspoonfuls of dough into 1-inch balls. Place 2 inches apart on prepared cookie sheets. Flatten cookies to ⅛-inch thickness with bottom of glass covered with waxed paper. Bake 7 to 9 minutes or until edges are very lightly browned.

# Mrs. J's Chip Cookies

**Makes about 8 dozen cookies**

4 cups crisp rice cereal
1 milk chocolate crunch bar
    (5 ounces), broken into
    squares
2 cups all-purpose flour
1 teaspoon baking powder
1 teaspoon baking soda
¼ teaspoon salt

1 cup (2 sticks) butter, softened
1 cup granulated sugar
1 cup packed light brown sugar
2 eggs
1 teaspoon vanilla
1 package (12 ounces)
    semisweet chocolate chips
1½ cups chopped walnuts

Preheat oven to 375°F. Line cookie sheets with parchment paper or leave ungreased. Process cereal in blender or food processor until pulverized. Add chocolate bar; continue processing until both chocolate and cereal are completely ground. Add flour, baking powder, baking soda and salt; process until blended. Beat butter and sugars in large bowl until well blended. Add eggs; beat until light. Blend in vanilla. Add flour mixture; blend until smooth. Stir in chocolate chips and walnuts until blended. Shape dough into 1-inch balls. Place 2 inches apart on prepared cookie sheets. Bake 10 to 12 minutes or until firm in center. *Do not overbake.* Remove to wire racks to cool.

# Soft Spicy Molasses Cookies

| | | |
|---|---|---|
| 2 cups all-purpose flour | ½ teaspoon baking soda | **Makes about 4 dozen cookies** |
| 1 cup sugar | ½ teaspoon ground ginger | |
| ¾ cup (1½ sticks) butter, softened | ½ teaspoon ground cinnamon | |
| ⅓ cup light molasses | ½ teaspoon ground cloves | |
| 3 tablespoons milk | ⅛ teaspoon salt | |
| 1 egg | Additional sugar for rolling | |

Combine flour, 1 cup sugar, butter, molasses, milk, egg, baking soda, ginger, cinnamon, cloves and salt in large bowl. Beat at low speed of electric mixer 2 to 3 minutes or until well blended, scraping bowl often. Cover; refrigerate until firm enough to handle, at least 4 hours or overnight.

Preheat oven to 350°F. Shape rounded teaspoonfuls of dough into 1-inch balls. Roll in sugar. Place 2 inches apart on ungreased cookie sheets. Bake 10 to 12 minutes or until slightly firm to the touch. Remove immediately from cookie sheets to wire racks.

*Note:*

Both light and dark molasses may be bleached with sulfer dioxide. Unsulfered molasses—processed without sulfer—has a milder flavor but either can be used in recipes.

# Mocha Mint Crisps

**Makes about 4 dozen cookies**

1 cup (2 sticks) butter or
    margarine, softened
1 cup sugar
1 egg
¼ cup light corn syrup
¼ teaspoon peppermint extract
1 teaspoon powdered instant
    coffee

1 teaspoon hot water
2 cups all-purpose flour
6 tablespoons HERSHEY'S
    Cocoa
2 teaspoons baking soda
¼ teaspoon salt
    Mocha Mint Sugar
    (recipe follows)

*1.* Beat butter and sugar in large bowl until fluffy. Add egg, corn syrup and peppermint extract; beat until well blended. Dissolve instant coffee in hot water; stir into butter mixture.

*2.* Stir together flour, cocoa, baking soda and salt; gradually add to butter mixture, beating until well blended. Cover; refrigerate dough until firm enough to shape into balls.

*3.* Heat oven to 350°F.

*4.* Shape dough into 1-inch balls. Roll balls in Mocha Mint Sugar. Place on ungreased cookie sheet, about two inches apart.

*5.* Bake 8 to 10 minutes or until no imprint remains when touched lightly. Cool slightly; remove from cookie sheet to wire rack. Cool completely.

**Mocha Mint Sugar:** *Stir together ¼ cup powdered sugar, 2 tablespoons finely crushed hard peppermint candies (about 6 candies) and 1½ teaspoons powdered instant coffee in small bowl.*

# Double Chocolate Chunk Cookies

2 squares (1 ounce each)
   unsweetened chocolate
3 large eggs
1 cup vegetable oil
¾ cup packed light brown sugar
1 teaspoon baking powder
1 teaspoon vanilla

¼ teaspoon baking soda
¼ teaspoon salt
2⅓ cups all-purpose flour
1 package (12 ounces)
   semisweet chocolate
   chunks

**Makes about 2 dozen cookies**

Preheat oven to 350°F. Lightly grease cookie sheets or line with parchment paper. Melt unsweetened chocolate in top of double boiler over hot, not boiling, water. Remove from heat; cool. Beat eggs in large bowl until foamy. Add oil and brown sugar; continue beating until light and frothy. Blend in baking powder, vanilla, baking soda, salt and melted unsweetened chocolate. Mix in flour until smooth. Stir in chocolate chunks. Shape dough into walnut-sized balls. Place 2 inches apart on prepared cookie sheets. Bake 10 to 12 minutes or until firm in center. Do not overbake. Remove to wire racks to cool.

<u>White Chocolate Chunk Cookies:</u> *Substitute one package (12 ounces) white chocolate chunks or two white chocolate candy bars (5 to 6 ounces each), cut into chunks, for semisweet chocolate chunks.*

*Note:*

Oils should be stored in a cool, dark place. Alway check oil for any off odors before using it (especially if you haven't used it in a while). Heat, light and time will turn oils rancid, and rancid oil will ruin any dish it is used in.

# Choco-Scutterbotch

Makes about 3 dozen cookies

⅔ cup shortening
½ cup firmly packed brown
    sugar
2 eggs
1 package DUNCAN HINES®
    Moist Deluxe® Classic
    Yellow Cake Mix
1 cup toasted rice cereal

½ cup milk chocolate chips
½ cup semisweet chocolate
    chips
½ cup butterscotch flavored
    chips
½ cup coarsely chopped
    walnuts or pecans

*1.* Preheat oven to 375°F.

*2.* Combine ⅔ cup shortening and brown sugar in large bowl. Beat at medium speed of electric mixer until well blended. Beat in eggs.

*3.* Add yellow cake mix gradually at low speed. Mix until well blended. Stir in cereal, chocolate chips, butterscotch chips and walnuts with spoon. Stir until well blended. Shape dough into 1¼-inch balls. Place 2 inches apart on *ungreased* baking sheets. Flatten slightly to form circles.

*4.* Bake at 375°F for 7 to 9 minutes or until lightly browned around edges. Cool 2 minutes before removing to wire racks.

# Almond Tea Cookies

1 Butter Flavor CRISCO® Stick or 1 cup Butter Flavor CRISCO® all-vegetable shortening
2 tablespoons milk
1 teaspoon almond extract

½ cup granulated sugar
1⅔ cups all-purpose flour
⅔ cup chopped slivered almonds
¼ teaspoon salt
Confectioners' sugar

Makes 3 dozen cookies

*1.* Heat oven to 350°F. Place sheets of foil on countertop for cooling cookies.

*2.* Combine 1 cup shortening, milk and almond extract in large bowl. Beat at medium speed with electric mixer until well blended. Beat in granulated sugar.

*3.* Combine flour, almonds and salt. Add gradually to creamed mixture at low speed. Shape dough into balls using 1 level measuring tablespoon for each. Place 2 inches apart on *ungreased* baking sheet.

*4.* Bake for 10 to 12 minutes or until set. Cookies will not brown. *Do not overbake.* Cool 2 minutes on baking sheet. Remove cookies to foil to cool completely.

*5.* Roll slightly warm cookies in confectioners' sugar. Roll in confectioners' sugar again when cookies are cool.

*Note:*

Don't use a baking sheet that's too big for your oven. Make sure there's a two-inch margin between the edges of the baking sheet and the oven walls and door to allow the heat to circulate evenly.

# Chewy Chocolate-Cinnamon Cookies

**Makes about 40 cookies**

6 tablespoons butter or margarine, softened
⅔ cup packed light brown sugar
3 tablespoons plus ¼ cup granulated sugar, divided
1 egg
1 teaspoon baking soda

½ cup light corn syrup
1 teaspoon vanilla extract
1½ cups all-purpose flour
⅓ cup HERSHEY'S Cocoa
¼ to ½ teaspoon ground cinnamon

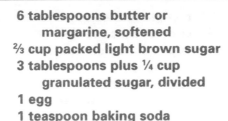

Baking Soda

*1.* Heat oven to 350°F. Spray cookie sheet with nonstick cooking spray.

*2.* Beat butter until creamy. Add brown sugar and 3 tablespoons granulated sugar; beat until blended. Add corn syrup, egg, baking soda and vanilla; beat well.

*3.* Stir together flour and cocoa; beat into butter mixture. If batter becomes to stiff, use wooden spoon to stir in remaining flour. Cover; refrigerate about 30 minutes, if necessary, until batter is firm enough to shape. Shape dough into 1-inch balls. Combine remaining ¼ cup granulated sugar and cinnamon; roll balls in mixture. Place balls 2 inches apart on prepared cookie sheet.

*4.* Bake 9 to 10 minutes or until cookies are set and tops are cracked. Cool slightly; remove from cookie sheet to wire rack. Cool completely.

# Peanut Butter Chocolate Chip Cookies

¼ cup (½ stick) butter or
    margarine, softened
¼ cup shortening
½ cup REESE'S® Creamy Peanut
    Butter
½ cup packed light brown sugar
½ cup granulated sugar
1 egg

1¼ cups all-purpose flour
¾ teaspoon baking soda
½ teaspoon baking powder
2 cups (12-ounce package)
    HERSHEY₅S Semi-Sweet
    Chocolate Chips
Granulated sugar

**Makes about 3 dozen cookies**

*1.* Heat oven to 375°F.

*2.* Beat butter, shortening, peanut butter, brown sugar, ½ cup granulated sugar and egg in large bowl until fluffy. Stir together flour, baking soda and baking powder; stir into butter mixture. Stir in chocolate chips (if necessary, work chocolate chips into batter with hands).

*3.* Shape dough into 1-inch balls; place on ungreased cookie sheet. With fork dipped in granulated sugar flatten slightly in criss-cross pattern.

*4.* Bake 9 to 11 minutes or just until set. Cool slightly; remove from cookie sheet to wire rack. Cool completely.

# White Chip Apricot Oatmeal Cookies

**Makes about 3½ dozen cookies**

¾ cup (1½ sticks) butter or
   margarine, softened
½ cup granulated sugar
½ cup packed light brown sugar
1 egg
1 cup all-purpose flour

1 teaspoon baking soda
2½ cups rolled oats
1⅔ cups (10-ounce package)
   HERSHEY᾿S Premier White
   Chips
¾ cup chopped dried apricots

*Note:*

Use kitchen scissors to cut up dried apricots quickly and easily. Dipping the scissors in hot water or sugar occasionally will help keep the apricots from sticking to the scissors.

*1.* Heat oven to 375°F.

*2.* Beat butter, granulated sugar and brown sugar in large bowl until fluffy. Add egg; beat well. Add flour and baking soda; beat until well blended. Stir in oats, white chips and apricots. Loosely form rounded teaspoonfuls dough into balls; place on ungreased cookie sheet.

*3.* Bake 7 to 9 minutes or just until lightly browned; do not overbake. Cool slightly; remove from cookie sheet to wire rack. Cool completely.

# Special
# Occasion
# Cookies

CHAPTER FIVE

# Valentine's Day Cookie Cards

**Makes 1 dozen cookies**

Butter Cookie Dough
(recipe follows)
1 container (16 ounces) vanilla
   frosting
1 container (16 ounces) pink
   cherry-flavored frosting

Assorted candies

Supplies
   Pastry bags and assorted
   decorating tips

*1.* Preheat oven to 350°F. Grease cookie sheets.

*2.* On lightly floured surface, roll out cookie dough to ⅛-inch thickness. Cut out 4½×3-inch rectangles. Place on prepared cookie sheets.

*3.* Bake 8 to 10 minutes or until edges are lightly browned. Remove to wire racks; cool completely.

*4.* Spread cookies with desired frostings; spoon remaining frostings into pastry bags fitted with decorating tips. Decorate cookies with frostings and candies as desired to resemble Valentine's Day cards.

## Butter Cookie Dough

¾ cup butter, softened
¼ cup granulated sugar
¼ cup packed light brown sugar
1 egg yolk

1¾ cups all-purpose flour
¾ teaspoon baking powder
⅛ teaspoon salt

*1.* Combine butter, granulated sugar, brown sugar and egg yolk in medium bowl. Add flour, baking powder and salt; mix well.

*2.* Cover; refrigerate about 4 hours or until firm.

# Black & White Hearts

| | |
|---|---|
| 1 cup (2 sticks) butter, softened | 1½ teaspoons vanilla |
| ¾ cup sugar | 3 cups all-purpose flour |
| 1 package (3 ounces) cream cheese, softened | 1 cup semisweet chocolate chips |
| 1 egg | 2 tablespoons shortening |

**Makes about 3½ dozen cookies**

*1.* Combine butter, sugar, cream cheese, egg and vanilla in large bowl. Beat at medium speed of electric mixer, scraping bowl often, until light and fluffy. Add flour; beat until well mixed. Divide dough in half; wrap each half in waxed paper. Refrigerate 2 hours or until firm.

*2.* Preheat oven to 375°F. Roll out dough to 1¼-inch thickness on lightly floured surface. Cut out with lightly floured heart-shaped cookie cutter. Place 1 inch apart on ungreased cookie sheets. Bake 7 to 10 minutes or until edges are very lightly browned. Remove immediately to wire racks to cool completely.

*3.* Melt chocolate chips and shortening in small saucepan over low heat 4 to 6 minutes or until melted. Dip half of each heart into melted chocolate. Refrigerate on cookie sheets or trays lined with waxed paper until chocolate is firm. Store, covered, in refrigerator.

*Note:*

After cutting out as many cookies as possible from the first rolling, gather the scraps of dough, pat them out and cut out another batch.
It's best not to reroll scraps of dough more than once, as the cookies may be tough.

# Valentine Stained Glass Hearts

**Makes about 2½ dozen medium cookies**

½ cup (1 stick) butter or
    margarine, softened
¾ cup granulated sugar
2 eggs
1 teaspoon vanilla extract

2⅓ cups all-purpose flour
1 teaspoon baking powder
Red hard candies, crushed
    (about ⅓ cup)
Frosting (optional)

Cream butter and sugar in mixing bowl. Beat in eggs and vanilla. Sift flour and baking powder together. Gradually stir in flour mixture until dough is very stiff. Cover and chill. Dough needs to chill 3 hours to overnight.

Preheat oven to 375°F. Roll out dough to ⅛-inch thickness on lightly floured surface. To prevent cookies from becoming tough and brittle, do not incorporate too much flour. Cut out cookies using large heart-shaped cookie cutter or use sharp knife and cut heart design. Transfer cookies to foil-lined baking sheet. Using small heart-shaped cookie cutter, cut out and remove heart design from center of each cookie. Fill cutout sections with crushed candy. Bake 7 to 9 minutes or until cookies are lightly browned and candy has melted. Do not overcook.

Remove from oven; immediately slide foil off baking sheet. Cool completely; carefully loosen cookies from foil. If desired, pipe decorative borders with frosting around edges.

Favorite recipe from **The Sugar Association, Inc.**

# Gift Tag Cookies

2 squares (1 ounce each) white
   chocolate
1 cup (2 sticks) butter, softened
1 cup granulated sugar
1 large egg
¾ teaspoon vanilla extract
2¼ cups all-purpose flour
1 teaspoon baking powder
¼ teaspoon salt
   Decorator's Icing
   (recipe follows)
1 cup "M&M's"® Chocolate
   Mini Baking Bits
   Black string licorice, cut into
   4-inch lengths

**Makes 1½ dozen
cookies**

In top of double boiler over hot water melt white chocolate. Remove from heat. In large bowl cream butter and sugar until light and fluffy; beat in egg, vanilla and melted white chocolate. In medium bowl combine flour, baking powder and salt; add to creamed mixture. Wrap and refrigerate dough 2 to 3 hours. Preheat oven to 350°F. Working with half the dough at a time on lightly floured surface, roll to ⅛-inch thickness. Cut into 3×5-inch rectangles; cut off 2 corners from one short side. Place about 2 inches apart on ungreased cookie sheets. Using drinking straw, cut out small hole from tapered end of rectangle. Bake 10 to 12 minutes. Cool 2 minutes on cookie sheets; cool completely on wire racks. Prepare Decorator's Icing; spread over cookies. Write names on cookies using "M&M's"® Chocolate Mini Baking Bits. Place one piece licorice through hole and tie. Store in tightly covered container.

**Decorator's Icing:** *In medium bowl combine 2½ cups powdered sugar and 5 tablespoons milk until smooth. Add 1 tablespoon additional milk if necessary to make icing pourable.*

*Note:*

**To make your icing as smooth and lump-free as possible, sift the powdered sugar before combining it with milk.**

# Heavenly Oatmeal Hearts

**Makes 2½ dozen heart cookies**

**Cookies**

¾ Butter Flavor CRISCO® Stick or ¾ cup Butter Flavor CRISCO® all-vegetable shortening plus additional for greasing

1¼ cups firmly packed light brown sugar

1 egg

⅓ cup milk

1½ teaspoons vanilla

3 cups quick oats, uncooked

1 cup all-purpose flour

1½ teaspoons cinnnamon

½ teaspoon baking soda

½ teaspoon salt

1 cup milk chocolate chips

1 cup white chocolate baking pieces

1 cup honey-roasted peanuts, chopped

**Drizzle**

½ cup milk chocolate chips

½ cup white chocolate baking pieces

1 teaspoon Butter Flavor CRISCO® Stick or 1 teaspoon Butter Flavor CRISCO® all-vegetable shortening

*Note:*

When measuring flour, lightly spoon it into the measuring cup, then level it off with a metal spatula or the flat edge of a knife. Don't tap or bang the measuring cup on the counter— this will pack the flour (which could affect the final product).

*1.* Heat oven to 375°F. Grease baking sheets. Place sheets of foil on countertop for cooling cookies.

*2.* For cookies, combine ¾ cup shortening, brown sugar, egg, milk and vanilla in large bowl. Beat at medium speed of electric mixer until well blended.

*3.* Combine oats, flour, cinnamon, baking soda and salt. Mix into creamed mixture at low speed just until blended. Stir in chips, baking pieces and nuts.

*4.* Place 3-inch heart-shaped cookie cutter on prepared baking sheet. Place ⅓ cup dough inside cutter. Press to edges and level. Remove cutter. Repeat to form remaining cookies, spacing 2½ inches apart.

*5.* Bake one baking sheet at a time at 375°F for 10 to 12 minutes or until lightly browned. *Do not overbake.* Cool 2 minutes on baking sheet. Remove cookies to foil to cool completely.

**6.** For drizzle, place both chips in separate heavy resealable sandwich bags. Add ½ teaspoon shortening to each bag. Seal. Microwave 1 bag at 50% (MEDIUM). Knead bag after 1 minute. Repeat until mixture is smooth. Repeat with remaining bag. Cut tiny piece off corner of each bag. Squeeze out and drizzle both mixtures over cookies. To serve, cut cookies in half, if desired.

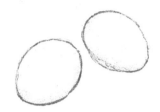

# Sweetheart Layer Bars

1 cup (2 sticks) butter or margarine, divided
1½ cups finely crushed unsalted thin pretzels or pretzel sticks
1 cup HERSHEY'S MINI KISSES™ Milk Chocolates or Semi-Sweet Chocolates

1 can (14 ounces) sweetened condensed milk (not evaporated milk)
¾ cup HERSHEY'S Cocoa
2 cups MOUNDS® Sweetened Coconut Flakes, tinted*

*To tint coconut: Place 1 teaspoon water and ½ teaspoon red food color in small bowl; stir in 2 cups coconut flakes. With fork, toss until evenly coated.

**Makes about 36 bars**

**1.** Heat oven to 350°F.

**2.** Place ¾ cup butter in 13×9×2-inch baking pan; place in oven just until butter melts. Remove from oven. Stir in crushed pretzels; press evenly into bottom of pan. Sprinkle Mini Kisses™ Chocolate over pretzel layer.

**3.** Place sweetened condensed milk, cocoa and remaining ¼ cup butter in small microwave-safe bowl. Microwave at HIGH (100%) 1 to 1½ minutes or until mixture is melted and smooth when stirred; carefully pour over pretzel layer in pan. Top with coconut; press firmly down onto chocolate layer.

**4.** Bake 25 to 30 minutes or until lightly browned around edges. Cool completely in pan on wire rack. Cut into heart-shaped pieces with cookie cutters or cut into bars.

# Chocolate and Peanut Butter Hearts

**Makes 4 dozen cookies**

**Note:**

If you're not sure if your baking powder is still potent, drop a generous pinch into a small cup of hot water. If it bubbles or fizzes, it's still good. If it sinks to the bottom of the cup, discard it.

Chocolate Cookie Dough
(recipe follows)
1 cup sugar
½ cup creamy peanut butter
½ cup shortening
1 egg

3 tablespoons milk
1 teaspoon vanilla
2 cups all-purpose flour
1 teaspoon baking powder
¼ teaspoon salt

**1.** Prepare and chill Chocolate Cookie Dough as directed.

**2.** Beat sugar, peanut butter and shortening until fluffy. Add egg, milk and vanilla; mix well. Combine flour, baking powder and salt. Beat flour mixture into peanut butter mixture until well blended. Shape dough into disc. Wrap in plastic wrap; refrigerate 1 to 2 hours or until firm.

**3.** Preheat oven to 350°F. Grease cookie sheets. Roll peanut butter dough on floured waxed paper to ⅛-inch thickness. Cut dough using 3-inch heart-shaped cookie cutter. Place cutouts on prepared cookie sheets. Repeat with chocolate dough.

**4.** Use smaller heart-shaped cookie cutter to remove small section from centers of hearts. Place small peanut butter hearts into large chocolate hearts; place small chocolate hearts into large peanut butter hearts. Press together lightly.

**5.** Bake 12 to 14 minutes or until edges are lightly browned. Remove to wire racks; cool completely.

## Chocolate Cookie Dough

1 cup (2 sticks) butter, softened
1 cup sugar
1 egg
1 teaspoon vanilla
2 ounces semisweet chocolate, melted

2¼ cups all-purpose flour
1 teaspoon baking powder
¼ teaspoon salt

*1.* Beat butter and sugar in large bowl at high speed of electric mixer until fluffy. Beat in egg and vanilla. Add melted chocolate; mix well.

*2.* Add flour, baking powder and salt; mix well. Cover; refrigerate about 2 hours or until firm.

# Strawberry Hearts

1 roll (17 to 18 ounces) refrigerated sugar cookie dough
2 packages (8 ounces each) cream cheese, softened

⅔ cup powdered sugar
1 teaspoon vanilla
2 cups sliced fresh strawberries

**Makes about 2 dozen hearts**

*1.* Remove dough from wrapper. Roll out dough, cut out hearts and bake as directed on package.

*2.* Combine cream cheese, powdered sugar and vanilla; mix well.

*3.* Spread evenly onto cooled hearts; top evenly with strawberries.

# Conversation Heart Cereal Treats

**Makes 12 bars**

**Prep and Cook Time:**
*18 minutes*

| 2 tablespoons margarine or butter | 3 cups frosted oat cereal with marshmallow bits |
|---|---|
| 20 large marshmallows | 12 large conversation hearts |

*1.* Line 8- or 9-inch square pan with aluminum foil, leaving 2-inch overhangs on 2 sides. Generously grease or spray with nonstick cooking spray.

*2.* Melt margarine and marshmallows in medium saucepan over medium heat 3 minutes or until melted and smooth, stirring constantly. Remove from heat.

*3.* Add cereal; stir until completely coated. Spread in prepared pan; press evenly onto bottom using greased rubber spatula. Press heart candies into top of treats while still warm, evenly spacing to allow 1 heart per bar. Let cool 10 minutes. Using foil overhangs as handles, remove treats from pan. Cut into 12 bars.

# Shamrock Ice Cream Sandwiches

**Makes 6 to 8 cookie sandwiches**

| Butter Cookie Dough (page 172) | 1 pint ice cream or frozen yogurt, any flavor |
|---|---|
| 3 or 4 drops green food color | |

*1.* Prepare cookie dough; mix in food color. Cover; refrigerate until firm, about 4 hours or overnight.

*2.* Preheat oven to 350°F.

*3.* Roll dough on lightly floured surface to ¼-inch thickness. Cut out cookies using 3½- to 5-inch shamrock-shaped cookie cutter. Place on ungreased cookie sheets.

*4.* Bake 8 to 10 minutes or until cookies are lightly browned around edges. Remove cookies to wire racks; cool completely.

*5.* Remove ice cream from freezer; let stand at room temperature to soften slightly, about 10 minutes. Spread 4 to 5 tablespoons ice cream onto flat sides of half the cookies. Place remaining cookies, flat sides down, on ice cream; press cookies together lightly.

*6.* Wrap each sandwich in foil; freeze until firm, about 2 hours or overnight.

**Tip:** *Filled cookies store well up to 1 week in freezer.*

**Valentine Ice Cream Sandwiches:** *Prepare and chill cookie dough as directed, substituting red food color for green food color. Cut out cookies with heart-shaped cookie cutter. Continue as directed.*

**Patriotic Ice Cream Sandwiches:** *Prepare and chill cookie dough as directed, substituting red food color for green food color. Cut out cookies with star-shaped cookie cutter. Continue as directed.*

**Pumpkin Ice Cream Sandwiches:** *Prepare and chill cookie dough as directed, substituting orange food color for green food color. Cut out cookies with pumpkin-shaped cookie cutter. Continue as directed.*

**Christmas Tree Ice Cream Sandwiches:** *Prepare, tint and chill cookie dough as directed. Cut out cookies with Christmas tree-shaped cookie cutter. Continue as directed.*

*Note:*

If you don't have a shamrock-shaped cookie cutter, you can easily make your own. Trace your design on stiff cardboard to create a pattern. Place the pattern on top of the dough and use a small sharp knife to cut out the shape.

# St. Pat's Pinwheels

**Makes about 3 dozen cookies**

*Note:*

Corn syrup adds moisture and chewiness to cookies as well as sweetness. It should be stored in a cool, dark place for up to 6 months. Keep the cap on the bottle tightly sealed and free from drips and spills.

1¼ cups granulated sugar
1 Butter Flavor CRISCO® Stick or 1 cup Butter Flavor CRISCO® all-vegetable shortening
2 eggs
¼ cup light corn syrup or regular pancake syrup

1 tablespoon vanilla
3 cups all-purpose flour plus 2 tablespoons, divided
¾ teaspoon baking powder
½ teaspoon baking soda
½ teaspoon salt
½ teaspoon peppermint extract
Green food color

*1.* Place sugar and 1 cup shortening in large bowl. Beat at medium speed of electric mixer until well blended. Add eggs, syrup and vanilla; beat until well blended and fluffy.

*2.* Combine 3 cups flour, baking powder, baking soda and salt. Add gradually to shortening mixture, beating at low speed until well blended.

*3.* Place half of dough in medium bowl. Stir in peppermint extract and food color, a few drops at a time, until desired shade of green. Shape each dough into disk. Wrap with plastic wrap. Refrigerate several hours or until firm.

*4.* Sprinkle about 1 tablespoon flour on large sheet of waxed paper. Place peppermint dough on floured paper; flatten slightly with hands. Turn dough over; cover with another large sheet of waxed paper. Roll dough into 14×9-inch rectangle. Set aside. Repeat with plain dough.

*5.* Remove top sheet of waxed paper from both doughs. Invert plain dough onto peppermint dough, aligning edges carefully. Remove waxed paper from plain dough. Trim dough to form rectangle. Roll dough tightly in jelly-roll fashion starting with long side and using bottom sheet of waxed paper as guide, removing waxed paper during rolling. Wrap roll in waxed paper; freeze at least 30 minutes or until very firm.

*6.* Heat oven to 375°F. Place sheets of foil on countertop for cooling cookies. Remove roll from freezer; remove wrapping. Cut roll into ⅜-inch-thick slices. Place slices 2 inches apart on ungreased baking sheet.

*7.* Bake one baking sheet at a time at 375°F for 7 to 9 minutes or until edges of cookies are very lightly browned. *Do not overbake.* Cool 2 minutes on baking sheet; remove to foil to cool completely.

# Shamrock Chocolate Cookies

| | | |
|---|---|---|
| ½ cup (1 stick) butter or margarine<br>¾ cup sugar<br>1 egg<br>1 teaspoon vanilla extract<br>1½ cups all-purpose flour | ⅓ cup HERSHEY'S Cocoa<br>½ teaspoon baking powder<br>½ teaspoon baking soda<br>¼ teaspoon salt<br>Shamrock Glaze<br>(recipe follows) | **Makes about 36 (2½-inch) cookies** |

*1.* Beat butter, sugar, egg and vanilla until fluffy. Combine flour, cocoa, baking powder, baking soda and salt; add to butter mixture, beating until well blended. Refrigerate about 1 hour or until firm.

*2.* Heat oven to 325°F. Roll dough, a small portion at a time, on lightly floured surface or between 2 pieces of wax paper to ¼-inch thickness. With cookie cutter, cut into shamrock shapes; place on ungreased cookie sheet.

*3.* Bake 5 to 7 minutes or until no indentation remains when lightly touched. Cool slightly; remove from cookie sheet. Cool on wire rack. Frost with Shamrock Glaze.

**Shamrock Glaze:** *Melt 3 tablespoons butter or margarine; stir in 2 cups powdered sugar and 1 teaspoon vanilla extract. Gradually add 2 to 3 tablespoons milk, beating to desired consistency. Stir in 2 or 3 drops green food color. Makes about 1 cup glaze.*

# Edible Easter Baskets

**Makes 3 dozen cookies**

1 package (about 18 ounces) refrigerated sugar cookie dough
1 cup "M&M's"® Milk Chocolate Mini Baking Bits, divided
1 teaspoon water
1 to 2 drops green food coloring

¾ cup sweetened shredded coconut
¾ cup any flavor frosting
Red licorice whips, cut into 3-inch lengths

*Note:*

**Store leftover shredded coconut in an airtight container for up to 1 week in the refrigerator or up to 6 months in the freezer.**

Lightly grease 36 (1¾-inch) mini muffin cups. Cut dough into 36 equal pieces; roll into balls. Place 1 ball in each muffin cup. Press dough onto bottom and up side of each muffin cup; chill 15 minutes. Press ⅓ cup "M&M's"® Milk Chocolate Mini Baking Bits into bottoms and sides of dough cups. Preheat oven to 350°F. Bake cookies 8 to 9 minutes. Cookies will be puffy. Remove from oven; gently press down center of each cookie. Return to oven 1 minute. Cool cookies in muffin cups 5 minutes. Remove to wire racks; cool completely. In medium bowl combine water and food coloring. Add coconut; stir until evenly tinted. In each cookie cup, layer 1 teaspoon frosting, 1 teaspoon tinted coconut and 1 teaspoon "M&M's"® Milk Chocolate Mini Baking Bits. Push both licorice ends into frosting to make basket handle. Store in tightly covered container.

# Fluffy Cottontails

½ cup (1 stick) unsalted butter, softened
½ cup shortening
¾ cup sugar
1 teaspoon vanilla
2 cups all-purpose flour

⅔ cup malted milk powder
¼ teaspoon salt
Malted milk balls
Miniature marshmallows
Assorted colored icings

Makes 2½ dozen cookies

*1.* Beat butter, shortening, sugar and vanilla in large bowl. Add flour, malted milk powder and salt until well blended.

*2.* Preheat oven to 350°F. Lightly grease cookie sheets. For bunny body, shape heaping teaspoonfuls of dough around malted milk balls. For bunny head, shape scant teaspoonfuls of dough into balls. Press body and head together on prepared cookie sheet. Shape ½ teaspoon dough into 2 ears; press gently into head.

*3.* Bake 8 minutes or until lightly browned. Let cookies cool 1 minute on cookie sheets. Cut marshmallows in half. Immediately place marshmallow halves on cookies to resemble bunny tails. Remove to wire racks to cool completely.

*4.* Decorate cookies with colored icings as desired. Let cookies stand until icing is set.

# Festive Easter Cookies

**Makes 4 dozen cookies**

1 cup (2 sticks) butter, softened
2 cups powdered sugar
1 egg
2 teaspoons grated lemon peel
1 teaspoon vanilla
3 cups all-purpose flour

½ teaspoon salt
Royal Icing (recipe follows)
Assorted food colors
Assorted sprinkles and
    candies

*Note:*

When purchasing lemons, choose ones that are firm and heavy for their size, with a sheen to the skin. It is easier to remove the peel from thick-skinned lemons, but thin-skinned ones usually yield more juice.

*1.* Beat butter and powdered sugar in large bowl at high speed of electric mixer until fluffy. Add egg, lemon peel and vanilla; mix well. Combine flour and salt in medium bowl. Add to butter mixture; mix well.

*2.* Divide dough in half. Wrap each half with plastic wrap. Refrigerate 3 hours or overnight.

*3.* Preheat oven to 375°F. Roll dough on floured surface to ⅛-inch thickness. Cut out dough using Easter cookie cutters, such as eggs, bunnies and tulips. Place cutouts on ungreased cookie sheets.

*4.* Bake 8 to 12 minutes or just until edges are very lightly browned. Remove to wire racks; cool completely. Prepare Royal Icing; tint with food colors as desired. Decorate with sprinkles and candies.

## Royal Icing

1 egg white,* at room
    temperature
2 to 2½ cups sifted powdered
    sugar

½ teaspoon almond extract

*Use only grade A clean, uncracked egg.

Beat egg white in small bowl with electric mixer at high speed until foamy. Gradually add 2 cups powdered sugar and almond extract. Beat at low speed until moistened. Beat at high speed until icing is stiff, adding additional powdered sugar if needed.

# Springtime Nests

| | | |
|---|---|---|
| 1 cup butterscotch chips<br>½ cup light corn syrup<br>½ cup creamy peanut butter<br>⅓ cup sugar | 2 cups corn flakes, slightly<br>   crushed<br>2½ cups chow mein noodles<br>   Jelly beans or malted milk<br>   egg candies | **Makes 1½ dozen<br>cookies** |

*1.* Combine butterscotch chips, corn syrup, peanut butter and sugar in large microwavable bowl. Microwave at HIGH (100% power) 1 to 1½ minutes or until melted and smooth, stirring at 30-second intervals.

*2.* Stir in corn flakes and chow mein noodles until evenly coated. Quickly shape scant ¼ cupfuls mixture into balls; make indentation in centers to make nests. Place nests on waxed paper to set. Place 3 jelly beans in each nest.

## The Perfect Cookie Package

*Homemade cookies are a thoughtful gift for any occasion. Simple cookies can be made extraordinary when tucked into unique packages with lavish decorations.*

**Cookie containers:**

- Baskets and boxes, available in a wide variety of materials and sizes

- Gift bags, available in many sizes and colors

- Metal containers (tins) with tight-fitting lids

**Decorative accessories:**

- Cellophane, indispensible for hard-to-wrap gifts such as plates of cookies

- Decorative papers, in a variety of colors and finishes, can add pizzazz to baskets and gift bags

- Gift tags, in metal or paper, help personalize packages and can also be used for storage tips and serving suggestions

- Raffia, ribbons and satin cord add a festive touch to any package

# Frosted Easter Cut-Outs

**Makes about
3½ dozen cookies**

*Note:*

Most home ovens are

off by as much as 25

degrees, which is why

using an oven

thermometer is so

important. Check the

thermometer after

preheating the oven for

15 minutes and adjust

the temperature

as needed.

**Cookies**
1¼ cups granulated sugar
1 Butter Flavor CRISCO® Stick
   or 1 cup Butter Flavor
   CRISCO® all-vegetable
   shortening
2 eggs
¼ cup light corn syrup or
   regular pancake syrup
1 tablespoon vanilla
3 cups plus 4 tablespoons
   all-purpose flour, divided

¾ teaspoon baking powder
½ teaspoon baking soda
½ teaspoon salt

**Icing**
1 cup confectioners' sugar
2 tablespoons milk
   Food color (optional)
   Decorating icing

*1.* Place sugar and 1 cup shortening in large bowl. Beat at medium speed of electric mixer until well blended. Add eggs, syrup and vanilla; beat until well blended and fluffy.

*2.* Combine 3 cups flour, baking powder, baking soda and salt. Add gradually to shortening mixture, beating at low speed until well blended.

*3.* Divide dough into 4 equal pieces; shape each into disk. Wrap with plastic wrap. Refrigerate 1 hour or until firm.

*4.* Heat oven to 375°F. Place sheets of foil on countertop for cooling cookies.

*5.* Sprinkle about 1 tablespoon flour on large sheet of waxed paper. Place disk of dough on floured paper; flatten slightly with hands. Turn dough over; cover with another large sheet of waxed paper. Roll dough to ¼-inch thickness. Remove top sheet of waxed paper. Cut into desired shapes with floured cookie cutter. Place 2 inches apart on ungreased baking sheet. Repeat with remaining dough.

**6.** Bake one baking sheet at a time at 375°F for 5 to 7 minutes or until edges of cookies are lightly browned. *Do not overbake.* Cool 2 minutes on baking sheet. Remove cookies to foil to cool completely.

**7.** For icing, combine confectioners' sugar and milk; stir until smooth. Add food color, if desired. Stir until blended. Spread icing on cookies; place on foil until icing is set. Decorate as desired with decorating icing.

# Chocolate Bunny Cookies

| | | |
|---|---|---|
| 1 (21-ounce) package DUNCAN HINES® Family-Style Chewy Fudge Brownie Mix<br>1 egg<br>¼ cup water<br>¼ cup vegetable oil | 1⅓ cups pecan halves (96)<br>1 container DUNCAN HINES® Creamy Home-Style Dark Chocolate Fudge Frosting<br>White chocolate chips | **Makes 4 dozen cookies** |

**1.** Preheat oven to 350°F. Grease baking sheets.

**2.** Combine brownie mix, egg, water and oil in large bowl. Stir with spoon until well blended, about 50 strokes. Drop by 2 level teaspoonfuls 2 inches apart on greased baking sheets. Place two pecan halves, flat-side up, on each cookie for ears. Bake at 350°F for 10 to 12 minutes or until set. Cool 2 minutes on baking sheets. Remove to cooling racks. Cool completely.

**3.** Spread Dark Chocolate Fudge frosting on one cookie. Place white chocolate chips, upside down, on frosting for eyes and nose. Dot each eye with frosting using toothpick. Repeat for remaining cookies. Allow frosting to set before storing cookies between layers of waxed paper in airtight container.

**Tip:** *For variety, frost cookies with Duncan Hines® Vanilla Frosting and use semisweet chocolate chips for the eyes and noses.*

# Grand Old Flag Cookie

**Makes 10 to 12 servings**

1 package (18 ounces) refrigerated sugar cookie dough
1 container (16 ounces) vanilla frosting
Blue food color
50 white chocolate chips

3 cherry- or strawberry-flavored chewy fruit snack rolls, divided
2 pretzel rods

**Supplies**
1 (15×10-inch) cake board, covered, or large platter

*Note:*

Frosting cookies can be a messy job. Keep your spatula clean between applications of frosting by dipping it into a glass of warm water. Dry it off before dipping it back into the container of frosting.

*1.* Preheat oven to 350°F. Grease 13×9-inch baking pan with nonstick cooking spray. Place dough in prepared pan; press evenly onto bottom of pan. Bake 15 to 18 minutes or until lightly browned. Cool in pan on wire rack 15 minutes. Remove cookie from pan to rack; cool completely.

*2.* Place cookie on prepared cake board. Tint ½ cup frosting blue. Spread blue frosting in 4-inch square in top left corner of cookie as background for stars. Frost remaining cookie with remaining white frosting. Arrange chips for stars over blue background, alternating 5 rows of 6 stars each with 4 rows of 5 stars each.

*3.* Cut fruit snack rolls into 3 (9-inch) strips and 3 (13-inch) strips; place on cookie as stripes. Wrap pretzel rods with remaining fruit roll lengths; place next to cookie for flag pole.

# High-Flying Flags

¾ cup (1½ sticks) unsalted
  butter, softened
¼ cup granulated sugar
¼ cup packed light brown sugar
1 egg yolk
1¾ cups all-purpose flour

¾ teaspoon baking powder
⅛ teaspoon salt
  Lollipop sticks
  Blue icing, white sugar stars,
  white icing and red string
  licorice

Makes 3 dozen cookies

*1.* Combine butter, granulated sugar, brown sugar and egg yolk in medium bowl; mix until well blended. Add flour, baking powder and salt; mix until well blended. Wrap dough in plastic wrap and chill 1 hour or until firm.

*2.* Preheat oven to 350°F. Grease cookie sheets. Roll dough on lightly floured surface to ¼-inch thickness. Cut out dough using 3-inch flag-shaped cookie cutter. Place lollipop stick underneath left side of each flag; press gently to adhere. Place flags 2 inches apart on prepared cookie sheets.

*3.* Bake 8 to 10 minutes or until edges are lightly browned. Remove to wire racks and cool completely.

*4.* Spread blue icing in square in upper left corner of each flag; place sugar stars on blue icing. Spread white icing over plain sections of remaining cookies. Place strips of red licorice on white icing; let set.

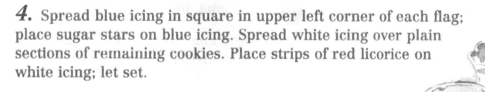

# Uncle Sam's Hat

**Makes 1 large cookie**

1 package (about 18 ounces) refrigerated chocolate chip cookie dough

2 cups powdered sugar
2 to 4 tablespoons milk
Red and blue food colors

*1.* Preheat oven to 350°F. Lightly grease 12-inch round pizza pan and cookie sheet. Remove dough from wrapper. Press dough evenly into prepared pizza pan. Cut dough into hat shape. Press scraps together and flatten heaping tablespoons dough onto prepared cookie sheet. Using 1½- to 2-inch star cookie cutter, cut out several stars; remove and discard dough scraps.

*2.* Bake stars 5 to 7 minutes and hat 7 to 9 minutes or until lightly browned at edges. Cool stars on cookie sheet 1 minute. Remove stars to wire rack; cool completely. Cool hat completely on pan on rack.

*3.* Combine powdered sugar and enough milk, one tablespoon at a time, to make medium-thick pourable glaze. Spread small amount of glaze over stars and place on waxed paper; let stand until glaze is set. Using red and blue food colors, tint ½ of glaze red, tint ¼ of glaze blue and leave remaining ¼ of glaze white.

*4.* Decorate hat with red, white and blue glazes; place stars on blue band of hat. Let stand until glaze is set.

# Frost-on-the-Pumpkin Cookies

2 cups all-purpose flour
1 teaspoon baking powder
1 teaspoon ground cinnamon
½ teaspoon baking soda
½ teaspoon ground nutmeg
1 cup butter, softened
¾ cup DOMINO® Granulated Sugar
¾ cup firmly packed DOMINO® Brown Sugar

1 cup canned pumpkin
1 egg
2 teaspoons vanilla
½ cup raisins
½ cup chopped walnuts
Cream Cheese Frosting (recipe follows)

**Makes 48 cookies**

Preheat oven to 350°F. In small mixing bowl, combine flour, baking powder, cinnamon, baking soda and nutmeg. Set aside. In large mixer bowl, beat butter for 1 minute. Add granulated sugar and brown sugar; beat until fluffy. Add pumpkin, egg and vanilla; beat well. Add flour mixture to pumpkin mixture; mix until well blended. Stir in raisins and walnuts. Drop by teaspoonfuls 2 inches apart onto greased cookie sheet.

Bake 10 to 12 minutes. Cool on cookie sheet for 2 minutes. Transfer to wire rack; cool completely. Frost with Cream Cheese Frosting. Garnish with chopped nuts, if desired.

**Cream Cheese Frosting:** *In medium mixing bowl, beat 3 ounces softened cream cheese, ¼ cup softened butter and 1 teaspoon vanilla until light and fluffy. Gradually add 2 cups DOMINO® Powdered Sugar, beating until smooth.*

*Note:*

Canned pumpkin can be kept in a cool, dry place for up to one year. Refrigerate any opened canned pumpkin in a tightly covered nonmetal container for up to five days.

# Irresistible Peanut Butter Jack O'Lanterns

**Makes about 3 dozen cookies**

**Cookies**
1¼ cups firmly packed light brown sugar
¾ cup JIF® Creamy Peanut Butter
½ CRISCO® Stick or ½ cup CRISCO® all-vegetable shortening
3 tablespoons milk
1 tablespoon vanilla
1 egg
1¾ cups all-purpose flour
¾ teaspoon baking soda
¾ teaspoon salt

**Icing**
1 cup (6 ounces) semisweet chocolate chips
2 teaspoons Butter Flavor CRISCO® Stick or
2 teaspoons Butter Flavor CRISCO® all-vegetable shortening

*1.* Heat oven to 375°F. Place sheets of foil on countertop for cooling cookies.

*2.* For cookies, place brown sugar, peanut butter, ½ cup shortening, milk and vanilla in large bowl. Beat at medium speed of electric mixer until well blended. Add egg; beat just until blended.

*3.* Combine flour, baking soda and salt. Add to shortening mixture; beat at low speed just until blended.

*4.* Pinch off walnut-sized pieces of dough; shape into balls. Place 3 inches apart on ungreased baking sheet. Flatten each ball with bottom of glass to approximately ⅜-inch thickness. Form into pumpkin shape, making indentation on top of round. Pinch off very small piece of dough and roll to form small stem. Attach to top of round. Score dough with vertical lines with small, sharp knife to resemble pumpkin.

*5.* Bake one baking sheet at a time at 375°F for 7 to 8 minutes or until cookies are set and just beginning to brown. *Do not overbake.* Cool on baking sheet 2 minutes. Remove cookies to foil to cool completely.

*6.* For icing, place chocolate chips and 2 teaspoons shortening in heavy resealable sandwich bag; seal bag. Microwave at 50% (MEDIUM) for 1 minute. Knead bag. If necessary, microwave at 50% for another 30 seconds at a time until mixture is smooth when bag
is kneaded. Cut small tip off corner of bag. Pipe lines and faces on cookies to resemble jack o'lanterns.

*Note:*

**Before starting to pipe the icing, practice a few times on waxed paper. Lightly mark designs on the cookies with a toothpick to use as a guide.**

# Ghostly Delights

| 1 package (18 ounces) refrigerated cookie dough, any flavor | 1 cup prepared vanilla frosting<br>¾ cup marshmallow creme<br>32 chocolate chips for decoration | Makes 16 cookies |

**Prep and Cook Time:**
*25 minutes*

*1.* Preheat oven to 350°F. Using about 1 tablespoon dough for body and about 1 teaspoon dough for head, form cookie dough into ghost shapes on greased cookie sheets. Bake 10 to 11 minutes or until browned. Cool 1 minute on cookie sheets; place warm cookies on serving plates.

*2.* While cookies are baking, combine frosting and marshmallow creme in small bowl until well blended.

*3.* Frost each ghost with frosting mixture. Press 2 chocolate chips, points up, into frosting mixture to create eyes on each ghost. Decorate with additional candy, if desired.

**Serving Suggestion:** *These cookies are excellent served with a tall glass of cold milk.*

# Jack-O-Lantern Bars

**Makes 24 bars**

**Prep Time:**
*20 minutes*

**Bake Time:**
*30 minutes*

**Cool Time:**
*1½ hours*

**Frost and Decorate Time:**
*20 minutes*

*Note:*
You can substitute
1 teaspoon cinnamon,
½ teaspoon nutmeg,
¼ teaspoon ground
ginger and ¼ teaspoon
ground cloves for the
pumpkin pie spice.

**Bars**
2 cups all-purpose flour
2 cups DOMINO® Granulated
    Sugar
2 teaspoons baking powder
2 teaspoons pumpkin pie spice
1 teaspoon baking soda
½ teaspoon salt
4 eggs, beaten
1 (15-ounce) can pumpkin
    (about 2 cups)
1 cup oil

**Frosting**
2 cups DOMINO® Confectioners
    Sugar
1 (3-ounce) package cream
    cheese, softened
⅓ cup butter or margarine,
    softened
1 tablespoon milk
1 teaspoon vanilla
3 drops yellow food color
2 drops red food color

**Decorations**
Fall color corn candy and
    melted chocolate

Heat oven to 350°F. Grease and flour 15×10×1-inch baking pan. Combine all dry ingredients for bars in large bowl; mix well. Add eggs, pumpkin and oil. Stir until well blended. Pour into pan. Bake for 25 to 30 minutes or until toothpick inserted in center comes out clean. Cool completely.

Mix frosting ingredients in small bowl until smooth. Frost cooled bars. Cut into squares. Decorate as desired.

**Quick Melted Chocolate for Piping:** *Place ¼ cup chocolate chips in small resealable plastic bag. Seal. Place in bowl of very warm water, being careful to keep interior of bag dry. Knead chocolate occasionally until melted. Dry bag thoroughly. Cut small opening in tip of bag. Squeeze chocolate out to pipe on decorations. Chocolate can also be melted in plastic bag in microwave oven. Microwave on MEDIUM for 30 seconds at a time, checking and kneading chocolate until melted.*

# Skeleton Cookies

30 to 40 drops black food
    coloring
1 (18-ounce) package
    refrigerated sugar cookie
    dough

Skeleton or gingerbread man
    cookie cutters
1 tube white frosting

**Makes about 2 dozen cookies**

*1.* Knead food coloring into cookie dough on lightly floured surface. Wrap in plastic wrap and refrigerate 2 hours or until very firm.

*2.* Preheat oven to 350°F. Roll out dough on floured surface to ⅛-inch thickness. Cut out cookies with cookie cutters. Bake 9 to 13 minutes or until edges are browning (centers will be somewhat soft). Cool 1 minute on cookie sheet. Remove from cookie sheet and cool completely on wire rack.

*3.* Draw skeleton figures on cookies with frosting.

**Tips:** *Cookies will appear a shade or two lighter after baking, so, while kneading in the black food coloring, add a few more drops of coloring after the desired shade has been reached.*

*The yield of this recipe is an approximation only and depends on the size of your cookie cutters and the thickness of the cookie dough.*

# Smucker's® Spider Web Tartlets

**Makes 8 servings**

1 (16-ounce) log refrigerated
    sugar cookie dough
¾ cup all-purpose flour
    Nonstick cooking spray or
    parchment paper

1 cup (12-ounce jar)
    SMUCKER'S® Apricot
    Preserves
1 tube black cake decorating
    gel

*1.* Preheat oven to 375°F. Unwrap cookie dough and place in medium mixing bowl. With floured hands, knead flour into cookie dough. Roll dough back into log shape; place on clean cutting board and cut into eight equal slices. With floured fingers, place dough circles on baking sheet lined with parchment paper or sprayed with nonstick spray.

*2.* Gently press dough circles, flattening to make each one approximately 4 inches in diameter. With thumb and forefinger, pinch edge of each dough circle to create ridge all around. Pinch each dough circle along ridge to make eight points.

*3.* Spread 2 tablespoons of SMUCKER'S® Preserves (or Simply Fruit) onto each dough circle, making sure to spread it all the way to edge and in each point. Refrigerate for 20 minutes. Bake 12 to 14 minutes or until edges are lightly browned.

*4.* Remove tartlets from baking sheet and cool on wire rack. When cool, use black decorating gel to make spider web design.

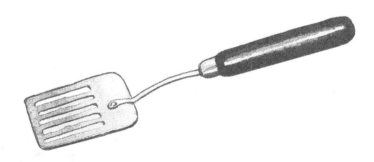

# Sugar & Spice Jack-O'-Lantern Cookies

Makes 2 to 3 dozen cookies

2⅓ cups all-purpose flour
  2 teaspoons ground cinnamon
1½ teaspoons baking powder
1½ teaspoons ground ginger
  ½ teaspoon salt
  ¼ teaspoon nutmeg
  ¾ cup butter, softened

½ cup packed brown sugar
½ cup molasses
1 egg
  Assorted Halloween cookie decorations, such as orange and black frostings and orange and black jimmies

*1.* Combine flour, cinnamon, baking powder, ginger, salt and nutmeg in medium bowl. Beat butter with sugar in large bowl of electric mixer at medium speed until light and fluffy. Add molasses and egg; beat until well blended. Gradually beat in flour mixture until just combined.

*2.* Form dough into 2 balls; press into 2-inch-thick discs. Wrap in plastic wrap; refrigerate at least 1 hour or until firm. (Dough may be prepared up to 2 days before baking.) Let stand at room temperature to soften slightly before rolling out.

*3.* Preheat oven to 350°F. Roll out dough on lightly floured surface to ¼-inch thickness. Cut out cookies with jack-o'-lantern cookie cutters or other shapes as desired. Place cutouts on *ungreased* cookie sheets. Bake about 12 to 14 minutes or until center of cookies are firm to the touch. Let cookies stand on cookie sheets 1 minute; cool completely on wire racks. Frost cookies and decorate as desired.

*Note:*

When creaming mixtures of butter and sugar, start the electric mixer at a low setting to blend the ingredients, then gradually increase the speed to medium or high to get more volume into the batter.

# Sweet Spiders

**Makes 20 cookies**

1 package (18 ounces) refrigerated sugar cookie dough
¼ cup unsweetened cocoa powder
3 to 4 tablespoons seedless red raspberry or cherry preserves*

Chocolate licorice
Decors, cinnamon candies, assorted icings, sprinkles and mini chocolate chips

*If there are large pieces of fruit in preserves, purée in food processor until smooth.

*Note:*

Unsweetened cocoa powder can be stored in a tightly closed container in a cool, dark place for up to two years.

**1.** Preheat oven to 350°F. Grease cookie sheets; set aside. Remove dough from wrapper according to package directions. Combine dough and cocoa powder in large bowl; mix until well blended.

**2.** Evenly divide dough into 20 pieces. Shape each piece into 2 (1-inch) balls and 1 (½-inch) ball. For each spider body, flatten 1 (1-inch) ball into 2-inch circle on prepared cookie sheet. Place ½ teaspoon preserves in center of circle. Flatten remaining 1-inch ball into 2-inch circle and place over preserves, sealing dough edges. Cut licorice into 1½-inch pieces; cut pieces in half lengthwise. Press licorice into spider body for legs.

**3.** For each spider head, slightly flatten ½-inch ball and lightly press into spider body. Press decors or cinnamon candies into head for eyes.

**4.** Bake 10 to 12 minutes or until dough is set. Cool on cookie sheets 10 minutes; transfer to wire racks to cool completely. Decorate as desired with assorted icings, decors, sprinkles and mini chocolate chips.

# Chocolate Halloween Ice Cream Sandwiches

2 cups all-purpose flour
½ cup unsweetened cocoa
    powder
2 teaspoons baking soda
½ teaspoon salt
1¼ cups sugar
⅔ cup butter, softened
¼ cup light corn syrup

1 egg
1 teaspoon vanilla
3 pints mint chocolate chip
    and/or vanilla ice cream
Black and orange jimmies,
    sugar or other Halloween
    cookie decorations
    (optional)

**Makes about 2 dozen sandwiches**

*1.* Preheat oven to 350°F. Combine flour, cocoa, baking soda and salt in medium bowl. Beat sugar and butter in large bowl of electric mixer on medium speed until light and fluffy. Beat in corn syrup, egg and vanilla until well blended. Gradually beat in flour mixture at low speed until blended. Cover and refrigerate dough about 15 minutes or until firm.

*2.* Roll dough into 1-inch balls using about 1 tablespoon dough per ball. Place balls 2 inches apart on *ungreased* cookie sheets. Press lightly with fingers to flatten slightly. Bake 10 to 12 minutes or until cookies are set. Immediately transfer to wire racks; cool completely.

*3.* Soften ice cream at room temperature about 10 minutes or in microwave oven at MEDIUM (50% power) 10 to 20 seconds. For each ice cream sandwich, place about ¼ cup (1 small scoop) ice cream on flat side of a cookie; top with another cookie, flat side down. Press gently so that ice cream meets edges of cookies. Immediately roll edges of ice cream in decorations, if desired. Wrap in plastic wrap; freeze until ready to serve.

*Note:*

Ice cream that is allowed to thaw and refreeze develops large ice crystals. Prevent this by returning softened ice cream to the freezer as quickly as possible and serve within a week.

# Yummy Mummy Cookies

**Makes about
30 cookies**

⅔ cup butter or margarine,
  softened
1 cup sugar
2 teaspoons vanilla extract
2 eggs
2½ cups all-purpose flour
½ cup HERSHEY⁶S Cocoa
¼ teaspoon baking soda
½ teaspoon salt
1 cup HERSHEY⁶S MINI CHIPS™
  Semi-Sweet Chocolate
  Chips

1 to 2 packages (10 ounces
  each) HERSHEY⁶S Premier
  White Chips
1 to 2 tablespoons shortening
  (do *not* use butter,
  margarine, spread or oil)
Additional HERSHEY⁶S MINI
  CHIPS™ Semi-Sweet
  Chocolate Chips

*Note:*

To test a raw egg for
freshness, place it in a
bowl of cold water. A
fresh egg will sink to
the bottom, while an
older egg will start to
skim the water's
surface. A stale egg
will float and should
be discarded.

*1.* Beat butter, sugar and vanilla in large bowl until creamy. Add eggs; beat well. Stir together flour, cocoa, baking soda and salt; gradually add to butter mixture, beating until blended. Stir in 1 cup small chocolate chips. Refrigerate dough 15 to 20 minutes or until firm enough to handle.

*2.* Heat oven to 350°F.

*3.* To form mummy body, using 1 tablespoon dough, roll into 3½-inch carrot shape; place on ungreased cookie sheet. To form head, using 1 teaspoon dough, roll into ball the size and shape of a grape; press onto wide end of body. Repeat procedure with remaining dough.

*4.* Bake 8 to 9 minutes or until set. Cool slightly; remove from cookie sheet to wire rack. Cool completely.

*5.* Place 1⅔ cups (10-ounce package) white chips and 1 tablespoon shortening in microwave-safe pie plate or shallow bowl. Microwave at HIGH (100%) 1 minute; stir until chips are melted.

*6.* Coat tops of cookies by placing one cookie at a time on table knife or narrow metal spatula; spoon white chip mixture evenly over cookie to coat. (If mixture begins to thicken, return to microwave for a few seconds). Place coated cookies on wax paper. Melt additional chips with shortening, if needed, for additional coating. As coating begins to set on cookies, using a toothpick, score lines and facial features into coating to resemble mummy. Place 2 small chocolate chips on each cookie for eyes. Store, covered, in cool, dry place.

# Brrrrownie Cats

| | | |
|---|---|---|
| 1 cup (2 sticks) unsalted butter<br>4 ounces unsweetened<br>chocolate<br>1½ cups sugar<br>3 eggs | 1 cup all-purpose flour<br>¼ teaspoon salt<br>Black frosting, jimmies and<br>other decorations as<br>desired | **Makes about 2 dozen<br>brownies** |

*1.* Preheat oven to 350°F. Grease 13×9-inch baking pan. Melt butter and chocolate in top of double boiler*, stirring occasionally.

*2.* Transfer butter mixture to large bowl. Stir in sugar until well blended. Beat in eggs, one at a time. Stir in flour and salt.

*3.* Spread batter into prepared pan. Bake 20 to 25 minutes or just until firm. Cool completely on wire rack.

*4.* Using Halloween cookie cutters, cut brownies in cat shapes. Decorate as desired.

*Or, place unwrapped chocolate squares in small microwavable bowl. Microwave at HIGH (100%) 1 to 1½ minutes, stirring after 1 minute.

# Gobble, Gobble Gobblers

**Makes 3 dozen cookies**

½ cup (1 stick) butter, softened
½ cup granulated sugar
½ cup firmly packed light brown sugar
2 large eggs
2¼ cups all-purpose flour
1½ teaspoons ground cinnamon

1 teaspoon baking powder
½ teaspoon ground ginger
⅛ teaspoon ground cloves
½ cup vanilla frosting
½ cup chocolate frosting
1 cup "M&M's"® Chocolate Mini Baking Bits

*Note:*

To soften butter quickly and easily, place one stick of butter on a microwavable plate and heat at LOW (30% power) about 30 seconds or just until softened.

In large bowl cream butter and sugars until light and fluffy; beat in eggs. In medium bowl combine flour, cinnamon, baking powder, ginger and cloves; add to creamed mixture. Wrap and refrigerate dough 2 to 3 hours. Preheat oven to 325°F. Lightly grease cookie sheets; set aside. Working with half the dough at a time on lightly floured surface, roll to ¼-inch thickness. Cut into turkey shapes using 3½-inch cookie cutters. Place about 2 inches apart on prepared cookie sheets. Bake 10 to 12 minutes. Cool 2 minutes on cookie sheets; cool completely on wire racks. In small bowl combine vanilla and chocolate frostings until well blended. Frost cookies and decorate with "M&M's"® Chocolate Mini Baking Bits. Store in tightly covered container.

# *Festive*
# Holiday
# Cookies

## CHAPTER SIX

# Premier Cheesecake Cranberry Bars

**Makes 2½ dozen bars**

2 cups all-purpose flour
1½ cups quick or old-fashioned oats
¼ cup packed light brown sugar
1 cup (2 sticks) butter or margarine, softened
2 cups (12-ounce package) NESTLÉ® TOLL HOUSE® Premier White Morsels
1 package (8 ounces) cream cheese, softened

1 can (14 ounces) NESTLÉ® CARNATION® Sweetened Condensed Milk
¼ cup lemon juice
1 teaspoon vanilla extract
1 can (16 ounces) whole-berry cranberry sauce
2 tablespoons cornstarch

**PREHEAT** oven to 350°F. Grease 13×9-inch baking pan.

**COMBINE** flour, oats and brown sugar in large bowl. Add butter; mix until crumbly. Stir in morsels. Reserve *2½ cups* morsel mixture for topping. With floured fingers, press *remaining* mixture into prepared pan.

**BEAT** cream cheese in large mixer bowl until creamy. Add sweetened condensed milk, lemon juice and vanilla extract; mix until smooth. Pour over crust. Combine cranberry sauce and cornstarch in medium bowl. Spoon over cream cheese mixture. Sprinkle *reserved* morsel mixture over cranberry mixture.

**BAKE** for 35 to 40 minutes or until center is set. Cool completely in pan on wire rack. Cover; refrigerate until serving time (up to 1 day). Cut into bars.

# Linzer Sandwich Cookies

1⅓ cups all-purpose flour
¼ teaspoon baking powder
¼ teaspoon salt
¾ cup granulated sugar
½ cup (1 stick) butter, softened

1 large egg
1 teaspoon vanilla
    Powdered sugar (optional)
    Seedless raspberry jam

**Makes about 2 dozen cookies**

Place flour, baking powder and salt in small bowl; stir to combine. Beat granulated sugar and butter in medium bowl with electric mixer at medium speed until light and fluffy. Beat in egg and vanilla. Gradually add flour mixture. Beat at low speed until dough forms. Divide dough in half; cover and refrigerate 2 hours or until firm.

Preheat oven to 375°F. Working with 1 portion at a time, roll out dough on lightly floured surface to ⅛-inch thickness. Cut dough into desired shapes with floured cookie cutters. Cut out equal numbers of each shape. (If dough becomes too soft, refrigerate several minutes before continuing.) Cut 1-inch centers out of half the cookies of each shape. Reroll trimmings and cut out more cookies. Place cookies 1½ to 2 inches apart on ungreased cookie sheets. Bake 7 to 9 minutes or until edges are lightly brown. Let cookies stand on cookie sheets 1 to 2 minutes. Remove cookies to wire racks; cool completely.

Sprinkle cookies with holes with powdered sugar, if desired. Spread 1 teaspoon jam on flat side of whole cookies, spreading almost to edges. Place cookies with holes, flat side down, over jam. Store tightly covered at room temperature or freeze up to 3 months.

*Note:*

The name "linzer" comes from Linz, Austria, where the linzertorte originated. Traditionally, this elegant tart has a buttery almond-flavored crust topped with raspberry jam and a lattice crust on top.

# Philadelphia® Snowmen Cookies

**Makes about 3 dozen cookies**

**Prep Time:**
*20 minutes*

**Bake Time:**
*21 minutes*

1 package (8 ounces) PHILADELPHIA® Cream Cheese, softened
1 cup powdered sugar
¾ cup (1½ sticks) butter *or* margarine

½ teaspoon vanilla
2¼ cups flour
½ teaspoon baking soda
Sifted powdered sugar
Miniature peanut butter cups (optional)

**MIX** cream cheese, 1 cup sugar, butter and vanilla with electric mixer on medium speed until well blended. Add flour and baking soda; mix well.

**SHAPE** dough into equal number of ½-inch and 1-inch diameter balls. Using 1 small and 1 large ball for each snowman, place balls, slightly overlapping, on ungreased cookie sheets. Flatten to ¼-inch thickness with bottom of glass dipped in additional flour. Repeat with remaining balls.

**BAKE** at 325°F for 19 to 21 minutes or until light golden brown. Cool on wire racks. Sprinkle each snowman with sifted powdered sugar. Decorate with icing as desired. Cut peanut butter cups in half for hats.

# Ornament Brownies

**Makes about
8 brownies**

6 squares (1 ounce each)
   semisweet chocolate,
   coarsely chopped
1 tablespoon freeze dried coffee
   granules
1 tablespoon boiling water
¾ cup all-purpose flour
¾ teaspoon ground cinnamon
½ teaspoon baking powder
¼ teaspoon salt

½ cup sugar
¼ cup butter, softened
2 eggs
   Prepared vanilla frosting or
      icing
   Assorted food colors
   Small candy canes, assorted
      candies and sprinkles for
      decoration

**1.** Preheat oven to 350°F. Grease 8-inch square baking pan; set aside. Melt chocolate in small heavy saucepan over low heat, stirring constantly; set aside. Dissolve coffee granules in boiling water in small cup; set aside.

**2.** Place flour, cinnamon, baking powder and salt in small bowl; stir to combine.

**3.** Beat sugar and butter in large bowl with electric mixer at medium speed until light and fluffy. Beat in eggs, 1 at a time. Beat in melted chocolate and coffee until well combined. Add flour mixture. Beat at low speed until well blended. Spread batter evenly in prepared pan.

**4.** Bake 30 to 35 minutes or until center is set. Remove to wire rack; cool completely. Cut into holiday shapes using 2-inch cookie cutters.

**5.** Tint frosting with food colors to desired color. Spread over each brownie shape. Break off top of small candy cane to create loop. Insert in top of brownie. Decorate with assorted candies and sprinkles as desired.

*Note:*

Don't throw away those brownie scraps after cutting out the holiday shapes! Crumble them and use them as an ice cream topping, or in a parfait with pound cake cubes, whipped cream and berries.

# Christmas Stained Glass Cookies

**Makes about 2½ dozen medium-sized cookies**

Colored hard candy
¾ cup butter or margarine, softened
¾ cup granulated sugar
2 eggs
1 teaspoon vanilla extract

3 cups all-purpose flour
1 teaspoon baking powder
Frosting (optional)
Small decorative candies (optional)

Separate colors of hard candy into resealable plastic freezer bags. Crush with mallet or hammer to equal about ⅓ cup crushed candy; set aside. In mixing bowl, cream butter and sugar. Beat in eggs and vanilla. In another bowl sift together flour and baking powder. Gradually stir flour mixture into butter mixture until dough is very stiff. Wrap in plastic wrap and chill about 3 hours.

Preheat oven to 375°F. Roll out dough to ⅛-inch thickness on lightly floured surface. Additional flour may be added to dough if necessary. Cut out cookies using large Christmas cookie cutters. Transfer cookies to foil-lined baking sheet. Using small Christmas cookie cutter of the same shape as large one, cut out and remove dough from center of each cookie.* Fill cut out sections with crushed candy. If using cookies as hanging ornaments, make holes at tops of cookies for string with drinking straw or chopstick. Bake 7 to 9 minutes or until cookies are lightly browned and candy is melted. Slide foil off baking sheets. When cool, carefully loosen cookies from foil. Use frosting and candy for additional decorations, if desired.

*For different designs, other cookie cutter shapes can be used to cut out center of cookies (i.e., small circle and star-shaped cutters can be used to cut out ornament designs on large Christmas tree cookies).

Favorite recipe from **The Sugar Association, Inc.**

# Danish Raspberry Cookies

2 squares (1 ounce each)
    unsweetened chocolate
½ cup (1 stick) butter, softened
½ cup sugar
1 egg
2 cups cake flour
1 teaspoon vanilla

¼ teaspoon salt
1 cup (6 ounces) milk chocolate
    or white chocolate chips or
    ½ cup of each
1 to 1¼ cups seedless raspberry
    preserves or jam

**Makes 8 dozen cookies**

*Note:*

Cake flour, also called pastry flour, is made from low-gluten soft wheat. It has a fine texture and is a good choice for pastries, cakes and quick breads.

Melt unsweetened chocolate in top of double boiler over hot, not boiling, water. Remove from heat; cool. Cream butter and sugar in large bowl until light. Add egg and melted chocolate; beat until fluffy. Stir in cake flour, vanilla and salt until well blended. Cover; refrigerate until firm, about 1 hour.

Preheat oven to 400°F. Lightly grease cookie sheets or line with parchment paper. Divide dough into 4 equal parts. Divide each part into 2 pieces. Roll each piece into rope 12 inches long on lightly floured board. (The ropes should be about the thickness of a finger.) Place 2 inches apart on prepared cookie sheets. With side of finger, make an indentation along length of each rope. Bake 8 minutes or until firm. Meanwhile, melt chocolate chips in small bowl over hot water. Stir until smooth. (If using both kinds of chips, melt separately.) Stir preserves; spoon into pastry bag fitted with ¼-inch tip or into small heavy-duty plastic bag. (If using plastic bag, snip off small corner from one side of bag.) Remove cookies from oven. Pipe preserves down length of each cookie strip. Return to oven for 2 minutes, then remove to wire racks. While cookies are still warm, drizzle melted chocolate over tops, then cut strips into 1-inch diagonal pieces. Refrigerate until chocolate is set.

# Holiday Cookies on a Stick

**Makes about 18 (3½-inch) cookies**

1 cup (2 sticks) butter or margarine, softened
¾ cup granulated sugar
¾ cup packed light brown sugar
1 teaspoon vanilla extract
2 eggs
2⅓ cups all-purpose flour
½ cup HERSHEY'S Cocoa
1 teaspoon baking soda
½ teaspoon salt
About 18 wooden ice cream sticks

1 tub (16 ounces) vanilla ready-to-spread frosting (optional)
Decorating icing in tube, colored sugar, candy sprinkles, HERSHEY'S Holiday Candy Coated Bits, HERSHEY'S MINI KISSES™ Semi-Sweet or Milk Chocolates

*1.* Heat oven to 350°F.

*2.* Beat butter, granulated sugar, brown sugar and vanilla in large bowl on medium speed of mixer until creamy. Add eggs; beat well. Stir together flour, cocoa, baking soda and salt; gradually add to butter mixture, beating until well blended.

*3.* Drop dough by scant ¼ cupfuls onto ungreased cookie sheet, about 3 inches apart. Shape into balls. Insert wooden stick about three-fourths of the way into side of each ball. Flatten slightly.

*4.* Bake 8 to 10 minutes or until set. (Cookies will spread during baking.) Cool 3 minutes; using wide spatula, carefully remove from cookie sheet to wire rack. Cool completely.

*5.* Spread with frosting, if desired. Decorate as desired with Christmas motifs, such as star, tree, candy cane, holly and Santa using decorating icing and garnishes.

# Icicle Ornaments

2½ cups all-purpose flour
¼ teaspoon salt
1 cup sugar
¾ cup (1½ sticks) unsalted
    butter, softened
2 squares (1 ounce each) white
    chocolate, melted
1 egg

1 teaspoon vanilla
    Coarse white decorating
        sugar, colored sugars and
        decors
Ribbon

**Makes about
2½ dozen cookies**

*1.* Combine flour and salt in medium bowl. Beat sugar and butter in large bowl at medium speed of electric mixer until fluffy. Beat in melted white chocolate, egg and vanilla. Gradually add flour mixture. Beat at low speed until well blended. Shape dough into disc. Wrap in plastic wrap; refrigerate 30 minutes or until firm.

*2.* Preheat oven to 350°F. Grease cookie sheets. Shape heaping tablespoonfuls of dough into 10-inch ropes. Fold each rope in half; twist to make icicle shape, leaving opening at top and tapering ends. Roll in coarse sugar; sprinkle with colored sugars and decors as desired. Place 1 inch apart on prepared cookie sheets.

*3.* Bake 8 to 10 minutes. (Do not brown.) Cool on cookie sheets 1 minute. Remove to wire racks; cool completely. Pull ribbon through opening in top of each icicle; tie small knot in ribbon ends.

# Pumpkin Cheesecake Bars

**Makes 4 dozen bars**

1 (16-ounce) package pound cake mix
3 eggs, divided
2 tablespoons butter or margarine, melted
4 teaspoons pumpkin pie spice, divided
1 (8-ounce) package cream cheese, softened

1 (14-ounce) can EAGLE® BRAND Sweetened Condensed Milk (NOT evaporated milk)
1 (15-ounce) can pumpkin
½ teaspoon salt
1 cup chopped nuts

*1.* Preheat oven to 350°F. In large mixing bowl, beat cake mix, 1 egg, butter and 2 teaspoons pumpkin pie spice on low speed of electric mixer until crumbly. Press onto bottom of ungreased 15×10×1-inch jelly-roll pan.

*2.* In large mixing bowl, beat cream cheese until fluffy. Gradually beat in Eagle Brand until smooth. Beat in remaining 2 eggs, pumpkin, remaining 2 teaspoons pumpkin pie spice and salt; mix well. Pour over crust; sprinkle with nuts.

*3.* Bake 30 to 35 minutes or until set. Cool. Chill; cut into bars. Store covered in refrigerator.

# Fruitcake Slices

1 cup (2 sticks) butter, softened
1 cup powdered sugar
1 egg
1 teaspoon vanilla
1½ cups coarsely chopped
    candied fruit (fruitcake mix)
½ cup coarsely chopped
    walnuts

2½ cups all-purpose unsifted
    flour, divided
¾ to 1 cup flaked coconut
    Maraschino cherry halves
    (optional)

**Makes about 4 dozen cookies**

Beat butter in large bowl with electric mixer at medium speed until smooth. Add powdered sugar; beat until well blended. Add egg and vanilla; beat until well blended.

Combine candied fruit and walnuts in medium bowl. Stir ¼ cup flour into fruit mixture. Add remaining 2¼ cups flour to butter mixture; beat at low speed until blended. Stir in fruit mixture with spoon.

Shape dough into 2 logs, each about 2 inches in diameter and 5½ inches long. Spread coconut evenly on sheet of waxed paper. Roll logs in coconut, coating evenly. Wrap each log in plastic wrap. Refrigerate 2 to 3 hours or overnight, or freeze up to 1 month. (Let frozen logs stand at room temperature about 10 minutes before slicing and baking.)

Preheat oven to 350°F. Grease cookie sheets. Cut logs into ¼-inch-thick slices; place 1 inch apart on cookie sheets.

Bake 13 to 15 minutes or until edges are golden brown. Transfer to wire racks to cool. Decorate with cherry halves, if desired. Store in airtight container.

*Note:*

Candying fruit is a process of dipping or cooking fruit in several boiling sugar syrups, then sometimes dipping it in granulated sugar after it has dried. The candying process preserves the fruit along with its color, shape and flavor.

# Banana Gingerbread Bars

**Makes about 32 bars**

1 package (14.5 ounces) gingerbread cake mix
½ cup lukewarm water
1 ripe, medium DOLE® Banana, mashed (about ½ cup)
1 egg

1 small DOLE® Banana, peeled and chopped
½ cup DOLE® Seedless Raisins
½ cup slivered almonds
1½ cups powdered sugar
Juice from 1 lemon

*Note:*

To ripen bananas, store them at room temperature. To speed ripening, place them in an unsealed paper bag at room temperature. And to prevent ripe bananas from spoiling, store them, tightly wrapped, in the refrigerator for up to three days.

• Preheat oven to 350°F.

• In large mixer bowl, combine gingerbread mix, water, mashed banana and egg. Beat on low speed of electric mixer 1 minute.

• Stir in chopped banana, raisins and almonds.

• Spread batter in greased 13×9-inch baking pan. Bake 20 to 25 minutes or until top springs back when lightly touched.

• In medium bowl, mix powdered sugar and 3 tablespoons lemon juice to make thin glaze. Spread over warm gingerbread. Cool before cutting into bars. Sprinkle with additional powdered sugar, if desired.

# Christmas Spritz Cookies

2¼ cups all-purpose flour
¼ teaspoon salt
1¼ cups powdered sugar
1 cup (2 sticks) butter, softened
1 egg
1 teaspoon almond extract
1 teaspoon vanilla

Green food coloring (optional)
Candied red and green
   cherries and assorted
   decorative candies
   (optional)
Icing (recipe follows, optional)

**Makes about 5 dozen cookies**

Preheat oven to 375°F. Place flour and salt in medium bowl; stir to combine. Beat powdered sugar and butter in large bowl until light and fluffy. Beat in egg, almond extract and vanilla. Gradually add flour mixture. Beat until well blended.

Divide dough in half. If desired, tint half of dough with green food coloring. Fit cookie press with desired plate (or change plates for different shapes after first batch). Fill press with dough; press dough 1 inch apart onto ungreased cookie sheets. Decorate cookies with cherries and assorted candies, if desired.

Bake 10 to 12 minutes or until just set. Remove cookies to wire racks; cool completely.

Prepare Icing, if desired. Pipe or drizzle on cooled cookies. Decorate with cherries and assorted candies, if desired. Store tightly covered at room temperature or freeze up to 3 months.

## Icing

1½ cups powdered sugar
2 tablespoons milk plus
   additional, if needed

⅛ teaspoon almond extract

Place all ingredients in medium bowl; stir until thick but spreadable. (If icing is too thick, stir in 1 teaspoon additional milk.)

# Winter Wonderland Snowmen Brownies

**Makes about 12 large brownies or 36 squares**

¾ cup HERSHEY'S Cocoa or
   HERSHEY'S Dutch
   Processed Cocoa
½ teaspoon baking soda
⅔ cup butter or margarine,
   melted and divided
½ cup boiling water
2 cups sugar

2 eggs
1 teaspoon vanilla extract
1½ cups all-purpose flour
1⅔ cups (10-ounce package)
   REESE'S® Peanut Butter
   Chips
Powdered sugar (optional)

*1.* Heat oven to 350°F. Line 13×9×2-inch baking pan with foil; grease foil.

*2.* Stir together cocoa and baking soda in large bowl; stir in ⅓ cup melted butter. Add boiling water; stir until mixture thickens. Stir in sugar, eggs, vanilla and remaining ⅓ cup butter; stir until smooth. Add flour; stir until blended. Stir in peanut butter chips. Pour into prepared pan.

*3.* Bake 35 to 40 minutes or until brownies begin to pull away from sides of foil. Cool completely in pan. Cover; refrigerate until firm. Remove from pan; remove foil. Cut into snowmen shapes with cookie cutters or cut into squares. Just before serving, sprinkle with powdered sugar, if desired.

# Hanukkah Cookies

**Makes 3½ dozen cookies**

½ cup unsalted butter, softened
1 package (3 ounces) cream
   cheese
½ cup sugar
¼ cup honey
1 egg

½ teaspoon vanilla
2½ cups all-purpose flour
⅓ cup finely ground walnuts
1 teaspoon baking powder
¼ teaspoon salt
Assorted colored icings

Beat butter, cream cheese, sugar, honey, egg and vanilla with electric mixer at medium speed until creamy. Stir in flour, walnuts, baking powder and salt until well blended. Form dough into ball; wrap in plastic wrap and flatten. Chill 2 hours or until firm.

Preheat oven to 350°F. Lightly grease cookie sheets. Roll out dough, small portion at a time, to ¼-inch thickness on floured surface with lightly floured rolling pin. (Keep remaining dough wrapped in refrigerator.) Cut out dough with 2½-inch dreidel-shaped cookie cutter and 6-pointed star cookie cutter. Transfer to prepared cookie sheets. Bake 8 to 10 minutes or until edges are lightly browned. Let cookies stand on cookie sheets 1 to 2 minutes; cool completely on wire racks. Decorate cookies with blue and white icings, sprinkles, sugars and decors as desired.

*Note:*

If your honey has crystallized, place the opened container in a pan of hot water and gently stir the honey until it liquifies. It can also be liquified by removing the lid and microwaving at HIGH for 20 to 60 seconds.

# Christmas Sugar Cookies

| | | Makes about 3 dozen (3-inch) cookies |
|---|---|---|
| 1 cup DOMINO® Granulated Sugar | ¼ teaspoon lemon extract | |
| ¾ cup butter or margarine, softened | 3 cups all-purpose flour | **Prep Time:** *20 minutes* |
| 1 egg | 1 teaspoon baking powder | |
| 1 teaspoon grated lemon peel | ½ teaspoon salt | **Chill Time:** *1 hour* |
| 1 teaspoon vanilla | Assorted Christmas candies and sprinkles | |
| | | **Bake Time:** *12 minutes* |

Cream sugar and butter in large bowl until light and fluffy. Add egg, lemon peel, vanilla and lemon extract; mix well. Add flour, baking powder and salt, beating at low speed until well mixed. Refrigerate dough 1 hour or until chilled.

Heat oven to 350°F. On well-floured surface, roll out half of dough to ⅛-inch thickness. Cut with cookie cutters; place on *ungreased* cookie sheets. Decorate with candies and sprinkles. Repeat with remaining half of dough. Bake 9 to 12 minutes or until lightly browned at edges.

# Candy Cane Cookies

**Makes about 4½ dozen cookies**

*Note:*

To package cookies for holiday gift giving, arrange one layer in a box and cover with waxed paper. Continue layering cookies and waxed paper, and top the final layer of cookies with enough waxed paper to hold them firmly in place.

1¼ cups granulated sugar
1 Butter Flavor CRISCO® Stick or 1 cup Butter Flavor CRISCO® all-vegetable shortening
2 eggs
¼ cup light corn syrup or regular pancake syrup
1 tablespoon vanilla
3 cups plus 4 tablespoons all-purpose flour, divided
¾ teaspoon baking powder
½ teaspoon baking soda
½ teaspoon salt
½ teaspoon red food color
¼ teaspoon peppermint extract

*1.* Combine sugar and 1 cup shortening in large bowl. Beat at medium speed of electric mixer until well blended. Add eggs, syrup and vanilla. Beat until well blended and fluffy.

*2.* Combine 3 cups flour, baking powder, baking soda and salt. Add gradually to creamed mixture at low speed. Mix until well blended.

*3.* Divide dough in half. Add red food color and peppermint extract to one half. Wrap each half in plastic wrap. Refrigerate several hours or overnight.

*4.* Heat oven to 375°F. Place sheets of foil on countertop for cooling cookies.

*5.* Roll 1 rounded teaspoonful plain dough with hands into a 6-inch rope on lightly floured surface. Repeat, using 1 teaspoonful red dough. Place ropes side by side. Twist together gently. Pinch ends to seal. Curve one end into the "hook" of a candy cane. Transfer to ungreased baking sheet with large pancake turner. Repeat with remaining dough. Place cookies 2 inches apart.

*6.* Bake one baking sheet at a time at 375°F for 7 to 9 minutes, or until just lightly browned. *Do not overbake.* Cool 2 minutes on baking sheet. Remove cookies to foil to cool completely.

# Holiday Peppermint Slices

**1 package (18 ounces)
refrigerated sugar cookie
dough
¼ teaspoon peppermint extract,
divided**

**Red food coloring
Green food coloring**

**Makes 2½ dozen
cookies**

*1.* Remove dough from wrapper according to package directions.
Cut dough into thirds.

*2.* Combine ⅓ of dough, ⅛ teaspoon peppermint extract and
enough red food coloring to make dough desired shade of red.
Knead dough until evenly tinted.

*3.* Repeat with second ⅓ of dough, remaining ⅛ teaspoon
peppermint extract and green food coloring.

*4.* To assemble, shape each portion of dough into 8-inch roll.
Place red roll beside green roll; press together slightly. Place
plain roll on top. Press rolls together to form one tri-colored
roll; wrap in plastic wrap. Refrigerate 2 hours or overnight.

*5.* Preheat oven to 350°F.

*6.* Cut dough into ¼-inch-thick slices. Place 2 inches apart on
ungreased cookie sheets. Bake 8 to 9 minutes or until set but
not browned. Cool 1 minute on cookie sheets. Cool completely
on wire racks.

# Jolly Snowman Cookies

**Makes 1 dozen cookies**

½ cup (1 stick) butter, softened
½ cup granulated sugar
1 teaspoon vanilla extract
1 cup all-purpose flour

¼ teaspoon salt
1 cup "M&M's"® Chocolate
   Mini Baking Bits, divided
White Icing (recipe follows)

Preheat oven to 375°F. In large bowl cream butter and sugar until light and fluffy; beat in vanilla. In medium bowl combine flour and salt; add to creamed mixture. Stir in ¾ cup "M&M's"® Chocolate Mini Baking Bits. Divide dough into 12 equal sections. Roll each section into 3 balls, large, medium and small for each snowman. Place 3 balls in row, ¼ inch apart on ungreased cookie sheet for each snowman; flatten balls slightly. Bake 12 minutes. Remove from oven. Cool on cookie sheets 1 to 2 minutes; cool completely on wire racks. Prepare White Icing; pour over cookies. Let cookies stand about 10 minutes or until almost set. Decorate with remaining ¼ cup "M&M's"® Chocolate Mini Baking Bits to look like snowmen. Store in tightly covered container.

<u>**White Icing:**</u> *In small bowl combine 1½ cups powdered sugar and 1 tablespoon milk until well blended. Add additional milk, 1 teaspoon at a time, if necessary to make frosting pourable.*

# Soft Molasses Spice Cookies

2¼ cups all-purpose flour
1 teaspoon baking soda
1 teaspoon ground cinnamon
½ teaspoon ground ginger
¼ teaspoon ground nutmeg
⅛ teaspoon salt
⅛ teaspoon ground cloves
½ cup plus 2 tablespoons butter, softened, divided

½ cup packed dark brown sugar
1 egg
½ cup molasses
1¼ teaspoons vanilla, divided
¼ cup plus 2 to 3 tablespoons milk, divided
¾ cup raisins (optional)
2 cups powdered sugar

**Makes about 3 dozen cookies**

*1.* Preheat oven to 350°F. Grease cookie sheets. Combine flour, baking soda, cinnamon, ginger, nutmeg, salt and cloves in medium bowl.

*2.* Beat ½ cup butter in large bowl with electric mixer at medium speed until smooth and creamy. Gradually beat in brown sugar until blended; increase speed to high and beat until light and fluffy. Beat in egg until fluffy. Beat in molasses and 1 teaspoon vanilla until smooth. Beat in flour mixture at low speed alternately with ¼ cup milk until blended. Stir in raisins, if desired.

*3.* Drop rounded tablespoonfuls of dough about 1½ inches apart onto prepared cookie sheets. Bake 12 minutes or until set. Let cookies stand on cookie sheets 5 minutes; transfer to wire racks to cool completely.

*4.* For icing, melt remaining 2 tablespoons butter in small saucepan over medium-low heat. Remove from heat; add powdered sugar and stir until blended. Add remaining 2 tablespoons milk and ¼ teaspoon vanilla; stir until smooth. If icing is too thick, add milk, 1 teaspoon at a time, until desired consistency.

*5.* Spread icing over tops of cookies. Let stand 15 minutes or until icing is set. Store in airtight container.

*Note:*

Brown sugar should always be firmly packed into a measuring cup before using. To test, fill the cup with brown sugar and turn upside down. If the sugar holds its shape, it's been correctly measured.

# Berlinerkranser (Little Wreaths)

**Makes 4 dozen cookies**

1 Butter Flavor CRISCO® Stick or 1 cup Butter Flavor CRISCO® all-vegetable shortening
1 cup confectioners' sugar
2 large hard boiled egg yolks, mashed

2 large eggs, separated
1 teaspoon vanilla
1 teaspoon almond extract
2¼ cups all-purpose flour
   Green colored sugar crystals
24 red candied cherries, cut into halves

*Note:*

Flavoring extracts are made by distilling the essential oils of fruits, nuts or plants, such as almonds or vanilla. The oils are mixed with an alcohol base which dissipates when heated.

*1.* Combine 1 cup shortening and confectioners' sugar in large bowl. Beat on medium speed with electric mixer until well blended. Beat in hard boiled egg yolks, uncooked egg yolks, vanilla and almond extract. Beat in flour, ¼ cup at a time, until well blended. Cover and refrigerate 3 hours.

*2.* Let dough stand at room temperature until it becomes easy to handle.

*3.* Heat oven to 350°F. Divide dough into 2 equal portions. Cut each portion into 24 equal pieces. Roll each piece of dough into 5-inch-long rope. Form each rope into wreath or loop 1½ inches apart on ungreased cookie sheet, overlapping both ends. Brush each wreath with beaten egg whites; sprinkle with colored sugar crystals. Lightly press cherry piece into top of each wreath.

*4.* Bake at 350°F for 10 to 12 minutes or until edges are lightly browned. Cool on cookie sheets 3 minutes; transfer to cooling racks.

<u>Tip:</u> *These wreath-shaped cookies are a Norwegian holiday favorite for the family to bake together.*

# Holiday Bits Cutout Cookies

1 cup (2 sticks) butter or
   margarine, softened
1 cup sugar
2 eggs
2 teaspoons vanilla extract

2½ cups all-purpose flour
½ teaspoon baking powder
½ teaspoon salt
   HERSHEY᾽S Holiday Candy
   Coated Bits

**Makes about
3½ dozen cookies**

**Prep Time:**
*30 minutes*

**Bake Time:**
*6 minutes*

**Chill Time:**
*1 hour*

*1.* Beat butter, sugar, eggs and vanilla in large bowl on low speed of mixer just until blended. Stir together flour, baking powder and salt; add to butter mixture, stirring until well blended.

*2.* Divide dough in half. Cover; refrigerate 1 to 2 hours or until firm enough to handle. Heat oven to 400°F. On lightly floured surface, roll each half of dough to about ¼-inch thickness.

*3.* Cut into tree, wreath, star or other shapes with 2½-inch cookie cutters. Place on ungreased cookie sheet. Press candy coated bits into cutouts.

*4.* Bake 6 to 8 minutes or until edges are firm and bottoms are very lightly browned. Remove from cookie sheet to wire rack. Cool completely.

**Tip:** *Brownies, bars and cookies make great gifts. Place them in a paper-lined tin or on a decorative plate covered with plastic wrap and tied with colorful ribbon. For a special touch, include the recipe.*

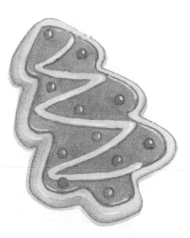

# Macadamia Nut White Chip Pumpkin Cookies

**Makes about 4 dozen cookies**

2 cups all-purpose flour
2 teaspoons ground cinnamon
1 teaspoon ground cloves
1 teaspoon baking soda
1 cup (2 sticks) butter or margarine, softened
½ cup granulated sugar
½ cup packed brown sugar
1 cup LIBBY'S® 100% Pure Pumpkin

1 large egg
2 teaspoons vanilla extract
2 cups (12-ounce package) NESTLÉ® TOLL HOUSE® Premier White Morsels
⅔ cup coarsely chopped macadamia nuts or walnuts, toasted

**PREHEAT** oven to 350°F.

**COMBINE** flour, cinnamon, cloves and baking soda in small bowl. Beat butter, granulated sugar and brown sugar in large mixer bowl until creamy. Beat in pumpkin, egg and vanilla extract until blended. Gradually beat in flour mixture. Stir in morsels and nuts. Drop by rounded tablespoon onto greased baking sheets; flatten slightly with back of spoon or greased bottom of glass dipped in granulated sugar.

**BAKE** for 11 to 14 minutes or until centers are set. Cool on baking sheets for 2 minutes; remove to wire racks to cool completely.

# Gingerbread Apple Bars

**Makes 1 dozen bars**

1 cup applesauce
½ cup raisins
⅓ cup unsulfured light molasses
1 teaspoon baking soda
2 eggs
¼ cup sugar
¼ cup CRISCO® Oil*

1½ cups all-purpose flour
1 teaspoon ground cinnamon
½ teaspoon ground ginger
¼ teaspoon ground cloves
⅛ teaspoon salt

*Use your favorite Crisco Oil product.

*1.* Heat oven to 350°F. Oil 8-inch square pan lightly.

*2.* Place applesauce and raisins in small saucepan. Cook and stir on low heat until mixture comes to a boil. Remove from heat. Stir in molasses and baking soda. Cool slightly.

*3.* Combine eggs and sugar in large bowl. Beat in ¼ cup oil gradually.

*4.* Combine flour, cinnamon, ginger, cloves and salt in small bowl. Add to egg mixture alternately with applesauce mixture, beginning and ending with flour mixture. Spoon into pan.

*5.* Bake at 350°F for 30 minutes or until toothpick inserted in center comes out clean. Cool in pan on cooling rack. Cut into bars. Serve warm or at room temperature.

## Special Delivery

*Cookies make great holiday gifts—always appreciated, never returned. Just keep a few things in mind when shipping cookies to friends and family out of town.*

- Soft, moist cookies can handle jostling better than crisp cookies that crumble easily.

- Brownies and bar cookies are generally sturdy, but don't ship ones with moist fillings and/or frostings.

- Wrap each type of cookie separately to retain flavors and textures.

- Place wrapped cookies as tightly as possible in snug rows inside a sturdy shipping box or container.

- Fill the bottom of the shipping container with an even layer of packing material. Don't use popped popcorn or puffed cereal, as they may attract insects. Place crumpled waxed paper, newspaper or paper towels in between layers of wrapped cookies. Fill any crevices with packing material, and add a final layer at the top of the box.

- Ship the container to arrive as soon as possible.

# Santa's Thumbprints

**Makes about 3 dozen cookies**

1 cup (2 sticks) margarine, softened
½ cup firmly packed brown sugar
1 whole egg
1 teaspoon vanilla

1½ cups QUAKER® Oats (quick or old fashioned, uncooked)
1½ cups all-purpose flour
1 cup finely chopped nuts
¼ cup jelly or preserves

Preheat oven to 350°F. Beat margarine and sugar until fluffy. Blend in egg and vanilla. Add combined oats and flour; mix well. Shape to form 1-inch balls; roll in chopped nuts. Place 2 inches apart on ungreased cookie sheets. Press center of each ball with thumb. Fill each thumbprint with about ¼ teaspoon jelly. Bake 12 to 15 minutes or until light golden brown. Cool completely on wire rack. Store loosely covered.

# Yuletide Linzer Bars

**Makes 36 bars**

1⅓ cups butter, softened
¾ cup sugar
1 egg
1 teaspoon grated lemon peel
2½ cups all-purpose flour
1½ cups whole almonds, ground

1 teaspoon ground cinnamon
¾ cup raspberry preserves
Powdered sugar

Preheat oven to 350°F. Grease 13×9-inch baking pan.

Beat butter and sugar in large bowl at medium speed of electric mixer until creamy. Beat in egg and lemon peel until blended. Mix in flour, almonds and cinnamon until well blended.

Press 2 cups dough onto bottom of prepared pan. Spread preserves over crust. Press remaining dough, a small amount at a time, evenly over preserves.

Bake 35 to 40 minutes until golden brown. Cool in pan on wire rack. Sprinkle with powdered sugar; cut into bars.

# Fruitcake Cookies

¾ cup sugar
½ cup (1 stick) butter, softened
½ cup milk
1 egg
2 tablespoons orange juice
1 tablespoon vinegar
2 cups all-purpose flour
1 teaspoon baking powder

½ teaspoon baking soda
¼ teaspoon salt
½ cup chopped walnuts
½ cup chopped candied mixed fruit
½ cup raisins
¼ cup chopped dried pineapple
Powdered sugar

**Makes about 2½ dozen cookies**

Preheat oven to 350°F. Grease cookie sheets. Beat sugar and butter in large bowl until creamy. Beat in milk, egg, orange juice and vinegar until blended. Mix in flour, baking powder, baking soda and salt. Stir in walnuts, mixed fruit, raisins and pineapple. Drop rounded tablespoonfuls of dough 2 inches apart onto prepared cookie sheets.

Bake 12 to 14 minutes or until lightly browned around edges. Cool 2 minutes on cookie sheets. Remove to wire racks; cool completely. Dust with powdered sugar. Store in airtight container.

*Note:*

To shape drop cookies into a uniform size, use a small ice cream scoop with a release mechanism. A variety of different scoops can be found at cookware and restaurant supply stores.

# White Chocolate Cranberry Cookie Bars

**Makes 2 dozen bars**

2 cups all-purpose flour
1 teaspoon baking powder
1 teaspoon salt
4 eggs
1¾ cups sugar
1 teaspoon vanilla extract

1 bag (12 ounces) white
   chocolate chips (2 cups),
   divided
½ cup (1 stick) IMPERIAL®
   Spread
1 cup dried cranberries

Preheat oven to 350°F. Grease 13×9-inch baking pan; set aside.

In medium bowl, combine flour, baking powder and salt; set aside. In small bowl, with wire whisk, beat eggs, sugar and vanilla; set aside.

In medium saucepan, melt 1 cup white chocolate chips with spread over low heat, stirring occasionally. Remove from heat; let cool slightly. While stirring chocolate mixture, slowly stir in egg mixture, then flour mixture until blended. Stir in remaining 1 cup chips and cranberries. Evenly pour into prepared pan.

Bake uncovered 40 minutes or until center springs back when lightly touched. On wire rack, cool completely. To serve, cut into bars.

# Chocolate Spritz

**Makes about 5 dozen cookies**

2 squares (1 ounce each)
   unsweetened chocolate
1 cup (2 sticks) butter, softened
½ cup granulated sugar
1 egg

1 teaspoon vanilla
¼ teaspoon salt
2¼ cups all-purpose flour
   Powdered sugar

Preheat oven to 400°F. Line cookie sheets with parchment paper or leave ungreased. Melt chocolate in top of double boiler over hot, not boiling, water. Remove from heat; cool. Beat butter, granulated sugar, egg, vanilla and salt in large bowl until light. Blend in melted chocolate and flour until stiff. Fit cookie press with your choice of plate. Load press with dough; press cookies out onto cookie sheets, spacing 2 inches apart.

Bake 5 to 7 minutes or just until very slightly browned around edges. Remove to wire racks to cool. Sprinkle with powdered sugar.

*Note:*

The dough for pressed cookies often needs to be chilled briefly to firm up before pressing. (However, it can't be too cold or it will be too difficult to press.)

# Old World Pfeffernüsse Cookies

| | |
|---|---|
| ¾ cup packed brown sugar | 1 teaspoon baking soda |
| ½ cup (1 stick) butter, softened | 1 teaspoon ground cinnamon |
| ½ cup molasses | ½ teaspoon ground cloves |
| 1 egg | ¼ teaspoon ground nutmeg |
| 1 tablespoon licorice-flavored liqueur (optional) | Dash black pepper |
| 3¼ cups all-purpose flour | Powdered sugar |

**Makes about 4 dozen cookies**

Preheat oven to 350°F. Grease cookie sheets. Beat brown sugar and butter in large bowl until creamy. Beat in molasses, egg and liqueur, if desired, until light and fluffy. Mix in flour, baking soda, cinnamon, cloves, nutmeg and pepper. Shape level tablespoonfuls of dough into balls. Place 2 inches apart on prepared cookie sheets.

Bake 12 to 14 minutes or until set. Cool 2 minutes on cookie sheets. Remove to wire racks; sprinkle with powdered sugar. Cool completely. Store in airtight containers.

# Basic Banana Holiday Cookies

**Makes 4½ dozen cookies**

**Prep Time:**
*15 minutes*

**Bake Time:**
*12 minutes*

*Note:*

Cookie recipes sometimes call for granulated sugar and brown sugar. Both sugars are sweeteners and tenderizers, while brown sugar imparts a rich molasses taste that's desirable in small amounts.

2¾ cups all-purpose flour
1 teaspoon baking soda
¼ teaspoon salt
1 cup margarine, softened
1¼ cups granulated sugar, divided

¼ cup packed brown sugar
1 large, ripe DOLE® Banana, mashed (about ½ cup)
1 egg
½ teaspoon ground cinnamon

• **Combine** flour, baking soda and salt in medium bowl; set aside.

• **Beat** together margarine, 1 cup granulated sugar and brown sugar in large bowl until creamy. Beat in banana and egg until blended. Stir in flour mixture until combined. Cover and chill 2 hours or overnight until dough is firm enough to handle.

• **Combine** remaining ¼ cup granulated sugar and cinnamon in small bowl.

• **Shape** dough into 1-inch balls. Roll in cinnamon mixture; place two inches apart on ungreased baking sheets.

• **Bake** at 350°F 10 to 12 minutes or until lightly browned. Carefully remove cookies to wire rack to cool completely.

**Chocolate Banana Stars:** *Prepare, shape and bake dough as directed except roll dough in 1 cup finely chopped DOLE® Almonds instead of cinnamon mixture. Immediately after baking, press unwrapped individual milk chocolate star candies into center of each cookie. Cool as directed.*

**Banana Chippers:** *Prepare and shape dough as directed except stir 1 package (10 ounces) peanut butter chips and 1 cup chopped pecans or walnuts into dough and omit cinnamon mixture. Bake and cool as directed.*

**Zana Kringles:** *Stir 1 teaspoon ground ginger into flour mixture and replace brown sugar with 2 tablespoons molasses. Prepare, shape, bake and cool as directed.*

# Holiday Wreath Cookies

1 package (20 ounces)
　refrigerated sugar cookie
　dough
2 cups shredded coconut
2 to 3 drops green food color

1 container (16 ounces) French
　vanilla frosting
Green sugar or small
　cinnamon candies

**Makes about 2 dozen cookies**

**Prep and Bake Time:**
*30 minutes*

*1.* Preheat oven to 350°F. Remove dough from wrapper according to package directions. Divide dough in half; wrap half of dough in plastic wrap and refrigerate. Roll out remaining half of dough on well-floured surface to ⅛-inch thickness. Cut with cookie cutters to resemble wreaths. Repeat with remaining half of dough.

*2.* Place cookies about 2 inches apart on ungreased baking sheets. Bake 7 to 9 minutes or until edges are lightly browned. Remove cookies from baking sheets to wire racks to cool completely.

*3.* Place coconut in resealable plastic food storage bag. Add food color; seal bag and shake until coconut is evenly tinted. Frost cookies with frosting and decorate with coconut, green sugar and cinnamon candies.

# Chocolate-Raspberry Kolacky

**Makes about 1½ dozen cookies**

2 squares (1 ounce each) semisweet chocolate, coarsely chopped
1½ cups all-purpose flour
¼ teaspoon baking soda
¼ teaspoon salt
½ cup (1 stick) butter, softened

3 ounces cream cheese or light cream cheese, softened
⅓ cup granulated sugar
1 teaspoon vanilla
Seedless raspberry jam
Powdered sugar

Place chocolate in 1-cup microwavable glass measure. Microwave at HIGH 1 to 1½ minutes or until chocolate is melted, stirring after 1 minute.

Combine flour, baking soda and salt in small bowl; stir well. Beat butter and cream cheese in large bowl with electric mixer at medium speed until well blended. Beat in granulated sugar until light and fluffy. Beat in vanilla and melted chocolate. Gradually add flour mixture. Beat at low speed just until blended. Divide dough in half; flatten each half into disc. Wrap separately in plastic wrap. Refrigerate 1 to 2 hours or until firm.

Preheat oven to 375°F. Lightly grease cookie sheets. Roll out each dough disc on well-floured surface to ¼- to ⅛-inch thickness. Cut out with 3-inch round cookie cutter. Place 2 inches apart on prepared cookie sheets. Place rounded ½ teaspoon jam in center of each circle. Bring three edges of dough circles up over jam; pinch edges together to seal, leaving center of triangle slightly open.

Bake 10 minutes or until set. Let cookies stand on cookie sheets 2 minutes. Remove cookies to wire racks; cool completely. Just before serving, sprinkle with powdered sugar. Store cookies tightly covered in refrigerator; let stand 30 minutes at room temperature before serving.

*Note:*

The easiest way to sprinkle powdered sugar over cookies is with a sugar dredger— a perforated screw-top container sold in kitchenware stores. But a salt shaker or a fine sieve can also be used to do the job.

**Note:** *These cookies do not freeze well.*

**Chocolate-Raspberry Kolacky Cups:** *Fit dough circles into greased mini-muffin cups; fill with heaping teaspoonful jam. Bake 10 minutes or until set. Let pans stand on wire racks; cool completely. Dust with powdered sugar before serving.*

# Christmas Spirits

| | | Makes about 48 cookies |
|---|---|---|
| 32 chocolate creme sandwich cookies<br>1¼ cups toasted California walnuts<br>¾ cup powdered sugar, divided | 2 tablespoons instant coffee powder, divided<br>2 tablespoons light corn syrup<br>⅓ cup brandy, coffee liqueur or rum | |

Break up cookies and place in food processor; process until cookies form fine crumbs (about 2 cups crumbs). Add walnuts, ½ cup powdered sugar and 1½ tablespoons coffee powder. Process until thoroughly combined. Add corn syrup; gradually mix in brandy until mixture forms a thick paste. Form into 1-inch balls.

Combine remaining ¼ cup powdered sugar and remaining ½ tablespoon coffee powder. Roll balls in sugar mixture to coat. Cookies may be stored loosely packed between sheets of waxed paper or aluminum foil in airtight container for up to 2 weeks.

Favorite recipe from **Walnut Marketing Board**

# Pumpkin Spiced and Iced Cookies

**Makes about 5½ dozen cookies**

*Note:*

If you use butter to grease your baking sheets, it's best to use unsalted butter. Salted butter may cause baked goods to stick.

2¼ cups all-purpose flour
1½ teaspoons pumpkin pie spice
1 teaspoon baking powder
½ teaspoon baking soda
½ teaspoon salt
1 cup (2 sticks) butter or margarine, softened
1 cup granulated sugar
1 can (15 ounces) LIBBY'S® 100% Pure Pumpkin

2 large eggs
1 teaspoon vanilla extract
2 cups (12-ounce package) NESTLÉ® TOLL HOUSE® Semi-Sweet Chocolate Morsels
1 cup chopped walnuts (optional)
Vanilla Glaze (recipe follows)

**PREHEAT** oven to 375°F. Grease baking sheets.

**COMBINE** flour, pumpkin pie spice, baking powder, baking soda and salt in medium bowl. Beat butter and granulated sugar in large mixer bowl until creamy. Beat in pumpkin, eggs and vanilla extract. Gradually beat in flour mixture. Stir in morsels and nuts. Drop by rounded tablespoon onto prepared baking sheets.

**BAKE** for 15 to 20 minutes or until edges are lightly browned. Cool on baking sheets for 2 minutes; remove to wire rack to cool completely. Spread or drizzle with Vanilla Glaze.

**Vanilla Glaze:** *COMBINE 1 cup powdered sugar, 1 to 1½ tablespoons milk and ½ teaspoon vanilla extract in small bowl; mix well.*

# Dutch St. Nicolas Cookies

Makes about
3½ dozen cookies

½ cup whole natural almonds
¾ cup butter or margarine,
   softened
½ cup packed brown sugar
2 tablespoons milk
1½ teaspoons ground cinnamon
¼ teaspoon ground nutmeg

¼ teaspoon ground ginger
¼ teaspoon ground cloves
2 cups sifted all-purpose flour
1½ teaspoons baking powder
½ teaspoon salt
¼ cup coarsely chopped citron

Spread almonds in single layer on baking sheet. Bake at 375°F,
10 to 12 minutes, stirring occasionally, until lightly toasted. Cool.
Chop finely. In large bowl, cream butter, sugar, milk and spices.
In small bowl, combine flour, baking powder and salt. Add flour
mixture to creamed mixture; blend well. Stir in almonds and
citron. Knead dough slightly to make ball. Cover; refrigerate until
firm. Roll out dough ¼ inch thick on lightly floured surface. Cut
out with cookie cutters. Place 2 inches apart on greased cookie
sheets. Bake at 375°F 7 to 10 minutes, until lightly browned.
Remove to wire racks to cool.

Favorite recipe from **Almond Board of California**

# Holiday Mini Kisses Treasure Cookies

**Makes about 3 dozen cookies**

1½ cups graham cracker crumbs
½ cup all-purpose flour
2 teaspoons baking powder
1 can (14 ounces) sweetened condensed milk (not evaporated milk)
½ cup (1 stick) butter, softened

1⅓ cups MOUNDS® Coconut Flakes
1 cup HERSHEY'S MINI KISSES™ Milk Chocolates or Semi-Sweet Chocolates
1⅓ cups (10-ounce package) HERSHEY'S Holiday Bits

*1.* Heat oven to 375°F. Stir together graham cracker crumbs, flour and baking powder in small bowl; set aside.

*2.* Beat sweetened condensed milk and butter until smooth; add reserved crumb mixture, mixing well. Stir in coconut, Mini Kisses™ and Holiday Bits. Drop by rounded tablespoons onto ungreased cookie sheet.

*3.* Bake 8 to 10 minutes or until lightly browned. Cool 1 minute; remove from cookie sheet to wire rack. Cool completely.

**Variation:** *Use 1¾ cups (10-ounce package) HERSHEY®S MINI KISSES™ Milk Chocolate or Semi-Sweet Baking Pieces and 1 cup coarsely chopped walnuts. Omit Holiday Bits. Proceed as directed above.*

# Snowmen

**Makes 1 dozen cookies**

1 package (20 ounces) refrigerated chocolate chip cookie dough
1½ cups sifted powdered sugar
2 tablespoons milk

Candy corn, gumdrops, chocolate chips, licorice and other assorted small candies

*1.* Preheat oven to 375°F. Remove dough from wrapper. Cut dough into 12 equal sections. Divide each section into 3 balls: large, medium and small for each snowman.

*2.* For each snowman, place 3 balls in row, ¼ inch apart, on ungreased cookie sheet.

*3.* Bake 10 to 12 minutes or until edges are very lightly browned. Cool 4 minutes on cookie sheets. Remove to wire racks; cool completely.

*4.* Mix powdered sugar and milk in medium bowl until smooth. Pour over cookies. Let cookies stand 20 minutes or until set.

*5.* Decorate with assorted candies to create snowman faces, hats and arms.

*Note:*

To minimize breakage, use a sealed airtight container when transporting holiday cookies. Transfer them to a serving plate once you reach your destination.

# Rum Fruitcake Cookies

| | |
|---|---|
| 1 cup sugar | 1 teaspoon baking soda |
| ¾ cup shortening | 1 teaspoon salt |
| 3 eggs | 2 cups (8 ounces) chopped |
| ⅓ cup orange juice | candied mixed fruit |
| 1 tablespoon rum extract | 1 cup raisins |
| 3 cups all-purpose flour | 1 cup nuts, coarsely chopped |
| 2 teaspoons baking powder | |

**Makes about 6 dozen cookies**

*1.* Preheat oven to 375°F. Lightly grease cookie sheets; set aside. Beat sugar and shortening in large bowl until fluffy. Add eggs, orange juice and rum extract; beat 2 minutes.

*2.* Combine flour, baking powder, baking soda and salt in medium bowl. Add candied fruit, raisins and nuts. Stir into creamed mixture. Drop dough by rounded teaspoonfuls 2 inches apart onto prepared cookie sheets. Bake 10 to 12 minutes or until golden. Let cookies stand on cookie sheets 2 minutes. Remove to wire racks; cool completely.

# Holiday Almond Wreaths

**Makes about 3 dozen cookies**

¾ cup FLEISCHMANN'S® Margarine, softened
½ cup sugar
¼ cup EGG BEATERS® Healthy Real Egg Product
1 teaspoon almond extract

2 cups all-purpose flour
½ cup ground almonds
Green and red glacé cherries, optional

Preheat oven to 400°F. In medium bowl, using electric mixer at medium speed, cream margarine and sugar. Add Egg Beaters® and almond extract. Stir in flour and ground almonds. Using pastry bag with ½-inch star tip, pipe dough into 1-inch wreaths 2 inches apart on ungreased cookie sheets. Decorate wreaths with green and red glacé cherries, if desired. Bake for 10 to 12 minutes or until golden brown. Cool on wire racks.

# Green's Mint Meringue Trees

**Makes 1½ dozen cookies**

2 large egg whites
¼ teaspoon mint extract
½ cup granulated sugar

Green food coloring
½ cup "M&M's"® Semi-Sweet Chocolate Mini Baking Bits

Preheat oven to 250°F. Line baking sheet with parchment paper; set aside. In large bowl beat egg whites until foamy. Add mint extract; beat until soft peaks form. Gradually add sugar; beat until stiff peaks form. Fold in a few drops food coloring to make desired shade of green. Using pastry bag with round or star tip, pipe 3-inch tree shapes onto prepared baking sheet. Decorate with "M&M's"® Semi-Sweet Chocolate Mini Baking Bits. Bake 12 to 15 minutes or until set. Cool on baking sheet 1 minute; cool completely on wire racks. Store in tightly covered container.

# Pumpkin White Chocolate Drops

2 cups (4 sticks) butter, softened
2 cups granulated sugar
1 can (16 ounces) solid pack pumpkin
2 eggs
4 cups all-purpose flour
2 teaspoons pumpkin pie spice

1 teaspoon baking powder
½ teaspoon baking soda
1 bag (12 ounces) white chocolate chips
1 container (16 ounces) cream cheese frosting
¼ cup packed brown sugar

**Makes about 6 dozen cookies**

*1.* Preheat oven to 375°F. Grease cookie sheets.

*2.* Beat butter and granulated sugar in large bowl until light and fluffy. Add pumpkin and eggs; beat until smooth. Add flour, pumpkin pie spice, baking powder and baking soda; beat just until well blended. Stir in white chocolate chips.

*3.* Drop dough by teaspoonfuls about 2 inches apart onto prepared cookie sheets. Bake about 16 minutes or until set and bottoms are brown. Cool 1 minute on cookie sheets. Remove to wire racks; cool.

*4.* Combine frosting and brown sugar in small bowl. Spread on warm cookies.

# Star Christmas Tree Cookies

**Makes 2 to 3 dozen cookies**

**Cookies**

½ cup vegetable shortening
⅓ cup butter or margarine, softened
2 egg yolks
1 teaspoon vanilla extract
1 package DUNCAN HINES® Moist Deluxe® Classic Yellow or Devil's Food Cake Mix
1 tablespoon water

**Frosting**

1 container (16 ounces) DUNCAN HINES® Creamy Home-Style Classic Vanilla Frosting
Green food coloring
Red and green sugar crystals for garnish
Assorted colored candies and decors for garnish

Preheat oven to 375°F. For cookies, combine shortening, butter, egg yolks and vanilla extract. Blend in cake mix gradually. Add 1 teaspoonful water at a time until dough is rolling consistency. Divide dough into 4 balls. Flatten one ball with hand; roll to ⅛-inch thickness on lightly floured surface. Cut with graduated star cookie cutters. Repeat using remaining dough. Bake large cookies together on *ungreased* baking sheet. Bake 6 to 8 minutes or until edges are light golden brown. Cool cookies 1 minute. Remove from baking sheet. Repeat with smaller cookies, testing for doneness at minimum baking time.

For frosting, tint Vanilla frosting with green food coloring. Frost cookies and stack, beginning with largest cookies on bottom and ending with smallest cookies on top. Rotate cookies when stacking to alternate corners. Decorate as desired with colored sugar crystals and assorted colored candies and decors.

# Chocolate Reindeer

1 cup (2 sticks) butter, softened
1 cup granulated sugar
1 egg
1 teaspoon vanilla
2 ounces semisweet chocolate, melted

2¼ cups all-purpose flour
1 teaspoon baking powder
¼ teaspoon salt
Royal Icing (page 186)
Assorted food colors
Assorted small candies

**Makes 16 (4-inch) cookies**

*1.* Beat butter and sugar in large bowl at high speed of electric mixer until fluffy. Beat in egg and vanilla. Add melted chocolate; mix well. Add flour, baking powder and salt; mix well. Divide dough in half; wrap each half in plastic wrap and refrigerate 2 hours or until firm.

*2.* Preheat oven to 325°F. Grease 2 cookie sheets; set aside.

*3.* Roll one half of dough on well-floured surface to ¼-inch thickness. Cut out cookies with reindeer cookie cutter. Place 2 inches apart on prepared cookie sheets. Chill 10 minutes.

*4.* Bake 13 to 15 minutes or until set. Cool completely on cookie sheets. Repeat steps with remaining dough.

*5.* Prepare Royal Icing. Tint with food colors as desired. Pipe icing on reindeer and decorate with small candies. For best results, let cookies dry overnight uncovered before storing in airtight container at room temperature.

*Note:*

Royal icing is a versatile decorating icing made with egg white (or meringue powder) and powdered sugar. It dries to a smooth, hard finish and is great for adding clear, crisp details to your cookies.

# Cranberry Brown Sugar Cookies

**Makes about 5 dozen cookies**

**Prep Time:**
*30 minutes*

**Bake Time:**
*10 minutes*

**Cool Time:**
*30 minutes*

2 cups firmly packed DOMINO® Dark Brown Sugar
1 cup butter or margarine, softened
2 eggs
½ cup sour cream
3½ cups all-purpose flour
1 teaspoon baking soda

1 teaspoon salt
1 teaspoon ground cinnamon
½ teaspoon ground nutmeg
¼ teaspoon ground cloves
1 cup dried cranberries (5 ounces)
1 cup golden raisins

Heat oven to 400°F. Lightly grease cookie sheets. Beat sugar and butter in large bowl until light and fluffy. Add eggs and sour cream; beat until creamy. Stir together flour, baking soda, salt, cinnamon, nutmeg and cloves in small bowl; gradually add to sugar mixture, beating until well mixed. Stir in cranberries and raisins. Drop by rounded teaspoonfuls onto cookie sheets. Bake 8 to 10 minutes or until lightly browned. Remove from cookie sheets to cooling racks. Cool.

**Reduced Fat Version:** *Substitute 70% spread margarine for butter, ½ cup refrigerated or frozen non-fat egg product, thawed, for the 2 eggs, and non-fat sour cream for the sour cream. Proceed as directed. Per cookie: 87 calories, 2 g fat.*

**Tips:** *1 cup chopped dried cherries may be substituted for 1 cup dried cranberries. If cranberries are exceptionally large, chop before adding to cookie dough.*

# Dress 'em Up Ginger People

¾ cup (1½ sticks) butter, softened
½ cup firmly packed light brown sugar
½ cup dark molasses
1 large egg
2¼ cups all-purpose flour
2 teaspoons ground cinnamon
1½ teaspoons ground ginger
1 teaspoon baking powder
½ teaspoon salt
⅛ teaspoon ground nutmeg
⅛ teaspoon ground cloves
¼ cup powdered sugar
1 teaspoon water
1 cup "M&M's"® Chocolate Mini Baking Bits

**Makes 4 dozen cookies**

In large bowl cream butter and sugar until light and fluffy; beat in molasses and egg. In medium bowl combine flour, cinnamon, ginger, baking powder, salt, nutmeg and cloves; add to creamed mixture. Wrap and refrigerate dough 1 hour. Preheat oven to 350°F. Working with one-third of dough at a time on lightly floured surface, roll to ⅛-inch thickness. Cut out gingerbread people using 3-inch cookie cutters. Place about 2 inches apart on ungreased cookie sheets. Bake 10 minutes. Cool 2 minutes on cookie sheets; cool completely on wire racks. In small bowl combine powdered sugar and water until smooth. Using icing to attach, decorate cookies with "M&M's"® Chocolate Mini Baking Bits. Store in tightly covered container.

*Note:*

The lids of molasses jars often stick and are nearly impossible to open. Instead of wiping off the jar rims, top the jars with a small piece of plastic wrap before screwing on the lids. No more struggling to unstick lids!

# Frosted Holiday Cut-Outs

**Makes about 3½ dozen cookies**

*Note:*

Make sure the cookies are completely cool before applying the icing. If they are still even a little warm, the icing will melt.

.

1¼ cups granulated sugar
1 Butter Flavor CRISCO® Stick
   or 1 cup Butter Flavor
   CRISCO® all-vegetable
   shortening
2 eggs
¼ cup light corn syrup or
   regular pancake syrup
1 tablespoon vanilla
3 cups plus 4 tablespoons
   all-purpose flour, divided

¾ teaspoon baking powder
½ teaspoon baking soda
½ teaspoon salt

Icing
1 cup confectioners' sugar
2 tablespoons milk
   Food color (optional)
   Decorating icing

*1.* Combine sugar and 1 cup shortening in large bowl. Beat at medium speed of electric mixer until well blended. Add eggs, syrup and vanilla; beat until well blended and fluffy. Combine 3 cups flour, baking powder, baking soda and salt in medium bowl. Gradually add to shortening mixture, beating at low speed until well blended. Divide dough into 4 equal pieces; shape each into disk. Wrap with plastic wrap. Refrigerate 1 hour or until firm.

*2.* Heat oven to 375°F. Place sheets of foil on countertop for cooling cookies. Sprinkle about 1 tablespoon flour on large sheet of waxed paper. Place disk of dough on floured paper; flatten slightly with hands. Turn dough over; cover with another large sheet of waxed paper. Roll dough to ¼-inch thickness. Remove top sheet of waxed paper. Cut into desired shapes with floured cookie cutters. Place 2 inches apart on ungreased baking sheet. Repeat with remaining dough.

*3.* Bake one baking sheet at a time at 375°F for 5 to 7 minutes or until edges of cookies are lightly browned. *Do not overbake.* Cool 2 minutes on baking sheet. Remove cookies to foil to cool completely.

*4.* For icing, combine confectioners' sugar and milk; stir until smooth. Add food color, if desired. Stir until blended. Spread icing on cookies; place on foil until icing is set. Decorate as desired with decorating icing.

<u>Kitchen Hint:</u> *Before you begin frosting and decorating the cookies, place waxed paper under the wire rack to keep your counters clean and make cleanup easier.*

# Holiday Chocolate Shortbread Cookies

| | | |
|---|---|---|
| 1 cup (2 sticks) butter, softened<br>1¼ cups powdered sugar<br>1 teaspoon vanilla extract<br>½ cup HERSHEY₅S Dutch Processed Cocoa or HERSHEY₅S Cocoa | 1¾ cups all-purpose flour<br>1⅔ cups (10-ounce package) HERSHEY₅S Premier White Chips | **Makes about 4½ dozen (2-inch diameter) cookies** |

**Prep Time:** *30 minutes*

**Bake Time:** *15 minutes*

**Cool Time:** *30 minutes*

*1.* Heat oven to 300°F. Beat butter, powdered sugar and vanilla in large bowl until creamy. Add cocoa; beat until well blended. Gradually add flour, stirring until smooth.

*2.* Roll or pat dough to ¼-inch thickness on lightly floured surface or between 2 pieces of wax paper. Cut into holiday shapes using star, tree, wreath or other cookie cutters. Reroll dough scraps, cutting cookies until all dough is used. Place on ungreased cookie sheet.

*3.* Bake 15 to 20 minutes or just until firm. Immediately place white chips, flat side down, in decorative designs on warm cookies. Cool slightly; remove from cookie sheet to wire rack. Cool completely. Store in airtight container.

<u>Note:</u> *For more even baking, place similar shapes and sizes of cookies on the same cookie sheet.*

# Holiday Hideaways

Makes about 4 dozen cookies

**Cookies**

⅔ Butter Flavor CRISCO® Stick or ⅔ cup Butter Flavor CRISCO® all-vegetable shortening

¾ cup sugar

1 egg

1 tablespoon milk

1 teaspoon vanilla

1¾ cups all-purpose flour

1 teaspoon baking powder

½ teaspoon salt

½ teaspoon baking soda

48 maraschino cherries, well drained on paper towels

**Dipping Chocolate**

1 cup white or dark melting chocolate, cut in small pieces

2 tablespoons Butter Flavor CRISCO® Stick or 2 tablespoons Butter Flavor CRISCO all-vegetable shortening

Finely chopped pecans

Slivered white chocolate

*Note:*

A small amount of vegetable shortening melted with chocolate chips creates a glaze that keeps its sheen at room temperature.

Heat oven to 350°F. Place sheets of foil on countertop for cooling cookies.

For cookies, cream ⅔ cup shortening, sugar, egg, milk and vanilla in large bowl at medium speed of electric mixer until well blended. Combine flour, baking powder, salt and baking soda; beat into creamed mixture at low speed. Press dough in very thin layer around well-drained cherries. Place 2 inches apart on ungreased cookie sheet. Bake 10 minutes. *Do not overbake.* Cool on cookie sheet 1 minute. Remove cookies to foil to cool completely.

For dipping chocolate, melt chocolate of choice and 2 tablespoons shortening in small saucepan over very low heat or at 50% power in microwave; stir until smooth. Transfer chocolate to glass measuring cup. Drop one cookie at a time into chocolate. Use fork to turn, covering cookie completely in chocolate. (If chocolate becomes too firm, microwave on low to reheat.) Lift cookie out of chocolate on fork, allowing excess to drip off. Place on waxed paper-lined cookie sheet. Before chocolate sets, sprinkle chopped pecans on top of white chocolate cookies or white chocolate on top of dark chocolate cookies. Chill in refrigerator to set chocolate.

# Chocolate Raspberry Thumbprints

| | | |
|---|---|---|
| 1½ cups (3 sticks) butter, softened<br>1 cup sugar<br>1 egg<br>1 teaspoon vanilla extract<br>3 cups all-purpose flour<br>¼ cup unsweetened cocoa<br>    powder | ½ teaspoon salt<br>1 cup (6 ounces) semisweet<br>    mini chocolate chips<br>⅔ cup raspberry preserves<br>    Powdered sugar (optional) | **Makes about<br>4½ dozen cookies** |

Preheat oven to 350°F. Grease cookie sheets. Beat butter and sugar in large bowl. Beat in egg and vanilla until light and fluffy. Mix in flour, cocoa and salt until well blended. Stir in chocolate chips. Roll level tablespoonfuls of dough into balls. Place 2 inches apart on prepared cookie sheets. Make deep indentation in center of each ball with thumb.

Bake 12 to 15 minutes until just set. Cool 2 minutes on cookie sheets. Remove to wire racks; cool completely. Fill centers with raspberry preserves and sprinkle with powdered sugar, if desired. Store between layers of waxed paper in airtight containers.

# Holiday Red Raspberry Chocolate Bars

**Makes 36 bars**

2½ cups all-purpose flour
1 cup sugar
¾ cup finely chopped pecans
1 egg, beaten
1 cup (2 sticks) cold butter or margarine
1 jar (12 ounces) seedless red raspberry jam

1⅔ cups HERSHEY᾿S Milk Chocolate Chips, HERSHEY᾿S Semi-Sweet Chocolate Chips, HERSHEY᾿S Raspberry Chips, or HERSHEY᾿S MINI KISSES™ Milk Chocolates

*1.* Heat oven to 350°F. Grease 13×9×2-inch baking pan.

*2.* Stir together flour, sugar, pecans and egg in large bowl. Cut in butter with pastry blender or fork until mixture resembles coarse crumbs; set aside 1½ cups crumb mixture. Press remaining crumb mixture on bottom of prepared pan; spread jam over top. Sprinkle with chocolate chips. Crumble remaining crumb mixture evenly over top.

*3.* Bake 40 to 45 minutes or until lightly browned. Cool completely in pan on wire rack; cut into bars.

# Holiday Sugar Cookies

**Makes about 3 dozen cookies**

1 cup (2 sticks) butter, softened
¾ cup sugar
1 egg
2 cups all-purpose flour
1 teaspoon baking powder

¼ teaspoon salt
¼ teaspoon ground cinnamon
Colored sprinkles or sugars (optional)

Beat butter and sugar in large bowl at medium speed of electric mixer until creamy. Add egg; beat until fluffy.

Stir in flour, baking powder, salt and cinnamon until well blended. Form dough into ball; wrap in plastic wrap and flatten. Refrigerate about 2 hours or until firm.

Preheat oven to 350°F. Roll out dough, small portion at a time, to ¼-inch thickness on lightly floured surface with lightly floured rolling pin. (Keep remaining dough wrapped in refrigerator.)

Cut out dough with 3-inch cookie cutters. Sprinkle with colored sprinkles or sugars, if desired. Transfer to ungreased cookie sheets.

Bake 7 to 9 minutes until edges are lightly browned. Let cookies stand on cookie sheets 1 minute; transfer to wire racks to cool completely. Store in airtight container.

# Santa's Chocolate Cookies

| | | |
|---|---|---|
| 1 cup butter<br>⅔ cup semisweet chocolate<br>    chips<br>¾ cup sugar<br>1 egg<br>½ teaspoon vanilla | 2 cups all-purpose flour<br>Apricot jam, melted<br>    semisweet chocolate,<br>    chopped almonds, frosting,<br>    coconut or colored<br>    sprinkles (optional) | **Makes about 3 dozen cookies** |

Preheat oven to 350°F. Melt butter and chocolate chips in small saucepan over low heat, or microwave at HIGH 1 minute or until completely melted. Combine chocolate mixture and sugar in large bowl. Add egg and vanilla; mix well. Add flour; mix well. Refrigerate 30 minutes or until firm.

Shape dough into 1-inch balls. Place 1 inch apart on ungreased cookie sheets. If desired, flatten balls with bottom of drinking glass, or make depression in centers and fill with apricot jam. Bake 8 to 10 minutes or until set. Remove to wire racks to cool completely. Decorate as desired with melted chocolate, almonds, frosting, coconut or colored sprinkles.

# Kringle's Cutouts

**Makes 3 to 4 dozen cookies (depending on size and shape)**

1¼ cups granulated sugar
1 Butter Flavor CRISCO® Stick
   or 1 cup Butter Flavor
   CRISCO® all-vegetable
   shortening
2 eggs
¼ cup light corn syrup or
   regular pancake syrup

1 teaspoon vanilla
3 cups plus 4 tablespoons
   all-purpose flour, divided
¾ teaspoon baking powder
½ teaspoon baking soda
½ teaspoon salt
   Colored sugar, decors and
   prepared frosting (optional)

*Note:*

**With frosting, less is more. Try to use only one or two colors per cookie—too much decorating makes the cookies lose their appeal. If time is short, special holiday-themed decors are a quick way to make cookies look festive.**

*1.* Combine sugar and 1 cup shortening in large bowl. Beat at medium speed of electric mixer until well blended. Add eggs, syrup and vanilla. Beat until well blended and fluffy.

*2.* Combine 3 cups flour, baking powder, baking soda and salt. Add gradually to creamed mixture at low speed. Mix until well blended.

*3.* Divide dough into 4 quarters. Cover and refrigerate at least two hours or overnight.

*4.* Heat oven to 375°F. Place sheets of foil on countertop for cooling cookies.

*5.* Spread 1 tablespoon flour on large sheet of waxed paper. Place one quarter of dough on floured paper. Flatten slightly with hands. Turn dough over. Cover with another large sheet of waxed paper. Roll dough to ¼-inch thickness. Remove top layer of waxed paper. Cut out with seasonal cookie cutters. Place cutouts 2 inches apart on ungreased baking sheets. Roll and cut out remaining dough. Sprinkle with colored sugar and decors or leave plain to frost when cool.

*6.* Bake at 375°F for 5 to 9 minutes, depending on size of cookies. (Bake small, thin cookies about 5 minutes; larger cookies about 9 minutes.) *Do not overbake.* Cool 2 minutes on baking sheet. Remove cookies to foil to cool completely.

# Especially for
# Kids

# Chocolate Snowball Cookies

1 cup (2 sticks) butter or margarine, softened
¾ cup packed light brown sugar
1 egg
1 teaspoon vanilla extract
2 cups all-purpose flour
½ cup HERSHEY'S Dutch Processed Cocoa or HERSHEY'S Cocoa

1 teaspoon baking powder
¼ teaspoon baking soda
3 tablespoons milk
¾ cup finely chopped macadamia nuts or almonds
¾ cup SKOR® English Toffee Bits
Powdered sugar

*Note:*

The term "Dutch process" on a cocoa package means it's been treated with an alkaline solution. This cocoa has a darker color and more mellow taste, but can be used interchangeably with regular powdered cocoa unless the recipe directs otherwise.

*1.* Beat butter, brown sugar, egg and vanilla in large bowl until blended. Stir together flour, cocoa, baking powder and baking soda; add with milk to butter mixture until well blended. Stir in nuts and toffee.

*2.* Refrigerate until firm enough to handle, at least 2 hours. Heat oven to 350°F. Shape dough into 1-inch balls; place 2 inches apart on ungreased cookie sheet.

*3.* Bake 8 to 10 minutes or until set. Remove from cookie sheet to wire rack. Cool completely; roll in powdered sugar.

# Cookie Pizza

1 package (20 ounces)
    refrigerated sugar or
    peanut butter cookie dough
All-purpose flour (optional)
1 cup (6 ounces) semisweet
    chocolate chips
1 tablespoon plus 2 teaspoons
    shortening, divided

¼ cup white chocolate chips
Gummy fruit, chocolate-
    covered peanuts, assorted
    roasted nuts, raisins, jelly
    beans and other assorted
    candies for toppings

**Makes 10 to 12 pizza slices**

*1.* Preheat oven to 350°F. Generously grease 12-inch pizza pan. Remove dough from wrapper according to package directions.

*2.* Sprinkle dough with flour to minimize sticking, if necessary. Press dough into bottom of prepared pan, leaving about ¾ inch between edge of dough and pan.

*3.* Bake 14 to 23 minutes or until golden brown and set in center. Cool completely in pan on wire rack, running spatula between cookie and pan after 10 to 15 minutes to loosen.

*4.* Melt semisweet chocolate chips and 1 tablespoon shortening in microwavable bowl at HIGH 1 minute; stir. Repeat process at 10- to 20-second intervals until smooth.

*5.* Melt white chocolate chips and remaining 2 teaspoons shortening in another microwavable bowl at MEDIUM-HIGH (70% power) 1 minute; stir. Repeat process at 10- to 20-second intervals until smooth.

*6.* Spread melted semisweet chocolate mixture over crust to within 1 inch of edge. Decorate with desired toppings.

*7.* Drizzle melted white chocolate over toppings to resemble melted mozzarella cheese. Cut and serve.

# Oatmeal Apple Cookies

**Makes about
2½ dozen cookies**

1¼ cups firmly packed brown
    sugar
¾ Butter Flavor CRISCO® Stick
    or ¾ cup Butter Flavor
    CRISCO® all-vegetable
    shortening plus additional
    for greasing
¼ cup milk
1 egg
1½ teaspoons vanilla
1 cup all-purpose flour

1¼ teaspoons ground cinnamon
½ teaspoon salt
¼ teaspoon baking soda
¼ teaspoon ground nutmeg
3 cups quick oats (not instant
    or old-fashioned), uncooked
1 cup diced peeled apples
¾ cup raisins (optional)
¾ cup coarsely chopped
    walnuts (optional)

*1.* Heat oven to 375°F. Grease baking sheet. Place sheets of foil on countertop for cooling cookies.

*2.* Combine brown sugar, ¾ cup shortening, milk, egg and vanilla in large bowl. Beat at medium speed of electric mixer until well blended and creamy.

*3.* Combine flour, cinnamon, salt, baking soda and nutmeg. Add gradually to creamed mixture at low speed. Mix just until blended. Stir in, one at a time, oats, apples, raisins and nuts with spoon. Drop by rounded tablespoonfuls 2 inches apart onto prepared baking sheet.

*4.* Bake at 375°F for 13 minutes or until set. *Do not overbake.* Cool 2 minutes on baking sheet. Remove cookies to foil to cool completely.

# Crispy's Irresistible Peanut Butter Marbles

1 package (18 ounces) refrigerated peanut butter cookie dough

2 cups "M&M's"® Milk Chocolate Mini Baking Bits, divided

1 cup crisp rice cereal, divided (optional)

1 package (18 ounces) refrigerated sugar cookie dough

¼ cup unsweetened cocoa powder

In large bowl combine peanut butter dough, 1 cup "M&M's"® Milk Chocolate Mini Baking Bits and ½ cup cereal, if desired. Remove dough to small bowl; set aside. In large bowl combine sugar dough and cocoa powder until well blended. Stir in remaining 1 cup "M&M's"® Milk Chocolate Mini Baking Bits and remaining ½ cup cereal, if desired. Remove half the dough to small bowl; set aside. Combine half the peanut butter dough with half the chocolate dough by folding together just enough to marble. Shape marbled dough into 8×2-inch log. Wrap log in plastic wrap. Repeat with remaining doughs. Refrigerate logs 2 hours. To bake, preheat oven to 350°F. Cut dough into ¼-inch-thick slices. Place about 2 inches apart on ungreased cookie sheets. Bake 12 to 14 minutes. Cool 1 minute on cookie sheets; cool completely on wire racks. Store in tightly covered container.

# Peanut Butter and Jelly Sandwich Cookies

**Makes 11 sandwich cookies**

1 package (18 ounces) refrigerated sugar cookie dough
1 tablespoon unsweetened cocoa powder

All-purpose flour (optional)
¾ cup creamy peanut butter
½ cup grape jam or jelly

*1.* Remove dough from wrapper according to package directions. Reserve ¼ section of dough; cover and refrigerate remaining ¾ section of dough. Combine reserved dough and cocoa in small bowl; cover and refrigerate.

*2.* Shape remaining ¾ section of dough into 5½-inch log. Sprinkle with flour to minimize sticking, if necessary. Remove chocolate dough from refrigerator; roll on sheet of waxed paper into 9½×6½-inch rectangle. Place dough log in center of rectangle.

*3.* Bring waxed paper edges and chocolate dough up and together over log. Press gently on top and sides of dough so entire log is wrapped in chocolate dough. Flatten log slightly to form square. Wrap in waxed paper. Freeze 10 minutes.

*4.* Preheat oven to 350°F. Remove waxed paper. Cut dough into ¼-inch slices. Place slices 2 inches apart on ungreased cookie sheets. Reshape dough edges into square, if necessary. Press dough slightly to form indentation so dough resembles slice of bread.

*5.* Bake 8 to 11 minutes or until lightly browned. Remove from oven and straighten cookie edges with spatula. Cool 2 minutes on cookie sheets. Remove to wire racks; cool completely.

**6.** To make sandwich, spread about 1 tablespoon peanut butter on bottom of 1 cookie. Spread about ½ tablespoon jam over peanut butter; top with second cookie, pressing gently. Repeat with remaining cookies.

**Tip:** *Cut each sandwich diagonally in half for a smaller cookie and fun look.*

# Marshmallow Krispie Bars

1 (21-ounce) package DUNCAN HINES® Family-Style Chewy Fudge Brownie Mix
1 package (10½ ounces) miniature marshmallows
1½ cups semisweet chocolate chips

1 cup creamy peanut butter
1 tablespoon butter or margarine
1½ cups crisp rice cereal

Makes about 2 dozen bars

**1.** Preheat oven to 350°F. Grease bottom only of 13×9-inch pan.

**2.** Prepare and bake brownies following package directions for cake-like recipe. Remove from oven. Sprinkle marshmallows on hot brownies. Return to oven. Bake for 3 minutes longer.

**3.** Place chocolate chips, peanut butter and butter in medium saucepan. Cook over low heat, stirring constantly, until chips are melted. Add rice cereal; mix well. Spread mixture over marshmallow layer. Refrigerate until chilled. Cut into bars.

**Tip:** *For a special presentation, cut bars into diamond shapes.*

*Note:*

Marshmallows were once created from the roots of the marshmallow plant, a pink-flowered European perennial herb. Now they are produced commercially from corn syrup, gelatin, additives and flavorings.

# Moons and Stars

**Makes about 4 dozen cookies**

1 cup (2 sticks) butter, softened
1 cup sugar
1 egg
2 teaspoons lemon peel
½ teaspoon almond extract

3 cups all-purpose flour
½ cup ground almonds
Assorted colored icings, hard candies and colored sprinkles

*Note:*

Ground almonds can be purchased in the baking section of the supermarket. Or, if you have whole or chopped almonds on hand, grind the nuts quickly in the food processor.

**1.** Preheat oven to 350°F. Grease cookie sheets.

**2.** Beat butter, sugar, egg, lemon peel and almond extract in large bowl at medium speed of electric mixer until light and fluffy.

**3.** Combine flour and almonds in medium bowl. Add flour mixture to butter mixture; stir just until combined.

**4.** Roll dough on lightly floured surface to ⅛- to ¼-inch thickness. Cut out cookies using moon and star cookie cutters. Place cookies 2 inches apart on prepared cookie sheets.

**5.** Bake 7 to 9 minutes or until set but not browned. Cool on cookie sheets 2 minutes. Remove to wire racks; cool completely.

**6.** Decorate cookies with icings, candies and sprinkles as desired.

# Frosty's Colorful Cookies

1¼ cups firmly packed light
   brown sugar
¾ Butter Flavor CRISCO® Stick
   or ¾ cup Butter Flavor
   CRISCO® all-vegetable
   shortening
2 tablespoons milk

1 tablespoon vanilla
1 egg
1¾ cups all-purpose flour
1 teaspoon salt
¾ teaspoon baking soda
2 cups candy-coated chocolate
   pieces

Makes about 3 dozen
cookies

*1.* Heat oven to 375°F. Place sheets of foil on countertop for cooling cookies.

*2.* Place brown sugar, ¾ cup shortening, milk and vanilla in large bowl. Beat at medium speed of electric mixer until well blended. Add egg; beat well.

*3.* Combine flour, salt and baking soda. Add to shortening mixture; beat at low speed just until blended. Stir in candy-coated chocolate pieces.

*4.* Drop dough by rounded measuring tablespoonfuls 3 inches apart onto ungreased baking sheets.

*5.* Bake one baking sheet at a time at 375°F for 8 to 10 minutes for chewy cookies, or 11 to 13 minutes for crisp cookies. *Do not overbake.* Cool 2 minutes on baking sheet. Remove cookies to foil to cool completely.

# Banana Split Cups

**Makes 3 dozen cookies**

1 package (18 ounces) refrigerated chocolate chip cookie dough
⅔ cup "M&M's"® Chocolate Mini Baking Bits, divided
1 ripe medium banana, cut into 18 slices and halved

¾ cup chocolate syrup, divided
2¼ cups any flavor ice cream, softened
Aerosol whipped topping
¼ cup chopped maraschino cherries

Lightly grease 36 (1¾-inch) mini muffin cups. Cut dough into 36 equal pieces; roll into balls. Place 1 ball in bottom of each muffin cup. Press dough onto bottoms and up sides of muffin cups; chill 15 minutes. Press ⅓ cup "M&M's"® Chocolate Mini Baking Bits into bottoms and sides of dough cups. Preheat oven to 350°F. Bake cookies 8 to 9 minutes. Cookies will be puffy. Remove from oven; gently press down center of each cookie. Return to oven 1 minute. Cool cookies in muffin cups 5 minutes. Remove to wire racks; cool completely. Place 1 banana half slice in each cookie cup; top with ½ teaspoon chocolate syrup. Place about ½ teaspoon "M&M's"® Chocolate Mini Baking Bits in each cookie cup; top with 1 tablespoon ice cream. Top each cookie cup with ½ teaspoon chocolate syrup, whipped topping, remaining "M&M's"® Chocolate Mini Baking Bits and 1 maraschino cherry piece. Store covered in freezer.

# Peanut Butter Secrets

Cookies
 1¼ cups firmly packed light
   brown sugar
 ¾ cup JIF® Creamy Peanut
   Butter
 ½ CRISCO® Stick or ½ cup
   CRISCO® all-vegetable
   shortening
 3 tablespoons milk
 1 tablespoon vanilla
 1 egg
 1¾ cups all-purpose flour
 ¾ teaspoon salt
 ¾ teaspoon baking soda

30 to 36 chocolate covered
   miniature peanut butter
   cups, unwrapped

Glaze
 1 cup semisweet chocolate
   chips
 2 tablespoons JIF® Creamy
   Peanut Butter
 1 teaspoon Butter Flavor
   CRISCO® Stick or
   1 teaspoon Butter Flavor
   CRISCO® all-vegetable
   shortening

**Makes about 3 dozen cookies**

*Note:*

With chocolate peanut

butter cups wrapped

in peanut butter

dough and dipped

in a chocolate-peanut

butter glaze, these

treats should please

even the pickiest of

peanut butter fanatics.

*1.* Heat oven to 375°F. Place sheets of foil on countertop for cooling cookies.

*2.* Combine brown sugar, peanut butter, ½ cup shortening, milk and vanilla in large bowl. Beat at medium speed of electric mixer until well blended. Add egg. Beat just until blended. Combine flour, salt and baking soda. Add to shortening mixture at low speed. Mix just until blended.

*3.* Form rounded tablespoonfuls around each peanut butter cup. Enclose entirely. Place 2 inches apart onto ungreased baking sheet. Flatten slightly in crisscross pattern with tines of fork.

*4.* Bake one sheet at a time at 375°F for 7 to 8 minutes, or until set and just beginning to brown. *Do not overbake.* Cool 2 minutes on baking sheet. Remove cookies to foil to cool completely.

*5.* For glaze, combine chips, peanut butter and 1 teaspoon shortening in microwave-safe cup. Microwave at 50% (MEDIUM). Stir after 1 minute. Repeat until smooth (or melt on rangetop in small saucepan on very low heat). Dip cookie tops in glaze.

# Triple Layer Chocolate Bars

**Makes 24 to 36 bars**

1½ cups graham cracker crumbs
½ cup HERSHEY᛬S Cocoa, divided
¼ cup sugar
½ cup (1 stick) butter or margarine, melted
1 can (14 ounces) sweetened condensed milk (not evaporated milk)

¼ cup all-purpose flour
1 egg
1 teaspoon vanilla extract
½ teaspoon baking powder
¾ cup chopped nuts
2 cups (12-ounce package) HERSHEY᛬S Semi-Sweet Chocolate Chips

*1.* Heat oven to 350°F. Stir graham cracker crumbs, ¼ cup cocoa and sugar in medium bowl; stir in butter, blending well. Press mixture firmly onto bottom of ungreased 13×9×2-inch baking pan.

*2.* Beat sweetened condensed milk, flour, egg, vanilla, baking powder and remaining ¼ cup cocoa in small bowl. Stir in nuts. Spread evenly over prepared crust. Sprinkle chocolate chips over top.

*3.* Bake 25 minutes or until set. Cool completely in pan on wire rack. Cut into bars. Store tightly covered at room temperature.

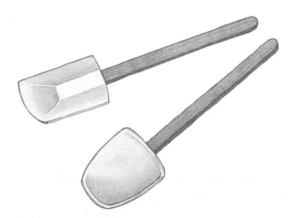

# "Everything but the Kitchen Sink" Bar Cookies

1 package (18 ounces)
   refrigerated chocolate chip
   cookie dough
1 jar (7 ounces) marshmallow
   creme

½ cup creamy peanut butter
1½ cups toasted corn cereal
½ cup miniature candy-coated
   chocolate pieces

**Makes 3 dozen bars**

*1.* Preheat oven to 350°F. Grease 13×9-inch baking pan. Remove dough from wrapper according to package directions.

*2.* Press dough into prepared baking pan. Bake 13 minutes.

*3.* Remove baking pan from oven. Drop teaspoonfuls of marshmallow creme and peanut butter over hot cookie base.

*4.* Bake 1 minute. Carefully spread marshmallow creme and peanut butter over cookie base.

*5.* Sprinkle cereal and chocolate pieces over melted marshmallow and peanut butter mixture.

*6.* Bake 7 minutes. Cool completely on wire rack. Cut into 2-inch bars.

*Note:*

Softening peanut butter makes it easier to use in recipes. Place a jar of peanut butter, without the lid, in the microwave. Heat at HIGH 30 to 40 seconds, stirring halfway through heating time.

# Kids' Favorite Jumbo Chippers

| Makes 3 dozen cookies | |
|---|---|
| 1 cup butter, softened | 1 teaspoon baking soda |
| ¾ cup granulated sugar | ¾ teaspoon salt |
| ¾ cup packed brown sugar | 1¼ cups "M&M's"® Milk Chocolate Candies |
| 2 eggs | 1 cup peanut butter flavored chips |
| 1 teaspoon vanilla | |
| 2¼ cups all-purpose flour | |

Preheat oven to 375°F. Beat butter, granulated sugar and brown sugar in large bowl until light and fluffy. Beat in eggs and vanilla. Add flour, baking soda and salt. Beat until well blended. Stir in "M&M's"® Chocolate Candies and peanut butter chips. Drop by rounded tablespoonfuls 3 inches apart onto ungreased cookie sheets. Bake 10 to 12 minutes or until edges are golden brown. Let cookies stand on cookie sheets 2 minutes. Remove cookies to wire racks; cool completely.

**Note:** *For a change of pace, substitute "M&M's"® Crispy Chocolate Candies, "M&M's"® Peanut Chocolate Candies, "M&M's"® Almond Chocolate Candies, or "M&M's"® Peanut Butter Chocolate Candies for the chocolate candies.*

# Lollipop Clowns

1 package (18 ounces)
   refrigerated red, green or
   blue cookie dough*
All-purpose flour (optional)
Assorted colored icings and
   hard candies

Supplies
18 (4-inch) lollipop sticks

*If colored dough is unavailable, sugar cookie dough can be tinted with paste food coloring.

Makes about
18 cookies

*1.* Preheat oven to 350°F.

*2.* Remove dough from wrapper according to package directions. Divide dough into 2 equal sections. Reserve 1 section; cover and refrigerate remaining section.

*3.* Roll reserved dough on lightly floured surface to ⅛-inch thickness. Sprinkle with flour to minimize sticking, if necessary.

*4.* Cut out cookies using 3½-inch round cookie cutter. Place lollipop sticks on cookies so that tips of sticks are imbedded in cookies. Carefully turn cookies so sticks are in back; place on ungreased cookie sheets.

*5.* Bake 8 to 10 minutes or until firm but not brown. Cool on cookie sheets 2 minutes. Remove to wire racks; cool completely.

*6.* Decorate cookies with icings to create clown faces and hair.

*Note:*

These happy clown faces make the perfect topping for a birthday cake. Stick a Lollipop Clown, one for each child, in the cake for a wonderful circus theme party.

# Anna's Icing Oatmeal Sandwich Cookies

**Makes about
16 sandwich cookies**

### Note:

For mess-free
measuring when
baking, place the
measuring cup on top
of a flexible paper plate
when spooning out dry
ingredients. Any spills
fall onto the plate,
which easily bends to
dump the ingredients
back into the container.

**Cookies**
¾ Butter Flavor CRISCO® Stick
   or ¾ cup Butter Flavor
   CRISCO® all-vegetable
   shortening plus additional
   for greasing
1¼ cups firmly packed light
   brown sugar
1 egg
⅓ cup milk
1½ teaspoons vanilla
3 cups quick oats, uncooked

1 cup all-purpose flour
½ teaspoon baking soda
½ teaspoon salt

**Frosting**
2 cups confectioners' sugar
¼ Butter Flavor CRISCO® Stick
   or ¼ cup Butter Flavor
   CRISCO® all-vegetable
   shortening
½ teaspoon vanilla
Milk

*1.* Heat oven to 350°F. Grease baking sheets with shortening. Place sheets of foil on countertop for cooling cookies.

*2.* For cookies, combine ¾ cup shortening, brown sugar, egg, milk and vanilla in large bowl. Beat at medium speed of electric mixer until well blended.

*3.* Combine oats, flour, baking soda and salt. Mix into creamed mixture at low speed just until blended.

*4.* Drop rounded measuring tablespoonfuls of dough 2 inches apart onto prepared baking sheets.

*5.* Bake one sheet at a time at 375°F for 10 to 12 minutes, or until lightly browned. *Do not overbake.* Cool 2 minutes on baking sheet. Remove cookies to foil to cool completely.

*6.* For frosting, combine confectioners' sugar, ¼ cup shortening and vanilla in medium bowl. Beat at low speed, adding enough milk for good spreading consistency. Spread on bottoms of half the cookies. Top with remaining cookies.

# Smushy Cookies

1 package (20 ounces)
   refrigerated cookie dough,
   any flavor
All-purpose flour (optional)

Fillings

Peanut butter, multi-colored
   miniature marshmallows,
   assorted colored sprinkles,
   chocolate-covered raisins
   and caramel candy squares

**Makes about 8 to
10 sandwich cookies**

*1.* Preheat oven to 350°F. Grease cookie sheets.

*2.* Remove dough from wrapper according to package directions. Cut into 4 equal sections. Reserve 1 section; refrigerate remaining 3 sections.

*3.* Roll reserved dough to ¼-inch thickness. Sprinkle with flour to minimize sticking, if necessary. Cut out cookies using 2½-inch round cookie cutter. Transfer to prepared cookie sheets. Repeat with remaining dough, working with 1 section at a time.

*4.* Bake 8 to 11 minutes or until edges are light golden brown. Remove to wire racks; cool completely.

*5.* To make sandwich, spread about 1½ tablespoons peanut butter on underside of 1 cookie to within ¼ inch of edge. Sprinkle with miniature marshmallows and candy pieces. Top with second cookie, pressing gently. Repeat with remaining cookies and fillings.

*6.* Just before serving, place sandwiches on paper towels. Microwave at HIGH 15 to 25 seconds or until fillings become soft.

**Tip:** *Invite the neighbor kids over on a rainy day to make these fun Smushy Cookies. Be sure to have lots of filling choices available so each child can create their own unique cookies.*

# Rocky Road Bars

**Makes 2½ dozen bars**

2 cups (12-ounce package)
    NESTLÉ® TOLL HOUSE®
    Semi-Sweet Chocolate
    Morsels, *divided*
1½ cups all-purpose flour
1½ teaspoons baking powder
1 cup granulated sugar

6 tablespoons (¾ stick) butter
    or margarine, softened
1½ teaspoons vanilla extract
2 large eggs
2 cups miniature marshmallows
1½ cups coarsely chopped
    walnuts

**PREHEAT** oven to 375°F. Grease 13×9-inch baking pan.

**MICROWAVE** *1 cup* morsels in medium, microwave-safe bowl on HIGH (100%) power for 1 minute; stir. Microwave at additional 10- to 20-second intervals; stir until smooth. Cool to room temperature. Combine flour and baking powder in small bowl.

**BEAT** sugar, butter and vanilla in large mixer bowl until crumbly. Beat in eggs. Add melted chocolate; beat until smooth. Gradually beat in flour mixture. Spread batter into prepared baking pan.

**BAKE** for 16 to 20 minutes or until wooden pick inserted in center comes out slightly sticky.

**REMOVE** from oven; sprinkle immediately with marshmallows, nuts and *remaining* morsels. Return to oven for 2 minutes or just until marshmallows begin to melt. Cool in pan on wire rack for 20 to 30 minutes. Cut into bars with wet knife. Serve warm.

# Cookie Cups

1 package (20 ounces)
    refrigerated sugar cookie
    dough
All-purpose flour (optional)

Prepared pudding, nondairy
    whipped topping,
    maraschino cherries, jelly
    beans, assorted sprinkles
    and small candies

**Makes 12 cookies**

*1.* Grease 12 (2¾-inch) muffin cups.

*2.* Remove dough from wrapper according to package directions. Sprinkle dough with flour to minimize sticking, if necessary.

*3.* Cut dough into 12 equal pieces; roll into balls. Place 1 ball in bottom of each muffin cup. Press dough halfway up sides of muffin cups, making indentation in centers.

*4.* Freeze muffin cups 15 minutes. Preheat oven to 350°F.

*5.* Bake 15 to 17 minutes or until golden brown. Cookies will be puffy. Remove from oven; gently press indentations with teaspoon.

*6.* Return to oven 1 to 2 minutes. Cool cookies in muffin cups 5 minutes. Remove to wire rack; cool completely.

*7.* Fill each cookie cup with desired fillings. Decorate as desired.

**Giant Cookie Cups Variation:** *Grease 10 (3¾-inch) muffin cups. Cut dough into 10 pieces; roll into balls. Complete recipe according to regular Cookie Cups directions. Makes 10 giant cookie cups.*

*Note:*

Add some pizzazz to your cookie cups by filling them with a mixture of prepared fruit-flavored gelatin combined with prepared pudding or nondairy whipped topping. (Purchase snack-size gelatins and puddings for convenience.)

# Chocolate Peanut Butter Cookies

| Makes about 3½ dozen cookies | 1 package DUNCAN HINES® Moist Deluxe® Devil's Food Cake Mix<br>¾ cup crunchy peanut butter | 2 eggs<br>2 tablespoons milk<br>1 cup candy-coated peanut butter pieces |
| --- | --- | --- |

**1.** Preheat oven to 350°F. Grease baking sheets.

**2.** Combine cake mix, peanut butter, eggs and milk in large mixing bowl. Beat at low speed with electric mixer until blended. Stir in peanut butter pieces.

**3.** Drop dough by slightly rounded tablespoonfuls onto prepared baking sheets. Bake 7 to 9 minutes or until lightly browned. Cool 2 minutes on baking sheets. Remove to cooling racks.

**Tip:** *You can use 1 cup peanut butter chips in place of candy-coated peanut butter pieces.*

# Dino-Mite Dinosaurs

| Makes 2 dozen cookies | 1 cup (2 sticks) butter, softened<br>1¼ cups granulated sugar<br>1 large egg<br>2 squares (1 ounce each) semi-sweet chocolate, melted<br>½ teaspoon vanilla extract<br>2⅓ cups all-purpose flour | 1 teaspoon baking powder<br>¼ teaspoon salt<br>1 cup white frosting<br>Assorted food colorings<br>1 cup "M&M's"® Chocolate Mini Baking Bits |
| --- | --- | --- |

In large bowl cream butter and sugar until light and fluffy; beat in egg, chocolate and vanilla. In medium bowl combine flour, baking powder and salt; add to creamed mixture. Wrap and refrigerate dough 2 to 3 hours. Preheat oven to 350°F. Working with half the dough at a time on lightly floured surface, roll to ¼-inch thickness. Cut into dinosaur shapes using 4-inch cookie cutters. Place about 2 inches apart on ungreased cookie sheets. Bake 10 to 12 minutes. Cool 2 minutes on cookie sheets; cool completely on wire racks. Tint frosting desired colors. Frost cookies and decorate with "M&M's"® Chocolate Mini Baking Bits. Store in tightly covered container.

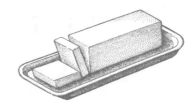

# Peanut Butter Cremes

¾ Butter Flavor CRISCO® Stick or ¾ cup Butter Flavor CRISCO® all-vegetable shortening
1 cup JIF® Creamy Peanut Butter
1 cup packed dark brown sugar

1 cup marshmallow creme
1 egg
2 teaspoons vanilla
1¾ cups all-purpose flour
1 teaspoon baking powder
1 teaspoon salt

Makes about 4 dozen cookies

*1.* Heat oven to 350°F. Place sheets of foil on countertop for cooling cookies.

*2.* Combine ¾ cup shortening, peanut butter, brown sugar and marshmallow creme in large bowl. Beat at medium speed of electric mixer until well blended. Beat in egg and vanilla.

*3.* Combine flour, baking powder and salt. Mix into shortening mixture at low speed until just blended.

*4.* Drop by rounded tablespoonfuls 2 inches apart onto ungreased baking sheets.

*5.* Bake one baking sheet at a time at 350°F for 11 minutes or until lightly browned. *Do not overbake.* Cool 2 minutes on baking sheets. Remove cookies to foil to cool completely.

# Chocolate Cookie Pops

**Makes about 1 dozen cookie pops**

### Note:
Wooden popsicle sticks can be purchased at some supermarkets and at craft and hobby stores.

2 cups all-purpose flour
½ cup unsweetened cocoa powder
½ teaspoon baking powder
½ teaspoon salt
1 cup (2 sticks) butter, softened
1 cup granulated sugar
½ cup packed light brown sugar
1 egg

1 teaspoon vanilla
   Additional granulated sugar
1 cup semisweet chocolate chips
2 teaspoons shortening, divided
1 cup white chocolate chips or chopped white chocolate candy bar

**1.** Preheat oven to 350°F. Combine flour, cocoa, baking powder and salt in small bowl; set aside. Beat butter, 1 cup granulated sugar and brown sugar in large bowl of electric mixer until light and fluffy. Beat in egg and vanilla until well blended. Gradually beat in flour mixture on low speed.

**2.** Drop dough by level ¼ cupfuls onto ungreased cookie sheets or parchment-lined cookie sheets, spacing 3 inches apart. Flatten dough until 2 inches in diameter with bottom of glass that has been dipped in additional granulated sugar. Insert popsicle stick 1½ inches into each cookie.

**3.** Bake 14 to 16 minutes or until cookies are set. Cool cookies 2 minutes on cookie sheets; transfer cookies to wire rack or slide parchment and cookies onto countertop. Cool completely.

**4.** For icing, place semisweet chocolate chips and 1 teaspoon shortening in small resealable plastic food storage bag; seal bag. Microwave at HIGH 30 seconds. Turn bag over; microwave 30 seconds to 1 minute or until chips are melted. Knead bag until chocolate is smooth. Repeat with white chocolate chips and remaining 1 teaspoon shortening.

**5.** Cut off small corner of each bag; pipe chocolate over cookies. Let stand until chocolate is set, about 30 minutes.

# Quick Peanut Butter Chocolate Chip Cookies

| | | |
|---|---|---|
| 1 package DUNCAN HINES® Moist Deluxe® Classic Yellow Cake Mix<br>½ cup creamy peanut butter | ½ cup butter or margarine, softened<br>2 eggs<br>1 cup milk chocolate chips | **Makes about 4 dozen cookies** |

*1.* Preheat oven to 350°F. Grease baking sheets.

*2.* Combine cake mix, peanut butter, butter and eggs in large bowl. Mix at low speed with electric mixer until blended. Stir in chocolate chips.

*3.* Drop by rounded teaspoonfuls onto prepared baking sheets. Bake at 350°F for 9 to 11 minutes or until lightly browned. Cool 2 minutes on baking sheets. Remove to cooling racks.

**Tip:** *Crunchy peanut butter can be substituted for regular peanut butter.*

## *Decorations Make all the Difference*

Kids love cookies with decorations—and they also love decorating cookies! The next time you host an impromptu (or planned) cookie decorating party, be prepared with plenty of options:

• Colorful small candies, available in bulk at supermarkets and party supply stores

• Tubes of decorator frosting in a variety of colors

• Powdered sugar glaze, made by blending 1 cup sifted powdered sugar with 5 teaspoons milk (add additional sugar to thicken or milk to thin glaze if necessary)

• Melted chocolate (white, milk or semisweet), which can be drizzled over cookies with a spoon or fork

• Tinted coconut, made by diluting a few drops of liquid food coloring with ½ teaspoon milk or water, then adding 1 cup flaked coconut and tossing with a fork until the coconut is evenly tinted

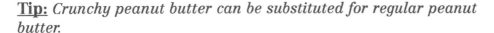

# Oatmeal Carmelita Bars

**Makes 3 dozen squares**

¾ Butter Flavor CRISCO® Stick or ¾ cup Butter Flavor CRISCO® all-vegetable shortening, melted, plus additional for greasing
1½ cups quick oats (not instant or old-fashioned), uncooked
¾ cup firmly packed brown sugar
½ cup plus 3 tablespoons all-purpose flour, divided
½ cup whole wheat flour
½ teaspoon baking soda
¼ teaspoon cinnamon
1⅓ cups milk chocolate chips
½ cup chopped walnuts
1 jar (12.5 ounces) or ¾ cup SMUCKER'S® Caramel Ice Cream Topping

*1.* Heat oven to 350°F. Grease bottom and sides of 9×9×2-inch baking pan with shortening. Place wire rack on countertop to cool bars.

*2.* Combine ¾ cup shortening, oats, sugar, ½ cup all-purpose flour, whole wheat flour, baking soda and cinnamon in large bowl. Mix at low speed of electric mixer until crumbs form. Reserve ½ cup for topping. Press remaining crumbs into prepared pan.

*3.* Bake at 350°F for 10 minutes. Sprinkle chocolate chips and nuts over crust.

*4.* Combine caramel topping and remaining 3 tablespoons all-purpose flour. Stir until well blended. Drizzle over chocolate chips and nuts. Sprinkle reserved ½ cup crumbs over caramel topping.

*5.* Return to oven. Bake for 20 to 25 minutes or until golden brown. *Do not overbake.* Run spatula around edge of pan before cooling. Cool completely in pan on wire rack. Cut into 1½×1½-inch squares.

# Crayon Cookies

1 cup (2 sticks) butter, softened
2 teaspoons vanilla
½ cup powdered sugar
2¼ cups all-purpose flour

¼ teaspoon salt
Assorted paste food colors
1½ cups chocolate chips
1½ teaspoons shortening

**Makes 20 cookies**

*1.* Preheat oven to 350°F. Grease cookie sheets.

*2.* Beat butter and vanilla in large bowl at high speed of electric mixer until fluffy. Add powdered sugar; beat at medium speed until blended. Combine flour and salt in small bowl. Gradually add to butter mixture.

*3.* Divide dough into 10 equal sections. Reserve 1 section; cover and refrigerate remaining 9 sections. Combine reserved section and desired food color in small bowl; blend well.

*4.* Cut dough in half. Roll each half into 5-inch log. Pinch one end to resemble crayon tip. Place cookies 2 inches apart on prepared cookie sheets. Repeat with remaining 9 sections of dough and desired food colors.

*5.* Bake 15 to 18 minutes or until edges are lightly browned. Cool completely on cookie sheets.

*6.* Combine chocolate chips and shortening in small microwavable bowl. Microwave at HIGH (100%) 1 to 1½ minutes, stirring after 1 minute, or until smooth. Decorate cookies with chocolate mixture to look like crayons.

*Note:*

Paste food colors come in a wider variety of colors than liquid. When they are stored tightly sealed in a cool, dry place, paste food colors will last indefinitely.

# Sugar Doodles

**Makes about 2½ dozen cookies**

*Note:*

For baking purposes, use a mild, flavorless oil such as vegetable, canola or safflower oil.

1 package (22.3 ounces) golden sugar cookie mix
2 eggs
⅓ cup oil
1 teaspoon water

½ cup (of each) HERSHEY'S Butterscotch Chips, HERSHEY'S Semi-Sweet Chocolate Chips and REESE'S® Peanut Butter Chips
5 tablespoons colored sugar
1 tablespoon granulated sugar

*1.* Heat oven to 375°F.

*2.* Empty cookie mix into large bowl. Break up any lumps. Add eggs, oil and water to mix; stir with spoon or fork until well blended. Stir in butterscotch chips, chocolate chips and peanut butter chips. Cover; refrigerate dough about 1 hour.

*3.* Shape dough into 1½-inch balls. Place colored sugar and granulated sugar in large reclosable plastic bag; shake well to blend. Place 2 balls into bag; reclose bag and shake well. Place balls 2 inches apart on ungreased cookie sheet. Repeat until all balls are coated with sugar mixture.

*4.* Bake 8 to 10 minutes or until set. Cool slightly; remove from cookie sheet to wire rack. Cool completely.

**Cocoa Sugar Doodles:** *Substitute 5 tablespoons granulated sugar and ¾ teaspoon HERSHEY'S Cocoa or HERSHEY'S Dutch Processed Cocoa for amounts of colored and granulated sugars above.*

**Rainbow Sugar Doodles:** *Substitute about 1¾ teaspoons each of blue, pink and yellow colored sugar for the 5 tablespoons colored sugar called for above.*

# Peanut Butter Bears

2 cups quick-cooking rolled oats
2 cups all-purpose flour
1 tablespoon baking powder
1 cup granulated sugar
¾ cup (1½ sticks) butter, softened

½ cup creamy peanut butter
½ cup packed brown sugar
½ cup cholesterol-free egg substitute
1 teaspoon vanilla
3 tablespoons miniature chocolate chips

**Makes 4 dozen cookies**

*1.* Stir together rolled oats, flour and baking powder; set aside.

*2.* Beat granulated sugar, butter, peanut butter and brown sugar in large bowl with mixer at medium-high speed until creamy. Add egg substitute and vanilla; beat until light and fluffy. Add rolled oat mixture. Beat on low speed until combined. Cover and refrigerate 1 to 2 hours or until easy to handle.

*3.* Preheat oven to 375°F.

*4.* For each bear, shape one 1-inch ball for body and one ¾-inch ball for head. Place body and head together on baking sheet; flatten slightly. Make 7 small balls for ears, arms, legs and mouth. Place on bear body and head. Place 2 chocolate chips on each head for eyes; place 1 chocolate chip on each body for belly-button.

*5.* Bake 9 to 11 minutes or until light brown. Cool 1 minute on cookie sheet. Remove to wire racks; cool completely.

# Bananaramas

**Makes about 4 dozen cookies**

1¼ cups firmly packed light brown sugar
¾ cup JIF® Creamy Peanut Butter
½ CRISCO® Stick or ½ cup CRISCO® all-vegetable shortening
1 cup mashed banana
3 tablespoons milk
1½ teaspoons vanilla
½ teaspoon almond extract
1 egg

2 cups all-purpose flour
¾ teaspoon baking soda
¾ teaspoon salt
1½ cups milk chocolate chunks or semisweet chocolate chunks*
1 cup peanuts or coarsely chopped pecans (optional)

*A combination of milk chocolate and semisweet chocolate chunks can be used.*

*1.* Heat oven to 350°F. Place sheets of foil on countertop for cooling cookies.

*2.* Place brown sugar, peanut butter, ½ cup shortening, banana, milk, vanilla and almond extract in large bowl. Beat at medium speed of electric mixer until well blended. Add egg; beat just until blended.

*3.* Combine flour, baking soda and salt. Add to shortening mixture; beat at low speed just until blended. Stir in chocolate chunks and nuts, if desired.

*4.* Drop dough by rounded measuring tablespoonfuls 2 inches apart onto ungreased baking sheets.

*5.* Bake one baking sheet at a time at 350°F for 11 to 13 minutes or until cookies are light brown around edges. *Do not overbake.* Cool 2 minutes on baking sheet. Remove cookies to foil to cool completely.

# Peanut Butter Critter Cookies

3 cups all-purpose flour
1 cup peanut butter chips, melted
¾ cup granulated sugar
¼ cup packed brown sugar
1 cup (2 sticks) butter, softened

1 egg
1½ teaspoons milk
1 teaspoon vanilla
Powdered sugar
Prepared icing

**Makes about 4 dozen cookies**

*1.* Combine flour, melted peanut butter chips, granulated sugar, brown sugar, butter, egg, milk and vanilla in large bowl. Beat at low speed of electric mixer 1 to 2 minutes, scraping bowl often, until well mixed. Divide dough in half. Wrap in plastic wrap; refrigerate 1 to 2 hours or until firm.

*2.* Preheat oven to 375°F. Roll out dough on well-floured surface to ⅛-inch thickness. Cut out desired shapes using 2½-inch cookie cutters. Place 1 inch apart on ungreased cookie sheets. Bake 5 to 8 minutes or until edges are lightly browned. Remove immediately to wire racks; cool completely. Sprinkle with powdered sugar or decorate with icing as desired.

*Note:*

If you run out of space when cooling cookies on wire racks, a perforated roasting rack can also be used.

# Jumbo 3-Chip Cookies

**Makes about 2 dozen cookies**

*Note:*

Most cookies freeze well for several months. Store unfrosted cookies in sealed plastic bags or airtight containers with plastic wrap or waxed paper between layers of cookies. Thaw cookies at room temperature for 10 to 15 minutes.

4 cups all-purpose flour
1 teaspoon baking powder
1 teaspoon baking soda
1½ cups (3 sticks) butter, softened
1¼ cups granulated sugar
1¼ cups packed brown sugar
2 large eggs
1 tablespoon vanilla extract

1 cup (6 ounces) NESTLÉ® TOLL HOUSE® Milk Chocolate Morsels
1 cup (6 ounces) NESTLÉ® TOLL HOUSE® Semi-Sweet Chocolate Morsels
½ cup NESTLÉ® TOLL HOUSE® Premier White Morsels
1 cup chopped nuts

**PREHEAT** oven to 375°F.

**COMBINE** flour, baking powder and baking soda in medium bowl. Beat butter, granulated sugar and brown sugar in large mixer bowl until creamy. Beat in eggs and vanilla extract. Gradually beat in flour mixture. Stir in morsels and nuts. Drop dough by level ¼-cup measure 2 inches apart onto ungreased baking sheets.

**BAKE** for 12 to 14 minutes or until light golden brown. Cool on baking sheets for 2 minutes; remove to wire racks to cool completely.

# Chocolate-Frosted Marshmallow Cookies

Makes about 5 dozen cookies

**Cookies**
- ½ cup (1 stick) butter
- 2 squares (1 ounce each) unsweetened chocolate
- 1 egg
- 1 cup packed brown sugar
- 1 teaspoon vanilla
- ½ teaspoon baking soda
- 1½ cups all-purpose flour
- ½ cup milk
- 1 package (16 ounces) large marshmallows, halved crosswise

**Frosting**
- 1½ squares (1½ ounces) unsweetened chocolate
- ¼ cup (½ stick) butter
- 1½ cups powdered sugar
- 1 egg white*
- 1 teaspoon vanilla

*Use clean, uncracked egg

Preheat oven to 350°F. Lightly grease cookie sheets or line with parchment paper. Melt butter and chocolate in small heavy saucepan over low heat; stir to blend. Remove from heat; cool. Beat egg, brown sugar, vanilla and baking soda in large bowl until light and fluffy. Blend in chocolate mixture and flour until smooth. Slowly beat in milk to make a light, cake-batter-like dough. Drop dough by teaspoonfuls 2 inches apart onto prepared cookie sheets.

Bake 10 to 12 minutes or until firm in center. Immediately place a halved marshmallow, cut side down, onto each baked cookie. Return to oven 1 minute or just until marshmallow is warm enough to stick to cookie. Remove to wire racks to cool.

For frosting, melt chocolate and butter in small heavy saucepan over low heat; stir to blend. Beat in powdered sugar. Beat in egg white and vanilla, adding a little water, if necessary, to make a smooth, slightly soft frosting. Spoon frosting over cookies to cover marshmallows.

# Chewy Choco-Peanut Pudgies

**Makes about 3 dozen cookies**

**Cookies**
1¼ cups firmly packed light brown sugar
¾ cup JIF® Creamy Peanut Butter
½ CRISCO® Stick or ½ cup CRISCO® all-vegetable shortening
3 tablespoons milk
1 tablespoon vanilla
1 egg
1¾ cups all-purpose flour
¾ teaspoon baking soda
¾ teaspoon salt

1½ cups coarsely chopped unsalted peanuts (raw or dry roasted)
½ cup granulated sugar

**Frosting**
½ cup semisweet chocolate chips
½ teaspoon Butter Flavor CRISCO® Stick or ½ teaspoon Butter Flavor CRISCO® all-vegetable shortening
½ teaspoon granulated sugar

*1.* Heat oven to 375°F. Place sheets of foil on countertop for cooling cookies.

*2.* For cookies, combine brown sugar, peanut butter, ½ cup shortening, milk and vanilla in large bowl. Beat at medium speed of electric mixer until well blended. Add egg. Beat just until blended.

*3.* Combine flour, baking soda and salt. Add to creamed mixture at low speed. Mix just until blended. Stir in nuts.

*4.* Form dough into 1¼-inch balls. Roll in ½ cup granulated sugar. Place 2 inches apart onto ungreased baking sheet; flatten slightly with fork.

*5.* Bake one baking sheet at a time at 375°F for 7 to 8 minutes, or until set and just beginning to brown. *Do not overbake.* Cool 2 minutes on baking sheet. Remove cookies to foil to cool completely.

**6.** For frosting, combine chocolate chips, ½ teaspoon shortening and ½ teaspoon granulated sugar in microwave-safe measuring cup. Microwave at 50% (MEDIUM). Stir after 1 minute. Repeat until smooth (or melt on rangetop in small saucepan on very low heat). Drizzle generously over cooled cookies.

# Nutty Footballs

| | |
|---|---|
| 1 cup (2 sticks) butter, softened | ¼ cup unsweetened cocoa |
| ½ cup sugar | powder |
| 1 egg | 1 cup finely chopped almonds |
| ½ teaspoon vanilla | Colored icings (optional) |
| 2 cups all-purpose flour | White icing |

**Makes 2 dozen cookies**

**1.** Beat butter and sugar in large bowl until creamy. Add egg and vanilla; mix until well blended. Stir together flour and cocoa; gradually add to butter mixture, beating until well blended. Add almonds; beat until well blended. Shape dough into disc. Wrap dough in plastic wrap and refrigerate 30 minutes.

**2.** Preheat oven to 350°F. Lightly grease cookie sheets. Roll out dough on floured surface to ¼-inch thickness. Cut dough with 2½- to 3-inch football-shaped cookie cutter.* Place 2 inches apart on prepared cookie sheets.

**3.** Bake 10 to 12 minutes or until set. Cool on cookie sheets 1 to 2 minutes. Remove to wire racks; cool completely. Decorate with colored icings, if desired. Pipe white icing onto footballs to make laces.

*If you do not have a football-shaped cookie cutter, shape 3 tablespoonfuls of dough into ovals. Place 3 inches apart on prepared cookie sheets. Flatten ovals to ¼-inch thickness; taper ends. Bake as directed.

# Mini Pizza Cookies

**Makes 8 cookies**

1 (20-ounce) tube refrigerated
    sugar cookie dough
2 cups (16 ounces) prepared
    pink frosting
  "M&M's"® Chocolate Mini
    Baking Bits

Variety of additional toppings
    such as shredded coconut,
    granola, raisins, nuts,
    small pretzels, snack
    mixes, sunflower seeds,
    popped corn and mini
    marshmallows

*Note:*

Don't take the dough
out of the refrigerator
until just before you're
ready to use it—cold
dough is easier to work
with and will stick less.

Preheat oven to 350°F. Lightly grease cookie sheets; set aside.
Divide dough into 8 equal portions. On lightly floured surface,
roll each portion of dough into ¼-inch-thick circle; place
about 2 inches apart onto prepared cookie sheets. Bake 10 to
13 minutes or until golden brown on edges. Cool completely on
wire racks. Spread top of each pizza with frosting; sprinkle with
"M&M's"® Chocolate Mini Baking Bits and 2 or 3 suggested
toppings.

# Caramel Marshmallow Bars

**Crumb Mixture**
- 1¼ cups all-purpose flour
- ½ cup sugar
- ½ cup butter, softened
- ¼ cup graham cracker crumbs
- ¼ teaspoon salt
- ½ cup chopped salted peanuts

**Filling**
- ¾ cup caramel ice cream topping
- ½ cup salted peanuts
- ½ cups miniature marshmallows
- ½ cup milk chocolate chips

**Makes about 2½ dozen bars**

Preheat oven to 350°F. Grease and flour 9-inch square baking pan. For crumb mixture, combine flour, sugar, butter, graham cracker crumbs and salt in small mixer bowl. Beat at low speed of electric mixer, scraping bowl often, until mixture is crumbly, 1 to 2 minutes. Stir in chopped nuts. Reserve ¾ cup crumb mixture. Press remaining crumb mixture onto bottom of prepared pan. Bake 10 to 12 minutes or until lightly browned.

For filling, spread caramel topping evenly over hot crust. Sprinkle with nuts, marshmallows and chocolate chips. Crumble ¾ cup reserved crumb mixture over chocolate chips. Continue baking 10 to 12 minutes or until marshmallows just start to brown. Cool on wire rack about 30 minutes. Cover; refrigerate 1 to 2 hours or until firm. Cut into bars.

<u>**Serving Suggestion:**</u> *For an extra special treat, serve these kid-pleasing bars with a scoop of ice cream.*

# Outrageous Cookie Bars

| Makes 2 to 3 dozen bars |
| --- |

½ cup (1 stick) butter or
margarine
1½ cups graham cracker crumbs
1 can (14 ounces) NESTLÉ®
CARNATION® Sweetened
Condensed Milk

2 cups (12-ounce package)
NESTLÉ® TOLL HOUSE®
Semi-Sweet Chocolate
Morsels
1 cup flaked coconut
1 cup chopped walnuts

**PREHEAT** oven to 350°F.

**MELT** butter in 13×9-inch baking pan in oven; remove from oven. Sprinkle graham cracker crumbs over butter. Stir well; press onto bottom of pan. Pour sweetened condensed milk evenly over crumbs. Sprinkle with morsels, coconut and nuts; press down firmly.

**BAKE** for 25 to 30 minutes or until light golden brown. Cool completely in pan on wire rack. Cut into bars.

# Worm Cookies

| Makes about 3 dozen cookies |
| --- |

1¾ cups all-purpose flour
¾ cup powdered sugar
¼ cup unsweetened cocoa
powder

⅛ teaspoon salt
1 cup (2 sticks) butter
1 teaspoon vanilla
1 tube white frosting

*1.* Combine flour, sugar, cocoa and salt. Beat butter and vanilla in large bowl with electric mixer at medium-low speed until fluffy. Gradually beat in flour mixture until well combined. Cover and chill dough at least 30 minutes before rolling.

*2.* Preheat oven to 350°F. Form dough into 1½ inch balls. Roll balls gently to form 5- to 6-inch logs about ½ inch thick. Shape into worms 2 inches apart on ungreased cookie sheets.

*3.* Bake 12 minutes or until set. Let stand on cookie sheets until cooled completely. Create eyes and stripes with white frosting.

# Chocolate Sandwich Cookies

**Cookies**
   2 cups all-purpose flour
   ⅓ cup unsweetened cocoa
      powder
   1 teaspoon baking soda
   ¼ teaspoon salt
   1 cup sugar
   6 tablespoons butter, softened
   1 egg
   1 cup milk

**Filling**
   ½ cup milk
   2 tablespoons all-purpose flour
   ½ cup butter, softened
   ½ cup sugar
   1 teaspoon vanilla

**Makes about
2½ dozen sandwich
cookies**

Preheat oven to 425°F. For cookies, stir together 2 cups flour, cocoa, baking soda and salt in medium bowl.

Beat 1 cup sugar and 6 tablespoons butter in large bowl until fluffy. Beat in egg. Add flour mixture and 1 cup milk alternately to butter mixture, beating after each addition. Drop dough by rounded teaspoonfuls onto greased cookie sheets. Bake about 7 minutes or until set. Remove to wire racks to cool.

For filling, stir together ½ cup milk and 2 tablespoons flour in small saucepan over low heat. Cook and stir until thick and bubbly; continue cooking 1 to 2 minutes more. Cool slightly. Beat ½ cup butter and ½ cup sugar in small bowl until fluffy. Add cooled flour mixture and vanilla. Beat until smooth. Spread filling on flat side of half the cooled cookies; top with remaining cookies.

Favorite recipe from **Wisconsin Milk Marketing Board**

# Granola & Chocolate Chip Cookies

**Makes about 3½ dozen cookies**

*Note:*

If the cookies have cooled too long on the baking sheet and are difficult to remove, reheat the baking sheet in the oven for one minute, then remove the cookies from the sheet.

1¼ cups firmly packed light brown sugar
¾ Butter Flavor CRISCO® Stick or ¾ cup Butter Flavor CRISCO® all-vegetable shortening
2 tablespoons milk
1 tablespoon vanilla
1 egg
1¼ cups all-purpose flour
1 teaspoon salt
¾ teaspoon baking soda
2 cups granola cereal
1 cup semisweet chocolate chips

*1.* Heat oven to 375°F. Place sheets of foil on countertop for cooling cookies.

*2.* Combine brown sugar, ¾ cup shortening, milk and vanilla in large bowl. Beat at medium speed of electric mixer until well blended. Beat egg into creamed mixture.

*3.* Combine flour, salt and baking soda. Mix into creamed mixture just until blended. Stir in granola and chocolate chips.

*4.* Drop by rounded measuring tablespoonfuls 3 inches apart onto ungreased baking sheet.

*5.* Bake one baking sheet at a time at 375°F. for 8 to 10 minutes for chewy cookies, or 11 to 13 minutes for crisp cookies. *Do not overbake.* Cool 2 minutes on baking sheet. Remove cookies to foil to cool completely.

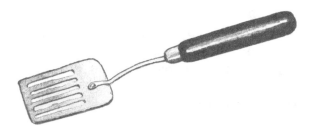

# Happy Face Oatmeal Monsters

1½ cups all-purpose flour
1 teaspoon baking soda
½ teaspoon salt
1 cup (2 sticks) butter, softened
1 cup packed brown sugar
2 eggs
1 teaspoon vanilla
2 cups uncooked quick oats

Granulated sugar
28 chocolate-covered candies or
   large chocolate chips
Cinnamon red hot candies or
   red licorice strings
Colored frosting in tube and
   flaked coconut (optional)

**Makes about
14 (4-inch) cookies**

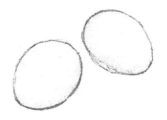

*1.* Preheat oven to 350°F.

*2.* Combine flour, baking soda and salt in small bowl; set aside. Beat butter and brown sugar in large bowl of electric mixer at medium speed until light and fluffy. Beat in eggs, one at a time, until well blended. Beat in vanilla. Gradually beat in flour mixture on low speed until blended. Stir in oats.

*3.* Drop dough by level ¼ cupfuls onto ungreased cookie sheets, spacing 3 inches apart. Flatten dough until 2 inches in diameter with bottom of glass that has been dipped in granulated sugar. Press chocolate candies into cookies to form "eyes" and use cinnamon candies or licorice for "mouth."

*4.* Bake 12 to 14 minutes or until cookies are set and edges are golden brown. Cool cookies 2 minutes on cookie sheets; transfer to wire racks. Cool completely.

*5.* If desired, decorate cookies with frosting and coconut to form "hair."

# Three-in-One Chocolate Chip Cookies

Varies by version

6 tablespoons butter or
  margarine, softened
½ cup packed light brown sugar
¼ cup granulated sugar
1 egg
1 teaspoon vanilla extract

1½ cups all-purpose flour
½ teaspoon baking soda
¼ teaspoon salt
2 cups (12-ounce package)
  HERSHEY₅S Semi-Sweet
  Chocolate Chips

Beat butter, brown sugar and granulated sugar in large bowl until fluffy. Add egg and vanilla; beat well. Stir together flour, baking soda and salt; gradually blend into butter mixture. Stir in chocolate chips. Shape and bake cookies into one of the three versions below.

**Giant Cookie:** *Prepare dough. Heat oven to 350°F. Line 12×⅝-inch round pizza pan with foil. Pat dough evenly into prepared pan to within ¾ inch of edge. Bake 15 to 18 minutes or until lightly browned. Cool completely; cut into wedges. Decorate or garnish as desired. Makes about 8 servings (one 12-inch cookie).*

**Medium-Size Refrigerator Cookies:** *Prepare dough. On wax paper, shape into 2 rolls, 1½ inches in diameter. Wrap in wax paper; cover with plastic wrap. Refrigerate several hours, or until firm enough to slice. Heat oven to 350°F. Remove rolls from refrigerator; remove wrapping. With sharp knife, cut into ¼-inch-thick slices. Place on ungreased cookie sheet, about 3 inches apart. Bake 8 to 10 minutes or until lightly browned. Cool slightly; remove from cookie sheet to wire rack. Cool completely. Makes about 2½ dozen (2½-inch) cookies.*

**Miniature Cookies:** *Prepare dough. Heat oven to 350°F. Drop dough by ¼ teaspoons onto ungreased cookie sheet, about 1½ inches apart. (Or, spoon dough into disposable plastic frosting* *bag; cut about ¼ inch off tip. Squeeze batter by ¼ teaspoons onto ungreased cookie sheet.) Bake 5 to 7 minutes or just until set. Cool slightly; remove from cookie sheet to wire rack. Cool completely. Makes about 18½ dozen (¾-inch) cookies.*

# Dandy Candy Oatmeal Cookies

**Makes 3½ dozen cookies**

1 jar (12 ounces) JIF® Creamy Peanut Butter
1 cup granulated sugar
1 cup firmly packed brown sugar
½ Butter Flavor CRISCO® Stick or ½ cup Butter Flavor CRISCO® all-vegetable shortening plus additional for greasing

3 eggs
¾ teaspoon vanilla
¾ teaspoon maple (or maple-blend) syrup
2 teaspoons baking soda
4½ cups quick oats, uncooked, divided
1 package (8 ounces) candy-coated chocolate pieces

*1.* Heat oven to 350°F. Grease baking sheet with shortening. Place sheets of foil on countertop for cooling cookies.

*2.* Combine peanut butter, granulated sugar, brown sugar and ½ cup shortening in large bowl. Beat at medium speed with electric mixer until well blended and fluffy. Add eggs, vanilla and maple syrup. Beat at high speed 3 to 4 minutes. Add baking soda and 2¼ cups oats; stir. Stir in candy. Stir in remaining 2¼ cups oats. Shape dough into 1½-inch balls. Flatten slightly. Place 2 inches apart on prepared baking sheet.

*3.* Bake for 9 to 10 minutes for chewy cookies or 11 to 12 minutes for crispy cookies. Cool 2 minutes. Remove cookies to foil to cool completely.

# Peanuts

**Makes about 2 dozen cookies**

½ cup (1 stick) butter, softened
¼ cup shortening
¼ cup creamy peanut butter
1 cup powdered sugar, sifted
1 egg yolk
1 teaspoon vanilla

1¾ cups all-purpose flour
1 cup finely ground honey-roasted peanuts, divided
Peanut Buttery Frosting (recipe follows)

## Note:

**Make cookie baking easier by lining your cookie sheet with a reusable, nonstick silicone baking mat. The mat insulates the pan so cookie bottoms won't burn or stick. And since there's no need to grease the cookie sheet, cleanup is a breeze!**

*1.* Beat butter, shortening and peanut butter in large bowl at medium speed of electric mixer. Gradually add powdered sugar, beating until smooth. Add egg yolk and vanilla; beat well. Add flour; mix well. Stir in ⅓ cup ground peanuts. Cover dough; refrigerate 1 hour. Prepare Peanut Buttery Frosting.

*2.* Preheat oven to 350°F. Grease cookie sheets. Shape dough into 1-inch balls. Place 2 balls, side by side and slightly touching, on prepared cookie sheet. Gently flatten balls with fingertips to form into "peanut" shape. Repeat steps with remaining dough.

*3.* Bake 16 to 18 minutes or until edges are lightly browned. Cool on cookie sheets 5 minutes. Remove cookies to wire racks; cool completely.

*4.* Place remaining ⅔ cup ground peanuts in shallow dish. Spread about 2 teaspoons Peanut Buttery Frosting evenly over top of each cookie. Coat with ground peanuts.

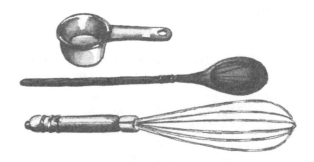

## Peanut Buttery Frosting

½ cup (1 stick) butter or margarine, softened
½ cup creamy peanut butter

2 cups powdered sugar, sifted
½ teaspoon vanilla
3 to 6 tablespoons milk

*1.* Beat butter and peanut butter in medium bowl at medium speed of electric mixer until smooth. Gradually add powdered sugar and vanilla until blended but crumbly.

*2.* Add milk, 1 tablespoon at a time, until smooth. Refrigerate until ready to use.

*Makes 1⅓ cups frosting*

# Colorful Cookie Buttons

Makes 3 dozen cookies

1½ cups (3 sticks) butter, softened
½ cup granulated sugar
½ cup firmly packed light brown sugar
2 large egg yolks

1 teaspoon vanilla extract
3½ cups all-purpose flour
1½ teaspoons baking powder
½ teaspoon salt
1 cup "M&M's"® Chocolate Mini Baking Bits

Preheat oven to 350°F. In large bowl cream butter and sugars until light and fluffy; beat in egg yolks and vanilla. In medium bowl combine flour, baking powder and salt; add to creamed mixture. Shape dough into 72 balls. For each cookie, place one ball on ungreased cookie sheet and flatten. Place 8 to 10 "M&M's"® Chocolate Mini Baking Bits on dough. Flatten second ball and place over "M&M's"® Chocolate Mini Baking Bits, pressing top and bottom dough together. Decorate top with remaining "M&M's"® Chocolate Mini Baking Bits. Repeat with remaining dough balls and "M&M's"® Chocolate Mini Baking Bits, placing cookies about 2 inches apart on cookie sheet. Bake 17 to 18 minutes. Cool 2 minutes on cookie sheets; cool completely on wire racks. Store in tightly covered container.

# Confetti Chocolate Chip Cookies

**Makes 2 dozen cookies**

1¼ cups firmly packed brown sugar
¾ Butter Flavor CRISCO® Stick or ¾ cup Butter Flavor CRISCO® all-vegetable shortening
2 tablespoons milk
1 tablespoon vanilla
1 egg

1½ cups all-purpose flour
1 teaspoon salt
¾ teaspoon baking soda
1 cup walnut pieces
½ cup semisweet chocolate chunks
½ cup large vanilla milk chunks
½ cup milk chocolate chips

*1.* Heat oven to 375°F. Place sheets of foil on countertop for cooling cookies.

*2.* Combine brown sugar, ¾ cup shortening, milk and vanilla in large bowl. Beat at medium speed with electric mixer until well blended. Beat in egg.

*3.* Combine flour, salt and baking soda. Add gradually to creamed mixture at low speed. Mix until blended.

*4.* Stir in walnuts, chocolate chunks, vanilla milk chunks and chocolate chips. Drop by rounded tablespoonfuls 3 inches apart onto *ungreased* baking sheet.

*5.* Bake for 8 to 10 minutes. Cookies will look light and moist. *Do not overbake.* Cool 2 minutes on baking sheet. Remove cookies to foil to cool completely.

# Peanut Butter S'Mores

1½ cups all-purpose flour
½ teaspoon baking powder
½ teaspoon baking soda
¼ teaspoon salt
½ cup (1 stick) butter, softened
½ cup granulated sugar
½ cup packed brown sugar
½ cup creamy or chunky peanut
   butter

1 egg
1 teaspoon vanilla
½ cup chopped roasted peanuts
   (optional)
4 (1.55-ounce) milk chocolate
   candy bars
16 large marshmallows

**Makes about
16 sandwich cookies**

*Note:*

**Store leftover**

**marshmallows in a**

**tightly sealed bag in**

**the freezer; this will**

**prevent them from**

**drying out.**

*1.* Preheat oven to 350°F.

*2.* Combine flour, baking powder, baking soda and salt in small bowl; set aside. Beat butter, granulated sugar and brown sugar in large bowl with electric mixer at medium speed until light and fluffy. Beat in peanut butter, egg and vanilla until well blended. Gradually beat in flour mixture at low speed until blended. Stir in peanuts, if desired.

*3.* Roll dough into 1-inch balls; place 2 inches apart on ungreased cookie sheets. Flatten dough with fork, forming criss-cross pattern. Bake about 14 minutes or until set and edges are light golden brown. Cool cookies 2 minutes on cookie sheets; transfer to wire cooling racks. Cool completely.

*4.* To assemble sandwiches, break each candy bar into four sections. Place 1 section of chocolate on flat side of 1 cookie. Place on microwavable plate; top with 1 marshmallow. Microwave at HIGH 10 to 12 seconds or until marshmallow is puffy. Immediately top with another cookie, flat side down. Press slightly on top cookie, spreading marshmallow to edges. Repeat with remaining cookies, marshmallows and candy pieces, one at a time. Cool completely.

# Chocolate Crackletops

**Makes about 5 dozen cookies**

2 cups all-purpose flour
2 teaspoons baking powder
2 cups granulated sugar
½ cup (1 stick) butter or margarine
4 squares (1 ounce each) unsweetened baking chocolate, chopped

4 large eggs, lightly beaten
2 teaspoons vanilla extract
1¾ cups "M&M's"® Chocolate Mini Baking Bits
Additional granulated sugar

*Note:*

To coarsely chop chocolate, use a large chef's knife on a cutting board. A gadget called an ice or chocolate chipper also works well.

Combine flour and baking powder; set aside. In 2-quart saucepan over medium heat combine 2 cups sugar, butter and chocolate, stirring until butter and chocolate are melted; remove from heat. Gradually stir in eggs and vanilla. Stir in flour mixture until well blended. Chill mixture 1 hour. Stir in "M&M's"® Chocolate Mini Baking Bits; chill mixture an additional 1 hour.

Preheat oven to 350°F. Line cookie sheets with foil. With sugar-dusted hands, roll dough into 1-inch balls; roll balls in additional granulated sugar. Place about 2 inches apart onto prepared cookie sheets. Bake 10 to 12 minutes. Do not overbake. Cool completely on wire racks. Store in tightly covered container.

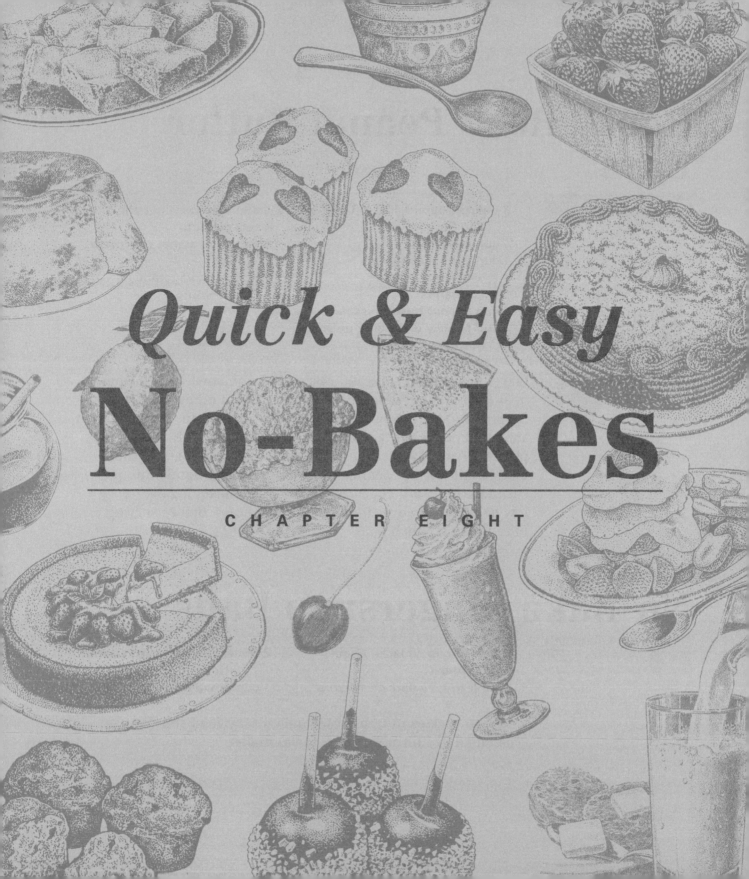

# Quick & Easy
# No-Bakes

CHAPTER EIGHT

# Rocky Road Peanut Butter Bars

**Makes 36 bars**

3 quarts popped JOLLY TIME®
   Pop Corn
½ cup raisins
1 cup light corn syrup
1 tablespoon butter or
   margarine
½ cup peanut butter pieces
⅓ cup chunky or creamy peanut
   butter

¾ cup miniature marshmallows
½ cup peanuts
½ cup semi-sweet chocolate
   pieces
1 teaspoon vegetable
   shortening

Place popped pop corn and raisins in large bowl. In saucepan, heat corn syrup and butter to boiling. Boil 3 minutes. Remove from heat. Stir in peanut butter pieces and peanut butter until smooth. Pour mixture over pop corn, tossing gently to coat all pieces. Press into greased 9-inch square baking pan. Sprinkle marshmallows and peanuts over top, pressing lightly into pop corn mixture. Melt chocolate pieces and shortening over very low heat. Drizzle over top. Cool several hours before serving. Cut into 2¼×1-inch bars.

# No-Bake Gingersnap Balls

**Makes 2 dozen cookies**

20 gingersnap cookies (about
   5 ounces)
3 tablespoons dark corn syrup

2 tablespoons creamy peanut
   butter
⅓ cup powdered sugar

*1.* Place cookies in large resealable plastic food storage bag; crush finely with rolling pin or meat mallet.

*2.* Combine corn syrup and peanut butter in medium bowl. Add crushed gingersnaps; mix well. (Mixture should hold together without being sticky. If mixture is too dry, stir in additional 1 tablespoon corn syrup.)

*3.* Shape mixture into 24 (1-inch) balls; roll in powdered sugar.

**Tip:** *Some gingersnaps are crisper than others, so you might need to add an extra tablespoonful, or two, of corn syrup to the crumb mixture in order to hold it together.*

# Peanut Butter Cereal Bars

| | | |
|---|---|---|
| 3 cups miniature marshmallows | 1 cup uncooked quick oats | **Makes 40 servings** |
| 3 tablespoons margarine | ⅓ cup mini semisweet | |
| ½ cup reduced-fat peanut butter | chocolate chips | |
| 3½ cups crisp rice cereal | | |

*1.* Lightly coat 13×9-inch baking pan with nonstick cooking spray; set aside.

*2.* Combine marshmallows and margarine in large microwavable bowl. Microwave at HIGH 15 seconds; stir. Continue to microwave 1 minute; stir until marshmallows are melted and mixture is smooth. Add peanut butter; stir. Add cereal and oats; stir until well coated. Spread into prepared pan. Immediately sprinkle chocolate chips on top; lightly press.

*3.* Cool completely in pan. Cut into 40 bars.

**Tip:** *To make spreading the cereal mixture easier and cleanup a snap, lightly spray your spoon with nonstick cooking spray before stirring.*

# Fudgey Cocoa No-Bake Treats

**Makes about 4 dozen**

**Prep Time:**
*20 minutes*

**Cook Time:**
*5 minutes*

**Cool Time:**
*30 minutes*

2 cups sugar
½ cup (1 stick) butter or
   margarine
½ cup milk
⅓ cup HERSHEY'S Cocoa
⅔ cup REESE'S® Crunchy
   Peanut Butter

3 cups quick-cooking
   rolled oats
½ cup chopped peanuts
   (optional)
2 teaspoons vanilla extract

*1.* Place piece of wax paper or foil on tray or cookie sheet. Combine sugar, butter, milk and cocoa in medium saucepan.

*2.* Cook over medium heat, stirring constantly, until mixture comes to a rolling boil.

*3.* Remove from heat; cool 1 minute.

*4.* Add peanut butter, oats, peanuts, if desired, and vanilla; stir to mix well. Quickly drop mixture by heaping teaspoons onto wax paper or foil. Cool completely. Store in cool, dry place.

# P.B. Graham Snackers

**Makes about 3 dozen**

2 cups confectioners' sugar
¾ cup JIF® Creamy Peanut
   Butter
½ Butter Flavor CRISCO® Stick
   or ½ cup Butter Flavor
   CRISCO® all-vegetable
   shortening

1 cup graham cracker crumbs
½ cup semisweet chocolate
   chips
½ cup graham cracker crumbs
   or crushed peanuts or
   colored sugar or sprinkles
   (optional)

*1.* Combine confectioners' sugar, peanut butter and ½ cup shortening in large bowl. Beat at low speed of electric mixer until well blended. Stir in 1 cup crumbs and chocolate chips. Cover and refrigerate 1 hour.

*2.* Form dough into 1-inch balls. Roll in ½ cup crumbs, peanuts, colored sugar or sprinkles. Cover and refrigerate until ready to serve.

# Haystacks

| | | |
|---|---|---|
| 2 cups butterscotch chips<br>½ cup JIF® Creamy Peanut Butter<br>¼ Butter Flavor CRISCO® Stick or ¼ cup Butter Flavor CRISCO® all-vegetable shortening | 6 cups corn flakes<br>⅔ cup miniature semisweet chocolate chips<br>Chopped peanuts or chocolate jimmies (optional) | Makes about 3 dozen cookies |

*Note:*

When melting shortening or butter in the microwave, covering the container with a piece of waxed paper helps prevent spatters.

*1.* Combine butterscotch chips, peanut butter and ¼ cup shortening in large microwave-safe bowl. Cover with waxed paper. Microwave at 50% (MEDIUM). Stir after 1 minute. Repeat until smooth (or melt on rangetop in small saucepan on very low heat, stirring constantly).

*2.* Pour corn flakes into large bowl. Pour hot butterscotch mixture over flakes. Stir with spoon until flakes are coated. Stir in chocolate chips.

*3.* Spoon scant ¼ cup mixture into mounds on waxed paper-lined baking sheets. Sprinkle with chopped nuts, if desired. Refrigerate until firm.

# No-Bake Pineapple Marmalade Squares

**Makes 16 servings**

1 cup graham cracker crumbs
½ cup plus 2 tablespoons sugar, divided
¼ cup light margarine, melted
1 cup fat free or light sour cream
4 ounces light cream cheese, softened

¼ cup orange marmalade or apricot fruit spread, divided
1 can (20 ounces) DOLE® Crushed Pineapple
1 envelope unflavored gelatin

• Combine graham cracker crumbs, 2 tablespoons sugar and margarine in 8-inch square glass baking dish; pat mixture firmly and evenly onto bottom of dish. Freeze 10 minutes.

• Beat sour cream, cream cheese, remaining ½ cup sugar and 1 tablespoon marmalade in medium bowl until smooth and blended; set aside.

• Drain crushed pineapple; reserve ¼ cup juice.

• Sprinkle gelatin over reserved juice in small saucepan; let stand 1 minute. Cook and stir over low heat until gelatin dissolves.

• Beat gelatin mixture into sour cream mixture until well blended. Spoon mixture evenly over crust.

• Stir together crushed pineapple and remaining 3 tablespoons marmalade in small bowl until blended. Evenly spoon over sour cream filling. Cover and refrigerate 2 hours or until firm.

# Peanut Butter Power Bars

PAM® No-Stick Cooking Spray
¾ cup firmly packed light brown sugar
½ cup honey
5 cups whole grain cereal flakes

1½ cups PETER PAN® Smart Choice Creamy Peanut Butter
⅓ cup diced mixed dried fruit

*1.* Spray 13×9×2-inch baking pan with PAM Cooking Spray.

*2.* In large saucepan, combine brown sugar and honey.

*3.* Cook over medium heat, stirring constantly, until mixture comes to a full rolling boil.

*4.* Remove from heat and add *remaining* ingredients; stir until mixture is well coated.

*5.* Press into baking pan; cool and cut into squares.

*Note:*

Soften hardened dried fruit by covering it with boiling water and letting it sit for 15 minutes. Drain fruit and dry with paper towels before using.

# Crispy Chocolate Logs

1 cup (6 ounces) semisweet chocolate chips
½ cup butter or margarine

1 package (10 ounces) marshmallows
6 cups crisp rice cereal

Lightly grease 13×9-inch baking pan. Melt chocolate chips and butter in large bowl over hot water, stirring constantly. Add marshmallows; stir until melted. Add cereal; stir until evenly coated with chocolate mixture. Press into prepared pan; cool until mixture is firm. Cut into 2×1½-inch logs.

# Walnut-Granola Clusters

**Makes 5 dozen**

¼ cup butter
1 (10½-ounce) package
   miniature marshmallows
½ teaspoon ground cinnamon
3 cups rolled oats

2 cups chopped California
   walnuts
1 cup flaked coconut
2 (1-ounce) squares semi-sweet
   chocolate

Microwave butter in large microwavable mixing bowl at HIGH (100% power) 40 seconds or until melted. Stir in marshmallows and cinnamon. Microwave 1½ minutes or until melted, stirring halfway through. Quickly stir in oats, walnuts and coconut. With wet hands, form mixture into small balls and place on wax paper-lined baking sheets.

Microwave chocolate in glass measuring cup at HIGH 2½ minutes or until melted; stir. Lightly drizzle chocolate over clusters. Store at room temperature, uncovered, 4 to 5 days.

Favorite recipe from **Walnut Marketing Board**

# No-Bake Peanutty Chocolate Drops

½ cup (1 stick) butter or
    margarine
⅓ cup unsweetened cocoa
2½ cups quick-cooking oats
1 (14-ounce) can EAGLE®
    BRAND Sweetened
    Condensed Milk
    (NOT evaporated milk)

1 cup chopped peanuts
½ cup peanut butter

**Makes about 5 dozen drops**

**Prep Time:**
*10 minutes*

**Chill Time:**
*2 hours*

*1.* Line baking sheets with waxed paper. In medium saucepan over medium heat, melt butter; stir in cocoa. Bring mixture to a boil.

*2.* Remove from heat; stir in remaining ingredients.

*3.* Drop by teaspoonfuls onto prepared baking sheets; chill 2 hours or until set. Store loosely covered in refrigerator.

*Note:*

Oats should be stored

in an airtight container

in a cool, dry place for

up to 6 months.

# Chocolate Cereal Bars

**Makes 24 squares**

6 cups crisp rice cereal
1 cup (6 ounces) semisweet
    chocolate chips
1 jar (7 ounces) marshmallow
    creme

2 tablespoons butter or
    margarine
1 teaspoon vanilla

*1.* Butter 13×9-inch baking pan; set aside. Place cereal in large heatproof bowl; set aside.

*2.* Melt chocolate chips, marshmallow creme and butter in small heavy saucepan over medium heat, stirring occasionally. Remove from heat.

*3.* Stir in vanilla. Pour chocolate mixture over cereal. Stir until blended. Press into prepared pan; cool.

*4.* Cut into squares.

## How Much of This = That?

| | |
|---|---|
| **Butter** | 1 cup = ½ pound or 2 sticks<br>½ cup = 1 stick or 8 tablespoons |
| **Chocolate** | 1 (6-ounce) package chocolate chips = 1 cup chips or 6 (1-ounce) squares semisweet chocolate |
| **Cocoa, unsweetened** | 1 (8-ounce) can = 2 cups |
| **Cream cheese** | 1 (3-ounce) package = 6 tablespoons |
| **Flour**<br>    white or all-purpose<br>    whole wheat | <br>1 pound = 3½ to 4 cups<br>1 pound = 3¾ to 4 cups |
| **Nuts** | 4 ounces = 1 cup chopped |
| **Shortening** | 1 pound = 2½ cups |
| **Sugar**<br>    granulated<br>    brown, packed<br>    powdered | <br>1 pound = 2½ cups<br>1 pound = 2¼ cups<br>1 pound = 3¾ to 4 cups, unsifted |

# No-Bake Banana Peanut Butter Fudge Bars

1 ripe, large DOLE® Banana
⅔ cup butter or margarine
2 teaspoons vanilla extract
2½ cups rolled oats

½ cup packed brown sugar
1 cup semisweet chocolate chips
½ cup peanut butter

Makes 24 bars

• Finely chop banana (1¼ cups). Melt butter in large skillet over medium heat; stir in vanilla. Add oats and brown sugar. Heat and stir 5 minutes. Set aside ¾ cup oat mixture. Press remaining oat mixture into greased 9-inch square baking pan. Sprinkle banana over crust.

• Melt chocolate chips and peanut butter together over low heat. Pour and spread over banana. Sprinkle with reserved oat mixture; press down lightly. Chill 2 hours before cutting. Store in refrigerator.

# No-Bake Cherry Crisps

1 cup peanut butter
1 cup powdered sugar
¼ cup (½ stick) butter, softened
1⅓ cups crisp rice cereal
½ cup maraschino cherries, drained, dried and chopped

¼ cup plus 2 tablespoons mini semisweet chocolate chips
¼ cup chopped pecans
1 to 2 cups flaked coconut (for rolling)

Makes about 3 dozen cookies

Beat powdered sugar, peanut butter and butter in large bowl. Stir in cereal, cherries, chocolate chips and pecans. Mix well. Shape teaspoonfuls of dough into 1-inch balls. Roll in coconut. Place on cookie sheets and refrigerate 1 hour. Store in refrigerator.

# Nathaniel's Jumble

**Makes 24 bars**

*Note:*

When a recipe calls for sifted powdered sugar, be sure to measure it after sifting. If the recipe says "powdered sugar, sifted", then the sugar should be measured before sifting.

1 cup creamy peanut butter
6 tablespoons margarine or butter, melted
2¼ cups sifted confectioners' sugar
4 cups popped NEWMAN'S OWN® Natural Flavor Microwave Popcorn

½ cup regular candy-coated chocolate pieces
4 ounces semisweet chocolate, melted
⅓ cup caramel ice cream syrup

## Layer 1
Combine peanut butter and margarine in large mixing bowl. With mixer at low speed, beat in confectioners' sugar, about ½ cup at a time, mixing well. After mixing, knead by hand. Spread into foil-lined 8-inch square pan.

## Layer 2
Place popcorn and chocolate pieces in medium bowl. Pour melted chocolate over popcorn mixture; gently mix with spoon until all popcorn is covered with chocolate. Spread popcorn mixture evenly over peanut butter layer; press slightly to adhere to bottom layer. Drizzle caramel over popcorn mixture.

Refrigerate or freeze until set.

# Oat & Dried Fruit Balls

**Makes about 5 dozen balls**

3 cups uncooked old-fashioned oats
1 cup flaked coconut
1 cup chopped dried mixed fruit
¼ cup sunflower seeds or chopped walnuts
1 cup sugar

½ cup milk
½ cup (1 stick) butter or margarine
6 tablespoons unsweetened cocoa powder
¼ teaspoon salt
1 teaspoon vanilla

Combine oats, coconut, dried fruit and sunflower seeds in large bowl; set aside. Combine sugar, milk, butter, cocoa and salt in 2-quart saucepan until blended. Heat to boiling. Boil 3 minutes, stirring constantly; remove from heat. Stir in vanilla. Pour hot sugar syrup into oat mixture; stir until well blended. When cool enough to handle, shape rounded tablespoonfuls into balls; place on waxed paper until completely cooled and firm.

# Fudgy Peanut Butter Jiffy Cookies

2 cups granulated sugar
½ cup evaporated milk
½ cup (1 stick) margarine or butter
¼ cup unsweetened cocoa powder

2½ cups QUAKER® Oats (quick or old fashioned, uncooked)
½ cup peanut butter
½ cup raisins or chopped dates
2 teaspoons vanilla

**Makes about 3 dozen cookies**

In large saucepan, combine sugar, milk, margarine and cocoa. Bring to a boil over medium heat, stirring frequently. Continue boiling 3 minutes. Remove from heat. Stir in oats, peanut butter, raisins and vanilla; mix well. Quickly drop by tablespoonfuls onto waxed paper or greased cookie sheet. Let stand until set. Store tightly covered at room temperature.

# Scotcheroos

**Makes 2½ dozen bars**

Nonstick cooking spray
1½ cups creamy peanut butter
1 cup granulated sugar
1 cup light corn syrup
6 cups toasted rice cereal
1⅔ cups (11-ounce package)
NESTLÉ® TOLL HOUSE®
Butterscotch Flavored
Morsels

1 cup (6 ounces) NESTLÉ®
TOLL HOUSE® Semi-Sweet
Chocolate Morsels

**COAT** 13×9-inch baking pan with cooking spray.

**COMBINE** peanut butter, sugar and corn syrup in large saucepan. Cook over medium-low heat, stirring frequently, until melted. Remove from heat. Add cereal; stir until thoroughly coated. Press onto bottom of prepared baking pan.

**MICROWAVE** butterscotch morsels and semi-sweet chocolate morsels in large, microwave-safe bowl on HIGH (100%) power for 1 minute; stir. Microwave at additional 10- to 20-second intervals, stirring until smooth. Spread over cereal mixture.

**REFRIGERATE** for 15 to 20 minutes or until topping is firm. Cut into bars.

# No-Bake Fudgy Brownies

1 (14-ounce) can EAGLE®
  BRAND Sweetened
  Condensed Milk
  (NOT evaporated milk)
2 (1-ounce) squares
  unsweetened chocolate,
  cut up

1 teaspoon vanilla extract
2 cups plus 2 tablespoons
  packaged chocolate cookie
  crumbs, divided
¼ cup miniature candy-coated
  milk chocolate candies or
  chopped nuts

**Makes 24 to 36 bars**

**Prep Time:**
*10 minutes*

**Chill Time:**
*4 hours*

*1.* Grease 8-inch square baking pan or line with foil; set aside.

*2.* In medium heavy saucepan over low heat, combine Eagle Brand and chocolate; cook and stir just until boiling. Reduce heat; cook and stir for 2 to 3 minutes more or until mixture thickens. Remove from heat. Stir in vanilla.

*3.* Stir in 2 cups cookie crumbs. Spread evenly in prepared pan. Sprinkle with remaining cookie crumbs and candies or nuts; press down gently with back of spoon.

*4.* Cover and chill 4 hours or until firm. Cut into squares. Store covered in refrigerator.

*Note:*

Store vanilla extract in
a cool, dark place—if
the bottle is sealed
airtight, the vanilla
will keep indefinitely.

# Peanut Butter Chocolate No-Bake Bars

**Makes 24 bars**

*Note:*

It's important to stir the chocolate pieces occasionally when melting them in the microwave, as they retain their original shape even when melted.

**Bars**
1 cup peanut butter
½ cup light corn syrup
½ cup powdered sugar
2 tablespoons margarine or butter
2 cups QUAKER® Oats (quick or old fashioned, uncooked)

**Topping**
1 cup (6 ounces) semisweet chocolate pieces
2 tablespoons peanut butter
¼ cup chopped peanuts (optional)

*1.* For bars, in medium saucepan, heat 1 cup peanut butter, corn syrup, powdered sugar and margarine over medium-low heat until margarine is melted, stirring frequently. Remove from heat. Stir in oats; mix well.

*2.* Spread onto bottom of *ungreased* 8- or 9-inch square pan; set aside.

*3.* For topping, place chocolate pieces in medium-size microwavable bowl. Microwave on HIGH 1 to 2 minutes, stirring every 30 seconds until smooth.

*4.* Stir in 2 tablespoons peanut butter until well blended.

*5.* Spread evenly over oats layer. Sprinkle with chopped nuts, if desired. Refrigerate 30 minutes or until chocolate is set.

*6.* Cut into bars with sharp knife. If bars are difficult to cut, let stand about 10 minutes. Store tightly covered at room temperature.

# 3-Minute No-Bake Cookies

2 cups granulated sugar
½ cup (1 stick) margarine or
   butter
½ cup 2% milk

⅓ cup unsweetened cocoa
   powder
3 cups QUAKER® Oats (quick or
   old fashioned, uncooked)

**Makes about 3 dozen cookies**

In large saucepan, combine sugar, margarine, milk and cocoa.
Bring to boil over medium heat, stirring frequently. Continue
boiling 3 minutes. Remove from heat. Stir in oats; mix well.
Quickly drop by tablespoonfuls onto waxed paper or greased
cookie sheet. Let stand until set. Store tightly covered at room
temperature.

# Crispy Cocoa Bars

¼ cup (½ stick) margarine
¼ cup HERSHEY'S Cocoa

5 cups miniature marshmallows
5 cups crisp rice cereal

**Makes 24 bars**

*1.* Spray 13×9×2-inch pan with vegetable cooking spray.

*2.* Melt margarine in large saucepan over low heat; stir in
cocoa and marshmallows. Cook over low heat, stirring constantly,
until marshmallows are melted and mixture is smooth and well
blended. Continue cooking 1 minute, stirring constantly. Remove
from heat.

*3.* Add cereal; stir until coated. Lightly spray spatula with
vegetable cooking spray; press mixture into prepared pan.
Cool completely. Cut into bars.

# No-Bake Chocolate Oat Bars

**Makes 32 bars**

1 cup (2 sticks) butter
½ cup packed brown sugar
1 teaspoon vanilla
3 cups uncooked quick oats

1 cup semisweet chocolate
  chips
½ cup crunchy or creamy
  peanut butter

Grease 9-inch square baking pan. Melt butter in large saucepan over medium heat. Add brown sugar and vanilla; mix well.

Stir in oats. Cook over low heat 2 to 3 minutes or until ingredients are well blended. Press half of mixture into prepared pan. Use back of large spoon to spread mixture evenly.

Meanwhile, melt chocolate chips in small heavy saucepan over low heat, stirring occasionally. Stir in peanut butter. Pour chocolate mixture over oat mixture in pan; spread evenly with knife or back of spoon. Crumble remaining oat mixture over chocolate layer, pressing down gently. Cover and refrigerate 2 to 3 hours or overnight.

Bring to room temperature before cutting into bars. (Bars can be frozen; let thaw about 10 minutes or more before serving.)

# Monkey Bars

**Makes 2 dozen bars**

3 cups miniature marshmallows
½ cup honey
⅓ cup butter
¼ cup peanut butter
2 teaspoons vanilla

¼ teaspoon salt
4 cups crispy rice cereal
2 cups rolled oats, uncooked
½ cup flaked coconut
¼ cup peanuts

Combine marshmallows, honey, butter, peanut butter, vanilla and salt in medium saucepan. Melt marshmallow mixture over low heat, stirring constantly. Combine rice cereal, oats, coconut and peanuts in 13×9×2-inch baking pan. Pour marshmallow mixture over dry ingredients. Mix until thoroughly coated. Press mixture firmly into pan. Cool completely before cutting.

<u>Microwave Directions:</u> *Microwave marshmallows, honey, butter, peanut butter, vanilla and salt in 2-quart microwave-safe bowl on HIGH 2½ to 3 minutes. Continue as above.*

Favorite recipe from **National Honey Board**

*Note:*

**Shredded coconut freezes well and doesn't need to be defrosted before using—stock up so you'll always have it on hand for baking emergencies!**

# Microwave Double Peanut Bars

| | | |
|---|---|---|
| ½ cup light brown sugar | ¾ cup raisins | |
| ½ cup light corn syrup or honey | ½ cup chopped peanuts | |
| ½ cup creamy peanut butter | | |
| 6 shredded wheat biscuits, coarsely crushed | | |

**Makes 2 dozen bars**

In 2-quart microwavable bowl, blend sugar, corn syrup and peanut butter. Microwave on HIGH (100% power) 1 to 1½ minutes until bubbly. Stir until smooth. Quickly stir in cereal, raisins and peanuts. Press evenly into greased 8- or 9-inch square baking pan. Cool. Cut into bars.

Favorite recipe from **Peanut Advisory Board**

# Chewy Chocolate No-Bakes

**Makes 3 dozen cookies**

*Note:*

If you only have regular-size marshmallows, it's easy to cut them down to the miniature size. Use scissors to snip them into smaller pieces, dipping the scissors into cold water occasionally if they get too sticky.

1 cup (6 ounces) semisweet chocolate pieces
16 large marshmallows
⅓ cup (5 tablespoons plus 1 teaspoon) margarine or butter
2 cups QUAKER® Oats (quick or old fashioned, uncooked)

1 cup (any combination of) raisins, diced dried mixed fruit, flaked coconut, miniature marshmallows or chopped nuts
1 teaspoon vanilla

In large saucepan over low heat, melt chocolate pieces, marshmallows and margarine, stirring until smooth. Remove from heat; cool slightly. Stir in remaining ingredients. Drop by rounded teaspoonfuls onto waxed paper. Chill 2 to 3 hours. Let stand at room temperature about 15 minutes before serving. Store in tightly covered container in refrigerator.

**Microwave Directions:** *Place chocolate pieces, marshmallows and margarine in large microwavable bowl. Microwave on HIGH 1 to 2 minutes or until mixture is melted and smooth, stirring every 30 seconds. Proceed as recipe directs.*

# No-Bake Butterscotch Haystacks

1 cup HERSHEY'S Butterscotch Chips
½ cup REESE'S® Peanut Butter Chips
1 tablespoon shortening (do not use butter, margarine, spread or oil)

1½ cups (3-ounce can) chow mein noodles, coarsely broken

**Makes about 2 dozen cookies**

**Prep Time:**
*15 minutes*

**Cook Time:**
*1 minute*

**Cool Time:**
*30 minutes*

*1.* Line cookie sheet with wax paper. Place butterscotch chips, peanut butter chips and shortening in medium microwave-safe bowl.

*2.* Microwave at HIGH (100%) 1 minute; stir. If necessary, microwave at HIGH an additional 15 seconds at a time, stirring after each heating, just until chips are melted and mixture is smooth when stirred.

*3.* Immediately add chow mein noodles; stir to coat. Drop mixture by heaping teaspoons onto prepared cookie sheet or into paper candy cups; let stand until firm. If necessary, cover and refrigerate until firm. Store in refrigerator in tightly covered container.

Chocolate Haystacks: *Substitute 1 cup HERSHEY'S Semi-Sweet Chocolate Chips or HERSHEY'S Milk Chocolate Chips for butterscotch chips. Proceed as directed above with peanut butter chips, shortening and chow mein noodles.*

# Citrus Cream Bars

**Makes about 2 dozen bars**

1¼ cups finely crushed chocolate sandwich cookies
⅔ cup butter, softened, divided
1½ cups powdered sugar
1 tablespoon milk

1½ teaspoons grated orange peel
½ teaspoon lemon peel
½ teaspoon vanilla
¼ cup semisweet chocolate chips, melted

*1.* Combine cookie crumbs and ⅓ cup butter in medium bowl. Press onto bottom of ungreased 9-inch square baking pan. Refrigerate until firm.

*2.* Combine powdered sugar, remaining ⅓ cup butter, milk, orange peel, lemon peel and vanilla in small bowl. Beat at medium speed of electric mixer, scraping bowl often, until light and fluffy. Spread over crust.

*3.* Drizzle melted chocolate over filling. Refrigerate until firm, about 2 hours. Cut into bars. Store leftovers in refrigerator.

# Peanut Butter-Hop-Scotch Treats

4 cups corn flakes
1½ cups "M&M's"® Chocolate
    Mini Baking Bits, divided
¾ cup butterscotch chips
½ cup creamy peanut butter

¼ cup light corn syrup
4 tablespoons butter, divided
6 squares (1 ounce each)
    semi-sweet chocolate

**Makes 3 dozen bars**

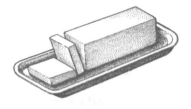

Lightly grease 13×9-inch baking pan; set aside. In large bowl combine cereal and 1 cup "M&M's"® Chocolate Mini Baking Bits; set aside. In heavy saucepan melt butterscotch chips, peanut butter, corn syrup and 2 tablespoons butter over low heat, stirring often until mixture is smooth. Pour melted mixture over cereal mixture, tossing lightly until thoroughly coated. Gently press into prepared pan with buttered fingers. In small saucepan melt remaining 2 tablespoons butter and chocolate over low heat. Spread chocolate mixture over cereal mixture; decorate with remaining ½ cup "M&M's"® Chocolate Mini Baking Bits. Store in tightly covered container.

*Note:*

The quality of commercially available chocolate varies a great deal. Good quality chocolate breaks evenly, is smooth, not grainy, and has a shiny, unmarked surface.

# Special Treat No-Bake Squares

**Makes about 3 dozen squares**

*Note:*

Store leftover shredded coconut in an airtight container for up to 1 week in the refrigerator or up to 6 months in the freezer.

½ cup plus 1 teaspoon butter, divided
¼ cup granulated sugar
¼ cup unsweetened cocoa powder
1 egg
¼ teaspoon salt
1½ cups graham cracker crumbs
¾ cup flaked coconut

½ cup chopped pecans
⅓ cup butter, softened
1 package (3 ounces) cream cheese, softened
1 teaspoon vanilla
1 cup powdered sugar
1 (2-ounce) dark sweet or bittersweet candy bar, broken into ½-inch pieces

Line 9-inch square baking pan with foil, shiny side up, allowing 2-inch overhang on sides. Set aside.

For crust, combine ½ cup butter, granulated sugar, cocoa, egg and salt in medium saucepan. Cook over medium heat, stirring constantly, until mixture thickens, about 2 minutes. Remove from heat; stir in graham cracker crumbs, coconut and pecans. Press evenly into prepared baking pan.

For filling, beat ⅓ cup softened butter, cream cheese and vanilla in small bowl until smooth. Gradually beat in powdered sugar. Spread over crust; refrigerate 30 minutes.

For glaze, combine candy bar pieces and remaining 1 teaspoon butter in small resealable plastic bag; seal. Microwave at HIGH (100%) 50 seconds. Turn bag over; heat at HIGH 40 to 50 seconds or until melted. Knead bag until candy bar is smooth. Cut tiny corner off bag; drizzle chocolate over filling. Refrigerate until firm, about 20 minutes. Remove bars from pan using foil. Cut into 1½-inch squares.

# No-Bake Chocolate Caramel Bars

2 cups semisweet chocolate chips (12-ounce bag)
¼ Butter Flavor CRISCO® Stick or ¼ cup Butter Flavor CRISCO all-vegetable shortening plus additional for greasing

5 cups crispy rice cereal
1⅓ cup caramel candy such as Milk Duds® (10-ounce box)
1 tablespoon water

**Makes about 2 dozen bars**

*1.* Grease 13×9×2-inch pan with shortening.

*2.* Combine chocolate chips and ¼ cup shortening in large microwave-safe bowl. Microwave on HIGH for 1 minute. Stir vigorously. If necessary, microwave on HIGH an additional 30 seconds at a time, stirring vigorously after each heating, just until chips are melted.

*3.* Pour cereal into melted chip mixture. Stir until thoroughly coated.

*4.* Combine caramel candy and water in medium microwave-safe bowl. Microwave on HIGH for 1 minute. Stir vigorously. If necessary, microwave on HIGH an additional 30 seconds at a time, stirring vigorously after each heating, until caramel is pourable. Fold caramel mixture into chocolate coated cereal. *Caution, caramel may be hot.*

*5.* Pour and spread into greased pan. *Do not press, surface should appear rough.* Cool in refrigerator for 30 minutes or until chocolate is set. Bring back up to room temperature. Cut into bars about 2×2 inches.

**Tip:** *Caramel bowl is easier to clean when caramel is warm.*

# No-Bake Chocolate Peanut Butter Bars

**Makes about 5 dozen bars**

2 cups peanut butter, *divided*
¾ cup (1½ sticks) butter, softened
2 cups powdered sugar, *divided*
3 cups graham cracker crumbs

2 cups (12-ounce package) NESTLÉ® TOLL HOUSE® Semi-Sweet Chocolate Mini Morsels, *divided*

### *Note:*

It's easy to make your own graham cracker crumbs in the food processor. Feed graham crackers, two or three at a time, into the food processor with the machine running. Turn it off when the crumbs have reached the desired consistency. (36 graham cracker squares will make about 3 cups crumbs.)

GREASE 13×9-inch baking pan.

BEAT 1¼ cups peanut butter and butter in large mixer bowl until creamy. Gradually beat in *1 cup* powdered sugar. With hands or wooden spoon, work in *remaining* powdered sugar, graham cracker crumbs and *½ cup* morsels. Press evenly into prepared pan. Smooth top with spatula.

MELT *remaining* peanut butter and *remaining* morsels in medium, *heavy-duty* saucepan over *lowest possible heat*, stirring constantly, until smooth. Spread over graham cracker crust in pan. Refrigerate for at least 1 hour or until chocolate is firm; cut into bars. Store in refrigerator.

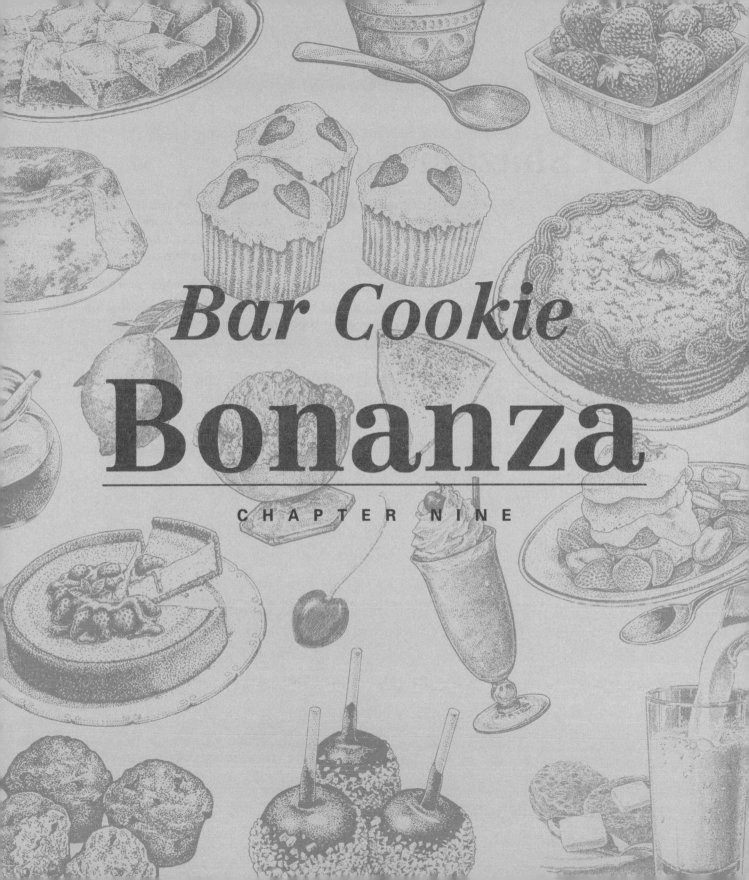

# Bar Cookie
# Bonanza

## CHAPTER NINE

# Oreo® Shazam Bars

**Makes 24 bars**

*Note:*

Always use the pan
size called for in the
recipe. A larger pan
may cause the bar
cookies to be thin and
brittle, and a smaller
pan may result in
thick, soggy bars.

28 OREO® Chocolate Sandwich
Cookies, divided
¼ cup margarine or butter,
melted
1 cup shredded coconut

1 cup white chocolate chips
½ cup chopped nuts
1 (14-ounce) can sweetened
condensed milk

*1.* Finely roll 20 cookies. Mix cookie crumbs and margarine or butter; spread over bottom of 9×9×2-inch baking pan, pressing lightly.

*2.* Chop remaining cookies. Layer coconut, chips, nuts and chopped cookies in prepared pan; drizzle evenly with condensed milk.

*3.* Bake at 350°F for 25 to 30 minutes or until golden and set. Cool completely. Cut into bars.

# Buttery Black Raspberry Bars

| | | |
|---|---|---|
| 1 cup butter or margarine | 1 cup chopped walnuts | **Makes 32 bars** |
| 1 cup sugar | ½ cup SMUCKER'S® Seedless | |
| 2 egg yolks | Black Raspberry Jam | |
| 2 cups all-purpose flour | | |

Beat butter until soft and creamy. Gradually add sugar, beating until mixture is light and fluffy. Add egg yolks; blend well. Gradually add flour; mix thoroughly. Fold in walnuts.

Spoon half of batter into greased 8-inch square pan; spread evenly. Top with jam; cover with remaining batter.

Bake at 325°F for 1 hour or until lightly browned. Cool and cut into 2×1-inch bars.

# Heath® Bits Bars

| | | |
|---|---|---|
| 2 packages (8 ounces each) HEATH® BITS, divided | 1 egg yolk | **Makes about 4 dozen bars** |
| 1 cup (2 sticks) butter, softened | 1 teaspoon vanilla extract | |
| 1 cup packed light brown sugar | 2 cups all-purpose flour | |
| | ½ cup finely chopped pecans | |

*1.* Heat oven to 350°F. Set aside ¾ cup Heath Bits.

*2.* Beat butter in large bowl until creamy; add brown sugar, egg yolk and vanilla; beat until blended. Using spoon, mix in flour, remaining Heath Bits and pecans. Press into ungreased 15½×10½×1-inch jelly-roll pan.

*3.* Bake 18 to 20 minutes or until browned. Remove from oven; immediately sprinkle reserved ¾ cup Heath Bits over top. Cool slightly. Cut into bars while warm. Cool completely.

# Apple Lemon Bars

**Makes 16 bars**

Cookie Crust (recipe follows)
1 cup diced, peeled Washington
    Golden Delicious apple
⅓ cup sugar
1 egg, beaten
2 tablespoons butter or
    margarine, melted

2 teaspoons grated lemon peel
¾ cup all-purpose flour
¼ teaspoon ground cinnamon
¼ teaspoon baking powder
¼ teaspoon salt
    Lemon Glaze (recipe follows)

Preheat oven to 350°F. Prepare Cookie Crust. Combine apple, sugar, egg, butter and lemon peel in large bowl; mix thoroughly. Combine flour, cinnamon, baking powder and salt in medium bowl; mix well. Stir flour mixture into apple mixture. Spread evenly over crust. Bake 25 minutes or until apples are tender. Cool in pan on wire rack. Brush with Lemon Glaze.

**Cookie Crust:** *Beat ½ cup butter or margarine, ¼ cup powdered sugar and 2 teaspoons grated lemon peel until creamy; blend in 1 cup flour. Press into bottom of ungreased 8-inch square baking pan. Bake at 350°F 15 to 18 minutes or until lightly browned.*

**Lemon Glaze:** *Combine ¾ cup powdered sugar and 1 tablespoon lemon juice; mix thoroughly.*

Favorite recipe from **Washington Apple Commission**

# Championship Chocolate Chip Bars

1½ cups all-purpose flour
½ cup packed light brown sugar
½ cup (1 stick) cold butter or margarine
2 cups (12-ounce package) HERSHEY᛫S Semi-Sweet Chocolate Chips, divided

1 can (14 ounces) sweetened condensed milk (*not* evaporated milk)
1 egg
1 teaspoon vanilla extract
1 cup chopped nuts

**Makes about 36 bars**

*1.* Heat oven to 350°F.

*2.* Stir together flour and brown sugar in medium bowl; with pastry blender, cut in butter until mixture resembles coarse crumbs. Stir in ½ cup chocolate chips; press mixture onto bottom of 13×9×2-inch baking pan. Bake 15 minutes.

*3.* Meanwhile, in large bowl, combine sweetened condensed milk, egg and vanilla. Stir in remaining 1½ cups chips and nuts. Spread over baked crust. Continue baking 25 minutes or until golden brown. Cool completely in pan on wire rack. Cut into bars.

*Note:*

Bar cookies like these are great for picnics, potlucks and other parties, since you can bake them and transport them in the same pan. Some baking pans are sold with lids that will allow you to store the bars airtight.

# Chocolate & Malt Bars

**Makes 2 dozen bars**

1 cup all-purpose flour
1 cup malted milk powder or
   malted milk drink mix
2 teaspoons baking powder
¼ teaspoon salt
½ cup granulated sugar
¼ cup firmly packed light brown
   sugar

¼ cup (½ stick) butter, softened
½ cup milk
½ teaspoon vanilla extract
2 large eggs
1 cup "M&M's"® Chocolate
   Mini Baking Bits, divided
Chocolate Malt Frosting
   (recipe follows)

Preheat oven to 350°F. Lightly grease 13×9-inch baking pan; set aside. In large bowl combine flour, malted milk powder, baking powder and salt; stir in sugars. Beat in butter, milk and vanilla; blend well. Add eggs; beat 2 minutes. Spread batter in prepared pan. Sprinkle with ¼ cup "M&M's"® Chocolate Mini Baking Bits. Bake about 20 minutes or until toothpick inserted in center comes out clean. Cool completely on wire rack. Prepare Chocolate Malt Frosting; spread over cake. Sprinkle with remaining ¾ cup "M&M's"® Chocolate Mini Baking Bits. Store in tightly covered container.

## Chocolate Malt Frosting

¼ cup (½ stick) butter, softened
4 teaspoons light corn syrup
½ teaspoon vanilla extract
¼ cup malted milk powder or
   malted milk drink mix

3 tablespoons unsweetened
   cocoa powder
1½ cups powdered sugar
3 to 4 tablespoons milk

In small bowl beat butter, corn syrup and vanilla; stir in malted milk powder and cocoa powder until well blended. Blend in powdered sugar and enough milk for good spreading consistency.

# West Haven Date Bars

1 cup boiling water
1 cup chopped pitted dates
1 cup sugar
½ cup (1 stick) butter, softened
2 eggs
1 teaspoon vanilla
1½ cups all-purpose flour

2 tablespoons unsweetened
    cocoa powder
1 teaspoon baking soda
1 cup (6 ounces) semisweet
    chocolate chips
½ cup chopped walnuts or
    pecans

**Makes about 3 dozen bars**

Preheat oven to 350°F. Lightly grease 13×9-inch pan. Pour boiling water over dates in small bowl; let stand until cooled. Cream sugar with butter in large bowl. Add eggs and vanilla; beat until light. Blend in flour, cocoa and baking soda to make a smooth dough. Stir in date mixture. Spread batter evenly in prepared pan. Sprinkle chocolate chips and nuts over top. Bake 25 to 30 minutes or just until center feels firm. Cut into 2×1½-inch bars while still warm.

# Blueberry Cheesecake Bars

**Makes about 16 bars**

1 package DUNCAN HINES®
Bakery-Style Blueberry
Streusel Muffin Mix
¼ cup cold butter or margarine
⅓ cup finely chopped pecans
1 package (8 ounces) cream
cheese, softened

½ cup sugar
1 egg
3 tablespoons lemon juice
1 teaspoon grated lemon peel

*1.* Preheat oven to 350°F. Grease 9-inch square baking pan.

*2.* Rinse blueberries from Mix with cold water and drain; set aside.

*3.* Place muffin mix in medium bowl; cut in butter with pastry blender or two knives. Stir in pecans. Press into bottom of prepared pan. Bake at 350°F for 15 minutes or until set.

*4.* Combine cream cheese and sugar in medium bowl. Beat until smooth. Add egg, lemon juice and lemon peel. Beat well. Spread over baked crust. Sprinkle with blueberries. Sprinkle topping packet from Mix over blueberries. Return to oven. Bake at 350°F for 35 to 40 minutes or until filling is set. Cool completely. Refrigerate until ready to serve. Cut into bars.

# Peanut Butter Shortbreads

**Makes 16 wedge-shaped cookies**

½ cup unsalted butter, softened
½ cup granulated sugar

¼ cup creamy peanut butter
2 cups all-purpose flour

Preheat oven to 300°F. In bowl, combine all ingredients with fingers until mixture resembles coarse meal. Press the mixture into an ungreased 8-inch round pan. With a fork, prick decorative wedges in the dough. Bake for about 1 hour or until very lightly browned. Cut into wedges while warm.

Favorite recipe from **Peanut Advisory Board**

# Toffee Bars

| | | Makes about 3 dozen bars |
|---|---|---|
| ½ cup (1 stick) butter, softened<br>½ cup packed light brown sugar<br>1 egg yolk<br>1 teaspoon vanilla<br>1 cup all-purpose flour | 1 cup (6 ounces) milk chocolate chips<br>½ cup chopped walnuts or pecans | |

Preheat oven to 350°F. Lightly grease 13×9-inch baking pan. Cream butter and brown sugar in large bowl. Blend in egg yolk and vanilla. Stir in flour until well blended. Press on bottom of prepared pan. Bake 15 minutes or until golden. Remove from oven; sprinkle chocolate chips over top. Let stand a few minutes until chips melt, then spread evenly over bars. Sprinkle nuts over chocolate. Score into 2×1½-inch bars while still warm. Cool completely in pan on wire rack before cutting and removing from pan.

# Creamy Lemon Bars

**Makes 15 servings**

**Prep Time:**
*25 minutes*

**Chill Time:**
*4 hours*

1½ cups graham cracker crumbs
½ cup sugar, divided
½ cup (1 stick) butter or
    margarine, melted
1 package (8 ounces)
    PHILADELPHIA® Cream
    Cheese, softened
2 tablespoons milk
1 tub (8 ounces) COOL WHIP®
    Whipped Topping, thawed

1 package (4.3 ounces) JELL-O®
    Lemon Flavor Cook & Serve
    Pudding & Pie Filling
    *(not Instant)*
¾ cup sugar
3 cups water, divided
3 egg yolks

**MIX** crumbs, ¼ cup of the sugar and butter in 13×9-inch pan. Press firmly onto bottom of pan. Refrigerate until ready to fill.

**BEAT** cream cheese, remaining ¼ cup sugar and milk until smooth. Gently stir in ½ of the whipped topping. Spread evenly over crust.

**STIR** pudding mix, ¾ cup sugar, ½ cup of the water and egg yolks in medium saucepan. Stir in remaining 2½ cups water. Stirring constantly, cook on medium heat until mixture comes to full boil. Cool 5 minutes, stirring twice. Pour over cream cheese layer.

**REFRIGERATE** 4 hours or until set. Just before serving, spread remaining whipped topping over pudding.

# Raspberry Crisp Bars

**Crust**
- ½ Butter Flavor CRISCO® Stick or ½ cup Butter Flavor CRISCO® all-vegetable shortening
- ⅓ cup confectioners' sugar
- 1 cup all-purpose flour

**Topping**
- ½ cup all-purpose flour
- 3 tablespoons firmly packed light brown sugar
- ¼ teaspoon baking powder
- ¼ teaspoon ground cinnamon
- 4 tablespoons Butter Flavor CRISCO® all-vegetable shortening
- 1 egg yolk
- ½ teaspoon vanilla
- ¾ cup SMUCKER'S® Raspberry Preserves or any flavor

**Makes 1 dozen bars**

*1.* Heat oven to 350°F.

*2.* For crust, combine ½ cup shortening and confectioners' sugar in large bowl. Beat at medium speed with electric mixer until well blended. Stir in 1 cup flour until mixture is just crumbly. Press into bottom of ungreased 8-inch square baking pan. Bake at 350°F for 10 to 12 minutes or until crust is set but not browned. Remove from oven and place on cooling rack.

*3.* For topping, combine ½ cup flour, brown sugar, baking powder and cinnamon in medium bowl; mix well. Cut in 4 tablespoons shortening with fork until mixture forms even crumbs. Add egg yolk and vanilla; mix well.

*4.* Spread preserves evenly over crust. Sprinkle topping evenly over preserves. Bake at 350°F for 30 minutes or until topping is golden. Place on cooling rack and allow to cool completely. Cut into bars.

*Note:*

Most recipes that call for eggs were developed using large eggs. Unless otherwise specified in the recipe, always use large eggs when baking.

# Deluxe Toll House® Mud Bars

**Makes 3 dozen bars**

1 cup plus 2 tablespoons
   all-purpose flour
½ teaspoon baking soda
½ teaspoon salt
¾ cup packed brown sugar
½ cup (1 stick) butter, softened
1 teaspoon vanilla extract

1 large egg
2 cups (12-ounce package)
   NESTLÉ® TOLL HOUSE®
   Semi-Sweet Chocolate
   Morsels, *divided*
½ cup chopped walnuts

*Note:*

Try cutting bar
cookies into triangles
or diamonds for
variety. To make
serving easy, remove
a corner piece first;
then remove the rest.

PREHEAT oven to 375°F. Grease 9-inch-square baking pan.

COMBINE flour, baking soda and salt in small bowl. Beat sugar, butter and vanilla extract in large mixer bowl until creamy. Beat in egg; gradually beat in flour mixture. Stir in *1¼ cups* morsels and nuts. Spread into prepared baking pan.

BAKE for 20 to 23 minutes. Remove pan to wire rack. Sprinkle with *remaining* morsels. Let stand for 5 minutes or until morsels are shiny; spread evenly. Cool in pan on wire rack. Cut into bars.

# Almond Toffee Bars

**Makes about 40 bars**

¾ cup butter or margarine,
   softened
¾ cup packed brown sugar
1½ cups all-purpose flour
½ teaspoon almond extract
½ teaspoon vanilla extract

¼ teaspoon salt
1 package (6 ounces) semi-
   sweet real chocolate pieces
¾ cup BLUE DIAMOND®
   Chopped Natural Almonds,
   toasted

Preheat oven to 350°F. Cream butter and sugar; blend in flour. Add extracts and salt, mixing well. Spread in bottom of ungreased 13×9×2-inch baking pan. Bake in 350°F oven for 15 to 20 minutes or until deep golden brown. Remove from oven and sprinkle with chocolate pieces. When chocolate has melted, spread evenly; sprinkle with almonds. Cut into bars; cool.

# Chocolate Nut Bars

1¾ cups graham cracker crumbs
½ cup (1 stick) butter or
    margarine, melted
1 (14-ounce) can EAGLE®
    BRAND Sweetened
    Condensed Milk
    NOT evaporated milk)

2 cups (12 ounces) semi-sweet
    chocolate chips, divided
1 teaspoon vanilla extract
1 cup chopped nuts

**Makes 24 to 36 bars**

**Prep Time:**
*10 minutes*

**Bake Time:**
*33 to 38 minutes*

*1.* Preheat oven to 375°F. In medium mixing bowl, combine crumbs and butter; press firmly on bottom of ungreased 13×9-inch baking pan. Bake 8 minutes. Reduce oven temperature to 350°F.

*2.* In small saucepan, melt Eagle Brand with 1 cup chips and vanilla. Spread chocolate mixture over prepared crust. Top with remaining 1 cup chips and nuts; press down firmly.

*3.* Bake 25 to 30 minutes. Cool. Chill, if desired. Cut into bars. Store loosely covered at room temperature.

# Peanut Butter Chip Triangles

**Makes 24 or 40 triangles**

**Prep Time:**
*20 minutes*

**Bake Time:**
*40 minutes*

**Cool Time:**
*2 hours*

1½ cups all-purpose flour
½ cup packed light brown sugar
½ cup (1 stick) cold butter or margarine
1⅔ cups (10-ounce package) REESE'S® Peanut Butter Chips, divided

1 can (14 ounces) sweetened condensed milk (not evaporated milk)
1 egg, slightly beaten
1 teaspoon vanilla extract
¾ cup chopped walnuts
Powdered sugar (optional)

**1.** Heat oven to 350°F. Stir together flour and brown sugar in medium bowl. Cut in butter with pastry blender or fork until mixture resembles coarse crumbs. Stir in ½ cup peanut butter chips. Press mixture into bottom of ungreased 13×9×2-inch baking pan. Bake 15 minutes.

**2.** Meanwhile, combine sweetened condensed milk, egg and vanilla in large bowl. Stir in remaining chips and walnuts. Spread evenly over hot baked crust.

**3.** Bake 25 minutes or until golden brown. Cool completely in pan on wire rack. Cut into 2- or 2½-inch squares; cut squares diagonally into triangles. Sift powdered sugar over top, if desired.

**Tip:** *To sprinkle powdered sugar over brownies, bars, cupcakes or other desserts, place sugar in a wire mesh strainer. Hold over top of desserts and gently tap sides of strainer.*

# Absolutely Wonderful Pecan Bars

1½ cups quick or old-fashioned oats
1½ cups all-purpose flour
2 cups DOMINO® Dark Brown Sugar, packed, divided
1½ cups butter (we do not recommend margarine), divided

1½ cups or 1 (7-ounce) package pecan halves
1 cup DOMINO® Granulated Sugar
⅓ cup heavy cream
2 teaspoons vanilla

**Makes 48 bars**

In large bowl, combine oats, flour and 1 cup brown sugar. Cut ½ cup butter into mixture until coarse and crumbly. Press into 13×9-inch baking pan. Sprinkle pecans evenly over crumb mixture.

In heavy saucepan, combine remaining 1 cup brown sugar, granulated sugar and 1 cup butter. Bring to a rolling boil over medium heat, stirring constantly. Boil 3 minutes; remove from heat. Stir in cream and vanilla until well blended; pour over pecans. Bake in preheated 350°F oven 35 to 40 minutes. Cool in pan; cut into bars.

*Note:*

To keep bar cookies as fresh as possible, only cut as many as you need at a time and keep the remaining bars covered tightly with aluminum foil. (With so many sides exposed, bar cookies have a tendency to dry out quickly.)

# Chocolate Mousse Squares

**Makes 16 squares**

¾ cup plus 2 tablespoons
    all-purpose flour, divided
⅔ cup plus 3 tablespoons
    granulated sugar, divided
¼ cup (½ stick) cold margarine
¼ cup HERSHEY₅S Cocoa
½ teaspoon powdered instant
    coffee

¼ teaspoon baking powder
½ cup liquid egg substitute
½ teaspoon vanilla extract
½ cup plain lowfat yogurt
½ teaspoon powdered sugar

*Note:*

It's easy to dress up bar cookies for guests. Place each bar inside a paper muffin cup and arrange the filled cups on a serving tray. Not only do the bars look prettier, but the paper cups make handling and eating them less messy.

*1.* Heat oven to 350°F.

*2.* Stir together ¾ cup flour and 3 tablespoons granulated sugar in medium bowl. Cut in margarine, with pastry blender or 2 knives, until fine crumbs form. Press mixture onto bottom of ungreased 8-inch square baking pan.

*3.* Bake 15 minutes or until golden. Reduce oven temperature to 300°F.

*4.* Meanwhile, stir together remaining ⅔ cup granulated sugar, cocoa, remaining 2 tablespoons flour, instant coffee and baking powder in medium bowl. Add egg substitute and vanilla; beat on medium speed of mixer until well blended. Add yogurt; beat just until blended. Pour over prepared crust.

*5.* Bake 30 minutes or until center is set. Cool completely in pan on wire rack. Cut into squares. If desired, place small paper cutouts over top. Sift powdered sugar over cutouts. Carefully remove cutouts. Store, covered, in refrigerator.

# Power Bars

Makes 32 (2-inch) bars

2 cups firmly packed brown sugar
¾ cup butter or margarine
2 cups all-purpose flour
2 cups old-fashioned or quick-cooking oats, uncooked

2 teaspoons baking soda
1 (21-ounce) can cherry pie filling
2 tablespoons granulated sugar
1 tablespoon cornstarch
½ teaspoon almond extract

Beat brown sugar and butter in medium bowl with electric mixer at medium speed until light and fluffy. Combine flour, oats and baking soda. Add flour mixture to sugar mixture; mix on low speed until crumbly.

Spread two-thirds of oat mixture into bottom of ungreased 13×9×2-inch baking pan. Press down to form crust.

Process cherry filling in food processor or blender until smooth. Pour into medium saucepan. Combine granulated sugar and cornstarch; stir into cherry filling. Cook, stirring constantly, over low heat until mixture is thick and bubbly. Stir in almond extract. Pour cherry mixture over oat layer; spread evenly. Top with remaining oat mixture.

Bake in preheated 325°F oven 45 minutes or until golden brown. Cool before cutting.

Favorite recipe from **Cherry Marketing Institute**

# Peanut Butter Caramel Macadamia Bars

**Makes 48 pieces**

**Prep Time:**
*25 minutes*

1 box (17¼ ounces) frozen puff
   pastry sheets, thawed
¾ cup sugar
½ cup PETER PAN® Honey
   Roasted Creamy
   Peanut Butter
½ cup unsalted butter

3 tablespoons light corn syrup
1 can (14 ounces) sweetened
   condensed milk
3 cups whole macadamia nuts
½ tablespoon vanilla
12 ounces bittersweet chocolate

Place each puff pastry sheet on ungreased cookie sheet; pierce all over with fork. Bake according to package directions; cool. While pastry is cooling, combine sugar, Peter Pan® Peanut Butter, butter, corn syrup and condensed milk in heavy saucepan over low heat. Stir constantly until butter has melted and sugar is dissolved. Simmer 15 minutes or until golden, stirring often. Remove from heat; stir in macadamia nuts and vanilla. Spread filling evenly over crusts; set aside. Melt chocolate according to package directions. Spread chocolate evenly over filling. Let cool and harden completely before cutting. Cut into bars, then in half diagonally to form triangles.

# Chocolate Fudge Pecan Bars

2⅔ cups all-purpose flour
1¼ cups packed light brown
    sugar, divided
1 cup (2 sticks) cold butter or
    margarine
4 eggs
1 cup light corn syrup
4 bars (1 ounce each)
    HERSHEY᙭S Unsweetened
    Baking Chocolate,
    unwrapped and melted

2 teaspoons vanilla extract
½ teaspoon salt
2 cups coarsely chopped
    pecans

**Makes about 36 bars**

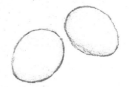

*1.* Heat oven to 350°F. Grease 15½×10½×1-inch jelly-roll pan.

*2.* Stir together flour and ¼ cup brown sugar in large bowl. With pastry blender, cut in butter until mixture resembles coarse crumbs; press onto bottom of prepared pan.

*3.* Bake 10 to 15 minutes or until set. Remove from oven. With back of spoon, lightly press crust into corners and against sides of pan.

*4.* Beat eggs, corn syrup, remaining 1 cup brown sugar, melted chocolate, vanilla and salt; stir in pecans. Pour mixture evenly over warm crust. Return to oven.

*5.* Bake 25 to 30 minutes or until chocolate filling is set. Cool completely in pan on wire rack. Cut into bars.

*Note:*

15×10×1-inch jelly-roll pans, used for making bar cookies or thin sheet cakes, are available in aluminum and steel. Jelly-roll pans are not a good choice for baking individual cookies because the sides interfere with air circulation during baking and result in uneven browning.

# Chewy Fruit & Nut Bars

**Makes 20 bars**

**Prep Time:**
*15 minutes plus refrigerating*

2 cups LORNA DOONE®
 Shortbread crumbs
5 tablespoons butter *or*
 margarine, melted
1 cup boiling water
2 packages (4-serving size each)
 JELL-O® Brand Apricot *or*
 Peach Flavor Gelatin

½ cup light corn syrup
1 cup chopped toasted
 PLANTERS® Slivered
 Almonds

**STIR** crumbs and butter in 9-inch square baking pan until crumbs are well moistened, reserving ½ cup crumb mixture. Firmly press remaining crumbs onto bottom of pan. Refrigerate until ready to fill.

**STIR** boiling water into gelatin in large bowl at least 2 minutes until completely dissolved. Stir in corn syrup. Refrigerate 15 minutes or until slightly thickened (consistency of unbeaten egg whites). Stir in almonds. Pour into pan over crust. Sprinkle with remaining crumbs.

**REFRIGERATE** 3 hours or until firm. Cut into bars.

**Great Substitute:** *Use JELL-O® Brand Orange Flavor Gelatin instead of Apricot Flavor. Reduce almonds to ½ cup and add ½ cup chopped dried apricots.*

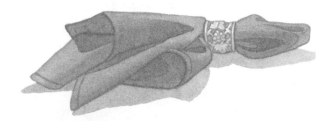

# Peanut Butter Cup Bars

1½ cups all-purpose flour
1 teaspoon baking powder
1 teaspoon salt
⅔ cup IMPERIAL® Spread,
   softened
2 cups sugar

4 eggs
1 cup semi-sweet chocolate
   chips, melted
½ cup SKIPPY® Creamy
   Peanut Butter

**Makes 2 dozen bars**

Preheat oven to 350°F. Grease 13×9-inch baking pan; set aside.

In medium bowl, combine flour, baking powder and salt; set aside.

In large bowl, with electric mixer, beat Imperial Spread and sugar on medium-high speed until light and fluffy, about 5 minutes. Beat in eggs, scraping sides occasionally. Gradually beat in flour mixture until blended. Remove 2 cups batter to medium bowl and stir in melted chocolate. Evenly spread batter into prepared pan. Add peanut butter to remaining batter in large bowl; beat until blended. Spoon over chocolate batter and spread into even layer.

Bake uncovered 35 minutes or until center is set. On wire rack, cool completely. To serve, cut into bars.

*Note:*

To melt 1 cup of

chocolate chips in

the microwave, place

the chips in a small

microwavable bowl.

Microwave on High

(100% power) 1 to

1½ minutes, stirring

after 1 minute. Stir the

chocolate at 30-second

intervals until smooth.

# Emily's Dream Bars

**Makes 4½ dozen bars**

1 cup JIF® Crunchy Peanut Butter
½ Butter Flavor CRISCO® Stick or ½ cup Butter Flavor CRISCO® all-vegetable shortening plus additional for greasing
½ cup firmly packed brown sugar
½ cup light corn syrup
1 egg
1 teaspoon vanilla
1 cup all-purpose flour

½ teaspoon baking powder
¼ cup milk
2 cups 100% natural oats, honey and raisins cereal
1 package (12 ounces) miniature semisweet chocolate chips (2 cups), divided
1 cup almond brickle chips
1 cup milk chocolate covered peanuts
1 package (2 ounces) nut topping (⅓ cup)

*Note:*

When you need to bring dessert for a large group, prepare bar cookies. They're a snap to make and you can always increase the number of servings, if necessary, by cutting smaller bars.

*1.* Heat oven to 350°F. Grease 13×9×2-inch pan with shortening. Place cooling rack on top of countertop.

*2.* Combine peanut butter, ½ cup shortening, brown sugar and corn syrup in large bowl. Beat at medium speed of electric mixer until creamy. Add egg and vanilla. Beat well.

*3.* Combine flour and baking powder. Add alternately with milk to creamed mixture at medium speed. Stir in cereal, 1 cup chocolate chips, almond brickle chips and chocolate covered nuts with spoon. Spread in prepared pan.

*4.* Bake at 350°F for 20 to 26 minutes or until golden brown and toothpick inserted in center comes out clean. *Do not overbake.* Sprinkle remaining 1 cup chocolate chips over top immediately after removing from oven. Remove pan to cooling rack. Let stand about 3 minutes or until chips become shiny and soft. Spread over top. Sprinkle with nut topping. Cool completely. Cut into 2×1- inch bars.

# Chocolate Caramel Nut Bars

1 cup (2 sticks) butter *or*
    margarine, softened
½ cup firmly packed brown
    sugar
2 cups flour
¼ teaspoon salt
1 package (12 ounces)
    BAKER'S® Semi-Sweet
    Chocolate Chunks

1 bag (14 ounces) caramels,
    unwrapped
⅓ cup whipping (heavy) cream
1 cup chopped walnuts *or*
    pecans

**Makes 3 dozen bars**

**Prep Time:**
*20 minutes*

**Bake Time:**
*15 minutes*

**HEAT** oven to 350°F.

**BEAT** butter and sugar in large bowl with electric mixer on medium speed until light and fluffy. Add flour and salt; beat on low speed until crumbly. Press into 15×10×1-inch baking pan.

**BAKE** 15 minutes or until edges are golden brown. Remove from oven. Sprinkle chocolate chunks over top. Cover with foil. Let stand 5 minutes or until chocolate is melted. Spread chocolate evenly over top.

**MICROWAVE** caramels and cream in microwavable bowl on HIGH 2 minutes or until caramels begin to melt. Stir in walnuts. Gently spread caramel mixture over chocolate. Cool in pan on wire rack.

**Storage Know-How:** *Store in tightly covered container up to 1 week.*

# Apple Crumb Squares

**Makes about 2 dozen bars**

2 cups QUAKER® Oats (quick or old fashioned, uncooked)
1½ cups all-purpose flour
1 cup packed brown sugar
¾ cup (12 tablespoons) butter or margarine, melted

1 teaspoon ground cinnamon
½ teaspoon baking soda
½ teaspoon salt (optional)
¼ teaspoon ground nutmeg
1 cup applesauce
½ cup chopped nuts

Preheat oven to 350°F. In large bowl, combine all ingredients except applesauce and nuts; mix until crumbly. Reserve 1 cup oats mixture. Press remaining mixture on bottom of greased 13×9-inch metal baking pan. Bake 13 to 15 minutes; cool. Spread applesauce over partially baked crust. Sprinkle reserved 1 cup oats mixture over top; sprinkle with nuts. Bake 13 to 15 minutes or until golden brown. Cool in pan on wire rack; cut into 2-inch squares.

# Granola Bars

**Makes 48 bars**

**Prep Time:**
*20 minutes*

**Bake Time:**
*25 to 30 minutes*

3 cups oats
1 (14-ounce) can EAGLE® BRAND Sweetened Condensed Milk (NOT evaporated milk)
1 cup peanuts

1 cup sunflower seeds
1 cup raisins
½ cup (1 stick) butter or margarine, melted
1½ teaspoons ground cinnamon

*1.* Preheat oven to 325°F. Line 15×10-inch jelly-roll pan with aluminum foil; grease foil.

*2.* In large mixing bowl, combine all ingredients; mix well. Press evenly into prepared pan.

*3.* Bake 25 to 30 minutes or until golden brown. Cool slightly; remove from pan and peel off foil. Cut into bars. Store loosely covered at room temperature.

# Plum Oat Squares

**Makes 12 squares**

1 cup uncooked rolled oats
⅓ cup whole wheat flour
⅓ cup packed brown sugar
1 teaspoon ground cinnamon
¼ teaspoon baking soda
¼ teaspoon ground nutmeg
1 egg, lightly beaten
2 tablespoons unsalted butter, melted

2 tablespoons unsweetened apple juice concentrate, thawed
1 teaspoon vanilla
2 fresh California plums, finely chopped

Preheat oven to 350°F. Grease 11×7-inch baking pan; set aside. Combine oats, flour, sugar, cinnamon, baking soda and nutmeg in large bowl. Combine egg, butter, juice and vanilla in small bowl until well blended. Stir into oat mixture until well blended. Fold in plums. Spread evenly into prepared pan. Bake 25 minutes or until wooden pick inserted in center comes out clean. Cool in pan on wire rack 10 minutes. Cut into squares. Serve warm or cool completely.

Favorite recipe from **California Tree Fruit Agreement**

# Butterscotch Pan Cookies

**Makes 48 bars**

1 package DUNCAN HINES®
    Moist Deluxe® French
    Vanilla Cake Mix
2 eggs
1 cup butter or margarine,
    melted

¾ cup firmly packed light brown
    sugar
1 teaspoon vanilla extract
1 package (12 ounces)
    butterscotch flavored chips
1½ cups chopped pecans

*1.* Preheat oven to 375°F. Grease 15½×10½×1-inch jelly-roll pan.

*2.* Combine cake mix, eggs, melted butter, brown sugar and vanilla extract in large bowl. Beat at low speed with electric mixer until smooth and creamy. Stir in butterscotch chips and pecans. Spread in prepared pan. Bake at 375°F for 20 to 25 minutes or until golden brown. Cool completely. Cut into bars.

<u>**Tip:**</u> *You can substitute chocolate or peanut butter flavored chips for the butterscotch flavored chips.*

# Peachy Oatmeal Bars

**Makes 2 to 2½ dozen bars**

Crumb Mixture
    1½ cups all-purpose flour
    1 cup uncooked old-fashioned
        oats
    ¾ cup (1½ sticks) butter, melted
    ½ cup sugar
    2 teaspoons almond extract

½ teaspoon baking soda
¼ teaspoon salt

Filling
    ¾ cup peach preserves
    ⅓ cup flaked coconut

Preheat oven to 350°F. Grease 9-inch square baking pan.

Combine flour, oats, butter, sugar, almond extract, baking soda and salt in large bowl. Beat with electric mixer at low speed 1 to 2 minutes until mixture is crumbly. Reserve ¾ cup crumb mixture; press remaining crumb mixture onto bottom of prepared baking pan.

Spread peach preserves to within ½ inch of edge of crumb mixture; sprinkle reserved crumb mixture and coconut over top. Bake 22 to 27 minutes or until edges are lightly browned. Cool completely. Cut into bars.

# Spring Macaroon Bars

Makes about 24 bars

| | |
|---|---|
| 1 cup graham cracker crumbs | ¼ teaspoon salt |
| 1 cup sugar, divided | 3 egg whites |
| ¼ cup (½ stick) butter or margarine, melted | 1 egg, slightly beaten |
| 3¾ cups (10-ounce package) MOUNDS® Sweetened Coconut Flakes | 1 teaspoon almond extract |
| | 12 red or green maraschino cherries, halved and drained |
| ¼ cup all-purpose flour | |

*1.* Heat oven to 350°F. Lightly grease 8-inch or 9-inch square baking pan.

*2.* Stir together crumbs, ¼ cup sugar and melted butter. Press onto bottom of prepared pan. Bake 5 minutes. Remove from oven; leave oven on.

*3.* Stir together coconut, remaining ¾ cup sugar, flour and salt. Stir in egg whites, egg and almond extract. Spread mixture carefully over crumb mixture. Press in cherry halves.

*4.* Bake 30 to 35 minutes or until lightly browned around edges. Cool completely in pan on wire rack. Cover; refrigerate 6 to 8 hours. Cut into bars. Cover; refrigerate leftover bars.

# Strawberry Cheesecake Squares

**Makes 16 bars**

2 large eggs, divided
1 cup "M&M's"® Chocolate Mini
   Baking Bits, divided
¾ cup graham cracker crumbs
⅓ cup plus 2 tablespoons
   granulated sugar, divided

2 tablespoons butter, melted
1 package (8 ounces) cream
   cheese, softened
1 teaspoon vanilla extract
½ cup seedless strawberry jam
Powdered sugar

*Note:*

Cookies that require
refrigeration, such as
these cheesecake
squares, should be
covered airtight so
they don't absorb
other food odors.

Preheat oven to 350°F. Lightly grease 8×8×2-inch baking pan; set aside. In small bowl separate 1 egg white, reserving egg yolk in another small bowl. In medium bowl combine ⅓ cup "M&M's"® Chocolate Mini Baking Bits, cracker crumbs and 2 tablespoons granulated sugar; stir in butter and 1 egg white. Press dough evenly onto bottom of prepared pan. Bake 8 minutes; cool 5 minutes on wire rack. In large bowl beat cream cheese and remaining ⅓ cup granulated sugar; add reserved egg yolk, remaining whole egg and vanilla until well blended. In small bowl stir jam until smooth. Spread jam evenly over crust. Spread cream cheese mixture evenly over jam layer. Bake 20 minutes. Sprinkle with ⅓ cup "M&M's"® Chocolate Mini Baking Bits; press down slightly. Bake 10 to 15 minutes more or until filling is set. Cool completely on wire rack. Sprinkle with powdered sugar and remaining ⅓ cup "M&M's"® Chocolate Mini Baking Bits. Cut into squares. Store in tightly covered container in refrigerator.

# Banana Cocoa Marbled Bars

½ cup uncooked rolled oats
1½ cups all-purpose flour
2 teaspoons baking powder
½ teaspoon baking soda
½ teaspoon salt
1 cup sugar
½ cup MOTT'S® Natural
    Apple Sauce

1 whole egg
1 egg white
2 tablespoons vegetable oil
⅓ cup low-fat buttermilk
2 tablespoons unsweetened
    cocoa powder
1 large ripe banana, mashed
    (⅔ cup)

**Makes 14 bars**

*1.* Preheat oven to 350°F. Spray 9-inch square baking pan with nonstick cooking spray.

*2.* Place oats in food processor or blender; process until finely ground.

*3.* In medium bowl, combine oats, flour, baking powder, baking soda and salt.

*4.* In large bowl, combine sugar, apple sauce, whole egg, egg white and oil.

*5.* Add flour mixture to apple sauce mixture; stir until well blended. (Mixture will look dry.)

*6.* Remove 1 cup of batter to small bowl. Add buttermilk and cocoa; mix well.

*7.* Add banana to remaining batter. Mix well; spread into prepared pan.

*8.* Drop tablespoonfuls of cocoa batter over banana batter. Run knife through batters to marble.

*9.* Bake 35 minutes or until toothpick inserted in center comes out clean. Cool on wire rack 15 minutes; cut into 14 bars.

# Chewy Red Raspberry Bars

**Makes 12 bars**

1 cup firmly packed light brown
  sugar
½ cup butter or margarine,
  room temperature
½ teaspoon almond extract
1 cup all-purpose flour

1 cup quick-cooking or
  old-fashioned oats
1 teaspoon baking powder
½ cup SMUCKER'S® Red
  Raspberry Preserves

Combine brown sugar and butter; beat until fluffy. Beat in almond extract. Mix in flour, oats and baking powder until crumbly. Reserve ¼ cup mixture; pat remaining mixture into bottom of greased 8-inch square baking pan. Dot preserves over crumb mixture in pan; sprinkle with reserved crumb mixture.

Bake at 350°F for 30 to 40 minutes or until brown. Cool on wire rack. Cut into bars.

# Nutty Chocolate Chunk Bars

**Makes 36 bars**

3 eggs
1 cup DOMINO® Granulated
  Sugar
1 cup DOMINO® Brown Sugar,
  packed
1 cup oat bran
1 cup crunchy peanut butter

¾ cup butter, softened
2 teaspoons baking soda
2 teaspoons vanilla
3½ cups quick-cooking oats
1 package (12 ounces) semi-
  sweet chocolate chunks
1 cup Spanish peanuts

In large bowl, beat eggs, granulated sugar and brown sugar. Add oat bran, peanut butter, butter, baking soda and vanilla. Mix well. Stir in oats, chocolate chunks and peanuts. Spread mixture into greased 15×10×2-inch pan. Bake in 350°F oven 20 to 25 minutes.

# Mississippi Mud Bars

¾ cup packed brown sugar
½ cup (1 stick) butter, softened
1 egg
1 teaspoon vanilla
½ teaspoon baking soda
¼ teaspoon salt
1 cup plus 2 tablespoons
   all-purpose flour

1 cup (6 ounces) semisweet
   chocolate chips, divided
1 cup (6 ounces) white
   chocolate chips, divided
½ cup chopped walnuts or
   pecans

**Makes about 3 dozen bars**

Preheat oven to 375°F. Line 9-inch square pan with foil; grease foil. Beat sugar and butter in large bowl until blended and smooth. Beat in egg and vanilla until light. Blend in baking soda and salt. Add flour, mixing until well blended. Stir in ¾ cup each semisweet and white chocolate chips and nuts. Spread dough in prepared pan. Bake 23 to 25 minutes or until center feels firm. (Do not overbake.) Remove from oven; sprinkle remaining ¼ cup each semisweet and white chocolate chips over top. Let stand until chips melt; spread evenly over bars. Cool in pan on wire rack until chocolate is set. Cut into 2¼×1-inch bars.

*Note:*

Bar cookies lend themselves to endless variations. Substitute different types of chips or nuts for the ones called for in the recipe. Or, make the cookies even more decadent by adding chopped candy bars.

# Maple Walnut Bars

**Makes 24 bars**

1 package DUNCAN HINES®
  Moist Deluxe® Classic
  Yellow Cake Mix, divided
⅓ cup butter or margarine,
  melted
4 eggs, divided

1⅓ cups MRS. BUTTERWORTH'S®
  Maple Syrup
⅓ cup packed light brown sugar
½ teaspoon vanilla extract
1 cup chopped walnuts

*1.* Preheat oven to 350°F. Grease 13×9-inch pan.

*2.* Reserve ⅔ cup cake mix; set aside. Combine remaining cake mix, melted butter and 1 egg in large bowl. Stir until thoroughly blended. (Mixture will be crumbly.) Press into prepared pan. Bake 15 to 20 minutes or until light golden brown.

*3.* Combine reserved cake mix, maple syrup, remaining 3 eggs, sugar and vanilla extract in large mixing bowl. Beat at low speed with electric mixer for 3 minutes. Pour over crust. Sprinkle with walnuts. Bake 30 to 35 minutes or until filling is set. Cool completely in pan. Cut into bars. Store in refrigerator.

# Spiced Date Bars

½ cup margarine, softened
1 cup packed brown sugar
2 eggs
¾ cup light sour cream
2 cups all-purpose flour
1 teaspoon baking soda

1 teaspoon ground cinnamon
½ teaspoon ground nutmeg
1 package (8 or 10 ounces)
   DOLE® Chopped Dates or
   Pitted Dates, chopped
Powdered sugar (optional)

**Makes 24 bars**

**Prep Time:**
*15 minutes*

**Bake Time:**
*30 minutes*

• Beat margarine and brown sugar until light and fluffy. Beat in eggs, one at a time. Stir in sour cream.

• Combine dry ingredients. Beat into sour cream mixture; stir in dates. Spread batter evenly into greased 13×9-inch baking pan.

• Bake at 350°F 25 to 30 minutes or until toothpick inserted in center comes out clean. Cool completely in pan on wire rack. Cut into bars. Dust with powdered sugar, if desired.

## The Baker's Pantry

*If you're going to bake often, your pantry should be stocked with the ingredients that are most commonly used in recipes. (Be careful not to buy too much though, as many items won't keep indefinitely.) This list will get you started—it covers the basics but is not all-inclusive.*

Baking powder
Baking soda
Butter and/or margarine
Chocolate (unsweetened
   and chocolate chips)
Coconut
Corn syrup
Cream cheese

Eggs
Flour (all-purpose)
Nuts
Oats (quick and
   old-fashioned)
Peanut butter
Raisins
Shortening

Spices (cinnamon, ginger,
   nutmeg)
Sugar (brown, granulated
   and powdered)
Sweetened condensed milk
Unsweetened cocoa powder
Vanilla extract
Vegetable oil

# Razzle-Dazzle Apple Streusel Bars

**Makes 2 dozen bars**

**Crust and Streusel**
2½ cups all-purpose flour
2 cups QUAKER® Oats (quick or old fashioned, uncooked)
1¼ cups sugar
2 teaspoons baking powder
1 cup (2 sticks) margarine or butter, melted

**Filling**
3 cups peeled, thinly sliced apples (about 3 medium)
2 tablespoons all-purpose flour
1 (12-ounce) jar (1 cup) raspberry or apricot preserves

*Note:*

All-purpose apples are good for both cooking and eating raw. Some of these varieties include Cortland, Fuji, Granny Smith, Jonathan, McIntosh, Northern Spy and Winesap.

Heat oven to 375°F. For crust and streusel, combine flour, oats, sugar and baking powder; mix well. Add margarine, mixing until moistened. Reserve 2 cups; set aside. Press remaining oat mixture onto bottom of 13×9-inch baking pan. Bake 15 minutes.

For filling, combine apples and flour. Stir in preserves. Spread onto crust to within ½ inch of edge. Sprinkle with reserved oat mixture, pressing lightly. Bake 30 to 35 minutes or until light golden brown. Cool completely; cut into bars. Store tightly covered.

# White Chip Lemon Bars

1¼ cups all-purpose flour, divided
1 cup granulated sugar, divided
⅓ cup butter, softened
¾ cup **HERSHEY'S** Premier
    White Chips

2 eggs, slightly beaten
¼ cup lemon juice
2 teaspoons freshly grated
    lemon peel
Powdered sugar

**Makes about 36 bars**

*1.* Heat oven to 350°F.

*2.* Stir together 1 cup flour and ¼ cup granulated sugar in medium bowl. Cut in butter with pastry blender until mixture resembles coarse crumbs. Press mixture onto bottom of 9-inch square baking pan.

*3.* Bake 15 minutes or until lightly browned. Remove from oven; sprinkle white chips over crust.

*4.* Stir together eggs, lemon juice, lemon peel, remaining ¼ cup flour and remaining ¾ cup sugar in medium bowl; carefully pour over chips and crust.

*5.* Bake 15 minutes or until set. Cool slightly in pan on wire rack; sift with powdered sugar. Cool completely. Cut into bars.

# Fruit and Chocolate Dream Bars

**Makes 2½ dozen bars**

Crust
  1¼ cups all-purpose flour
  ½ cup granulated sugar
  ½ cup (1 stick) butter or
    margarine

Topping
  ⅔ cup all-purpose flour
  ½ cup chopped pecans

⅓ cup packed brown sugar
6 tablespoons butter or
  margarine, softened
½ cup raspberry or strawberry
  jam
1¾ cups (11.5-ounce package)
  NESTLÉ® TOLL HOUSE®
  Milk Chocolate Morsels

**PREHEAT** oven to 375°F. Grease 9-inch-square baking pan.

**For Crust**
**COMBINE** flour and granulated sugar in medium bowl. Cut in butter with pastry blender or two knives until mixture resembles coarse crumbs. Press onto bottom of prepared baking pan.

**BAKE** for 18 to 22 minutes or until set but not brown.

**For Topping**
**COMBINE** flour, nuts and brown sugar in small bowl. Cut in butter with pastry blender or two knives until mixture resembles coarse crumbs.

**SPREAD** jam over hot crust. Sprinkle with morsels and topping.

**BAKE** for 15 to 20 minutes or until golden brown. Cool completely in pan on wire rack.

# S'More Cookie Bars

¾ cup (1½ sticks) IMPERIAL®
  Spread, melted
3 cups graham cracker crumbs
1 package (6 ounces)
  semi-sweet chocolate chips
  (1 cup)

1 cup butterscotch chips
1 cup mini marshmallows
1 can (14 ounces) sweetened
  condensed milk

Preheat oven to 350°F.

In 13×9-inch baking pan, combine Imperial Spread with crumbs; press to form even layer. Evenly sprinkle with chocolate chips, then butterscotch chips, then marshmallows. Pour condensed milk evenly over mixture.

Bake 25 minutes or until bubbly. On wire rack, let cool completely. To serve, cut into squares. For firmer bars, refrigerate 1 hour.

*Note:*

Aluminum pans are generally a baker's first choice. If you use a glass pan, lower the oven temperature by 25 degrees to prevent burning. The cookies should also be checked for doneness about 5 minutes early.

# Coconut Butterscotch Bars

**Makes 36 bars**

½ cup (1 stick) butter or margarine, softened
½ cup powdered sugar
1 cup all-purpose flour
1 can (14 ounces) sweetened condensed milk (not evaporated milk)

1⅓ cups MOUNDS® Coconut Flakes
1 cup HERSHEY'S Butterscotch Chips
1 teaspoon vanilla extract

*Note:*

To cut bar cookies as neatly as possible, use a sharp knife. Make sure to cut all the way through to the bottom of the pan so you can remove the cookies easily.

*1.* Heat oven to 350°F.

*2.* Beat butter and powdered sugar in bowl until blended. Add flour; mix well. Pat mixture onto bottom of ungreased 9-inch square baking pan. Bake 12 to 15 minutes or until lightly browned. Combine sweetened condensed milk, coconut, butterscotch chips and vanilla; spread over baked layer.

*3.* Bake 25 to 30 minutes or until golden brown around edges. (Center will not appear set.) Cool completely in pan on wire rack. Cut into bars.

# Lemon Bars

1 package DUNCAN HINES®
   Moist Deluxe® Lemon
   Supreme Cake Mix
3 eggs, divided
⅓ cup butter-flavor shortening
½ cup granulated sugar

¼ cup lemon juice
2 teaspoons grated lemon peel
½ teaspoon baking powder
¼ teaspoon salt
   Confectioners' sugar

**Makes 30 to 32 bars**

*1.* Preheat oven to 350°F.

*2.* Combine cake mix, 1 egg and shortening in large mixing bowl. Beat at low speed with electric mixer until crumbs form. Reserve 1 cup. Pat remaining mixture lightly into *ungreased* 13×9-inch pan. Bake at 350°F for 15 minutes or until lightly browned.

*3.* Combine remaining 2 eggs, granulated sugar, lemon juice, lemon peel, baking powder and salt in medium mixing bowl. Beat at medium speed with electric mixer until light and foamy. Pour over hot crust. Sprinkle with reserved crumb mixture.

*4.* Bake at 350°F for 15 minutes or until lightly browned. Sprinkle with confectioners' sugar. Cool in pan. Cut into bars.

**Tip:** *These bars are also delicious using Duncan Hines® Moist Deluxe® Classic Yellow Cake Mix.*

# Double Decker Bars

| Makes 24 bars | | |
|---|---|---|
| | 3 ripe DOLE® Bananas, divided | 1 teaspoon vanilla extract |
| | ½ cup margarine | 2 cups all-purpose flour |
| **Prep Time:** | 1 cup granulated sugar | 2 teaspoons baking powder |
| *20 minutes* | 1 cup packed brown sugar | ¼ teaspoon salt |
| | 2 eggs | 2 tablespoons milk |
| **Bake Time:** | ¼ cup plus 3 tablespoons | 2½ cups powdered sugar |
| *35 minutes* | peanut butter, divided | |

• Blend 1 banana in blender (½ cup). Beat margarine, granulated sugar and brown sugar in large bowl. Beat in puréed banana, eggs, 3 tablespoons peanut butter and vanilla.

• Combine flour, baking powder and salt in medium bowl. Gradually beat dry ingredients into banana mixture.

• Spread half of batter in greased 13×9-inch baking pan. Finely chop 1 banana; sprinkle over batter in pan. Cover with remaining batter.

• Bake at 350°F, 30 to 35 minutes. Cool completely.

**Peanut Butter Frosting**
• Blend remaining banana in blender (¼ cup). Combine banana, remaining peanut butter and milk. Slowly beat in powdered sugar until thick and smooth. Frost bars.

# Reese's® Nut Brittle Cookie Bars

1⅔ cups all-purpose flour
2 tablespoons sugar
¾ teaspoon baking powder
½ cup (1 stick) cold butter
    (no substitutes)
1 egg, slightly beaten

2 tablespoons evaporated milk
1⅔ cups (10-ounce package)
    REESE'S® Peanut Butter
    Chips, divided
Nut Filling (recipe follows)

**Makes about 48 bars**

*Note:*

Once opened,
unused evaporated
milk should be stored
in an airtight container
in the refrigerator for
up to five days.

*1.* Heat oven to 375°F.

*2.* Stir together flour, sugar and baking powder in medium bowl. Cut in butter with pastry blender until mixture forms coarse crumbs. Stir in egg and evaporated milk; mix until mixture holds together. Press evenly onto bottom and up sides of 15½×10½×1-inch ungreased jelly-roll pan.

*3.* Bake 8 to 10 minutes or until golden; cool in pan on wire rack. Sprinkle 1 cup peanut butter chips over crust. Prepare Nut Filling; carefully spoon over baked crust and chips. (Do not spread; mixture will spread during baking.)

*4.* Bake 12 to 15 minutes or until filling is caramel colored. Remove from oven; sprinkle remaining ⅔ cup peanut butter chips over top. Cool completely in pan on wire rack; cut into bars.

**Nut Filling:** *Combine 1½ cups sugar, ½ cup (1 stick) butter, ½ cup evaporated milk and ½ cup light corn syrup in 3-quart saucepan. Cook over medium heat, stirring constantly, until mixture boils. Stir in 1½ cups sliced almonds. Continue cooking and stirring over medium heat until mixture reaches 240°F on candy thermometer or until small amount of mixture, when dropped into very cold water, forms a soft ball which flattens when removed from water. (Bulb of candy thermometer should not rest on bottom of saucepan.) Remove from heat; use immediately.*

# Raspberry & White Chip Nut Bars

**Makes about 24 bars**

1⅔ cups (10-ounce package) HERSHEY'S Premier White Chips, divided
¾ cup (1½ sticks) butter or margarine
2¼ cups all-purpose flour
¾ cup sugar
3 eggs

¾ teaspoon baking powder
1⅔ cups (10-ounce package) HERSHEY'S Raspberry Chips, divided
½ cup chopped pecans
Double Drizzle (recipe follows)

*1.* Heat oven to 350°F. Grease 13×9×2-inch baking pan.

*2.* Reserve 2 tablespoons white chips for drizzle. Place remaining white chips and butter in medium microwave-safe bowl. Microwave at HIGH (100%) 1½ minutes; stir. If necessary, microwave at HIGH an additional 15 seconds at a time, stirring after each heating, just until chips are melted when stirred. Combine flour, sugar, eggs and baking powder in large bowl. Add white chip mixture; beat well. Reserve 2 tablespoons raspberry chips for drizzle. Chop remaining raspberry chips in food processor (use pulsing motion); stir into batter with pecans. Spread batter into prepared pan.

*3.* Bake 25 minutes or until edges pull away from sides of pan and top surface is golden. Cool completely in pan on wire rack. Prepare Double Drizzle; using one flavor at a time, drizzle over top of bars. Cut into bars.

**Double Drizzle:** *Place 2 tablespoons HERSHEY'S Premier White Chips and ½ teaspoon shortening (do not use butter, margarine, spread or oil) in small microwave-safe bowl. Microwave at HIGH (100%) 1 minute; stir. If necessary, microwave at HIGH an additional 15 seconds at a time, stirring after each heating, just until chips are melted when stirred. Repeat procedure with raspberry chips.*

**Peanut Butter and Chocolate Bars:** *Omit HERSHEY'S Premier White Chips; replace with REESE'S® Peanut Butter Chips. Omit HERSHEY'S Raspberry Chips; replace with HERSHEY'S Semi-Sweet Chocolate Chips. Omit chopped pecans; replace with ½ cup chopped peanuts.*

**Butterscotch and Chocolate Bars:** *Omit HERSHEY'S Premier White Chips; replace with HERSHEY'S Butterscotch Chips. Omit HERSHEY'S Raspberry Chips; replace with HERSHEY'S Semi-Sweet Chocolate Chips. Omit chopped pecans; replace with ½ cup chopped walnuts.*

# Double Chocolate Chewies

| | |
|---|---|
| 1 package DUNCAN HINES® Moist Deluxe® Butter Recipe Fudge Cake Mix | 1 package (6 ounces) semisweet chocolate chips |
| 2 eggs | 1 cup chopped nuts |
| ½ cup butter or margarine, melted | Confectioners' sugar (optional) |

**Makes 36 bars**

*1.* Preheat oven to 350°F. Grease 13×9×2-inch pan.

*2.* Combine cake mix, eggs and melted butter in large bowl. Stir until thoroughly blended. (Mixture will be stiff.) Stir in chocolate chips and nuts. Press mixture evenly in prepared pan. Bake at 350°F for 25 to 30 minutes or until toothpick inserted in center comes out clean. *Do not overbake.* Cool completely. Cut into bars. Dust with confectioners' sugar, if desired.

**Tip:** *For a special effect, cut a paper towel into ¼-inch-wide strips. Place strips in diagonal pattern on top of cooled bars before cutting. Place confectioners' sugar in tea strainer. Tap strainer lightly to dust surface with sugar. Carefully remove strips.*

# Golden Peanut Butter Bars

**Makes 24 to 36 bars**

**Prep Time:**
*20 minutes*

**Bake Time:**
*40 minutes*

2 cups all-purpose flour
¾ cup firmly packed light
    brown sugar
1 egg, beaten
½ cup (1 stick) cold butter or
    margarine
1 cup finely chopped peanuts

1 (14-ounce) can EAGLE®
    BRAND Sweetened
    Condensed Milk
    (NOT evaporated milk)
½ cup peanut butter
1 teaspoon vanilla extract

*Note:*

Since nuts have a high
oil content, they turn
rancid quickly at room
temperature. If you buy
a large amount of nuts
for baking, freeze them
in airtight containers
or resealable plastic
freezer bags, each one
clearly marked with
the contents and date.

*1.* Preheat oven to 350°F. In large mixing bowl, combine flour, brown sugar and egg; cut in cold butter until crumbly. Stir in peanuts. Reserve 2 cups crumb mixture. Press remaining mixture on bottom of 13×9-inch baking pan.

*2.* Bake 15 minutes or until lightly browned.

*3.* Meanwhile, in another large mixing bowl, beat Eagle Brand, peanut butter and vanilla. Spread over prepared crust; top with reserved crumb mixture.

*4.* Bake an additional 25 minutes or until lightly browned. Cool. Cut into bars. Store covered at room temperature.

# Chewy Chocolate Chip Cookie Squares

Butter Flavor CRISCO® Stick or Butter Flavor CRISCO® all-vegetable shortening for greasing
2¼ cups firmly packed brown sugar
½ Butter Flavor CRISCO® Stick or ½ Butter Flavor CRISCO® all-vegetable shortening, melted

2 cups self-rising all-purpose flour*
2 eggs
1 teaspoon vanilla
1 cup semisweet chocolate chips
¾ cup chopped pecans

*Substitute 2 cups all-purpose flour plus 1 tablespoon baking powder and ¼ teaspoon salt in place of self-rising flour, if desired.

**Makes 4 dozen squares**

*1.* Heat oven to 325°F. Grease 13×9×2-inch pan with shortening. Place cooling rack on countertop.

*2.* Combine brown sugar and ½ cup shortening in large bowl. Beat at low speed with electric mixer until well blended. Add, one at a time, flour, eggs and vanilla. Beat until blended. Add chocolate chips and pecans. Beat just until blended. Spread in greased pan.

*3.* Bake for 30 to 35 minutes or until toothpick inserted in center comes out clean. *Do not overbake.* Cool in pan on cooling rack. Cut into squares about 1½×1½ inches.

# Peanut Butter 'n' Fudge Filled Bars

**Makes 32 bars**

1 cup (2 sticks) margarine or
    butter, softened
2 cups firmly packed brown
    sugar
¼ cup peanut butter
2 eggs
2 cups QUAKER® Oats (quick or
    old fashioned, uncooked)
2 cups all-purpose flour

1 teaspoon baking soda
¼ teaspoon salt (optional)
1 (14-ounce) can sweetened
    condensed milk (not
    evaporated milk)
1 (12-ounce) package (2 cups)
    semisweet chocolate pieces
2 tablespoons peanut butter
½ cup chopped peanuts

Heat oven to 375°F. Beat margarine, sugar and ¼ cup peanut
butter until creamy. Add eggs; beat well. Add combined oats,
flour, baking soda and salt; mix well. Reserve 1 cup oat mixture
for topping; set aside. Spread remaining oat mixture onto bottom
of ungreased 13×9-inch baking pan. In medium saucepan,
combine condensed milk, chocolate pieces and remaining
2 tablespoons peanut butter. Cook over low heat until chocolate
is melted, stirring constantly. Remove from heat; stir in peanuts.
Spread mixture evenly over crust. Drop reserved oat mixture by
teaspoonfuls over chocolate mixture. Bake 30 to 35 minutes or
until light golden brown. Cool completely; cut into bars. Store
tightly covered.

# Apricot Crumb Squares

**Makes 15 squares**

1 package (18.25 ounces) light
    yellow cake mix
1 teaspoon ground cinnamon
½ teaspoon ground nutmeg
6 tablespoons cold margarine,
    cut into pieces
¾ cup uncooked multigrain
    oatmeal cereal or
    old-fashioned oats

1 whole egg
2 egg whites
1 tablespoon water
1 jar (10 ounces) apricot
    fruit spread
2 tablespoons packed light
    brown sugar

Preheat oven to 350°F. Combine cake mix, cinnamon and nutmeg in medium bowl. Cut in margarine with pastry blender or 2 knives until coarse crumbs form. Stir in cereal. Reserve 1 cup mixture. Mix egg, egg whites and water into remaining mixture.

Spread batter evenly in ungreased 13×9-inch baking pan; top with fruit spread. Sprinkle reserved 1 cup cereal mixture over fruit spread; top with brown sugar.

Bake 35 to 40 minutes or until top is golden brown. Cool in pan on wire rack; cut into squares.

## *Note:*

Store eggs in the coldest part of the refrigerator (not in the door, which is the warmest part). When you get your ingredients ready for baking, make sure the eggs don't sit out at room temperature for more than two hours.

# Brown Sugar Shortbread

**Makes 8 servings**

1 cup (2 sticks) I CAN'T
BELIEVE IT'S NOT
BUTTER!® Spread
¾ cup firmly packed light
brown sugar

2 cups all-purpose flour
⅓ cup semisweet chocolate
chips, melted

*Note:*

**The history of shortbread goes back to ancient Scotland. Shortbread traditionally has a tender, crumbly texture that is drier than other bar cookies. It was called "short" because of the large amount of "shortening" used to make it.**

Preheat oven to 325°F. Grease 9-inch round cake pan; set aside.

In large bowl, with electric mixer, beat I Can't Believe It's Not Butter! Spread and brown sugar until light and fluffy, about 5 minutes. Gradually add flour and beat on low until blended. Spread mixture into prepared pan and press into even layer. With knife, score surface into 8 pie-shaped wedges.

Bake 30 minutes or until lightly golden. On wire rack, cool 20 minutes; remove from pan and cool completely. To serve, pour melted chocolate into small plastic storage bag. Snip corner and drizzle chocolate over shortbread. Cut into wedges.

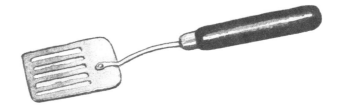

# Swirl of Chocolate Cheesecake Triangles

**Crust**
- 2 cups graham cracker crumbs
- ½ cup (1 stick) butter or margarine, melted
- ⅓ cup granulated sugar

**Filling**
- 2 packages (8 ounces *each*) cream cheese, softened
- 1 cup granulated sugar

- ¼ cup all-purpose flour
- 1 can (12 fluid ounces) NESTLÉ® CARNATION® Evaporated Milk
- 2 large eggs
- 1 tablespoon vanilla extract
- 1 cup (6 ounces) NESTLÉ® TOLL HOUSE® Semi-Sweet Chocolate Morsels

**Makes 30 triangles**

**PREHEAT** oven to 325°F.

**For Crust**
**COMBINE** graham cracker crumbs, butter and sugar in medium bowl; press onto bottom of ungreased 13×9-inch baking pan.

**For Filling**
**BEAT** cream cheese, sugar and flour in large mixer bowl until smooth. Gradually beat in evaporated milk, eggs and vanilla extract.

**MICROWAVE** morsels in medium, microwave-safe bowl on HIGH (100%) power for 1 minute; stir. Microwave at additional 10- to 20-second intervals, stirring until smooth. Stir *1 cup* cream cheese mixture into chocolate. Pour *remaining* cream cheese mixture over crust. Pour chocolate mixture over cream cheese mixture. Swirl mixtures with spoon, pulling plain cream cheese mixture up to surface.

**BAKE** for 40 to 45 minutes or until set. Cool completely in pan on wire rack; refrigerate until firm. Cut into 15 rectangles; cut each rectangle in half diagonally to form triangles.

# Layered Chocolate Cheese Bars

**Makes about 24 bars**

**Prep Time:**
*15 minutes*

1½ cups graham cracker crumbs
¾ cup sugar, divided
¼ cup (½ stick) butter *or*
    margarine, melted
1 package (4 ounces)
    BAKER'S® GERMAN'S®
    Sweet Chocolate

1 package (8 ounces)
    PHILADELPHIA®
    Cream Cheese, softened
1 egg
1 cup BAKER'S® ANGEL FLAKE®
    Coconut
1 cup chopped nuts

**HEAT** oven to 350°F.

**MIX** crumbs and ¼ cup of the sugar. Add butter, mix well. Press evenly onto bottom of 13×9-inch baking pan. Bake 10 minutes.

**MEANWHILE** microwave chocolate in microwaveable bowl on HIGH 1½ to 2 minutes or until almost melted, stirring halfway through heating time. Stir until chocolate is completely melted.

**ADD** cream cheese, egg and remaining ½ cup sugar; mix well. Spread evenly over baked crust. Top with coconut and nuts, pressing into cheese mixture.

**BAKE** for 30 minutes. Cool; cut into bars.

*Note:*

**Supermarkets sell regular and unsalted butter. Unsalted butter has a more delicate flavor and is preferred by many cooks, especially for sauces and baking. Although it varies by manufacturer, salted butter has about 1½ teaspoons added salt per pound.**

# Fabulous Fruit Bars

Makes 16 servings

1½ cups all-purpose flour, divided
1½ cups sugar, divided
½ cup MOTT'S® Apple Sauce, divided
½ teaspoon baking powder
2 tablespoons margarine
½ cup chopped peeled apple

½ cup chopped dried apricots
½ cup chopped cranberries
1 whole egg
1 egg white
1 teaspoon lemon juice
½ teaspoon vanilla extract
1 teaspoon ground cinnamon

*1.* Preheat oven to 350°F. Spray 13×9-inch baking pan with nonstick cooking spray.

*2.* In medium bowl, combine 1¼ cups flour, ½ cup sugar, ⅓ cup apple sauce and baking powder. Cut in margarine with pastry blender or fork until mixture resembles coarse crumbs.

*3.* In large bowl, combine apple, apricots, cranberries, remaining apple sauce, whole egg, egg white, lemon juice and vanilla.

*4.* In small bowl, combine remaining 1 cup sugar, ¼ cup flour and cinnamon. Add to fruit mixture, stirring just until mixed.

*5.* Press half of crumb mixture evenly into bottom of prepared pan. Top with fruit mixture. Sprinkle with remaining crumb mixture.

*6.* Bake 40 minutes or until lightly browned. Broil, 4 inches from heat, 1 to 2 minutes or until golden brown. Cool on wire rack 15 minutes; cut into 16 bars.

# Rocky Road Tasty Team Treats

**Makes about 36 bars**

1½ cups finely crushed thin pretzels or pretzel sticks
¾ cup (1½ sticks) butter or margarine, melted
1 can (14 ounces) sweetened condensed milk (not evaporated milk)

1¾ cups (10-ounce package) HERSHEY₅S MINI KISSES™ Semi-Sweet Chocolates
3 cups miniature marshmallows
1⅓ cups coarsely chopped pecans or pecan pieces

*1.* Heat oven to 350°F. Grease bottom and sides of 13×9×2-inch baking pan.

*2.* Combine pretzels and melted butter in small bowl; press evenly onto bottom of prepared pan. Spread sweetened condensed milk evenly over pretzel layer; layer evenly with Mini Kisses™ Chocolates, marshmallows and pecans, in order. Press down firmly on pecans.

*3.* Bake 20 to 25 minutes or until lightly browned. Cool completely in pan on wire rack. Cut into bars.

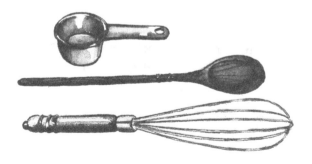

# Yummy Oatmeal Apple Cookie Squares

Makes 3½ dozen bars

1 Butter Flavor CRISCO® Stick or 1 cup Butter Flavor CRISCO® all-vegetable shortening plus additional for greasing
1 cup granulated sugar
1 cup firmly packed brown sugar
2 eggs
⅓ cup apple juice
2 teaspoons vanilla
1½ cups all-purpose flour
2 teaspoons ground cinnamon
1 teaspoon baking powder
1 teaspoon baking soda
¼ teaspoon nutmeg
4 cups quick oats (not instant or old-fashioned)
2 cups peeled, diced apples
½ cup raisins (optional)

*1.* Heat oven to 350°F. Grease 15½×10½×1-inch pan with shortening.

*2.* Combine 1 cup shortening, granulated sugar and brown sugar in large bowl. Beat at medium speed of electric mixer until well blended. Beat in eggs, apple juice and vanilla.

*3.* Combine flour, cinnamon, baking powder, baking soda and nutmeg. Mix into creamed mixture at low speed until blended. Stir in oats, apples and raisins with spoon. Spread in pan.

*4.* Bake at 350°F for 30 to 35 minutes or until browned and toothpick inserted in center comes out clean. *Do not overbake.* Cool in pan on cooling rack. Cut into 2½×1½-inch bars.

*Note:*

Quick oats and old-fashioned oats are essentially the same; the quick oats simply cook faster because they have been rolled into thinner flakes.

# Mint Chocolate Banana Bars

**Makes 16 servings**

**Prep Time:**
*15 minutes*

**Bake Time:**
*25 minutes*

1 cup packed brown sugar
¼ cup margarine, softened
¾ cup mashed DOLE® Banana
   (approximately 2 large
   bananas)
1 egg
1 teaspoon vanilla extract

1½ cups all-purpose flour
1 teaspoon baking powder
14 pieces chocolate mint
   candies, broken into
   small pieces
½ cup toasted walnuts

• Cream together sugar and margarine. Mix in bananas, egg and vanilla. Stir in flour and baking powder until just moistened.

• Gently fold in mint candies.

• Pour into 8-inch square *ungreased* baking dish. Top with toasted walnuts.

• Bake at 350°F, 25 to 30 minutes or until golden brown.

# Walnut Apple Dumpling Bars

**Makes 24 bars**

6 tablespoons (¾ stick) butter
   or margarine
1 cup packed light brown sugar
1 cup all-purpose flour
1½ teaspoons ground cinnamon
1 teaspoon baking powder
2 eggs
1½ cups coarsely chopped
   California walnuts

1 Granny Smith or Pippin
   apple, coarsely grated*
   (about 1 cup lightly packed)
Powdered sugar

*It's not necessary to peel or core apple. Use a hand-held grater, turning the apple as you go, until only core remains.*

Preheat oven to 350°F.

Melt butter in 3-quart saucepan. Add sugar. Stir until sugar is melted and mixture begins to bubble; cool. In small bowl combine flour, cinnamon and baking powder; mix to blend thoroughly. Beat eggs into butter mixture in saucepan, 1 at a time, then add flour mixture. Add walnuts and apple. Turn into buttered and floured 9-inch square baking pan; smooth top. Bake 25 to 35 minutes until toothpick inserted in center comes out clean and edges begin to pull away from sides of pan. Cool completely on rack. Cut into 3×1-inch bars. Garnish with powdered sugar.

Favorite recipe from **Walnut Marketing Board**

*Note:*

If you chop nuts by hand, use a sharp knife on a cutting board to do the job. Don't chop more than 1 cup at a time or the nuts may go flying in every direction.

# White Chocolate Cheesecake Squares

**Makes 4 dozen squares**

*Note:*

These rich cheesecake bars make the perfect dessert for a party since they can be prepared in advance. Keep them tightly covered and refrigerate for up to five days or freeze for up to one month.

⅓ Butter Flavor CRISCO® Stick or ⅓ cup Butter Flavor CRISCO® all-vegetable shortening, melted, plus additional for greasing
1¾ cups finely chopped chocolate cookie crumbs
24 ounces white chocolate, divided

2 (8-ounce) packages cream cheese, softened
½ cup sour cream
4 eggs
2 teaspoons vanilla
¼ cup whipping cream
2 teaspoons almond extract

*1.* Heat oven to 300°F. Grease bottom and sides of 13×9×2-inch baking pan (preferably glass) with shortening.

*2.* Combine ⅓ cup melted shortening and chocolate crumbs in medium bowl. Stir until well blended. Reserve 2 tablespoons. Press remaining mixture into prepared pan.

*3.* Place 16 ounces white chocolate in microwave-safe bowl. Microwave at 50% (MEDIUM) for 1 minute. Stir. Repeat until smooth. (Or, use heavy saucepan over low heat.) Cool slightly.

*4.* Combine cream cheese and sour cream in large bowl. Beat at medium speed of electric mixer until light and fluffy. Add eggs, one at a time. Beat well after each addition. Add vanilla and melted chocolate. Stir until just blended. Pour over crust and distribute evenly.

*5.* Bake at 300°F for 30 minutes. Turn off oven. Leave pan in oven 30 minutes. Remove from oven. Cool completely.

*6.* Place remaining 8 ounces white chocolate in small microwave-safe bowl. Microwave at 50% (MEDIUM) for 1 minute. Stir. Repeat until smooth (or melt in heavy saucepan over low heat). Add whipping cream and almond extract. Mix well. Pour over baked cheesecake. Sprinkle with reserved crumbs. Cover with foil. Refrigerate 8 hours or overnight.

*7.* Cut cheesecake into 1½-inch squares. Cover tightly and refrigerate.

# Zesty Fresh Lemon Bars

**Makes about 3 dozen bars**

**Crust**
- ½ cup butter or margarine, softened
- ½ cup granulated sugar
- Grated peel of ½ SUNKIST® lemon
- 1¼ cups all-purpose flour

**Filling**
- 1 cup packed brown sugar
- 1 cup chopped walnuts
- 2 eggs, slightly beaten

- ¼ cup all-purpose flour
- Grated peel of ½ SUNKIST® lemon
- ¼ teaspoon baking powder

**Glaze**
- 1 cup powdered sugar
- 1 tablespoon butter or margarine, softened
- 2 tablespoons fresh-squeezed SUNKIST® lemon juice

To prepare crust, preheat oven to 350°F. In medium bowl, beat ½ cup butter, granulated sugar and lemon peel. Gradually stir in 1¼ cups flour to form soft dough. Press evenly on bottom of ungreased 13×9×2-inch pan. Bake 15 minutes.

To prepare filling, in medium bowl, combine all filling ingredients. Spread over baked crust. Bake 20 minutes. Meanwhile, prepare glaze.

To prepare glaze, in small bowl, gradually blend small amount of powdered sugar into 1 tablespoon butter. Add lemon juice and remaining powdered sugar; stir to blend well. Drizzle glaze over hot lemon filling. Cool in pan on wire rack; cut into bars. Store tightly covered at room temperature.

# Chocolate Amaretto Squares

| Makes about 16 squares |
| --- |

*Note:*

Amaretto is a liqueur with the flavor of almonds (although it is often made with the kernels of apricot pits). Originally created in Italy, almond-flavored liqueur is now produced by American distilleries as well.

½ cup (1 stick) butter (do *not* use margarine), melted
1 cup sugar
2 eggs
½ cup all-purpose flour
⅓ cup HERSHEY'S Cocoa or HERSHEY'S Dutch Processed Cocoa

1¼ cups ground almonds
2 tablespoons almond-flavored liqueur *or* ½ teaspoon almond extract
Sliced almonds (optional)

*1.* Heat oven to 325°F. Grease 8-inch square baking pan.

*2.* Beat butter and sugar in medium bowl until creamy. Add eggs, flour and cocoa; beat well. Stir in ground almonds and almond liqueur. Pour batter into prepared pan.

*3.* Bake 35 to 40 minutes or just until set. Cool completely in pan on wire rack. Cut into squares. Garnish with sliced almonds, if desired.

# Brownies & Blondies Galore

CHAPTER TEN

# Hershey's Premium Double Chocolate Brownies

**Makes about 36 brownies**

¾ cup HERSHEY'S Cocoa
½ teaspoon baking soda
⅔ cup butter or margarine, melted and divided
½ cup boiling water
2 cups sugar
2 eggs
1 teaspoon vanilla extract

1⅓ cups all-purpose flour
¼ teaspoon salt
2 cups (12-ounce package) HERSHEY'S Semi-Sweet Chocolate Chips
½ cup coarsely chopped nuts (optional)

*1.* Heat oven to 350°F. Grease 13×9×2-inch baking pan.

*2.* Stir together cocoa and baking soda in large bowl; stir in ⅓ cup butter. Add boiling water; stir until mixture thickens. Stir in sugar, eggs, remaining ⅓ cup butter and vanilla; stir until smooth. Gradually add flour and salt to cocoa mixture, beating until well blended. Stir in chocolate chips and nuts, if desired; pour batter into prepared pan.

*3.* Bake 35 to 40 minutes or until brownies begin to pull away from sides of pan. Cool completely in pan on wire rack. Cut into bars.

# Mini Kisses Blondies

**Makes about 36 bars**

½ cup (1 stick) butter or margarine, softened
1⅓ cups packed light brown sugar
2 eggs
2 teaspoons vanilla extract
¼ teaspoon salt

2 cups all-purpose flour
1½ teaspoons baking powder
1¾ cups (10-ounce package) HERSHEY'S MINI KISSES™ Semi-Sweet Chocolates
½ cup chopped nuts

*1.* Heat oven to 350°F. Lightly grease 13×9×2-inch baking pan.

*2.* Beat butter and brown sugar in large bowl until fluffy. Add eggs, vanilla and salt; beat until blended. Add flour and baking powder; beat just until blended. Stir in Mini Kisses™ Chocolates. Spread batter into prepared pan. Sprinkle nuts over top.

*3.* Bake 28 to 30 minutes or until set and golden brown. Cool completely in pan on wire rack. Cut into bars.

# Banana Rum Brownies

| | | Makes 16 servings |
|---|---|---|
| 1 box (about 21 ounces) brownie mix<br>¼ cup chocolate milk or regular milk | 1 tablespoon rum extract<br>3 DOLE® Bananas, cubed<br>½ cup toasted chopped pecans | **Prep Time:**<br>*15 minutes*<br><br>**Bake Time:**<br>*40 minutes* |

• Prepare brownie mix as directed on package in large bowl; set aside.

• Heat milk and extract in medium saucepan until hot. Add bananas and stir for 1 minute to heat through.

• Pour banana mixture and nuts into brownie mix and stir. Pour into lightly greased 9-inch square pan.

• Bake at 350°F 35 to 40 minutes or until toothpick inserted in center comes out clean. Sprinkle with powdered sugar, if desired. Cut into bars.

# Toffee Brownie Bars

**Makes 48 bars**

*Note:*

These bars can be made ahead and frozen in an airtight container for several weeks.

**Crust**
¾ cup butter or margarine, softened
¾ cup firmly packed brown sugar
1 egg yolk
¾ teaspoon vanilla extract
1½ cups all-purpose flour

**Filling**
1 (21-ounce) package DUNCAN HINES® Family-Style Chewy Fudge Brownie Mix

1 egg
⅓ cup water
⅓ cup vegetable oil

**Topping**
1 package (12 ounces) milk chocolate chips, melted
¾ cup finely chopped pecans

*1.* Preheat oven to 350°F. Grease 15½×10½×1-inch pan.

*2.* For crust, combine butter, brown sugar, egg yolk and vanilla extract in large bowl. Stir in flour. Spread in prepared pan. Bake at 350°F for 15 minutes or until golden.

*3.* For filling, prepare brownie mix following package directions. Spread over hot crust. Bake at 350°F for 15 minutes or until surface appears set. Cool 30 minutes.

*4.* For topping, spread melted chocolate on top of brownie layer; sprinkle with pecans. Cool completely.

# Brownie Raspberry Bars

Makes 3 to 4 dozen bars

1 cup (6 ounces) semi-sweet
    chocolate chips
¼ cup (½ stick) butter or
    margarine
2 cups biscuit baking mix
1 (14-ounce) can EAGLE®
    BRAND Sweetened
    Condensed Milk
    (NOT evaporated milk)
1 egg

1 teaspoon vanilla extract
1 cup chopped nuts
1 (8-ounce) package cream
    cheese, softened
½ cup powdered sugar
½ cup red raspberry preserves
    Red food coloring, if desired
    Chocolate Drizzle
    (recipe follows)

*1.* Preheat oven to 350°F. In heavy saucepan over low heat, melt chips with butter.

*2.* In large mixing bowl, combine chocolate mixture, biscuit mix, Eagle Brand, egg and vanilla; mix well. Stir in nuts. Spread in well-greased 15×10×1-inch baking pan. Bake 20 minutes or until center is set. Cool completely.

*3.* In small mixing bowl, beat cream cheese, powdered sugar, preserves and food coloring, if desired, until smooth; spread over brownies. Garnish with Chocolate Drizzle. Chill. Cut into bars. Store covered in refrigerator.

<u>Chocolate Drizzle:</u> *In heavy saucepan over low heat, melt ½ cup semi-sweet chocolate chips with 1 tablespoon shortening. Immediately drizzle over bars.*

# Supreme Chocolate Saucepan Brownies

**Makes about 24 brownies**

1 cup (2 sticks) butter or margarine
2 cups sugar
½ cup HERSHEY'S Cocoa
4 eggs, beaten
⅔ cup all-purpose flour
½ teaspoon salt

¼ teaspoon baking soda
2 teaspoons vanilla extract
2 cups (12-ounce package) HERSHEY'S Semi-Sweet Chocolate Chips
½ cup macadamia nuts, coarsely chopped

*1.* Heat oven to 350°F. Grease 13×9×2-inch baking pan.

*2.* Melt butter in medium saucepan over low heat. Add sugar and cocoa; stir to blend. Remove from heat. Stir in eggs. Stir together flour, salt and baking soda; stir into chocolate mixture. Stir in vanilla, chocolate chips and nuts. Spread in prepared pan.

*3.* Bake 30 to 35 minutes or until brownies begin to pull away from sides of pan and begin to crack slightly; do not underbake. Cool completely; cut into bars.

# Chocolate Peanut Brownie Bars

2 eggs
1 cup sugar
⅔ cup butter, melted
1 teaspoon vanilla
¾ cup flour
⅓ cup unsweetened cocoa
    powder
1 teaspoon baking powder

½ teaspoon salt
1½ cups coarsely chopped,
    peeled and cored apples
    or Bartlett pears
1 cup chopped dry-roasted
    peanuts, divided
½ cup peanut butter morsels

**Makes 16 bars**

Preheat oven to 350°F. Beat eggs in large bowl until fluffy. Blend in sugar, butter and vanilla, beating until sugar is dissolved.

Combine flour, cocoa, baking powder and salt in separate bowl. Stir into egg mixture until dry ingredients are just moistened. Carefully fold in apples or pears, ½ cup peanuts and peanut butter morsels.

Pour into greased 8-inch baking pan; sprinkle with remaining ½ cup peanuts. Bake 30 to 35 minutes or until toothpick inserted into center comes out clean. Remove to wire rack to cool completely. Cut into squares.

Favorite recipe from **Texas Peanut Producers Board**

*Note:*
Unsweetened cocoa powder can be stored in a tightly closed container in a cool, dark place for up to two years.

# Double Decadence Chocolate Chip Brownies

**Makes 2 dozen brownies**

1 cup granulated sugar
1 stick plus 3 tablespoons margarine or butter, softened
2 eggs
1 teaspoon vanilla
2 cups (12-ounce package) semisweet chocolate pieces, divided

1¼ cups all-purpose flour
1 cup QUAKER® Oats (quick or old fashioned, uncooked)
1 teaspoon baking powder
½ cup chopped nuts (optional)
Powdered sugar

Heat oven to 350°F. Lightly grease 13×9-inch baking pan. Beat sugar, margarine, eggs and vanilla until smooth. Add 1 cup chocolate, melted;* mix well. Add flour, oats, baking powder, remaining 1 cup chocolate pieces and nuts, mixing well. Spread into prepared pan. Bake 25 to 30 minutes or until brownies just begin to pull away from sides of pan. Cool completely. Sprinkle with powdered sugar, if desired. Cut into bars.

*To melt 1 cup chocolate pieces: Microwave at HIGH 1 to 2 minutes, stirring every 30 seconds until smooth. Or, heat in heavy saucepan over low heat, stirring until smooth.

# Blonde Brickle Bars

Makes 12 bars

1⅓ cups all-purpose flour
½ teaspoon baking powder
¼ teaspoon salt
2 eggs
½ cup granulated sugar
½ cup packed light brown sugar
⅓ cup butter or margarine,
    melted

1 teaspoon vanilla extract
¼ teaspoon almond extract
1⅓ cups (8-ounce package)
    HEATH® BITS, divided
½ cup chopped slivered
    almonds, toasted
    (see Note)
Vanilla ice cream (optional)

*1.* Heat oven to 350°F. Grease 8-inch square baking pan.

*2.* Mix flour with baking powder and salt; set aside. Beat eggs in medium bowl. Gradually beat in granulated sugar and brown sugar until thick and creamy. Add butter, vanilla and almond extract; beat well. Stir in flour mixture until blended. Fold in ⅔ cup Heath Bits and almonds. Pour batter into prepared pan.

*3.* Bake 25 to 30 minutes or until bar begins to pull away from sides of pan. Remove from oven; immediately sprinkle remaining ⅔ cup bits over top. Cool to room temperature; cut into bars. Serve with scoop of ice cream, if desired.

*Note:*

To toast almonds, heat oven to 350°F. Spread almonds in a thin layer in a shallow baking pan. Bake for 6 to 8 minutes, stirring occasionally, until light brown. Cool almonds completely before chopping.

# Mint in the Mix Brownies

**Makes 16 brownies**

¾ cup (1½ sticks) butter
4 squares (1 ounce each)
    semi-sweet chocolate
1 package (3 ounces) cream
    cheese, softened
1 cup plus 2 tablespoons
    granulated sugar, divided
3 large eggs, divided
1 cup plus 1 tablespoon
    all-purpose flour, divided

¼ teaspoon mint extract
½ teaspoon baking powder
¼ teaspoon salt
1 teaspoon vanilla extract
1 cup "M&M's"® Semi-Sweet
    Chocolate Mini Baking Bits,
    divided
Chocolate Glaze
    (recipe follows)

Preheat oven to 325°F. Lightly grease 8×8×2-inch baking pan; set aside. In small saucepan melt butter and chocolate over low heat. Remove from heat; set aside. In small bowl beat cream cheese and 2 tablespoons sugar until well blended. Beat in 1 egg, 1 tablespoon flour and mint extract; set aside. In large bowl beat remaining 2 eggs and remaining 1 cup sugar until light; blend in 1 cup flour, baking powder and salt. Stir in chocolate mixture, vanilla and ½ cup "M&M's"® Semi-Sweet Chocolate Mini Baking Bits. Spread chocolate mixture in prepared pan. Drop spoonfuls of cream cheese mixture over chocolate mixture; swirl with knife to marble. Bake 50 to 55 minutes or until firm in center. Cool completely on wire rack. Prepare Chocolate Glaze. Drizzle over brownies; sprinkle with remaining ½ cup "M&M's"® Semi-Sweet Chocolate Mini Baking Bits. Cut into bars. Store in tightly covered container.

**Chocolate Glaze:** *In small saucepan over low heat combine 4 teaspoons water and 1 tablespoon butter until it comes to a boil. Stir in 4 teaspoons unsweetened cocoa powder. Gradually stir in ½ cup powdered sugar until smooth. Remove from heat; stir in ¼ teaspoon vanilla extract. Let glaze cool slightly.*

# Marbled Peanut Butter Brownies

⅔ cup all-purpose or
  whole-wheat flour
½ teaspoon baking powder
¼ teaspoon salt
¾ cup firmly packed brown
  sugar
½ cup SMUCKER'S® Creamy
  Natural Peanut Butter

¼ cup butter or margarine,
  softened
2 eggs
1 teaspoon vanilla
3 (1-ounce) squares semisweet
  chocolate or ½ cup
  semisweet chocolate chips,
  melted and cooled

**Makes 24 bars**

Combine flour, baking powder and salt; set aside.

In small bowl of electric mixer, combine brown sugar, peanut butter and butter; beat until light and creamy. Add eggs and vanilla; beat until fluffy. Stir in flour mixture just until blended. Spread in greased 8-inch square baking pan. Drizzle chocolate over batter, then swirl into batter with table knife to marbleize.

Bake in preheated 350°F oven 25 to 30 minutes or until toothpick inserted in center comes out clean. Cool in pan on wire rack. Cut into bars.

*Note:*

Make sure that melted chocolate has cooled to room temperature before adding it to a batter. Warm chocolate can melt the fat in the mixture, which may affect the texture of the final product.

# Peanut Butter Layered Brownies

| Makes 2 dozen brownies |
| --- |

**Prep Time:**
*30 minutes*

**Bake Time:**
*35 minutes*

*Note:*

Lining baking pans with foil makes cutting brownies and bars much easier and cuts down on cleanup time. Leave at least 3 inches of foil hanging over each end, then use the foil to lift the brownies or bars out of the pan.

**Brownies**
- 4 squares BAKER'S® Unsweetened Baking Chocolate
- ¾ cup (1½ sticks) butter or margarine
- 2 cups granulated sugar
- 4 eggs
- 1 teaspoon vanilla
- 1 cup flour

**Peanut Butter Layer**
- 1 cup creamy peanut butter
- ½ cup powdered sugar
- 1 teaspoon vanilla

**Chocolate Glaze**
- 4 squares BAKER'S® Semi-Sweet Baking Chocolate
- 3 tablespoons butter or margarine

### Brownies

HEAT oven to 350°F. Line 13×9-inch baking pan with foil; grease foil.

MICROWAVE chocolate and butter in large microwavable bowl on HIGH 2 minutes or until butter is melted. Stir until chocolate is completely melted. Stir sugar into chocolate mixture until well blended. Mix in eggs and vanilla. Stir in flour until well blended. Spread in prepared pan.

BAKE 30 to 35 minutes or until toothpick inserted in center comes out with fudgy crumbs. DO NOT OVERBAKE. Cool in pan on wire rack.

### Peanut Butter Layer

MIX peanut butter, powdered sugar and vanilla in large bowl until well blended and smooth. Spread over brownies.

### Chocolate Glaze

MICROWAVE chocolate and butter in small microwavable bowl on HIGH 2 minutes or until butter is melted. Stir until chocolate is completely melted. Spread over peanut butter layer. Refrigerate 30 minutes or until firm. Lift out of pan onto cutting board.

**Tip:** *For 13×9-inch glass baking dish, bake at 325°F.*

# Ricotta Cheese Brownies

**Brownie Layer**
- ½ **cup butter or margarine**
- ⅓ **cup unsweetened cocoa**
- 1 **cup sugar**
- 2 **eggs, slightly beaten**
- 1 **teaspoon vanilla**
- ½ **cup all-purpose flour**
- ½ **teaspoon baking powder**
- ¼ **teaspoon salt**

**Cheese Layer**
- ¾ **cup (6 ounces) SARGENTO®**
  **Part-Skim Ricotta Cheese**
- ¼ **cup sugar**
- 1 **egg, slightly beaten**
- 2 **tablespoons butter or**
  **margarine, softened**
- 1 **tablespoon all-purpose flour**
- ½ **teaspoon vanilla**

**Makes 16 brownies**

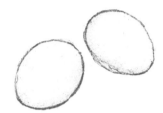

Melt butter in small saucepan; remove from heat. Stir in cocoa; cool. In large bowl of electric mixer, beat sugar, eggs and vanilla on medium speed until light and fluffy. In small bowl, stir together flour, baking powder and salt. Add to egg mixture; beat until blended. Add cocoa mixture; beat until thoroughly combined. Reserve 1 cup batter; spread remaining batter into greased 8-inch square baking pan.

In small bowl of electric mixer, beat Ricotta cheese, sugar, egg, butter, flour and vanilla on medium speed until well blended. Spread over batter in pan. Drop teaspoonfuls of reserved chocolate batter over Ricotta mixture; spread batter with spatula to cover Ricotta mixture. Bake at 350°F 40 minutes. Cool.

# Mississippi Mud Brownies

**Makes 20 to 24 brownies**

1 (21-ounce) package DUNCAN HINES® Family-Style Chewy Fudge Brownie Mix
2 eggs
⅓ cup water
⅓ cup vegetable oil plus additional for greasing

1 jar (7 ounces) marshmallow creme
1 container DUNCAN HINES® Milk Chocolate Frosting, melted

*1.* Preheat oven to 350°F. Grease bottom only of 13×9-inch pan.

*2.* Combine brownie mix, eggs, water and oil in large bowl. Stir with spoon until well blended, about 50 strokes. Spread in pan. Bake at 350°F for 25 to 28 minutes or until set.

*3.* Spread marshmallow creme gently over hot brownies. Pour 1¼ cups melted milk chocolate frosting over marshmallow creme. Swirl with knife to marble. Cool completely. Cut into bars.

**Note:** *Store leftover melted frosting in original container. Refrigerate.*

# Frosted Maraschino Brownies

24 maraschino cherries, drained
1 (23.6-ounce) package brownie mix, plus ingredients to prepare mix
2 cups powdered sugar
½ cup plus 1 tablespoon butter or margarine, softened, divided

3 tablespoons milk
2 tablespoons instant vanilla pudding mix
1 ounce sweet baking chocolate

**Makes about 24 brownies**

Preheat oven to temperature directed on brownie mix. Pat cherries with paper towel to remove excess juice; set aside. Prepare and bake brownie mix according to package directions in 13×9-inch baking pan; cool completely in pan on wire rack.

For frosting, beat sugar, ½ cup butter, milk and pudding mix in medium bowl until smooth. Cover; refrigerate until slightly thickened. Spread over cooled brownie in pan. Arrange cherries in rows over frosting. In small saucepan, over low heat, melt chocolate and remaining 1 tablespoon butter; stir to blend. Cool slightly. Drizzle chocolate mixture over frosting. When chocolate is set, cut brownies into bars.

Favorite recipe from **Cherry Marketing Institute**

*Note:*

Maraschino cherries are most often made from Royal Ann cherries, although any variety can be used. The cherries are pitted and soaked in a flavored sugar syrup, then dyed red or green.

# Easy Double Chocolate Chip Brownies

**Makes 2 dozen brownies**

2 cups (12-ounce package) NESTLÉ® TOLL HOUSE® Semi-Sweet Chocolate Morsels, *divided*
½ cup (1 stick) butter or margarine, cut into pieces

3 large eggs
1¼ cups all-purpose flour
1 cup granulated sugar
1 teaspoon vanilla extract
¼ teaspoon baking soda
½ cup chopped nuts

**PREHEAT** oven to 350°F. Grease 13×9-inch baking pan.

**MELT** *1 cup* morsels and butter in large, *heavy-duty* saucepan over low heat; stir until smooth. Remove from heat. Stir in eggs. Stir in flour, sugar, vanilla extract and baking soda. Stir in *remaining* morsels and nuts. Spread into prepared baking pan.

**BAKE** for 18 to 22 minutes or until wooden pick inserted in center comes out slightly sticky. Cool completely in pan on wire rack.

# Sour Cream Brownies

**Brownies**
- 1 cup water
- 1 cup butter
- 3 tablespoons unsweetened cocoa powder
- 2 cups all-purpose flour
- 2 cups granulated sugar
- 1 teaspoon baking soda
- ½ teaspoon salt
- 1 (8-ounce) container dairy sour cream
- 2 eggs

**Frosting**
- 4 cups sifted powdered sugar
- 3 tablespoons unsweetened cocoa powder
- ½ cup butter, softened
- 6 tablespoons milk
- 1 cup chopped nuts

**Makes about 40 brownies**

*Note:*

Using sifted powdered sugar in the frosting will prevent it from being lumpy.

For brownies, preheat oven to 350°F. Grease 15×10×1-inch baking pan; set aside. Combine water, butter and cocoa in medium saucepan. Cook, stirring constantly, until mixture comes to a boil. Remove from heat; set aside. Combine flour, granulated sugar, baking soda and salt in medium bowl; set aside.

Beat sour cream and eggs at medium speed of electric mixer. Gradually add hot cocoa mixture, beating well. Blend in flour mixture; beat until smooth. Pour batter into prepared pan. Bake 25 to 30 minutes or until brownie springs back when lightly touched. Cool completely in pan on wire rack.

For frosting, combine powdered sugar and cocoa in large bowl; set aside. Beat butter in medium bowl at medium speed of electric mixer until creamy. Add powdered sugar mixture alternately with milk, beating well after each addition. Spread over cooled brownies. Sprinkle nuts over frosting.

Favorite recipe from **Wisconsin Milk Marketing Board**

# Divine Truffle Brownies

**Makes 16 brownies**

**Prep Time:**
*15 minutes*

**Bake Time:**
*40 minutes*

*Note:*

Cream is categorized
according to the
amount of milk fat
it contains.
Heavy whipping
cream contains
36 to 40 percent
milk fat.

1 package (8 squares) BAKER'S®
Semi-Sweet Baking
Chocolate *or* 1 package
(6 squares) BAKER'S®
Bittersweet Baking
Chocolate Squares, divided

¼ cup (½ stick) butter *or*
margarine
¾ cup sugar, divided
3 eggs, divided
¾ cup flour
⅔ cup heavy (whipping) cream

**HEAT** oven to 350°F (325°F for glass baking dish). Line 8-inch baking pan with foil, extending over edges to form handles. Grease foil.

**MICROWAVE** 2 squares of the chocolate and butter in medium microwavable bowl on HIGH 1½ minutes or until butter is melted. Stir until chocolate is melted.

**STIR** ½ cup of the sugar into chocolate mixture. Mix in 1 egg. Stir in flour until well blended. Spread batter in prepared pan.

**MICROWAVE** remaining chocolate (6 squares if using semi-sweet, 4 squares if using bittersweet) and cream in microwavable bowl on HIGH 1½ minutes. Stir until chocolate is completely melted.

**BEAT** remaining ¼ cup sugar and 2 eggs in small bowl with electric mixer on high speed 1 minute until thick and lemon yellow colored; beat in chocolate/cream mixture. Pour over batter in pan.

**BAKE** 35 to 40 minutes or until truffle topping is set and edges begin to pull away from sides of pan. Cool in pan. Run knife around edge of pan to loosen brownies from sides. Lift from pan using foil as handles. Cut into squares.

# Rocky Road Brownies

**Brownie**
- ½ **cup butter or margarine**
- 3 **ounces unsweetened baking chocolate**
- 1 **cup all-purpose flour**
- ¾ **teaspoon baking powder**
- ½ **teaspoon salt**
- 3 **eggs**
- 1½ **cups DOMINO® Granulated Sugar**
- 1½ **teaspoons vanilla**

**Topping**
- ½ **cup chopped peanuts**
- ½ **cup semi-sweet chocolate chips**
- ½ **cup miniature marshmallows**
- ¼ **cup chocolate fudge topping, warmed**

**Makes 2 dozen brownies**

**Prep Time:**
*30 minutes*

**Bake Time:**
*42 minutes*

Heat oven to 350°F. Generously grease 9-inch square baking pan. Melt butter and unsweetened chocolate over low heat in medium saucepan, stirring frequently; cool. Combine flour, baking powder and salt in small bowl; set aside. Beat eggs in large bowl until light. Add sugar, 2 tablespoons at a time, beating until mixture is thick. Add vanilla. Gradually add chocolate mixture to egg mixture. Stir in flour mixture just until blended. Spread evenly into pan. Bake at 350°F for 25 to 30 minutes or until edges slightly pull away from sides of pan. Remove from oven. Sprinkle peanuts, chocolate chips and marshmallows over top; drizzle with chocolate fudge topping. Continue baking 8 to 12 minutes or until lightly browned. Cool completely. Cut into bars.

# Three Great Tastes Blond Brownies

**Makes about 72 bars**

2 cups packed light brown sugar
1 cup (2 sticks) butter or margarine, melted
2 eggs
2 teaspoons vanilla extract
2 cups all-purpose flour
1 teaspoon salt

⅔ cup (of each) HERSHEY'S Semi-Sweet Chocolate Chips, REESE'S® Peanut Butter Chips, and HERSHEY'S Premier White Chips
Chocolate Chip Drizzle (recipe follows)

*1.* Heat oven to 350°F. Grease 15½×10½×1-inch jelly-roll pan.

*2.* Stir together brown sugar and butter in large bowl; beat in eggs and vanilla until smooth. Add flour and salt, beating just until blended; stir in chocolate, peanut butter and white chips. Spread batter into prepared pan.

*3.* Bake 25 to 30 minutes or until wooden pick inserted in center comes out clean. Cool completely in pan on wire rack. Cut into bars. With tines of fork, drizzle Chocolate Chip Drizzle randomly over bars.

**Chocolate Chip Drizzle:** *In small microwave-safe bowl, place ¼ cup HERSHEY'S Semi-Sweet Chocolate Chips and ¼ teaspoon shortening (do not use butter, margarine, spread or oil). Microwave at HIGH (100%) 30 seconds to 1 minute; stir until chips are melted and mixture is smooth.*

# Nuggets o' Gold Brownies

Makes 20 brownies

3 ounces unsweetened baking
    chocolate
¼ cup WESSON® Vegetable Oil
2 eggs
1 cup sugar
1 teaspoon vanilla extract

¼ teaspoon salt
½ cup all-purpose flour
1 (3.8-ounce) BUTTERFINGER®
    Candy Bar, coarsely
    chopped

In microwave-safe measuring cup, heat chocolate 2 minutes on
HIGH in microwave oven. Stir and continue heating in 30-second
intervals until chocolate is completely melted. Stir in oil and set
aside to cool. In mixing bowl, beat eggs until foamy. Whisk in
sugar, then add vanilla and salt. Stir in chocolate mixture, then
mix in flour until all ingredients are moistened. Gently fold in
candy. Pour batter into greased 9-inch baking pan and bake
at 350°F for 25 to 30 minutes or until edges begin to pull away
from sides of pan. Cool before cutting.

## Emergency Baking Substitutions

*Even with a well-stocked pantry, sometimes you run out of an ingredient at the last minute and don't
have time to run to the store. Knowing a few easy substitutions can save the day.*

| IF YOU DON'T HAVE: | USE: |
| --- | --- |
| ½ cup firmly packed brown sugar | ½ cup granulated sugar mixed with 2 tablespoons molasses |
| 1 cup cake flour | 1 cup minus 2 tablespoons all-purpose flour |
| 1 ounce (1 square) unsweetened baking chocolate | 3 tablespoons unsweetened cocoa plus 1 tablespoon shortening |
| 3 ounces (3 squares) semisweet baking chocolate | 3 ounces (½ cup) semisweet chocolate chips |
| 1 cup heavy cream (for baking, not whipping) | ¾ cup whole milk plus ¼ cup butter |
| 1 cup whole milk | 1 cup skim milk plus 2 tablespoons melted butter |
| 1 cup buttermilk | 1 tablespoon lemon juice or vinegar plus milk to equal 1 cup (stir; let stand 5 minutes) |
| 1 cup sour cream | 1 cup plain yogurt |

# Cream Cheese Brownies

**Makes 2 dozen brownies**

**Prep Time:**
*15 minutes*

**Bake Time:**
*40 minutes*

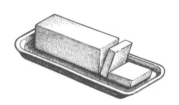

4 squares BAKER'S®
   Unsweetened Baking
   Chocolate
¾ cup (1½ sticks) butter or
   margarine
2½ cups sugar, divided

5 eggs, divided
1¼ cups flour, divided
1 package (8 ounces)
   PHILADELPHIA® Cream
   Cheese, softened

**HEAT** oven to 350°F. Line 13×9-inch baking pan with foil; grease foil.

**MICROWAVE** chocolate and butter in large microwavable bowl on HIGH 2 minutes or until butter is melted. Stir until chocolate is completely melted.

**STIR** 2 cups of the sugar into chocolate mixture until well blended. Mix in 4 of the eggs. Stir in 1 cup of the flour until well blended. Spread in prepared pan. Beat cream cheese, remaining ½ cup sugar, 1 egg and ¼ cup flour in same bowl with wire whisk until well blended. Spoon mixture over brownie batter. Swirl batters with knife to marbleize.

**BAKE** 40 minutes or until toothpick inserted in center comes out with fudgy crumbs. DO NOT OVERBAKE. Cool in pan on wire rack. Lift out of pan onto cutting board.

**Tip:** *For 13×9-inch glass baking dish, bake at 325°F.*

# Decadent Blonde Brownies

1½ cups all-purpose flour
1 teaspoon baking powder
½ teaspoon salt
¾ cup granulated sugar
¾ cup packed light brown sugar
½ cup (1 stick) butter, softened
2 large eggs
2 teaspoons vanilla

1 package (10 ounces)
   semisweet chocolate
   chunks*
1 jar (3½ ounces) macadamia
   nuts, coarsely chopped,
   to measure ¾ cup

*If chocolate chunks are not available, cut
1 (10-ounce) thick chocolate candy bar into
¼-inch pieces to equal 1½ cups.

**Makes 2 dozen brownies**

*Note:*

**Macadamia nuts are native to Australia, but most of the commercial crop is now grown in Hawaii. This small, round nut has a hard brown shell with cream-colored meat and a buttery rich, slightly sweet flavor.**

*1.* Preheat oven to 350°F. Grease 13×9-inch baking pan. Combine flour, baking powder and salt in small bowl; set aside.

*2.* Beat granulated sugar, brown sugar and butter in large bowl with electric mixer at medium speed until light and fluffy. Beat in eggs and vanilla. Add flour mixture. Beat at low speed until well blended. Stir in chocolate chunks and macadamia nuts. Spread batter evenly into prepared pan. Bake 25 to 30 minutes or until golden brown. Remove pan to wire rack; cool completely. Cut into 3¼×1½-inch bars.

# Candy Bar Brownies

**Makes 18 brownies**

1 (21-ounce) package DUNCAN HINES® Family-Style Chewy Fudge Brownie Mix
4 bars (5.3 ounces each) milk chocolate candy bars

⅓ cup mini candy-coated milk chocolate pieces

*Note:*

**For another delicious candy topping, try sprinkling the melted chocolate with ½ cup chopped chocolate-covered toffee chips instead of the candy-coated chocolate pieces.**

*1.* Preheat oven to 350°F. Grease bottom only of 13×9×2-inch baking pan.

*2.* Prepare and bake brownies following package directions for basic recipe chewy brownies. Break chocolate candy bars along scored lines. Place pieces immediately on hot brownies. Cover pan with aluminum foil for 3 to 5 minutes or until chocolate is shiny and soft. Spread gently to cover surface of brownies. Sprinkle with candy-coated chocolate pieces. Cool completely. Cut into bars.

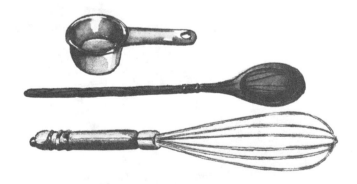

# Chewy Macadamia Nut Blondies

¾ Butter Flavor CRISCO® Stick or ¾ cup Butter Flavor CRISCO® all-vegetable shortening
1 cup firmly packed light brown sugar
1 large egg

1 teaspoon vanilla
1 teaspoon almond extract
1 cup all-purpose flour
½ teaspoon baking soda
⅛ teaspoon salt
6 ounces white chocolate chips
1 cup chopped macadamia nuts

**Makes about 16 bars**

*1.* Heat oven to 325°F.

*2.* Combine ¾ cup shortening and sugar in large bowl. Beat at medium speed with electric mixer until well blended. Beat in egg, vanilla and almond extract until well blended.

*3.* Combine flour, baking soda and salt in small bowl. Add to creamed mixture until just incorporated. *Do not overmix.* Fold in white chocolate chips and nuts until just blended.

*4.* Spray 9-inch square baking pan with CRISCO® No-Stick Cooking Spray. Pour batter into prepared pan. Bake at 325°F for 25 to 30 minutes or until toothpick inserted in center comes out almost dry and top is golden. *Do not overbake or overbrown.*

*5.* Place on cooling rack; cool completely. Cut into bars.

# Sensational Peppermint Pattie Brownies

**Makes about 36 brownies**

24 small (1½-inch) YORK®
   Peppermint Patties
1½ cups (3 sticks) butter or
   margarine, melted
3 cups sugar
1 tablespoon vanilla extract

5 eggs
2 cups all-purpose flour
1 cup HERSHEY⋅S Cocoa
1 teaspoon baking powder
1 teaspoon salt

*1.* Heat oven to 350°F. Remove wrappers from peppermint patties. Grease 13×9×2-inch baking pan.

*2.* Stir together butter, sugar and vanilla in large bowl. Add eggs; beat until well blended. Stir together flour, cocoa, baking powder and salt; gradually add to butter mixture, blending well. Reserve 2 cups batter. Spread remaining batter into prepared pan. Arrange peppermint patties about ½ inch apart in single layer over batter. Spread reserved batter over patties.

*3.* Bake 50 to 55 minutes or until brownies pull away from sides of pan. Cool completely in pan on wire rack.

# Brownie Mint Sundae Squares

1 (21.5- or 23.6-ounce) package
    fudge brownie mix
¾ cup coarsely chopped
    walnuts
1 (14-ounce) can EAGLE®
    BRAND Sweetened
    Condensed Milk
    (NOT evaporated milk)

2 teaspoons peppermint extract
    Green food coloring,
    if desired
2 cups (1 pint) whipping cream,
    whipped
½ cup mini chocolate chips
    Chocolate ice cream topping,
    if desired

**Makes 10 to 12 servings**

*1.* Line 13×9-inch baking pan with aluminum foil; grease foil. Prepare brownie mix as package directs; stir in walnuts. Spread in prepared pan. Bake as directed. Cool completely.

*2.* In large mixing bowl, combine Eagle Brand, peppermint extract and food coloring, if desired. Fold in whipped cream and chips. Pour over brownie layer; cover.

*3.* Freeze 6 hours or until firm. To serve, lift brownies from pan with foil; cut into squares. Serve with chocolate ice cream topping, if desired. Freeze leftovers.

## *Note:*

Peppermint extract, like other extracts, is sensitive to heat and light. To prevent evaporation and loss of flavor, keep bottles of extracts tightly closed and store them in a cool, dark place.

# Creamy Filled Brownies

**Makes about 24 brownies**

½ cup (1 stick) butter or margarine
⅓ cup HERSHEY'S Cocoa
2 eggs
1 cup sugar
½ cup all-purpose flour
¼ teaspoon baking powder
¼ teaspoon salt

1 teaspoon vanilla extract
1 cup finely chopped nuts
Creamy Filling (recipe follows)
MiniChip Glaze (recipe follows)
½ cup sliced almonds or chopped nuts (optional)

***1.*** Heat oven to 350°F. Line 15½×10½×1-inch jelly roll pan with foil; grease foil.

***2.*** Melt butter in small saucepan; remove from heat. Stir in cocoa until smooth. Beat eggs in medium bowl; gradually add sugar, beating until fluffy. Stir together flour, baking powder and salt; add to egg mixture. Add cocoa mixture and vanilla; beat well. Stir in nuts. Spread batter into prepared pan.

***3.*** Bake 12 to 14 minutes or until top springs back when touched lightly in center. Cool completely in pan on wire rack; remove from pan to cutting board. Remove foil; cut brownie in half crosswise. Spread one half with Creamy Filling; top with second half. Spread MiniChip Glaze over top; sprinkle with almonds, if desired. After glaze has set cut into bars.

**Creamy Filling:** *Beat 1 package (3 ounces) softened cream cheese, 2 tablespoons softened butter or margarine and 1 teaspoon vanilla extract in small bowl. Gradually add 1½ cups powdered sugar, beating until of spreading consistency.*

**MiniChip Glaze:** *Heat ¼ cup sugar and 2 tablespoons water to boiling in small saucepan. Remove from heat. Immediately add ½ cup HERSHEY'S MINICHIPS™ Semi-Sweet Chocolate, stirring until melted.*

*Note:*

When adding eggs to a batter, break them one at a time into a small bowl before adding them to the mixing bowl. Breaking eggs directly into the batter runs the risk of ruining the whole mixture with one bad egg.

**Filling Variations:** *Coffee: Add 1 teaspoon powdered instant coffee. Orange: Add ½ teaspoon freshly grated orange peel and 1 or 2 drops orange food color. Almond: Add ¼ teaspoon almond extract.*

# Orange Cappuccino Brownies

¾ cup (1½ sticks) butter
2 squares (1 ounce each)
   semisweet chocolate,
   coarsely chopped
2 squares (1 ounce each)
   unsweetened chocolate,
   coarsely chopped
1¾ cups granulated sugar
1 tablespoon instant espresso
   powder or instant coffee
   granules

3 eggs
¼ cup orange-flavored liqueur
2 teaspoons grated orange peel
1 cup all-purpose flour
1 package (12 ounces)
   semisweet chocolate chips
2 tablespoons shortening

> Makes about 2 dozen brownies

Preheat oven to 350°F. Grease 13×9-inch baking pan.

Melt butter and chopped chocolates in large heavy saucepan over low heat, stirring constantly. Stir in granulated sugar and espresso powder. Remove from heat. Cool slightly. Beat in eggs, 1 at a time. Whisk in liqueur and orange peel. Beat flour into chocolate mixture just until blended. Spread batter evenly in prepared pan.

Bake 25 to 30 minutes or until center is just set. Remove pan to wire rack. Meanwhile, melt chocolate chips and shortening in small heavy saucepan over low heat, stirring constantly. Immediately, spread hot chocolate mixture over warm brownies. Cool completely in pan on wire rack. Cut into 2-inch squares.

# Almond Brownies

**Makes 16 brownies**

*Note:*

Remove brownies from the oven while still moist. A toothpick inserted into the center of the pan should have a few crumbs clinging.

½ cup (1 stick) butter
2 squares (1 ounce each) unsweetened baking chocolate
2 large eggs
1 cup firmly packed light brown sugar
¼ teaspoon almond extract

½ cup all-purpose flour
1½ cups "M&M's"® Chocolate Mini Baking Bits, divided
½ cup slivered almonds, toasted and divided
Chocolate Glaze (recipe follows)

Preheat oven to 350°F. Grease and flour 8×8×2-inch baking pan; set aside. In small saucepan melt butter and chocolate over low heat; stir to blend. Remove from heat; let cool. In medium bowl beat eggs and brown sugar until well blended; stir in chocolate mixture and almond extract. Add flour. Stir in 1 cup "M&M's"® Chocolate Mini Baking Bits and ¼ cup almonds. Spread batter evenly in prepared pan. Bake 25 to 28 minutes or until firm in center. Cool completely on wire rack. Prepare Chocolate Glaze. Spread over brownies; decorate with remaining ½ cup "M&M's"® Chocolate Mini Baking Bits and remaining ¼ cup almonds. Cut into bars. Store in tightly covered container.

<u>**Chocolate Glaze:**</u> *In small saucepan over low heat combine 4 teaspoons water and 1 tablespoon butter until it comes to a boil. Stir in 4 teaspoons unsweetened cocoa powder. Gradually stir in ½ cup powdered sugar until smooth. Remove from heat; stir in ¼ teaspoon vanilla extract. Let glaze cool slightly.*

# Cheesecake Marble Brownies

6 squares (1 ounce each)
semi-sweet chocolate
¾ cup (1½ sticks) IMPERIAL®
Spread, softened, divided
1¾ cups all-purpose flour, divided
1 teaspoon baking powder
½ teaspoon salt

2 cups sugar, divided
4 eggs, divided
1½ teaspoons vanilla extract, divided
1 package (8 ounces) cream cheese, softened

**Makes 24 brownies**

Preheat oven to 350°F. Grease 13×9-inch baking pan; set aside.

In medium saucepan, melt chocolate with ½ cup Imperial Spread over low heat, stirring occasionally. Remove from heat and let cool slightly. In medium bowl, blend 1½ cups flour, baking powder and salt; set aside.

In medium bowl, with wire whisk, beat 1¼ cups sugar, 3 eggs and ½ teaspoon vanilla. Stir egg mixture, then flour mixture, into cooled chocolate mixture. Spread into prepared pan.

In medium bowl, with electric mixer, beat cream cheese, remaining ¾ cup sugar and ¼ cup Imperial Spread until smooth. Beat in remaining egg and 1 teaspoon vanilla, then remaining ¼ cup flour. Spoon over chocolate batter and gently spread in even layer. With tip of knife, gently marble in cream cheese mixture.

Bake 30 minutes or until set. On wire rack, cool completely. To serve, cut into bars.

# Layers of Love Chocolate Brownies

**Makes 16 brownies**

¾ cup all-purpose flour
¾ cup NESTLÉ® TOLL HOUSE®
    Baking Cocoa
¼ teaspoon salt
½ cup (1 stick) butter, cut in
    pieces
½ cup granulated sugar
½ cup packed brown sugar
3 large eggs, *divided*

2 teaspoons vanilla extract
1 cup chopped pecans
¾ cup NESTLÉ® TOLL HOUSE®
    Premier White Morsels
½ cup caramel ice cream
    topping
¾ cup NESTLÉ® TOLL HOUSE®
    Semi-Sweet Chocolate
    Morsels

**PREHEAT** oven to 350°F. Grease 8-inch-square baking pan.

**COMBINE** flour, cocoa and salt in small bowl. Beat butter, granulated sugar and brown sugar in large mixer bowl until creamy. Add *2 eggs,* one at a time, beating well after each addition. Add vanilla extract; mix well. Gradually beat in flour mixture. Reserve *¾ cup* batter. Spread *remaining* batter into prepared baking pan. Sprinkle pecans and white morsels over batter. Drizzle caramel topping over top. Beat *remaining* egg and *reserved* batter in same large bowl until light in color. Stir in semi-sweet morsels. Spread evenly over caramel topping.

**BAKE** for 30 to 35 minutes or until center is set. Cool completely in pan on wire rack. Cut into squares.

# Fudge Topped Brownies

2 cups sugar
1 cup (2 sticks) butter or
    margarine, melted
1 cup all-purpose flour
⅔ cup unsweetened cocoa
½ teaspoon baking powder
2 eggs
½ cup milk
3 teaspoons vanilla extract,
    divided

1 cup chopped nuts, if desired
2 cups (12 ounces) semi-sweet
    chocolate chips
1 (14-ounce) can EAGLE®
    BRAND Sweetened
    Condensed Milk
    (NOT evaporated milk)
Dash salt

Makes 3 to 3½ dozen
brownies

*1.* Preheat oven to 350°F. In large mixing bowl, combine sugar, butter, flour, cocoa, baking powder, eggs, milk and 1½ teaspoons vanilla; mix well. Stir in nuts, if desired. Spread in greased 13×9-inch baking pan. Bake 40 minutes or until brownies begin to pull away from sides of pan.

*2.* Meanwhile, in heavy saucepan over low heat, melt chips with Eagle Brand, remaining 1½ teaspoons vanilla and salt. Remove from heat. Immediately spread over hot brownies. Cool. Chill. Cut into bars. Store covered at room temperature.

*Note:*

To prevent overdone
edges and an
underdone center
in brownies, wrap
foil strips around just
the outside edges of
the baking pan.

# Green's Butterscotch Blondies

**Makes 3 dozen blondies**

½ cup (1 stick) butter, softened
¾ cup granulated sugar
¾ cup firmly packed light brown sugar
2 large eggs
1½ teaspoons vanilla extract
1½ cups all-purpose flour
1 teaspoon baking powder

½ teaspoon salt
1¼ cups "M&M's"® Semi-Sweet Chocolate Mini Baking Bits, divided
½ cup butterscotch chips
½ cup chopped pecans
¼ cup caramel ice cream topping

*Note:*

For even layers of brownies and bars, pour the batter or dough into the center of the pan. Use a rubber spatula to spread the batter out to the sides and into the corners of the pan.

Preheat oven to 350°F. Lightly grease 13×9-inch baking pan; set aside. In large bowl beat butter and sugars until light and fluffy; beat in eggs and vanilla. In medium bowl combine flour, baking powder and salt; add to creamed mixture. Stir in 1 cup "M&M's"® Semi-Sweet Chocolate Mini Baking Bits, butterscotch chips and pecans. Spread in prepared pan. Drop spoonfuls of caramel topping on batter; swirl with knife to marble. Sprinkle with remaining ¼ cup "M&M's"® Semi-Sweet Chocolate Mini Baking Bits. Bake about 25 minutes or until golden brown. Remove pan to wire rack; cool completely. Cut into bars. Store in tightly covered container.

# Cindy's Fudgy Brownies

**Makes 24 brownies**

1 (21-ounce) package
  DUNCAN HINES® Family-
  Style Chewy Fudge
  Brownie Mix
1 egg

⅓ cup water
⅓ cup vegetable oil
¾ cup semisweet chocolate
  chips
½ cup chopped pecans

*1.* Preheat oven to 350°F. Grease bottom only of 13×9×2-inch baking pan.

*2.* Combine brownie mix, egg, water and oil in large bowl. Stir with spoon until well blended, about 50 strokes. Stir in chocolate chips. Spread in prepared pan. Sprinkle with pecans. Bake at 350°F for 25 to 28 minutes or until set. Cool completely. Cut into bars.

**Tip:** *Overbaking brownies will cause them to become dry. Follow the recommended baking times given in recipes closely.*

# Macaroon Brownies

**Makes 24 brownies**

1 (21-ounce) package DUNCAN HINES® Family-Style Chewy Fudge Brownie Mix
2 egg whites

½ cup granulated sugar
¼ teaspoon almond extract
1 cup finely chopped almonds
1 cup flaked coconut

*1.* Preheat oven to 350°F. Grease bottom only of 13×9-inch pan.

*2.* Prepare brownies as directed on package for cake-like brownies. Bake at 350°F for 25 minutes or until set. Place egg whites in medium mixing bowl. Beat at high speed with electric mixer until foamy and double in volume. Beat in sugar gradually, beating until meringue forms firm peaks. Add almond extract. Fold in almonds and coconut. Spread over warm brownies. Bake at 350°F for 12 to 14 minutes or until meringue is set and lightly browned. Cool completely in pan. Cut into bars.

**Tip:** *Spread the meringue to the edges of the pan to prevent meringue from shrinking.*

# Fabulous Blonde Brownies

**Makes 3 dozen**

1¾ cups all-purpose flour
1 teaspoon baking powder
¼ teaspoon salt
1 cup (6 ounces) white chocolate chips
1 cup (4 ounces) blanched whole almonds, chopped

1 cup toffee baking pieces
1½ cups packed light brown sugar
⅔ cup butter, softened
2 eggs
2 teaspoons vanilla

Preheat oven to 350°F. Lightly grease 13×9-inch baking pan. Combine flour, baking powder and salt in small bowl; mix well. Combine white chocolate chips, almonds and toffee pieces in medium bowl; mix well.

Beat brown sugar and butter in large bowl with electric mixer at medium speed until light and fluffy. Beat in eggs and vanilla. Add flour mixture; beat at low speed until well blended. Stir in ¾ cup of white chocolate chip mixture. Spread evenly in prepared pan.

Bake 20 minutes. Immediately sprinkle remaining white chocolate chip mixture evenly over brownies. Press lightly. Bake 15 to 20 minutes or until toothpick inserted into center comes out clean. Cool brownies completely in pan on wire rack. Cut into 2×1½-inch bars.

# Quick No-Bake Brownies

| | | |
|---|---|---|
| 1 cup finely chopped nuts, divided<br>2 (1-ounce) squares unsweetened chocolate<br>1 (14-ounce) can EAGLE® BRAND Sweetened Condensed Milk (NOT evaporated milk) | 2 to 2½ cups vanilla wafer crumbs (about 48 to 60 wafers) | **Makes 24 brownies**<br><br>**Prep Time:**<br>*15 minutes*<br><br>**Chill Time:**<br>*4 hours* |

*1.* Grease 9-inch square pan with butter. Sprinkle ¼ cup nuts evenly over bottom of pan. In heavy saucepan over low heat, melt chocolate with Eagle Brand. Cook and stir until mixture thickens, about 10 minutes.

*2.* Remove from heat; stir in crumbs and ½ cup nuts. Spread evenly in prepared pan.

*3.* Top with remaining ¼ cup nuts. Chill 4 hours or until firm. Cut into squares. Store loosely covered at room temperature.

# White Chip Island Blondies

**Makes about 16 bars**

*Note:*

For neat, attractive slices, turn cooled bars or brownies upside down onto a cutting board—the top doesn't crumble when the bars are cut from the bottom.

1 cup plus 2 tablespoons all-purpose flour
1 teaspoon baking powder
¼ teaspoon salt
¾ cup packed light brown sugar
⅓ cup butter or margarine, softened
½ teaspoon vanilla extract

1 large egg
1 cup (6 ounces) NESTLÉ® TOLL HOUSE® Premier White Morsels
½ cup coarsely chopped macadamia nuts
½ cup toasted coconut

**PREHEAT** oven to 350°F. Grease 9-inch-square baking pan.

**COMBINE** flour, baking powder and salt in medium bowl. Beat sugar, butter and vanilla extract in large mixer bowl until creamy. Beat in egg. Gradually beat in flour mixture. Stir in morsels, nuts and coconut. Press into prepared baking pan.

**BAKE** for 20 to 25 minutes or until golden brown. Cool completely in pan on wire rack. Cut into bars.

# Triple Chocolate Brownies

3 squares (1 ounce each)
    unsweetened chocolate,
    coarsely chopped
2 squares (1 ounce each)
    semisweet chocolate,
    coarsely chopped
½ cup (1 stick) butter
1 cup all-purpose flour

½ teaspoon salt
¼ teaspoon baking powder
1½ cups sugar
3 large eggs
1 teaspoon vanilla
¼ cup sour cream
½ cup milk chocolate chips
    Powdered sugar (optional)

**Makes 2 dozen brownies**

Preheat oven to 350°F. Lightly grease 13×9-inch baking pan.

Place unsweetened chocolate, semisweet chocolate and butter in medium microwavable bowl. Microwave at HIGH 2 minutes or until butter is melted; stir until chocolate is completely melted. Cool to room temperature.

Place flour, salt and baking powder in small bowl; stir to combine.

Beat sugar, eggs and vanilla in large bowl with electric mixer at medium speed until slightly thickened. Beat in chocolate mixture until well combined. Add flour mixture; beat at low speed until blended. Add sour cream; beat at low speed until combined. Stir in milk chocolate chips. Spread mixture evenly into prepared pan.

Bake 20 to 25 minutes or until toothpick inserted into center comes out almost clean. (Do not overbake.) Cool brownies completely in pan on wire rack. Cut into 2-inch squares. Place powdered sugar in fine-mesh strainer; sprinkle over brownies, if desired.

Store tightly covered at room temperature or freeze up to 3 months.

# Scrumptious Minted Brownies

**Makes 36 brownies**

1 (21-ounce) package DUNCAN HINES® Family-Style Chewy Fudge Brownie Mix
1 egg

⅓ cup water
⅓ cup vegetable oil
48 chocolate crème de menthe candy wafers, divided

*1.* Preheat oven to 350°F. Grease bottom only of 13×9-inch pan.

*2.* Combine brownie mix, egg, water and oil in large bowl. Stir with spoon until well blended, about 50 strokes. Spread in prepared pan. Bake at 350°F for 25 minutes or until set. Place 30 candy wafers evenly over hot brownies. Let stand for 1 minute to melt. Spread candy wafers to frost brownies. Score frosting into 36 bars by running tip of knife through melted candy. (Do not cut through brownies.) Cut remaining 18 candy wafers in half lengthwise; place halves on each scored bar. Cool completely. Cut into bars.

# Fruit & Pecan Brownies

**Makes 16 brownies**

2 squares (1 ounce each) unsweetened chocolate
1 cup sugar
½ cup (1 stick) butter, softened
2 eggs
1 teaspoon vanilla

½ cup all-purpose flour
1 cup chopped dried mixed fruit
1 cup coarsely chopped pecans, divided
1 cup (6 ounces) semisweet chocolate chips, divided

Preheat oven to 350°F. Butter 8-inch square pan. Melt unsweetened chocolate in top of double boiler over hot, not boiling, water. Remove from heat; cool. Cream sugar and butter in large bowl until smooth. Mix in eggs, beating until light and fluffy. Blend n melted chocolate and vanilla. Stir in flour, fruit, ½ cup pecans and ½ cup chocolate chips. Spread batter evenly in prepared pan. Sprinkle with remaining ½ cup pecans and ½ cup chocolate chips. Bake 25 to 30 minutes or just until center feels firm. Do not overbake. Remove from oven; cover while still warm with waxed paper or foil. Cool completely in pan on wire rack. Cut into 2-inch squares.

# Honey Brownies

| | | Makes 16 brownies |
|---|---|---|
| 1 cup (6 ounces) semisweet chocolate chips | ½ cup all-purpose flour | |
| 6 tablespoons butter | ½ teaspoon baking powder | |
| 2 eggs | Dash salt | |
| ⅓ cup honey | 1 cup chopped walnuts | |
| 1 teaspoon vanilla | | |

Preheat oven to 350°F. Lightly grease 8-inch square baking pan. Melt chocolate chips and butter in medium heavy saucepan over low heat. Remove from heat; cool slightly. Stir in eggs, honey and vanilla. Combine flour, baking powder, salt and walnuts in small bowl. Stir into chocolate mixture. Spread batter evenly in prepared pan. Bake 20 to 25 minutes or just until center feels springy. Cool in pan on wire rack. Cut into 2-inch squares.

# Mocha Fudge Brownies

**Makes 16 brownies**

3 squares (1 ounce each)
   semisweet chocolate
¾ cup sugar
½ cup (1 stick) butter, softened
2 eggs
2 teaspoons instant espresso
   coffee powder

1 teaspoon vanilla
½ cup all-purpose flour
½ cup chopped toasted almonds
1 cup (6 ounces) milk chocolate
   chips, divided

Preheat oven to 350°F. Grease 8-inch square pan. Melt semisweet chocolate in top of double boiler over hot, not boiling, water. Remove from heat; cool. Cream sugar and butter in medium bowl. Beat in eggs until light and fluffy. Add melted chocolate, coffee powder and vanilla. Blend in flour, almonds and ½ cup chocolate chips. Spread batter evenly in prepared pan. Bake 25 minutes or just until firm in center. Remove from oven; sprinkle with remaining ½ cup chocolate chips. Let stand a few minutes until chips melt, then spread evenly over brownies. Cool completely in pan on wire rack. Cut into 2-inch squares.

# Irresistible Peanut Butter Chip Brownies

1 cup (2 sticks) butter or
   margarine, softened
1 package (3 ounces) cream
   cheese, softened
2 cups sugar
3 eggs
1 teaspoon vanilla extract
1 cup all-purpose flour

¾ cup HERSHEY'S Cocoa
½ teaspoon salt
¼ teaspoon baking powder
1⅔ cups (10-ounce package)
   REESE'S® Peanut Butter
   Chips
Brownie Frosting
   (recipe follows, optional)

**Makes about 36 bars**

*1.* Heat oven to 325°F. Grease bottom of 13×9×2-inch baking pan.

*2.* Beat butter, cream cheese and sugar until fluffy. Beat in eggs and vanilla. Combine flour, cocoa, salt and baking powder; gradually add to butter mixture, beating well. Stir in chips. Spread batter into pan.

*3.* Bake 35 to 40 minutes or until brownies begin to pull away from sides of pan. Cool completely. Frost with Brownie Frosting, if desired. Cut into bars.

**Brownie Frosting:** *Beat 3 tablespoons softened butter or margarine and 3 tablespoons HERSHEY'S Cocoa until blended. Gradually add 1⅓ cups powdered sugar and ¾ teaspoon vanilla extract alternately with 1 to 2 tablespoons milk, beating to spreading consistency. Makes about 1 cup.*

*Note:*

Deliciously rich brownies are a great make-ahead treat. Unfrosted, brownies can keep up to four days tightly covered at room temperature, or they can be frozen for up to four months.

# Chocolate Chip & Sour Cream Brownies

**Makes about 30 brownies**

1 cup packed light brown sugar
½ cup (1 stick) butter, softened
1 egg
1 cup sour cream
1 teaspoon vanilla
½ cup unsweetened cocoa powder

½ teaspoon baking soda
¼ teaspoon salt
2 cups all-purpose flour
1 cup (6 ounces) semisweet chocolate chips
Powdered sugar

Preheat oven to 350°F. Butter 13×9-inch baking pan. Cream brown sugar and butter in large bowl until blended. Add egg, sour cream and vanilla; beat until light. Add cocoa, baking soda and salt; beat until smooth. Blend in flour until well mixed. Stir in chocolate chips; spread batter evenly in prepared pan. Bake 25 to 30 minutes or until center springs back when touched. Cool in pan on wire rack. Sift powdered sugar over the top. Cut into 2½×1½-inch bars.

# White Chocolate Brownies

6 tablespoons butter
5 squares (1 ounce each)
    white chocolate, divided
1 large egg
½ cup granulated sugar
¾ cup all-purpose flour

¾ teaspoon vanilla extract
¼ teaspoon salt
1¼ cups "M&M's"® Semi-Sweet
    Chocolate Mini Baking Bits,
    divided
½ cup chopped walnuts

**Makes 16 brownies**

Preheat oven to 325°F. Lightly grease 8×8×2-inch baking pan;
set aside. In small saucepan melt butter and 4 squares white
chocolate over low heat; stir to blend. Remove from heat; let
cool slightly. In medium bowl beat egg and sugar until light;
stir in white chocolate mixture, flour, vanilla and salt. Spread
batter evenly in prepared pan. Sprinkle with ¾ cup "M&M's"®
Semi-Sweet Chocolate Mini Baking Bits and walnuts. Bake
35 to 37 minutes or until firm in center. Cool completely on
wire rack. Place remaining 1 square white chocolate in small
microwave-safe bowl. Microwave at HIGH 20 seconds; stir.
Repeat as necessary until white chocolate is completely melted,
stirring at 10-second intervals. Drizzle over brownies and sprinkle
with remaining ½ cup "M&M's"® Semi-Sweet Chocolate Mini
Baking Bits. Cut into bars. Store in tightly covered container.

# Caramel Fudge Brownies

**Makes 3 dozen brownies**

*Note:*

The flavor of vanilla extract greatly diminishes when cooked, so it's best to add vanilla to a hot mixture off the heat or after it has cooled slightly.

1 jar (12 ounces) hot caramel
　　ice cream topping
1¼ cups all-purpose flour, divided
¼ teaspoon baking powder
　　Dash salt
4 squares (1 ounce each)
　　unsweetened chocolate,
　　coarsely chopped

¾ cup (1½ sticks) butter
2 cups sugar
3 eggs
2 teaspoons vanilla
¾ cup semisweet chocolate
　　chips
¾ cup chopped pecans

*1.* Preheat oven to 350°F. Lightly grease 13×9-inch baking pan.

*2.* Combine caramel topping and ¼ cup flour in small bowl; set aside. Combine remaining 1 cup flour, baking powder and salt in small bowl; mix well.

*3.* Place unsweetened chocolate and butter in medium microwavable bowl. Microwave at HIGH (100%) 2 minutes or until butter is melted; stir until chocolate is completely melted.

*4.* Stir sugar into melted chocolate. Add eggs and vanilla; stir until combined. Add flour mixture, stirring until well blended. Spread chocolate mixture evenly in prepared pan.

*5.* Bake 25 minutes. Immediately after removing brownies from oven, spread caramel mixture over brownies. Sprinkle top evenly with chocolate chips and pecans.

*6.* Return pan to oven; bake 20 to 25 minutes or until topping is golden brown and bubbling. *Do not overbake.* Cool brownies completely in pan on wire rack. Cut into 2×1½-inch bars.

*7.* Store tightly covered at room temperature or freeze up to 3 months.

# Hershey's Best Brownies

1 cup (2 sticks) butter or
  margarine
2 cups sugar
2 teaspoons vanilla extract
4 eggs
¾ cup HERSHEY'S Cocoa or
  HERSHEY'S Dutch
  Processed Cocoa

1 cup all-purpose flour
½ teaspoon baking powder
¼ teaspoon salt
1 cup chopped nuts (optional)

**Makes about
36 brownies**

*1.* Heat oven to 350°F. Grease 13×9×2-inch baking pan.

*2.* Place butter in large microwave-safe bowl. Microwave at HIGH (100%) 2 to 2½ minutes or until melted. Stir in sugar and vanilla. Add eggs, one at a time, beating well with spoon after each addition. Add cocoa; beat until well blended. Add flour, baking powder and salt; beat well. Stir in nuts, if desired. Pour batter into prepared pan.

*3.* Bake 30 to 35 minutes or until brownies begin to pull away from sides of pan. Cool completely in pan on wire rack. Cut into bars.

# Festive Fruited White Chip Blondies

**Makes about 16 bars**

½ cup (1 stick) butter or
    margarine
1⅔ cups (10-ounce package)
    HERSHEY'S Premier White
    Chips, divided
2 eggs
¼ cup granulated sugar

1¼ cups all-purpose flour
⅓ cup orange juice
¾ cup cranberries, chopped
¼ cup chopped dried apricots
½ cup coarsely chopped nuts
¼ cup packed light brown sugar

*Note:*

To prevent chopped dried fruit from sinking to the bottom of the batter, toss it with a small amount of flour from the recipe (a few teaspoons) before stirring it into the batter.

*1.* Heat oven to 325°F. Grease and flour 9-inch square baking pan.

*2.* Melt butter in medium saucepan; stir in 1 cup white chips. In large bowl, beat eggs until foamy. Add granulated sugar; beat until thick and pale yellow in color. Add flour, orange juice and white chip mixture; beat just until combined. Spread one-half of batter, about 1¼ cups, into prepared pan.

*3.* Bake 15 minutes or until edges are lightly browned; remove from oven.

*4.* Stir cranberries, apricots and remaining ⅔ cup white chips into remaining one-half of batter; spread over top of hot baked mixture. Stir together nuts and brown sugar; sprinkle over top.

*5.* Bake 25 to 30 minutes or until edges are lightly browned. Cool completely in pan on wire rack. Cut into bars.

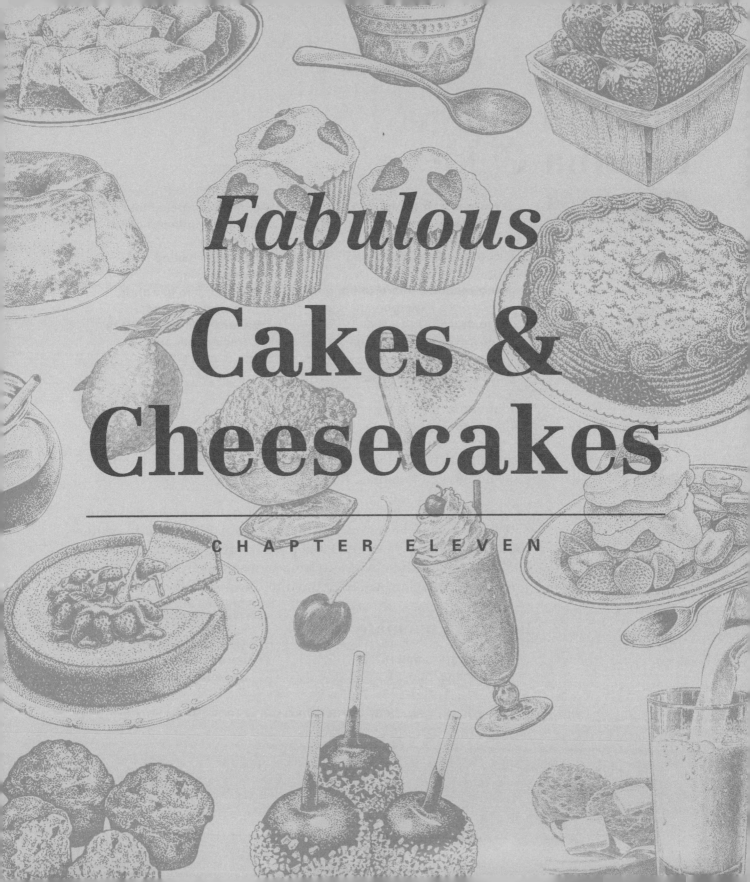

# *Fabulous*
# Cakes &
# Cheesecakes

## CHAPTER ELEVEN

# Almond Fudge Banana Cake

**Makes 16 to 20 servings**

3 extra-ripe, medium DOLE®
    Bananas
1½ cups sugar
  ½ cup margarine, softened
  3 eggs
  3 tablespoons amaretto liqueur
    *or* ½ to 1 teaspoon almond
    extract
  1 teaspoon vanilla extract

1½ cups all-purpose flour
  ½ cup unsweetened cocoa
    powder
  1 teaspoon baking soda
  ½ teaspoon salt
  ½ cup chopped almonds,
    toasted, ground
    Banana Chocolate Glaze
    (recipe follows)

• Mash bananas; set aside.

• Beat sugar and margarine until light and fluffy. Beat in eggs, liqueur and vanilla.

• Combine dry ingredients. Stir in almonds. Add to sugar mixture alternately with bananas. Beat well.

• Pour batter into greased 10-inch Bundt pan. Bake in preheated 350°F oven 45 to 50 minutes or until toothpick inserted in center comes out almost clean and cake pulls away from side of pan. Cool 10 minutes. Remove cake from pan to wire rack to cool completely. Drizzle glaze over top and down side of cake.

## Banana Chocolate Glaze

1 extra-ripe, small DOLE®
  Banana, puréed

1 square (1 ounce) semisweet
  chocolate, melted

• With wire whisk, beat puréed banana into melted chocolate.

# Raspberry Swirl Cheesecakes

1½ cups fresh or thawed lightly
   sweetened loose-pack
   frozen red raspberries
1 (14-ounce) can EAGLE®
   BRAND Sweetened
   Condensed Milk (NOT
   evaporated milk), divided
2 (8-ounce) packages cream
   cheese, softened

3 eggs
2 (6-ounce) chocolate crumb pie
   crusts
   Chocolate Leaves (recipe
   follows), if desired
   Fresh raspberries, if desired

**Makes 16 servings
(2 cheesecakes)**

**Prep Time:**
*15 minutes*

**Bake Time:**
*25 minutes*

**Chill Time:**
*4 hours*

*1.* Preheat oven to 350°F. In blender container, blend 1½ cups raspberries until smooth; press through sieve to remove seeds. Stir ⅓ cup Eagle Brand into sieved raspberries; set aside.

*2.* In large mixing bowl, beat cream cheese, eggs and remaining Eagle Brand. Spoon into crusts. Drizzle with raspberry mixture. With table knife, gently swirl raspberry mixture through cream cheese mixture.

*3.* Bake 25 minutes or until center is nearly set when shaken. Cool; chill at least 4 hours. Garnish with chocolate leaves and fresh raspberries, if desired. Store leftovers covered in refrigerator.

<u>**Chocolate Leaves:**</u> *Place 1 (1-ounce) square semi-sweet or white chocolate in microwave-safe bowl. Microwave at HIGH (100% power) 1 to 2 minutes, stirring every minute until smooth. With small, clean paintbrush, paint several coats of melted chocolate on undersides of nontoxic leaves, such as mint, lemon or strawberry. Wipe off any chocolate from top sides of leaves. Place leaves, chocolate sides up, on waxed paper-lined baking sheet or on curved surface, such as rolling pin. Refrigerate leaves until chocolate is firm. To use, carefully peel leaves away from chocolate.*

# Glazed Pear Shortcake

**Makes one 8-inch round shortcake (8 to 10 servings)**

1 can (16 ounces) Bartlett pear halves in heavy syrup
2 cups all-purpose flour
¾ cup sugar
2 teaspoons baking powder
¼ teaspoon salt
½ cup Butter Flavor CRISCO® Stick or ½ cup Butter Flavor CRISCO® all-vegetable shortening plus additional for greasing

⅔ cup diluted evaporated milk (⅓ cup evaporated milk, ⅓ cup water)
1 teaspoon ground cinnamon

*1.* Heat oven to 375°F. Grease 8-inch round cake pan. Flour lightly.

*2.* Drain pears, reserving syrup. Pat pears dry with paper towels. Cut each pear half into 4 to 5 slices, cutting up to, but not through, stem ends. Holding stem end in place, gently fan out slices.

*3.* Combine flour, sugar, baking powder and salt in medium bowl. Cut in ½ cup shortening using pastry blender (or 2 knives) until mixture is crumbly.

*4.* Pour milk mixture over flour mixture. Toss lightly with fork just until blended. *Do not overmix.* Spoon into pan. Smooth top. Arrange pears over batter with stem ends in center. Brush with a portion of reserved syrup. Sprinkle with cinnamon.

*5.* Bake at 375°F for 40 to 45 minutes or until toothpick inserted in center comes out clean. *Do not overbake.* Cool 15 minutes. Brush with reserved syrup. (You will not use all of syrup.) Invert cake on plate. Remove pan. Place cake, pear side up, on wire rack. Cool completely. Place cake on serving plate.

# Marble Chiffon Cake

Makes 12 to
16 servings

2 tablespoons plus 1½ cups
   sugar, divided
2 tablespoons plus ½ cup
   vegetable oil, divided
⅓ cup HERSHEY'S Cocoa
1 cup cold water, divided
2 cups all-purpose flour

1 tablespoon baking powder
1 teaspoon salt
7 eggs, separated
2 teaspoons vanilla extract
½ teaspoon cream of tartar
Vanilla Glaze (optional,
   recipe follows)

*1.* Heat oven to 325°F. Combine 2 tablespoons sugar, 2 tablespoons oil, cocoa and ¼ cup cold water in small bowl; stir until smooth.

*2.* Stir together flour, remaining 1½ cups sugar, baking powder and salt in small bowl. Add remaining ½ cup oil, ¾ cup cold water, egg yolks and vanilla. Beat on low speed of mixer until combined; continue beating on high speed 5 minutes.

*3.* Beat egg whites with cream of tartar in large bowl, with clean set of beaters, until stiff peaks form. Pour batter in thin stream over beaten whites, gently folding with rubber spatula just until blended. Remove one-third batter to separate bowl; gently fold in chocolate mixture. Pour half of light batter into ungreased 10-inch tube pan; top with half of chocolate batter. Repeat layers. With spatula or knife swirl gently through batters to marble.

*4.* Bake 65 to 70 minutes or until top springs back when touched lightly. Invert pan on heatproof funnel; cool cake completely. Loosen cake from pan; invert onto serving plate. Spread Vanilla Glaze over top of cake, allowing glaze to drizzle down sides.

<u>Vanilla Glaze:</u> *Melt ¼ cup (½ stick) butter or margarine in saucepan over low heat; remove from heat. Gradually stir in 2 cups powdered sugar, 2 to 3 tablespoons hot water and 1 teaspoon vanilla extract; beat with wire whisk until smooth and slightly thickened. Makes about 1¼ cups glaze.*

*Note:*

**Chiffon cakes are a hybrid—they share characteristics of both shortened cakes (fat in the form of vegetable oil and a chemical leavener, baking powder) and foam cakes (beaten eggs provide some of the leavening).**

# Angel Food Cake

**Makes one 10-inch tube cake**

1¼ cups cake flour, sifted
1⅓ cups plus ½ cup sugar, divided
12 egg whites
1¼ teaspoons cream of tartar

¼ teaspoon salt (optional)
1½ teaspoon vanilla
Fresh strawberries for garnish (optional)

*1.* Preheat oven to 350°F. Sift together flour with ½ cup sugar twice.

*2.* Beat egg whites with cream of tartar, salt and vanilla in large bowl at high speed with electric mixer until stiff peaks form.

*3.* Gradually add remaining 1⅓ cups sugar, beating well after each addition. Fold in flour mixture. Pour into *ungreased* 10-inch tube pan.

*4.* Bake 35 to 40 minutes or until cake springs back when lightly touched.

*5.* Invert pan; place on top of clean empty bottle. Allow cake to cool completely in pan before removing from pan. Serve with strawberries, if desired.

# Sour Cream Pound Cake

**Makes 12 to 16 servings**

3 cups sugar
1 cup (2 sticks) butter, softened
1 teaspoon vanilla
1 teaspoon lemon extract

6 eggs
3 cups cake flour
¼ teaspoon baking soda
1 cup dairy sour cream

Heat oven to 325°F. Butter and flour 10-inch tube pan. In large bowl, beat sugar and butter until light and fluffy. Add vanilla and lemon extract; mix well. Add eggs, one at a time, beating well after each addition. In medium bowl, combine flour and baking soda. Add to butter mixture alternately with sour cream, beating well after each addition. Pour batter into pan. Bake 1 hour and 20 minutes or until toothpick inserted in center comes out clean. Cool in pan 15 minutes; invert onto wire rack and cool completely. Store tightly covered.

Favorite recipe from **Southeast United Dairy Industry Association, Inc.**

# Pebbles and Stones Chocolate Cake

**Makes 12 servings**

| | |
|---|---|
| 2 cups semisweet chocolate morsels, divided | 1½ cups all-purpose flour |
| ½ cup WESSON® Vegetable Oil | ¾ teaspoon baking soda |
| ½ cup sour cream, at room temperature | ½ teaspoon salt |
| | PAM® No-Stick Cooking Spray |
| 2 eggs, lightly beaten | 4 tablespoons instant coffee |
| 2 cups granulated sugar | 1 cup warm milk |
| | ½ cup chopped nuts |

In a small microwave-safe bowl, microwave 1 cup morsels on HIGH for 1 minute; stir. Cook at additional 10-second intervals, stirring between intervals until smooth. Cool to room temperature. In a large mixing bowl, beat melted chocolate, Wesson® Oil, sour cream and eggs until well blended. Add sugar, flour, baking soda and salt; mix batter well. Preheat oven to 350°F. Spray a 13×9×2-inch baking pan with PAM® Cooking Spray; lightly dust pan with flour. Set aside. In a small bowl, dissolve coffee in warm milk; slowly mix into batter. Pour into baking pan and bake 40 to 50 minutes or until wooden pick inserted into center comes out clean. Remove and sprinkle with *remaining* morsels and nuts. Cool cake completely.

# Harvest Honey Spice Cake

**Makes 12 servings**

1 cup honey
⅓ cup vegetable oil
⅓ cup strong brewed coffee
3 eggs
2½ cups all-purpose flour
1½ teaspoons baking soda
1½ teaspoons ground cinnamon
¾ teaspoon ground nutmeg

½ teaspoon salt
2 cups peeled chopped tart apples
½ cup toasted slivered almonds
½ cup dried cranberries
Powdered sugar
Toasted sliced almonds, for garnish

*Note:*

Cakes are "silent" when they've baked enough. Pull a cake from the oven 10 minutes before the end of the suggested baking time. Does it crackle and pop? If so, bake another 5 minutes.

Using electric mixer, beat together honey, oil and coffee. Beat in eggs.

Combine dry ingredients; gradually add to honey-egg mixture, mixing until well blended. Stir in apples, almonds and cranberries.

Pour into lightly greased and floured Bundt or tube pan. Bake at 350°F for 35 to 40 minutes or until toothpick inserted near center comes out clean. Remove from oven; cool on wire rack. Dust with powdered sugar; garnish with sliced almonds, if desired.

Favorite recipe from **National Honey Board**

# Molten Mocha Cakes

1 package BAKER'S® Semi-
    Sweet Baking Chocolate
1 cup (2 sticks) butter
2 cups powdered sugar
½ cup GENERAL FOODS
    INTERNATIONAL
    COFFEES®, any flavor

5 eggs
4 egg yolks
¾ cup flour
    Powdered sugar (optional)
    Raspberries (optional)

**Makes 8 cakes**

**Prep Time:**
*15 minutes*

**Bake Time:**
*15 minutes*

**HEAT** oven to 425°F. Butter eight ¾-cup custard cups or soufflé dishes. Place on cookie sheet.

**MICROWAVE** chocolate and butter in large microwavable bowl on HIGH 2 minutes or until butter is melted. Stir with wire whisk until chocolate is completely melted. Stir in sugar and flavored instant coffee until well blended. Whisk in eggs and egg yolks. Stir in flour. Divide batter among custard cups.

**BAKE** 14 to 15 minutes or until sides are firm but centers are soft. Let stand 1 minute, then run small knife around cakes to loosen. Invert cakes onto dessert dishes. Sprinkle with powdered sugar and garnish with raspberries, if desired.

<u>**Make-Ahead:**</u> *Bake as directed above. Cool slightly, then cover custard cups with plastic wrap. Refrigerate up to 2 days. Place custard cups on cookie sheet. Reheat in 425°F oven for 12 to 13 minutes.*

# Maple Walnut Pound Cake

| Makes 1 (9- or 10-inch) cake |
| --- |

1 cup butter or margarine, softened
1½ cups granulated sugar
½ cup packed brown sugar
2¼ cups flour
1 teaspoon baking powder
½ teaspoon salt
¼ cup milk

1 tablespoon maple flavoring
5 eggs
1½ cups chopped California walnuts
Maple Glaze (recipe follows)
Walnut halves or chopped California walnuts, for garnish

Preheat oven to 300°F. Grease 9- or 10-inch tube pan. Cream butter and sugars in large bowl until fluffy. Combine flour, baking powder and salt in medium bowl. Combine milk and maple flavoring in glass measuring cup; add to butter mixture alternately with flour mixture. Beat in eggs, 1 at a time, beating well after each addition. Mix in 1½ cups chopped walnuts. Pour into prepared pan. Bake in lower third of oven 1 hour to 1 hour and 15 minutes or until toothpick inserted near center comes out clean. Cool in pan 15 minutes. Remove from pan to wire rack to cool completely. Meanwhile, prepare Maple Glaze. Drizzle with glaze and garnish with walnuts.

<u>Maple Glaze:</u> *Mix 1 cup sifted powdered sugar and 1 tablespoon milk in small bowl to make a glaze of thick pouring consistency. Add additional 1 teaspoon milk if necessary. Stir in ¼ teaspoon maple flavoring.*

Favorite recipe from **Walnut Marketing Board**

# Butterscotch Pumpkin Cake

**Makes 24 servings**

1⅔ cups (11-ounce package) NESTLÉ® TOLL HOUSE® Butterscotch Flavored Morsels, *divided*
2 cups all-purpose flour
1¾ cups granulated sugar
1 tablespoon baking powder
1½ teaspoons ground cinnamon
1 teaspoon salt
½ teaspoon ground nutmeg
1 cup LIBBY'S® 100% Pure Pumpkin
½ cup vegetable oil
3 large eggs
1 teaspoon vanilla extract
Powdered sugar (optional)
Butterscotch Sauce (recipe follows)

*Note:*

Briefly cooling a cake in the pan is an important step. It allows the steam to build between the cake and the pan, which helps release the cake.

**PREHEAT** oven to 350°F. Grease 12-cup bundt pan.

**MICROWAVE** *1 cup* morsels in small, microwave-safe bowl on MEDIUM-HIGH (70%) power for 1 minute; stir. Microwave at additional 10- to 20-second intervals, stirring until smooth. Cool to room temperature.

**COMBINE** flour, granulated sugar, baking powder, cinnamon, salt and nutmeg in medium bowl. Stir together melted morsels, pumpkin, vegetable oil, eggs and vanilla extract in large bowl with wire whisk. Stir in flour mixture. Spoon batter into prepared bundt pan.

**BAKE** for 40 to 50 minutes or until wooden pick inserted in cake comes out clean. Cool in pan on wire rack for 30 minutes; remove to wire rack to cool completely. Sprinkle with powdered sugar. Serve with Butterscotch Sauce.

**Butterscotch Sauce:** *HEAT ⅓ cup NESTLÉ® CARNATION® Evaporated Milk in medium,* heavy-duty *saucepan over medium heat* just to a boil; *remove from heat. Add* remaining *morsels; stir until smooth. Return to heat. Stirring constantly, bring mixture just to a boil. Cool to room temperature. Stir before serving.*

# Velvet Chocolate Cheesecake

**Makes 10 servings**

**Prep Time:**
*20 minutes*

**Bake Time:**
*1 hour*

30 CHIPS AHOY!® Chocolate Chip
  Cookies, divided
¼ cup margarine or butter,
  melted
1⅓ cups sugar, divided
2 (8-ounce) packages
  PHILADELPHIA® Cream
  Cheese, softened
⅓ cup unsweetened cocoa

2 eggs
1½ teaspoons vanilla extract,
  divided
1 cup BREAKSTONE'S® or
  KNUDSEN® Sour Cream
COOL WHIP® Whipped
  Topping and maraschino
  cherries, for garnish

*1.* Finely crush 20 cookies. Mix cookie crumbs and margarine
or butter; press on bottom of 8-inch springform pan. Stand
remaining cookies around side of pan; set aside.

*2.* Reserve 2 tablespoons sugar. Beat cream cheese in medium
bowl with electric mixer at medium speed until creamy; beat in
remaining sugar, cocoa, eggs and 1 teaspoon vanilla until fluffy.
Pour into prepared crust. Cover tops of cookies with band of
aluminum foil before baking to avoid overbrowning.

*3.* Bake at 375°F for 50 minutes or until cheesecake is puffed
and toothpick inserted ½ inch from edge comes out clean;
remove from oven.

*4.* Blend reserved sugar, sour cream and remaining vanilla;
spread evenly over cheesecake. Return to oven; bake 10 minutes
more. Cool completely at room temperature. Refrigerate for
3 hours or overnight. Remove side of pan. Garnish with whipped
topping and maraschino cherries if desired.

# Southern Jam Cake

**Makes 12 to 16 servings**

Cake
- ¾ cup butter or margarine, softened
- 1 cup granulated sugar
- 3 eggs
- 1 cup (12-ounce jar) SMUCKER'S® Seedless Blackberry Jam
- 2½ cups all-purpose flour
- 1 teaspoon baking soda
- 1 teaspoon ground cinnamon
- 1 teaspoon ground cloves
- 1 teaspoon ground allspice
- 1 teaspoon ground nutmeg
- ¾ cup buttermilk

Caramel Icing (optional)
- 2 tablespoons butter
- ½ cup firmly packed brown sugar
- 3 tablespoons milk
- 1¾ cups powdered sugar

Grease and flour tube pan. Combine ¾ cup butter and granulated sugar; beat until light and fluffy. Add eggs one at a time, beating well after each addition. Fold in jam.

Combine flour, baking soda, cinnamon, cloves, allspice and nutmeg; mix well. Add to batter alternately with buttermilk, stirring just enough to blend after each addition. Spoon mixture into prepared pan.

Bake at 350°F for 50 minutes or until toothpick inserted near center comes out clean. Cool in pan for 10 minutes. Remove from pan; cool completely.

In saucepan, melt 2 tablespoons butter; stir in brown sugar. Cook, stirring constantly, until mixture boils; remove from heat. Cool 5 minutes. Stir in milk; blend in powdered sugar. Frost cake.

*Note:*

When blending flour into a creamed butter and sugar mixture, don't beat longer than necessary. Beating develops the protein in flour, making baked goods tougher.

# Chocolate Sheet Cake

**Makes one 15×10-inch cake**

1¼ cups (2½ sticks) butter
    or margarine, divided
1 cup water
½ cup unsweetened cocoa,
    divided
2 cups all-purpose flour
1½ cups firmly packed light
    brown sugar
1 teaspoon baking soda
1 teaspoon ground cinnamon

½ teaspoon salt
1 (14-ounce) can EAGLE®
    BRAND Sweetened
    Condensed Milk (NOT
    evaporated milk), divided
2 eggs
1 teaspoon vanilla extract
1 cup powdered sugar
1 cup coarsely chopped nuts

*Note:*

Avoid opening the oven door during the first half of the baking time. The oven temperature must remain constant in order for the cake to rise properly.

*1.* Preheat oven to 350°F. In small saucepan over medium heat, melt 1 cup butter; stir in water and ¼ cup cocoa. Bring to a boil; remove from heat. In large mixing bowl, combine flour, brown sugar, baking soda, cinnamon and salt. Add cocoa mixture; beat well. Stir in ⅓ cup Eagle Brand, eggs and vanilla. Pour into greased 15×10×1-inch jelly-roll pan. Bake 15 minutes or until cake springs back when lightly touched.

*2.* In small saucepan over medium heat, melt remaining ¼ cup butter; add remaining ¼ cup cocoa and remaining Eagle Brand. Stir in powdered sugar and nuts. Spread over warm cake.

# Lemonade Torte for a Long Hot Summer

1½ cups sugar, divided
¾ cup blanched almonds
1½ cups whole-wheat bread crumbs
1 tablespoon grated lemon peel
¼ teaspoon baking powder
¼ teaspoon ground cinnamon

6 large egg whites
1 cup NEWMAN'S OWN® Old-Fashioned Roadside Lemonade
2 tablespoons confectioners' sugar

**Makes 8 servings**

Preheat oven to 350°F. Butter and flour 9-inch springform pan.

In food processor, process 1 cup sugar with almonds. In medium bowl, mix ground almond mixture with bread crumbs, lemon peel, baking powder and cinnamon. Set aside.

In large mixing bowl, with mixer at high speed, beat egg whites with remaining ½ cup sugar until stiff peaks form. Gently fold crumb mixture into beaten egg whites. Pour mixture into springform pan and bake on lower oven rack for 1 hour.

In small saucepan over medium-high heat, cook Newman's Own® Old-Fashioned Roadside Lemonade 10 minutes or until reduced by half.

Remove torte from oven. Pour reduced lemonade gradually over top of hot torte. Let torte stand in pan on wire rack until cool. Remove side of springform pan and dust top of torte with confectioners' sugar.

*Note:*

Egg whites reach the fullest volume if they are allowed to stand at room temperature for 30 minutes before beating.

# Reese's® Chocolate Peanut Butter Cheesecake

**Makes 12 servings**

1¼ cups graham cracker crumbs
⅓ cup plus ¼ cup sugar
⅓ cup HERSHEY'S Cocoa
⅓ cup butter or margarine, melted
3 packages (8 ounces each) cream cheese, softened
1 can (14 ounces) sweetened condensed milk (not evaporated milk)
1⅔ cup (10-ounce package) REESE'S® Peanut Butter Chips, melted

4 eggs
2 teaspoons vanilla extract
Chocolate Drizzle (recipe follows)
Whipped topping
HERSHEY'S MINI KISSES™ Semi-Sweet or Milk Chocolates

*1.* Heat oven to 300°F. Combine graham cracker crumbs, ⅓ cup sugar, cocoa and butter; press onto bottom of 9-inch springform pan.

*2.* Beat cream cheese and remaining ¼ cup sugar until fluffy. Gradually beat in sweetened condensed milk, then melted chips, until smooth. Add eggs and vanilla; beat well. Pour over crust.

*3.* Bake 60 to 70 minutes or until center is almost set. Remove from oven. With knife, loosen cake from side of pan. Cool. Remove side of pan. Refrigerate until cold. Garnish with Chocolate Drizzle, whipped topping and Mini Kisses™. Store, covered, in refrigerator.

<u>**Chocolate Drizzle:**</u> *Melt 2 tablespoons butter in small saucepan over low heat; add 2 tablespoons HERSHEY'S Cocoa and 2 tablespoons water. Cook and stir until slightly thickened. Do not boil. Cool slightly. Gradually add 1 cup powdered sugar and ½ teaspoon vanilla extract, beating with whisk until smooth. Makes about ¾ cup. (If desired, spoon drizzle into small heavy seal-top plastic bag. With scissors, make small diagonal cut in bottom corner of bag. Squeeze drizzle over top of cake.)*

# Gingerbread Upside-Down Cake

1 can (20 ounces) DOLE®
    Pineapple Slices
½ cup margarine, softened,
    divided
1 cup packed brown sugar,
    divided
10 maraschino cherries

1 egg
½ cup dark molasses
1½ cups all-purpose flour
1 teaspoon baking soda
1 teaspoon ground ginger
½ teaspoon ground cinnamon
½ teaspoon salt

**Makes 8 to
10 servings**

• Preheat oven to 350°F. Drain pineapple slices; reserve ½ cup
syrup. In 10-inch cast iron skillet, melt ¼ cup margarine.
Remove from heat. Add ½ cup brown sugar and stir until
blended. Arrange pineapple slices in skillet. Place 1 cherry
in center of each slice.

• In large mixer bowl, beat remaining ¼ cup margarine and
½ cup brown sugar until light and fluffy. Beat in egg and
molasses. In small bowl, combine flour, baking soda, ginger,
cinnamon and salt.

• In small saucepan, bring reserved pineapple syrup to a boil.
Add dry ingredients to creamed mixture alternately with hot
syrup. Spread evenly over pineapple slices in skillet. Bake
30 to 40 minutes or until wooden pick inserted in center
comes out clean. Let stand in skillet on wire rack 5 minutes.
Invert onto serving plate.

# Traditional Ricotta Cheesecake

**Makes 8 servings**

### Crust
1 cup finely crushed graham crackers
¼ cup sugar
¼ cup melted margarine

### Filling
2 cups (15 ounces) SARGENTO® Light Ricotta Cheese
½ cup sugar
½ cup half-and-half
2 tablespoons all-purpose flour
1 tablespoon fresh lemon juice
1 teaspoon finely grated lemon peel
¼ teaspoon salt
2 eggs

### Topping
1 cup light sour cream
2 tablespoons sugar
1 teaspoon vanilla

Combine graham crackers, ¼ cup sugar and margarine; mix well. Press evenly over bottom and 1½ inches up side of 8- or 9-inch springform pan. Chill while preparing filling.

In bowl of electric mixer, combine ricotta cheese, ½ cup sugar, half and-half, flour, lemon juice, lemon peel and salt; blend until smooth. Add eggs, one at a time; blend until smooth. Pour into crust. Bake at 350°F 50 minutes or until center is just set. Remove from oven.

Beat sour cream with 2 tablespoons sugar and vanilla. Gently spoon onto warm cheesecake; spread evenly over surface. Return to oven 10 minutes. Turn off oven; cool in oven with door propped open 30 minutes. Remove to wire cooling rack; cool completely. Chill at least 3 hours.

# Peanut Butter Pudding Cake

**Makes 12 servings**

1 cup roasted peanuts,
   chopped, divided
1 cup all-purpose flour
½ cup butter, softened
1 package (8 ounces) cream
   cheese
⅓ cup creamy peanut butter
1 cup confectioners' sugar
1 container (4.5 ounces) frozen
   whipped topping, thawed

1 package (3 ounces) instant
   vanilla pudding
1 package (3 ounces) instant
   chocolate pudding
2¾ cups milk
1 container (9 ounces) frozen
   whipped topping, thawed
1 square (1 ounce) chocolate,
   grated

*1.* In a small bowl, thoroughly mix ⅔ cup peanuts, flour and softened butter. Press onto bottom of 12×8-inch baking dish. Bake for 20 minutes at 350°F. Cool thoroughly.

*2.* Beat cream cheese and peanut butter until smooth. Add sugar and mix well. Fold in 4½ ounces frozen whipped topping. Spread over cooled peanut layer.

*3.* Mix puddings with milk until thickened. Spread over peanut butter layer.

*4.* Top with 9 ounces frozen whipped topping. Sprinkle with chocolate and remaining ⅓ cup peanuts. Chill 2 to 3 hours.

Favorite recipe from **Peanut Advisory Board**

# Upside-Down German Chocolate Cake

**Makes 12 to 16 servings**

1½ cups flaked coconut
1½ cups chopped pecans
1 package **DUNCAN HINES®**
   Moist Deluxe® German
   Chocolate or Classic
   Chocolate Cake Mix

1 package (8 ounces) cream
   cheese, softened
½ cup butter or margarine,
   melted
1 pound (3½ to 4 cups)
   confectioners' sugar

*1.* Preheat oven to 350°F. Grease and flour 13×9-inch pan.

*2.* Spread coconut evenly on bottom of prepared pan. Sprinkle with pecans. Prepare cake mix as directed on package. Pour over coconut and pecans. Combine cream cheese and melted butter in medium mixing bowl. Beat at low speed with electric mixer until creamy. Add sugar; beat until blended and smooth. Drop by spoonfuls evenly over cake batter. Bake at 350°F for 45 to 50 minutes or until toothpick inserted halfway to bottom of cake comes out clean. Cool completely in pan. To serve, cut into individual pieces; turn upside down onto plate.

**Tip:** *This cake can be served warm, if desired. Also, store leftover coconut in the refrigerator and use within four weeks.*

# Chocolate Lovers' Cake

**Makes 12 servings**

**Cake**
- ¾ cup (1½ sticks) I CAN'T BELIEVE IT'S NOT BUTTER!® Spread
- 6 squares (1 ounce each) bittersweet chocolate, coarsely chopped *or* 1 cup semisweet chocolate chips
- 4 eggs, separated
  Pinch salt
- ¾ cup sugar
- ⅓ cup all-purpose flour

**Glaze**
- 5 tablespoons I CAN'T BELIEVE IT'S NOT BUTTER!® Spread
- 10 squares (1 ounce each) bittersweet chocolate, coarsely chopped *or* 1⅔ cups semisweet chocolate chips

For cake, preheat oven to 350°F. Grease 9-inch round cake pan, then line with parchment or waxed paper; set aside.

In small saucepan, melt I Can't Believe It's Not Butter! Spread and chocolate over low heat, stirring occasionally; set aside to cool slightly. In medium bowl, with electric mixer, beat egg whites with salt until stiff peaks form; set aside.

In medium bowl, with electric mixer, beat egg yolks and sugar until light and ribbony, about 2 minutes. While beating, slowly add chocolate mixture until blended. Beat in flour. With spatula, fold in egg whites just until blended. Pour into prepared pan.

Bake 30 minutes. (Note: Toothpick inserted in center will *not* come out clean.) Remove cake to wire rack and run knife around rim to loosen cake from sides; cool 15 minutes. Remove cake from pan and cool completely.

For glaze, in small saucepan, melt I Can't Believe It's Not Butter! Spread and chocolate in a small saucepan, over low heat, stirring occasionally. Spread warm glaze over cake.

## *Note:*

To avoid cakes that peak in the center, make sure the oven is set at the appropriate temperature and don't overbeat the batter.

# Pumpkin Cake with Orange Glaze

**Makes one 10-inch bundt cake (12 to 16 servings)**

### Cake

2 cups firmly packed light brown sugar

¾ Butter Flavor CRISCO® Stick or ¾ cup Butter Flavor CRISCO® all-vegetable shortening plus additional for greasing

4 eggs

1 can (16 ounces) solid-pack pumpkin (not pumpkin pie filling)

¼ cup water

2½ cups cake flour

1 tablespoon plus 1 teaspoon baking powder

1 tablespoon pumpkin pie spice

1½ teaspoons baking soda

1 teaspoon salt

½ cup chopped walnuts

½ cup raisins

### Glaze

1 cup confectioners' sugar

1 tablespoon plus 1 teaspoon orange juice

¾ teaspoon grated orange peel

Additional chopped walnuts

*Note:*

Cake flour, also called pastry flour, is made from low-gluten soft wheat. It has a fine texture and is a good choice for making tender cakes, pastries and quick breads.

*1.* Heat oven to 350°F. Grease 10-inch (12-cup) Bundt pan. Flour lightly.

*2.* For cake, combine brown sugar and ¾ cup shortening in large bowl. Beat at low speed with electric mixer until creamy. Add eggs, 1 at a time, beating well after each addition. Stir in pumpkin and water.

*3.* Combine flour, baking powder, pumpkin pie spice, baking soda and salt in medium bowl. Add to pumpkin mixture. Beat at low speed with electric mixer until blended. Beat 2 minutes at medium speed. Fold in ½ cup nuts and raisins. Spoon into prepared pan.

*4.* Bake at 350°F for 55 to 60 minutes or until toothpick inserted near center comes out clean. Cool 10 minutes before removing from pan. Place cake, fluted side up, on serving plate. Cool completely.

*5.* For glaze, combine confectioners' sugar, orange juice and orange peel in small bowl. Stir with spoon to blend. Spoon over top of cake, letting excess glaze run down side. Sprinkle with additional nuts before glaze hardens.

# Banana Jewel Cake

| | |
|---|---|
| 1 box (18 ounces) vanilla-flavored cake mix | ¼ cup sugar |
| 1 cup water | 1½ cups DOLE® Fresh Cranberries |
| ¼ cup orange juice | 3 DOLE® Bananas, sliced |
| 2 tablespoons grated orange peel | |

**Makes 12 servings**

**Prep Time:**
*15 minutes*

**Bake Time:**
*35 minutes*

• Prepare cake mix as directed, except add only 1 cup water. Pour into 13×9-inch baking pan.

• Heat orange juice and grated peel in medium saucepan until hot. Add sugar and stir to dissolve. Add cranberries and simmer until skins burst. Add bananas. Continue cooking for 1 minute. Remove from heat.

• Evenly spoon cranberry-banana mixture over cake. *Do not stir.*

• Bake at 350°F, 35 to 40 minutes or until lightly browned. Garnish with fresh cranberries and orange twist, if desired.

# Cappuccino Cake

**Makes 12 to 16 servings**

½ cup (3 ounces) semisweet chocolate chips
½ cup chopped hazelnuts, walnuts or pecans
1 (18.25-ounce) package yellow cake mix
¼ cup instant espresso coffee powder
2 teaspoons ground cinnamon

1¼ cups water
3 large eggs
⅓ cup FILIPPO BERIO® Pure or Extra Light Tasting Olive Oil
Powdered sugar
1 (15-ounce) container ricotta cheese
2 teaspoons granulated sugar
Additional ground cinnamon

Preheat oven to 325°F. Grease 10-inch (12-cup) Bundt pan or 10-inch tube pan with olive oil. Sprinkle lightly with flour.

In small bowl, combine chocolate chips and hazelnuts. Spoon evenly into bottom of prepared pan.

In large bowl, combine cake mix, coffee powder and 2 teaspoons cinnamon. Add water, eggs and olive oil. Beat with electric mixer at low speed until dry ingredients are moistened. Beat at medium speed 2 minutes. Pour batter over topping in pan.

Bake 60 minutes or until toothpick inserted in center comes out clean. Cool on wire rack 15 minutes. Remove from pan. Place cake, fluted side up, on serving plate. Cool completely. Sprinkle with powdered sugar.

In medium bowl, combine ricotta cheese and granulated sugar. Sprinkle with cinnamon. Serve alongside slices of cake. Serve cake with cappuccino, espresso or your favorite coffee, if desired.

# Tropical Snack Cake

1½ cups all-purpose flour
1 cup QUAKER® Oats (quick or
    old fashioned, uncooked)
¼ cup granulated sugar *or*
    2 tablespoons fructose
2 teaspoons baking powder
½ teaspoon baking soda
¼ teaspoon salt (optional)
1 can (8 ounces) crushed
    pineapple in juice,
    undrained

½ cup fat-free milk
⅓ cup mashed ripe banana
¼ cup egg substitute *or* 2 egg
    whites
2 tablespoons vegetable oil
2 teaspoons vanilla

Heat oven to 350°F. Grease and flour 8×8-inch square baking
pan. Combine first 6 ingredients; mix well. Set aside. Blend
pineapple, milk, banana, egg substitute, oil and vanilla until
mixed thoroughly. Add to dry ingredients, mixing just until
moistened. Pour into prepared pan. Bake 45 to 50 minutes or
until golden brown and wooden pick inserted in center comes
out clean. Cool slightly before serving.

*Note:*

Occasionally a cake
batter using an
acidic fruit, such as
pineapple, will look
curdled. The problem
usually corrects itself
once all the flour has
been added, and the
texture of the cake
after baking will
be fine.

# Tuxedo Cheesecake

**Makes 14 to 16 servings**

**Crust**
1¾ cups (about 18) crushed creme-filled chocolate cookies
2 tablespoons butter or margarine, melted

**Filling**
1 cup (6 ounces) NESTLÉ® TOLL HOUSE® Premier White Morsels

3 packages (8 ounces *each*) cream cheese, softened
¾ cup granulated sugar
2 teaspoons vanilla extract
3 large eggs
1 bar (2 ounces *total*) NESTLÉ® TOLL HOUSE® Semi-Sweet Chocolate or Premier White Chocolate Baking Bars, made into curls or grated

**PREHEAT** oven to 350°F.

**For Crust**
**COMBINE** cookie crumbs and butter together in medium bowl. Press onto bottom of ungreased 9-inch springform pan. Bake for 10 minutes.

**For Filling**
**MICROWAVE** morsels in small, microwave-safe bowl on MEDIUM-HIGH (70%) power for 1 minute; stir. Microwave at additional 10- to 20-second intervals, stirring until smooth; cool to room temperature.

**BEAT** cream cheese, sugar and vanilla extract in large mixer bowl until smooth. Beat in eggs; gradually beat in melted white morsels. Spread over chocolate crust.

**BAKE** for 40 to 50 minutes or until edges are set but center still moves slightly. Cool in pan on wire rack; refrigerate until firm. Remove side of springform pan.

**SPRINKLE** chocolate curls over cheesecake before serving.

# Carrot Cake

Makes 8 servings

4 eggs
1¼ cups vegetable oil
2 cups all-purpose flour
1½ cups sugar
2 teaspoons baking powder
2 teaspoons ground cinnamon
1 teaspoon baking soda

¼ teaspoon salt
2½ cups shredded carrots
  (about 7 medium)
1 cups coarsely chopped
  pecans or walnuts
Cream Cheese Icing
  (recipe follows)

Preheat oven to 350°F. Grease and flour bottom and sides of 13×9-inch baking pan.

Beat eggs and oil in small bowl. Combine flour, sugar, baking powder, cinnamon, baking soda and salt in large bowl. Add egg mixture; mix well. Stir in carrots and pecans. Pour into prepared pan.

Bake 40 to 45 minutes or until wooden pick inserted into center comes out clean. Cool cake completely in pan on wire rack.

Prepare Cream Cheese Icing. Spread over cooled cake. Garnish, if desired.

## Cream Cheese Icing

1 package (8 ounces) cream
  cheese, softened
½ cup (1 stick) butter or
  margarine, softened

1 teaspoon vanilla
4 cups powdered sugar

Beat cream cheese, butter and vanilla in large bowl with electric mixer at medium speed until smooth, scraping down side of bowl occasionally. Gradually add powdered sugar. Beat at low speed until well blended, scraping down side of bowl occasionally.

*Makes about 1½ cups*

# Strawberry Chocolate Chip Shortcake

**Makes 12 servings**

1 cup sugar, divided
½ cup (1 stick) butter or
    margarine, softened
1 egg
2 teaspoons vanilla extract,
    divided
1½ cups all-purpose flour
½ teaspoon baking powder
1 cup HERSHEY₅S MINI CHIPS™
    Semi-Sweet Chocolate or
    HERSHEY₅S Semi-Sweet
    Chocolate Chips, divided

1 container (16 ounces) dairy
    sour cream
2 eggs
2 cups frozen non-dairy
    whipped topping, thawed
Fresh strawberries, rinsed
    and halved

*Note:*

**Strawberries should
be stored in the
refrigerator, with green
caps attached, until
ready to use. Rinse
gently under cold
water just before
preparing, and use
fresh strawberries as
soon as possible for
maximum freshness.**

*1.* Heat oven to 350°F. Grease 9-inch springform pan.

*2.* Beat ½ cup sugar and butter in large bowl. Add 1 egg and 1 teaspoon vanilla; beat until creamy. Gradually add flour and baking powder, beating until smooth; stir in ½ cup small chocolate chips. Press mixture onto bottom of prepared pan.

*3.* Stir together sour cream, remaining ½ cup sugar, 2 eggs and remaining 1 teaspoon vanilla in medium bowl; stir in remaining ½ cup small chocolate chips. Pour over mixture in pan.

*4.* Bake 50 to 55 minutes until almost set in center and edges are lightly browned. Cool completely on wire rack; remove side of pan. Spread whipped topping over top. Cover; refrigerate. Just before serving, arrange strawberry halves on top of cake; garnish as desired. Refrigerate leftover dessert.

# Peppery Poundcake

1 cup (2 sticks) butter *or*
   margarine
1 cup granulated sugar
1 cup packed light brown sugar
4 eggs
3 cups sifted cake flour
2 teaspoons baking powder
½ teaspoon allspice

¼ teaspoon salt
1 cup milk
3 teaspoons vanilla extract
½ teaspoon TABASCO® brand
   Pepper Sauce
Confectioners' sugar
   (optional)

**Makes 8 to
10 servings**

Preheat oven to 350°F. Grease 9-inch tube pan. Beat butter,
granulated and brown sugars in medium bowl until light and
fluffy. Add eggs, one at a time, beating well after each addition.

Sift flour, baking powder, allspice and salt into medium bowl.
Beat flour mixture and milk alternately into butter mixture;
beat in vanilla and TABASCO® Sauce. Pour into prepared pan.
Bake 50 to 60 minutes or until cake tester inserted near center
comes out clean. Cool in pan on wire rack 20 to 30 minutes;
remove from pan and cool completely. Before serving, dust
with confectioners' sugar, if desired.

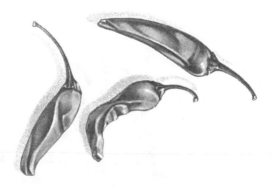

# Oatmeal Chocolate Chip Cake

**Makes 18 servings**

1¾ cups boiling water
1 cup uncooked quick-cooking oats
1 cup granulated sugar
1 cup packed brown sugar
2 tablespoons margarine, cut into small pieces
½ cup unsweetened applesauce
2 eggs

1¾ cups all-purpose flour
2 tablespoons unsweetened cocoa powder
1 teaspoon salt
1 teaspoon baking soda
½ cup semisweet mini chocolate chips, divided
2 tablespoons chopped walnuts

Pour boiling water over oats; let stand 10 minutes. Add sugars and margarine; stir until margarine melts. Add applesauce. Add eggs, 1 at a time, mixing well after each addition. Sift or stir flour, cocoa, salt and baking soda together; add to mixture. Mix well. Add ¼ cup chocolate chips; stir.

Pour batter into 13×9-inch pan coated with nonstick cooking spray and dusted with flour. Sprinkle remaining ¼ cup chips and walnuts on top. Bake in preheated 350°F oven 25 to 30 minutes.

Favorite recipe from **North Dakota Wheat Commission**

# Classic New York Cheesecake

**Crust**
- 1 cup HONEY MAID® Graham Cracker Crumbs
- 3 tablespoons sugar
- 3 tablespoons butter *or* margarine, melted

**Filling**
- 4 packages (8 ounces each) PHILADELPHIA® Cream Cheese, softened
- 1 cup sugar
- 3 tablespoons flour
- 1 tablespoon vanilla
- 1 cup BREAKSTONE'S® *or* KNUDSEN® Sour Cream
- 4 eggs

**Makes 12 servings**

**Prep Time:**
*15 minutes plus refrigerating*

**Bake Time:**
*1 hour 10 minutes*

## Crust
MIX crumbs, 3 tablespoons sugar and butter; press onto bottom of 9-inch springform pan. Bake at 325°F for 10 minutes if using a silver springform pan. (Bake at 300°F for 10 minutes if using a dark nonstick springform pan.)

## Filling
BEAT cream cheese, 1 cup sugar, flour and vanilla with electric mixer on medium speed until well blended. Blend in sour cream. Add eggs, 1 at a time, mixing on low speed after each addition just until blended. Pour over crust.

BAKE at 325°F for 1 hour to 1 hour 5 minutes or until center is almost set if using a silver springform pan. (Bake at 300°F for 1 hour to 1 hour 5 minutes or until center is almost set if using a dark nonstick springform pan.) Run knife or metal spatula around rim of pan to loosen cake; cool before removing rim of pan. Refrigerate 4 hours or overnight.

# Zesty Lemon Pound Cake

**Makes 16 servings**

1 cup (6 ounces) NESTLÉ®
TOLL HOUSE® Premier
White Morsels or 3 bars
(6-ounce box) NESTLÉ®
TOLL HOUSE® Premier
White Baking Bars, broken
into pieces
2½ cups all-purpose flour
1 teaspoon baking powder
½ teaspoon salt

1 cup (2 sticks) butter, softened
1½ cups granulated sugar
2 teaspoons vanilla extract
3 large eggs
3 to 4 tablespoons (about
3 medium lemons) grated
lemon peel
1⅓ cups buttermilk
1 cup powdered sugar
3 tablespoons fresh lemon juice

*Note:*

One medium lemon
will yield about 3 to 4
tablespoons of juice
and 1 to 2 teaspoons
of grated peel.

**PREHEAT** oven to 350°F. Grease and flour 12-cup bundt pan.

**MELT** morsels in medium, microwave-safe bowl on MEDIUM-HIGH (70%) power for 1 minute; stir. Microwave at additional 10- to 20-second intervals, stirring until smooth; cool slightly.

**COMBINE** flour, baking powder and salt in small bowl. Beat butter, granulated sugar and vanilla extract in large mixer bowl until creamy. Beat in eggs, one at a time, beating well after each addition. Beat in lemon peel and melted morsels. Gradually beat in flour mixture alternately with buttermilk. Pour into prepared bundt pan.

**BAKE** for 50 to 55 minutes or until wooden pick inserted in cake comes out clean. Cool in pan on wire rack for 10 minutes. Combine powdered sugar and lemon juice in small bowl. Make holes in cake with wooden pick; pour *half* of lemon glaze over cake. Let stand for 5 minutes. Invert onto plate. Make holes in top of cake; pour *remaining* glaze over cake. Cool completely before serving.

# Mocha Marble Cheesecake

**12 ounces cream cheese, softened**
**½ cup sugar**
**1 teaspoon vanilla**
**2 eggs**

**½ cup white crème de cacao**
**1 teaspoon instant coffee granules**
**1 (6-ounce) READY CRUST® Graham Cracker Pie Crust**

**Makes 8 servings**

**Prep Time:**
*10 minutes*

**Bake Time:**
*30 to 35 minutes*

**Chill Time:**
*3 hours*

*1.* Preheat oven to 325°F. Beat cream cheese in medium bowl until smooth. Add sugar and vanilla. Add eggs, one at a time, beating until well blended.

*2.* Reserve ½ cup cream cheese mixture; set aside. Pour remaining mixture into crust. Mix crème de cacao and coffee granules with reserved cream cheese mixture.

*3.* Place crust on baking sheet. Pour coffee mixture over cheesecake filling. Gently cut through coffee layer with knife to create marbled appearance. Bake 30 to 35 minutes or until just set in center. Cool on wire rack. Chill 3 hours. Refrigerate leftovers.

# Spicy Applesauce Cake

**Makes 9 servings**

2¼ cups all-purpose flour
2 teaspoons baking soda
1 teaspoon ground cinnamon
1 teaspoon ground nutmeg
½ teaspoon ground cloves
1 cup firmly packed brown
   sugar
½ cup FILIPPO BERIO® Olive Oil

1½ cups applesauce
1 cup raisins
1 cup coarsely chopped
   walnuts
   Powdered sugar or
   sweetened whipped cream
   (optional)

Preheat oven to 375°F. Grease 9-inch square pan with olive oil. In medium bowl, combine flour, baking soda, cinnamon, nutmeg and cloves.

In large bowl, mix brown sugar and olive oil with electric mixer at medium speed until blended. Add applesauce; mix well. Add flour mixture all at once; beat on low speed until well blended. Stir in raisins and nuts. Spoon batter into prepared pan.

Bake 20 to 25 minutes or until lightly browned. Cool completely on wire rack. Cut into squares. Serve plain, dusted with powdered sugar or frosted with whipped cream, if desired.

# Fruity Jell-O® Cake

**Makes 24 servings**

**Prep Time:**
*15 minutes*

**Bake Time:**
*55 minutes*

2 cups chopped strawberries
1 can (20 ounces) crushed
   pineapple, drained
1 package (8-serving size) or
   2 packages (4-serving size
   each) JELL-O® Brand
   Strawberry Flavor Gelatin

3 cups miniature marshmallows
1 package (2-layer size) white
   cake mix
2 eggs

**HEAT** oven to 350°F.

**ARRANGE** fruit on bottom of 13×9-inch pan. Sprinkle with gelatin. Cover with marshmallows.

**PREPARE** cake mix as directed on package, omitting oil and using 2 eggs and water as specified. Spread batter over mixture in pan.

**BAKE** 50 to 55 minutes. Remove to rack; cool 15 minutes. Serve warm with thawed COOL WHIP® Whipped Topping, if desired.

# Applesauce Molasses Snacking Cake

| |
|---|
| 1½ cups all-purpose flour |
| 1 cup whole wheat flour |
| 1 teaspoon baking soda |
| 1 teaspoon ground cinnamon |
| ¼ teaspoon ground allspice |
| 1 cup firmly packed dark brown sugar |
| ½ cup FLEISCHMANN'S® Original Margarine, softened |
| 1¼ cups sweetened applesauce |
| ½ cup EGG BEATERS® Healthy Real Egg Product |
| ⅓ cup light molasses |
| ½ cup seedless raisins |
| Powdered sugar, optional |

**Makes 4 dozen bars**

**Prep Time:**
*25 minutes*

**Bake Time:**
*25 minutes*

In medium bowl, combine all-purpose flour, whole wheat flour, baking soda, cinnamon and allspice; set aside.

In large bowl, with electric mixer at medium speed, beat brown sugar and margarine until creamy. Add applesauce, Egg Beaters® and molasses; beat until smooth. Gradually add flour mixture, beating until well blended. Stir in raisins. Spread batter into ungreased 15×10×1-inch baking pan. Bake at 350°F for 20 to 25 minutes or until toothpick inserted in center comes out clean. Cool in pan on wire rack. Dust with powdered sugar before serving if desired. Cut into 48 (2×1-inch) bars.

# Pumpkin Cheesecake

**Makes 16 servings**

*Note:*

The texture and flavor of cheesecakes improve with chilling. Bake cheesecake one to two days before serving; keep wrapped and refrigerated.

**Crust**
1½ cups graham cracker crumbs
⅓ cup butter or margarine, melted
¼ cup granulated sugar

**Filling**
3 packages (8 ounces *each*) cream cheese, softened
1 cup granulated sugar
¼ cup packed light brown sugar
2 large eggs
1 can (15 ounces) LIBBY'S® 100% Pure Pumpkin

⅔ cup (5 fluid-ounce can) NESTLÉ® CARNATION® Evaporated Milk
2 tablespoons cornstarch
1¼ teaspoons ground cinnamon
½ teaspoon ground nutmeg

**Topping**
1 container (16 ounces) sour cream, at room temperature
⅓ cup granulated sugar
1 teaspoon vanilla extract

**PREHEAT** oven to 350°F.

### For Crust
**COMBINE** graham cracker crumbs, butter and granulated sugar in medium bowl. Press onto bottom and 1 inch up side of 9-inch springform pan. Bake for 6 to 8 minutes (do not allow to brown). Cool on wire rack for 10 minutes.

### For Filling
**BEAT** cream cheese, granulated sugar and brown sugar in large mixer bowl until fluffy. Beat in eggs, pumpkin and milk. Add cornstarch, cinnamon and nutmeg; beat well. Pour into crust.

**BAKE** for 55 to 60 minutes or until edge is set but center still moves slightly.

### For Topping
**MIX** sour cream, granulated sugar and vanilla extract in small bowl; mix well. Spread over surface of warm cheesecake. Bake for 5 minutes. Cool on wire rack. Refrigerate for several hours or overnight. Remove side of springform pan.

# Peanut Butter Cheesecake

Makes 1 cheesecake

### Crust
1¼ cup graham cracker crumbs
¼ cup sugar
¼ cup (½ stick) butter, melted

### Peanut Butter Mixture
⅔ cup powdered sugar
½ cup peanut butter
¼ cup brown sugar

### Cheese Filling
2 (8 ounce) packages cream
   cheese, softened
1 cup sugar
2 tablespoons lemon juice
2 teaspoons vanilla
2 large eggs

For crust, mix graham cracker crumbs with sugar. Add butter and press into 9-inch glass pie pan. Bake at 325°F for 8 minutes.

For peanut butter mixture, blend powdered sugar and peanut butter with fork until balls form. Blend in brown sugar. Save 2 tablespoons for garnish. Spread remaining mixture over crust.

For cheese filling, mix cream cheese with sugar, lemon juice, vanilla and eggs. Beat 5 minutes. Pour over peanut butter mixture and garnish with remaining peanut butter mixture. Bake at 350°F until done, about 35 minutes. Cool 3 hours.

Favorite recipe from **Peanut Advisory Board**

# Miss Kathleen's Texas Sheet Cake

**Makes 12 to 14 servings**

**Cake**

PAM® No-Stick Cooking Spray
2 cups all-purpose flour
2 cups sugar
½ teaspoon salt
1 cup water
⅔ cup WESSON® Canola Oil
4 tablespoons cocoa powder
½ cup sour cream
2 eggs, at room temperature, beaten
1 teaspoon baking soda

**Frosting**

½ cup (1 stick) butter or margarine, softened
⅓ cup milk
4 tablespoons cocoa powder
1 box (16 ounces) powdered sugar
1 cup chopped nuts

## Cake

Preheat oven to 400°F. Spray a 18×10½×1-inch jelly-roll pan with PAM® Cooking Spray; lightly dust with flour. Set aside. In a large mixing bowl, sift together flour, sugar and salt; set aside. In saucepan, combine water, Wesson® Oil and cocoa powder; heat to boiling over LOW heat. Stir occasionally until cocoa is dissolved. While oil mixture is heating, blend together sour cream, eggs and baking soda; mix well. When oil mixture is hot and cocoa has dissolved, add to flour mixture; mix slightly. Pour sour cream mixture into flour mixture; stir until well blended and smooth. Pour batter into jelly-roll pan. Bake for 20 minutes or until wooden pick inserted into center comes out clean.

## Frosting

Meanwhile, in a medium saucepan, combine butter, milk and cocoa powder. Bring to a light boil over LOW heat, stirring occasionally. Remove pan from heat; sift in sugar. Beat well until smooth; fold in nuts. Spread frosting over cake *immediately* after baking.

# Mahogany Sour Cream Cake

4 squares BAKER'S®
　　Unsweetened Baking
　　Chocolate
½ cup water
1 container (8 ounces)
　　BREAKSTONE'S® *or*
　　KNUDSEN® Sour Cream
1¾ cups flour
1½ teaspoons CALUMET®
　　Baking Powder

1 teaspoon baking soda
½ teaspoon salt
⅔ cup butter or margarine,
　　softened
1 cup granulated sugar
⅔ cup firmly packed brown
　　sugar
3 eggs
2 teaspoons vanilla

**Makes 12 to 16 servings**

**Prep Time:**
*30 minutes*

**Bake Time:**
*40 minutes*

**HEAT** oven to 350°F. Grease and flour two 9-inch round cake pans.

**MICROWAVE** chocolate and water in medium microwavable bowl on HIGH 1 to 2 minutes until chocolate is almost melted, stirring halfway through heating time. Stir until chocolate is completely melted; cool thoroughly. Stir in sour cream.

**MIX** flour, baking powder, soda and salt; set aside. Beat butter and sugars in large bowl with electric mixer on medium speed until light and fluffy. Add eggs, 1 at a time, beating well after each addition. Add vanilla. Add flour mixture alternately with chocolate mixture, beating well after each addition until smooth. Pour into prepared pans.

**BAKE** 35 to 40 minutes or until toothpick inserted in center comes out clean. Cool cakes in pans 10 minutes; remove from pans. Cool completely on wire rack. Fill and frost as desired.

# Mini Cheesecakes

**Makes 2 dozen mini cheesecakes**

**Prep Time:**
*20 minutes*

**Bake Time:**
*20 minutes*

1½ cups graham cracker or chocolate wafer crumbs
¼ cup sugar
¼ cup (½ stick) butter or margarine, melted
3 (8-ounce) packages cream cheese, softened

1 (14-ounce) can EAGLE® BRAND Sweetened Condensed Milk (NOT evaporated milk)
3 eggs
2 teaspoons vanilla extract

*1.* Preheat oven to 300°F. In small mixing bowl, combine crumbs, sugar and butter; press equal portions firmly on bottoms of 24 lightly greased or paper-lined muffin cups.

*2.* In large mixing bowl, beat cream cheese until fluffy. Gradually beat in Eagle Brand until smooth. Add eggs and vanilla; mix well. Spoon equal amounts of mixture (about 3 tablespoons) into prepared cups. Bake 20 minutes or until cakes spring back when lightly touched. Cool.* Chill. Garnish as desired. Refrigerate leftovers.

*If greased muffin cups are used, cool baked cheesecakes. Freeze 15 minutes; remove with narrow spatula. Proceed as directed above.

**Chocolate Mini Cheesecakes:** *Melt 1 cup (6 ounces) semi-sweet chocolate chips; mix into batter. Proceed as directed above, baking 20 to 25 minutes.*

# Chocolate Chip Cheesecake

1½ cups finely crushed crème-
    filled chocolate sandwich
    cookie crumbs (about
    18 cookies)
2 to 3 tablespoons butter or
    margarine, melted
3 (8-ounce) packages cream
    cheese, softened
1 (14-ounce) can EAGLE®
    BRAND Sweetened
    Condensed Milk
    (NOT evaporated milk)

3 eggs
2 teaspoons vanilla extract
1 cup mini semi-sweet
    chocolate chips, divided
1 teaspoon all-purpose flour

Makes one 9-inch
cheesecake

*Note:*

For the best

distribution of

chocolate chips

throughout this

cheesecake, do

not oversoften

or overbeat the

cream cheese.

*1.* Preheat oven to 300°F. In small mixing bowl, combine cookie crumbs and butter; press firmly on bottom of ungreased 9-inch springform pan.

*2.* In large mixing bowl, beat cream cheese until fluffy. Gradually beat in Eagle Brand until smooth. Add eggs and vanilla; mix well.

*3.* In small mixing bowl, toss ½ cup chips with flour to coat; stir into cheese mixture. Pour into crust. Sprinkle remaining ½ cup chips evenly over top.

*4.* Bake 1 hour or until cake springs back when lightly touched. Cool to room temperature. Chill thoroughly. Garnish as desired. Refrigerate leftovers.

# Chocolate Truffle Cake with Strawberry Sauce

**Makes 12 servings**

## Note:

Dusting the inside of the cake pan with flour helps the cake to develop a thin, crisp crust and prevents the cake from absorbing the fat used to grease the pan.

### Truffle Cake

1¾ cups (11.5-ounce package) NESTLÉ® TOLL HOUSE® Milk Chocolate Morsels, *divided*
½ cup (1 stick) butter
3 large eggs
⅔ cup granulated sugar
1 teaspoon vanilla extract
¼ teaspoon salt
⅔ cup all-purpose flour

### Glaze

¼ cup NESTLÉ® TOLL HOUSE® Butterscotch Flavored Morsels
¼ cup creamy peanut butter

### Sauce

2 cups fresh or frozen strawberries, thawed
2 tablespoons granulated sugar
Garnish suggestions: whipped topping, fresh strawberries, fresh mint leaves

### For Truffle Cake

**PREHEAT** oven to 350°F. Grease and flour 9-inch springform pan. Melt *1 cup* milk chocolate morsels and butter in small, microwave-safe bowl on MEDIUM-HIGH (70%) power for 1 minute; stir. Microwave at additional 10- to 20-second intervals, stirring until smooth. Cool for 10 minutes.

**BEAT** eggs, ⅔ cup sugar, vanilla extract and salt in large mixer bowl. Blend in chocolate mixture. Stir in flour; mix well. Pour into prepared pan.

**BAKE** for 30 to 35 minutes or until wooden pick inserted in center comes out clean. Cool completely in pan on wire rack. Remove side of pan.

### For Glaze

**MELT** *remaining* milk chocolate morsels, butterscotch morsels and peanut butter in small, microwave-safe bowl on MEDIUM-HIGH (70%) power for 1 minute; stir. Microwave at additional 10- to 20-second intervals, stirring until smooth. Cool slightly. Spread glaze over top and side of cooled cake. Refrigerate for 30 minutes or until glaze is set.

### For Strawberry Sauce

**PLACE** strawberries and 2 tablespoons sugar in blender; cover. Blend until smooth. Refrigerate until serving time. To serve, cut into wedges. Garnish with Strawberry Sauce, whipped topping, strawberries and mint leaves.

# Cherry-Mallow Cake

| | | |
|---|---|---|
| 4 cups miniature marshmallows (about ¾ of 10½-ounce package)<br>1 (18.25-ounce) package yellow cake mix | 1 (21-ounce) can cherry pie filling | **Makes 15 servings** |

Spray 13×9×2-inch baking pan with vegetable cooking spray. Place marshmallows evenly in bottom of pan.

Prepare cake mix according to package directions. Pour batter over marshmallows. Spoon cherry filling evenly over cake batter.

Bake in preheated 350°F oven 30 to 40 minutes. Top of cake will be bubbly and marshmallows will be sticky. Let cool before serving.

Favorite recipe from **Cherry Marketing Institute**

# Chocolate Bar Cake

**Makes 10 to 12 servings**

1 HERSHEY'S Milk Chocolate Bar (7 ounces), broken into pieces
½ cup (1 stick) butter or margarine, softened
1 cup boiling water
2 cups all-purpose flour
1½ cups sugar
½ cup HERSHEY'S Cocoa
2 teaspoons baking soda
1 teaspoon salt
2 eggs
½ cup dairy sour cream
1 teaspoon vanilla extract
Vanilla Glaze (recipe follows)

*1.* Heat oven to 350°F. Grease and flour 12-cup fluted tube pan.

*2.* Stir together chocolate, butter and water in small bowl until chocolate is melted. Stir together flour, sugar, cocoa, baking soda and salt in large bowl; gradually add chocolate mixture, beating on medium speed of mixer until well blended. Add eggs, sour cream and vanilla; blend well. Beat 1 minute. Pour batter into prepared pan.

*3.* Bake 50 to 55 minutes or until wooden pick inserted in center comes out clean. Cool 10 minutes; remove from pan to wire rack. Cool completely. Prepare Vanilla Glaze; drizzle over cake.

<u>Vanilla Glaze:</u> *Microwave ¼ cup (½ stick) butter or margarine in medium microwave-safe bowl at HIGH (100%) 30 seconds or until melted. Gradually stir in 2 cups powdered sugar, 2 tablespoons hot water and 1 teaspoon vanilla extract; beat with wire whisk until smooth and slightly thickened. Add additional water, 1 teaspoon at a time, if needed.*

# Chocolate Cherry Cheesecake

1 (8-ounce) package cream cheese, softened
¾ cup sugar
2 eggs
2 (1-ounce) squares semi-sweet chocolate, melted

1 teaspoon vanilla
1 (6-ounce) READY CRUST® Chocolate Pie Crust
1 (21-ounce) can cherry pie filling

Makes 8 servings

**Prep Time:**
*15 minutes*

**Bake Time:**
*35 minutes*

**Chill Time:**
*3 hours*

*1.* Preheat oven to 325°F. Beat cream cheese in medium bowl until fluffy. Add sugar, eggs, chocolate and vanilla; mix well. Place crust on baking sheet. Pour mixture into crust.

*2.* Bake 35 minutes or until filling springs back when touched lightly. Cool on wire rack.

*3.* Spread cherry pie filling over top. Chill 3 hours. Refrigerate leftovers.

## Common Weights & Measures

*For accurate results, always use dry measures (plastic or metal) for dry ingredients and clearly marked glass or plastic measuring cups for liquids.*

½ tablespoon = 1½ teaspoons

1 tablespoon = 3 teaspoons

¼ cup = 4 tablespoons

⅓ cup = 5 tablespoons plus 1 teaspoon

½ cup = 8 tablespoons

¾ cup = 12 tablespoons

1 cup = 16 tablespoons

½ pint = 1 cup or 8 fluid ounces

1 pint = 2 cups or 16 fluid ounces

1 quart = 4 cups or 2 pints or 32 fluid ounces

1 gallon = 16 cups or 4 quarts

1 pound = 16 ounces

# Fudgy Banana Oat Cake

**Makes 15 servings**

*Note:*

Bananas add body and natural sweetness to cakes. Be careful not to overbeat this fruit batter or it will become gummy.

Topping:
- 1 cup QUAKER® Oats (quick or old fashioned, uncooked)
- ½ cup firmly packed brown sugar
- ¼ cup (½ stick) margarine or butter, chilled

Filling:
- 1 cup (6 ounces) semisweet chocolate pieces
- ⅔ cup sweetened condensed milk (not evaporated milk)
- 1 tablespoon margarine or butter

Cake:
- 1 package (18.25 ounces) devil's food cake mix
- 1¼ cups mashed ripe bananas (about 3 large)
- ⅓ cup vegetable oil
- 3 eggs
- Banana slices (optional)
- Whipped cream (optional)

Heat oven to 350°F. Lightly grease bottom only of 13×9-inch baking pan. For topping, combine oats and brown sugar. Cut in margarine until mixture is crumbly; set aside.

For filling, in small saucepan, heat chocolate pieces, sweetened condensed milk and margarine over low heat until chocolate is melted, stirring occasionally. Remove from heat; set aside.

For cake, in large mixing bowl, combine cake mix, bananas, oil and eggs. Blend at low speed of electric mixer until dry ingredients are moistened. Beat at medium speed 2 minutes. Spread batter evenly into prepared pan. Drop chocolate mixture by teaspoonfuls evenly over batter. Sprinkle with reserved oat mixture. Bake 40 to 45 minutes or until cake pulls away from sides of pan and topping is golden brown. Cool cake in pan on wire rack. Garnish with banana slices and sweetened whipped cream, if desired.

# Hershey's Red Velvet Cake

½ cup (1 stick) butter or
    margarine, softened
1½ cups sugar
2 eggs
1 teaspoon vanilla extract
1 cup buttermilk or sour milk*
2 tablespoons (1-ounce bottle)
    red food color
2 cups all-purpose flour
⅓ cup HERSHEY'S Cocoa
1 teaspoon salt

1½ teaspoons baking soda
1 tablespoon white vinegar
1 can (16 ounces) ready-to-
    spread vanilla frosting
HERSHEY'S MINI CHIPS™
    Semi-Sweet Chocolate
    Chips or HERSHEY'S Milk
    Chocolate Chips (optional)

*To sour milk: Use 1 tablespoon white vinegar
plus milk to equal 1 cup.

*1.* Heat oven to 350°F. Grease and flour 13×9×2-inch
baking pan.**

*2.* Beat butter and sugar in large bowl; add eggs and vanilla,
beating well. Stir together buttermilk and food color. Stir together
flour, cocoa and salt; add alternately to butter mixture with
buttermilk mixture, mixing well. Stir in baking soda and vinegar.
Pour into prepared pan.

*3.* Bake 30 to 35 minutes or until wooden pick inserted in center
comes out clean. Cool completely in pan on wire rack. Frost;
garnish with chocolate chips, if desired.

**This recipe can be made in 2 (9-inch) cake pans. Bake at 350°F for 30 to 35 minutes.

# Philadelphia® 3-Step® Chocolate Chip Cheesecake

**Makes 8 servings**

**Prep Time:**
*10 minutes plus refrigerating*

**Bake Time:**
*40 minutes*

2 packages (8 ounces each)
   PHILADELPHIA® Cream
   Cheese, softened
½ cup sugar
½ teaspoon vanilla
2 eggs

¾ cup miniature semi-sweet
   chocolate chips, divided
1 HONEY MAID® Graham or
   OREO® Pie Crust (6 ounces)

*1.* BEAT cream cheese, sugar and vanilla with electric mixer on medium speed until well blended. Add eggs; mix just until blended. Stir in ½ cup of the chips.

*2.* POUR into crust. Sprinkle with remaining ¼ cup chips.

*3.* BAKE at 350°F for 40 minutes or until center is almost set. Cool. Refrigerate 3 hours or overnight.

**Peanut Butter Chocolate Chip Cheesecake:** *Prepare as directed, adding ⅓ cup peanut butter to cream cheese mixture before beating in eggs.*

**Banana Chocolate Chip Cheesecake:** *Prepare as directed, adding ½ cup mashed ripe banana to cream cheese mixture before beating in eggs.*

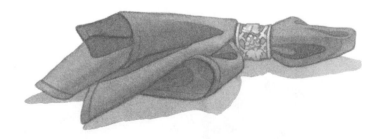

# Delicate White Chocolate Cake

1 package DUNCAN HINES®
   Moist Deluxe® White
   Cake Mix
1 package (4-serving size)
   vanilla-flavor instant
   pudding and pie filling mix
4 egg whites
1 cup water
½ cup vegetable oil
5 ounces finely chopped white
   chocolate

1 cup cherry preserves
8 drops red food coloring
   (optional)
2 cups whipping cream, chilled
2 tablespoons confectioners'
   sugar
   Maraschino cherries for
   garnish
1 ounce white chocolate
   shavings for garnish

Makes 12 to
16 servings

*Note:*

To line cake pans with

waxed paper, simply

trace the bottom of the

cake pan onto a piece

of waxed paper and cut

to fit. (If you make the

same cake often, cut

out a stack of circles

at the same time.)

*1.* Preheat oven to 350°F. Cut waxed paper circles to fit bottoms of three 9-inch round cake pans. Grease bottoms and sides of pans. Line with waxed paper circles.

*2.* Combine cake mix, pudding mix, egg whites, water and oil in large mixing bowl. Beat at medium speed with electric mixer for 2 minutes. Fold in chopped white chocolate. Pour into prepared pans. Bake at 350°F for 18 to 22 minutes or until toothpick inserted in center comes out clean. Cool in pans 15 minutes. Invert onto cooling racks. Peel off waxed paper. Cool completely.

*3.* Combine cherry preserves and food coloring, if desired. Stir to blend color.

*4.* Beat whipping cream in large bowl until soft peaks form. Add sugar gradually. Beat until stiff peaks form.

*5.* To assemble, place one cake layer on serving plate. Spread ½ cup cherry preserves over cake. Place second cake layer on top. Spread with remaining preserves. Place third cake layer on top. Frost sides and top of cake with whipped cream. Decorate with maraschino cherries and white chocolate shavings. Refrigerate until ready to serve.

# Grandma's Favorite Molasses Fruitcake

**Varies by version**

2 SUNKIST® oranges
1 cup light molasses
1 package (15 ounces) raisins
1 package (8 ounces) dates, chopped
2 containers (16 ounces each) glacé fruit mix
1¼ cups granulated sugar
1 cup butter or margarine, softened
6 eggs

3 cups all-purpose flour
1½ teaspoons ground cinnamon
1 teaspoon baking soda
1 teaspoon ground nutmeg
½ teaspoon ground allspice
½ teaspoon ground cloves
1 cup freshly squeezed SUNKIST® orange juice
2 cups nut halves
Powdered sugar

Cut oranges into large chunks. In blender or food processor, finely chop oranges to measure 1⅓ cups. In large saucepan, combine chopped oranges, molasses, raisins and dates; bring to a boil. Reduce heat and simmer 5 to 10 minutes. Remove from heat; stir in fruit mix. Set aside.

Preheat oven to 300°F. In large bowl, cream together sugar and butter. Beat in eggs, 1 at a time. Sift together flour, cinnamon, baking soda, nutmeg, allspice and cloves. Add to creamed mixture alternately with orange juice. Stir batter into molasses-fruit mixture. Add nuts. Divide batter; spoon 8 cups batter into well-greased 10-inch Bundt or tube pan. With remaining 6 cups batter, make 2 dozen cupcakes or 8 dozen mini fruitcakes (see variations). Bake cake 2 hours or until toothpick inserted in center comes out clean. Cool 10 minutes. Remove from pan; cool on wire rack. To serve, sprinkle with powdered sugar. Garnish with orange pieces and candied cherries, if desired.

**"Cupcake" Fruitcakes:** *With 6 cups batter, spoon about ¼ cup batter into each of 24 paper-lined muffin cups (2½×1¼ inch). Press candied cherry or nut half into top of each, if desired. Bake at 300°F 40 to 45 minutes. Makes 2 dozen cupcake-size fruitcakes.*

**"Mini" Fruitcakes:** *With 6 cups batter, spoon about 1 tablespoon batter into each of 96 paper-lined "miniature" muffin cups (1¾×1 inch). Press candied cherry or nut half into top of each, if desired. Bake at 300°F 30 to 35 minutes Makes 8 dozen miniature fruitcakes.*

# Velvety Chocolate Cake

1 package (4 ounces) BAKER'S® GERMAN'S® Sweet Baking Chocolate, broken in pieces
6 tablespoons butter *or* margarine

3 tablespoons flour
3 eggs, separated
¼ cup sugar

**Makes 8 servings**

**Prep Time:**
*15 minutes*

**Bake Time:**
*20 minutes*

**HEAT** oven to 350°F.

**MICROWAVE** chocolate and butter in microwavable bowl on HIGH 1 to 2 minutes or until butter is melted. Stir until chocolate is completely melted. Stir in flour. Add egg yolks, 1 at a time, stirring until blended.

**BEAT** egg whites until foamy. Gradually add sugar, beating until soft peaks form. Gently fold chocolate mixture into egg whites, blending thoroughly. Pour into greased and floured 8-inch round cake pan.

**BAKE** 20 minutes or until cake tester inserted in center comes out clean. Cool in pan 10 minutes. (Cake may settle as it cools.) Remove from pan; cool completely, upside down, on wire rack. Frost top and sides, if desired. Serve with fresh raspberry purée, if desired.

**Variation:** *Prepare as directed, substituting 4 squares BAKER'S® Semi-Sweet Baking Chocolate for the sweet chocolate.*

**High Altitude Instructions:** *Increase flour to ¼ cup and eggs to 4. Bake 20 to 25 minutes.*

# Texas Peanuts 'n' Caramel Cake

**Makes 8 servings**

*Note:*

Make sure the cake layers have completely cooled before frosting them. To keep the cake plate clean, place small strips of waxed paper under the edges of the cake; remove them after the cake has been frosted.

**Cake**
1½ cups plus ⅔ cup sugar, divided
⅔ cup boiling water
½ cup vegetable shortening
1 teaspoon vanilla extract
2 eggs
2½ cups all-purpose or cake flour
1 tablespoon baking powder
¾ cup cold water
¾ cup dry-roasted unsalted peanuts, finely chopped

**Filling and Frosting**
½ cup reduced-fat unsalted peanut butter
½ cup currant jelly
1 container (12 ounces) low-calorie frozen whipped topping, thawed
½ cup dry-roasted unsalted peanuts, coarsely chopped

In large saucepan over medium heat, melt ⅔ cup sugar, stirring occasionally, until deep golden brown. Remove from heat and add boiling water. Return to heat; stir constantly until sugar is dissolved. Continue to cook until reduced and syrup measures ½ cup. Remove from heat and cool.

In large mixing bowl, beat together shortening and remaining 1½ cups sugar until light and fluffy. Beat in vanilla, then eggs, 1 at a time. Stir flour and baking powder into creamed mixture alternately with cold water. Add sugar syrup and beat 4 minutes. Stir in finely chopped peanuts.

Divide mixture into two greased and floured 9-inch round pans. Bake in preheated 350°F oven 25 to 30 minutes or until toothpick inserted in center of cake comes out clean. Cool 5 to 10 minutes in pans; remove from pans and cool completely on wire rack.

To assemble cake, spread peanut butter over top of 1 layer, then spread jelly over peanut butter. Place second cake layer on top and frost sides and top of cake with whipped topping. Sprinkle coarsely chopped peanuts on top. Refrigerate until ready to serve.

Favorite recipe from **Texas Peanut Producers Board**

# Blueberry Cheesecake

1 (8-ounce) package cream
   cheese, softened
½ cup sugar
2 eggs, beaten
1 (6-ounce) READY CRUST®
   Graham Cracker Pie Crust

1 (21-ounce) can blueberry
   pie filling
Frozen whipped topping,
   thawed

**Makes 8 servings**

**Prep Time:**
*10 minutes*

**Bake Time:**
*25 to 30 minutes*

**Chill Time:**
*3 hours*

*1.* Preheat oven to 325°F. Beat cream cheese, sugar and eggs in small bowl until fluffy. Place crust on baking sheet. Pour mixture into crust.

*2.* Bake 25 to 30 minutes or until center is almost set. Cool.

*3.* Spread blueberry filling on top. Garnish with whipped topping. Chill 3 hours. Refrigerate leftovers.

# Orange Mousse Cake

1 cup cold milk
1 package (4-serving size)
   JELL-O® Vanilla Flavor
   Instant Pudding & Pie
   Filling

1 tub (8 ounces) COOL WHIP®
   Whipped Topping, thawed
2 teaspoons grated orange peel
1 package (9 ounces) chocolate
   wafer cookies

**Makes 8 servings**

**Prep Time:**
*15 minutes*

POUR milk into medium bowl. Add pudding mix. Beat with wire whisk 1 minute. Gently stir in half of the whipped topping and orange peel.

SPREAD about 1 tablespoon pudding mixture on each cookie and stack in groups of 6 cookies. Lay stacks down, side by side, on tray to form rectangle. Frost top and sides with remaining whipped topping. To serve, slice diagonally.

# Oreo® White Chocolate Mousse Cake

**Makes 16 servings**

**Prep Time:**
*20 minutes*

**Chill Time:**
*6 hours and 30 minutes*

1 (1-pound 4-ounce) package Holiday OREO® Chocolate Sandwich Cookies, divided
6 tablespoons margarine or butter, melted
1 envelope KNOX® Unflavored Gelatine
1¼ cups milk

1 (11-ounce) package white chocolate chips
1 pint heavy cream, whipped, or 4 cups COOL WHIP® Whipped Topping, thawed
Fresh raspberries, for garnish

*1.* Finely crush 24 cookies. Mix crushed cookies and margarine or butter; press on bottom and 1 inch up side of 9-inch springform pan. Set aside.

*2.* Sprinkle gelatine over milk in large saucepan; let stand 1 minute. Stir over low heat about 3 minutes or until gelatine completely dissolves.

*3.* Add white chocolate chips to gelatine mixture; continue heating until chocolate chips are melted and smooth. Refrigerate 30 minutes or until slightly thickened.

*4.* Coarsely chop 24 cookies. Gently fold chopped cookies and whipped cream into cooled chocolate mixture. Spoon into prepared crust. Refrigerate 6 hours or overnight.

*5.* Halve remaining cookies; garnish with cookie halves and raspberries if desired.

# Perfect
# Pies &
# Tarts

CHAPTER TWELVE

# Luscious Brownie Chip Pie

**Makes 8 servings**

25 CHIPS AHOY!® Chocolate Chip
　Cookies, divided
½ cup margarine or butter,
　melted, divided
½ cup light corn syrup
3 eggs

½ cup sugar
⅓ cup unsweetened cocoa
2 teaspoons vanilla extract
　Whipped cream, for garnish
　Chocolate curls, for garnish

*Note:*

To make decorative
chocolate curls, bring
a bar of semisweet
or milk chocolate to
room temperature.
Run a clean, odor-free
vegetable peeler along
the surface of the
chocolate to
create curls.

*1.* Cut 5 cookies in half; set aside. Roll remaining cookies between two pieces of waxed paper until fine crumbs form. Combine cookie crumbs and ¼ cup melted margarine or butter; press on bottom and up side of 9-inch pie plate.

*2.* Heat remaining ¼ cup margarine or butter and corn syrup in saucepan until warm; remove from heat. Beat in eggs, sugar, cocoa and vanilla; pour into crust. Bake at 350°F 15 minutes; insert cookie halves around edge of pie crust.

*3.* Bake 15 to 20 minutes more or until set, tenting with foil during last 5 to 10 minutes if excessive browning occurs. Cool. Garnish with whipped cream and chocolate curls.

# Apple Custard Tart

1 folded refrigerated unbaked
  pastry crust (one-half of
  15-ounce package)
1 (14-ounce) can EAGLE®
  BRAND Sweetened
  Condensed Milk
  (NOT evaporated milk)
1½ cups sour cream
¼ cup thawed frozen apple juice
  concentrate

1 egg
1½ teaspoons vanilla extract
¼ teaspoon ground cinnamon
  Apple Cinnamon Glaze
  (recipe follows)
2 medium all-purpose apples,
  cored, pared and thinly
  sliced
1 tablespoon butter or
  margarine

**Makes 1 tart**

Prep Time:
*10 minutes*

Bake Time:
*40 minutes*

Cool Time:
*1 hour*

Chill Time:
*4 hours*

*1.* Let refrigerated pastry crust stand at room temperature according to package directions. Preheat oven to 375°F. On floured surface, roll pastry crust from center to edge, forming circle about 13 inches in diameter. Ease pastry into 11-inch tart pan with removable bottom. Trim pastry even with rim of pan. Place pan on baking sheet. Bake crust 15 minutes or until lightly golden.

*2.* Meanwhile, in medium mixing bowl, beat Eagle Brand, sour cream, apple juice concentrate, egg, vanilla and cinnamon in small bowl until smooth. Pour into baked pie crust. Bake 25 minutes or until center appears set when shaken. Cool 1 hour on wire rack. Prepare Apple Cinnamon Glaze.

*3.* In large skillet, cook apples in butter until tender-crisp. Arrange apples on top of tart; drizzle with Apple Cinnamon Glaze. Chill in refrigerator at least 4 hours. Store leftovers loosely covered in refrigerator.

**Apple Cinnamon Glaze:** *In small saucepan, combine ⅓ cup thawed frozen apple juice concentrate, 1 teaspoon cornstarch and ½ teaspoon ground cinnamon. Mix well. Cook and stir over low heat until thick and bubbly.*

# by's® Famous Pumpkin Pie

**Makes 8 servings**

¾ cup granulated sugar
½ teaspoon salt
1 teaspoon ground cinnamon
½ teaspoon ground ginger
¼ teaspoon ground cloves
2 large eggs
1 can (15 ounces) LIBBY'S®
   100% Pure Pumpkin

1 can (12 fluid ounces)
   NESTLÉ® CARNATION®
   Evaporated Milk*
1 *unbaked* 9-inch (4-cup
   volume) deep-dish pie shell
Whipped cream

*For lower fat/calorie pie, substitute
CARNATION® Evaporated Lowfat Milk or
Evaporated Fat Free Milk.*

**MIX** sugar, salt, cinnamon, ginger and cloves in small bowl. Beat eggs in large bowl. Stir in pumpkin and sugar-spice mixture. Gradually stir in evaporated milk.

**POUR** into pie shell.

**BAKE** in preheated 425°F. oven for 15 minutes. Reduce temperature to 350°F.; bake 40 to 50 minutes or until knife inserted near center comes out clean. Cool on wire rack for 2 hours. Serve immediately or refrigerate. Top with whipped cream before serving.

**Note:** *Do not freeze, as this will cause the crust to separate from the filling.*

**Substitution:** *Substitute 1¾ teaspoons pumpkin pie spice for the cinnamon, ginger and cloves; however, the taste will be slightly different.*

**For 2 Shallow Pies:** *Substitute two 9-inch (2-cup volume) pie shells. Bake in preheated 425°F. oven for 15 minutes. Reduce temperature to 350°F.; bake for 20 to 30 minutes or until pies test done.*

# Rustic Apple Croustade

Makes 8 servings

1⅓ cups all-purpose flour
¼ teaspoon salt
2 tablespoons butter or margarine
2 tablespoons vegetable shortening
4 to 5 tablespoons ice water
⅓ cup packed light brown sugar

1 tablespoon cornstarch
1 teaspoon cinnamon, divided
3 large Jonathan or MacIntosh apples peeled, cored and thinly sliced (4 cups)
1 egg white, beaten
1 tablespoon granulated sugar

*1.* Combine flour and salt in small bowl. Cut in butter and shortening with pastry blender or two knives until mixture resembles coarse crumbs. Mix in ice water, 1 tablespoon at a time, until mixture comes together and forms a soft dough. Wrap in plastic wrap; refrigerate 30 minutes.

*2.* Preheat oven to 375°F. Roll out pastry on floured surface to ⅛-inch thickness. Cut into 12-inch circle. Transfer pastry to nonstick jelly-roll pan.

*3.* Combine brown sugar, cornstarch and ¾ teaspoon cinnamon in medium bowl; mix well. Add apples; toss well. Spoon apple mixture into center of pastry, leaving 1½-inch border. Fold pastry over apples, folding edges in gently and pressing down lightly. Brush egg white over pastry. Combine remaining ¼ teaspoon cinnamon and granulated sugar in small bowl; sprinkle evenly over tart.

*4.* Bake 35 to 40 minutes or until apples are tender and crust is golden brown. Let stand 20 minutes before serving. Cut into wedges.

*Note:*

A rustic pie crust that doesn't call for a pie pan is easy to form; it just takes a little practice. Fold over 1 inch of pie crust toward the center to form the rim of the tart, then pleat the dough as necessary.

# Michigan Blueberry Pie

**Makes 1 (9-inch) pie**

**Crust**
   Classic Crisco® Double Crust
   (page 512)

**Filling**
   3 packages (12 ounces each)
      frozen blueberries, thawed
      and drained, reserving
      liquid
   ¼ cup quick-cooking tapioca
   1½ cups sugar

   ¼ cup cornstarch
   2 tablespoons grated orange
      peel
   1 tablespoon butter or
      margarine
   1 tablespoon cinnamon

**Glaze**
   Milk
   Sugar (optional)

*1.* For crust, prepare as directed. Press bottom crust into 9-inch pie plate. Do not bake. Heat oven to 425°F.

*2.* For filling, pour reserved liquid into medium saucepan. Stir in tapioca. Let stand 5 minutes. Stir in 1½ cups sugar and cornstarch. Cook and stir on medium heat until mixture comes to a boil and thickens. Stir in orange peel, butter and cinnamon. Fold in blueberries. Bring to a boil. Pour into unbaked pie crust. Moisten pastry edge with water.

*3.* Roll top crust same as bottom. Lift onto filled pie. Trim ½ inch beyond edge of pie plate. Fold top edge under bottom crust. Flute.

*4.* For glaze, brush with milk. Sprinkle with sugar, if desired. Cut slits in top crust to allow steam to escape.

*5.* Bake at 425°F for 45 minutes, or until filling in center is bubbly and crust is golden brown. *Do not overbake.* Cover edge with foil, if necessary, to prevent overbrowning. Serve barely warm or at room temperature.

# Chocolate Pecan Pie

Pastry for single-crust pie
2 cups chopped pecans
   (about 8 ounces)
1 cup dark corn syrup
¾ cup sugar
½ cup (1 stick) I CAN'T BELIEVE
   IT'S NOT BUTTER!® Spread

⅔ cup semi-sweet chocolate
   chips (about 4 ounces)
3 eggs
1 teaspoon vanilla extract
   Pinch salt
1 cup pecan halves (about
   4 ounces)

**Makes 12 servings**

Preheat oven to 350°F.

On lightly floured surface, roll pastry into 14-inch circle. Lift and press into 9-inch deep-dish pie plate. Fold excess pastry under and press together to form a thick crust, then flute edges. Fill with chopped pecans; chill.

Meanwhile, in large saucepan, bring corn syrup and sugar to a boil over medium heat, stirring occasionally. Remove from heat and add I Can't Believe It's Not Butter! Spread and chocolate. Let stand 1 minute, then stir until chocolate is melted and mixture is smooth. In large bowl, with wire whisk, beat eggs, vanilla and salt. While beating egg mixture, very slowly drizzle in chocolate mixture. Pour into pie crust over chopped pecans. Arrange pecan halves on top. With fork, gently press pecan halves into filling to completely coat.

Bake 50 minutes or until center is set, covering edge of crust with aluminum foil after 30 minutes. On wire rack, cool completely.

# Mocha Truffle Pie

| Makes 12 servings | | |
|---|---|---|

**Prep Time:**
*15 minutes*

**Chill Time:**
*4 hours*

1 package (8 squares) BAKER'S® Semi-Sweet Baking Chocolate, broken in half
1 cup whipping (heavy) cream
¼ cup plus 2 tablespoons GENERAL FOODS INTERNATIONAL COFFEES®, any flavor, divided

2 tablespoons sugar
1 teaspoon vanilla
1 OREO® Pie Crust *or* HONEY MAID® Graham Pie Crust (6 ounces or 9 inch)
1 tub (8 ounces) COOL WHIP® Whipped Topping, thawed

**PLACE** chocolate in medium bowl; set aside. Mix cream, ¼ cup of the flavored instant coffee and sugar in small saucepan. Bring to gentle boil, stirring constantly. Remove from heat. Pour over chocolate in bowl. Let stand 2 minutes.

**WHISK** until chocolate is melted and mixture is smooth. Whisk in vanilla. Pour into crust; cover. Refrigerate 4 hours or overnight.

**STIR** remaining 2 tablespoons flavored instant coffee into whipped topping in tub until blended. Spread over top of pie. Refrigerate until ready to serve.

**Make-Ahead:** *Pie can be prepared, covered and frozen. Thaw in refrigerator for 2 hours before serving.*

# Traditional Cherry Pie

4 cups frozen tart cherries
1⅓ cups granulated sugar
3 tablespoons quick-cooking
   tapioca or cornstarch
½ teaspoon almond extract

Pastry for double crust
   9-inch pie
2 tablespoons butter or
   margarine

In medium bowl, combine cherries, sugar, tapioca and almond extract; mix well. (It is not necessary to thaw cherries before using.) Let cherry mixture stand 15 minutes.

Line 9-inch pie plate with pastry; fill with cherry mixture. Dot with butter. Cover with top crust, cutting slits for steam to escape.

Bake in preheated oven 400°F 50 to 55 minutes or until crust is golden brown and filling is bubbly.

Favorite recipe from **Cherry Marketing Institute**

# Old-Fashioned Caramel Pie

3 large eggs
1 cup (12-ounce jar)
   SMUCKER'S®
   Caramel Topping
1 cup quick-cooking or
   old-fashioned oats

½ cup sugar
½ cup milk
¼ cup butter, melted
1 teaspoon vanilla
⅛ teaspoon salt
1 (9-inch) pie shell, baked

In large bowl, beat eggs. Add remaining ingredients; blend well. Pour into baked pie shell.

Bake at 350°F for 1 hour or until set.

# Brownie Ice Cream Pie

**Makes 8 servings**

1 (21-ounce) package
   DUNCAN HINES® Chewy
   Fudge Brownie Mix
2 eggs
½ cup vegetable oil
¼ cup water
¾ cup semisweet chocolate
   chips

1 (9-inch) unbaked pastry crust
1 (10-ounce) package frozen
   sweetened sliced
   strawberries
Vanilla ice cream

*1.* Preheat oven to 350°F.

*2.* Combine brownie mix, eggs, oil and water in large bowl. Stir with spoon until well blended, about 50 strokes. Stir in chocolate chips. Spoon into crust. Bake at 350°F for 40 to 45 minutes or until set. Cool completely. Purée strawberries in food processor or blender. Cut pie into wedges. Serve with ice cream and puréed strawberries.

# Peachy Blueberry Pie

Classic Crisco® Double Crust
(page 512)
4 cups peeled and thinly sliced
fresh ripe peaches
1½ cups fresh blueberries,
washed and well drained

1 cup plus 2 tablespoons
granulated sugar, divided
2 tablespoons cornstarch
2 teaspoons vanilla
¼ cup milk

Makes 1 (9-inch) pie
(8 servings)

*1.* For crust, prepare as directed. Press bottom crust into 9-inch pie plate. Do not bake. Heat oven to 350°F.

*2.* Combine peaches, blueberries, 1 cup sugar, cornstarch and vanilla in large bowl. Mix gently until cornstarch is dissolved and fruit is well coated. Pour into unbaked pie crust. Moisten pastry edge with water. Cover pie with top crust. Trim ½ inch beyond edge of pie plate. Fold top edge under bottom crust; flute. Cut slits in top crust to allow steam to escape.

*3.* Bake at 350°F for about 35 minutes. Remove from oven; brush top with milk and sprinkle with remaining 2 tablespoons sugar. Return to oven and continue to bake for an additional 15 to 20 minutes or until peach-blueberry mixture bubbles and crust is golden. Let rest 10 minutes before serving.

## *Note:*

When a fruit pie is done, the juices should be bubbling and the fruit should be tender. To test, insert a wooden skewer into a piece of fruit in the pie. If the skewer goes through quickly, the pie is done.

# Peanut Butter Cup Cookie Ice Cream Pie

**Makes 8 servings**

**Prep Time:**
*15 minutes*

½ cup creamy peanut butter
¼ cup honey
1 quart (2 pints) vanilla ice cream, softened
1 cup KEEBLER® Chips Deluxe™ With Peanut Butter Cups Cookies, chopped

1 (6-ounce) READY CRUST® Chocolate Pie Crust
½ cup chocolate syrup
Whipped cream

*1.* Place large bowl in freezer. Mix peanut butter and honey in medium bowl. Place ice cream in bowl from freezer; add peanut butter mixture and cookies. Mix on low speed with electric mixer until blended.

*2.* Spoon half of ice cream mixture into crust. Spread chocolate syrup over ice cream mixture in crust. Spoon remaining ice cream mixture over chocolate syrup.

*3.* Garnish with whipped cream and additional chocolate syrup. Freeze leftovers.

# Apple Strudel Tarts with Vanilla Sauce

**Makes 6 tarts**

3 cups apples, peeled, cored
    and chopped
¼ cup sugar
¼ cup raisins
2 tablespoons margarine or
    butter
1½ teaspoons ground cinnamon,
    divided

6 sheets phyllo dough, thawed
2 tablespoons margarine or
    butter, melted
2 cups milk
¼ cup vanilla pudding mix

For filling, combine chopped apples, sugar, raisins, 2 tablespoons margarine and 1 teaspoon cinnamon in large skillet. Cook over medium heat, stirring frequently, until apples are tender.

Preheat oven to 350°F. Grease 6 custard cups or 6-cup muffin pan; set aside. Brush 1 sheet phyllo dough with melted margarine. Top with another phyllo dough sheet. Repeat brushing and layering with remaining phyllo dough and melted margarine. Cut phyllo stack lengthwise into 6 strips. Cut stack crosswise into thirds, making 18 pieces total. Press 3 pieces into each custard or muffin cup, placing pieces at angles so that each cup is covered with dough. Spoon apple mixture evenly into each cup. Bake 20 minutes or until golden brown. Cool 5 minutes in cups; carefully remove tarts to serving dishes.

For sauce, combine milk, pudding mix and remaining ½ teaspoon cinnamon in medium saucepan. Cook over medium-low heat, stirring frequently, until slightly thickened. Serve tarts warm with sauce.

Favorite recipe from **New York Apple Association, Inc.**

## *Note:*

**Prevent phyllo dough sheets from drying out by keeping extra sheets covered with a slightly damp dish cloth or plastic wrap. Phyllo sheets are fragile and may tear during preparation; this will not affect the final results.**

# Lemon Buttermilk Pie

**Makes 8 servings**

1 (9-inch) unbaked pie crust*
1½ cups sugar
½ cup (1 stick) butter, softened
3 eggs
1 cup buttermilk
1 tablespoon cornstarch

1 tablespoon fresh lemon juice
⅛ teaspoon salt

*If using a commercial frozen pie crust, purchase a deep-dish crust and thaw before using.

Heat oven to 350°F. Prick crust all over with fork. Bake until light golden brown, about 8 minutes; cool on wire rack. *Reduce oven temperature to 325°F.* In large bowl, beat sugar and butter until creamy. Add eggs, one at a time, beating well after each addition. Add buttermilk, cornstarch, lemon juice and salt; mix well. Pour filling into crust. Bake 55 to 60 minutes or just until knife inserted near center comes out clean. Cool; cover and chill.

Favorite recipe from **Southeast United Dairy Industry Association, Inc.**

# Mini Chocolate Pies

**Makes 6 servings**

**Prep Time:**
*5 minutes*

**Cook Time:**
*10 minutes*

**Cool Time:**
*5 minutes*

**Chill Time:**
*2 hours*

1 package (4-serving size)
   vanilla cook & serve
   pudding and pie filling mix*
1 cup HERSHEY₅S MINI CHIPS™
   Semi-Sweet Chocolate
   Chips
1 package (4 ounces) single
   serve graham cracker crusts
   (6 crusts)

Whipped topping
Additional MINI CHIPS™
   Semi-Sweet Chocolate
   Chips

*Do not use instant pudding mix.

*1.* Prepare pudding and pie filling mix as directed on package; remove from heat. Immediately add 1 cup small chocolate chips; stir until melted. Cool 5 minutes, stirring occasionally.

*2.* Pour filling into crusts; press plastic wrap directly onto surface. Refrigerate several hours or until firm. Garnish with whipped topping and small chocolate chips.

# Honey Pumpkin Pie

**Makes 8 servings**

1 can (16 ounces) solid pack
    pumpkin
1 cup evaporated low-fat milk
¾ cup honey
3 eggs, slightly beaten
2 tablespoons all-purpose flour

1 teaspoon ground cinnamon
½ teaspoon ground ginger
½ teaspoon rum extract
    Pastry for single 9-inch pie
    crust

Combine all ingredients except pastry in large bowl; beat until well blended. Pour into pastry-lined 9-inch pie plate. Bake at 400°F 45 minutes or until knife inserted near center comes out clean.

Favorite recipe from **National Honey Board**

# Quaker's Best Oatmeal Pie

**Makes 8 servings**

- 6 egg whites, lightly beaten *or* ¾ cup egg substitute
- ⅔ cup firmly packed brown sugar
- ⅓ cup granulated sugar
- ¾ cup fat-free milk
- 1 teaspoon vanilla
- 1¼ cups QUAKER® Oats (quick or old fashioned, uncooked)
- ¾ cup raisins or other dried fruit such as cherries, cranberries or chopped apricots
- ½ cup flaked or shredded coconut
- ½ cup chopped nuts (optional)
- 1 prepared 9-inch pie crust, unbaked

Heat oven to 375°F. Beat egg whites and sugars until well blended. Add milk and vanilla; mix well. Stir in oats, raisins, coconut and nuts; mix well. Pour filling into prepared pie crust. Bake 35 to 45 minutes or until center of pie is set. Cool completely on wire rack. Serve with ice cream or whipped cream. Store, covered, in refrigerator.

# Coconut Peach Crunch Pie

**Makes 8 servings**

**Prep Time:**
*15 minutes*

**Bake Time:**
*35 to 40 minutes*

- 1 (6-ounce) READY CRUST® Shortbread Pie Crust
- 1 egg yolk, beaten
- 1 (21-ounce) can peach pie filling
- 1 cup flaked coconut
- ½ cup all-purpose flour
- ½ cup sugar
- ¼ cup wheat germ
- ¼ cup margarine, melted

*1.* Preheat oven to 375°F. Brush bottom and sides of crust with egg yolk; bake on baking sheet 5 minutes or until golden brown.

*2.* Spoon peach filling into crust. Combine coconut, flour, sugar, wheat germ and margarine in small bowl. Mix until well blended. Spread over peach filling.

*3.* Bake on baking sheet 30 to 35 minutes or until filling is bubbly and topping is light brown. Cool on wire rack.

# Mixed Berry Tart with Ginger-Raspberry Glaze

| | |
|---|---|
| 1 refrigerated pie crust, at room temperature | 2 cups fresh or frozen blueberries |
| ¾ cup no-sugar-added seedless raspberry fruit spread | 2 cups fresh or frozen blackberries |
| ½ teaspoon grated fresh ginger *or* ¼ teaspoon ground ginger | 1 peach, peeled and thinly sliced |

**Makes 8 servings**

*1.* Preheat oven 450°F. Coat 9-inch pie pan or tart pan with nonstick cooking spray. Carefully place pie crust on bottom of pan. Turn edges of pie crust inward to form ½-inch-thick edge. Press edges firmly against side of pan. Using fork, pierce several times over entire bottom of pan to prevent crust from puffing up while baking. Bake 12 minutes or until golden brown. Cool completely on wire rack.

*2.* For glaze, heat fruit spread in small saucepan over high heat; stir until completely melted. Immediately remove from heat; stir in ginger and set aside to cool slightly.

*3.* Reserve 2 tablespoons glaze. Combine blueberries, blackberries and remaining glaze; set aside.

*4.* Brush reserved glaze evenly over bottom of cooled crust. Decoratively arrange peach slices on top of crust and mound berries on top of peach slices. Refrigerate at least 2 hours.

# Sweet 'n' Spicy Pecan Pie

**Makes 8 servings**

Prepared pie crust for one
9-inch pie
3 eggs
1 cup dark corn syrup
½ cup dark brown sugar
¼ cup (½ stick) butter *or*
margarine, melted

1 tablespoon TABASCO® brand
Pepper Sauce
1½ cup pecans, coarsely chopped
Whipped cream (optional)

Preheat oven to 425°F. Place pie crust in 9-inch pie plate; flute edge of crust.

Beat eggs lightly in large bowl. Stir in corn syrup, brown sugar, butter and TABASCO® Sauce; mix well. Place pecans in prepared pie crust; pour filling over pecans. Bake 15 minutes.

Reduce oven to 350°F. Bake pie 40 minutes or until knife inserted 1 inch from edge comes out clean. Cool pie on wire rack. Serve with whipped cream, if desired.

# Chocolate Chunk Cookie Pie

**Makes 8 servings**

**Prep Time:**
*20 minutes*

**Bake Time:**
*70 minutes*

½ package (15 ounces)
refrigerated pie crust
¾ cup (1½ sticks) butter *or*
margarine, softened
½ cup granulated sugar
½ cup firmly packed brown
sugar

2 eggs
1 teaspoon vanilla
½ cup flour
1 cup BAKER'S® Semi-Sweet
Chocolate Chunks
1 cup chopped nuts (optional)

**HEAT** oven to 325°F. Prepare pie crust as directed on package, using 9-inch pie plate.

**BEAT** butter and sugars in large bowl with electric mixer on medium speed until light and fluffy. Add eggs and vanilla; beat well. Beat in flour on low speed. Stir in chocolate chunks and nuts. Spread in prepared crust.

**BAKE** 65 to 70 minutes or until toothpick inserted into center comes out clean. Cool completely on wire rack.

**Special Extra:** *Serve with thawed COOL WHIP® Whipped Topping or vanilla ice cream.*

# Southern Peanut Pie

| | | Makes 6 servings |
|---|---|---|
| 3 eggs | ¼ teaspoon salt | |
| 1½ cups dark corn syrup | 1½ cups chopped roasted | |
| ½ cup granulated sugar | peanuts | |
| ¼ cup butter, melted | 1 (9-inch) unbaked deep-dish | |
| ½ teaspoon vanilla extract | pastry shell | |

Beat eggs until foamy. Add corn syrup, sugar, butter, vanilla and salt; continue to beat until thoroughly blended. Stir in peanuts. Pour into unbaked pastry shell. Bake in preheated 375°F oven 50 to 55 minutes. Serve warm or cold. Garnish with whipped cream or ice cream, if desired.

Favorite recipe from **Texas Peanut Producers Board**

# Peach Yogurt Pie with Raspberry Sauce

**Makes 1 (9-inch) pie
(8 servings)**

**Crust**
- 1 cup graham cracker crumbs
- ¼ cup sugar
- 3 tablespoons CRISCO® Oil*
- 1¼ teaspoons water

**Filling**
- 1 quart peach flavor frozen yogurt, softened

**Sauce**
- 1 package (12 ounces) frozen unsweetened raspberries, thawed
- ⅓ cup sugar
- 1 teaspoon cornstarch
- ⅛ teaspoon salt
- ¼ teaspoon almond extract

*Use your favorite Crisco Oil product.

*1.* Heat oven to 350°F. Place cooling rack on countertop.

*2.* For crust, combine graham cracker crumbs, sugar, oil and water in 9-inch pie plate. Mix with fork. Press firmly against bottom and up side of pie plate.

*3.* Bake at 350°F for 8 minutes. *Do not overbake.* Remove pie plate to cooling rack. Cool completely.

*4.* For filling, spread softened yogurt into cooled crust. Freeze 2½ to 3 hours or until firm.

*5.* For sauce, combine raspberries, sugar, cornstarch and salt in small saucepan. Cook and stir over medium heat until mixture comes to a boil and is thickened. Press through sieve to remove seeds. Stir in almond extract. Cool to room temperature. Refrigerate. Drizzle over pie just before serving. Garnish, if desired.

**Kitchen Hint:** *For a richer version of this pie, try substituting chocolate flavor frozen yogurt for the peach flavor frozen yogurt called for in the recipe.*

# S'more Pie

1 (12-ounce) chocolate candy
    bar, broken into pieces
30 regular marshmallows
¾ cup milk
2½ cups whipped cream, divided
1 (6-ounce) jar hot fudge
    topping, warmed

1 (9-ounce) READY CRUST®
    2 Extra Servings Graham
    Cracker Pie Crust
Chocolate syrup, for garnish

**Makes 8 servings**

**Prep Time:**
*15 minutes*

**Chill Time:**
*3 hours*

*1.* Place chocolate bar, marshmallows and milk in medium saucepan. Cook over low heat, stirring constantly, until marshmallows and chocolate are melted. Cool to room temperature.

*2.* Fold 1½ cups whipped cream into chocolate mixture. Spread thin layer of warm hot fudge over bottom of crust. Gently spoon chocolate mixture into crust. Top with remaining 1 cup whipped cream and garnish with chocolate syrup.

*3.* Refrigerate 3 hours or until set. Refrigerate leftovers.

*Note:*

To add even more
flavor to this pie,
use a chocolate
almond or chocolate
peanut candy bar in
place of a plain
chocolate bar.

# Mississippi Mud Pie

**Makes 8 servings**

1 *prepared* 9-inch (6 ounces) chocolate crumb crust
1 cup powdered sugar
1 cup (6 ounces) NESTLÉ® TOLL HOUSE® Semi-Sweet Chocolate Morsels
¼ cup (½ stick) butter or margarine, cut up
¼ cup heavy whipping cream
2 tablespoons light corn syrup
1 teaspoon vanilla extract
¾ cup chopped nuts, *divided* (optional)
2 pints coffee ice cream, softened slightly, *divided*
Whipped cream (optional)

*Note:*

To soften ice cream quickly, place a 1-quart container of hard-packed ice cream in the microwave and heat at MEDIUM (50% power) about 20 seconds or just until softened.

**HEAT** sugar, morsels, butter, cream and corn syrup in small, *heavy-duty* saucepan over low heat, stirring constantly, until butter is melted and mixture is smooth. Remove from heat. Stir in vanilla extract. Cool until slightly warm.

**DRIZZLE** ⅓ *cup* chocolate sauce in bottom of crust; sprinkle with ¼ *cup* nuts. Layer *1 pint* ice cream, scooping thin slices with a large spoon; freeze for 1 hour. Repeat with ⅓ *cup* sauce, ¼ *cup* nuts and *remaining* ice cream. Drizzle with *remaining* sauce; top with *remaining* nuts. Freeze for 2 hours or until firm. Top with whipped cream before serving.

# Peppermint Ice Cream Pie

1½ cups rolled oats
¾ cup flaked coconut
¾ cup finely chopped California
     walnuts
½ cup margarine or butter
¾ cup sugar
½ cup unsweetened cocoa
     powder

2 cups vanilla ice cream,
     slightly softened
2 cups pink or green
     peppermint ice cream,
     slightly softened
¼ cup coarsely crushed striped
     round peppermint candies

**Makes 8 servings**

For crust, combine oats, coconut and nuts in medium bowl. Melt margarine in small saucepan over low heat. Stir in sugar and cocoa powder until smooth; pour over oat mixture, mixing well. Reserve 1 cup crust mixture. Press remaining crust mixture onto bottom and up side of 9-inch pie plate.

Freeze 5 to 10 minutes or until crust is firm. Scoop half of each ice-cream flavor into crust, placing scoops alternately side by side. Using metal spatula, smooth surface and swirl gently to marble. Sprinkle with ½ cup reserved crust mixture. Repeat with remaining ice cream and crust mixture. Sprinkle with crushed peppermint candies. Freeze 4 hours or until firm. Wrap tightly in plastic wrap; freeze up to 1 month. Let stand 10 to 15 minutes before serving.

Favorite recipe from **Walnut Marketing Board**

# Chocolate Caramel Pie

**Makes 6 to 8 servings**

1½ cups chocolate cookie crumbs
¾ cup chopped pecans
⅓ cup butter or margarine, melted
1 envelope unflavored gelatin
2¼ cups whipping cream, divided
2 egg yolks, beaten lightly

1½ cups (9 ounces) semisweet chocolate chips
1 teaspoon vanilla
24 caramels
Caramel Flowers (recipe follows, optional)

Preheat oven to 325°F. Combine cookie crumbs, pecans and margarine in small bowl; press onto bottom and side of 9-inch pie plate. Bake 10 minutes. Cool crust completely in pan on wire rack.

Sprinkle gelatin over ¼ cup cold water in small saucepan. Let stand 3 minutes for gelatin to soften. Heat over low heat, stirring constantly, until gelatin is completely dissolved, about 5 minutes.

Heat ¼ cup whipping cream in small microwavable bowl at HIGH (100%) 45 seconds or until warm; add to gelatin mixture.

Heat 1½ cups whipping cream in medium saucepan until hot. Place egg yolks in small bowl. Stir some of the hot cream into egg yolks. Stir back into hot cream. Cook, whisking constantly, about 5 minutes or until mixture thickens. Add gelatin mixture to saucepan; remove from heat. Add chocolate chips and vanilla; stir until chocolate is melted. Pour mixture into large bowl; refrigerate 15 minutes or until thickened.

Meanwhile, combine caramels and remaining ½ cup whipping cream in small saucepan. Simmer over low heat, stirring occasionally, until completely melted and smooth. Pour caramel mixture into crust; let stand about 10 minutes.

*Note:*

To be sure gelatin is completely dissolved, run a finger over the spoon to test for undissolved granules. If it is smooth, the gelatin is completely dissolved; if it feels granular, continue heating until it feels smooth.

Beat thickened gelatin mixture with electric mixer at medium speed until smooth. Pour over caramel layer; refrigerate 3 hours or until firm. Garnish with Caramel Flowers, if desired.

**Caramel Flowers:** *Place unwrapped, softened caramel between two sheets of waxed paper. With rolling pin, roll out caramel to 2-inch oval. (Press down firmly with rolling pin.) Remove caramel from waxed paper. Starting at one corner, roll caramel into cone to resemble flower.*

# Butter Pecan Pie

| | | |
|---|---|---|
| 1 cup coarsely chopped pecans<br>¼ cup butter or margarine<br>1 container DUNCAN HINES®<br>    Creamy Home-Style<br>    Buttercream Frosting<br>1 package (8 ounces) cream<br>    cheese, softened | 1 cup frozen non-dairy whipped<br>    topping, thawed<br>1 prepared 9-inch graham<br>    cracker crumb pie crust<br>Pecan halves for garnish | **Makes 8 to<br>10 servings** |

*1.* Place pecans and butter in 10-inch skillet over medium heat. Cook, stirring constantly, until butter is lightly browned. Pour into heatproof large bowl. Add Vanilla frosting and cream cheese. Stir until thoroughly blended.

*2.* Fold in whipped topping. Pour into prepared crust. Garnish with pecan halves, if desired. Refrigerate for 4 hours or until firm.

# Ritzy Banana Cream Pie

**Makes 8 servings**

**Prep Time:**
*15 minutes plus refrigerating*

37 RITZ® Crackers
½ cup (1 stick) butter *or* margarine, divided
1 package (6 ounces) BAKER'S® Bittersweet Baking Chocolate, divided
2 large ripe bananas, sliced, divided
1½ cups cold milk

2 packages (4-serving size each) JELL-O® Banana Cream Flavor Instant Pudding & Pie Filling
1 tub (8 ounces) COOL WHIP® Whipped Topping, thawed
Chocolate-Dipped RITZ® Crackers(recipe follows), for garnish

**CRUSH** crackers in zipper-style bag with rolling pin or in food processor. Melt 6 tablespoons butter. Mix cracker crumbs and butter. Press onto bottom and up side of 9-inch pie plate. Refrigerate until firm.

**MICROWAVE** 4 squares of the chocolate and remaining 2 tablespoons butter in small microwavable bowl on HIGH 2 minutes or until butter is melted. Stir until chocolate is completely melted. Carefully spread chocolate mixture over bottom and side of crust. Arrange ½ of banana slices on bottom and side of chocolate-coated crust.

**POUR** milk into medium bowl. Add pudding mixes. Beat with wire whisk 2 minutes or until well blended. (Mixture will be thick.) Gently fold in ½ tub whipped topping. Spoon into crust. Top with remaining banana slices. Spread remaining whipped topping on pie.

**REFRIGERATE** 4 hours or until set. Just before serving, garnish with Chocolate-Dipped RITZ® Crackers.

**Chocolate-Dipped RITZ® Crackers:** *Microwave remaining 2 squares chocolate in small microwavable bowl on HIGH 1 to 2 minutes or until chocolate is almost melted. Stir until chocolate is completely melted. Dip each cracker halfway into melted chocolate; let excess chocolate drip off. Place on wax paper-lined cookie sheet. Refrigerate until chocolate is firm.*

**Great Substitutes:** *For variety try JELL-O® Vanilla or Chocolate Flavor Instant Pudding instead of Banana Cream Flavor.*

# Silky Cocoa Cream Pie

Makes 8 servings

1 cup sugar
½ cup HERSHEY'S Cocoa
3 tablespoons cornstarch
¼ teaspoon salt
2 cups cold milk
2 egg yolks, beaten

1 tablespoon butter
1 teaspoon vanilla
1 baked (8-inch) pastry shell,
   cooled
Sweetened whipped cream

*1.* Mix sugar, cocoa, cornstarch and salt in saucepan. Gradually stir in milk. Cook over medium heat, stirring constantly, until mixture is thickened and bubbly. Boil 1 minute; remove from heat.

*2.* Gradually stir about half of the hot filling into yolks. Return all to saucepan; heat to gentle boil. Cook and stir 1 minute. Remove from heat; stir in butter and vanilla. Pour into crust.

*3.* Press plastic wrap directly onto pie surface. Cool. Refrigerate 3 to 6 hours until set. Remove plastic wrap; garnish with whipped cream. Cover; refrigerate leftover pie.

# Classic Crisco® Single Crust

| Makes 8- to 9-inch single crust | 1⅓ cups all-purpose flour<br>½ teaspoon salt<br>½ CRISCO® Stick or ½ cup<br>   CRISCO® Shortening | 3 tablespoons cold water |
|---|---|---|

*1.* Spoon flour into measuring cup and level. Combine flour and salt in medium bowl.

*2.* Cut in ½ cup shortening using pastry blender or 2 knives until all flour is blended to form pea-size chunks.

*3.* Sprinkle with water, 1 tablespoon at a time. Toss lightly with fork until dough forms a ball.

*4.* Press dough between hands to form 5- to 6-inch "pancake." Flour rolling surface and rolling pin lightly. Roll dough into circle. Trim 1 inch larger than upside-down pie plate. Loosen dough carefully.

*5.* Fold dough into quarters. Unfold and press into pie plate. Fold edge under. Flute.

# Classic Crisco® Double Crust

| Makes 2 (9-inch) crusts | 2 cups all-purpose flour<br>1 teaspoon salt<br>¾ CRISCO® Stick or ¾ cup<br>   CRISCO® all-vegetable<br>   shortening | 5 tablespoons cold water<br>(or more as needed) |
|---|---|---|

*1.* Spoon flour into measuring cup and level. Combine flour and salt in medium bowl.

*2.* Cut in ¾ cup shortening using pastry blender or 2 knives until all flour is blended to form pea-size chunks.

*3.* Sprinkle with water, 1 tablespoon at a time. Toss lightly with fork until dough forms a ball. Divide dough in half.

*4.* Press each half of dough between hands to form 5- to 6-inch "pancake." Flour rolling surface and rolling pin lightly. Roll each half of dough into circle. Trim one circle of dough 1 inch larger than upside-down pie plate. Carefully remove trimmed dough. Set aside to reroll and use for pastry cutout garnish, if desired.

*5.* Fold one circle of dough into quarters. Unfold and press into pie plate. Trim edge even with plate.

# No Bake Peanut Butter Pie

**Makes 1 pie**

4 ounces cream cheese
1 cup confectioners' sugar, sifted
1 cup crunchy peanut butter
½ cup milk

8 ounces frozen whipped topping, thawed
1 deep-dish graham cracker or chocolate-flavored crust

In large mixer bowl combine cream cheese and confectioners' sugar; mix well. Add peanut butter and mix. Slowly add milk and mix well. Fold in whipped topping. Pour into pie shell and cover. Freeze for at least 30 minutes. If desired, drizzle each serving with chocolate syrup.

Favorite recipe from **Peanut Advisory Board**

# Chocolate Macaroon Heath® Pie

**Makes 6 to 8 servings**

½ cup (1 stick) butter or margarine, melted
3 cups MOUNDS® Sweetened Coconut Flakes
2 tablespoons all-purpose flour

1⅓ cups (8-ounce package) HEATH® BITS
½ gallon chocolate ice cream, softened

*1.* Heat oven to 375°F.

*2.* Combine butter, coconut and flour in medium bowl. Press into 9-inch pie pan.

*3.* Bake 10 minutes or until edge is light golden brown. Cool completely.

*4.* Set aside ⅓ cup Heath® Bits. Combine ice cream and remaining Heath® Bits. Spread into cooled crust. Sprinkle with ⅓ cup reserved bits. Freeze at least 5 hours. Remove from freezer about 10 minutes before serving.

# Creamy Holiday Tarts

**Makes 12 servings**

**Prep Time:**
*10 minutes*

1 (4-serving-size) package vanilla flavor instant pudding and pie filling mix
1 (14-ounce) can sweetened condensed milk
¾ cup raisins
¾ cup cold water
1 teaspoon ground nutmeg

1 teaspoon brandy extract
1 cup whipping cream, whipped, divided
2 (4-ounce) packages READY CRUST® Mini-Graham Cracker Crusts
Additional raisins and ground nutmeg, for garnish

*1.* Mix together pudding mix, sweetened condensed milk, raisins, water, nutmeg and brandy extract in large bowl. Chill 15 minutes.

*2.* Fold 1 cup whipped cream into pudding mixture. Spoon into crusts.

*3.* Garnish with remaining whipped cream. Sprinkle with additional raisins and nutmeg. Refrigerate leftovers.

# Tinker Bell Peanut Butter Pie

| | | |
|---|---|---|
| 1 jar (18 ounces) PETER PAN® Creamy Peanut Butter<br>2 packages (8 ounces each) cream cheese, at room temperature<br>1¾ cups sugar<br>2 tablespoons unsalted butter<br>2 teaspoons vanilla extract | 2 cups heavy whipping cream<br>2 ready-to-use graham cracker pie crusts<br>4 squares (1 ounce each) semi-sweet baking chocolate<br>½ cup brewed coffee<br>Whipped cream (optional) | **Makes 2 pies (8 to 10 servings each)** |

In large bowl, beat together first 5 ingredients until smooth. In small bowl, beat whipping cream until stiff peaks form. Fold whipped cream into peanut butter mixture; divide mixture evenly between crusts. Refrigerate until chilled. In top of double boiler, melt chocolate with coffee. Cool mixture. Evenly drizzle chocolate mixture over pies and chill until ready to serve. Garnish with whipped cream.

*Note:*

For best results when beating heavy or whipping cream, chill the cream, bowl and beaters first—the cold keeps the fat in the cream solid, thus increasing the volume.

# Sweet Potato Pies

**Makes 16 servings**

## Note:

Sweet potatoes should be heavy for their size, firm, smooth and free of bruises or blemishes. Check for decay, which often begins at the tips. Choose potatoes of similar size and shape when they are to be cooked whole.

2 *unbaked* 9-inch (2-cup volume) pie shells
2 large or 3 medium (about 1½ to 2 pounds) sweet potatoes
½ cup (1 stick) butter or margarine, softened
1 cup granulated sugar
2 tablespoons packed brown sugar

⅔ cup (5 fluid-ounce can) NESTLÉ® CARNATION® Evaporated Milk
2 large eggs, beaten
1 teaspoon lemon juice
1 teaspoon vanilla extract
1 teaspoon ground cinnamon
¼ teaspoon ground nutmeg
⅛ teaspoon salt

**COOK** sweet potatoes in boiling water for 45 to 50 minutes or until tender. Drain, cool slightly and peel.

**PREHEAT** oven to 425°F.

**MASH** warm sweet potatoes and butter in large bowl. Stir in granulated sugar, brown sugar, evaporated milk and eggs. Stir in lemon juice, vanilla extract, cinnamon, nutmeg and salt. Pour into prepared pie shells.

**BAKE** for 15 minutes. Reduce heat to 350°F.; bake for 30 to 40 minutes or until knife inserted near center comes out clean. Cool on wire rack for 2 hours. Serve immediately or refrigerate.

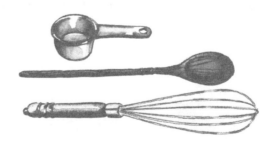

# Mocha Decadence Pie

Makes 8 servings

**4 ounces semisweet chocolate**
**2 cups heavy cream, divided**
**½ cup plus 1 tablespoon sugar, divided**
**3 eggs**

**2 teaspoons instant coffee granules**
**1 teaspoon vanilla, divided**
**1 packaged graham cracker crust (6 ounces)**

Place chocolate in small microwavable dish. Microwave at HIGH 1½ minutes or until melted, stirring after 1 minute. Set aside.

Combine 1 cup heavy cream and ½ cup sugar in medium saucepan over medium heat. Cook until sugar is dissolved, stirring constantly. Beat eggs in small bowl. Stir ¼ cup cream mixture into eggs. Stir back into cream mixture. Stir constantly 4 to 5 minutes or until thickened. Pour into large bowl. Beat in melted chocolate, coffee granules and ½ teaspoon vanilla on low speed of electric mixer. Increase speed to medium. Beat 2 minutes. Pour into pie shell. Cool 15 minutes. Cover and refrigerate 3 hours or overnight.

Beat remaining 1 cup cream in medium bowl with electric mixer on high speed 1 minute. Add remaining 1 tablespoon sugar and remaining ½ teaspoon vanilla. Beat until mixture forms soft peaks. Top each slice of pie with whipped cream.

# Peanut Butter and Chocolate Mousse Pie

**Makes 6 to 8 servings**

1⅔ cups (10-ounce package) REESE'S® Peanut Butter Chips, divided
1 package (3 ounces) cream cheese, softened
¼ cup powdered sugar
⅓ cup plus 2 tablespoons milk
1 (9-inch) pie crust, baked and cooled

1 teaspoon unflavored gelatin
1 tablespoon cold water
2 tablespoons boiling water
½ cup sugar
⅓ cup HERSHEY'S Cocoa
1 cup (½ pint) cold whipping cream
1 teaspoon vanilla extract

***1.*** Melt 1½ cups peanut butter chips. Beat cream cheese, powdered sugar and ⅓ cup milk in medium bowl until smooth. Add melted chips; beat well. Beat in remaining 2 tablespoons milk. Spread into cooled crust.

***2.*** Sprinkle gelatin over cold water in small bowl; let stand 1 minute to soften. Add boiling water; stir until gelatin is completely dissolved. Cool slightly. Combine sugar and cocoa in medium bowl; add whipping cream and vanilla. Beat on medium speed of mixer until stiff; pour in gelatin mixture, beating until well blended. Spoon into crust over peanut butter layer. Refrigerate several hours. Garnish with remaining chips. Cover; refrigerate leftover pie.

# Hoosier Harvest Apple Pie

Classic Crisco® Double Crust
(page 512)
½ cup firmly packed brown
sugar
½ cup granulated sugar
2 tablespoons all-purpose flour
½ teaspoon cinnamon
1 tablespoon Butter Flavor
CRISCO® Stick or
1 tablespoon Butter Flavor
CRISCO® all-vegetable
shortening

6 cups peeled, sliced tart
baking apples, about
2 pounds
3 tablespoons apple cider
or juice
Milk
Granulated sugar

**Makes 8 servings**

Prep Time:
*25 minutes*

Total Time:
*2 hours*

*1.* For crust, prepare as directed. Press bottom crust into 9-inch pie plate. Do not bake. Heat oven to 375°F.

*2.* Combine brown sugar, ½ cup granulated sugar, flour and cinnamon. Cut in 1 tablespoon shortening with fork until crumbs form. Toss apples with crumb mixture. Pour into unbaked pie crust. Sprinkle cider over filling. Moisten pastry edge with water.

*3.* Cover pie with top crust. Trim ½ inch beyond edge of pie plate. Fold top edge under bottom crust; flute with fingers or fork. Brush top of pie crust with milk. Sprinkle with additional granulated sugar. Cut slits in top crust to allow steam to escape.

*4.* Bake at 375°F for 40 to 50 minutes. Cover edge of pie with foil last 10 minutes, if necessary, to prevent overbrowning. *Do not overbake.* Cool until barely warm or to room temperature before serving.

# Decadent Triple Layer Mud Pie

**Makes 8 servings**

**Prep Time:**
*10 minutes*

2 squares BAKER'S® Semi-Sweet Baking Chocolate, melted
¼ cup sweetened condensed milk
1 prepared chocolate flavor crumb crust (6 ounces *or* 9 inches)

¾ cup chopped pecans, toasted
2 cups cold milk
2 packages (4-serving size each) JELL-O® Chocolate Flavor Instant Pudding & Pie Filling
1 tub (8 ounces) COOL WHIP® Whipped Topping, thawed

**POUR** chocolate and sweetened condensed milk into bowl; stir until smooth. Pour into crust. Press nuts evenly into chocolate in crust. Refrigerate 10 minutes.

**POUR** milk into large bowl. Add pudding mixes. Beat with wire whisk 1 minute. (Mixture will be thick.) Spoon 1½ cups pudding over pecans in crust.

**STIR** half of the whipped topping into remaining pudding. Spread over pudding in crust. Top with remaining whipped topping.

**REFRIGERATE** 3 hours. Garnish as desired.

# Picture Perfect Creamy Banana Pie

**Makes 8 servings**

**Prep Time:**
*25 minutes*

**Chill Time:**
*4 hours*

½ cup sugar, divided
1 envelope unflavored gelatin
2 tablespoons cornstarch
1¾ cups lowfat milk
2 eggs, separated
¼ cup margarine

2 teaspoons vanilla extract
3 DOLE® Bananas, divided
1 (9-inch) chocolate cookie crust

• Combine ¼ cup sugar with gelatin and cornstarch in medium saucepan. Stir in milk and slightly beaten egg yolks. Cook over medium heat, stirring, until mixture boils and thickens. Remove from heat. Stir in margarine and vanilla.

• Pour custard into large bowl. Cover surface with plastic wrap. Refrigerate 15 minutes.

• Place 2 bananas in blender or food processor container. Cover; blend until smooth. Stir into custard.

• Beat egg whites until foamy. Gradually add remaining sugar. Beat until stiff peaks form. Fold into custard mixture. Pour into prepared crust.

• Chill 4 hours or until firm. Garnish with whipped cream, if desired. Slice remaining banana. Arrange banana slices over top of pie.

*Note:*

Separate eggs while they are cold because the yolk is firm and less likely to break. Let the whites sit out at room temperature for 30 minutes before beating in order to achieve their highest volume.

# Blueberry Crumble Pie

1 (6-ounce) READY CRUST®
   Graham Cracker Pie Crust
1 egg yolk, beaten
1 (21-ounce) can blueberry
   pie filling

⅓ cup all-purpose flour
⅓ cup quick-cooking oats
¼ cup sugar
3 tablespoons margarine,
   melted

**Makes 8 servings**

Prep Time:
*15 minutes*

Bake Time:
*40 minutes*

*1.* Preheat oven to 375°F. Brush bottom and sides of crust with egg yolk; bake on baking sheet 5 minutes or until light brown.

*2.* Pour blueberry pie filling into crust. Combine flour, oats and sugar in small bowl; mix in margarine. Spoon over pie filling.

*3.* Bake on baking sheet about 35 minutes or until filling is bubbly and topping is browned. Cool on wire rack.

# Nestlé® Toll House® Chocolate Chip Pie

**Makes 8 servings**

1 *unbaked* 9-inch (4-cup volume) deep-dish pie shell*
2 large eggs
½ cup all-purpose flour
½ cup granulated sugar
½ cup packed brown sugar
¾ cup (1½ sticks) butter, softened

1 cup (6 ounces) NESTLÉ® TOLL HOUSE® Semi-Sweet Chocolate Morsels
1 cup chopped nuts
Sweetened whipped cream or ice cream (optional)

*If using frozen pie shell, use deep-dish style, thawed completely. Bake on baking sheet; increase baking time slightly.*

PREHEAT oven to 325°F.

BEAT eggs in large mixer bowl on high speed until foamy. Beat in flour, granulated sugar and brown sugar. Beat in butter. Stir in morsels and nuts. Spoon into pie shell.

BAKE for 55 to 60 minutes or until knife inserted halfway between outside edge and center comes out clean. Cool on wire rack. Serve warm with whipped cream.

# Chess Pie

**Makes 1 (10-inch) pie**

Crust
    Classic Crisco® Single Crust
    (page 512)

Filling
    3 cups sugar
    ½ cup butter or margarine, softened

5 eggs, lightly beaten
3 tablespoons cornmeal
2 teaspoons vanilla
⅛ teaspoon salt
1 cup milk

*1.* For crust, prepare as directed. Do not bake. Heat oven to 325°F.

*2.* For filling, combine sugar and butter in large bowl. Beat at low speed of electric mixer until blended. Beat in eggs, cornmeal, vanilla and salt. Add milk. Beat at low speed until blended. Pour into unbaked pie crust.

*3.* Bake at 325°F for 1 hour to 1 hour 20 minutes or until filling is set. Cover edge of pie with foil, if necessary, to prevent overbrowning. *Do not overbake.* Cool to room temperature before serving. Refrigerate leftover pie.

# Bourbon Pecan Pie

| | |
|---|---|
| Pastry for single-crust 9-inch pie | 3 eggs |
| ¼ cup butter or margarine, softened | 1½ cups light or dark corn syrup |
| ½ cup sugar | 2 tablespoons bourbon |
| | 1 teaspoon vanilla extract |
| | 1 cup pecan halves |

**Makes 6 to 8 servings**

Preheat oven to 350°F. Roll out pastry and line 9-inch pie pan; flute edge. Beat butter in large bowl of electric mixer on medium speed until creamy. Add sugar; beat until fluffy. Add eggs, one at a time, beating well after each addition. Add corn syrup, bourbon and vanilla; beat until well blended. Pour filling into pastry shell. Arrange pecan halves on top. Bake on lowest oven rack 50 to 55 minutes or until knife inserted slightly off center comes out clean (filling will be puffy). Place on rack and cool. Serve at room temperature or refrigerate up to 24 hours.

<u>Tip:</u> *Use your favorite recipe for pastry or purchase a 1½-inch-deep, 9-inch frozen pie shell.*

# Chocolate Bavarian Pie

**Makes 6 to 8 servings**

1 envelope unflavored gelatin
1¾ cups milk, divided
⅔ cup sugar
6 tablespoons HERSHEY⨯S
   Cocoa
1 tablespoon light corn syrup
2 tablespoons butter (do *not*
   use margarine, spread
   or oil)

¾ teaspoon vanilla extract
1 cup (½ pint) cold whipping
   cream
1 baked 9-inch pie crust *or*
   crumb crust

*Note:*

For optimum volume, beat whipping cream in a deep, narrow bowl. Generally 1 cup of cream will yield 2 cups of whipped cream, so be sure to choose a bowl that will accommodate the increased volume. Do not overbeat or the cream will clump together and form butter.

*1.* Sprinkle gelatin over 1 cup milk in medium saucepan; let stand 2 minutes to soften.

*2.* Stir together sugar and cocoa. Add to mixture in saucepan. Add corn syrup. Cook, stirring constantly over medium-high heat until mixture comes to a boil. Remove from heat. Add butter; stir until melted. Stir in remaining ¾ cup milk and vanilla. Pour into large bowl. Cool; refrigerate until almost set.

*3.* Beat whipping cream in small bowl on high speed of mixer until stiff. Beat chocolate mixture on medium speed of mixer until smooth. On low speed, add half the whipped cream to chocolate mixture, beating just until blended. Pour into prepared crust. Refrigerate 3 hours or until firm. Just before serving, garnish with remaining whipped cream. Cover; refrigerate leftover pie.

# Mixed Berry Pie

Classic Crisco® Double Crust
(page 512)
2 cups canned or frozen
    blackberries, thawed
    and well drained
1½ cups canned or frozen
    blueberries, thawed
    and well drained

½ cup canned or frozen
    gooseberries, thawed
    and well drained
⅛ teaspoon almond extract
¼ cup sugar
3 tablespoons cornstarch

**Makes 1 (9-inch) pie**

*1.* For crust, prepare as directed. Press bottom crust into 9-inch pie plate. Do not bake. Heat oven to 425°F.

*2.* For filling, combine blackberries, blueberries, gooseberries and almond extract in large bowl. Combine sugar and cornstarch. Add to berries. Toss well to mix. Spoon into unbaked pie crust.

*3.* Cut top crust into leaf shapes and arrange on top of pie, or cover pie with top crust. Flute edge. Cut slits into top crust, if using, to allow steam to escape.

*4.* Bake at 425°F for 40 minutes or until filling in center is bubbly and crust is golden brown. *Do not overbake.* Cool until barely warm or at room temperature before serving.

# White Chocolate Coconut Cream Pie

**Makes 8 servings**

**Prep Time:**
*45 minutes plus refrigerating*

1 package (6 ounces) BAKER'S® Premium White Baking Chocolate Squares, divided
1 tablespoon butter *or* margarine
1 NILLA® Pie Crust (9 inch)
1¾ cups cold milk *or* half-and-half
1 package (4-serving size) JELL-O® Coconut Cream Flavor Instant Pudding & Pie Filling

½ cup BAKER'S® ANGEL FLAKE® Coconut
1½ cups cold whipping (heavy) cream, divided

**MICROWAVE** 3 squares chocolate and butter in small microwavable bowl on HIGH 1½ minutes or until butter is melted. Stir until chocolate is completely melted. Spread onto bottom of crust. Refrigerate 15 minutes or until chocolate is firm.

**POUR** milk into large bowl. Add pudding mix and coconut. Beat with wire whisk 2 minutes or until well blended. Spoon into crust. Refrigerate until ready to top.

**MICROWAVE** remaining chocolate and ¼ cup of the cream in large microwavable bowl on HIGH 2 minutes. Stir until chocolate is completely melted. Cool 20 minutes or until room temperature, stirring occasionally.

**BEAT** remaining 1¼ cups cream in chilled large bowl with electric mixer on medium speed until soft peaks form. Gently stir ½ of the whipped cream into cooled chocolate mixture. Gently stir in remaining whipped cream just until blended. Spoon over filling in crust.

**REFRIGERATE** 4 hours or until ready to serve.

<u>Special Extra:</u> *Garnish with toasted BAKER'S® ANGEL FLAKE® Coconut.*

# Heavenly Chocolate Mousse Pie

| | | |
|---|---|---|
| 4 (1-ounce) squares unsweetened chocolate, melted<br>1 (14-ounce) can EAGLE® BRAND Sweetened Condensed Milk (NOT evaporated milk) | 1½ teaspoons vanilla extract<br>1 cup (½ pint) whipping cream, whipped<br>1 (6-ounce) chocolate crumb pie crust | **Makes 1 pie**<br><br>**Prep Time:**<br>*20 minutes*<br><br>**Chill Time:**<br>*15 minutes* |

*1.* In medium mixing bowl, beat melted chocolate with Eagle Brand and vanilla until well blended.

*2.* Chill 15 minutes or until cooled; stir until smooth. Fold in whipped cream.

*3.* Pour into crust. Chill thoroughly. Garnish as desired. Refrigerate leftovers.

## The Pie Primer

**Chiffon pies** are single-crust chilled pies with a light, airy filling made by folding whipped cream or stiffly beaten egg whites into a gelatin-, cream- or cream cheese-based mixture.

**Cream pies** are single-crust chilled pies with a rich, sweet puddinglike filling. They are usually topped with meringue, whipped cream or fruit.

**Custard pies** are single-crust baked pies with a sweet, rich custard filling made from eggs and milk. Since they are all made with eggs or dairy products, chiffon, cream and custard pies should be kept refrigerated. (Be careful to refrigerate custard pies only after they have cooled to room temperature.)

**Frozen pies** have a single crust. They are filled with an ice cream, cream cheese or chiffon filling. Once they have frozen solid, they can be wrapped and stored up tp one week.

**Fruit pies** may have single or double crusts. They are filled with fresh, canned or frozen fruit and baked. Fruit pies may be stored at room temperature for a day or two. After that they should also be refrigerated. (If desired, fruit pies can be reheated in a 300°F oven for 10 to 15 minutes before serving.)

# Classic Lemon Meringue Pie

**Makes 1 (9-inch) pie**

**Crust**
Classic Crisco® Single Crust
(page 512)

**Filling**
1½ cups sugar
¼ cup cornstarch
3 tablespoons all-purpose flour
¼ teaspoon salt
1½ cups hot water
3 egg yolks, beaten
2 tablespoons butter or
     margarine

1½ teaspoons grated lemon peel
⅓ cup plus 1 tablespoon fresh
     lemon juice

**Meringue**
½ cup sugar, divided
1 tablespoon cornstarch
½ cup cold water
4 egg whites
¾ teaspoon vanilla

*1.* For crust, prepare as directed. Heat oven to 425°F. Prick bottom and side of crust thoroughly with fork (50 times) to prevent shrinkage. Bake at 425°F for 10 to 15 minutes or until lightly browned. Cool crust while preparing filling. Reduce oven temperature to 350°F.

*2.* For filling, combine 1½ cups sugar, ¼ cup cornstarch, flour and salt in medium saucepan. Add 1½ cups hot water gradually, stirring constantly. Cook and stir on medium heat until mixture comes to a boil and thickens. Reduce heat to low. Cook and stir constantly 8 minutes. Remove from heat. Add about one third of hot mixture slowly to egg yolks. Mix well. Return mixture to saucepan. Bring mixture to a boil on medium-high heat. Reduce heat to low. Cook and stir 4 minutes. Remove from heat. Stir in butter and lemon peel. Add lemon juice slowly. Mix well. Spoon into baked pie crust.

*3.* For meringue, combine 2 tablespoons sugar, 1 tablespoon cornstarch and ½ cup cold water in small saucepan. Stir until cornstarch dissolves. Cook and stir on medium heat until mixture is clear. Cool.

*4.* Combine egg whites and vanilla in large bowl. Beat at high speed of electric mixer until soft peaks form. Beat in remaining 6 tablespoons sugar, 1 tablespoon at a time. Beat well after each addition. Combine meringue with cornstarch mixture and continue beating until stiff peaks form. Spread over filling, covering completely and sealing to edge of pie.

*5.* Bake at 350°F for 12 to 15 minutes or until meringue is golden. *Do not overbake.* Cool to room temperature before serving. Refrigerate leftover pie.

# Carnation® Key Lime Pie

**Makes 8 servings**

1 *prepared* 9-inch (6 ounces)
    graham cracker crumb crust
1 can (14 ounces) NESTLÉ®
    CARNATION® Sweetened
    Condensed Milk
½ cup (about 3 medium limes)
    fresh lime juice

1 teaspoon grated lime peel
2 cups frozen whipped topping,
    thawed
    Lime peel twists or lime slices
    (optional)

**BEAT** sweetened condensed milk and lime juice in small mixer bowl until combined; stir in lime peel. Pour into crust; spread with whipped topping. Refrigerate for 2 hours or until set. Garnish with lime peel twists.

# Red, White & Blueberry Cream Pie

**Makes 8 servings**

**Prep Time:**
*10 minutes*

**Chill Time:**
*3 hours*

1¼ cup fresh blueberries, rinsed, drained and divided
1 (6-ounce) READY CRUST® Graham Cracker Pie Crust
1 (8-ounce) package cream cheese, softened

1 (14-ounce) can sweetened condensed milk
⅓ cup lemon juice
1 teaspoon vanilla extract
Sliced fresh strawberries

**1.** Place ¾ cup blueberries in crust.

**2.** Beat cream cheese in large bowl until fluffy. Gradually beat in sweetened condensed milk until smooth. Stir in lemon juice and vanilla. Spread into crust.

**3.** Chill 3 hours or until set. Top with remaining ½ cup blueberries and strawberries. Refrigerate leftovers.

# Cream Cheese Brownie Pie

**Makes 10 servings**

**Prep Time:**
*30 minutes*

**Bake Time:**
*45 minutes*

½ package (15 ounces) refrigerated pie crust
1 package (8 ounces) PHILADELPHIA® Cream Cheese, softened
¼ cup sugar
3 eggs, divided
6 squares BAKER'S® Semi-Sweet Baking Chocolate

½ cup (1 stick) butter *or* margarine
⅔ cup sugar
1 teaspoon vanilla
1 cup flour
2 squares BAKER'S® Semi-Sweet Baking Chocolate, melted (optional)

HEAT oven to 350°F. Prepare crust as directed on package, using 9-inch pie plate. Mix cream cheese, ¼ cup sugar and 1 egg in medium bowl until well blended; set aside.

**MICROWAVE** chocolate and butter in large microwavable bowl on HIGH 2 minutes or until butter is melted. Stir until chocolate is completely melted.

**STIR** ⅔ cup sugar into chocolate mixture until well blended. Mix in 2 eggs and vanilla. Stir in flour until well blended. Spread half of the brownie batter into prepared crust. Carefully spread cream cheese mixture over top. Top with remaining brownie batter.

**BAKE** 45 minutes or until toothpick inserted in center comes out with fudgy crumbs. Cool completely on wire rack. Drizzle with melted chocolate, if desired.

<u>**To soften cream cheese in the microwave:**</u> *Place 1 completely unwrapped (8-ounce) package of cream cheese in microwavable bowl. Microwave on HIGH 15 seconds. Add 15 seconds for each additional package of cream cheese.*

# Chocolate Triple Layer Pie

| | | Makes 8 servings |
|---|---|---|
| 2 cups cold milk<br>2 (4-serving-size) packages<br>    chocolate flavor instant<br>    pudding & pie filling | 1 (6-ounce) READY CRUST®<br>    Graham Cracker Pie Crust<br>1 (8-ounce) tub frozen whipped<br>    topping, thawed, divided | **Prep Time:**<br>*15 minutes*<br><br>**Chill Time:**<br>*4 hours* |

*1.* Pour milk into large bowl. Add pudding mixes. Beat with wire whisk 1 minute. (Mixture will be thick.) Spoon 1½ cups of the pudding into crust.

*2.* Gently stir half of whipped topping into remaining pudding. Spread over pudding in crust. Top with remaining whipped topping.

*3.* Refrigerate 4 hours or until set. Refrigerate leftovers.

# High Country Peach Pie

**Makes 1 (9-inch) pie**

**Crust**

Classic Crisco® Double Crust
(page 512)
1 egg white, lightly beaten

**Filling**

1 cup sugar
⅓ cup unbleached all-purpose
    flour
3 tablespoons vanilla or French
    vanilla flavor instant
    pudding and pie filling
    mix (not sugar-free)

2 tablespoons honey
5 cups sliced, peeled peaches
2 tablespoons Butter Flavor
    CRISCO® Stick or
    2 tablespoons Butter Flavor
    CRISCO® all-vegetable
    shortening

**Glaze**

Milk

*Note:*

Let fruit pies cool to lukewarm before serving. The bubbling juices in a hot pie thicken as the pie cools, preventing slices from being runny.

**1.** For crust, prepare as directed. Press bottom crust into 9-inch pie plate. Brush with egg white. Do not bake. Heat oven to 425°F.

**2.** For filling, combine sugar, flour, pudding mix and honey in large bowl. Fold in peaches.

**3.** Melt 1 tablespoon shortening. Pour over peaches.

**4.** Lift peaches from liquid with slotted spoon, reserving ¼ cup liquid. Place peaches and reserved liquid in unbaked pie crust. Dot with remaining 1 tablespoon shortening. Discard remaining liquid. Moisten pastry edge with water.

**5.** Roll top crust same as bottom. Cut 5 peach leaf designs in center of pastry. Reserve cutouts. Lift top crust onto filled pie. Trim ½ inch beyond edge of pie plate. Fold top edge under bottom crust. Flute.

*6.* For glaze, brush with milk. Cut veins in leaf cutouts. Place between "leaf" vents. Brush leaves with milk. Cover edge of crust with foil to prevent overbrowning.

*7.* Bake at 425°F for 10 minutes. Reduce oven temperature to 400°F. Bake 30 minutes. Remove foil. Bake 5 minutes or until filling in center is bubbly and crust is golden brown. *Do not overbake.* Serve barely warm.

# Chocolate Chip Walnut Pie

**Makes 1 (9-inch) pie**

**¾ cup packed light brown sugar**
**½ cup all-purpose flour**
**½ teaspoon baking powder**
**¼ teaspoon ground cinnamon**
**2 eggs, slightly beaten**
**1 cup HERSHEY'S Semi-Sweet Chocolate Chips, MINI CHIPS™ or Milk Chocolate Chips**

**1 cup coarsely chopped walnuts**
**1 baked (9-inch) pie crust**
**Spiced Cream (recipe follows)**

*1.* Heat oven to 350°F.

*2.* Combine brown sugar, flour, baking powder and cinnamon in medium bowl. Add eggs; stir until well blended. Add chocolate chips and walnuts. Pour into baked pie crust.

*3.* Bake 25 to 30 minutes or until lightly browned and set. Serve slightly warm or at room temperature with Spiced Cream. Refrigerate leftovers.

<u>**Spiced Cream:**</u> *Combine ½ cup chilled whipping cream, 1 tablespoon powdered sugar, ¼ teaspoon vanilla extract, ¼ teaspoon ground cinnamon and dash ground nutmeg in small bowl; beat until stiff.*

# Walnut Crunch Pumpkin Pie

**Makes 8 servings**

1 *unbaked* 9-inch (4-cup volume) deep-dish pie shell
1¼ cups coarsely chopped walnuts
¾ cup packed brown sugar
1 can (15 ounces) LIBBY'S® 100% Pure Pumpkin
1 can (12 fluid ounces) NESTLÉ® CARNATION® Evaporated Milk
¾ cup granulated sugar
2 large eggs, lightly beaten
1½ teaspoons pumpkin pie spice
¼ teaspoon salt
3 tablespoons butter, melted

**PREHEAT** oven to 425°F.

**COMBINE** walnuts and brown sugar in small bowl. Place *¾ cup* of nut-sugar mixture on bottom of pie shell. Combine pumpkin, evaporated milk, granulated sugar, eggs, pumpkin pie spice and salt in medium bowl; mix well. Pour batter over nuts.

**BAKE** for 15 minutes. Reduce temperature to 350°F.; bake for 40 to 50 minutes or until knife inserted near center comes out clean. Cool on wire rack.

**COMBINE** butter and *remaining* nut-sugar mixture; stir until moistened. Sprinkle over cooled pie. Broil about 5 inches from heat for 2 to 3 minutes or until bubbly. Cool before serving.

# Delightfully
# Cool
# Creations

CHAPTER THIRTEEN

# Caribbean Freeze

**Makes 6 servings
(¾ cup each)**

⅔ cup sugar
3 tablespoons HERSHEY᠍S
   Cocoa
1¾ cups water

3 tablespoons frozen pineapple
   juice concentrate, thawed
1 tablespoon golden rum or
   ½ teaspoon rum extract

*1.* Stir together sugar and cocoa in medium saucepan; stir in water. Cook over medium heat, stirring occasionally, until mixture comes to a boil. Reduce heat; simmer 3 minutes, stirring occasionally. Cool completely.

*2.* Stir concentrate and rum into chocolate mixture. Cover; refrigerate until cold, about 6 hours.

*3.* Pour cold mixture into 1-quart container of ice cream freezer. Freeze according to manufacturer's directions. Garnish as desired.

# Fruit Mousse

**Makes 6 servings**

1 cup heavy cream
1 teaspoon vanilla
1 package (3 ounces) cream
   cheese, softened

½ cup no-sugar-added
   strawberry or seedless
   raspberry fruit spread

Combine cream and vanilla in small bowl of electric mixer; beat at high speed until stiff peaks form. Transfer to separate bowl. In same small mixer bowl, beat cream cheese until creamy. Blend in fruit spread. Fold in whipped cream mixture. Spoon into individual dessert dishes; chill at least 2 hours or up to 24 hours before serving.

**Variation:** *Layer mousse with unsweetened fresh sliced strawberries or raspberries in parfait glasses; chill up to 4 hours before serving.*

# Chocolate Peanut Butter Parfaits

| | |
|---|---|
| 3 tablespoons milk | 1 package (4-serving size) |
| 3 tablespoons peanut butter | JELL-O® Chocolate Flavor |
| 1 cup thawed COOL WHIP® | Instant Pudding & Pie |
|    Whipped Topping | Filling |
| 2 cups cold milk | ¼ cup chopped peanuts |

**Makes 6 servings**

Prep Time:
*5 minutes*

**STIR** 3 tablespoons milk into peanut butter in medium bowl until smooth. Gently stir in whipped topping.

**POUR** 2 cups milk into medium bowl. Add pudding mix. Beat with wire whisk 2 minutes. Alternately spoon whipped topping mixture and pudding into 6 parfait glasses.

**REFRIGERATE** until ready to serve. Sprinkle with peanuts.

# Englishman's Trifle

**Makes 4 servings**

**Prep Time:**
*20 minutes*

1 box (10 ounces) BIRDS EYE®
  frozen Strawberries*
1 package (3.4 ounces) vanilla
  instant pudding
1½ cups milk
1 cup thawed frozen whipped
  topping

8 thin slices fresh or thawed
  frozen pound cake
½ cup toasted sliced almonds
¼ cup mini semisweet
  chocolate chips (optional)

*Or, substitute Birds Eye® frozen Raspberries.

• Thaw strawberries according to package directions.

• Prepare pudding with 1½ cups milk according to package directions. Let stand 5 minutes; gently stir in whipped topping.

• Place 1 slice cake in each of 4 individual serving bowls. Spoon half the strawberries over cake. Top with half the pudding mixture, almonds and chocolate chips.

• Repeat layers of cake, strawberries, pudding, almonds and chips. Cover and chill until ready to serve.

# Peach Sorbet

**Makes 8 servings**

7 fresh California peaches,
  peeled, halved, pitted
  and quartered

¾ cup sugar
3 tablespoons light corn syrup
1 teaspoon lemon juice

Add peaches to food processor or blender; process to measure 3½ cups purée. Combine peach purée, sugar, corn syrup and lemon juice in saucepan. Cook and stir over low heat until sugar dissolves; cool. Prepare in ice cream maker according to manufacturer's directions. Pack into freezing containers. Freeze until firm.

Favorite recipe from **California Tree Fruit Agreement**

# Cherries in the Snow Dessert

1 package DUNCAN HINES®
   Angel Food Cake Mix
1 package (8 ounces) cream
   cheese, softened
1 cup confectioners' sugar

1 container (12 ounces) frozen
   whipped topping, thawed
1 can (21 ounces) cherry pie
   filling

**Makes 16 to 20 servings**

*1.* Preheat oven to 375°F. Prepare, bake and cool cake following package directions. Cut cake into 16 slices.

*2.* Combine cream cheese and confectioners' sugar in small bowl. Beat at medium speed with electric mixer until smooth.

*3.* To assemble, spread half the whipped topping in bottom of 13×9×2-inch pan. Arrange 8 cake slices on whipped topping; press lightly. Spread with cream cheese mixture. Arrange remaining cake slices on cream cheese mixture; press lightly. Spread with remaining whipped topping. Spoon cherry pie filling evenly over top. (Pan will be filled to the brim.) Refrigerate for 2 hours or until ready to serve. Cut into squares.

*Note:*

**Make sure the cake cools completely before cutting it into slices. (Preparing the cake one day in advance will make it easier to cut.)**

# Orange Mousse with Strawberry Sauce

**Makes 12 servings**

**Prep Time:**
*15 minutes plus refrigerating*

1½ cups boiling water
1 package (8-serving size) *or*
  2 packages (4-serving size
  each) JELL-O® Brand
  Orange Flavor Gelatin
2 teaspoons grated orange peel
  (optional)
1 cup cold water

¾ cup cold orange juice
1 tub (8 ounces) COOL WHIP®
  Whipped Topping, thawed
1 package (10 ounces) frozen
  strawberries *or* raspberries
  in syrup, thawed, puréed in
  blender

**STIR** boiling water into gelatin and orange peel in large bowl at least 2 minutes until gelatin is completely dissolved. Stir in cold water and orange juice. Refrigerate about 1¼ hours or until slightly thickened (consistency of unbeaten egg whites).

**STIR** in whipped topping with wire whisk until smooth. Pour into 6-cup mold which has been sprayed with no stick cooking spray.

**REFRIGERATE** 3 hours or until firm. Unmold. Serve with puréed strawberries.

<u>**How To Unmold:**</u> *Dip mold in warm water for about 15 seconds. Gently pull gelatin from around edges with moist fingers. Place moistened serving plate on top of mold. Invert mold and plate; holding mold and plate together, shake slightly to loosen. Gently remove mold and center gelatin on plate.*

<u>**For individual servings:**</u> *Pour mousse mixture into 12 (6-ounce) custard cups, filling each about ¾ full.*

<u>**Lemon Mousse:**</u> *Substitute JELL-O® Brand Lemon Flavor Gelatin and lemon peel for the Orange Flavor Gelatin and orange peel.*

# Amy's Lemonade Mousse

1 quart cold fat-free (skim) milk
2 packages (1 ounce each)
    fat-free, sugar-free vanilla
    instant pudding mix
2 packages (½ ounce each)
    sugar-free powdered
    lemonade mix, undiluted

1 container (8 ounces) frozen
    fat-free whipped dessert
    topping, thawed
Fresh or frozen mixed berries

**Makes 8 servings**

*1.* Pour milk into large mixing bowl. Add pudding mix and whisk for 2 minutes until smooth. Whisk in powdered lemonade mix. After mixture thickens, whisk in whipped topping until smooth. Pour into 8 parfait glasses. Chill.

*2.* Garnish with berries.

# California Plum Sorbet

12 fresh California plums,
    halved, pitted and sliced
1 cup orange juice

3 tablespoons sugar
1 tablespoon grated orange
    peel

**Makes 6 servings**

*1.* Add plums, orange juice, sugar and orange peel to food processor or blender; process until smooth. Pour into loaf pan; freeze about 4 hours.

*2.* Process again 30 minutes before serving. Freeze until ready to serve.

Favorite recipe from **California Tree Fruit Agreement**

# All-American Pineapple & Fruit Trifle

**Makes 8 to 10 servings**

1 DOLE® Fresh Pineapple
1 cup frozen sliced peaches, thawed
1 cup frozen strawberries, thawed, sliced
1 cup frozen raspberries, thawed
1 (10-inch) angel food cake

1 package (4-serving size) vanilla flavor sugar free instant pudding and pie filling mix
⅓ cup cream sherry
½ cup thawed frozen whipped topping

*Note:*

Cream sherry, also called golden sherry, is a sweet Oloroso sherry. This variety is aged longer than medium or dry sherries; it is darker and fuller flavored.

• Twist crown from pineapple. Cut pineapple in half lengthwise. Refrigerate one half for another use, such as fruit salad. Cut fruit from shell. Cut fruit into thin wedges. Reserve 3 wedges for garnish; combine remaining pineapple with peaches and berries.

• Cut cake in half. Freeze one half for another use. Tear remaining cake into chunks.

• Prepare pudding mix according to package directions.

• In 2-quart glass serving bowl, arrange half of cake chunks; sprinkle with half of sherry. Top with half each fruit mixture and pudding. Repeat layers. Cover; chill 1 hour or overnight.

• Just before serving, garnish with whipped topping and reserved pineapple wedges.

# Double Chocolate Delight

Makes 6 to 8 servings

3 tablespoons butter or
   margarine, melted
2 tablespoons sugar
1 cup graham cracker crumbs
½ cup milk
1 HERSHEY'S Milk Chocolate
   Bar (7 ounces), broken into
   pieces

½ cup HERSHEY'S MINI CHIPS™
   Semi-Sweet Chocolate
   Chips
1 cup (½ pint) cold whipping
   cream
Sweetened whipped cream
Sliced sweetened
   strawberries

*1.* Stir together butter and sugar in small bowl. Add graham cracker crumbs; mix well. Press mixture firmly onto bottom of 8-inch square pan. Refrigerate 1 to 2 hours or until firm.

*2.* Meanwhile, heat milk in small saucepan just until it begins to boil; remove from heat. Immediately add chocolate bar pieces and small chocolate chips; stir until chocolate melts and mixture is smooth. Pour into medium bowl; cool to room temperature.

*3.* Beat whipping cream in small bowl on high speed of mixer until stiff; fold gently into chocolate mixture. Pour onto prepared crust; freeze several hours or until firm. Cut into squares. Just before serving, garnish with sweetened whipped cream and strawberries.

# Frozen Mocha Cheesecake Loaf

**Makes 8 to 10 servings**

**Prep Time:**
*20 minutes*

**Freeze Time:**
*6 hours*

### Note:

Instant powdered coffees are the result of removing water from brewed coffee through drying. Instant and freeze-dried coffees should be stored in a cool place.

2 cups finely crushed crème-filled chocolate sandwich cookies (about 20 cookies)
3 tablespoons butter or margarine, melted
1 (8-ounce) package cream cheese, softened
1 (14-ounce) can EAGLE® BRAND Sweetened Condensed Milk (NOT evaporated milk)

1 tablespoon vanilla extract
2 cups (1 pint) whipping cream, whipped
2 tablespoons instant coffee dissolved in 1 tablespoon hot water
½ cup chocolate-flavored syrup

*1.* Line 9×5-inch loaf pan with foil, extending foil above sides of pan. In small mixing bowl, combine cookie crumbs and butter; press firmly on bottom and halfway up sides of prepared pan.

*2.* In large mixing bowl, beat cream cheese until fluffy. Gradually add Eagle Brand until smooth; add vanilla. Fold in whipped cream.

*3.* Remove half the mixture and place in medium bowl; fold in coffee liquid and chocolate syrup. Spoon half the chocolate mixture into prepared pan, then half the vanilla mixture. Repeat. With table knife, cut through cream mixture to marble.

*4.* Cover; freeze 6 hours or until firm. To serve, remove from pan; peel off foil. Cut into slices and garnish as desired. Freeze leftovers.

# Peppermint Rice Cloud

| | | |
|---|---|---|
| 2 cups cooked rice<br>1½ cups miniature marshmallows<br>1 cup low-fat milk<br>⅓ cup crushed peppermint<br>candy | 1 teaspoon vanilla extract<br>1 cup heavy cream, whipped<br>1 (9-inch) prepared chocolate<br>crumb crust<br>¼ cup fudge sauce, warmed | **Makes 6 servings** |

Combine rice, marshmallows, milk and candy in 2-quart saucepan. Cook over medium heat 6 to 8 minutes or until thick and creamy, stirring constantly. Remove from heat; stir in vanilla. Cool completely. Fold in whipped cream. Spoon into crust. Refrigerate at least 3 hours. To serve, drizzle with fudge sauce.

Favorite recipe from **USA Rice Federation**

# Cocoa Mint Sherbet

| | | |
|---|---|---|
| ¾ cup sugar<br>¼ cup HERSHEY₅S Cocoa<br>1½ cups (12-ounce can)<br>evaporated nonfat milk | ¼ teaspoon mint extract | **Makes 6 servings**<br>(¼ cup each) |

Stir together sugar and cocoa in medium saucepan; add evaporated milk. Cook over medium heat, stirring constantly, until sugar dissolves and mixture is smooth. Remove from heat; stir in mint extract. Pour into 8-inch square pan. Place in freezer, stirring occasionally, until frozen.

# Vanilla Flan

**Makes 8 servings**

¾ cup granulated sugar
1 can (12 fluid ounces)
   NESTLÉ® CARNATION®
   Evaporated Milk
1 can (14 ounces)
   NESTLÉ® CARNATION®
   Sweetened Condensed Milk

3 large eggs
1 tablespoon vanilla extract

**PREHEAT** oven to 325°F.

**HEAT** sugar in small, *heavy-duty* saucepan over medium-low heat, stirring constantly, for 3 to 4 minutes or until dissolved and caramel colored. Quickly pour onto bottom of deep-dish 9-inch pie plate; swirl around bottom and side to coat.

**COMBINE** evaporated milk, sweetened condensed milk, eggs and vanilla extract in medium bowl. Pour into prepared pie plate. Place pie plate in large roasting pan; fill roasting pan with warm water to about 1-inch depth.

**BAKE** for 45 to 50 minutes or until knife inserted near center comes out clean. Remove flan from water. Cool on wire rack. Refrigerate for 4 hours or overnight.

**TO SERVE:** Run small spatula around edge of pie plate. Invert serving plate over pie plate. Turn over; shake gently to release. Caramelized sugar forms sauce.

# Chocolate Rice Pudding

2 cups water
1 cup uncooked UNCLE BEN'S®
    ORIGINAL CONVERTED®
    Brand Rice
2 tablespoons butter
¼ cup sugar

2 teaspoons cornstarch
2 cups milk
½ teaspoon vanilla
2 egg yolks
½ cup semisweet chocolate
    chips

**Makes 6 servings**

*1.* Bring water to a boil in large saucepan. Stir in rice and butter. Reduce heat; cover and simmer 20 minutes. Remove from heat. Let stand covered until all liquid is absorbed, about 5 minutes.

*2.* Combine sugar and cornstarch in small bowl; add to hot rice in saucepan. Stir in milk.

*3.* Bring mixture to a boil, stirring occasionally. Boil 1 minute, stirring constantly. Remove from heat; stir in vanilla.

*4.* Beat egg yolks in small bowl. Stir about 1 cup of hot rice mixture into beaten egg yolks.

*5.* Stir egg yolk mixture back into remaining rice mixture in saucepan.

*6.* Cook rice mixture over medium heat, stirring frequently, just until mixture starts to bubble. Remove from heat; add chocolate chips and stir until melted.

*7.* Spoon into individual serving dishes. Chill.

*8.* Garnish, if desired.

# Two Great Tastes Pudding Parfaits

**Makes 4 to 6 servings**

1 package (6-serving size, 4.6 ounces) vanilla cook & serve pudding and pie filling mix*
3½ cups milk
1 cup REESE'S® Peanut Butter Chips
1 cup HERSHEY'S MINI KISSES™ Semi-Sweet or Milk Chocolates

Whipped topping (optional)
Additional MINI KISSES™ Chocolates or grated chocolate

*Do not use instant pudding mix.

*1.* Combine pudding mix and 3½ cups milk in large heavy saucepan (rather than amount listed in package directions). Cook over medium heat, stirring constantly, until mixture comes to a full boil. Remove from heat; divide hot mixture between 2 heatproof medium bowls.

*2.* Immediately stir peanut butter chips into mixture in one bowl and Mini Kisses™ Chocolates into second bowl. Stir both mixtures until chips are melted and mixture is smooth. Cool slightly, stirring occasionally.

*3.* Alternately layer peanut butter and chocolate mixtures in parfait dishes, wine glasses or dessert dishes. Place plastic wrap directly onto surface of each dessert; refrigerate about 6 hours. Garnish with whipped topping, if desired, and Mini Kisses™ Chocolates.

# Frozen Chocolate Cheesecake

Makes 8 servings

1½ cups chocolate or vanilla wafer cookie crumbs

⅓ cup butter or margarine, melted

10 ounces (1¼ packages) cream cheese, softened

½ cup sugar

1 cup (6 ounces) semisweet chocolate chips, melted

1 teaspoon vanilla

1⅓ cups thawed frozen nondairy whipped topping

¾ cup chopped pecans

Grated chocolate or chocolate curls (optional)

Preheat oven to 325°F.

Combine cookie crumbs and butter in small bowl; press onto bottom and side of 9-inch pie plate. Bake 10 minutes. Cool crust completely in pan on wire rack.

Combine cream cheese and sugar in large bowl. Gradually stir melted chocolate chips and vanilla into cheese mixture. Gently fold whipped topping into cheese mixture; fold in pecans. Pour cheese filling into prepared crust and freeze until firm. Garnish with grated chocolate or chocolate curls, if desired.

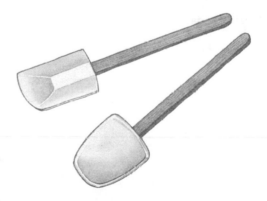

# Cran-Raspberry Hazelnut Trifle

**Makes 8 servings**

**Prep Time:**
*20 minutes*

## Note:

**A trifle is a layered dessert of English origin that has been on American menus since colonial times. Traditionally trifles were made with sponge cake or ladyfingers, but pound cake and even chopped cookies are commonly used today.**

2 cups hazelnut-flavored liquid
   dairy creamer
1 package (3.4 ounces) instant
   vanilla pudding and pie
   filling mix
1 package (about 11 ounces)
   frozen pound cake, thawed

1 can (21 ounces) raspberry
   pie filling
1 can (16 ounces) whole berry
   cranberry sauce

*1.* Combine dairy creamer and pudding in medium bowl; beat with wire whisk 1 to 2 minutes or until thickened.

*2.* Cut pound cake into ¾-inch cubes. Combine pie filling and cranberry sauce in medium bowl; blend well.

*3.* Layer ⅓ of cake cubes, ¼ of fruit sauce and ⅓ of pudding mixture in 1½- to 2-quart straight-sided glass serving bowl. Repeat layers twice; top with remaining fruit sauce. Cover; refrigerate until serving time.

**<u>Serving Suggestion:</u>** *Garnish trifle with whipped topping and fresh mint sprigs.*

# Smucker's® English Berry Pudding

**Makes 8 servings**

12 to 16 slices white bread, crusts removed, cut into half or quarter triangles
1 cup SMUCKER'S® Red Raspberry Preserves

2 cups *each* raspberries, blueberries and sliced strawberries (fresh or frozen)

Line deep 1½- to 2-quart bowl with plastic wrap. Line bottom and side of bowl with half of triangle bread slices. Completely cover surface so no gaps remain between bread slices.

Heat SMUCKER'S® Raspberry Preserves and 6 cups mixed berries in saucepan over high heat. Bring to a boil and simmer 5 minutes to release juices. Spoon half of berry mixture into bread-lined bowl. Cover with half of remaining bread triangles and remaining berry mixture. Cover second layer of berries with remaining bread. Use more bread if needed to completely seal bowl. Cover pudding with plastic wrap.

Place plate over bowl to weigh it down. Refrigerate pudding 12 to 24 hours before serving.

To serve, remove plate and plastic wrap. Unmold bowl onto serving plate. Remove bowl and carefully peel plastic wrap from pudding. Serve pudding dusted with powdered sugar, with whipped cream, frozen yogurt or whipped topping.

# Chocolate Toffee Layered Dessert

**Makes 12 servings**

**Prep Time:**
*20 minutes*

**Chill Time:**
*1 hour*

3 cups cold milk
2 packages (4-serving size) JELL-O® Chocolate Flavor Instant Pudding & Pie Filling
1 tub (8 ounces) COOL WHIP® Whipped Topping, thawed

1 package (12 ounces) marble pound cake, cut into ½-inch cubes
½ cup chocolate flavored syrup
4 packages (1.4 ounces each) chocolate-covered English toffee bars, chopped

**POUR** milk into large bowl. Add pudding mixes. Beat with wire whisk 1 minute. Gently stir in 2 cups of the whipped topping.

**ARRANGE** ½ of the cake cubes in 3½-quart serving bowl. Drizzle with ½ of the chocolate flavored syrup. Layer with ½ of the chopped toffee bars and ½ of the pudding mixture. Repeat layers ending with pudding mixture.

**REFRIGERATE** 1 hour or until ready to serve. Top with remaining whipped topping.

# Sweetheart Chocolate Mousse

**Makes about 8 servings**

1 envelope unflavored gelatin
2 tablespoons cold water
¼ cup boiling water
1 cup sugar
½ cup HERSHEY'S Cocoa

2 cups (1 pint) cold whipping cream
2 teaspoons vanilla extract
Fresh raspberries or sliced strawberries

*1.* Sprinkle gelatin over cold water in small bowl; let stand 2 minutes to soften. Add boiling water; stir until gelatin is completely dissolved and mixture is clear. Cool slightly.

*2.* Mix sugar and cocoa in large bowl; add whipping cream and vanilla. Beat on medium speed, scraping bottom of bowl occasionally, until mixture is stiff. Pour in gelatin mixture; beat until well blended.

*3.* Spoon into dessert dishes. Refrigerate at least 30 minutes before serving. Garnish with fruit.

# Peach Tapioca

| | | Makes 4 servings |
|---|---|---|
| 2 cups reduced-fat (2%) milk<br>3 tablespoons quick cooking<br>tapioca<br>1 egg, lightly beaten<br>1½ cups peeled, coarsely<br>chopped peaches* | 3 tablespoons no-sugar-added<br>apricot spread<br>1 teaspoon vanilla extract<br><br>*If fresh peaches are not in season, use frozen peaches and add 1 to 2 packets sugar substitute or equivalent of 4 teaspoons sugar to milk mixture. | |

*1.* Combine milk, tapioca and egg in 1½-quart saucepan; let stand 5 minutes. Stir in peaches and apricot spread.

*2.* Cook and stir over medium heat until mixture comes to a rolling boil; cook 1 minute more. Remove from heat and stir in vanilla.

*3.* Cool slightly; stir. Place plastic wrap directly on surface of pudding; chill.

<u>Note:</u> *To quickly peel whole peaches, plunge into boiling water for about 1 minute.*

# Chocolate Hazelnut Terrine With Raspberry Sauce

**Makes 16 servings**

### Dark Chocolate Layer
2 cups (12-ounce package) NESTLÉ® TOLL HOUSE® Semi-Sweet Chocolate Morsels
⅓ cup butter, cut into pieces
¼ cup hazelnut liqueur
1½ cups heavy whipping cream

### Milk Chocolate Layer
1¾ cups (11.5-ounce package) NESTLÉ® TOLL HOUSE® Milk Chocolate Morsels
⅓ cup butter, cut into pieces

### Raspberry Sauce
1 package (10 ounces) frozen raspberries in syrup, thawed, puréed and strained
½ cup water
1 tablespoon cornstarch
1 teaspoon granulated sugar

LINE 9×5-inch loaf pan with plastic wrap.

**For Dark Chocolate Layer**
MICROWAVE semi-sweet morsels and ⅓ cup butter in medium, microwave-safe bowl on HIGH (100%) power for 1 minute; stir. Microwave at additional 10- to 20-second intervals, stirring until smooth. Stir in liqueur; cool to room temperature.

WHIP cream in small mixer bowl until stiff peaks form. Fold *2 cups* whipped cream into chocolate mixture. Spoon into prepared loaf pan. Refrigerate *remaining* whipped cream.

**For Milk Chocolate Layer**
MICROWAVE milk chocolate morsels and ⅓ cup butter in medium, microwave-safe bowl on MEDIUM-HIGH (70%) power for 1 minute; stir. Microwave at additional 10- to 20-second intervals, stirring until smooth. Cool to room temperature. Stir *remaining* whipped cream into chocolate mixture. Spread over dark chocolate layer. Cover; refrigerate for at least 2 hours or until firm.

**For Raspberry Sauce**

**COOK** raspberry purée, water, cornstarch and sugar over medium heat, stirring constantly, until mixture comes to a boil; boil for 1 minute. Cover; refrigerate.

**TO SERVE:** Invert terrine onto serving platter; remove plastic wrap. Cut into ½-inch-thick slices; serve in pool of Raspberry Sauce.

# Ambrosia

| | |
|---|---|
| 1 can (20 ounces) DOLE® Pineapple Chunks | 1 cup miniature marshmallows |
| 1 can (11 ounces) DOLE® Mandarin Oranges | 1 cup flaked coconut |
| 1 firm, large DOLE® Banana, sliced (optional) | ½ cup pecan halves or coarsely chopped nuts |
| 1½ cups DOLE® Seedless Grapes | 1 cup vanilla yogurt or sour cream |
| | 1 tablespoon brown sugar |

Makes 4 servings

• Drain pineapple chunks and oranges. In large bowl, combine pineapple chunks, oranges, banana, grapes, marshmallows, coconut and nuts. In 1-quart measure, combine yogurt and brown sugar. Stir into fruit mixture. Refrigerate, covered, 1 hour or overnight.

# Lemon Ginger Squares

**Makes 15 to 18 servings**

**Prep Time:**
*15 minutes*

2¼ cups gingersnap cookie crumbs
¼ cup sugar
⅓ cup butter or margarine, melted
⅔ cup boiling water
1 package (4-serving size) Lemon Flavor JELL-O® Brand Gelatin

½ cup cold water
Ice cubes
1 tub (12 ounces) COOL WHIP® Whipped Topping, thawed

**MIX** 2 cups cookie crumbs, sugar and butter with fork in 13×9-inch baking pan until crumbs are well moistened. Press firmly onto bottom of pan. Refrigerate until ready to fill.

**STIR** boiling water into gelatin in large bowl 2 minutes until completely dissolved. Mix cold water and ice cubes to make 1¼ cups. Add to gelatin, stirring until slightly thickened (consistency of unbeaten egg whites). Remove any remaining ice. Stir in 3½ cups whipped topping with wire whisk until smooth. Pour over crust.

**REFRIGERATE** 3 hours or until firm. Just before serving, spread remaining whipped topping over gelatin mixture. Sprinkle with remaining cookie crumbs. Cut into squares. Garnish as desired.

# Brownie Berry Parfaits

1 box (10 ounces) BIRDS EYE®
   frozen Raspberries*
4 large prepared brownies, cut
   into cubes
1 pint vanilla or chocolate ice
   cream

4 tablespoons chocolate syrup
2 tablespoons chopped walnuts

*Or, substitute Birds Eye® frozen Strawberries.

**Makes 4 servings**

**Prep Time:**
*10 minutes*

- Thaw raspberries according to package directions.

- Divide half the brownie cubes among four parfait glasses. Top with half the ice cream and raspberries. Repeat layers with remaining brownie cubes, ice cream and raspberries.

- Drizzle chocolate syrup over each dessert; sprinkle with walnuts.

# Mango-Peach Frozen Yogurt

2 medium (8 ounces each) ripe
   mangoes, peeled and cubed

2 cups peach low-fat yogurt
½ cup honey

**Makes 6 servings**

In blender or food processor container, blend mango cubes until smooth. Add yogurt and honey; blend until well combined. Transfer mixture to ice cream maker; freeze according to manufacturer's directions.

Favorite recipe from **National Honey Board**

# Neopolitan Chip Bomb

**Makes 12 servings**

**Prep Time:**
*25 minutes plus freezing*

**30 CHIPS AHOY!® Chocolate Chip Cookies, divided**
**½ gallon vanilla, chocolate and strawberry ice cream, softened**

**1 tub (8 ounces) COOL WHIP® Whipped Topping, thawed**

CUT 6 cookies in half. Reserve 1 whole cookie and cookie halves for garnish.

LINE 2½-quart bowl with plastic wrap. Separate 3 flavors of ice cream. Press 1 flavor into bowl. Arrange layer of cookies over ice cream. Repeat procedure to make 2 more layers, ending with cookies. Cover with plastic wrap.

FREEZE 4 hours or overnight. Invert bomb onto large serving plate. Remove plastic wrap. Frost with whipped topping. Garnish with reserved cookies. Let stand at room temperature about 10 minutes for easier cutting and serving.

<u>Great Substitute:</u> *Try other flavors of ice cream.*

# Peter Pan's Cloud Dessert

½ cup PETER PAN® Smart
    Choice Creamy Peanut
    Butter, Creamy or Chunky
2 (4-ounce) containers
    SWISS MISS® Fat Free
    Vanilla Pudding

3 cups reduced fat nondairy
    whipped topping
Chopped peanuts (optional)

**Makes 8 servings**

*1.* In medium bowl, combine Peter Pan Peanut Butter and pudding; fold in whipped topping.

*2.* Divide evenly into dessert cups and garnish with peanuts.

*3.* Refrigerate until chilled.

## Cool, creamy… and confusing

*Cold concoctions are delicious, but sometimes their names can cause brain freeze. Here are a few descriptions to help sort them out:*

Bavarian: a cold dessert made of custard, whipped cream, gelatin and flavorings such as fruit or chocolate, often prepared in a decorative mold.

Bombe: a frozen dessert made of layers of ice cream or sherbet prepared in a mold, often with a custard in the center.

Granité: a frozen mixture of water, sugar and liquid flavoring such as fruit juice or coffee. Granité (called granita in Italy and ice in the U.S.) is usually stirred frequently during the freezing process to produce a somewhat granular texture.

Mousse: a sweet dessert made by folding something foamy, such as beaten egg whites or whipped cream, into a cooked egg yolk or gelatin mixture that is often flavored with puréed fruit or chocolate. (Savory mousses are flavored with meat, poultry, seafood, vegetables, etc.)

Sorbet: a frozen mixture of fruit juice, fruit purée, water and sugar. Sorbet is the French term for sherbet but, unlike sherbet, it contains no milk products—it is actually more similar to an ice than to sherbet.

# Chocolate Truffle Loaf

**Makes 16 servings**

2 packages (8 squares each)
BAKER'S® Semi-Sweet
Chocolate
½ cup (1 stick) margarine or
butter

¼ cup milk
2 eggs, lightly beaten
1 teaspoon vanilla
1 tub (8 ounces) COOL WHIP®
Whipped Topping, thawed

**HEAT** 15 squares of the chocolate, margarine and milk in large heavy saucepan on very low heat until chocolate is melted and mixture is smooth, stirring constantly. Stir in eggs with wire whisk; cook 1 minute, stirring constantly. Remove from heat. Stir in vanilla.

**REFRIGERATE** about 20 minutes or until just cool, stirring occasionally. Gently stir in 2¾ cups of the whipped topping. Pour into 8×4-inch loaf pan which has been lined with plastic wrap.

**REFRIGERATE** 6 hours or overnight or freeze 3 hours until firm. Invert pan onto serving plate; remove plastic wrap. Melt remaining 1 square chocolate; drizzle over dessert. Garnish with remaining whipped topping. Store leftover dessert in refrigerator.

# Creamy Peach-Raspberry Melba

**Makes 8 servings**

Prep Time:
*15 minutes plus
refrigerating*

¾ cup boiling water
1 package (4-serving size)
JELL-O® Brand Raspberry
Flavor Gelatin
½ cup cold water
Ice cubes

¼ teaspoon almond extract
1 tub (8 ounces) COOL WHIP®
Whipped Topping, thawed
1 medium peach, peeled and
diced

**STIR** boiling water into gelatin in medium bowl at least 2 minutes until completely dissolved. Mix cold water and ice to make 1 cup. Add to gelatin, stirring until ice is melted. Stir in almond extract. Refrigerate 20 minutes or until slightly thickened (consistency of unbeaten egg whites). Gently stir in whipped topping. Gently stir in peach. Spoon into dessert dishes.

**REFRIGERATE** at least 30 minutes or until set. Garnish with additional whipped topping, if desired.

<u>Special Extra:</u> *Garnish with fresh raspberries.*

# Creamy Banana Pudding

| | | |
|---|---|---|
| 1 (14-ounce) can EAGLE® BRAND Sweetened Condensed Milk (NOT evaporated milk)<br>1½ cups cold water<br>1 (4-serving-size) package instant vanilla pudding and pie filling mix | 2 cups (1 pint) whipping cream, whipped<br>36 vanilla wafers<br>3 medium bananas, sliced and dipped in lemon juice from concentrate | **Makes 8 to 10 servings**<br><br>**Prep Time:**<br>*15 minutes* |

*1.* In large mixing bowl, combine Eagle Brand and water. Add pudding mix; beat until well blended. Chill 5 minutes.

*2.* Fold in whipped cream. Spoon 1 cup pudding mixture into 2½-quart glass serving bowl.

*3.* Top with one-third each of vanilla wafers, bananas and pudding mixture. Repeat layering twice, ending with pudding mixture. Chill thoroughly. Garnish as desired. Refrigerate leftovers.

# Easy Fresh Lemon Ice Cream

**Makes 6 to 9 servings (about 3 cups)**

2 cups heavy cream or
  whipping cream or
  half-and-half
1 cup sugar
  Grated peel of 1 SUNKIST®
  lemon

⅓ cup fresh squeezed SUNKIST®
  lemon juice
6 to 10 SUNKIST® lemon boats
  or shells (optional, see
  Note)

In large bowl, combine cream and sugar; stir to dissolve sugar. Blend in lemon peel and juice. (Mixture will thicken slightly.) Pour into shallow pan and freeze until firm, about 4 hours. Serve in lemon boats or shells, or in dessert dishes. Garnish with fresh mint leaves and strawberries, if desired.

**Lemon and Fruit Variation:** *Stir ½ cup mashed strawberries, bananas or kiwifruit into the slightly thickened lemon mixture before freezing. Makes about 3½ cups.*

**Note:** *To make lemon boats, cut large lemon in half lengthwise. Carefully ream out juice (save for use in other recipes). Scrape shells clean with spoon. Edges may be notched or scalloped. To prevent tipping, cut thin slice from bottom of each shell. To make lemon shells, cut lemon in half crosswise; proceed as above.*

# Mini Kisses Pumpkin Mousse Cups

1¾ cups (10-ounce package)
  HERSHEY₅S MINI KISSES™
  Semi-Sweet Chocolates,
  divided
24 marshmallows
½ cup milk

½ cup canned pumpkin
1 teaspoon vanilla extract
1 teaspoon pumpkin pie spice
⅓ cup powdered sugar
1 cup (½ pint) cold whipping
  cream

**Makes 10 servings**

*1.* Line 10 muffin cups (2½ inches in diameter) with paper bake cups. Reserve ½ cup Mini Kisses™ Chocolates. Place remaining 1¼ cups chocolates in small microwave-safe bowl; microwave at HIGH (100%) 1 minute or until melted when stirred. Mixture should be thick.

*2.* Very thickly coat inside pleated surfaces and bottoms of bake cups with melted chocolate using soft pastry brush. Refrigerate 10 minutes; recoat any thin spots with melted chocolate.* Refrigerate until firm, about 2 hours. Gently peel off paper; refrigerate until ready to fill.

*3.* Place marshmallows, milk and pumpkin in medium microwave-safe bowl. Microwave at HIGH 1 minute; stir. Microwave additional 30 seconds at a time, stirring after each heating, until mixture is melted and smooth. Stir in vanilla and pumpkin pie spice. Cool completely.

*4.* Beat powdered sugar and whipping cream until stiff; fold into pumpkin mixture. Fill cups with pumpkin mousse; garnish with reserved Mini Kisses™ Chocolates. Cover; refrigerate 2 hours or until firm.

*If reheating is needed, microwave chocolate at HIGH 15 seconds; stir.*

*Note:*

Pumpkin pie spice
is usually a blend of
cinnamon, ginger,
nutmeg and cloves
or allspice. It's
readily available in
supermarkets, but in
a pinch, combine two
teaspoons cinnamon,
1 teaspoon ginger and
¼ teaspoon ground
nutmeg or cloves.
Store in a small jar.

# Banana Pudding

**Makes 8 servings**

60 to 70 vanilla wafers*
1 cup granulated sugar
3 tablespoons cornstarch
¼ teaspoon salt
2 cans (12 fluid ounces *each*) NESTLÉ® CARNATION® Evaporated Milk
2 large eggs, lightly beaten
3 tablespoons butter, cut into pieces

1½ teaspoons vanilla extract
5 ripe but firm large bananas, cut into ¼-inch slices
1 container (8 ounces) frozen non-dairy whipped topping, thawed

*A 12-ounce box of vanilla wafers contains about 88 wafers.

**LINE** bottom and side of 2½-quart glass bowl with about 40 wafers.

## Note:

Cornstarch, a smooth powder that is made from the endosperm (center) of dried corn kernels, has about twice the thickening ability of flour. Unlike flour, cornstarch becomes clear when cooked, which is why it is often used in dessert sauces and puddings.

**COMBINE** sugar, cornstarch and salt in medium saucepan. Gradually stir in evaporated milk to dissolve cornstarch. Whisk in eggs. Add butter. Cook over medium heat, stirring constantly, until the mixture begins to thicken. Reduce heat to low; bring to a simmer and cook for 1 minute, stirring constantly. Remove from heat. Stir in vanilla extract. Let cool slightly.

**POUR** *half* of pudding over wafers. Top with *half* of bananas. Layer *remaining* wafers over bananas. Combine *remaining* pudding and bananas; spoon over wafers. Refrigerate for at least 4 hours. Top with whipped topping.

# Peaches & Cream Gingersnap Cups

**Makes 2 servings**

1½ tablespoons gingersnap
    crumbs (2 cookies)
¼ teaspoon ground ginger
2 ounces cream cheese,
    softened
1 container (6 ounces) peach
    yogurt

¼ teaspoon vanilla
⅓ cup chopped fresh peach
    or drained canned peach
    slices in juice

*1.* Combine gingersnap crumbs and ginger in small bowl; set aside.

*2.* Beat cream cheese in small bowl at medium speed of electric mixer until smooth. Add yogurt and vanilla. Beat at low speed until smooth and well blended. Stir in chopped peach.

*3.* Divide peach mixture between two 6-ounce custard cups. Cover and refrigerate 1 hour. Top each serving with half of gingersnap crumb mixture just before serving. Garnish as desired.

**Variation:** *Instead of crushing the gingersnaps, you can serve them whole with the peaches & cream cups.*

# Luscious Cold Chocolate Soufflés

**Makes 6 servings**

1 envelope unflavored gelatin
¼ cup cold water
2 tablespoons reduced-calorie tub margarine
1½ cups cold nonfat milk, divided
½ cup sugar
⅓ cup HERSHEY₀S Cocoa or HERSHEY₀S Dutch Processed Cocoa

2½ teaspoons vanilla extract, divided
1 envelope (1.3 ounces) dry whipped topping mix

*1.* Measure lengths of foil to fit around 6 small soufflé dishes (about 4 ounces each); fold in thirds lengthwise. Tape securely to outsides of dishes to form collars, allowing collars to extend 1 inch above rims of dishes. Lightly oil insides of foil.*

*2.* Sprinkle gelatin over water in small microwave-safe bowl; let stand 2 minutes to soften. Microwave at HIGH (100%) 40 seconds; stir thoroughly. Stir in margarine until melted; let stand 2 minutes or until gelatin is completely dissolved.

*3.* Stir together 1 cup milk, sugar, cocoa and 2 teaspoons vanilla in small bowl. Beat on low speed of mixer while gradually pouring in gelatin mixture. Beat until well blended.

*4.* Prepare topping mix as directed on package, using remaining ½ cup milk and remaining ½ teaspoon vanilla; carefully fold into chocolate mixture until well blended. Spoon into prepared soufflé dishes, filling ½ inch from tops of collars. Cover; refrigerate until firm, about 3 hours. Carefully remove foil. Garnish as desired.

*Six (6-ounce) custard cups may be used in place of soufflé dishes; omit foil collars.*

# Frozen Chocolate-Covered Bananas

2 ripe medium bananas
4 wooden sticks
½ cup low-fat granola cereal
without raisins

⅓ cup hot fudge sauce, at room
temperature

**Makes 4 servings**

*1.* Line baking sheet or 15×10-inch jelly-roll pan with waxed paper; set aside.

*2.* Peel bananas; cut each in half crosswise. Insert wooden stick into center of cut end of each banana about 1½ inches into banana half. Place on prepared baking sheet; freeze until firm, at least 2 hours.

*3.* Place granola in large plastic food storage bag; crush slightly using rolling pin or meat mallet. Transfer granola to shallow plate. Place fudge sauce in a shallow dish.

*4.* Working with 1 banana at a time, place frozen banana in fudge sauce; turn banana and spread fudge sauce evenly onto banana with small rubber scraper. Immediately place banana on plate with granola; turn to coat lightly. Return to baking sheet in freezer. Repeat with remaining bananas.

*5.* Freeze until fudge sauce is very firm, at least 2 hours. Place on small plates; let stand 5 minutes before serving.

# Easy Eclair Dessert

**Makes 18 servings**

**Prep Time:**
*20 minutes*

**Chill Time:**
*4 hours*

27 whole graham crackers, halved
3 cups cold milk
2 packages (4-serving size) JELL-O® Vanilla Flavor Instant Pudding & Pie Filling

1 tub (12 ounces) COOL WHIP® Whipped Topping, thawed
1 container (16 ounces) ready-to-spread chocolate fudge frosting
Strawberries

**ARRANGE** ⅓ of the crackers on bottom of 13×9-inch baking pan, breaking crackers to fit, if necessary.

**POUR** milk into large bowl. Add pudding mixes. Beat with wire whisk 2 minutes. Gently stir in whipped topping. Spread ½ of the pudding mixture over crackers. Place ½ of the remaining crackers over pudding; top with remaining pudding mixture and crackers.

**REMOVE** top and foil from frosting container. Microwave frosting in container on HIGH 1 minute or until pourable. Spread evenly over crackers.

**REFRIGERATE** 4 hours or overnight. Cut into squares to serve. Garnish with strawberries.

<u>Tips:</u> *You can make pistachio, banana-flavored or even double chocolate eclairs by simply changing the pudding flavors.*

# Chocolate Pudding Parfaits

**Makes 3 to 4 servings**

2 ounces semisweet chocolate,
    chopped
2 ounces white chocolate,
    chopped
½ cup sugar

2 tablespoons all-purpose flour
1 tablespoon cornstarch
2¼ cups milk
2 egg yolks, beaten
2 teaspoons vanilla, divided

*1.* Place semisweet chocolate and white chocolate in separate heatproof bowls; set aside.

*2.* Combine sugar, flour and cornstarch in saucepan. Gradually whisk in milk. Cook, stirring constantly, over medium heat until mixture comes to a boil. Boil 2 minutes, stirring constantly.

*3.* Remove saucepan from heat. Stir small amount of hot mixture into beaten egg yolks; return to hot mixture in pan. Cook and stir until thickened.

*4.* Spoon half of egg mixture over each chocolate in bowls; stir until chocolates are completely melted. Blend 1 teaspoon vanilla into each bowl.

*5.* Alternate layers of puddings in parfait glasses; cover. Refrigerate.

*Note:*

In sweet sauces and puddings, mixing cornstarch with the granulated sugar in the recipe before adding cold liquid helps to prevent lumps.

# Apple-Lemon Sherbet

**Makes 8 servings**

1 (16-ounce) jar MOTT'S® Apple
    Sauce
½ cup frozen apple juice
    concentrate, thawed

¼ cup lemon juice
1 egg white*

*Use clean, uncracked egg.

*1.* In food processor or blender, process apple sauce until smooth. Add juice concentrate, lemon juice and egg white; process until frothy.

*2.* Pour into ice cream maker freezer container; freeze according to manufacturer's directions. Or, pour into 8- or 9-inch square pan. Cover; freeze about 2 hours or until almost firm. Transfer to food processor or blender; process until smooth.

# Pudding in a Cloud Dessert

**Makes 8 (½-cup)
servings**

**Prep Time:**
*10 minutes*

2 (4-ounce) containers SWISS
    MISS® Vanilla Pudding
3 cups reduced-fat non-dairy
    whipped topping

Fresh mint leaves (optional)

In medium bowl, fold together pudding and whipped topping. Divide evenly into dessert cups. Refrigerate until chilled. Garnish with mint leaves, if desired.

# Chocolate Truffle Mousse

1 cup whipping cream, divided
1 egg yolk
2 tablespoons corn syrup
2 tablespoons butter
4 squares (1 ounce each)
    semisweet chocolate,
    coarsely chopped
4 squares (1 ounce each)
    milk chocolate,
    coarsely chopped

5 teaspoons powdered sugar
½ teaspoon vanilla
    Sweetened whipped cream,
    fresh raspberries and mint
    leaves (optional)

**Makes 6 servings**

Whisk ½ cup cream, egg yolk, corn syrup and butter in medium heavy saucepan over medium heat until mixture simmers. Continue whisking while mixture simmers 2 minutes. Remove from heat; add chocolates, stirring until smooth. Cool to room temperature.

Beat remaining ½ cup cream in medium bowl with electric mixer at high speed until soft peaks form. Add powdered sugar and vanilla; beat until stiff peaks form.

Stir whipped cream into chocolate mixture. Pour into medium serving bowl. Chill 4 hours or overnight. Garnish with sweetened whipped cream, fresh raspberries and mint leaves, if desired.

# Dulce de Leche Frozen Dessert

**Makes 8 servings**

**Prep Time:**
*20 minutes*

**Freeze Time:**
*6 hours*

3 cups half-and-half or milk
6 tablespoons KRAFT® Caramel
    Topping, divided
1 package (4-serving size)
    JELL-O® Butterscotch Flavor
    Instant Pudding & Pie
    Filling

1 package (4-serving size)
    JELL-O® Vanilla Flavor
    Instant Pudding & Pie
    Filling
1 tub (8 ounces) COOL WHIP®
    Whipped Topping, thawed

*Note:*

Dulce de leche literally means "sweet milk." It is a caramel made by cooking milk with sugar until the mixture is reduced to a thick amber syrup. Dulce de leche is an extremely poplular South American dessert, eaten on its own or used as an ingredient, ice cream flavor, filling or spread.

**POUR** half-and-half into large bowl. Stir in 2 tablespoons caramel topping until dissolved. Add pudding mixes. Beat with wire whisk 1 minute or until well blended. Gently stir in whipped topping until well mixed.

**SPOON** ½ of the pudding mixture into 8×4-inch loaf pan which has been lined with plastic wrap. Drizzle remaining caramel topping over mixture. Carefully spoon remaining pudding mixture over caramel and smooth with spatula.

**FREEZE** about 6 hours or overnight or until firm. Carefully invert pan onto serving platter and remove plastic wrap. Let stand at room temperature about 15 minutes before slicing.

**Variation:** *To prepare individual Dulce de Leche frozen pops or cups, spoon ½ of the pudding mixture into 10 to 12 paper-lined muffin cups. Place teaspoonful of caramel topping in center of each cup and cover with remaining pudding mixture. For pops, stick wooden popsicle sticks into each cup and freeze.*

# Speedy Pineapple-Lime Sorbet

| | | |
|---|---|---|
| 1 ripe pineapple, cut into cubes (about 4 cups)<br>⅓ cup frozen limeade concentrate, thawed | 1 to 2 tablespoons fresh lime juice<br>1 teaspoon grated lime peel | **Makes 8 (½-cup) servings** |

*1.* Arrange pineapple in single layer on large sheet pan; freeze at least 1 hour or until very firm. Use metal spatula to transfer pineapple to resealable plastic freezer food storage bags; freeze up to 1 month.

*2.* Combine frozen pineapple, limeade concentrate, lime juice and lime peel in food processor; process until smooth and fluffy. If pineapple doesn't become smooth and fluffy, let stand 30 minutes to soften slightly; then repeat processing. Serve immediately.

Note: *Sorbet is best if served immediately, but it may be made ahead, stored in the freezer and softened several minutes before serving.*

# Quick Creamy Chocolate Pudding

**Makes 4 to 5 servings**

⅔ cup sugar
¼ cup HERSHEY'S Cocoa
3 tablespoons cornstarch
¼ teaspoon salt
2¼ cups milk

2 tablespoons butter or
   margarine
1 teaspoon vanilla extract
   Whipped topping (optional)
   Chopped nuts (optional)

*Note:*

To prevent sticking and scorching, use a heavy-bottomed saucepan and stir the pudding constantly with a wooden spoon.

*1.* Stir together sugar, cocoa, cornstarch and salt in medium saucepan; gradually stir in milk. Cook over medium heat, stirring constantly, until mixture boils; boil and stir 1 minute. Remove from heat; stir in butter and vanilla.

*2.* Pour into individual dessert dishes. Press plastic wrap directly onto surface; refrigerate. Remove plastic wrap. Garnish with whipped topping and nuts, if desired.

**Microwave Directions:** *Stir together sugar, cocoa, cornstarch and salt in large microwave-safe bowl; gradually stir in milk. Microwave at HIGH (100%) 7 to 10 minutes or until mixture comes to a full boil, stirring every 2 minutes. Stir in butter and vanilla. Proceed as directed above.*

# Frozen Peanut Butter-Banana Dessert

2 large ripe bananas, cut into
½-inch slices
½ cup no-sugar-added natural
peanut butter (creamy or
chunky)

½ cup half-and-half

**Makes 4 servings**

Place bananas in single layer in plastic freezer bag; freeze until firm, at least 8 hours. Combine peanut butter and half-and-half in food processor container fitted with steel blade; cover and process until smooth. Add frozen bananas; let stand 10 minutes to soften slightly. Process until smooth, scraping down side of container frequently. (Dessert will be soft-set.) Serve immediately or cover and freeze in airtight container until serving time. Freeze leftovers.

<u>Note:</u> *Place frozen dessert in refrigerator 15 to 20 minutes before serving or let stand at room temperature 10 minutes before serving to soften slightly.*

# Creamy Strawberry-Orange Pops

**Makes 6 servings**

1 (8-ounce) container sugar-free strawberry yogurt
¾ cup orange juice
2 teaspoons vanilla
2 cups frozen whole strawberries

1 packet sugar substitute or equivalent of 2 teaspoons sugar
6 (7-ounce) paper cups
6 wooden sticks

*1.* Combine yogurt, orange juice and vanilla in food processor or blender. Cover and blend until smooth.

*2.* Add frozen strawberries and sugar substitute. Blend until smooth. Pour into 6 paper cups, filling each about ¾ full. Place in freezer for 1 hour. Insert wooden stick into center of each cup. Freeze completely. Peel cup off each pop to serve.

# Quick Chocolate Mousse

**Makes 8 to 10 servings**

**Prep Time:**
*5 minutes*

1 (14-ounce) can EAGLE® BRAND Sweetened Condensed Milk (NOT evaporated milk)
1 (4-serving-size) package instant chocolate pudding and pie filling mix

1 cup cold water
1 cup (½ pint) whipping cream, whipped

*1.* In large mixing bowl, beat Eagle Brand, pudding mix and water; chill 5 minutes.

*2.* Fold in whipped cream. Spoon into serving dishes; chill. Garnish as desired.

# Peach Melba Freeze

**Makes 8 servings**

1 container (8 ounces) peach lowfat yogurt
¼ cup peach fruit spread
1 tub (8 ounces) COOL WHIP LITE® Whipped Topping, thawed

½ cup fresh raspberries
1 package (10 ounces) frozen raspberries in lite syrup, thawed
2 teaspoons cornstarch

**STIR** yogurt and fruit spread in large bowl. Gently stir in whipped topping and fresh raspberries with wire whisk until blended.

**RINSE** and dry COOL WHIP tub. Spray with no stick cooking spray. Spoon yogurt mixture into tub. Cover with plastic wrap. Freeze 4 hours or until firm.

**MIX** raspberries in lite syrup and cornstarch in small saucepan. Stirring constantly, bring to boil on medium heat; boil 1 minute. Strain to remove seeds, if desired. Refrigerate sauce until ready to serve.

**RUN** small warm wet knife or spatula around edge of tub to unmold dessert. Place serving dish on top of tub. Invert, holding tub and dish together; shake gently to loosen. Carefully remove tub; cut dessert into wedges. Serve with raspberry sauce.

# Mocha Mousse

**Makes 8 servings**

1½ cups (12-ounce can) evaporated skim milk, divided
⅓ cup sugar
¼ cup HERSHEY'S Cocoa

1 envelope unflavored gelatin
¾ teaspoon powdered instant coffee
1 teaspoon vanilla extract

*1.* Pour ¾ cup evaporated milk into large bowl; place in freezer until milk begins to freeze around edges.

*2.* Stir together sugar, cocoa, gelatin and instant coffee in small saucepan. Stir in remaining ¾ cup evaporated milk. Let stand 2 minutes. Cook over medium heat, stirring constantly, until mixture is smooth and gelatin has completely dissolved. Pour into medium bowl; stir in vanilla. Cool to room temperature, stirring occasionally.

*3.* Beat cold evaporated milk on high speed of mixer until soft peaks form. Add cocoa mixture, stirring gently until well blended. Pour into individual dessert dishes. Refrigerate about 1 hour before serving.

# Strawberry-Banana Granité

**Makes 5 servings**

2 ripe medium bananas, peeled and sliced (about 2 cups)
2 cups unsweetened frozen strawberries *(do not thaw)*
¼ cup no-sugar-added strawberry pourable fruit*

Whole fresh strawberries (optional)
Fresh mint leaves (optional)

*\*3 tablespoons no-sugar-added strawberry fruit spread combined with 1 tablespoon warm water may be substituted.*

Place banana slices in plastic bag; freeze until firm. Place frozen banana slices and frozen strawberries in food processor container. Let stand 10 minutes for fruit to soften slightly. Add pourable fruit. Remove plunger from top of food processor to allow air to be incorporated. Process until smooth, scraping down side of container frequently. Serve immediately. Garnish with fresh strawberries and mint leaves, if desired. Freeze leftovers.

<u>Note:</u> *Granité may be transferred to airtight container and frozen up to 1 month. Let stand at room temperature 10 minutes to soften slightly before serving.*

# Chocolate-Amaretto Ice

¾ cup sugar
½ cup HERSHEY₀S Cocoa
2 cups (1 pint) light cream or
  half-and-half

2 tablespoons amaretto
  (almond flavored liqueur)
Sliced almonds (optional)

**Makes 4 servings**

*1.* Stir together sugar and cocoa in small saucepan; gradually stir in light cream. Cook over low heat, stirring constantly, until sugar dissolves and mixture is smooth and hot. Do not boil.

*2.* Remove from heat; stir in liqueur. Pour into 8-inch square pan. Cover; freeze until firm, stirring several times before mixture freezes. Scoop into dessert dishes. Serve frozen. Garnish with sliced almonds, if desired.

# All-American Trifle

**Makes 16 servings**

**Prep Time:**
*20 minutes*

**Chill Time:**
*4 hours*

4 cups boiling water
1 package (8-serving size) or
    2 packages (4-serving size)
    JELL-O® Brand Gelatin
    Dessert, any red flavor
1 package (8-serving size) or
    2 packages (4-serving size)
    JELL-O® Brand Berry Blue
    Flavor Gelatin Dessert

2 cups cold water
4 cups cubed pound cake
2 cups sliced strawberries
1 tub (8 ounces) COOL WHIP®
    Whipped Topping, thawed

*Note:*

**Trifles are generally prepared in a glass bowl to display all the layers. They are the refrigerated for several hours before serving to allow the flavors to blend.**

**STIR** 2 cups of the boiling water into each flavor of gelatin in separate bowls at least 2 minutes until completely dissolved. Stir 1 cup cold water into each bowl. Pour into separate 13×9-inch pans. Refrigerate 3 hours until firm. Cut each pan into ½-inch cubes.

**PLACE** red gelatin cubes in 3½-quart bowl or trifle bowl. Layer with cake cubes, strawberries and ½ of the whipped topping. Cover with blue gelatin cubes. Garnish with remaining whipped topping.

**REFRIGERATE** at least 1 hour or until ready to serve.

# Creamy Cappuccino Frozen Dessert

1 package (8 ounces) cream
   cheese, softened
1 can (14 ounces) sweetened
   condensed milk
½ cup chocolate syrup
1 tablespoon instant coffee
   powder

1 tablespoon hot water
1½ cups thawed frozen whipped
   topping
1 prepared chocolate crumb
   crust (6 ounces)
¼ cup chopped pecans, toasted
   Additional chocolate syrup

**Makes 16 servings**

**Make-Ahead Time:**
*1 day or up to
1 week before
serving*

**Final Prep/Stand
Time:**
*15 minutes*

*1.* Beat cream cheese in large mixing bowl on medium speed of electric mixer 2 to 3 minutes or until fluffy. Add sweetened condensed milk and ½ cup syrup; beat on low speed until well blended.

*2.* Dissolve coffee powder in hot water in small bowl. Slowly stir into cream cheese mixture. Fold in whipped topping; spoon mixture into crust. Sprinkle with pecans. Cover and freeze overnight.

*3.* Let dessert stand in refrigerator 10 to 15 minutes before serving. Cut into wedges. Drizzle with additional syrup.

# Angel Strawberry Bavarian

**Makes 12 to 16 servings**

1 package DUNCAN HINES®
Angel Food Cake Mix
1 package (10 ounces) frozen
sweetened sliced
strawberries, thawed
1 package (4-serving size)
strawberry-flavored gelatin
1 cup boiling water

2½ cups whipping cream, chilled,
divided
2½ tablespoons confectioners'
sugar
¾ teaspoon vanilla extract
4 fresh strawberries, sliced and
fanned for garnish
Mint leaves for garnish

*1.* Preheat oven to 375°F.

*2.* Prepare, bake and cool cake as directed on package. Cut cake into 1-inch cubes. Drain thawed strawberries, reserving juice.

*3.* Combine gelatin and boiling water in small bowl. Stir until gelatin is dissolved. Add enough water to strawberry juice to measure 1 cup; stir into gelatin. Refrigerate until gelatin is slightly thickened. Beat gelatin until foamy.

*4.* Beat 1 cup whipping cream until stiff peaks form in large bowl. Fold into gelatin along with strawberries.

*5.* Alternate layers of cake cubes and strawberry mixture into 10-inch tube pan. Press lightly. Cover. Refrigerate overnight.

*6.* Unmold cake onto serving plate. Beat remaining 1½ cups whipping cream, sugar and vanilla extract until stiff peaks form. Frost sides and top of cake. Refrigerate until ready to serve. Garnish with fresh strawberries and mint leaves.

# Delectable
# Desserts

## CHAPTER FOURTEEN

# Fruit Dessert Pizza

**Makes 10 servings**

**Prep Time:**
*15 minutes*

**Bake Time:**
*12 minutes*

1 package (18 ounces) refrigerated sugar cookie dough
2 DOLE® Bananas, divided
1 package (8 ounces) light cream cheese
¼ cup sugar
2 tablespoons orange juice
1 package (16 ounces) frozen peaches, thawed *or* 1 can (15 ounces) sliced peaches, drained

2 cups DOLE® Fresh Pineapple Chunks
½ cup orange marmalade or apricot preserves
Mint leaves (optional)

• Press small pieces of cookie dough onto greased 12-inch pizza pan. Bake at 350°F 10 to 12 minutes or until browned and puffed. Cool completely in pan on wire rack.

• Cut 1 banana into blender container. Cover; blend until smooth (½ cup). Beat cream cheese, sugar, orange juice and blended banana in bowl until smooth. Spread over cooled cookie.

• Slice remaining banana. Arrange banana slices, peaches and pineapple chunks over cream cheese. Brush orange marmalade over fruit. Garnish with mint leaves, if desired. Serve.

# Quick Tiramisu

1 package (18 ounces) NESTLÉ®
   TOLL HOUSE® Refrigerated
   Sugar Cookie Bar Dough
1 package (8 ounces) ⅓ less fat
   cream cheese
½ cup granulated sugar
¾ teaspoon TASTER'S CHOICE®
   100% Pure Instant Coffee
   dissolved in ¾ cup cold
   water, *divided*

1 container (8 ounces) frozen
   nondairy whipped topping,
   thawed
1 tablespoon NESTLÉ® TOLL
   HOUSE® Baking Cocoa

**Makes 6 to 8 servings**

**PREHEAT** oven to 325°F.

**DIVIDE** cookie dough into 20 pieces. Shape into 2½×1-inch
oblong shapes. Place on ungreased baking sheets.

**BAKE** for 10 to 12 minutes or until light golden brown around
edges. Cool on baking sheets for 1 minute; remove to wire racks
to cool completely.

**BEAT** cream cheese and sugar in large mixer bowl until smooth.
Beat in *¼ cup* Taster's Choice. Fold in whipped topping. Layer
6 cookies in 8-inch-square baking dish. Sprinkle each cookie
with *1 teaspoon* Taster's Choice. Spread *one-third* cream cheese
mixture over cookies. Repeat layers 2 more times with *12* cookies,
*remaining* coffee and *remaining* cream cheese mixture. Cover;
refrigerate for 2 to 3 hours. Crumble *remaining* cookies over
top. Sift cocoa over cookies. Cut into squares.

*Note:*

Traditionally, tiramisu
is made of sponge cake
or ladyfingers dipped
in a mixture of
espresso and marsala,
then layered with
mascarpone cheese
(a rich and creamy
Italian cheese), grated
chocolate and whipped
cream. Newer versions
of this dessert use
products that are more
commonly available in
supermarkets.

# Ice Cream Cookie Sandwich

**Makes 10 to 12 servings**

2 pints chocolate chip ice cream, softened
1 package DUNCAN HINES® Moist Deluxe® Dark Chocolate Fudge Cake Mix

½ cup butter or margarine, softened

*1.* Line bottom of one 9-inch round cake pan with aluminum foil. Spread ice cream in pan; return to freezer until firm. Run knife around edge of pan to loosen ice cream. Remove from pan; wrap in foil and return to freezer.

*2.* Preheat oven to 350°F. Line bottom of two 9-inch round cake pans with aluminum foil. Place cake mix in large bowl. Add butter; mix thoroughly until crumbs form. Place half the cake mix in each prepared pan; press lightly. Bake at 350°F for 15 minutes or until browned around edges; do not overbake. Cool 10 minutes; remove from pans. Remove foil from cookie layers; cool completely.

*3.* To assemble, place one cookie layer on serving plate. Top with ice cream. Peel off foil. Place second cookie layer on top. Wrap in foil and freeze 2 hours. To keep longer, store in airtight container. Let stand at room temperature for 5 to 10 minutes before cutting.

# Passionate Sorbet

**Makes 6 servings**

2 cups MAUNA LA'I® Paradise Passion® Juice Drink
¼ cup sugar

½ envelope of unflavored gelatin

*1.* Combine Mauna La'i Paradise Passion Juice Drink and sugar in medium saucepan. Sprinkle gelatin over juice drink and let stand 1 to 2 minutes to soften. Cook on low heat until gelatin and sugar dissolve, stirring occasionally. Pour into 9×9-inch pan and freeze until just firm.

*2.* Remove from freezer and cut into small pieces. Place frozen pieces in food processor. Process until light and creamy. Return to pan. Cover and freeze until firm. To serve, scrape off thin layers with spoon.

# "Best" Baked Apples

| 4 baking apples, cored<br>½ cup apple cider | 4 tablespoons maple syrup<br>Ground cinnamon |
|---|---|

**Makes 4 servings**

**Prep Time:**
*20 minutes*

Peel 1 inch around tops of apples. Place apples in microwavable casserole dish. Pour cider around apples. Fill each apple with 1 tablespoon syrup and dust lightly with cinnamon. Cover and microwave on HIGH 10 minutes or until fork-tender.

Favorite recipe from **New York Apple Association, Inc.**

# Irish Chocolate Mint Dessert

**Makes 24 servings**

1½ cups (3 sticks) plus
  6 tablespoons butter
  or margarine, divided
2 cups granulated sugar
2 teaspoons vanilla extract
4 eggs
¾ cup HERSHEY₅S Cocoa
1 cup all-purpose flour

½ teaspoon baking powder
2⅔ cups powdered sugar
1 tablespoon plus 1 teaspoon
  water
1 teaspoon mint extract
4 drops green food color
1 cup HERSHEY₅S Semi-Sweet
  Chocolate Chips

*1.* Heat oven to 350°F. Grease 13×9×2-inch baking pan.

*2.* Place 1 cup (2 sticks) butter in large microwave-safe bowl; cover. Microwave at HIGH (100%) 2 minutes or until melted. Stir in granulated sugar and vanilla. Add eggs; beat well. Add cocoa, flour and baking powder; beat until well blended. Pour batter into prepared pan.

*3.* Bake 30 to 35 minutes or until wooden pick inserted in center comes out clean. Cool completely in pan on wire rack.

*4.* Prepare mint cream center by combining powdered sugar, ½ cup (1 stick) butter, water, mint extract and food color. Beat until smooth. Spread evenly on brownies. Cover; refrigerate until cold.

*5.* Prepare chocolate glaze by placing remaining 6 tablespoons butter and chocolate chips in small microwave-safe bowl. Microwave at HIGH (100%) 1 minute or until mixture is smooth when stirred. Cool slightly; pour over chilled dessert. Cover; refrigerate at least 1 hour before serving. Cover; refrigerate leftover dessert.

# Blueberry Bread Pudding

1 package BOB EVANS® Frozen
    White Dinner Roll Dough,
    prepared according to
    package directions (day old)
5 eggs
1 cup whipping cream
¾ cup milk
½ cup granulated sugar

Pinch salt
1 cup packed brown sugar
½ cup water
1 cup butter, melted
2 tablespoons vanilla extract
1 teaspoon ground cinnamon
1 cup fresh blueberries

*Note:*

When selecting
blueberries, look for
plump, fresh berries
of good blue color
with a waxy bloom;
they should not have
stems attached.
Avoid juice-stained
containers and soft
berries.

Preheat oven to 350°F. Cut prepared dinner rolls into cubes; place in large bowl. Whisk together eggs, cream, milk, granulated sugar and salt; pour over bread cubes and toss to coat. Pour mixture into greased 11×7-inch baking dish; bake 1 hour.

To prepare sauce, stir brown sugar and water in medium saucepan until sugar is dissolved. Cook, uncovered, over medium heat until reduced by half. Remove from heat; stir in butter, vanilla and cinnamon until well blended. To serve, pour sauce over bread pudding and garnish with blueberries. Refrigerate leftovers.

# Cherry Crisp

**Makes 6 servings**

1 (21-ounce) can cherry pie
  filling
½ teaspoon almond extract
½ cup all-purpose flour
½ cup firmly packed brown
  sugar
1 teaspoon ground cinnamon

3 tablespoons butter or
  margarine, softened
½ cup chopped walnuts
¼ cup flaked coconut
  Ice cream or whipped cream
  (optional)

*Note:*

Cinnamon can vary in
flavor depending on
where it is grown.
Some of the world's
sweetest and strongest
comes from China and
Vietnam. Like most
spices, ground
cinnamon will lose its
strength over time, so
if yours has been in
the cabinet for a while,
sniff or taste it before
using to make sure it is
still flavorful.

Pour cherry pie filling into ungreased 8×8×2-inch baking pan.
Stir in almond extract.

Place flour, brown sugar and cinnamon in medium mixing bowl;
mix well. Add butter; stir with fork until mixture is crumbly. Stir
in walnuts and coconut. Sprinkle mixture over cherry pie filling.

Bake in preheated 350°F oven 25 minutes or until golden brown
on top and filling is bubbly. Serve warm or at room temperature.
If desired, top with ice cream or whipped cream.

**Tip:** *This recipe can be doubled. Bake in two 8×8×2-inch baking
pans or one 13×9×2-inch pan.*

Favorite recipe from **Cherry Marketing Institute**

# Black & White Bombe

1 package (12 ounces) pound
cake, cut into 10 slices
2 cups milk
1 package (4-serving size)
JELL-O® Devil's Food Flavor
Instant Pudding & Pie
Filling
2 tubs (8 ounces each) COOL
WHIP® Whipped Topping,
thawed

1 package (4-serving size)
JELL-O® White Chocolate
Flavor Instant Pudding &
Pie Filling
2 squares BAKER'S® Semi-
Sweet Baking Chocolate,
melted (optional)

**Makes 10 servings**

**Prep Time:**
*20 minutes*

**CUT** cake slices in half to form triangles. Line 2-quart bowl with plastic wrap. Arrange cake triangles in bottom and up side of bowl, reserving 5 triangles for top.

**POUR** 1 cup milk into large bowl. Add devil's food pudding mix. Beat with wire whisk 1 minute. Gently stir in half of one tub of the whipped topping. Spoon into bowl over cake slices.

**POUR** remaining milk into large bowl; add white chocolate pudding mix. Beat with wire whisk 1 minute. Gently stir in half of one tub of the whipped topping. Spoon into bowl. Press remaining cake slices on top.

**REFRIGERATE** 4 hours or overnight. Invert mold onto plate. Remove plastic wrap. Frost with remaining tub whipped topping. Drizzle with chocolate, if desired.

# Chocolate Cinnamon Bread Pudding

**Makes 6 to 9 servings**

4 cups soft white bread cubes
   (5 slices)
½ cup chopped nuts
3 eggs
¼ cup unsweetened cocoa
2 teaspoons vanilla extract
1 teaspoon ground cinnamon
½ teaspoon salt
2¾ cups water

1 (14-ounce) can EAGLE®
   BRAND Sweetened
   Condensed Milk
   (NOT evaporated milk)
2 tablespoons butter or
   margarine, melted
Cinnamon Cream Sauce
   (recipe follows)

*1.* Preheat oven to 350°F. Place bread cubes and nuts in buttered 9-inch square baking pan. In large mixing bowl, beat eggs, cocoa, vanilla, cinnamon and salt. Add water, Eagle Brand and butter; mix well. Pour evenly over bread, moistening completely.

*2.* Bake 40 to 45 minutes or until knife inserted in center comes out clean. Cool slightly. Serve warm topped with Cinnamon Cream Sauce. Refrigerate leftovers.

**Cinnamon Cream Sauce:** *In medium saucepan over medium-high heat, combine 1 cup whipping cream, ⅔ cup firmly packed light brown sugar, 1 teaspoon vanilla extract and ½ teaspoon ground cinnamon. Bring to a boil; reduce heat and boil rapidly 6 to 8 minutes or until thickened, stirring occasionally. Serve warm.*

# Apple Crisp

10 Golden Delicious apples
  (about 5 pounds), peeled,
  cored and sliced (about
  12 cups)
1 cup firmly packed brown
  sugar, divided

2 teaspoons ground cinnamon
¾ cup all-purpose flour
½ cup (1 stick) IMPERIAL®
  Spread
¾ cup uncooked quick or
  old-fashioned oats

Preheat oven to 375°F.

In large bowl, combine apples, ½ cup sugar and cinnamon. Turn into 13×9-inch baking pan or 3-quart shallow casserole; set aside.

In medium bowl, combine flour and remaining ½ cup sugar. With pastry blender or 2 knives, cut in Spread until mixture is size of coarse crumbs. Stir in oats. With hands, gently squeeze mixture to form crumbs; sprinkle over apple mixture.

Bake, uncovered, 1 hour or until apples are tender and topping is golden. Serve warm or at room temperature and, if desired, with vanilla ice cream or frozen yogurt.

# Chocolate-Raspberry Cupcakes

**Makes 24 cupcakes**

2 cups all-purpose flour
⅔ cup unsweetened cocoa powder
1¾ teaspoons baking soda
½ teaspoon baking powder
½ teaspoon salt
1¾ cups granulated sugar
⅔ cup vegetable shortening
1 cup cold water

2 teaspoons vanilla extract
3 large eggs
⅓ cup seedless raspberry jam
1½ cups "M&M's"® Semi-Sweet Chocolate Mini Baking Bits, divided
1 container (16 ounces) white frosting
Red food coloring

Preheat oven to 350°F. Lightly grease 24 (2¾-inch) muffin cups or line with paper or foil liners; set aside. In large bowl combine flour, cocoa powder, baking soda, baking powder and salt; stir in sugar. Beat in shortening until well combined. Gradually beat in water; stir in vanilla. Beat in eggs. Stir in raspberry jam. Divide batter evenly among prepared muffin cups. Sprinkle batter with 1 cup "M&M's"® Semi-Sweet Chocolate Mini Baking Bits. Bake 20 to 25 minutes or until toothpick inserted in centers comes out clean. Cool completely on wire racks. Combine frosting and red food coloring to make frosting pink. Spread frosting over cupcakes; decorate with remaining ½ cup"M&M's"® Semi-Sweet Chocolate Mini Baking Bits. Store in tightly covered container.

# Peanut Butter & Chocolate Dipped Strawberries

1¼ cup **PETER PAN®** Creamy
   Peanut Butter
18 to 25 large dipping
   strawberries with
   long stems

2 container (8 ounces) hard
   shell chocolate

**Makes 18 to 25 dipped strawberries**

**Prep Time:**
*10 minutes*

**Cook Time:**
*20 minutes*

Line *two* baking sheets with waxed paper; set aside. In a small microwavable bowl, heat Peter Pan Peanut Butter 10 to 15 seconds or until slightly "liquidy" soft; stir. Dip *each* strawberry into peanut butter, using a dip-roll motion, covering three fourths of the strawberry. Place strawberries on one baking sheet. Let stand for 20 to 30 minutes or refrigerate for 10 minutes to allow peanut butter to set quickly. Once set, heat chocolate according to package directions. Dip *each* strawberry into chocolate, leaving a small rim of peanut butter above chocolate. Set dipped strawberries on the *second* lined baking sheet; let harden.

<u>Serving Suggestion:</u> *For a fancy look without the fuss, drizzle melted white chocolate across the dark chocolate.*

# Deep Dark Chocolate Soufflé

**Makes 6 servings**

1 tablespoon sugar
½ cup HERSHEY₂S Dutch
   Processed Cocoa
¼ cup all-purpose flour
¼ cup (½ stick) butter or
   margarine, softened

1 cup milk
½ cup plus 2 tablespoons sugar,
   divided
1 teaspoon vanilla extract
4 eggs, separated
   Ice cream

## Note:

Egg whites should be beaten only until stiff peaks form. Overbeating will result in a soufflé that fails to rise properly. It's also important to fold beaten egg whites into the soufflé mixture just until combined—too much agitation can cause the egg whites to break down and the souffle to fall.

*1.* Heat oven to 350°F. Butter 6-cup soufflé dish; lightly coat with 1 tablespoon sugar.

*2.* Stir together cocoa and flour in medium bowl. Add butter; blend well. Heat milk in medium saucepan until very hot. *Do not boil.* Reduce heat to low. Add cocoa mixture; beat with whisk until smooth and thick. Remove from heat; stir in ½ cup sugar and vanilla. Cool slightly. Add egg yolks, one at a time, beating well after each addition. Cool to room temperature.

*3.* Beat egg whites in large bowl until foamy; gradually add remaining 2 tablespoons sugar, beating until stiff peaks form. Stir small amount of beaten whites into chocolate mixture; fold chocolate mixture into remaining whites. Carefully pour into prepared dish.

*4.* Bake 40 to 45 minutes or until puffed. Serve immediately with ice cream.

# Peanut Maple Triangle Puffs

½ cup creamy peanut butter
1¼ cups powdered sugar, divided
¼ oup plus 3 tablespoons maple-
flavored syrup, divided

1 package (17½ ounces) frozen
puff pastry, thawed

Makes 28 puffs

**Prep and Bake Time:**
*30 minutes*

*1.* Preheat oven to 400°F. Combine peanut butter, ¼ cup powdered sugar and ¼ cup syrup in small bowl until well blended; set aside.

*2.* Cut each puff pastry dough sheet into 3-inch squares. Place rounded teaspoon peanut butter mixture in center of each square. Fold squares over to form triangle. Seal edges with fork.

*3.* Place triangles about 2 inches apart on ungreased baking sheets; spray with cooking spray. Bake 6 to 8 minutes or until golden brown. Remove from baking sheets to wire rack to cool.

*4.* Combine remaining 1 cup powdered sugar, 3 tablespoons syrup and 1 to 2 tablespoons water in small bowl. Glaze puffs just before serving.

**Tip:** *For longer storage, do not glaze puffs; store loosely covered so pastry dough remains crisp. Glaze before serving.*

# Oreo® Cookie Bread Pudding

**Makes 6 servings**

**Prep Time:**
*10 minutes*

**Cook Time:**
*45 minutes*

4 cups day-old French bread or
   regular bread cubes
16 OREO® Chocolate Sandwich
   Cookies, coarsely broken
   (about 2 cups cookie
   pieces)
2 cups milk

½ cup sugar
¼ cup margarine or butter,
   melted
2 eggs
1 teaspoon vanilla extract
Ice cream, optional

*1.* Mix bread cubes and cookie pieces in large bowl; set aside.

*2.* Blend milk, sugar, margarine or butter, eggs and vanilla; pour over bread mixture, stirring to coat evenly. Pour into greased 1½-quart round casserole.

*3.* Bake at 350°F for 45 to 50 minutes or until set. Serve warm or at room temperature topped with ice cream if desired.

# Fresh Cherry Jubilee

**Makes about
8 servings**

½ cup sugar
1 tablespoon cornstarch
¼ cup water
¼ cup orange juice
3 cups pitted Northwest fresh
   sweet cherries

½ teaspoon grated orange peel
¼ cup brandy (optional)
1 quart vanilla ice cream

Combine sugar and cornstarch in skillet. Blend in water
and orange juice. Cook and stir over medium-high heat until
thickened and smooth. Add cherries and orange peel; simmer
10 minutes. Gently heat brandy, pour over sauce and flame, if
desired. Serve over ice cream.

Favorite recipe from **Northwest Cherry Growers**

# Apple and Walnut Strudel

| | |
|---|---|
| 1 package (about 17 ounces) frozen puff pastry | 1 can (21 ounces) apple pie filling, divided |
| 1 cup sour cream | 1 cup coarsely chopped walnuts, divided |
| 1 egg, separated | |
| 1 tablespoon water | |

**Makes 16 servings**

*1.* Thaw puff pastry according to package directions.

*2.* Preheat oven to 375°F. Spray 2 baking sheets with nonstick
cooking spray.

*3.* Combine sour cream and egg yolk in small bowl; set aside.
In separate small bowl, mix egg white and water; set aside.

*4.* On lightly floured board, roll 1 sheet pastry into 12×10-inch
rectangle. Spread half of apple filling vertically down center
third of pastry. Spread ½ cup sour cream mixture over apples;
sprinkle with ½ cup walnuts.

*5.* Fold one long side of pastry over filling then fold other side
over filling, overlapping edges. Press edges together to seal. Place
on baking sheet, seam side down, tucking ends under. Using
sharp knife, make 7 diagonal slits on top, then brush with egg
white mixture. Repeat with remaining pastry, apple filling, sour
cream mixture and walnuts. Bake 30 to 35 minutes or until
golden brown.

# Chocolate Cheesecake Cupcakes

**Makes 16 cupcakes**

**Cupcakes**
2 cups (12-ounce package)
   NESTLÉ® TOLL HOUSE®
   Semi-Sweet Chocolate
   Morsels, *divided*
1½ cups all-purpose flour
1 teaspoon baking soda
½ teaspoon salt
½ cup granulated sugar
⅓ cup vegetable oil
1 large egg
1 teaspoon vanilla extract
1 cup water

**Filling**
2 packages (3 ounces *each*)
   cream cheese, softened
¼ cup granulated sugar
1 large egg
⅛ teaspoon salt

### For Cupcakes

**PREHEAT** oven to 350°F. Grease or paper-line 16 muffin cups.

**MICROWAVE** *½ cup* morsels in small, microwave-safe bowl on HIGH (100%) power for 45 seconds; stir. Microwave at additional 10- to 20-second intervals, stirring until smooth; cool to room temperature.

**COMBINE** flour, baking soda and salt in small bowl. Beat sugar, oil, egg and vanilla extract in large mixer bowl until blended. Beat in melted chocolate; gradually beat in flour mixture alternately with water (batter will be thin).

### For Filling

**BEAT** cream cheese, sugar, egg and salt in small mixer bowl until creamy. Stir in *1 cup* morsels.

### To Assemble

**SPOON** batter into prepared muffin cups, filling ½ full. Spoon filling by rounded tablespoon over batter. Spoon *remaining* batter over filling. Bake for 20 to 25 minutes or until wooden pick inserted in center comes out clean. While still hot, sprinkle with *remaining ½ cup* morsels. Let cool for 5 minutes or until morsels are shiny; spread to frost. Remove to wire racks to cool completely.

# Gingered Pumpkin Custard

**Makes 6 to 8 servings**

¾ cup sugar
2 eggs
1½ teaspoons ground cinnamon
½ teaspoon salt
½ teaspoon nutmeg
1 can (15 ounces) solid-pack
    pumpkin

1¼ cups half-and-half
3 tablespoons chopped candied
    ginger
Sweetened whipped cream

*1.* Preheat oven to 375°F. Grease 1½-quart oval casserole dish or 8-inch glass baking dish.

*2.* Combine sugar, eggs, cinnamon, salt and nutmeg in medium bowl; mix well. Add pumpkin and cream. Mix until well blended. Pour into prepared dish. Sprinkle ginger evenly over top of pumpkin mixture.

*3.* Bake 45 minutes or until knife inserted in center comes out clean. Cool on wire rack at least 20 minutes before serving. Serve warm or at room temperature, garnished with whipped cream.

<u>Variation:</u> *For individual servings, pour custard mixture into 6 or 8 ramekins or custard cups. Place on a baking sheet. Bake until knife inserted in center comes out clean, 35 to 40 minutes.*

*Note:*

Candied ginger, also called crystallized ginger, has been cooked in a sugar syrup and coated with coarse sugar. It is found in Asian markets and some supermarkets.

# Hint of Lemon Bread Pudding

**Makes 6 servings**

4 cups day-old bread cubes
(about 6 slices)
3 cups milk
3 eggs, slightly beaten
½ cup sugar
½ cup raisins

2 tablespoons butter or
margarine, melted
Grated peel of 1 SUNKIST®
lemon
¼ teaspoon salt
Ground nutmeg

*Note:*

Leftover bread pudding can be stored in the refrigerator for up to two days. Reheat, covered, in a 350°F oven or in a microwave oven until warm.

In large shallow baking pan, arrange bread cubes in single layer; bake at 350°F 10 minutes to lightly dry bread. Meanwhile, combine remaining ingredients except nutmeg; stir to dissolve sugar.

In large bowl, pour milk mixture over dried bread cubes and stir well. Let soak 10 minutes. Pour into well-buttered 1½-quart casserole. Sprinkle with nutmeg. Set casserole in shallow baking pan filled with 1 inch hot water. Bake, uncovered, at 350°F 1 hour or until knife inserted in center comes out clean. Remove from water bath and cool 10 minutes. Serve warm. Refrigerate leftovers.

# Colorful Caramel Apples

Makes 6 apples

1 package (14 ounces)
   caramels, unwrapped
2 tablespoons water
6 wooden craft sticks
6 medium apples, rinsed and
   completely dried
1 cup chopped nuts, divided

1 cup "M&M's"® Semi-Sweet
   Chocolate Mini Baking Bits,
   divided
2 squares (1 ounce each)
   semi-sweet chocolate
2 squares (1 ounce each) white
   chocolate

Line baking sheet with waxed paper; set aside. In medium saucepan over medium heat combine caramels and water; cook, stirring constantly, until melted. Remove from heat. Insert 1 craft stick into stem end of each apple. Dip apples, one at a time, into caramel mixture, coating completely. Remove excess caramel mixture by scraping apple bottom across rim of saucepan. Place on waxed paper. Place ¾ cup nuts in shallow dish; set aside. Place ¾ cup "M&M's"® Semi-Sweet Chocolate Mini Baking Bits in separate shallow dish; set aside. Place semi-sweet chocolate in small microwave-safe bowl. Microwave at HIGH 1 minute; stir. Repeat as necessary until chocolate is completely melted, stirring at 10-second intervals. Drizzle chocolate over apples. Roll apples in nuts and "M&M's"® Semi-Sweet Chocolate Mini Baking Bits. Refrigerate apples 10 minutes. Place white chocolate in small microwave-safe bowl. Microwave at HIGH 1 minute; stir. Repeat as necessary until white chocolate is completely melted, stirring at 10-second intervals. Drizzle white chocolate over apples. Sprinkle apples with remaining ¼ cup nuts and remaining ¼ cup "M&M's"® Semi-Sweet Chocolate Mini Baking Bits. Refrigerate until firm.

# Honey-Spiced Fruit Compote

**Makes 6 servings**

1¼ cups honey
1 cup orange juice
1 tablespoon grated
   orange peel
2 cups diced dried fruits, such
   as pears, apricots, apples
   or peaches

2 cinnamon sticks *or*
   ½ teaspoon ground
   cinnamon
½ teaspoon whole cloves
½ cup port wine

Combine honey, orange juice and orange peel in large saucepan. Bring to a boil over medium-high heat. Add fruit. Add cinnamon and cloves, tied in cheesecloth. Reduce heat to low; simmer 5 minutes. Remove from heat; add wine. Marinate overnight to allow flavors to blend; remove spice bag. Serve warm or cold.

Favorite recipe from **National Honey Board**

# Traditional Rice Pudding

**Makes 6 servings**

1 bag SUCCESS® Rice
⅓ cup sugar
1½ tablespoons cornstarch
2 cups skim milk
2 eggs, slightly beaten

2 tablespoons reduced-calorie
   margarine
1 teaspoon vanilla
½ teaspoon cinnamon

Prepare rice according to package directions. Cool.

Combine sugar and cornstarch in medium saucepan. Add milk and eggs; mix well. Stir in rice. Bring to a boil over medium-high heat, stirring constantly. Remove from heat. Add margarine and vanilla; stir until margarine is melted. Pour into serving bowl; sprinkle with cinnamon. Garnish, if desired.

# Bananas with Caramel Sauce

**Makes 4 servings**

| | |
|---|---|
| 3 or 4 bananas, peeled | ¼ cup GRANDMA'S® Molasses |
| 2 tablespoons orange or lemon juice | ¼ teaspoon cinnamon |
| 2 tablespoons butter | ¼ teaspoon nutmeg |
| ¼ cup whipping cream | ¼ cup walnut halves |

*1.* Slice bananas in half lengthwise, then crosswise. Place bananas in large bowl; brush with orange juice. Set aside. Place butter in 9-inch microwave-safe pie plate.

*2.* Microwave at HIGH power for 30 seconds or until melted. Stir in cream, molasses, cinnamon and nutmeg. Microwave at HIGH for 1½ to 2 minutes or until thickened, stirring once. Add bananas and walnuts; mix well to coat. Microwave at HIGH for 30 seconds or until bananas are tender. Serve immediately over waffles, ice cream or orange slices.

# White Chocolate Bread Pudding

**Makes 6 servings**

5 cups (about 7 ounces) ¾-inch fresh Italian bread cubes
¼ cup (½ stick) I CAN'T BELIEVE IT'S NOT BUTTER!® Spread, melted
6 ounces white chocolate, coarsely chopped
1 cup whipping or heavy cream

1 cup milk
3 eggs
½ cup sugar
1 tablespoon crème de cacao liqueur *or* 1 teaspoon vanilla extract
¼ teaspoon salt

Grease 8-inch square baking dish; set aside.

In medium bowl, toss bread with melted I Can't Believe It's Not Butter!; arrange in prepared dish and set aside.

***Note:***

**Crème de cacao is a dark chocolate-flavored liqueur with a hint of vanilla.**

In medium saucepan, melt chocolate with cream and milk over low heat, stirring occasionally. In large bowl, with wire whisk, beat eggs, sugar, liqueur and salt. While beating slowly, drizzle in chocolate mixture. Pour over bread, pressing cubes down to coat evenly. Cover and refrigerate 2 hours.

Preheat oven to 350°F. Remove dish from refrigerator and remove cover. Press bread cubes down to coat with filling. Bake 30 minutes. Cover with aluminum foil and bake an additional 10 minutes or until knife inserted in center comes out clean and custard is set. Serve warm.

# Grasshopper Dessert

Makes 12 servings

**Crust**
- 1 package DUNCAN HINES® Moist Deluxe® Dark Chocolate Fudge Cake Mix, divided
- 1 egg
- ½ cup (1 stick) butter or margarine, softened

**Filling**
- 3 cups miniature marshmallows
- ½ cup milk
- ⅓ cup green crème de menthe
- 2 tablespoons white crème de cacao
- 1½ cups whipping cream, chilled

*1.* Preheat oven to 350°F. Grease and flour 13×9-inch pan. Remove ½ cup cake mix and spread into 8-inch *ungreased* baking pan. Toast in oven 7 minutes. Cool.

*2.* For crust, combine remaining cake mix, egg and butter in large bowl. Mix until crumbs form. Press lightly into prepared pan. Bake 15 minutes. Cool.

*3.* For filling, heat marshmallows and milk in medium saucepan over low heat. Stir constantly until marshmallows melt. Refrigerate until thickened. Stir crème de menthe and crème de cacao into marshmallow mixture.

*4.* Beat whipping cream until stiff in large bowl. Fold in marshmallow mixture. Pour into crust. Dust top with cooled toasted cake mix. Refrigerate until ready to serve. Cut into squares.

<u>Tip:</u> *To quickly chill marshmallow mixture, pour mixture into medium bowl; place in larger bowl of ice water and refrigerate. Stir occasionally.*

# Chocolate Candy Bar Dessert

**Makes 15 servings**

**Prep Time:**
*25 minutes*

**Chill Time:**
*2 hours*

2 cups chocolate wafer cookie crumbs
½ cup sugar, divided
½ cup (1 stick) butter or margarine, melted
1 package (8 ounces) PHILADELPHIA® Cream Cheese, softened
1 tub (12 ounces) COOL WHIP® Whipped Topping, thawed

1 cup chopped chocolate-covered candy bars
3 cups cold milk
2 packages (4-serving size) JELL-O® Chocolate Flavor Instant Pudding & Pie Filling

**MIX** cookie crumbs, ¼ cup of the sugar and butter in 13×9-inch pan. Press firmly onto bottom of pan. Refrigerate until ready to fill.

**BEAT** cream cheese and remaining ¼ cup sugar in medium bowl with wire whisk until smooth. Gently stir in ½ of the whipped topping. Spread evenly over crust. Sprinkle chopped candy bars over cream cheese layer.

**POUR** milk into large bowl. Add pudding mixes. Beat with wire whisk 1 minute. Pour over chopped candy bar layer. Let stand 5 minutes or until thickened. Spread remaining whipped topping over pudding layer.

**REFRIGERATE** 2 hours or until set.

# Strawberry Shortcake

**Shortcakes**
- 2¼ cups all-purpose flour
- 2 tablespoons granulated sugar
- 1 tablespoon baking powder
- ½ teaspoon salt
- ½ CRISCO® Stick or ½ cup CRISCO® all-vegetable shortening
- ¾ cup milk

- 1 large egg, beaten

**Filling**
- 1 quart strawberries, hulled and sliced
- Granulated sugar to taste
- 1 cup whipping cream, whipped stiff

**Makes 6 servings**

**Prep Time:**
*25 minutes*

**Total Time:**
*35 minutes*

*1.* Heat oven to 425°F. Combine flour, sugar, baking powder and salt in medium bowl. Cut in ½ cup shortening using pastry blender (or two knives) until flour is blended to form pea-size chunks. Make well in center. Combine milk and egg. Pour into well. Stir with fork 25 to 30 strokes.

*2.* Turn dough onto lightly floured surface. Roll dough ½ inch thick. Cut with floured 4-inch cutter. Place 2 inches apart on ungreased baking sheet.

*3.* Bake at 425°F for 11 to 13 minutes or until lightly browned. *Do not overbake.* Cool. Cut open with bread knife.

*4.* For filling, combine strawberries and sugar. Spoon over bottom halves of shortcakes. Top with whipped cream and shortcake tops.

**Tip:** *The shortcakes are best if made within a few hours of serving.*

# Chocolate Tiramisu Cupcakes

**Makes 30 cupcakes**

**Cupcakes**

1 package (18.25 ounces) chocolate cake mix
1¼ cups water
3 large eggs
⅓ cup vegetable oil or melted butter
2 tablespoons instant espresso powder
2 tablespoons brandy (optional)

**Frosting**

8 ounces mascarpone cheese or cream cheese
1½ to 1¾ cups powdered sugar
2 tablespoons coffee-flavored liqueur
1 tablespoon unsweetened cocoa powder

*1.* Preheat oven to 350°F. Line 30 regular-size (2½-inch) muffin cups with paper muffin cup liners.

*2.* Beat all cupcake ingredients with electric mixer at low speed 30 seconds. Beat at medium speed 2 minutes.

*3.* Spoon batter into prepared cups filling ⅔ full. Bake 20 to 22 minutes or until toothpick inserted in centers comes out clean. Cool in pans on wire racks 10 minutes. Remove cupcakes to racks; cool completely. (At this point, cupcakes may be frozen up to 3 months. Thaw at room temperature before frosting.)

*4.* For frosting, beat mascarpone cheese and 1½ cups powdered sugar with electric mixer at medium speed until well blended. Add liqueur; beat until well blended. If frosting is too soft, beat in additional powdered sugar or chill until spreadable.

*5.* Frost cooled cupcakes with frosting. Place cocoa in strainer; shake over cupcakes. Store at room temperature up to 24 hours or cover and refrigerate for up to 3 days before serving.

# Warm Fresh Fruit Sauté

¼ cup unsalted butter
3 tablespoons orange-flavored
  liqueur or freshly squeezed
  orange juice
3 tablespoons water
1½ tablespoons sugar
¾ cup Chilean seedless red
  or green grapes, cut into
  halves

2 Chilean peaches or nectarines
  (about ½ pound), thinly
  sliced
½ cup Chilean raspberries or
  sliced strawberries
Mint leaves (optional)
Lemon Crème Fraîche (recipe
  follows) or vanilla ice cream

**Makes 4 servings**

Melt butter in large skillet over medium-high heat. Stir in liqueur, water and sugar. Bring mixture to a simmer. Add grapes and peaches; reduce heat to medium. Cook, basting with sauce until fruits are just warmed through, about 2 to 3 minutes, being careful not to overcook. Add berries during last 30 seconds of cooking. (If using frozen berries, add them partially frozen.) Serve warm fruit in shallow bowls or on small plates; garnish with mint, if desired. Spoon on Lemon Crème Fraîche or serve with small scoop of vanilla ice cream.

<u>Lemon Crème Fraîche:</u> *In small bowl, stir together 1 cup whipping cream (not ultra-pasteurized), 1 tablespoon fresh lemon juice and finely grated peel of 1 lemon. Let mixture stand at room temperature until slightly thickened, 4 to 8 hours. Refrigerate until serving. Mixture will thicken more when chilled. Sweeten to taste with sugar or mild honey.*

Favorite recipe from **Chilean Fresh Fruit Association**

*Note:*

Crème fraîche is a
cultured, thickened
French cream with a
smooth texture and
subtle nutty taste. It
is used as a dessert
topping and in cooked
sauces and soups,
where it has the
advantage of not
curdling when boiled.

# Banana Split Dessert Pizza

**Makes one 12-inch pizza**

1 (14-ounce) can EAGLE® BRAND Sweetened Condensed Milk (NOT evaporated milk)
½ cup sour cream
¼ cup plus 2 tablespoons lemon juice from concentrate, divided
1 teaspoon vanilla extract
½ cup (1 stick) butter or margarine, softened
¼ cup firmly packed light brown sugar

1 cup unsifted all-purpose flour
¾ cup chopped nuts
3 medium bananas, sliced
1 (8-ounce) can sliced pineapple, drained and cut in half
Maraschino cherries and additional nuts
1 (1-ounce) square semi-sweet chocolate
1 tablespoon butter or margarine

*1.* Preheat oven to 375°F. Lightly grease 12-inch pizza pan or baking sheet; set aside. For filling, in medium mixing bowl, combine Eagle Brand, sour cream, ¼ cup lemon juice and vanilla; mix well. Chill.

*2.* In large mixing bowl, beat ½ cup butter and brown sugar until fluffy. Stir in flour and nuts; mix well. Press dough into 12-inch circle on prepared pan, forming rim around edge. Prick with fork. Bake 10 to 12 minutes or until golden brown. Cool.

*3.* Arrange 2 sliced bananas on cooled crust. Spoon filling evenly over bananas. Dip remaining banana slices in remaining 2 tablespoons lemon juice; arrange on top of pizza along with pineapple, cherries and additional nuts.

*4.* In heavy saucepan over low heat, melt chocolate with 1 tablespoon butter; drizzle over pizza. Chill thoroughly. Refrigerate leftovers.

# Apple Pan Dowdy

Makes 8 servings

5 apples, peeled, cored and
    sliced
1 cup bread flour
2 teaspoons baking powder
¾ teaspoon salt, divided
2 tablespoons shortening
¼ cup sugar

¼ cup GRANDMA'S® Molasses
½ teaspoon each cinnamon
    and nutmeg
¾ cup milk
½ cup hot water
    Whipped cream (optional)

Heat oven to 350°F. Grease 12×9-inch baking dish and layer
apples on bottom. In mixing bowl, sift flour, baking powder and
¼ teaspoon salt. Stir slightly. Beat shortening into flour mixture.
Add sugar, molasses, cinnamon, nutmeg and remaining
½ teaspoon salt. Pour in milk and water; mix until smooth. Pour
mixture over apples. Bake for 35 to 40 minutes. Turn onto plate
with apple side up. Serve with whipped cream, if desired.

## Desserts Made Dazzling

*Even the most humble of desserts can be made dressed to impress. A little whipped cream,
a few berries or a quick drizzle of chocolate is all it takes to go from simple to spectacular.*

**Chocolate curls**
Pull a vegetable peeler across a 1-ounce
square of chocolate. (Soften chocolate for a
few seconds in the microwave if necessary.)
Refrigerate the curls on a waxed paper-lined
baking sheet about 15 minutes or until firm.

**Chocolate drizzle or shapes**
Melt chocolate in a resealable plastic bag,
cut a tiny corner from the bag and drizzle
chocolate over desserts. Or, pipe chocolate
from the bag into shapes and patterns on
waxed paper. Let stand until firm.

**Fresh berries**
To dress up desserts instantly, pile berries
high inside the center of a bundt or tube
cake (or sprinkle them over almost anything).

**Whipped cream**
Chill the cream, bowl and beaters before
whipping to get the most volume. For extra
decadence, make chocolate whipped cream:
add 1 cup heavy cream to a mixture of
2 tablespoons each powdered sugar and
cocoa powder until well blended. Refrigerate
the mixture 30 minutes before whipping.

# Vanilla-Strawberry Cupcakes

**Makes 28 cupcakes**

### Cupcakes

2 cups all-purpose flour
2 teaspoons baking powder
¼ teaspoon salt
1¾ cups granulated sugar
½ cup (1 stick) butter, softened
¾ cup 2% or whole milk
1½ teaspoons vanilla
3 large egg whites
½ cup strawberry preserves

### Frosting

1 package (8 ounces) cream cheese (do not use fat-free), chilled and cut into cubes
4 tablespoons butter, softened
2 teaspoons vanilla
2 cups powdered sugar
1 to 1½ cups small fresh strawberry slices

*1.* Preheat oven to 350°F. Line 28 regular-size (2½-inch) muffin pan cups with paper muffin cup liners.

*2.* For cupcakes, combine flour, baking powder and salt in medium bowl; mix well and set aside. Beat granulated sugar and ½ cup butter with electric mixer at medium speed 1 minute. Add milk and 1½ teaspoons vanilla. Beat at low speed 30 seconds. Gradually beat in flour mixture; beat at medium speed 2 minutes. Add egg whites; beat 1 minute.

*3.* Spoon batter into prepared muffin cups filling ½ full. Drop 1 teaspoon preserves on top of batter; swirl into batter with toothpick. Bake 20 to 22 minutes or until toothpick inserted into centers comes out clean. Cool in pans on wire racks 10 minutes. Remove cupcakes to racks; cool completely. (At this point, cupcakes may be frozen up to 3 months. Thaw at room temperature before frosting.)

*4.* For frosting, process cream cheese, 4 tablespoons butter and 2 teaspoons vanilla in food processor or just until combined. Add powdered sugar; pulse just until sugar is incorporated. (Do not overmix or frosting will be too soft to spread).

*5.* Spread frosting over cooled cupcakes; decorate with sliced strawberries. Serve within 1 hour or refrigerate up to 8 hours before serving.

# Mocha Meringue Pudding

**Makes 6 servings**

3 cups cooked rice
3½ cups low-fat milk, divided
⅔ cup sugar, divided
½ teaspoon salt
3 eggs, separated
1½ teaspoons vanilla extract, divided

4 bars (1.55 ounces *each*) milk chocolate, broken in squares
1 tablespoon instant coffee

Combine rice, 3 cups milk, ⅓ cup sugar and salt in large saucepan. Cook over medium heat 20 to 25 minutes or until thick and creamy, stirring frequently. Beat egg yolks and remaining ½ cup milk in small bowl. Stir into rice mixture and cook 3 minutes more. Remove from heat. Stir in 1 teaspoon vanilla. Spread into buttered 9×9-inch baking pan. Arrange chocolate bars over rice mixture. Beat egg whites in medium bowl with electric mixer until soft peaks form. Add remaining ⅓ cup sugar, 1 tablespoon at a time; beat about 4 minutes or until stiff glossy peaks form. Fold in coffee and remaining ½ teaspoon vanilla. Spread over pudding. Bake at 350°F 15 minutes or until golden brown. Serve warm.

Favorite recipe from **USA Rice Federation**

# Double Chocolate Bread Pudding

**Makes 15 servings**

**Prep Time:**
*15 minutes*

**Bake Time:**
*45 minutes*

5 cups milk
2 packages (4-serving size)
   JELL-O® Chocolate Fudge
   Flavor Cook & Serve
   Pudding & Pie Filling
   *(not Instant)*

5 cups cubed French bread
1 cup BAKER'S® Semi-Sweet
   Real Chocolate Chunks

**HEAT** oven to 350°F.

**POUR** milk into large bowl. Add pudding mixes. Beat with wire whisk 1 minute. Stir in bread. Pour pudding mixture into 13×9-inch baking dish. Sprinkle evenly with chocolate chunks.

**BAKE** 45 minutes or until mixture comes to boil. Remove from oven. Let stand 10 minutes. Serve warm.

# Strawberries with Honeyed Yogurt Sauce

**Makes 4 servings**

1 quart fresh strawberries
1 cup plain low-fat yogurt
1 tablespoon orange juice

1 to 2 teaspoons honey
Ground cinnamon

Rinse and hull strawberries. Combine yogurt, juice, honey and cinnamon to taste in small bowl; mix well. Serve sauce over berries.

# Easy Peach Cobbler

**8 cups peeled and sliced peaches, nectarines or apples (½-inch-thick slices)**
**1 cup granulated sugar**
**⅔ cup plus 2 tablespoons BISQUICK®, divided**
**1 tablespoon ground cinnamon**

**2 tablespoons firmly packed brown sugar**
**¼ cup (½ stick) I CAN'T BELIEVE IT'S NOT BUTTER!® Spread**
**2 tablespoons milk**

**Makes 6 servings**

Preheat oven to 400°F.

In large bowl, combine peaches, granulated sugar, 2 tablespoons baking mix and cinnamon. In 11×7-inch baking dish, arrange peach mixture; set aside.

In medium bowl, mix remaining ⅔ cup baking mix with brown sugar. With pastry blender or 2 knives, cut in I Can't Believe It's Not Butter! Spread until mixture is size of small peas. Stir in milk just until moistened. Drop by teaspoonfuls onto peach mixture.

Bake 30 minutes or until peaches are tender and topping is golden. Let stand 5 minutes before serving. Serve warm and, if desired, with vanilla ice cream.

*Note:*

To peel a large quantity of peaches, blanch them in boiling water for about 30 seconds. Remove the peaches from the water with a slotted spoon and plunge them into cold water. Pull off the skins with a paring knife.

# White & Chocolate Covered Strawberries

**Makes 2 to 3 dozen berries**

1⅔ cups (10-ounce package) HERSHEY₀S Premier White Chips
2 tablespoons shortening (do not use butter, margarine, spread or oil), divided

1 cup HERSHEY₀S Semi-Sweet Chocolate Chips
4 cups (2 pints) fresh strawberries, rinsed, patted dry and chilled

*1.* Cover tray with wax paper.

*2.* Place white chips and 1 tablespoon shortening in medium microwave-safe bowl. Microwave at HIGH (100%) 1 minute; stir until chips are melted and mixture is smooth. If necessary, microwave at HIGH an additional 30 seconds at a time, just until smooth when stirred.

*3.* Holding by top, dip ⅔ of each strawberry into white chip mixture; shake gently to remove excess. Place on prepared tray; refrigerate until coating is firm, at least 30 minutes.

*4.* Repeat microwave procedure with chocolate chips in clean microwave-safe bowl. Dip lower ⅓ of each berry into chocolate mixture. Refrigerate until firm. Cover; refrigerate leftover strawberries.

# Apple Clafouti

2 jars (23 ounces each)
    MOTT'S® Chunky Apple
    Sauce
⅔ cup raisins
1 teaspoon ground cinnamon
1 cup all-purpose flour

1 teaspoon baking powder
½ teaspoon salt
3 egg whites
¼ cup low fat buttermilk
¼ cup honey
    Powdered sugar

**Makes 12 servings**

*1.* Preheat oven to 400°F. Spray two 9-inch glass pie plates with nonstick cooking spray.

*2.* In large bowl, combine apple sauce, raisins and cinnamon.

*3.* In small bowl, combine flour, baking powder and salt.

*4.* In medium bowl, whisk together egg whites, buttermilk and honey until slightly frothy.

*5.* Add flour mixture to egg white mixture; whisk until well blended. Pour ½ cup batter into each prepared pie plate.

*6.* Bake 4 to 5 minutes or until lightly browned. Pour half of apple sauce mixture over each baked layer. Spoon remaining batter over apple sauce mixture; spread evenly.

*7.* Reduce oven temperature to 350°F. Bake 15 to 20 minutes or until tops are puffy and lightly browned.

*8.* Cool completely on wire racks; sprinkle tops with powdered sugar. Slice each dessert into 6 wedges. Refrigerate leftovers.

# Blueberry Crisp Cupcakes

**Makes 30 cupcakes**

**Cupcakes**

    2 cups all-purpose flour
    2 teaspoons baking powder
    ¼ teaspoon salt
    1¾ cups granulated sugar
    ½ cup (1 stick) butter, softened
    ¾ cup milk
    1½ teaspoons vanilla
    3 large egg whites
    3 cups fresh or frozen
        (unthawed) blueberries

**Streusel**

    ⅓ cup all-purpose flour
    ¼ cup uncooked old-fashioned
        or quick oats
    ¼ cup packed light brown sugar
    ½ teaspoon ground cinnamon
    ¼ cup (½ stick) butter, softened
    ½ cup chopped walnuts or
        pecans

*1.* Preheat oven to 350°F. Line 30 regular-size (2½-inch) muffin cups with paper muffin cup liners.

*2.* For cupcakes, combine 2 cups flour, baking powder and salt in medium bowl; mix well and set aside. Beat granulated sugar and ½ cup butter with electric mixer at medium speed 1 minute. Add milk and vanilla. Beat at low speed 30 seconds. Gradually beat in flour mixture; beat at medium speed 2 minutes. Add egg whites; beat 1 minute. Spoon batter into prepared muffin cups filling ½ full. Spoon blueberries over batter. Bake 10 minutes.

*3.* Meanwhile for streusel, combine ⅓ cup flour, oats, brown sugar and cinnamon in small bowl; mix well. Cut in ¼ cup butter with pastry blender or two knives until mixture is well combined. Stir in chopped nuts.

*4.* Sprinkle streusel over partially baked cupcakes. Return to oven; bake 18 to 20 minutes or until golden brown and toothpick inserted into centers comes out clean. Cool in pans on wire racks 10 minutes. Remove cupcakes to racks; cool completely. (Cupcakes may be frozen up to 3 months.)

# Fruit-Filled Chocolate Chip Meringue Nests

**Makes 10 servings**

Meringues
- 4 large egg whites
- ½ teaspoon salt
- ½ teaspoon cream of tartar
- 1 cup granulated sugar
- 2 cups (12-ounce package) NESTLÉ® TOLL HOUSE® Semi-Sweet Chocolate Morsels

Chocolate Sauce
- ⅔ cup (5 fluid-ounce can) NESTLÉ® CARNATION® Evaporated Milk
- 1 cup (6 ounces) NESTLÉ® TOLL HOUSE® Semi-Sweet Chocolate Morsels
- 1 tablespoons granulated sugar
- 1 teaspoons vanilla extract
  Pinch salt

- 3 cups fresh fruit or berries (whole blackberries, blueberries or raspberries, sliced kiwi, peaches or strawberries)

*Note:*

For meringue to have a smooth texture, the sugar must dissolve completely. This is achieved by adding the sugar in small increments (one tablespoon at a time) while beating the egg whites.

### For Meringues

**PREHEAT** oven to 300°F. Lightly grease baking sheets.

**BEAT** egg whites, salt and cream of tartar in large mixer bowl until soft peaks form. Gradually add sugar; beat until sugar is dissolved. Gently fold in morsels. Spread meringue into ten 3-inch nests with deep wells about 2 inches apart on prepared baking sheets.

**BAKE** for 35 to 45 minutes or until meringues are dry and crisp. Cool on baking sheets for 5 minutes; remove to wire racks to cool completely.

### For Chocolate Sauce

**HEAT** evaporated milk to a boil in small, *heavy-duty* saucepan. Stir in morsels. Cook, stirring constantly, until mixture is slightly thickened and smooth. Remove from heat; stir in sugar, vanilla extract and salt.

**FILL** meringues with fruit and drizzle with Chocolate Sauce; serve immediately.

# Chocolate Ice Cream Cups

| Makes about 1½ dozen cups | 1 (12-ounce) package<br>semi-sweet chocolate chips<br>(2 cups)<br>1 (14-ounce) can EAGLE®<br>BRAND Sweetened<br>Condensed Milk<br>(NOT evaporated milk) | 1 cup finely ground pecans<br>Ice cream, any flavor |

*1.* In heavy saucepan over low heat, melt chocolate chips with Eagle Brand; remove from heat. Stir in pecans. In individual paper-lined muffin cups, spread about 2 tablespoons chocolate mixture. With lightly greased spoon, spread chocolate on bottom and up side of each cup.

*2.* Freeze 2 hours or until firm. Before serving, remove paper liners. Fill chocolate cups with ice cream. Store unfilled cups tightly covered in freezer.

<u>Note:</u> *It is easier to remove the paper liners if the chocolate cups sit at room temperature for about 5 minutes first.*

# Bananas Foster

| Makes 4 servings | 6 tablespoons I CAN'T BELIEVE<br>IT'S NOT BUTTER!® Spread<br>3 tablespoons firmly packed<br>brown sugar<br>4 medium ripe bananas, sliced<br>diagonally | 2 tablespoons dark rum or<br>brandy (optional)<br>Vanilla ice cream |

In 12-inch skillet, bring I Can't Believe It's Not Butter! Spread, brown sugar and bananas to a boil. Cook 2 minutes, stirring gently. Carefully add rum to center of pan and cook 15 seconds. Serve hot banana mixture over scoops of ice cream and top, if desired, with sweetened whipped cream.

**Tip:** *Recipe can be halved.*

# Strawberry Honey Parfaits

**Makes 4 servings**

1⅓ cups low-fat sour cream
¼ cup honey
2 teaspoons lime juice or
    1 teaspoon grated lime peel
4 cups strawberries

¼ cup coarsely chopped
    amaretti (Italian crunchy
    almond cookies) or biscotti
4 mint sprigs (optional)

Mix sour cream, honey and lime juice in medium bowl until well blended. Reserve 4 strawberries for garnish; coarsely chop remaining strawberries, about 3½ cups. Gently fold chopped strawberries into sour cream mixture; spoon into 4 (10- to 12-ounce) goblets or serving bowls. Sprinkle with 1 tablespoon cookie crumbs. Garnish with strawberries and mint sprigs, if desired. Serve immediately or refrigerate up to 6 hours.

Favorite recipe from **National Honey Board**

# Trifle Spectacular

**Makes 10 to 12 servings**

1 package DUNCAN HINES®
Moist Deluxe® Devil's Food
Cake Mix
1 can (14 ounces) sweetened
condensed milk
1 cup cold water
1 package (4-serving size)
vanilla-flavor instant
pudding and pie filling mix
2 cups whipping cream,
whipped

2 tablespoons orange juice,
divided
2½ cups sliced fresh
strawberries, divided
1 pint fresh raspberries, divided
2 kiwifruit, peeled and sliced,
divided
1½ cups frozen whipped topping,
thawed for garnish
Mint leaves for garnish
(optional)

*Note:*

**Since the different layers contribute to the beauty of this recipe, the fruit pieces should be arranged attractively along the side of the trifle dish.**

*1.* Preheat oven to 350°F. Grease and flour two 9-inch round cake pans.

*2.* Prepare, bake and cool cake following package directions for original recipe. Cut one cake layer into 1-inch cubes. Freeze other cake layer for later use.

*3.* Combine sweetened condensed milk and water in large bowl. Stir until blended. Add pudding mix. Beat until thoroughly blended. Chill 5 minutes. Fold whipped cream into pudding mixture.

*4.* To assemble, spread 2 cups pudding mixture into 3-quart trifle dish (or 3-quart clear glass bowl with straight sides). Arrange half the cake cubes over pudding mixture. Sprinkle with 1 tablespoon orange juice. Layer with 1 cup strawberry slices, half the raspberries and one-third of kiwifruit slices. Repeat layers. Top with remaining pudding mixture. Garnish with whipped topping, remaining ½ cup strawberry slices, kiwifruit slices and mint leaves, if desired.

# Smucker's® Double Apple Turnovers

½ cup SMUCKER'S® Cider
   Apple Butter
½ cup apple cider or juice
½ teaspoon ground cinnamon
   Grated peel of 1 orange
¼ cup golden raisins

4 large firm apples, peeled,
   cored and chopped
1 package frozen phyllo dough
   Nonstick cooking spray
   Granulated sugar for garnish

**Makes 6 turnovers**

**Prep Time:**
*30 minutes*

**Cook Time:**
*40 minutes*

Preheat oven to 375°F. Combine SMUCKER'S® Cider Apple Butter, cider, cinnamon and orange peel in a saucepan; simmer for 5 minutes. Add raisins and heat for 2 minutes more. Add apples; cook over medium heat for about 10 minutes or until apples begin to soften and most of the liquid evaporates. Cool in refrigerator.

Unwrap phyllo dough. Remove one sheet of dough, keeping remaining sheets covered with damp cloth. Coat dough with cooking spray, then cover with second sheet of dough. Spray top sheet with cooking spray.

Spoon about ⅓ cup of the apple filling on lower right corner of the dough. Fold dough over filling to form large rectangle. Then fold turnover as if it were a flag, making a triangular packet with each turn. Repeat with remaining dough and filling to make 6 turnovers. Place turnovers on baking sheet. Sprinkle with granulated sugar before baking. Bake 25 minutes or until turnovers are golden.

# Blue's Best Banana Bread Pudding

**Makes 8 to 10 servings**

4 large eggs, beaten
½ cup granulated sugar
¼ cup firmly packed light brown sugar
3 cups milk
1½ tablespoons vanilla extract
1 teaspoon ground cinnamon

8 slices bread, crusts removed
¼ cup (½ stick) butter, softened
1 large ripe banana, sliced
¾ cup "M&M's"® Chocolate Mini Baking Bits, divided
1¼ cups caramel ice cream topping, warmed

Lightly grease 8×8×2-inch baking pan; set aside. In large bowl combine eggs, sugars, milk, vanilla and cinnamon; set aside. Spread both sides of each bread slice with butter. Layer half of bread slices in prepared pan. Layer banana slices over bread. Layer with remaining bread slices. Pour egg mixture over bread; let stand 15 minutes. Preheat oven to 350°F. Sprinkle pudding with ¼ cup "M&M's"® Chocolate Mini Baking Bits. Bake 50 to 55 minutes. Serve warm with caramel topping and remaining ½ cup "M&M's"® Chocolate Mini Baking Bits. Store covered in refrigerator.

# Cookies & Cream Cupcakes

**Makes 24 cupcakes**

2¼ cups all-purpose flour
1 tablespoon baking powder
½ teaspoon salt
1⅔ cups sugar
½ cup (1 stick) butter, softened
1 cup milk
2 teaspoons vanilla

3 egg whites
1 cup crushed chocolate sandwich cookies (about 10 cookies) plus additional for garnish
1 container (16 ounces) vanilla frosting

*1.* Preheat oven to 350°F. Line 24 regular-size (2½-inch) muffin pan cups with paper muffin cup liners.

*2.* Sift flour, baking powder and salt together in large bowl. Stir in sugar. Add butter, milk and vanilla; beat with electric mixer at low speed 30 seconds. Beat at medium speed 2 minutes. Add egg whites; beat 2 minutes. Stir in 1 cup crushed cookies.

*3.* Spoon batter evenly into prepared muffin pans. Bake 20 to 25 minutes or until toothpick inserted into centers comes out clean. Cool in pans on wire racks 10 minutes. Remove to racks; cool completely.

*4.* Frost cupcakes; garnish with additional crushed cookies.

# Fabulous Fondue

| | | |
|---|---|---|
| 1 cup semisweet chocolate chips<br>¼ cup milk<br>2 to 3 tablespoons chopped pecans or walnuts | 1 large banana, sliced<br>2 medium apples, sliced<br>2 medium oranges, peeled and cut into segments | **Makes 6 servings**<br><br>**Prep and Cook Time:**<br>*15 minutes* |

*1.* Heat chocolate chips in small saucepan over very low heat until melted and smooth. Stir in milk and pecans; cook 1 minute.

*2.* Pour fondue into serving dish; serve immediately with fruit for dipping.

<u>Serving Suggestion:</u> *The possibilities for fondue dippers are endless! If fresh fruit is not available, try canned fruit or dried fruit. Cut a prepared pound cake or angel food cake into chunks for dipping, or set out a basket filled with a variety of small cookies.*

# Chocolate Toffee Bar Dessert

**Makes 15 servings**

**Prep Time:**
*20 minutes*

**Bake Time:**
*10 minutes*

**Chill Time:**
*3 hours*

1 cup flour
½ cup pecans, toasted and finely chopped
¼ cup sugar
½ cup (1 stick) butter or margarine, melted
1 cup toffee bits, divided
2 cups cold milk

2 packages (4-serving size each) JELL-O® Chocolate Flavor Instant Pudding & Pie Filling
1 tub (8 ounces) COOL WHIP® Whipped Topping, thawed, divided

**HEAT** oven to 400°F.

**MIX** flour, pecans, sugar, butter and ½ cup toffee bits in large bowl until well mixed. Press firmly onto bottom of 13×9-inch pan. Bake 10 minutes or until lightly browned. Cool.

**POUR** milk into large bowl. Add pudding mixes. Beat with wire whisk 1 minute or until well blended. Spread 1½ cups pudding on bottom of crust.

**GENTLY** stir ½ of the whipped topping into remaining pudding. Spread over pudding in pan. Top with remaining whipped topping. Sprinkle with remaining toffee bits.

**REFRIGERATE** 3 hours or overnight.

**Great Substitute:** *JELL-O® Butterscotch Flavor Instant Pudding can be substituted for Chocolate Flavor with delicious results.*

# Lemon Cake Top Pudding

4 eggs, separated
1 cup sugar, divided
3 tablespoons butter or
    margarine, softened
3 tablespoons all-purpose flour
¼ teaspoon salt

⅓ cup fresh squeezed SUNKIST®
    lemon juice
1 cup milk
    Grated peel of ½ SUNKIST®
    lemon
¼ cup sliced natural almonds

**Makes 6 servings**

In small bowl of electric mixer, beat egg whites until foamy; gradually add ¼ cup sugar, beating until soft peaks form. Set aside. In large bowl, using same beaters, beat egg yolks and butter well. Gradually add remaining ¾ cup sugar, beating until well blended (about 5 minutes). Add flour, salt and lemon juice; mix well. Blend in milk and lemon peel. Gently fold in beaten egg whites. Sprinkle almonds over bottom of buttered 1½-quart casserole; pour in batter. Set casserole in shallow baking pan filled with ½ inch hot water. Bake, uncovered, at 325°F 55 to 60 minutes or until lightly browned. Serve warm or chilled. Refrigerate leftovers.

*Note:*

Lemons should be firm and heavy for their size, with a sheen to the skin. Avoid those that have any sign of green, which indicates that they are unripe.

# Plantation Gingerbread

**Makes 4 servings**

2 cups all-purpose flour
2 teaspoon cinnamon
1½ teaspoons ginger
1 teaspoon baking powder
½ teaspoon baking soda
½ teaspoon salt

1 cup GRANDMA'S® Molasses
⅓ cup melted shortening
½ cup buttermilk
1 egg
½ cup MOTT'S® Apple Sauce
½ cup raisins

Heat oven to 350°F. In large bowl, combine dry ingredients. In another large bowl, combine molasses and shortening until well blended. Add molasses mixture, buttermilk and egg to flour mixture. Stir in apple sauce and raisins. Bake in greased 9-inch square pan for about 35 minutes or until toothpick inserted in center comes out clean.

# Blueberry Streusel Cobbler

**Makes 8 to 12 servings**

**Prep Time:**
*15 minutes*

**Bake Time:**
*1 hour and 10 minutes*

1 pint fresh or frozen
   blueberries
1 (14-ounce) can EAGLE®
   BRAND Sweetened
   Condensed Milk
   (NOT evaporated milk)
2 teaspoons grated lemon peel
¾ cup (1½ sticks) plus
   2 tablespoons cold butter
   or margarine, divided

2 cups biscuit baking mix,
   divided
½ cup firmly packed light brown
   sugar
½ cup chopped nuts
   Vanilla ice cream
   Blueberry Sauce
   (recipe follows)

*1.* Preheat oven to 325°F. In medium mixing bowl, combine blueberries, Eagle Brand and lemon peel.

*2.* In large mixing bowl, cut ¾ cup butter into 1½ cups biscuit mix until crumbly; add blueberry mixture. Spread in greased 9-inch square baking pan.

*3.* In small mixing bowl, combine remaining ½ cup biscuit mix and brown sugar; cut in remaining 2 tablespoons butter until crumbly. Add nuts. Sprinkle over cobbler.

*4.* Bake 1 hour and 10 minutes or until golden. Serve warm with vanilla ice cream and Blueberry Sauce. Refrigerate leftovers.

<u>Blueberry Sauce:</u> *In large saucepan over medium heat, combine ½ cup granulated sugar, 1 tablespoon cornstarch, ½ teaspoon ground cinnamon and ¼ teaspoon ground nutmeg. Gradually add ½ cup water. Cook and stir until thickened. Stir in 1 pint blueberries; cook and stir until hot. Makes about 1⅔ cups.*

# Famous Chocolate Refrigerator Roll

| | | |
|---|---|---|
| 1 teaspoon vanilla extract<br>2 cups heavy cream, whipped,<br>    or 1 (8-ounce) container<br>    COOL WHIP® Whipped<br>    Topping, thawed | 1 (9-ounce) package NABISCO®<br>    Famous Chocolate Wafers<br>Chocolate curls, for garnish | **Makes 12 servings**<br><br>**Prep Time:**<br>*30 minutes*<br><br>**Chill Time:**<br>*4 hours* |

*1.* Stir vanilla into whipped cream or topping.

*2.* Spread ½ tablespoon whipped cream or topping on each wafer. Begin stacking wafers together and stand on edge on serving platter to make 14-inch log.

*3.* Frost with remaining whipped cream. Chill for 4 to 6 hours.*
To serve, garnish with chocolate curls; slice roll at 45° angle.

*\*Or, freeze until firm; cover with plastic wrap. Thaw in refrigerator for 1 hour before serving.*

# Fruit Medley Dessert

**Makes 8 servings**

1 package (18 ounces) NESTLÉ®
   TOLL HOUSE® Refrigerated
   Sugar Cookie Bar Dough
1 container (32 ounces) lowfat
   vanilla yogurt or 1 quart
   vanilla frozen yogurt

4 cups fresh fruit (blueberries,
   raspberries, sliced apples,
   cherries, nectarines,
   peaches and/or
   strawberries)

**PREHEAT** oven to 325°F.

**ROLL** chilled dough on floured surface to ¼-inch thickness. Cut out 24 shapes using 3-inch cookie cutters. Place on ungreased baking sheets.

**BAKE** for 10 to 14 minutes or until edges are light golden brown. Cool on baking sheets for 2 minutes; remove to wire racks to cool completely.

**PLACE** two cookies on each plate. Top with ½ cup yogurt and ½ cup fruit mixture. Place third cookie on top.

# Ice Cream Cookie Dessert

**Makes 12 to 16 servings**

1 (1¼-pound) package
   chocolate sandwich cookies
1 stack (18 cookies) chocolate
   fudge mint cookies
½ gallon vanilla or mint
   chocolate chip ice cream,
   softened

2 cups (two 12-ounce jars)
   SMUCKER'S® Hot Fudge
   Topping
1 (12-ounce) carton whipped
   topping, thawed

Crush cookies until fine. Reserve 1 cup crumbs for topping. Press remaining cookie crumbs in 13×9-inch pan. Spoon ice cream on top of crumbs and freeze.

Heat hot fudge topping as directed on jar; spread over ice cream. Freeze for 1 hour.

Spread with whipped topping; top with reserved cookie crumbs. Freeze until ready to serve.

# Cherry Apricot Cornmeal Cobbler

| | | Makes 8 servings |
|---|---|---|
| 2 cups sliced pitted halved fresh apricots | 1½ tablespoons plus 1 teaspoon brown sugar, divided | |
| ⅓ cup granulated sugar | 2 teaspoons baking powder | |
| 2 cups pitted fresh cherries | ½ teaspoon ground cinnamon | |
| 1 cup plus 1 tablespoon all-purpose flour, divided | ¼ teaspoon salt | |
| ½ cup yellow cornmeal | 5 tablespoons butter | |
| | ¾ cup low-fat milk | |

Preheat oven to 375°F. Combine apricots and granulated sugar in small bowl. Combine cherries and 1 tablespoon flour in second bowl. Combine remaining 1 cup flour, cornmeal, 1½ tablespoons brown sugar, baking powder, cinnamon and salt in large bowl. Cut in butter until mixture resembles coarse crumbs. Add milk; blend just until ingredients are evenly moistened.

Place fruit in 1½-quart baking dish; top with batter. Sprinkle with remaining 1 teaspoon brown sugar. Bake 25 to 30 minutes or until golden brown. Let cool slightly before serving.

# Apple-Walnut "Pizza Pie"

**Makes 6 to 8 servings**

**Pizza Crust**
- 2½ cups all-purpose flour
- 4 tablespoons granulated sugar
- 1¼ teaspoons salt
- ½ cup CRISCO® Canola Oil
- 4 tablespoons milk
- ½ teaspoons almond extract

**Pizza Topping**
- 4 medium Granny Smith apples (peeled, cored, quartered, and sliced thin)
- ½ cup chopped walnuts
- ⅓ cup firmly packed light brown sugar
- 3 tablespoons raisins
- 1½ teaspoons ground cinnamon
- ½ tablespoon vanilla
- 6 tablespoons SMUCKER'S® Cider Apple Butter
- ½ cup grated coconut

*Note:*

Apple butter is a preserve made by slowly cooking apples, sugar, spices and cider together. It is thick and dark brown in color. It is great as a spread on breads and is also a tasty accompaniment to peanut butter.

*1.* Heat oven to 400°F. For pizza crust, combine flour, granulated sugar and salt in large bowl; mix well. Whisk together oil, milk and almond extract in small bowl until well blended. Slowly pour oil mixture into flour mixture while stirring with fork until well mixed and crumbly.

*2.* Spray 12¼-inch pizza pan with CRISCO® No-Stick Cooking Spray. Press crumb mixture with fingers firmly onto bottom and side of pan. Bake at 400°F for about 10 minutes or until golden brown; remove from oven. *Reduce oven temperature to 350°F.*

*3.* For pizza topping, combine apples, walnuts, brown sugar, raisins, cinnamon and vanilla in large bowl; mix well.

*4.* Spread SMUCKER'S® Cider Apple Butter evenly over baked pizza crust. Place apple mixture on top. Sprinkle with coconut "cheese". Bake at 350°F for 25 to 30 minutes. Remove from oven and serve warm or at room temperature. Cut into "pizza slices" and garnish with whipped cream.

# Double Chocolate Cocoa Cupcakes

¾ cup shortening
1¼ cups granulated sugar
2 eggs
1 teaspoon vanilla extract
1¾ cups all-purpose flour
½ cup HERSHEY⋅S Cocoa
1 teaspoon baking soda

½ teaspoon salt
1 cup milk
1 cup HERSHEY⋅S MINI CHIPS™
   Semi-Sweet Chocolate
   Chips
Powdered sugar

Makes about 2 dozen cupcakes

*1.* Heat oven to 375°F. Line muffin cups (2½ inches in diameter) with paper bake cups.

*2.* Beat shortening and granulated sugar in large bowl until fluffy. Add eggs and vanilla; beat well. Stir together flour, cocoa, baking soda and salt; add alternately with milk to shortening mixture, beating well after each addition. Stir in small chocolate chips. Fill prepared muffin cups about ¾ full with batter.

*3.* Bake 20 to 25 minutes or until cupcake springs back when touched lightly in center. Remove from pans to wire racks. Cool completely. Sift powdered sugar over tops of cupcakes.

# Baked Custard

**Makes 6 servings**

4 large eggs
½ cup granulated sugar
½ teaspoon salt
1 can (12 fluid ounces)
NESTLÉ® CARNATION®
Evaporated Milk

1 cup water
1 teaspoon vanilla extract
Ground nutmeg

**PREHEAT** oven to 350°F.

**COMBINE** eggs, sugar and salt in large mixer bowl. Add evaporated milk, water and vanilla extract; beat until mixed. Pour into six 6-ounce custard cups. Sprinkle with nutmeg. Place cups in 13×9-inch baking pan; fill pan with hot water to 1-inch depth.

**BAKE** for 35 to 40 minutes or until knife inserted near center comes out clean. Remove cups to wire rack to cool completely. Refrigerate until ready to serve.

# Chocolate-Caramel Fondue

**Makes 2½ cups**

**Prep Time:**
*15 minutes*

3 (1-ounce) squares
unsweetened chocolate,
chopped
1 (14-ounce) can EAGLE®
BRAND Sweetened
Condensed Milk
(NOT evaporated milk)

1 (12¼-ounce) jar caramel
ice cream topping
Dippers: Fresh fruit, cookies,
pound cake pieces or
angel food cake pieces

*1.* In medium saucepan, melt chocolate with Eagle Brand and caramel topping.

*2.* Pour into serving bowl or individual cups. Serve with desired dippers.

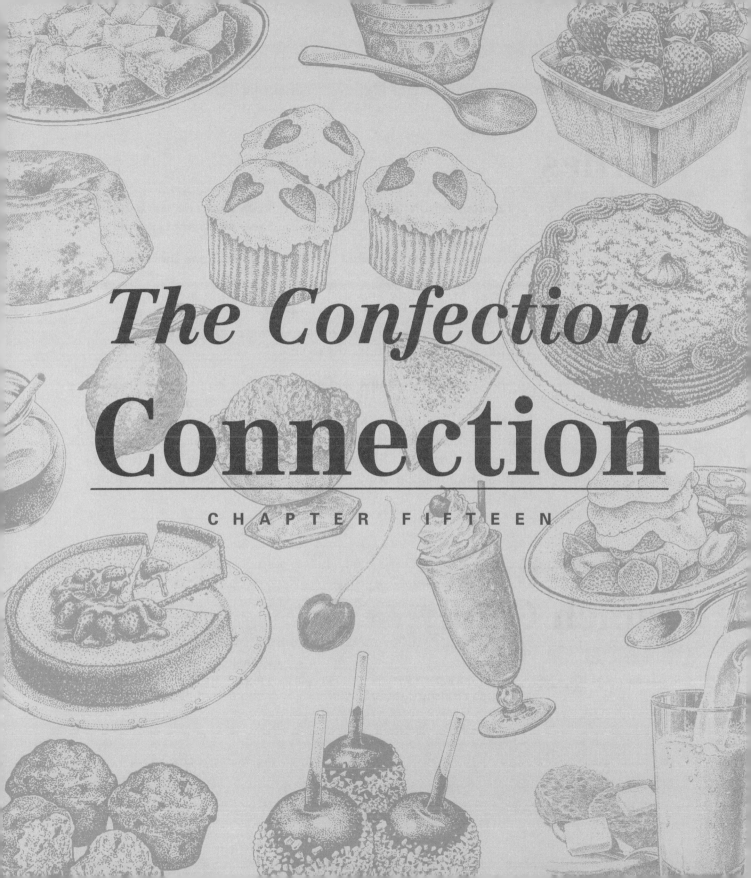

# The Confection
# Connection

CHAPTER FIFTEEN

# Truffles

| Makes about 3 dozen candies | 1 container DUNCAN HINES®<br>Creamy Home-Style Milk<br>Chocolate Frosting<br>2½ cups confectioners' sugar | 1 cup pecan halves, divided<br>1 cup semisweet chocolate<br>chips<br>3 tablespoons shortening |

*1.* Combine frosting and sugar in large mixing bowl. Stir with wooden spoon until thoroughly blended. Chop ⅓ cup pecan halves; set aside. Cover remaining pecan halves with 1 tablespoon frosting mixture each.

*2.* Place chocolate chips and shortening in 2-cup glass measuring cup. Microwave at MEDIUM (50% power) for 2 minutes; stir. Microwave 1 minute at MEDIUM; stir until smooth. Dip one candy ball into chocolate mixture until completely covered. Remove with fork to cooling rack. Sprinkle top with chopped pecans. Repeat until all candy balls are covered. Allow to stand until chocolate mixture is set.

# Peanut Butter Crunch Candy

| Makes 18 servings | 1½ cups sugar<br>¾ cup dark corn syrup<br>1½ cups crunchy peanut butter | 1 teaspoon vanilla<br>6 cups corn flakes<br>½ cup salted peanuts |

Bring sugar and corn syrup to a rolling boil. Remove from heat and add peanut butter and vanilla. Stir to blend. Pour over corn flakes and peanuts and mix until all cereal is coated. Pat into 2 greased 8×8×2-inch pans. While still warm, cut into squares.

Favorite recipe from **Peanut Advisory Board**

# Peppermint Patties

| | | Makes about 8 dozen patties |
|---|---|---|
| 1 (14-ounce) can EAGLE® BRAND Sweetened Condensed Milk (NOT evaporated milk)<br>1 tablespoon peppermint extract<br>Green or red food coloring, if desired | 6 cups powdered sugar<br>Additional powdered sugar<br>1½ pounds chocolate-flavored candy coating,* melted<br><br>*Also called confectionery coating or almond bark. | |

*1.* In large mixing bowl, combine Eagle Brand, peppermint extract and food coloring, if desired. Add 6 cups powdered sugar; beat at low speed of electric mixer until smooth and well blended. Turn mixture onto surface sprinkled with additional powdered sugar.

*2.* Knead lightly to form smooth ball. Shape into 1-inch balls. Place 2 inches apart on waxed-paper-lined baking sheets. Flatten each ball into 1½-inch patty.

*3.* Let dry 1 hour or longer; turn over and let dry at least 1 hour. With fork, dip each patty into melted candy coating (draw fork lightly across rim of pan to remove excess coating). Invert onto waxed-paper-lined baking sheets; let stand until firm. Store covered at room temperature or in refrigerator.

# Chocolate Chip Cookie Brittle

| Makes about 50 pieces | |
| --- | --- |

**1 cup (2 sticks) butter or margarine, softened**
**1 cup granulated sugar**
**1½ teaspoons vanilla extract**
**1 teaspoon salt**
**2 cups all-purpose flour**

**2 cups (12-ounce package) NESTLÉ® TOLL HOUSE® Semi-Sweet Chocolate Morsels, *divided***
**1 cup chopped nuts**

## *Note:*

When purchasing butter, check the freshness date stamped on the package. Store butter in the coldest part of the refrigerator or in the freezer. Either way, wrap it tightly since it picks up other flavors.

**PREHEAT** oven to 375°F.

**BEAT** butter, sugar, vanilla extract and salt in large mixer bowl. Gradually beat in flour. Stir in *1½ cups* morsels and nuts. Press into ungreased 15×10-inch jelly-roll pan.

**BAKE** for 20 to 25 minutes or until golden brown and set. Cool until just slightly warm.

**MICROWAVE** *remaining* morsels in small, *heavy-duty* plastic bag on HIGH (100%) power for 30 to 45 seconds; knead. Microwave at additional 10- to 20-second intervals, kneading until smooth. Cut tiny corner from bag; squeeze to drizzle over cookie. Allow chocolate to cool and set; break cookies into irregular pieces.

**Tip:** *Omitting nuts could cause cookie to become dry.*

# Candied Orange Peel

4 to 5 SUNKIST® oranges*
12 cups cold water, divided
2 cups sugar, divided
½ cup honey

1¾ cups boiling water

*Six Sunkist® lemons or Sunkist® grapefruit may be substituted.

Makes about 1 pound

Wash fruit; score peel into lengthwise quarters. Remove sections of peel; cut into ⅜-inch-wide strips to measure 3 cups peel. Bring 6 cups cold water and peel to boil; boil 10 minutes. Drain and rinse. Repeat process with 6 cups fresh water.

In large saucepan, bring to a boil 1½ cups sugar, honey and boiling water; boil 1 minute. Add peel and briskly simmer 40 to 45 minutes; stir frequently to avoid sticking. Drain well. In large bowl, toss drained peel with remaining ½ cup sugar to coat well. Spread on wire racks over waxed paper to dry. (May need to redip in sugar as peel dries.) Store in tightly covered container.

# Fireballs

1 (12-ounce) package
    semisweet chocolate chips
¼ cup butter or margarine
½ cup walnuts, toasted and
    finely chopped

2 tablespoons dark rum
1½ teaspoons TABASCO® brand
    Pepper Sauce
⅓ cup granulated sugar

Makes about 34 balls

Melt chocolate and butter in small saucepan over low heat. Stir in walnuts, rum and TABASCO® Sauce. Refrigerate mixture about 15 minutes. Shape chocolate mixture into 1-inch balls; roll balls in granulated sugar to coat. Refrigerate until ready to serve.

# Rich Cocoa Fudge

**Makes about 3 dozen pieces or 1¾ pounds**

**Prep Time:**
*25 minutes*

**Cook Time:**
*25 minutes*

**Cool Time:**
*2½ hours*

3 cups sugar
⅔ cup HERSHEY᾿S Cocoa or
   HERSHEY᾿S Dutch
   Processed Cocoa

⅛ teaspoon salt
1½ cups milk
¼ cup (½ stick) butter
1 teaspoon vanilla extract

*1.* Line 8- or 9-inch square pan with foil, extending foil over edges of pan. Butter foil.

*2.* Stir together sugar, cocoa and salt in heavy 4-quart saucepan; stir in milk. Cook over medium heat, stirring constantly, until mixture comes to full rolling boil. Boil, without stirring, until mixture reaches 234°F on candy thermometer or until small amount of mixture, dropped into very cold water, forms a soft ball which flattens when removed from water. (Bulb of candy thermometer should not rest on bottom of saucepan.) Remove from heat.

*3.* Add butter and vanilla. DO NOT STIR. Cool at room temperature to 110°F (lukewarm). Beat with wooden spoon until fudge thickens and just begins to lose some of its gloss. Quickly spread into prepared pan; cool completely. Cut into squares. Store in tightly covered container at room temperature.

**Nutty Rich Cocoa Fudge:** *Beat cooked fudge as directed. Immediately stir in 1 cup chopped almonds, pecans or walnuts and quickly spread into prepared pan.*

**Marshmallow Nut Cocoa Fudge:** *Increase cocoa to ¾ cup. Cook fudge as directed. Add 1 cup marshmallow creme with butter and vanilla. DO NOT STIR. Cool to 110°F (lukewarm). Beat 8 minutes; stir in 1 cup chopped nuts. Pour into prepared pan. (Fudge does not set until poured into pan.)*

**Tip:** *For best results, do not double this recipe.*

# Walnut Cherry Fudge Logs

3 cups semisweet chocolate
  chips
1 (14-ounce) can sweetened
  condensed milk

1 cup dried tart cherries
1 teaspoon vanilla
1 (6-ounce) package walnut
  pieces, chopped

**Makes 8 dozen candies**

Melt chocolate chips with sweetened condensed milk in medium saucepan over low heat. Remove from heat.

Stir in cherries and vanilla. Refrigerate 30 minutes.

Divide mixture in half; place each portion on 20-inch piece of waxed paper. Shape each portion into 12-inch log. Press walnuts onto log. Wrap tightly; refrigerate for 2 hours or until firm.

Remove waxed paper; cut into ¼-inch slices to serve. Store, covered, in refrigerator.

**<u>Almond Cherry Fudge Logs:</u>** *Omit vanilla and walnuts. Add 1 teaspoon almond extract and 1½ cups sliced almonds, toasted and chopped. Proceed as directed above.*

Favorite recipe from **Cherry Marketing Institute**

# Chocolate Chip Nougat

**Makes about
12 dozen pieces**

3 cups sugar, divided
⅔ cup plus 1¼ cups light corn
   syrup, divided
2 tablespoons water
¼ cup egg whites (about
   2 large), at room
   temperature
¼ cup (½ stick) butter or
   margarine, melted

2 teaspoons vanilla extract
2 cups chopped walnuts
¼ teaspoon red food color
   (optional)
1 cup HERSHEY⋅S MINI CHIPS™
   Semi-Sweet Chocolate or
   HERSHEY⋅S Semi-Sweet
   Chocolate Chips

*Note:*

Heavy saucepans with

flat bottoms will

prevent candy from

scorching during

cooking. Pans should

be large enough to

prevent syrups from

boiling and foaming

over the rims. Always

use the size pan

suggested in the recipe

and never double

cooked candy recipes.

*1.* Line 15½×10½×1-inch jelly roll pan with foil, extending foil over edges of pan; butter foil.

*2.* Combine 1 cup sugar, ⅔ cup corn syrup and water in a small saucepan; cook over medium heat, stirring constantly, until sugar dissolves. Continue cooking, without stirring. When mixture reaches 230°F on candy thermometer, continue cooking, but start to beat egg whites.

*3.* Beat egg whites in large bowl with mixer until stiff, but not dry. Continue cooking syrup until mixture reaches 238°F (soft-ball stage) or when syrup, dropped into small amount of very cold water, forms a soft ball which flattens when removed from water. (Bulb of candy thermometer should not rest on bottom of saucepan.) Remove from heat. Gradually pour hot mixture in a thin stream over whites, beating on high speed. Continue beating 4 to 5 minutes or until mixture becomes very thick. Cover; set aside.

*4.* Stir together remaining 2 cups sugar and remaining 1¼ cups corn syrup in heavy medium-size saucepan. Cook over medium heat, stirring constantly, until sugar dissolves. Cook, without stirring, to 275°F (soft-crack stage), or until syrup, when dropped into very cold water, separates into threads that are hard but not brittle. Immediately pour hot sugar mixture all at once over egg white mixture; blend with wooden spoon. Stir in butter and vanilla. Add walnuts; mix thoroughly. Stir in red food color, if desired.

*5.* Pour into prepared pan; sprinkle evenly with chocolate chips. Cool completely; do not disturb chips while cooling. Use foil to lift it out of pan; remove foil. Cut into 1-inch pieces. Store in tightly covered container in cool, dry place.

# Semi-Sweet Chocolate Fudge

| | | |
|---|---|---|
| 4 cups sugar<br>1 jar (7 ounces) marshmallow creme<br>1½ cups (12-ounce can) evaporated milk | 1 tablespoon butter or margarine<br>4 cups (24-ounce package) HERSHEY₅S Semi-Sweet Chocolate Chips | **Makes about 8 dozen squares** |

*1.* Line 13×9×2-inch pan with foil.

*2.* Place sugar, marshmallow creme, evaporated milk and butter in heavy 4-quart saucepan. Cook over medium heat, stirring constantly, until mixture comes to a full rolling boil; boil and stir 5 minutes. Remove from heat; immediately add chocolate chips, stirring until smooth. Pour into prepared pan; cool until firm.

*3.* Remove from pan; peel off foil. Cut into squares. Store in airtight container in cool, dry place.

# Chocolate Butter Crunch

**Makes about 1½ pounds**

1 cup (2 sticks) butter or margarine
1¼ cups sugar
¼ cup water

2 tablespoons light corn syrup
1 cup ground almonds, divided
½ teaspoon vanilla extract
¾ cup milk chocolate chips

Line 15×10-inch jelly-roll pan with foil, extending edges over sides of pan. Generously grease foil and narrow metal spatula with butter. Melt butter in 2-quart saucepan over medium heat. Add sugar, water and corn syrup. Bring to a boil, stirring constantly. Carefully clip candy thermometer to side of pan (do not let bulb touch bottom of pan). Cook until thermometer registers 290°F, stirring frequently. Stir in ⅔ cup almonds and vanilla. Pour into prepared pan. Spread mixture into corners with greased spatula. Let stand 1 minute. Sprinkle with chocolate chips. Let stand 2 to 3 minutes more until chocolate melts; spread chocolate over candy. Sprinkle with remaining ⅓ cup almonds. Cool completely. Lift candy out of pan using foil; remove foil. Break candy into pieces. Store in airtight container.

# Dreamy Divinity

**Makes 50 pieces (1½ pounds)**

3½ cups DOMINO® Granulated Sugar
⅔ cup water
⅔ cup light corn syrup
⅓ teaspoon salt

3 egg whites, beaten until stiff
1½ teaspoons vanilla extract
Food coloring, candied cherries and chopped nuts (optional)

Combine sugar, water, corn syrup and salt in saucepan. Heat, stirring occasionally, until sugar dissolves. Wipe down sugar crystals from side of pan as necessary with pastry brush dipped in water. Boil syrup mixture, without stirring, until mixture reaches 265°F or hard-ball stage on candy thermometer.

Gradually beat hot syrup into beaten egg whites. Add vanilla. Tint with food coloring, if desired. Continue beating until candy holds shape. Drop by teaspoonfuls onto buttered baking sheet or plate. Garnish with cherries and nuts as desired. When firm, store in airtight container.

# Loony Lollies

| ½ cup powdered sugar<br>1 tablespoon milk<br>4 giant flat lollipops | ½ cup "M&M's"® Chocolate<br>Mini Baking Bits | Makes 4 lollipops |
|---|---|---|

In small bowl combine powdered sugar and milk until smooth. Place icing in resealable plastic sandwich bag; seal bag. Cut tiny piece off one corner of bag (not more than ⅛ inch). Using icing to attach, decorate lollipops with "M&M's"® Chocolate Mini Baking Bits. Let set 10 to 15 minutes. Store in tightly covered container.

# Honey Fruit Truffles

| Makes about 12 truffles | | |
|---|---|---|
| | 6 ounces unsweetened chocolate, finely chopped<br>½ cup honey<br>2 tablespoons butter or margarine | 2 tablespoons heavy cream<br>½ cup chopped dried apricots<br>½ cup unsweetened cocoa powder |

Combine chocolate, honey, butter and cream in top of double boiler. Cook over medium heat, stirring constantly, until chocolate is melted and smooth. Stir in apricots. Refrigerate 1 hour, or until mixture is firm. Form into ¾-inch balls; roll in cocoa powder. Store in airtight container until ready to serve.

<u>Microwave method</u>

In medium, microwave-safe container, combine chocolate, honey, butter and cream. Microwave on HIGH (100%) for 1 minute; stir until smooth. Stir in apricots and proceed as directed.

Favorite recipe from **National Honey Board**

# Chocolate Raspberry Fudge

| Makes about 4 dozen pieces or about 2 pounds fudge | | |
|---|---|---|
| | 2¼ cups sugar<br>½ cup plus 2 tablespoons (5-ounce can) evaporated milk<br>¼ cup (½ stick) butter or margarine | 1⅔ cups (10-ounce package) HERSHEY⁏S Raspberry Chips<br>1 jar (7 ounces) marshmallow creme<br>1 teaspoon vanilla extract |

*1.* Line 8- or 9-inch square pan with foil, extending foil over edges of pan. Butter foil lightly.

*2.* Stir together sugar, evaporated milk and butter in heavy 3-quart saucepan. Cook over medium heat, stirring constantly, until mixture comes to full rolling boil; boil 5 minutes, stirring constantly. Remove from heat. Gradually add raspberry chips, stirring until melted. Add marshmallow creme and vanilla; stir until smooth. Pour into prepared pan; cool until firm.

*3.* Use foil to lift fudge out of pan; peel off foil. Cut fudge into squares. Store in tightly covered container in cool, dry place.

<u>Note:</u> *For best results, do not double this recipe.*

# Bittersweet Chocolate Mints

| | | |
|---|---|---|
| **3 squares (1 ounce each)<br>unsweetened chocolate,<br>coarsely chopped**<br>**½ cup semisweet chocolate<br>chips** | **3 packets sugar substitute**<br>**1 teaspoon peppermint extract** | **Makes about<br>¼ pound** |

*1.* Line 9×5-inch loaf pan with buttered foil; set aside.

*2.* Melt chocolate and chips in medium bowl over hot, not boiling, water, stirring constantly.

*3.* Stir in sugar substitute and peppermint extract; mix well. Pour into prepared pan. Score mints with knife into 1-inch squares. Refrigerate until firm.

*4.* Cut into squares. Store in refrigerator until just before serving.

# Baker's® One Bowl Chocolate Fudge

**Makes about 4 dozen**

**Prep Time:**
*15 minutes plus refrigerating*

2 packages (8 squares each)
   BAKER'S® Semi-Sweet
   Baking Chocolate
1 can (14 ounces) sweetened
   condensed milk

2 teaspoon vanilla
1 cup chopped nuts *or* toasted
   BAKER'S® ANGEL FLAKE®
   Coconut

**MICROWAVE** chocolate and milk in microwavable bowl on HIGH 2 minutes or until chocolate is almost melted, stirring halfway through heating time.

**STIR** in vanilla and nuts. Spread in foil-lined 8-inch square pan. Refrigerate 2 hours or until firm. Cut into squares.

**Double Chocolate Orange Nut Fudge:** *Prepare Fudge as directed, using 1 cup toasted chopped walnuts for nuts. Spread in pan. Before refrigerating Fudge, melt 1 package (6 squares) BAKER'S® Premium White Baking Chocolate as directed on package. Stir in ½ cup sweetened condensed milk and 1 teaspoon grated orange peel. Spread over Fudge in pan.*

**Tip:** *Lining the pan with foil makes cutting the fudge easier with little clean-up. Be sure to use enough foil to extend over the pan's edges—it becomes the handles for lifting fudge out of the pan and onto the cutting board.*

# Cookies and Cream Cheesecake Bonbons

24 chocolate cream-filled
   cookies, divided
1 package (8 ounces) cream
   cheese, softened
1 cup nonfat dry milk powder

1 teaspoon vanilla
1 package (1 pound) powdered
   sugar (about 4 cups)
Fresh raspberries and
   raspberry leaves for garnish

**Makes about 3 dozen bonbons**

*1.* Coarsely chop 12 cookies; set aside.

*2.* Place remaining 12 cookies in food processor; process until fine crumbs form. Place crumbs on baking sheet lined with waxed paper; set aside.

*3.* Beat cream cheese, dry milk and vanilla in medium bowl with electric mixer at medium speed until smooth. Beat in powdered sugar, 1 cup at a time, at low speed until mixture is smooth. Stir in reserved chopped cookies. Refrigerate 2 hours or until firm.

*4.* Shape rounded tablespoonfuls cream cheese mixture into balls. Roll balls in reserved cookie crumbs. Garnish, if desired. Store in airtight container in refrigerator.

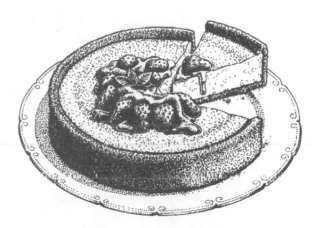

# Nutty Nougat Caramel Bites

**Makes about 15 dozen pieces**

**Cookie Base**
2¼ cups all-purpose flour
1 teaspoon baking soda
1 teaspoon salt
1 cup (2 sticks) butter, softened
¾ cup packed brown sugar
¼ cup granulated sugar
1 package (3.4 ounces) butterscotch-flavored instant pudding mix
2 large eggs, lightly beaten
1 teaspoon vanilla extract
1⅓ cups (about 8 ounces) NESTLÉ® TOLL HOUSE® Butterscotch Flavored Morsels

**Nougat Filling**
¼ cup (½ stick) butter
1 cup granulated sugar
¼ cup NESTLÉ® CARNATION® Evaporated Milk

1 jar (7 ounces) marshmallow creme
¼ cup creamy peanut butter
1 teaspoon vanilla extract
1½ cups (about 8 ounces) coarsely chopped salted peanuts

**Caramel Layer**
1 package (14 ounces) caramels, unwrapped
¼ cup heavy whipping cream

**Icing**
1 cup (6 ounces) NESTLÉ® TOLL HOUSE® Milk Chocolate Morsels
⅓ cup NESTLÉ® TOLL HOUSE® Butterscotch Flavored Morsels
¼ cup creamy peanut butter

### For Cookie Base
**PREHEAT** oven to 350°F. Line 17×11×1-inch baking pan with parchment paper.

**COMBINE** flour, baking soda and salt in small bowl. Beat butter, brown sugar and granulated sugar in large mixer bowl until creamy. Add pudding mix, eggs and vanilla extract; mix well. Gradually beat in flour mixture. Stir in 1⅓ cups butterscotch morsels. Spread and pat dough evenly into prepared baking pan.

**BAKE** for 10 to 11 minutes or until light golden brown. Carefully hold pan 2 to 3 inches above a heat-resistant surface and allow pan to drop. (This creates a chewier cookie base.) Cool completely in pan on wire rack.

### For Nougat Filling

**MELT** butter in medium, *heavy-duty* saucepan over medium heat. Add granulated sugar and evaporated milk; stir. Bring to a boil, stirring constantly. Boil, stirring constantly, for 5 minutes. Remove from heat.

**STIR** in marshmallow creme, peanut butter and vanilla extract. Add peanuts; stir well. Spread nougat mixture over cookie base. Refrigerate for 15 minutes or until set.

### For Caramel Layer

**COMBINE** caramels and cream in medium, *heavy-duty* saucepan. Cook over low heat, stirring constantly, until caramels are melted and mixture is smooth. Spread caramel mixture over nougat layer. Refrigerate for 15 minutes or until set.

### For Icing

**MELT** milk chocolate morsels, ⅓ cup butterscotch morsels and peanut butter in medium, microwave-safe bowl on MEDIUM-HIGH (70%) power for 1 minute; stir. Microwave at additional 10- to 20-second intervals, stirring until smooth. Spread icing over caramel layer. Refrigerate for at least 1 hour.

**TO SERVE,** let stand at room temperature for 5 to 10 minutes. Cut into 1-inch pieces. Store in airtight container in refrigerator.

# Cherry Almond Clusters

| Makes 2 dozen candies | 1 (8-ounce) package semisweet baking chocolate, coarsely chopped | 1 cup slivered almonds, toasted<br>1 cup dried tart cherries |

Place chocolate in microwave-safe bowl. Microwave on HIGH (100%) 2 minutes, stirring after 1 minute. Stir until chocolate is completely melted. Add almonds and dried cherries; mix until completely coated with chocolate. Drop by teaspoons onto waxed paper. Refrigerate until firm.

<u>Note:</u> *To toast almonds, spread almonds on ungreased baking sheet. Bake in preheated 350°F oven 5 to 7 minutes, stirring occasionally.*

Favorite recipe from **Cherry Marketing Institute**

# Toffee Diamonds

| Makes 4 dozen diamonds | 1 cup (2 sticks) I CAN'T BELIEVE IT'S NOT BUTTER!® Spread, softened<br>2 cups all-purpose flour<br>1 cup firmly packed brown sugar | 1 egg, separated<br>½ teaspoon vanilla extract<br>1 cup chopped walnuts |

Preheat oven to 325°F. Grease 15½×10½-inch jelly-roll pan; set aside.

In large bowl, with electric mixer, beat I Can't Believe It's Not Butter!® Spread, flour, sugar, egg yolk and vanilla until well blended. Evenly spread dough into prepared pan. With fork, beat egg white slightly. With pastry brush, brush egg white over top of flour mixture; sprinkle with walnuts.

Bake 30 minutes or until golden. Remove from oven and immediately cut into diamonds. Remove from pan to wire rack; cool completely.

# Chocolate Peanut Butter Fudge

| | |
|---|---|
| 3 cups powdered sugar | 1½ teaspoons vanilla |
| 1½ cups SMUCKER'S® Creamy Natural Peanut Butter | 1 cup (6 ounces) semi-sweet chocolate chips |
| ½ cup butter or margarine, melted | ⅓ cup butter or margarine |
| ½ cup firmly packed brown sugar | |

**Makes 60 bars**

Combine powdered sugar, peanut butter, ½ cup butter, brown sugar and vanilla; mix well. Press mixture into 13×9-inch pan.

Melt chocolate chips and ⅓ cup butter. Spread over peanut butter mixture. Refrigerate until firm. Cut into 1-inch squares.

# Bittersweet Chocolate Truffle Squares

**Makes 4 dozen squares**

**Prep Time:**
*15 minutes*

**Chill Time:**
*4 hours*

¾ cup whipping (heavy) cream
¼ cup (½ stick) butter *or* margarine, cut into chunks
3 tablespoons sugar
2 packages (6 squares each) BAKER'S® Bittersweet Baking Chocolate, broken into chunks

½ teaspoon vanilla
1 cup finely chopped toasted almonds

LINE 8-inch square baking pan with foil.

MICROWAVE cream, butter and sugar in large microwavable bowl on HIGH 3 minutes until mixture comes to full boil, stirring halfway through heating time. Add chocolate and vanilla; stir until chocolate is completely melted.

REFRIGERATE about 2 hours or until firm enough to handle. Sprinkle almonds in bottom of prepared pan. Spread chocolate mixture evenly over almonds. Refrigerate 2 hours or until firm. Cut into squares.

**Make-Ahead:** *Can be prepared up to 3 weeks ahead for gift-giving. Store in an airtight container between layers of wax paper in the refrigerator.*

**Bittersweet Chocolate Truffle Balls:** *Prepare as directed, shaping mixture into 1-inch balls. Roll in cocoa, BAKER'S® ANGEL FLAKE® Coconut, cookie crumbs or nuts. Store in refrigerator. Makes about 2 dozen.*

# Candy Crunch

| | | |
|---|---|---|
| 4 cups (half of 15-ounce bag) pretzel sticks or pretzel twists<br>1 (14-ounce) can EAGLE® BRAND Sweetened Condensed Milk (NOT evaporated milk) | 2 (10- to 12-ounce) packages premium white chocolate chips<br>1 cup dried fruit, such as dried cranberries, raisins or mixed dried fruit bits | **Makes about 1¾ pounds** |

**Prep Time:**
*15 minutes*

**Chill Time:**
*1 to 2 hours*

*1.* Line 15×10-inch baking pan with foil. Place pretzels in large mixing bowl.

*2.* In large saucepan over medium-low heat, heat Eagle Brand until warm, about 5 minutes. Remove from heat and immediately stir in white baking pieces until melted. Pour over pretzels, stirring to coat.

*3.* Immediately spread mixture in prepared pan. Sprinkle with dried fruit; press down lightly with back of spoon.

*4.* Chill 1 to 2 hours or until set. Break into chunks. Store loosely covered at room temperature.

*Note:*

White chocolate is not considered real chocolate since it contains no chocolate liquor (the main component in unsweetened chocolate). It is a combination of cocoa butter, sugar, milk solids, vanilla and emulsifiers, commonly available in chips and baking bars.

# Chocolate Peppermint Wafers

**Makes about 3 dozen candies**

3 bars (6-ounce box) NESTLÉ® TOLL HOUSE® Premier White Baking Bars, broken into pieces

12 (about ⅓ cup) coarsely crushed unwrapped hard peppermint candies

1 cup (6 ounces) NESTLÉ® TOLL HOUSE® Semi-Sweet Chocolate Morsels

1 tablespoon vegetable shortening

LINE 8-inch-square baking pan with foil.

**MICROWAVE** baking bars in medium, microwave-safe bowl on MEDIUM-HIGH (70%) power for 1 minute; stir. Microwave at additional 10- to 20-second intervals, stirring until smooth. Stir in candy. Thinly spread into prepared baking pan. Refrigerate for 10 minutes or until firm.

**REMOVE** foil from candy; break into bite-size pieces.

**LINE** baking sheets with wax paper.

**MICROWAVE** morsels and vegetable shortening in small, microwave-safe bowl on HIGH (100%) power for 1 minute; stir. Microwave at additional 10- to 20-second intervals, stirring until smooth.

**DIP** candy pieces ¾ of the way into melted chocolate; shake off excess. Place on prepared baking sheets. Refrigerate until ready to serve.

**Tip:** *To crush candies, place in* heavy-duty *resealable plastic food storage bag; close. Crush with rolling pin or mallet.*

# English Toffee

1 cup butter or margarine
1 cup granulated sugar
1 cup BLUE DIAMOND®
    Chopped Natural Almonds,
    divided

⅓ cup semi-sweet real
    chocolate pieces

**Makes about
1½ pounds**

Combine butter and sugar in heavy skillet; cook, stirring, until boiling point is reached. Boil mixture over medium heat, stirring constantly, to soft crack stage, 270° to 280°F, or until a little mixture dropped in cold water becomes hard and brittle. Remove from heat and stir in ½ cup of the almonds. Pour into buttered 11×7-inch pan; let stand 10 minutes or until top is set. Sprinkle chocolate over top of candy. When chocolate has melted, smooth with spatula; sprinkle remaining almonds over chocolate. Let stand until set; break into bite-size pieces.

## *Taking a temperature—without a thermometer*

*Temperature is a guide as to when a sugar and water syrup has reached its proper stage. If you don't have a candy thermometer, use the cold water test: Let a drop or two of hot syrup fall into a cup of very cold water, then remove it with your fingers. If it hasn't reached the desired stage, continue cooking and test again. These are the stages in making candy:*

**Soft-ball (234° to 240°F):** Cooled syrup can be rolled into a soft ball that flattens when removed from water.

**Firm-ball (244° to 248°F):** Syrup can be molded into a ball that retains its shape a little longer than the soft-ball. It will feel firm but still sticky.

**Hard-ball (250° to 266°F):** Syrup can be rolled into a firm ball that gives some resistance when pressed.

**Soft-crack (270° to 290°F):** Syrup can be stretched into strands that are hard but elastic.

**Hard-crack (300° to 310°F):** Syrup forms strands that are hard and brittle and can easily be snapped in half.

# Mocha Truffles

**Makes about 16 truffles**

¼ cup whipping cream
3 tablespoons sugar
3 tablespoons butter
1½ teaspoons powdered instant coffee
½ cup HERSHEY⅋S Semi-Sweet Chocolate Chips

½ teaspoon vanilla extract
Chopped nuts or HERSHEY⅋S Semi-Sweet Baking Chocolate, grated

*1.* Combine whipping cream, sugar, butter and instant coffee in small saucepan. Cook over low heat, stirring constantly, just until mixture boils.

*2.* Remove from heat; immediately add chocolate chips. Stir until chips are melted and mixture is smooth when stirred; add vanilla. Pour into small bowl; refrigerate, stirring occasionally, until mixture begins to set. Cover; refrigerate several hours or overnight to allow mixture to ripen and harden.

*3.* Shape small amounts of mixture into 1-inch balls, working quickly to prevent melting; roll in nuts or chocolate. Cover; store in refrigerator. Serve cold.

# Festive Black or White Peanut Clusters

**Makes 2 dozen**

1 cup (6 ounces) semisweet chocolate chips or white chocolate chips

½ cup creamy peanut butter
1 teaspoon shortening
1 cup roasted peanuts

**Microwave Directions**

Place chocolate in 1½-quart microwavable dish. Microwave on HIGH 2 to 3 minutes or until melted. Add peanut butter and shortening; microwave on HIGH 1 to 2 minutes or until mixture is smooth and creamy. Blend well. Stir in peanuts. Drop by teaspoonfuls onto waxed paper-lined cookie sheet; chill until set. Store in refrigerator.

Favorite recipe from **Texas Peanut Producers Board**

# Fudgy Banana Rocky Road Clusters

| | | |
|---|---|---|
| 1 package (12 ounces) semisweet chocolate chips (2 cups) ⅓ cup peanut butter | 3 cups miniature marshmallows 1 cup unsalted peanuts 1 cup banana chips | Makes 2½ to 3 dozen clusters |

Line baking sheets with waxed paper. Grease waxed paper.

Place chocolate chips and peanut butter in large microwavable bowl. Microwave at HIGH 2 minutes or until chips are melted and mixture is smooth, stirring twice. Fold in marshmallows, peanuts and banana chips.

Drop rounded tablespoonfuls candy mixture onto prepared baking sheets; refrigerate until firm. Store in airtight container in refrigerator.

**Tip:** *If you prefer more nuts, use chunky peanut butter.*

# Choco-Peanut Pinwheels

| Makes about 1½ pounds | 1 cup (6 ounces) peanut butter-flavored chips<br>1 (14-ounce) can EAGLE® BRAND Sweetened Condensed Milk (NOT evaporated milk), divided | 1 cup (6 ounces) semi-sweet chocolate chips<br>1 teaspoon vanilla extract |
| --- | --- | --- |

*1.* Cut waxed paper into 15×10-inch rectangle; butter paper.

*2.* In heavy saucepan over low heat, melt peanut butter chips with ⅔ cup Eagle Brand. Cool slightly. With fingers, press evenly into thin layer to cover waxed paper. Let stand at room temperature 15 minutes.

*3.* In heavy saucepan over low heat, melt chocolate chips with remaining Eagle Brand. Remove from heat; stir in vanilla. Spread evenly over peanut butter layer. Let stand at room temperature 30 minutes.

*4.* Beginning at 15-inch side, roll up tightly, jelly-roll fashion, without waxed paper. Wrap tightly in plastic wrap.

*5.* Chill 2 hours or until firm. Cut into ¼-inch slices to serve. Store covered at room temperature.

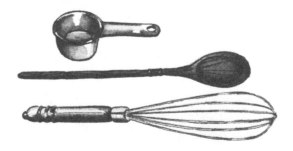

# Carnation® Famous Fudge

1½ cups granulated sugar
⅔ cup (5 fluid-ounce can)
   NESTLÉ® CARNATION®
   Evaporated Milk
2 tablespoons butter or
   margarine
¼ teaspoon salt

2 cups miniature marshmallows
1½ cups (9 ounces) NESTLÉ®
   TOLL HOUSE® Semi-Sweet
   Chocolate Morsels
½ cup chopped pecans or
   walnuts (optional)
1 teaspoon vanilla extract

**Makes about
49 pieces**

LINE 8-inch-square baking pan with foil.

COMBINE sugar, evaporated milk, butter and salt in medium, *heavy-duty* saucepan. Bring to a *full rolling boil* over medium heat, stirring constantly. Boil, stirring constantly, for 4 to 5 minutes. Remove from heat.

STIR in marshmallows, morsels, nuts and vanilla extract. Stir vigorously for 1 minute or until marshmallows are melted. Pour into prepared baking pan; refrigerate for 2 hours or until firm. Lift from pan; remove foil. Cut into pieces.

**For Milk Chocolate Fudge:** *SUBSTITUTE 1¾ cups (11.5-ounce package) NESTLÉ® TOLL HOUSE® Milk Chocolate Morsels for Semi-Sweet Morsels.*

**For Butterscotch Fudge:** *SUBSTITUTE 1⅔ cups (11-ounce package) NESTLÉ® TOLL HOUSE® Butterscotch Flavored Morsels for Semi-Sweet Morsels.*

**For Peanutty Chocolate Fudge:** *SUBSTITUTE 1⅔ cups (11-ounce package) NESTLÉ® TOLL HOUSE® Peanut Butter & Milk Chocolate Morsels for Semi-Sweet Morsels and ½ cup chopped peanuts for pecans or walnuts.*

*Note:*

Don't allow fudge to sit out at room temperature too long before cutting it—it is much easier to cut into neat squares when the fudge is firm and cold.

# Fudge Rum Balls

**Makes 6 dozen**

1 package DUNCAN HINES®
    Moist Deluxe® Butter Recipe
    Fudge Cake Mix
1 cup finely chopped pecans or
    walnuts
1 tablespoon rum extract

2 cups sifted confectioners'
    sugar
¼ cup unsweetened cocoa
    powder
Pecans or walnuts,
    finely chopped

*1.* Preheat oven to 375°F. Grease and flour 13×9×2-inch baking pan. Prepare, bake and cool cake following package directions.

*2.* Crumble cake into large bowl. Stir with fork until crumbs are fine and uniform in size. Add 1 cup nuts, rum extract, confectioners' sugar and cocoa. Stir until well blended.

*3.* Shape heaping tablespoonfuls of mixture into balls. Garnish by rolling balls in finely chopped nuts. Press firmly to adhere nuts to balls.

<u>**Tip:**</u> *Substitute rum for rum extract.*

# Peter Pan's Coconut Clusters

**Makes 18 candy clusters**

1 (8-ounce) package hard shell
    chocolate
½ cup PETER PAN® Creamy
    Peanut Butter

2 cups shredded coconut
¾ cup peanuts, coarsely
    chopped

*1.* In microwave-safe bowl, melt chocolate pieces and Peter Pan Peanut Butter in microwave on HIGH for 30-second intervals, until chocolate is melted. Stir after *each* interval; blend well.

*2.* Add coconut and peanuts; stir gently until well coated.

*3.* Drop by teaspoonfuls onto waxed paper-lined baking sheet. Let candy clusters harden completely before serving.

# Fast and Easy Microwave Peanut Brittle

**Makes 1 pound**

1 cup granulated sugar
½ cup light corn syrup
2 tablespoons water
⅛ teaspoon salt

1¼ cups Spanish peanuts
1 tablespoon butter or
   margarine
1 teaspoon baking soda

## Microwave Directions

In 2½-quart microwavable mixing bowl, combine sugar, corn syrup, water and salt; stir well. Cook uncovered on HIGH 5 minutes. Stir in peanuts and cook uncovered 3 to 5 minutes or until syrup reaches hard crack stage and is lightly golden in color. (The hard crack stage is achieved when a little candy syrup dropped into ice water separates into hard, brittle threads.) Remove from microwave; stir in butter and baking soda. Pour mixture onto oiled baking sheet, spreading to ¼-inch thickness. When cool, break into pieces and store in airtight container.

Favorite recipe from **The Sugar Association, Inc.**

# Almond Butterscotch Brittle

| Makes about 1¼ pounds | |
|---|---|
| 2 cups packed light brown sugar<br>⅔ cup light corn syrup<br>¼ cup water | ¼ cup half and half<br>¼ cup butter<br>1 cup BLUE DIAMOND® Chopped Natural Almonds |

Butter 13×9×2-inch baking pan. In large saucepan combine brown sugar, corn syrup, water and half and half; bring to boil, stirring constantly until sugar dissolves. Cook, stirring often, until candy thermometer reaches 260°F or until small amount of mixture dropped into very cold water forms a hard ball. Add butter and cook, stirring, until 280°F is reached or until small amount of mixture dropped into very cold water separates into threads which are hard but not brittle, in the soft crack stage. Remove from heat; quickly stir in almonds. Pour into prepared pan. When set, turn out of pan and break into bite-size pieces.

# Hershey's Buckeyes

| Makes about 5 dozen candies | |
|---|---|
| 1⅓ cups REESE'S® Crunchy Peanut Butter<br>¾ cup (1½ sticks) butter or margarine, softened<br>3 cups powdered sugar<br>2 cups (12-ounce package) HERSHEY'S Semi-Sweet Chocolate Chips | 1 tablespoon shortening (do *not* use butter, margarine, spread or oil) |

**Prep Time:**
*30 minutes*

**Chill Time:**
*1½ hours*

**Cook Time:**
*1½ minutes*

**Cool Time:**
*1 hour*

*1.* Beat peanut butter and butter in large bowl until blended. Gradually add powdered sugar, beating until well blended. Cover; refrigerate until firm enough to shape, about 30 minutes.

*2.* Shape into 1-inch balls. Cover; refrigerate until firm, about 1 hour.

*3.* Place chocolate chips and shortening in medium microwave-safe bowl. Microwave at HIGH (100%) 1½ minutes; stir. If necessary, microwave at HIGH an additional 15 seconds at a time, stirring after each heating, just until chips are melted when stirred.

*4.* Dip each ball into chocolate mixture, coating ¾ of ball. Place on wax paper, uncoated side up. Let stand until chocolate hardens. Store, covered, in refrigerator.

# Dark Chocolate Truffles

1⅔ cups chopped semisweet
   chocolate or semisweet
   chocolate chips
6 tablespoons whipping cream
1 tablespoon cold butter, cut
   into pieces

1 teaspoon vanilla extract
½ cup chopped macadamia
   nuts, chopped toffee or
   chocolate decors

**Makes 18 truffles**

Place chocolate in small bowl. Heat whipping cream and butter in small saucepan over medium-high heat until butter melts, stirring constantly. Pour over chocolate; stir once. Cover and let stand 3 to 5 minutes. Uncover; stir until chocolate is melted and mixture is smooth. Stir in vanilla; cover and refrigerate 15 minutes or until mixture is firm enough to hold its shape. Place level tablespoonfuls mixture on plate. Cover; refrigerate 2 hours or until fudgy, but not soft. Place nuts in shallow bowl. Roll each tablespoon chocolate mixture into ball; roll in nuts to evenly coat. Store tightly covered in refrigerator up to 3 weeks. Serve chilled or let stand at room temperature 15 to 20 minutes before serving.

# Peanut Butter Cups

| Makes 12 cups | | |
|---|---|---|

2 cups (12 ounces) semisweet chocolate chips
1 cup (6 ounces) milk chocolate chips
1½ cups powdered sugar
1 cup crunchy or smooth peanut butter

½ cup vanilla wafer crumbs (about 11 wafers)
6 tablespoons butter or margarine, softened

Line 12 (2½-inch) muffin cups with double-thickness paper cups or foil cups; set aside.

Melt both chips in heavy, small saucepan over very low heat, stirring constantly. Spoon about 1 tablespoonful chocolate into each cup. With back of spoon, bring chocolate up side of each cup. Refrigerate until firm, about 20 minutes.

Combine sugar, peanut butter, crumbs and butter in medium bowl. Spoon 2 tablespoons peanut butter mixture into each chocolate cup. Spread with small spatula.

Spoon about 1 tablespoon remaining chocolate over each peanut butter cup. Refrigerate until firm.

**Tip:** *To remove paper cups, cut slit in bottom of paper and peel paper up from bottom. Do not peel paper down from top edge.*

# Orange Creams

| Makes about 36 creams | | |
|---|---|---|

2¼ to 2½ cups powdered sugar
3 tablespoons frozen orange juice concentrate*
1 tablespoon grated orange peel

Additional powdered sugar for rolling

*\*Or, substitute any flavor frozen juice concentrate.*

*1.* Line baking sheet with buttered waxed paper; set aside.

*2.* Combine 2¼ cups sugar, orange juice concentrate and orange peel in small bowl, adding more sugar if needed to make a stiff dough. Form dough into ball; wrap in plastic wrap. Refrigerate 30 minutes.

*3.* Roll out dough to ¼-inch thickness on surface covered with powdered sugar. Cut into 1½-inch shapes. Arrange on prepared baking sheet. Refrigerate, uncovered, overnight.

*4.* Store in refrigerator in tightly sealed container between layers of waxed paper.

<u>Hint:</u> *Keep refrigerated to make serving easier.*

# Rocky Road Clusters

| | | Makes about 2 dozen candies |
|---|---|---|
| 2 cups (12-ounce package) NESTLÉ® TOLL HOUSE® Semi-Sweet Chocolate Morsels<br>1 can (14 ounces) NESTLÉ® CARNATION® Sweetened Condensed Milk | 2½ cups miniature marshmallows<br>1 cup coarsely chopped nuts<br>1 teaspoon vanilla extract | |

**LINE** baking sheets with waxed paper.

**COMBINE** morsels and sweetened condensed milk in large, microwave-safe bowl. Microwave on HIGH (100%) power for 1 minute; stir. Microwave at additional 10- to 20-second intervals, stirring until smooth. Stir in marshmallows, nuts and vanilla extract.

**DROP** by heaping tablespoon in mounds onto prepared baking sheets. Refrigerate until firm.

# Fruit Bon Bons

Makes about 5 dozen candies

1 (14-ounce) can EAGLE®
   BRAND Sweetened
   Condensed Milk
   (NOT evaporated milk)
2 (7-ounce) packages flaked
   coconut (5⅓ cups)
1 (6-ounce) package
   fruit-flavored gelatin,
   any flavor, divided

1 cup ground blanched
   almonds
1 teaspoon almond extract
   Food coloring, if desired

*Note:*

Make Fruit Bon Bons part of a holiday-themed gift basket of homemade treats. Vary the gelatin color according to the holiday: use red for Valentine's Day, orange for Halloween and red and green for Christmas.

*1.* In large mixing bowl, combine Eagle Brand, coconut, ⅓ cup gelatin, almonds, almond extract and enough food coloring to tint mixture desired shade, if desired. Chill 1 hour or until firm enough to handle.

*2.* Using about ½ tablespoon mixture for each, shape into 1-inch balls. Sprinkle remaining gelatin onto waxed paper; roll each ball in gelatin to coat.

*3.* Place on waxed-paper-lined baking sheets; chill.

*4.* Store covered at room temperature or in refrigerator.

**Strawberry Bon Bons:** *Using strawberry-flavored gelatin, prepare bon bon mixture as directed above. Form into strawberry shapes. In medium mixing bowl, combine 2¼ cups sifted powdered sugar, 3 tablespoons whipping cream and a few drops green food coloring (or use green tube decorator icing). Using pastry bag with open star tip, pipe small amount on top of each strawberry for stem.*

# Quick Holiday Raspberry Fudge

3⅓ cups (two 10-ounce packages) HERSHEY᳓S Raspberry Chips or 3⅓ cups HERSHEY᳓S Semi-Sweet Chocolate Chips

1 can (14 ounces) sweetened condensed milk (not evaporated milk)
1½ teaspoons vanilla extract or raspberry-flavored liqueur

**Makes about 4 dozen pieces or 2 pounds**

**Prep Time:**
*5 minutes*

**Cook Time:**
*1 minute*

**Chill Time:**
*2 hours*

*1.* Line 8-inch square pan with foil, extending foil over edges of pan.

*2.* Place raspberry chips and sweetened condensed milk in medium microwave safe bowl. Microwave at HIGH (100%) 1 minute; stir. If necessary, microwave an additional 30 seconds at a time, stirring after each heating, just until chips are melted and mixture is smooth when stirred; stir in vanilla. Spread evenly into prepared pan.

*3.* Cover; refrigerate 2 hours or until firm. Remove from pan; place on cutting board. Peel off foil; cut into squares. Store loosely covered at room temperature.

<u>Note:</u> *For best results, do not double this recipe.*

# Chocolate Caramel Drops

**Makes about 2 dozen**

**Prep Time:**
*20 minutes plus standing*

24 caramels (about 7 ounces), unwrapped
2 tablespoons heavy (whipping) cream

1 cup pecan halves
4 squares BAKER'S®
   Semi-Sweet Baking
   Chocolate, melted

**MICROWAVE** caramels and cream in large microwavable bowl on HIGH 1½ minutes; stir. Microwave 1½ minutes; stir until caramels are completely melted. Cool.

**PLACE** pecan halves on lightly greased cookie sheets in clusters of 3. Spoon caramel mixture over nuts, leaving ends showing. Spread melted chocolate over caramel mixture. Let stand until chocolate is set.

<u>**Top of Stove Preparation:**</u> *Heat caramels and cream in heavy 2-quart saucepan on very low heat until caramels are melted, stirring constantly. Continue as directed above.*

# Truffle Treats

6 squares BAKER'S® Semi-
Sweet Baking Chocolate
¼ cup (½ stick) margarine
2⅔ cups (7 ounces) BAKER'S®
ANGEL FLAKE® Coconut
1 package (8 ounces)
PHILADELPHIA® Cream
Cheese, softened

2½ cups cold half-and-half *or* milk
1 package (6-serving size)
JELL-O® Chocolate Flavor
Instant Pudding
& Pie Filling
2 tablespoons unsweetened
cocoa
1 tablespoon powdered sugar

**Makes about
20 pieces**

**Prep Time:**
*15 minutes plus
freezing*

**PLACE** chocolate in heavy saucepan over very low heat; stir constantly until just melted. Remove 2 tablespoons of the melted chocolate; set aside.

**STIR** margarine into remaining chocolate in saucepan until melted. Gradually stir in coconut, tossing to coat evenly. Press mixture into 13×9-inch baking pan which has been lined with foil.

**BEAT** cream cheese at medium speed of electric mixer until smooth; beat in reserved 2 tablespoons chocolate. Gradually mix in half-and-half. Add pudding mix. Beat at low speed until well blended, about 1 minute. Pour over crust. Freeze until firm, about 4 hours or overnight.

**MIX** together cocoa and sugar in small bowl; sift over truffle mixture. Lift with foil from pan onto cutting board; let stand 10 minutes to soften slightly. Cut into diamonds, squares or triangles.

*Note:*

Lining a pan with foil allows you to lift out the whole candy onto a cutting board. Then you can make firm, downward cuts with a knife—very difficult to do when cutting in the pan. You'll have neat pieces, no scratches on the bottom of the pan and no mess to clean up!

# Pecan Rolls

**Makes 6 (5-inch) rolls**

1¼ cups sugar
¼ cup corn syrup
¼ cup water
1 egg white
⅛ teaspoon cream of tartar
1 teaspoon vanilla

1 package (14 ounces)
   caramels, unwrapped
3 tablespoons water
2 cups coarsely chopped
   pecans

*Note:*

**Never try to rush a candy mixture by cooking it at a higher temperature than the recipe directs.**

*1.* Line 9×5-inch loaf pan with buttered waxed paper; set aside. Combine sugar, corn syrup and water in heavy, small saucepan. Cook over medium heat, stirring constantly, until sugar dissolves and mixture comes to a boil. Wash down side of pan frequently with pastry brush dipped in hot water to remove sugar crystals. Carefully clip candy thermometer to side of pan (do not let bulb touch bottom of pan.) Continue to cook until mixture reaches the hard-ball stage (255°F).

*2.* Meanwhile, beat egg white and cream of tartar with heavy-duty electric mixer until stiff but not dry. Slowly pour hot syrup into egg white mixture, beating constantly. Add vanilla; beat until candy forms soft peaks and starts to lose its gloss. Spoon mixture into prepared pan. Cut into 3 strips lengthwise, then crosswise in center. Freeze until firm.

*3.* Line baking sheet with waxed paper; set aside. Melt caramels with water in heavy, small saucepan over low heat, stirring occasionally. Arrange pecans on waxed paper. Working quickly, drop 1 piece of frozen candy mixture into melted caramels to coat. Roll in pecans to coat completely and shape into log. Place on prepared baking sheet to set. Repeat with remaining candy pieces, reheating caramels if mixture becomes too thick.

*4.* Cut logs into ½-inch slices. Refrigerate in airtight container between layers of waxed paper or freeze up to 3 months.

**Tip:** *For perfect slices, freeze finished rolls before cutting.*

# Easy Toffee Candy

1¼ cups (2½ sticks) butter,
   *divided*
35 to 40 soda crackers
1 cup packed dark brown sugar
1 can (14 ounces) NESTLÉ®
   CARNATION® Sweetened
   Condensed Milk

1½ cups (9 ounces) NESTLÉ®
   TOLL HOUSE® Semi-Sweet
   Chocolate Morsels
¾ cup finely chopped walnuts

Makes about
50 pieces

**PREHEAT** oven to 425°F. Line 15×10-inch jelly-roll pan with *heavy-duty* foil.

**MELT** *¼ cup (½ stick)* butter in medium saucepan. Pour into prepared jelly-roll pan. Arrange crackers over butter, breaking crackers to fit empty spaces.

**MELT** *remaining* butter in same saucepan; add sugar. Bring to a boil over medium heat. Reduce heat to low; cook, stirring occasionally, for 2 minutes. Remove from heat; stir in sweetened condensed milk. Pour over crackers.

**BAKE** for 10 to 12 minutes or until mixture is bubbly and slightly darkened. Remove from oven; cool for 1 minute.

**SPRINKLE** with morsels. Let stand for 5 minutes or until morsels are shiny and soft; spread evenly. Sprinkle with nuts; press into chocolate. Cool in pan on wire rack for 30 minutes. Refrigerate for about 30 minutes or until chocolate is set. Remove foil; cut into pieces.

# Tiger Stripes

| Makes 36 pieces |
| --- |

1 package (12 ounces)
    semisweet chocolate chips
3 tablespoons chunky peanut
    butter, divided

2 (2-ounce) white chocolate
    baking bars

Line 8-inch square pan with foil. Grease lightly. Melt semisweet chocolate and 2 tablespoons peanut butter in small saucepan over low heat; stir well. Pour half of chocolate mixture into prepared pan. Let stand 10 to 15 minutes to cool slightly. Melt white baking bars with remaining 1 tablespoon peanut butter over low heat in small saucepan. Spoon half of white chocolate mixture over dark chocolate mixture. Drop remaining dark and white chocolate mixtures by spoonfuls over mixture in pan. Using small metal spatula or knife, pull through the chocolates to create tiger stripes. Freeze about 1 hour or until firm. Remove from pan; peel off foil. Cut into 36 pieces. Refrigerate until ready to serve.

# Almond Butter Crunch

| Makes about ¾ pound |
| --- |

1 cup BLUE DIAMOND®
    Blanched Slivered Almonds
½ cup butter

½ cup sugar
1 tablespoon light corn syrup

Line bottom and side of 8- or 9-inch cake pan with aluminum foil (not plastic wrap or wax paper). Butter foil heavily; set aside. Combine almonds, butter, sugar and corn syrup in 10-inch skillet. Bring to a boil over medium heat, stirring constantly. Boil, stirring constantly, until mixture turns golden brown, about 5 to 6 minutes. Working quickly, spread candy in prepared pan. Cool about 15 minutes or until firm. Remove candy from pan by lifting edges of foil. Peel off foil. Cool thoroughly. Break into pieces.

# Peanut Butter Bon Bons

**Makes 100 candies**

2 cups creamy peanut butter
½ cup butter or margarine
4½ cups sifted powdered sugar
3 cups rice cereal, crushed
    (measure before crushing)
6 ounces butterscotch chips
    (1 cup)*

6 ounces semi-sweet chocolate chips (1 cup)*

*Substitute 1 pound of chocolate candy coating for butterscotch and chocolate chips, if desired.

Melt peanut butter and butter or margarine over low heat. In a separate bowl, mix powdered sugar and rice cereal. Pour peanut butter mixture over cereal mixture. Mix with spoon; then blend together with hands and form into small balls. If mixture is too dry, add 1 to 2 tablespoons of water. Chill balls on waxed paper-lined cookie sheets. Melt chips in double boiler. Dip balls in melted chocolate and place on lined cookie sheets. Chill and store in airtight container.

Favorite recipe from **Peanut Advisory Board**

# Chocolate Buttercream Cherry Candies

**Makes about 48 candies**

About 48 maraschino cherries with stems, well drained
¼ cup (½ stick) butter, softened
2 cups powdered sugar
¼ cup HERSHEY:S Cocoa or HERSHEY:S Dutch Processed Cocoa

1 to 2 tablespoons milk, divided
½ teaspoon vanilla extract
¼ teaspoon almond extract
White Chip Coating (recipe follows)
Chocolate Chip Drizzle (recipe follows)

*Note:*

**Sifting the powdered sugar before using it will prevent the buttercream from being lumpy. (Be sure to measure the sugar before sifting.)**

*1.* Cover tray with wax paper. Lightly press cherries between layers of paper towels to remove excess moisture.

*2.* Beat butter, powdered sugar, cocoa and 1 tablespoon milk in small bowl until well blended; stir in vanilla and almond extract. If necessary, add remaining milk, one teaspoon at a time, until mixture will hold together but is not wet.

*3.* Mold scant teaspoon mixture around each cherry, covering completely; place on prepared tray. Cover; refrigerate 3 hours or until firm.

*4.* Prepare White Chip Coating. Holding each cherry by stem, dip into coating. Place on tray; refrigerate until firm.

*5.* About 1 hour before serving, prepare Chocolate Chip Drizzle; with tines of fork drizzle randomly over candies. Refrigerate until drizzle is firm. Store in refrigerator.

<u>**White Chip Coating:**</u> *Place 1⅔ cups (10-ounce package) HERSHEY:S Premier White Chips in small microwave-safe bowl; drizzle with 2 tablespoons vegetable oil. Microwave at HIGH (100%) 1 minute; stir. If necessary, microwave at HIGH an additional 15 seconds at a time, stirring after each heating just until chips are melted and mixture is smooth. If mixture thickens while coating, microwave at HIGH 15 seconds; stir until smooth.*

**Chocolate Chip Drizzle:** *Place ¼ cup HERSHEY®S Semi-Sweet Chocolate Chips and ¼ teaspoon shortening (do not use butter, margarine, spread or oil) in another small microwave-safe bowl. Microwave at HIGH (100%) 30 seconds to 1 minute; stir until chips are melted and mixture is smooth.*

# Toasted Almond Bark

| ½ cup slivered almonds<br>12 ounces white chocolate,<br>coarsely chopped | 1 tablespoon shortening | Makes about 1 pound |
|---|---|---|

*1.* Preheat oven to 325°F.

*2.* Spread almonds on baking sheet. Bake 12 minutes or until golden brown, stirring occasionally.

*3.* Meanwhile, butter another baking sheet. Spread warm almonds on buttered baking sheet.

*4.* Melt white chocolate with shortening in heavy, small saucepan over very low heat, stirring constantly.

*5.* Spoon evenly over almonds, spreading about ¼ inch thick. Refrigerate until almost firm.

*6.* Cut into squares, but do not remove from baking sheet. Refrigerate until firm.

# Milk Chocolate Almond Brickle

| Makes about 50 pieces | |
|---|---|
| 1¼ cups almonds, toasted and coarsely chopped<br>1 cup (2 sticks) butter<br>1½ cups packed brown sugar | 1¾ cups (11.5-ounce package) NESTLÉ® TOLL HOUSE® Milk Chocolate Morsels |

**SPRINKLE** nuts over bottom of well-greased 13×9-inch baking pan.

**MELT** butter in medium, *heavy-duty* saucepan over medium heat. Stir in sugar. Bring to a boil, stirring constantly. Boil, stirring constantly, for 7 minutes. Pour hot mixture over nuts; let stand for 5 minutes. Sprinkle with morsels. Let stand for 5 minutes or until morsels are shiny and soft; spread evenly.

**REFRIGERATE** for about 20 minutes. Break into bite-size pieces.

# Peanut Butter Blocks

| Makes about 3 pounds | | |
|---|---|---|
| **Prep Time:**<br>*15 minutes*<br><br>**Chill Time:**<br>*2 hours* | 1 (14-ounce) can EAGLE® BRAND Sweetened Condensed Milk (NOT evaporated milk)<br>1¼ cups creamy peanut butter<br>⅓ cup water<br>1 tablespoon vanilla extract | ½ teaspoon salt<br>1 cup cornstarch, sifted<br>1 pound vanilla-flavored candy coating*<br>2 cups peanuts, finely chopped<br><br>*Also called confectionery coating or almond bark. |

***1.*** In heavy saucepan, combine Eagle Brand, peanut butter, water, vanilla and salt; stir in cornstarch. Over medium heat, cook and stir until thickened and smooth.

*2.* Add candy coating; cook and stir until melted and smooth. Spread evenly in waxed-paper-lined 9-inch square pan. Chill 2 hours or until firm. Cut into squares; roll firmly in peanuts to coat. Store covered at room temperature or in refrigerator.

**Microwave Method:** *In 1-quart glass measure, combine Eagle Brand, peanut butter, water, vanilla and salt; stir in cornstarch. Microwave at HIGH (100% power) 2 minutes; mix well. In microwave-safe 2-quart glass measure, melt candy coating at MEDIUM (50% power) 3 to 5 minutes, stirring after each minute. Add peanut butter mixture; mix well. Proceed as directed above.*

# Triple Chocolate Squares

**Makes 64 squares**

1½ cups BLUE DIAMOND®
   Blanched Almond Paste,
   divided
8 ounces semisweet chocolate,
   melted

¾ cup softened butter, divided
8 ounces milk chocolate,
   melted
8 ounces white chocolate,
   melted

Line bottom and sides of 8-inch square pan with aluminum foil. Beat ½ cup almond paste with semisweet chocolate. Beat in ¼ cup butter. Spread evenly in bottom of prepared pan. Chill to harden. Beat ½ cup almond paste with milk chocolate. Beat in ¼ cup butter. Spread mixture evenly over chilled semisweet chocolate layer. Chill to harden. Beat remaining ½ cup almond paste with white chocolate. Beat in remaining ¼ cup butter. Spread mixture evenly over chilled milk chocolate layer. Chill. Remove candy from pan by lifting edges of foil. Peel off foil and cut candy into 1-inch squares.

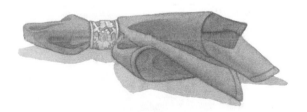

# Acknowledgments

The publisher would like to thank the companies and organizations listed below for the use of their recipes in this publication.

Almond Board of California

Arm & Hammer Division, Church & Dwight Co., Inc.

Birds Eye®

Blue Diamond Growers®

Bob Evans®

California Tree Fruit Agreement

Cherry Marketing Institute

Chilean Fresh Fruit Association

CHIPS AHOY!® Chocolate Chip Cookies

ConAgra Foods®

Dole Food Company, Inc.

Domino® Foods, Inc.

Duncan Hines® and Moist Deluxe® are registered trademarks of Aurora Foods Inc.

Eagle Brand®

Egg Beaters®

Filippo Berio® Olive Oil

Grandma's® is a registered trademark of Mott's, Inc.

Hershey Foods Corporation

JOLLY TIME® Pop Corn

Keebler® Company

Kraft Foods Holdings

© Mars, Incorporated 2003

Mauna La'i® is a registered trademark of Mott's, Inc.

McIlhenny Company (TABASCO® brand Pepper Sauce)

Mott's® is a registered trademark of Mott's, Inc.

Nabisco Biscuit and Snack Division

National Honey Board

Nestlé USA

Newman's Own, Inc.®

New York Apple Association, Inc.

North Dakota Wheat Commission

Northwest Cherry Growers

OREO® Chocolate Sandwich Cookies

Peanut Advisory Board

The Quaker® Oatmeal Kitchens

Riviana Foods Inc.

Sargento® Foods Inc.

The J.M. Smucker Company

Sokol and Company

Southeast United Dairy Industry Association, Inc.

The Sugar Association, Inc.

Property of © 2003 Sunkist Growers, Inc. All rights reserved

Texas Peanut Producers Board

Uncle Ben's Inc.

Unilever Bestfoods North America

USA Rice Federation

Walnut Marketing Board

Washington Apple Commission

Wisconsin Milk Marketing Board

# Index

**A**

**Almonds**
Almond Brownies, 412
Almond Butter Crunch, 676
Almond Butterscotch Brittle, 666
Almond Cherry Fudge Logs, 643
Almond Cream Cheese Cookies, 104
Almond Cream Cookies, 16
Almond Fudge Banana Cake, 432
Almond Kissed Cookies, 109
Almond Tea Cookies, 167
Almond Toffee Bars, 336
Bittersweet Chocolate Truffle Squares, 656
Butter Almond Classic Cookies, 145
Cherry Almond Clusters, 654
Chewy Fruit & Nut Bars, 344
Chocolate Almond Buttons, 127
Chocolate Amaretto Squares, 382
Chocolate Banana Stars, 232
Chocolate Butter Crunch, 646
Chocolate Chip Almond Oatmeal Cookies, 40
Cinnamon Crinkles, 161
Cocoa Almond Cut-Out Cookies, 82
Double Nut Chocolate Chip Cookies, 133
English Toffee, 659
Fabulous Blonde Brownies, 418
Fruit Bon Bons, 670
Holiday Almond Wreaths, 240
Macaroon Brownies, 418
Milk Chocolate Almond Brickle, 680
Nut Filling, 365
Nutty Footballs, 285

**Almonds** *(continued)*
Nutty Rich Cocoa Fudge, 642
Snow-Covered Almond Crescents, 153
Strawberry Bon Bons, 670
Toasted Almond Bark, 679
Triple Chocolate Squares, 681
Yuletide Linzer Bars, 228
Ambrosia, 555
Amy's Lemonade Mousse, 541
Angel Food Cake, 436
Angel Strawberry Bavarian, 582
Anna's Icing Oatmeal Sandwich Cookies, 268

**Apple**
Apple and Walnut Strudel, 599
Apple Cinnamon Glaze, 487
Apple Clafouti, 619
Apple Crisp, 593
Apple Crumb Squares, 348
Apple Custard Tart, 487
Apple Lemon Bars, 328
Apple-Lemon Sherbet, 570
Apple Pan Dowdy, 613
Apple Strudel Tarts with Vanilla Sauce, 497
Apple-Walnut "Pizza Pie," 634
Applesauce Molasses Snacking Cake, 465
Applesauce Raisin Chews, 33
"Best" Baked Apples, 587
Chocolate Peanut Brownie Bars, 389
Colorful Caramel Apples, 603
Fabulous Fondue, 627
Gingerbread Apple Bars, 226
Harvest Honey Spice Cake, 438
Hoosier Harvest Apple Pie, 519
Oatmeal Apple Cookies, 256
Razzle-Dazzle Apple Streusel Bars, 358
Rustic Apple Croustade, 489
Smucker's® Double Apple Turnovers, 625

**Apple** *(continued)*
Soft Apple Cider Cookies, 18
Spicy Applesauce Cake, 464
Walnut Apple Dumpling Bars, 379
Yummy Oatmeal Apple Cookie Squares, 377
Applesauce Molasses Snacking Cake, 465
Applesauce Raisin Chews, 33
**Apricot**
Apricot Crumb Squares, 371
Cherry Apricot Cornmeal Cobbler, 633
Peek-A-Boo Apricot Cookies, 77
Scrumptious Fruit and Nut Cookies, 45
White Chip Apricot Oatmeal Cookies, 170
Autumn Leaves, 87

**B**
Baked Custard, 636
Baker's® One Bowl Chocolate Fudge, 650
Baker's® Premium Chocolate Chunk Cookies, 21
Bananaramas, 280
**Bananas**
Almond Fudge Banana Cake, 432
Ambrosia, 555
Banana Chippers, 233
Banana Chocolate Chip Cheesecake, 478
Banana Chocolate Glaze, 432
Banana Cocoa Marbled Bars, 353
Banana Gingerbread Bars, 216
Banana Jewel Cake, 453
Banana Jumbles, 8
Banana Oatmeal Cookies with Banana Frosting, 27

**Bananas** *(continued)*
Banana Peanut Jumbles, 17
Banana Pudding, 564
Banana Rum Brownies, 385
Banana Sandies, 138
Banana Spice Lemon Drops, 36
Banana Split Cups, 262
Banana Split Dessert Pizza, 612
Bananaramas, 280
Bananas Foster, 622
Bananas with Caramel Sauce, 605
Basic Banana Holiday Cookies, 232
Blue's Best Banana Bread Pudding, 626
Chocolate Banana Stars, 232
Creamy Banana Pudding, 561
Double Decker Bars, 364
Fabulous Fondue, 627
Frozen Chocolate-Covered Bananas, 567
Frozen Peanut Butter-Banana Dessert, 575
Fruit Dessert Pizza, 584
Fudgy Banana Oat Cake, 476
Fudgy Banana Rocky Road Clusters, 661
Mint Chocolate Banana Bars, 378
No-Bake Banana Peanut Butter Fudge Bars, 309
Picture Perfect Creamy Banana Pie, 520
Ritzy Banana Cream Pie, 510
Strawberry-Banana Granité, 578
Zana Kringles, 233
**Bar Cookies** *(see also pages 325–382)*
Banana Gingerbread Bars, 216
Caramel Marshmallow Bars, 287
Chocolate Cereal Bars, 308
Citrus Cream Bars, 320
Conversation Hearts Cereal Treats, 180
Cookie Pizza, 255
Crispy Chocolate Logs, 305
Crispy Cocoa Bars, 315
"Everything but the Kitchen Sink" Bar Cookies, 265

**Bar Cookies** *(continued)*
Gingerbread Apple Bars, 226
Grand Old Flag Cookie, 190
Holiday Red Raspberry Chocolate Bars, 250
Jack-O-Lantern Bars, 196
Marshmallow Crispy Bars, 259
Microwave Double Peanut Bars, 317
Monkey Bars, 316
Nathaniel's Jumble, 310
No-Bake Banana Peanut Butter Fudge Bars, 309
No-Bake Chocolate Caramel Bars, 323
No-Bake Chocolate Oat Bars, 316
No-Bake Chocolate Peanut Butter Bars, 324
No-Bake Pineapple Marmalade Squares, 304
Oatmeal Carmelita Bars, 276
Outrageous Cookie Bars, 288
Peanut Butter Cereal Bars, 301
Peanut Butter Chocolate No-Bake Bars, 314
Peanut Butter-Hop-Scotch Treats, 321
Peanut Butter Power Bars, 305
Premier Cheesecake Cranberry Bars, 206
Pumpkin Cheesecake Bars, 214
Rocky Road Bars, 270
Rocky Road Peanut Butter Bars, 300
Scotcheroos, 312
Special Treat No-Bake Squares, 322
Sweetheart Layer Bars, 177
Three-in-One Chocolate Chip Cookies, 292
Triple Layer Chocolate Bars, 264
Uncle Sam's Hat, 192
White Chocolate Cranberry Cookie Bars, 230
Yuletide Linzer Bars, 228
Basic Banana Holiday Cookies, 232
Berlinerkranser (Little Wreaths), 224
Berry Treasures, 66
"Best" Baked Apples, 587

Biscochitos, 93
Bittersweet Chocolate Mints, 649
Bittersweet Chocolate Truffle Balls, 656
Bittersweet Chocolate Truffle Squares, 656
Black & White Bombe, 591
Black and White Chocolate Chunk Cookies, 28
Black and White Cutouts, 78
Black & White Hearts, 173
Black and White Sandwiches, 79
Blonde Brickle Bars, 391
**Blondies**
Blonde Brickle Bars, 391
Chewy Macadamia Nut Blondies, 407
Decadent Blonde Brownies, 405
Fabulous Blonde Brownies, 418
Festive Fruited White Chip Blondies, 430
Green's Butterscotch Blondies, 416
Mini Kisses Blondies, 384
Three Great Tastes Blond Brownies, 402
White Chip Island Blondies, 420
Blue's Best Banana Bread Pudding, 626
**Blueberry**
Blueberry Bread Pudding, 589
Blueberry Crisp Cupcakes, 620
Blueberry Crumble Pie, 521
Blueberry Sauce, 631
Blueberry Streusel Cobbler, 630
Michigan Blueberry Pie, 490
Mixed Berry Pie, 525
Mixed Berry Tart with Ginger-Raspberry Glaze, 501
Peachy Blueberry Pie, 495
Red, White & Blueberry Cream Pie, 530
Smucker's® English Berry Pudding, 551
Bourbon Pecan Pie, 523
Brownie Berry Parfaits, 557
Brownie Frosting, 425
Brownie Ice Cream Pie, 494

Brownie Mint Sundae Squares, 409
Brownie Raspberry Bars, 387
**Brownies**
Almond Brownies, 412
Banana Rum Brownies, 385
Brownie Berry Parfaits, 557
Brownie Ice Cream Pie, 494
Brownie Mint Sundae Squares, 409
Brownie Raspberry Bars, 387
Brrrrownie Cats, 203
Candy Bar Brownies, 406
Caramel Fudge Brownies, 428
Cheesecake Marble Brownies, 413
Chocolate Peanut Brownie Bars, 389
Cindy's Fudgy Brownies, 417
Cream Cheese Brownie Pie, 530
Cream Cheese Brownies, 404
Creamy Filled Brownies, 410
Divine Truffle Brownies, 400
Double Decadence Chocolate Chip Brownies, 390
Easy Double Chocolate Chip Brownies, 398
Frosted Maraschino Brownies, 397
Fruit & Pecan Brownies, 422
Fudge Topped Brownies, 415
Hershey's Best Brownies, 429
Hershey's Premium Double Chocolate Brownies, 384
Honey Brownies, 423
Irresistible Peanut Butter Chip Brownies, 425
Layers of Love Chocolate Brownies, 414
Luscious Brownie Chip Pie, 486
Macaroon Brownies, 418
Marbled Peanut Butter Brownies, 393, 426
Mississippi Mud Brownies, 396
Mocha Fudge Brownies, 424
No-Bake Fudgy Brownies, 313
Nuggets o' Gold Brownies, 403
Orange Cappuccino Brownies, 411
Ornament Brownies, 209

**Brownies** *(continued)*
Peanut Butter Layered Brownies, 394
Quick No-Bake Brownies, 419
Ricotta Cheese Brownies, 395
Rocky Road Brownies, 401
Scrumptious Minted Brownies, 422
Sensational Peppermint Pattie Brownies, 408
Sour Cream Brownies, 399
Supreme Chocolate Saucepan Brownies, 388
Toffee Brownie Bars, 386
Triple Chocolate Brownies, 421
White Chocolate Brownies, 427
Winter Wonderland Snowmen Brownies, 218
Brown Sugar Shortbread, 372
Brrrrownie Cats, 203
Butter Almond Classic Cookies, 145
Butter Cookie Dough, 172
Butterfly Cookies, 69
Butter Pecan Pie, 509
**Butterscotch**
Almond Butterscotch Brittle, 666
Butterscotch and Chocolate Bars, 367
Butterscotch Fudge, 663
Butterscotch Pan Cookies, 350
Butterscotch Pumpkin Cake, 441
Butterscotch Sauce, 441
Butterscotch Thins, 111
Choco-Scutterbotch, 166
Coconut Butterscotch Bars, 362
Fudgy Oatmeal Butterscotch Cookies, 39
Green's Butterscotch Blondies, 416
Haystacks, 303
No-Bake Butterscotch Haystacks, 319
Nutty Nougat Caramel Bites, 652
Oatmeal Scotchies, 47
Peanut Butter Bon Bons, 677
Peanut Butter-Hop-Scotch Treats, 321

**Butterscotch** *(continued)*
Scotcheroos, 312
S'More Cookie Bars, 361
Springtime Nests, 187
Buttery Almond Cutouts, 81
Buttery Black Raspberry Bars, 327

**C**
**Cakes**
Almond Fudge Banana Cake, 432
Angel Food Cake, 436
Applesauce Molasses Snacking Cake, 465
Banana Jewel Cake, 453
Butterscotch Pumpkin Cake, 441
Cappuccino Cake, 454
Carrot Cake, 457
Cherry-Mallow Cake, 473
Chocolate Bar Cake, 474
Chocolate Lovers' Cake, 451
Chocolate Sheet Cake, 444
Chocolate Truffle Cake with Strawberry Sauce, 472
"Cupcake" Fruitcakes, 480
Delicate White Chocolate Cake, 479
Fruity Jell-O® Cake, 464
Fudgy Banana Oat Cake, 476
Gingerbread Upside-Down Cake, 447
Glazed Pear Shortcake, 434
Grandma's Favorite Molasses Fruitcake, 480
Harvest Honey Spice Cake, 438
Hershey's Red Velvet Cake, 477
Lemonade Torte for a Long Hot Summer, 445
Mahogany Sour Cream Cake, 469
Maple Walnut Pound Cake, 440
Marble Chiffon Cake, 435
"Mini" Fruitcakes, 481
Miss Kathleen's Texas Sheet Cake, 468
Molten Mocha Cakes, 439
Oatmeal Chocolate Chip Cake, 460
Orange Mousse Cake, 483

**Cakes** *(continued)*
Oreo® White Chocolate Mousse Cake, 484
Peanut Butter Pudding Cake, 449
Pebbles and Stones Chocolate Cake, 437
Peppery Poundcake, 459
Pumpkin Cake with Orange Glaze, 452
Sour Cream Pound Cake, 436
Southern Jam Cake, 443
Spicy Applesauce Cake, 464
Strawberry Chocolate Chip Shortcake, 458
Texas Peanuts 'n' Caramel Cake, 482
Tropical Snack Cake, 455
Upside-Down German Chocolate Cake, 450
Velvety Chocolate Cake, 481
Zesty Lemon Pound Cake, 462
California Plum Sorbet, 541
Candied Orange Peel, 641
Candy Bar Brownies, 406
Candy Cane Cookies, 220
Candy Crunch, 657
Cappuccino Cake, 454
Cappuccino Cookies, 97
**Caramel**
Bananas with Caramel Sauce, 605
Blue's Best Banana Bread Pudding, 626
Caramel Flowers, 509
Caramel Fudge Brownies, 428
Caramel Marshmallow Bars, 287
Chocolate Caramel Drops, 672
Chocolate-Caramel Fondue, 636
Chocolate Caramel Nut Bars, 347
Chocolate Caramel Pie, 508
Chocolate-Caramel Sugar Cookies, 133
Colorful Caramel Apples, 603
Dulce de Leche Frozen Dessert, 572
No-Bake Chocolate Caramel Bars, 323

**Caramel** *(continued)*
Nutty Nougat Caramel Bites, 652
Oatmeal Carmelita Bars, 276
Old-Fashioned Caramel Pie, 493
Peanut Butter Caramel Macadamia Bars, 342
Pecan Rolls, 674
Texas Peanuts 'n' Caramel Cake, 482
Cardamom-Chocolate Sandwiches, 121
Caribbean Freeze, 536
Carnation® Famous Fudge, 663
Carnation® Key Lime Pie, 529
Carrot Cake, 457
**Cashews**
Cashew-Lemon Shortbread Cookies, 151
Cherry Cashew Cookies, 56
Championship Chocolate Chip Bars, 329
**Cheesecake**
Banana Chocolate Chip Cheesecake, 478
Blueberry Cheesecake, 483
Blueberry Cheesecake Bars, 332
Cheesecake Marble Brownies, 413
Chocolate Cheesecake Cupcakes, 600
Chocolate Cherry Cheesecake, 475
Chocolate Chip Cheesecake, 471
Chocolate Mini Cheesecakes, 470
Classic New York Cheesecake, 461
Frozen Chocolate Cheesecake, 549
Frozen Mocha Cheesecake Loaf, 544
Mini Cheesecakes, 470
Mocha Marble Cheesecake, 463
Peanut Butter Cheesecake, 467
Peanut Butter Chocolate Chip Cheesecake, 478

**Cheesecake** *(continued)*
Philadelphia® 3-Step® Chocolate Chip Cheesecake, 478
Pumpkin Cheesecake, 466
Raspberry Swirl Cheesecakes, 433
Reese's® Chocolate Peanut Butter Cheesecake, 446
Strawberry Cheesecake Squares, 352
Swirl of Chocolate Cheesecake Triangles, 373
Traditional Ricotta Cheesecake, 448
Tuxedo Cheesecake, 456
Velvet Chocolate Cheesecake, 442
White Chocolate Cheesecake Squares, 380
Cheesecake Marble Brownies, 413
**Cherries**
Almond Cherry Fudge Logs, 643
Cherries in the Snow Dessert, 539
Cherry Almond Clusters, 654
Cherry Apricot Cornmeal Cobbler, 633
Cherry Cashew Cookies, 56
Cherry Coconut Cookies, 160
Cherry Crisp, 590
Cherry-Mallow Cake, 473
Chocolate Buttercream Cherry Candies, 678
Chocolate Cherry Cheesecake, 475
Chocolate Cherry Cookies, 140
Fresh Cherry Jubilee, 598
Frosted Maraschino Brownies, 397
Holiday Hideaways, 248
No-Bake Cherry Crisps, 309
Power Bars, 341
Traditional Cherry Pie, 493
Walnut Cherry Fudge Logs, 643
Chess Pie, 522
Chewy Brownie Cookies, 32
Chewy Chocolate Chip Cookie Squares, 369
Chewy Chocolate-Cinnamon Cookies, 168

Chewy Chocolate No-Bakes, 318
Chewy Choco-Peanut Pudgies, 284
Chewy Fruit & Nut Bars, 344
Chewy Lemon-Honey Cookies, 15
Chewy Macadamia Nut Blondies, 407
Chewy Oatmeal Trail Mix Cookies, 35
Chewy Red Raspberry Bars, 354
Choco-Coco Pecan Crisps, 113
**Chocolate** *(see also* **Chocolate, Baking; Chocolate Chips; Cocoa; White Chocolate***)*
Almond Kissed Cookies, 109
Banana Rum Brownies, 385
Black & White Bombe, 591
Brownie Mint Sundae Squares, 409
Candy Bar Brownies, 406
Chocolate and Peanut Butter Hearts, 178
Chocolate Banana Stars, 232
Chocolate Bunny Cookies, 189
Chocolate Candy Bar Dessert, 608
Chocolate Caramel Pie, 508
Chocolate Macaroon Heath® Pie, 514
Chocolate Mint Ravioli Cookies, 89
Chocolate Oat Chewies, 147
Chocolate Peanut Butter Cookies, 272
Chocolate Peanut Butter Parfaits, 537
Chocolate Tiramisu Cupcakes, 610
Chocolate Toffee Bar Dessert, 628
Chocolate Toffee Layered Dessert, 552
Chocolate Triple Layer Pie, 531
Christmas Spirits, 235
Cindy's Fudgy Brownies, 417
Citrus Cream Bars, 320
Cookies and Cream Cheesecake Bonbons, 651
Cookies & Cream Cupcakes, 626
Creamy Cappuccino Frozen Dessert, 581

**Chocolate** *(continued)*
Decadent Triple Layer Mud Pie, 520
Double Chocolate Bread Pudding, 616
Double Chocolate Chewies, 367
Double Chocolate Delight, 543
Easy Eclair Dessert, 568
Famous Chocolate Refrigerator Roll, 631
Flourless Peanut Butter Cookies, 131
Frosted Maraschino Brownies, 397
Frozen Chocolate-Covered Bananas, 567
Frozen Mocha Cheesecake Loaf, 544
Fudge Rum Balls, 664
Fudgy Oatmeal Butterscotch Cookies, 39
Grasshopper Dessert, 607
Holiday Mini Kisses Treasure Cookies, 238
Ice Cream Cookie Dessert, 632
Ice Cream Cookie Sandwich, 586
Marshmallow Crispy Bars, 259
Mint Chocolate Banana Bars, 378
Mississippi Mud Brownies, 396
Mocha Meringue Pudding, 615
Orange Mousse Cake, 483
Oreo® Cookie Bread Pudding, 598
Oreo® Shazam Bars, 326
Peanut Blossom Cookies, 139
Peanut Butter & Chocolate Dipped Strawberries, 595
Peanut Butter Cup Cookie Ice Cream Pie, 496
Peanut Butter S'Mores, 297
Peppermint Patties, 639
Pinwheel Cookies, 108
Quick Chocolate Mousse, 576
Scrumptious Minted Brownies, 422
Simpler Than Sin Peanut Chocolate Cookies, 141
S'More Pie, 505
Sweetheart Layer Bars, 177
Swiss Chocolate Crispies, 152
Toffee Brownie Bars, 386

**Chocolate** *(continued)*
Trifle Spectacular, 624
Triple Chocolate Cookies, 25
Truffles, 638
Tuxedo Cheesecake, 456
Upside-Down German Chocolate Cake, 450
White Chocolate Cheesecake Squares, 380
**Chocolate, Baking**
Almond Brownies, 412
Baker's® One Bowl Chocolate Fudge, 650
Banana Chocolate Glaze, 432
Bittersweet Chocolate Mints, 649
Bittersweet Chocolate Truffle Balls, 656
Bittersweet Chocolate Truffle Squares, 656
Black & White Bombe, 591
Brrrrownie Cats, 203
Caramel Fudge Brownies, 428
Cheesecake Marble Brownies, 413
Cherry Almond Clusters, 654
Chocolate Almond Buttons, 127
Chocolate Bar Cake, 474
Chocolate Bursts, 50
Chocolate Caramel Drops, 672
Chocolate-Caramel Fondue, 636
Chocolate-Caramel Sugar Cookies, 133
Chocolate Cherry Cheesecake, 475
Chocolate Cherry Cookies, 140
Chocolate Cookie Dough, 179
Chocolate Crackletops, 298
Chocolate-Dipped Cinnamon Thins, 101
Chocolate-Dipped RITZ® Crackers, 511
Chocolate-Frosted Marshmallow Cookies, 283
Chocolate Fudge Pecan Bars, 343
Chocolate Leaves, 433
Chocolate Lovers' Cake, 451
Chocolate Mint Sandwiches, 110
Chocolate-Nut Cookies, 62

**Chocolate, Baking** (*continued*)

Chocolate Pudding Parfaits, 569

Chocolate-Raspberry Kolacky, 234

Chocolate-Raspberry Kolacky Cups, 235

Chocolate Reindeer, 243

Chocolate Spritz, 230

Chocolate Sugar Cookies, 132

Chocolate Truffle Loaf, 560

Chocolate Truffle Mousse, 571

Chocolate Walnut Truffles, 664

Cinnamon-Chocolate Cutouts, 67

Colorful Caramel Apples, 603

Cream Cheese Brownie Pie, 530

Cream Cheese Brownies, 404

Dark Chocolate Truffles, 667

Death By Chocolate Cookies, 48

Decadent Triple Layer Mud Pie, 520

Divine Truffle Brownies, 400

Double Chocolate Chunk Cookies, 165

Double Chocolate Orange Nut Fudge, 650

Double-Dipped Hazelnut Crisps, 76

Everything-But-The-Kitchen-Sink Cookies, 49

Frosted Maraschino Brownies, 397

Fruit & Pecan Brownies, 422

Fudge Frosting, 58

Heavenly Chocolate Mousse Pie, 527

Honey Fruit Truffles, 648

Layered Chocolate Cheese Bars, 374

Mahogany Sour Cream Cake, 469

Marbled Peanut Butter Brownies, 393, 426

Mint in the Mix Brownies, 392

Mocha Decadence Pie, 517

Mocha Fudge Brownies, 424

Mocha Melt Cookies, 38

Mocha Pecan Pinwheels, 106

Mocha Truffle Pie, 492

**Chocolate, Baking** (*continued*)

Molten Mocha Cakes, 439

Nathaniel's Jumble, 310

No-Bake Fudgy Brownies, 313

Nuggets o' Gold Brownies, 403

Orange Cappuccino Brownies, 411

Ornament Brownies, 209

Peanut Butter Caramel Macadamia Bars, 342

Peanut Butter-Hop-Scotch Treats, 321

Peanut Butter Layered Brownies, 394

Peanut Butter Pudding Cake, 449

Peek-A-Boo Apricot Cookies, 77

Quick No-Bake Brownies, 419

Ritzy Banana Cream Pie, 510

Rocky Road Brownies, 401

Special Treat No-Bake Squares, 322

Tinker Bell Peanut Butter Pie, 515

Triple Chocolate Brownies, 421

Triple Chocolate Squares, 681

Truffle Treats, 673

Velvety Chocolate Cake, 481

Walnut-Granola Clusters, 306

White Chocolate Chunk Cookies, 165

Chocolate-Amaretto Ice, 579

Chocolate Amaretto Squares, 382

Chocolate Bavarian Pie, 524

Chocolate Buttercream Cherry Candies, 678

Chocolate-Caramel Fondue, 636

Chocolate-Caramel Sugar Cookies, 133

**Chocolate Chips**

Almond Brownies, 412

Almond Cherry Fudge Logs, 643

Almond Toffee Bars, 336

Baker's® Premium Chocolate Chunk Cookies, 21

Banana Chippers, 233

Banana Chocolate Chip Cheesecake, 478

Bananaramas, 280

Black and White Chocolate Chunk Cookies, 28

**Chocolate Chips** (*continued*)

Black and White Cutouts, 78

Black & White Hearts, 173

Black and White Sandwiches, 79

Blue's Best Banana Bread Pudding, 626

Brownie Ice Cream Pie, 494

Brownie Raspberry Bars, 387

Butterscotch and Chocolate Bars, 367

Cardamom-Chocolate Sandwiches, 121

Carnation® Famous Fudge, 663

Championship Chocolate Chip Bars, 329

Chewy Brownie Cookies, 32

Chewy Chocolate Chip Cookie Squares, 369

Chewy Chocolate No-Bakes, 318

Chewy Choco-Peanut Pudgies, 284

Chewy Oatmeal Trail Mix Cookies, 35

Chocolate & Malt Bars, 330

Chocolate & Peanut Butter Tweed Cookies, 117

Chocolate Bursts, 50

Chocolate Butter Crunch, 646

Chocolate Caramel Nut Bars, 347

Chocolate Caramel Pie, 508

Chocolate Cereal Bars, 308

Chocolate Cheesecake Cupcakes, 600

Chocolate Cherry Cookies, 140

Chocolate Chip Almond Oatmeal Cookies, 40

Chocolate Chip Cheesecake, 471

Chocolate Chip Cookie Brittle, 640

Chocolate Chip Drizzle, 402, 679

Chocolate Chip Glaze, 86

Chocolate Chip Nougat, 644

Chocolate Chip Walnut Pie, 533

Chocolate Chunkaholic Cookies, 21

Chocolate Chunk Cookie Pie, 502

Chocolate Chunk Cookies, 126

**Chocolate Chips** *(continued)*
Chocolate Cookie Pops, 274
Chocolate Crackletops, 298
Chocolate Drizzle, 387
Chocolate Glaze, 82
Chocolate Haystacks, 319
Chocolate Hazelnut Terrine
   with Raspberry Sauce, 554
Chocolate Ice Cream Cups, 622
Chocolate Mini Cheesecakes,
   470
Chocolate Nut Bars, 337
Chocolate-Nut Cookies, 62
Chocolate Peanut Butter
   Fudge, 655
Chocolate Pecan Pie, 491
Chocolate Peppermint Wafers,
   658
Chocolate-Raspberry Cupcakes,
   594
Chocolate Raspberry Fudge,
   648
Chocolate Raspberry
   Thumbprints, 249
Chocolate Rice Pudding, 547
Chocolate Toffee Chip Popcorn
   Cookies, 14
Chocolate Truffle Cake with
   Strawberry Sauce, 472
Choco-Peanut Pinwheels, 662
Choco-Scutterbotch, 166
Chunky Milk Chocolate Chip
   Cookies, 6
Cinnamon Nut Chocolate
   Spirals, 119
Colorful Caramel Apples, 603
Colorful Cookie Buttons, 295
Confetti Chocolate Chip
   Cookies, 296
Cookie Pizza, 255
Cowboy Cookies, 14
Crayon Cookies, 277
Cream Cheese Chocolate Chip
   Pastry Cookies, 114
Crispy Chocolate Logs, 305
Crispy's Irresistible Peanut
   Butter Marbles, 257
Crunchy Chocolate Chip
   Cookies, 55
Dandy Candy Oatmeal Cookies,
   293
Decadent Blonde Brownies,
   405

**Chocolate Chips** *(continued)*
Deluxe Toll House® Mud Bars,
   336
Devil's Food Fudge Cookies,
   148
Dino-Mite Dinosaurs, 272
Double Chocolate Bread
   Pudding, 616
Double Chocolate Chewies, 367
Double Chocolate Chunk
   Cookies, 28, 165
Double Chocolate Cocoa
   Cupcakes, 635
Double Chocolate Dream
   Cookies, 30
Double Chocolate Peanut
   Butter Thumbprint Cookies,
   158
Double Decadence Chocolate
   Chip Brownies, 390
Double Nut Chocolate Chip
   Cookies, 133
Dress 'em Up Ginger People,
   245
Easy Double Chocolate Chip
   Brownies, 398
Easy Toffee Candy, 675
Edible Easter Baskets, 184
Emily's Dream Bars, 346
Fabulous Fondue, 627
Festive Black or White Peanut
   Clusters, 660
Fireballs, 641
Frosty's Colorful Cookies, 261
Frozen Chocolate Cheesecake,
   549
Fruit and Chocolate Dream
   Bars, 360
Fruit & Pecan Brownies, 422
Fruit-Filled Chocolate Chip
   Meringue Nests, 621
Fudge Cookies, 58
Fudge Topped Brownies, 415
Fudgy Banana Oat Cake, 476
Fudgy Banana Rocky Road
   Clusters, 661
Fudgy Oatmeal Butterscotch
   Cookies, 39
Gift Tag Cookies, 175
Gobble, Gobble, Gobblers,
   204
Granola & Chocolate Chip
   Cookies, 290

**Chocolate Chips** *(continued)*
Green's Butterscotch Blondies,
   416
Happy Face Oatmeal Monsters,
   291
Heavenly Oatmeal Hearts, 176
Hershey's Buckeyes, 666
Hershey's Classic Chocolate
   Chip Cookies, 9
Hershey's Mint Chocolate
   Cookies, 23
Hershey's Premium Double
   Chocolate Brownies, 384
Holiday Red Raspberry
   Chocolate Bars, 250
Honey Brownies, 423
Irish Chocolate Mint Dessert,
   588
Irresistible Peanut Butter Jack
   O'Lanterns, 194
Jolly Snowman Cookies, 222
Jumbo 3-Chip Cookies, 282
Kids' Favorite Jumbo Chippers,
   266
"M&M'S" Jam Sandwiches, 80
Marshmallow Crispy Bars, 259
Milk Chocolate Almond Brickle,
   680
Milk Chocolate Fudge, 663
MiniChip Glaze, 410
Mini Chip Slice and Bake
   Cookies, 120
Mini Chip Snowball Cookies,
   154
Mini Chocolate Pies, 498
Mini Kisses Blondies, 384
Mini Kisses Pumpkin Mousse
   Cups, 563
Mini Morsel Meringue Cookies,
   41
Mint Chocolate Pinwheels,
   100
Mint in the Mix Brownies,
   392
Mississippi Mud Bars, 355
Mississippi Mud Pie, 506
Mocha Fudge Brownies, 424
Mocha Truffles, 660
Mrs. J's Chip Cookies, 162
Nestlé® Toll House® Chocolate
   Chip Pie, 522
No-Bake Banana Peanut Butter
   Fudge Bars, 309

**Chocolate Chips** (*continued*)
No-Bake Chocolate Caramel Bars, 323
No-Bake Chocolate Oat Bars, 316
No-Bake Chocolate Peanut Butter Bars, 324
Nutty Chocolate Chunk Bars, 354
Nutty Nougat Caramel Bites, 652
Oatmeal Carmelita Bars, 276
Oatmeal Chocolate Chip Cake, 460
Oatmeal Toffee Lizzies, 136
"Orange and Spice Make Everything Nice" Cookies, 43
Orange Cappuccino Brownies, 411
Outrageous Cookie Bars, 288
P.B. Swirls, 107
Peanut Butter and Chocolate Bars, 367
Peanut Butter 'n' Fudge Filled Bars, 370
Peanut Butter Bon Bons, 677
Peanut Butter Chocolate Chip Cheesecake, 478
Peanut Butter Chocolate Chip Cookies, 169
Peanut Butter Chocolate No-Bake Bars, 314
Peanut Butter Cup Bars, 345
Peanut Butter Cups, 668
Peanut Butter-Hop-Scotch Treats, 321
Peanut Butter Oatmeal Treats, 20
Peanut Butter Secrets, 263
Peanut Chip Cookies, 60
Peanutty Chocolate Fudge, 663
Pebbles and Stones Chocolate Cake, 437
"Perfectly Chocolate" Chocolate Chip Cookies, 9
Philadelphia® 3-Step® Chocolate Chip Cheesecake, 478
Pistachio Chip Cookies, 39
Pumpkin Spiced and Iced Cookies, 236
Quick Holiday Raspberry Fudge, 671

**Chocolate Chips** (*continued*)
Quick Peanut Butter Chocolate Chip Cookies, 275
Red's Ultimate "M&M's" Cookies, 60
Rocky Road Bars, 270
Rocky Road Clusters, 669
Rocky Road Tasty Team Treats, 376
Santa's Chocolate Cookies, 251
Scotcheroos, 312
Scrumptious Fruit and Nut Cookies, 45
Semi-Sweet Chocolate Fudge, 645
S'More Cookie Bars, 361
Spicy Lemon Crescents, 144
Strawberry Cheesecake Squares, 352
Strawberry Chocolate Chip Shortcake, 458
Super-Duper Chocolate Pecan Cookies, 143
Supreme Chocolate Saucepan Brownies, 388
Swirl of Chocolate Cheesecake Triangles, 373
Three-in-One Chocolate Chip Cookies, 292
Tiger Stripes, 676
Toffee Bars, 333
Toffee Brownie Bars, 386
Triple Chocolate Cookies, 25
Triple Layer Chocolate Bars, 264
Tropical Gardens Cookies, 150
Truffles, 638
Two Great Tastes Pudding Parfaits, 548
Viennese Hazelnut Butter Thins, 116
Walnut Cherry Fudge Logs, 643
Walnut Minichips Biscotti, 128
Walnut-Orange Chocolate Chippers, 19
West Haven Date Bars, 331
White & Chocolate Covered Strawberries, 618
White Chocolate Brownies, 427
White Chocolate Chunk Brownie Drops, 12
Yummy Mummy Cookies, 202

Chocolate Cinnamon Bread Pudding, 592
Chocolate Crackles, 124
Chocolate-Dipped Cinnamon Thins, 101
Chocolate-Dipped RITZ® Crackers, 511
Chocolate-Frosted Marshmallow Cookies, 283
Chocolate Glaze, 82, 392, 412
Chocolate Halloween Ice Cream Cookie Sandwiches, 201
Chocolate Malt Frosting, 330
Chocolate Malted Cookies, 146
Chocolate Mousse Squares, 340
Chocolate-Nut Cookies, 62
Chocolate Peanut Brownie Bars, 389
Chocolate-Peanut Butter Checkerboards, 96
Chocolate-Raspberry Cupcakes, 594
Chocolate Sandwich Cookies, 289
Chocolate Sheet Cake, 444
Chocolate Snowball Cookies, 254
Choco-Peanut Pinwheels, 662
Choco-Scutterbotch, 166
Christmas Spirits, 235
Christmas Spritz Cookies, 217
Christmas Stained Glass Cookies, 210
Christmas Sugar Cookies, 219
Christmas Tree Ice Cream Sandwiches, 181
Chunky Milk Chocolate Chip Cookies, 6
Chunky Peanut Butter Cookies, 41
Cider Glaze, 18
Cindy's Fudgy Brownies, 417
Cinnamon-Chocolate Cutouts, 67
Cinnamon Cream Sauce, 592
Cinnamon Crinkles, 161
Cinnamon Nut Chocolate Spirals, 119
Cinnamon Roll Cookies, 122
Cinnamon Stars, 78
Citrus Cream Bars, 320
Classic Crisco® Double Crust, 512
Classic Crisco® Single Crust, 512

Classic Lemon Meringue Pie, 528
Classic New York Cheesecake, 461
Classic Peanut Butter Cookies, 160
**Cocoa**
Almond Fudge Banana Cake, 432
Banana Cocoa Marbled Bars, 353
Brownie Frosting, 425
Chewy Brownie Cookies, 32
Chewy Chocolate-Cinnamon Cookies, 168
Choco-Coco Pecan Crisps, 113
Chocolate Almond Buttons, 127
Chocolate-Amaretto Ice, 579
Chocolate Amaretto Squares, 382
Chocolate Bar Cake, 474
Chocolate Bavarian Pie, 524
Chocolate Buttercream Cherry Candies, 678
Chocolate Cinnamon Bread Pudding, 592
Chocolate Cookie Pops, 274
Chocolate Crackles, 124
Chocolate Drizzle, 446
Chocolate Glaze, 392, 412
Chocolate Halloween Ice Cream Cookie Sandwiches, 201
Chocolate Malt Frosting, 330
Chocolate Malted Cookies, 146
Chocolate Mousse Squares, 340
Chocolate Peanut Brownie Bars, 389
Chocolate-Peanut Butter Checkerboards, 96
Chocolate-Raspberry Cupcakes, 594
Chocolate Sandwich Cookies, 289
Chocolate Sheet Cake, 444
Chocolate Snowball Cookies, 254
Cocoa Almond Cut-Out Cookies, 82
Cocoa Gingerbread Cookies, 68
Cocoa Mint Sherbet, 545
Cocoa Sugar Doodles, 278
Creamy Filled Brownies, 410
Crispy Cocoa Bars, 315

**Cocoa** *(continued)*
Deep Dark Chocolate Soufflé, 596
Double Chocolate Cocoa Cupcakes, 635
Double Chocolate Dream Cookies, 30
Double Chocolate Peanut Butter Thumbprint Cookies, 158
Fudge Topped Brownies, 415
Fudgey Cocoa No-Bake Treats, 302
Fudgey German Sandwich Cookies, 157
Fudgy Peanut Butter Jiffy Cookies, 311
Fudgy Raisin Pixies, 150
Hershey's Best Brownies, 429
Hershey's Premium Double Chocolate Brownies, 384
Hershey's Red Velvet Cake, 477
Holiday Chocolate Shortbread Cookies, 247
Holiday Cookies on a Stick, 212
Honey Fruit Truffles, 648
Irish Chocolate Mint Dessert, 588
Irresistible Peanut Butter Chip Brownies, 425
Kentucky Oatmeal-Jam Cookies, 42
Layers of Love Chocolate Brownies, 414
Luscious Brownie Chip Pie, 486
Luscious Cold Chocolate Soufflés, 566
Marble Chiffon Cake, 435
Marshmallow Nut Cocoa Fudge, 642
Marshmallow Sandwich Cookies, 155
Miss Kathleen's Texas Sheet Cake, 468
Mocha Mint Crisps, 164
No-Bake Peanutty Chocolate Drops, 307
Nutty Rich Cocoa Fudge, 642
Oat & Dried Fruit Balls, 310
Peanut Butter and Chocolate Mousse Pie, 518

**Cocoa** *(continued)*
Peanut Butter and Chocolate Spirals, 99
Peppermint Ice Cream Pie, 507
"Perfectly Chocolate" Chocolate Chip Cookies, 9
Quick Creamy Chocolate Pudding, 574
Reese's® Chewy Chocolate Cookies, 54
Reese's® Chocolate Peanut Butter Cheesecake, 446
Rich Cocoa Fudge, 642
Ricotta Cheese Brownies, 395
Scrumptious Fruit and Nut Cookies, 45
Sensational Peppermint Pattie Brownies, 408
Shamrock Chocolate Cookies, 183
Silky Cocoa Cream Pie, 511
Sour Cream Brownies, 399
Supreme Chocolate Saucepan Brownies, 388
Sweetheart Chocolate Mousse, 552
Sweetheart Layer Bars, 177
Sweet Spiders, 200
3-Minute No-Bake Cookies, 315
Triple Layer Chocolate Bars, 264
Velvet Chocolate Cheesecake, 442
Winter Wonderland Snowmen Brownies, 218
Yummy Mummy Cookies, 202
**Coconut**
Ambrosia, 555
Cherry Coconut Cookies, 160
Choco-Coco Pecan Crisps, 113
Chocolate Macaroon Heath® Pie, 514
Chocolate Oat Chewies, 147
Coconut and Pecan Filling, 157
Coconut Butterscotch Bars, 362
Coconut Peach Crunch Pie, 500
Fruit Bon Bons, 670
Holiday Mini Kisses Treasure Cookies, 238
Holiday Wreath Cookies, 233
Layered Chocolate Cheese Bars, 374

**Coconut** *(continued)*
   Macaroon Brownies, 418
   No-Bake Cherry Crisps, 309
   Oat & Dried Fruit Balls, 310
   Oatmeal Macaroons, 17
   Oreo® Shazam Bars, 326
   Outrageous Cookie Bars, 288
   Spring Macaroon Bars, 351
   Strawberry Bon Bons, 670
   Sweetheart Layer Bars, 177
   Truffle Treats, 673
   Upside-Down German
     Chocolate Cake, 450
   Walnut-Granola Clusters, 306
   White Chocolate Coconut
     Cream Pie, 526
**Coffee**
   Cappuccino Cake, 454
   Cappuccino Cookies, 97
   Chocolate Tiramisu Cupcakes,
     610
   Chocolate Walnut Truffles, 664
   Christmas Spirits, 235
   Creamy Cappuccino Frozen
     Dessert, 581
   Frozen Mocha Cheesecake
     Loaf, 544
   Mocha Decadence Pie, 517
   Mocha Fudge Brownies, 424
   Mocha Marble Cheesecake, 463
   Mocha Melt Cookies, 38
   Mocha Meringue Pudding, 615
   Mocha Mint Crisps, 164
   Mocha Mint Sugar, 164
   Mocha Mousse, 578
   Mocha Pecan Pinwheels, 106
   Mocha Truffle Pie, 492
   Mocha Truffles, 660
   Molten Mocha Cakes, 439
   Orange Cappuccino Brownies,
     411
   Quick Tiramisu, 585
   Tinker Bell Peanut Butter Pie,
     515
Colorful Caramel Apples, 603
Colorful Cookie Buttons, 295
Confetti Chocolate Chip Cookies,
   296
Confetti Cookies, 103
Conversation Hearts Cereal
   Treats, 180
Cookie Crust, 328
Cookie Cups, 271

Cookie Pizza, 255
Cookie Pops, 71
Cookies and Cream Cheesecake
   Bonbons, 651
Cookies & Cream Cupcakes, 626
Cowboy Cookies, 14
**Cranberries**
   Banana Jewel Cake, 453
   Cranberry Brown Sugar
     Cookies, 244
   Cran-Raspberry Hazelnut
     Trifle, 550
   Premier Cheesecake Cranberry
     Bars, 206
   White Chocolate Cranberry
     Cookie Bars, 230
Cran-Raspberry Hazelnut Trifle,
   550
Crayon Cookies, 277
Cream Cheese Brownie Pie, 530
Cream Cheese Brownies, 404
Cream Cheese Chocolate Chip
   Pastry Cookies, 114
Cream Cheese Frosting, 193
Cream Cheese Icing, 457
Creamy Banana Pudding, 561
Creamy Cappuccino Frozen
   Dessert, 581
Creamy Filled Brownies, 410
Creamy Filling, 410
Creamy Holiday Tarts, 514
Creamy Lemon Bars, 334
Creamy Mint Filling, 110
Creamy Peach-Raspberry Melba,
   560
Creamy Strawberry-Orange Pops,
   576
Crispy Chocolate Logs, 305
Crispy Cocoa Bars, 315
Crispy's Irresistible Peanut
   Butter Marbles, 257
Crunchy Chocolate Chip Cookies,
   55
"Cupcake" Fruitcakes, 480
**Cutout Cookies** *(see also pages
   63–94)*
   Black & White Hearts, 173
   Chocolate and Peanut Butter
     Hearts, 178
   Chocolate-Raspberry Kolacky,
     234
   Chocolate-Raspberry Kolacky
     Cups, 235

**Cutout Cookies** *(continued)*
   Chocolate Reindeer, 243
   Christmas Stained Glass
     Cookies, 210
   Christmas Sugar Cookies, 219
   Christmas Tree Ice Cream
     Sandwiches, 181
   Dino-Mite Dinosaurs, 272
   Dress 'em Up Ginger People,
     245
   Dutch St. Nicolas Cookies, 237
   Festive Easter Cookies, 186
   Frosted Easter Cut-Outs, 188
   Frosted Holiday Cutouts, 246
   Gift Tag Cookies, 175
   Gobble, Gobble, Gobblers, 204
   Hanukkah Cookies, 218
   High-Flying Flags, 191
   Holiday Bits Cutout Cookies,
     225
   Holiday Chocolate Shortbread
     Cookies, 247
   Holiday Sugar Cookies, 250
   Holiday Wreath Cookies, 233
   Kringle's Cutouts, 252
   Linzer Sandwich Cookies, 207
   Lollipop Clowns, 267
   Moons and Stars, 260
   Nutty Footballs, 285
   Patriotic Ice Cream
     Sandwiches, 181
   Peanut Butter Critter Cookies,
     281
   Pumpkin Ice Cream
     Sandwiches, 181
   Shamrock Chocolate Cookies,
     183
   Shamrock Ice Cream
     Sandwiches, 180
   Skeleton Cookies, 197
   Smushy Cookies, 269
   Star Christmas Tree Cookies,
     242
   Strawberry Hearts, 179
   Sugar & Spice Jack-O'-Lantern
     Cookies, 199
   Valentine Ice Cream
     Sandwiches, 181
   Valentine's Day Cookies Cards,
     172
   Valentine Stained Glass Hearts,
     174
Cut-Out Sugar Cookies, 70

**D**

Dandy Candy Oatmeal Cookies, 293
Danish Raspberry Cookies, 211
Dark Chocolate Truffles, 667
**Dates**
  "Cupcake" Fruitcakes, 480
  Date Pinwheel Cookies, 115
  Grandma's Favorite Molasses Fruitcake, 480
  "Mini" Fruitcakes, 481
  Old-Fashioned Harvest Cookies, 46
  Spiced Date Bars, 357
  West Haven Date Bars, 331
Death By Chocolate Cookies, 48
Decadent Blonde Brownies, 405
Decadent Triple Layer Mud Pie, 520
Decorator Icing, 68
Decorator's Icing, 175
Deep Dark Chocolate Soufflé, 596
Delicate White Chocolate Cake, 479
Deluxe Toll House® Mud Bars, 336
Devil's Food Fudge Cookies, 148
Dino-Mite Dinosaurs, 272
Divine Truffle Brownies, 400
Domino® Sugar Cookies, 102
Double Chocolate Bread Pudding, 616
Double Chocolate Chewies, 367
Double Chocolate Chunk Cookies, 28, 165
Double Chocolate Cocoa Cupcakes, 635
Double Chocolate Delight, 543
Double Chocolate Dream Cookies, 30
Double Chocolate Orange Nut Fudge, 650
Double Chocolate Peanut Butter Thumbprint Cookies, 158
Double Decadence Chocolate Chip Brownies, 390
Double Decker Bars, 364
Double-Dipped Hazelnut Crisps, 76
Double Drizzle, 366
Double Lemon Delights, 7
Double Nut Chocolate Chip Cookies, 133

Double Peanut Butter Cookies, 144
Dreamy Divinity, 646
Dress 'em Up Ginger People, 245
**Drop Cookies** *(see also pages 5–62)*
  Anna's Icing Oatmeal Sandwich Cookies, 268
  Bananaramas, 280
  Chewy Chocolate No-Bakes, 318
  Chocolate Cookie Pops, 274
  Chocolate-Frosted Marshmallow Cookies, 283
  Chocolate Haystacks, 319
  Chocolate Peanut Butter Cookies, 272
  Chocolate Sandwich Cookies, 289
  Confetti Chocolate Chip Cookies, 296
  Cranberry Brown Sugar Cookies, 244
  Frost-on-the-Pumpkin Cookies, 193
  Frosty's Colorful Cookies, 261
  Fruitcake Cookies, 229
  Fudgey Cocoa No-Bake Treats, 302
  Fudgy Peanut Butter Jiffy Cookies, 311
  Granola & Chocolate Chip Cookies, 290
  Happy Face Oatmeal Monsters, 291
  Haystacks, 303
  Holiday Mini Kisses Treasure Cookies, 238
  Jumbo 3-Chip Cookies, 282
  Kids' Favorite Jumbo Chippers, 266
  Macadamia Nut White Chip Pumpkin Cookies, 226
  No-Bake Butterscotch Haystacks, 319
  No-Bake Peanutty Chocolate Drops, 307
  Oatmeal Apple Cookies, 256
  Peanut Butter Cremes, 273
  Pumpkin Spiced and Iced Cookies, 236
  Pumpkin White Chocolate Drops, 241

**Drop Cookies** *(continued)*
  Quick Peanut Butter Chocolate Chip Cookies, 275
  Rum Fruitcake Cookies, 239
  Soft Molasses Spice Cookies, 223
  Three-in-One Chocolate Chip Cookies, 292
  3-Minute No-Bake Cookies, 315
Drop Sugar Cookies, 13
Dulce de Leche Frozen Dessert, 572
Dutch St. Nicolas Cookies, 237

**E**

Easy Double Chocolate Chip Brownies, 398
Easy Eclair Dessert, 568
Easy Fresh Lemon Ice Cream, 562
Easy Lemon Cookies, 44
Easy Lemon Pudding Cookies, 134
Easy Peach Cobbler, 617
Easy Toffee Candy, 675
Edible Easter Baskets, 184
Emily's Dream Bars, 346
English Thumbprint Cookies, 135
English Toffee, 659
Englishman's Trifle, 538
European Kolacky, 64
"Everything but the Kitchen Sink" Bar Cookies, 265
Everything-But-The-Kitchen-Sink Cookies, 49

**F**

Fabulous Blonde Brownies, 418
Fabulous Fondue, 627
Fabulous Fruit Bars, 375
Famous Chocolate Refrigerator Roll, 631
Fast and Easy Microwave Peanut Brittle, 665
Festive Black or White Peanut Clusters, 660
Festive Easter Cookies, 186
Festive Fruited White Chip Blondies, 430
Festive Lebkuchen, 84
Fireballs, 641
Flourless Peanut Butter Cookies, 131

Fluffy Cottontails, 185
Fresh Cherry Jubilee, 598
Fresh Orange Cookies, 24
Frosted Butter Cookies, 94
Frosted Easter Cut-Outs, 188
Frosted Holiday Cutouts, 246
Frosted Maraschino Brownies, 397
Frosted Sugar Cookies, 84
**Frostings & Glazes**
  Apple Cinnamon Glaze, 487
  Banana Chocolate Glaze, 432
  Brownie Frosting, 425
  Chocolate Chip Drizzle, 402, 679
  Chocolate Chip Glaze, 86
  Chocolate Drizzle, 387, 446
  Chocolate Glaze, 82, 392, 412
  Chocolate Malt Frosting, 330
  Cider Glaze, 18
  Cream Cheese Frosting, 193
  Cream Cheese Icing, 457
  Decorator Icing, 68
  Decorator's Icing, 175
  Double Drizzle, 366
  Fudge Frosting, 58
  Icing, 217
  Lemon Glaze, 15, 328
  Maple Glaze, 440
  MiniChip Glaze, 410
  Orange Glaze, 24
  Peanut Buttery Frosting, 295
  Royal Icing, 186
  Shamrock Glaze, 183
  Vanilla Frosting, 85
  Vanilla Glaze, 236, 435, 474
  White Icing, 222
Frost-on-the-Pumpkin Cookies, 193
Frosty's Colorful Cookies, 261
Frozen Chocolate Cheesecake, 549
Frozen Chocolate-Covered Bananas, 567
Frozen Mocha Cheesecake Loaf, 544
Frozen Peanut Butter-Banana Dessert, 575
Fruit and Chocolate Dream Bars, 360
Fruit & Pecan Brownies, 422
Fruit Bon Bons, 670
Fruitcake Cookies, 229

Fruitcake Slices, 215
Fruit Dessert Pizza, 584
Fruit-Filled Chocolate Chip Meringue Nests, 621
Fruit Medley Dessert, 632
Fruit Mousse, 536
Fruity Jell-O® Cake, 464
Fudge Cookies, 58
Fudge Frosting, 58
Fudge Rum Balls, 664
Fudge Topped Brownies, 415
Fudgey Cocoa No-Bake Treats, 302
Fudgey German Sandwich Cookies, 157
Fudgy Banana Oat Cake, 476
Fudgy Banana Rocky Road Clusters, 661
Fudgy Oatmeal Butterscotch Cookies, 39
Fudgy Peanut Butter Jiffy Cookies, 311
Fudgy Raisin Pixies, 150

**G**
Ghostly Delights, 195
Giant Cookie Cups, 271
Giant Peanut Butter Cup Cookies, 37
Gift Tag Cookies, 175
Gingerbread Apple Bars, 226
Gingerbread Cookies, 73
Gingerbread Teddies, 159
Gingerbread Upside-Down Cake, 447
Gingered Pumpkin Custard, 601
Ginger Snap Oats, 57
Glazed Pear Shortcake, 434
Gobble, Gobble, Gobblers, 204
Golden Peanut Butter Bars, 368
Grandma's Favorite Molasses Fruitcake, 480
Grand Old Flag Cookie, 190
Granola & Chocolate Chip Cookies, 290
Granola Bars, 348
Grasshopper Dessert, 607
Greek Lemon-Herb Cookies, 125
Green's Butterscotch Blondies, 416
Green's Mint Meringue Trees, 240

**H**
Hanukkah Cookies, 218
Happy Face Oatmeal Monsters, 291
Harvest Honey Spice Cake, 438
Haystacks, 303
**Hazelnuts**
  Chocolate Hazelnut Terrine with Raspberry Sauce, 554
  Cran-Raspberry Hazelnut Trifle, 550
  Double-Dipped Hazelnut Crisps, 76
  Viennese Hazelnut Butter Thins, 116
Heath® Bits Bars, 327
Heath Bits Peanut Butter Cookies, 52
Heavenly Chocolate Mousse Pie, 527
Heavenly Oatmeal Hearts, 176
Hershey's Best Brownies, 429
Hershey's Buckeyes, 666
Hershey's Classic Chocolate Chip Cookies, 9
Hershey's Mint Chocolate Cookies, 23
Hershey's Premium Double Chocolate Brownies, 384
Hershey's Red Velvet Cake, 477
High Country Peach Pie, 532
High-Flying Flags, 191
Hint of Lemon Bread Pudding, 602
Holiday Almond Wreaths, 240
Holiday Bits Cutout Cookies, 225
Holiday Chocolate Shortbread Cookies, 247
Holiday Cookies on a Stick, 212
Holiday Hideaways, 248
Holiday Mini Kisses Treasure Cookies, 238
Holiday Peppermint Cookies, 221
Holiday Red Raspberry Chocolate Bars, 250
Holiday Sugar Cookies, 250
Holiday Wreath Cookies, 233
Honey Brownies, 423
Honey Carrot Cookies, 131
Honey Fruit Truffles, 648
Honey Ginger Snaps, 156
Honey Pumpkin Pie, 499

Honey-Spiced Fruit Compote, 604
Hoosier Harvest Apple Pie, 519

**I**
Ice Cream Cookie Dessert, 632
Ice Cream Cookie Sandwich, 586
Icicle Ornaments, 213
Icing, 217
Irish Chocolate Mint Dessert, 588
Irresistible Peanut Butter Chip Brownies, 425
Irresistible Peanut Butter Jack O'Lanterns, 194

**J**
Jack-O-Lantern Bars, 196
Jammy Pinwheels, 112
Jam-Up Oatmeal Cookies, 75
Jeremy's Famous Turtles, 142
Jolly Snowman Cookies, 222
Jumbo 3-Chip Cookies, 282

**K**
Kentucky Oatmeal-Jam Cookies, 42
Kids' Favorite Jumbo Chippers, 266
Kringle's Cutouts, 252

**L**
Layered Chocolate Cheese Bars, 374
Layers of Love Chocolate Brownies, 414
**Lemon**
Amy's Lemonade Mousse, 541
Apple Lemon Bars, 328
Apple-Lemon Sherbet, 570
Banana Spice Lemon Drops, 36
Chewy Lemon-Honey Cookies, 15
Cashew-Lemon Shortbread Cookies, 151
Classic Lemon Meringue Pie, 528
Creamy Lemon Bars, 334
Double Lemon Delights, 7
Easy Fresh Lemon Ice Cream, 562
Easy Lemon Cookies, 44
Easy Lemon Pudding Cookies, 134

**Lemon** *(continued)*
Greek Lemon-Herb Cookies, 125
Hint of Lemon Bread Pudding, 602
Lemonade Torte for a Long Hot Summer, 445
Lemon Bars, 363
Lemon Buttermilk Pie, 498
Lemon Cake Top Pudding, 629
Lemon Cookies, 138
Lemon Crème Fraîche, 611
Lemon Ginger Squares, 556
Lemon Glaze, 15, 328
Lemon Pecan Cookies, 29
Lemony Butter Cookies, 83
Lemon Yogurt Cookies, 152
Lip-Smacking Lemon Cookies, 104
Mini Lemon Sandwich Cookies, 91
Spicy Lemon Crescents, 144
White Chip Lemon Bars, 359
Zesty Fresh Lemon Bars, 381
Zesty Lemon Pound Cake, 462
Lemonade Torte for a Long Hot Summer, 445
Lemony Butter Cookies, 83
Libby's® Famous Pumpkin Pie, 488
Linzer Sandwich Cookies, 207
Lip-Smacking Lemon Cookies, 104
Lollipop Clowns, 267
Lone Star Peanut Butter Cutouts, 74
Loony Lollies, 647
Luscious Brownie Chip Pie, 486
Luscious Cold Chocolate Soufflés, 566

**M**
**Macadamia Nuts**
Chewy Macadamia Nut Blondies, 407
Macadamia Nut White Chip Pumpkin Cookies, 226
Peanut Butter Caramel Macadamia Bars, 342
Scrumptious Fruit and Nut Cookies, 45
Southern Belle White Chocolate Cookies, 26

Macaroon Brownies, 418
Mahogany Sour Cream Cake, 469
"M&M'S" Jam Sandwiches, 80
Mango-Peach Frozen Yogurt, 557
**Maple**
Maple Glaze, 440
Maple Walnut Bars, 356
Maple Walnut Pound Cake, 440
Peanut Maple Triangle Puffs, 597
Marble Chiffon Cake, 435
Marbled Peanut Butter Brownies, 393, 426
**Marshmallow**
Ambrosia, 555
Butterscotch Fudge, 663
Caramel Marshmallow Bars, 287
Carnation® Famous Fudge, 663
Cherry-Mallow Cake, 473
Chewy Chocolate No-Bakes, 318
Chocolate Cereal Bars, 308
Chocolate-Frosted Marshmallow Cookies, 283
Chocolate Raspberry Fudge, 648
Conversation Hearts Cereal Treats, 180
Crispy Chocolate Logs, 305
Crispy Cocoa Bars, 315
"Everything but the Kitchen Sink" Bar Cookies, 265
Fruity Jell-O® Cake, 464
Fudgy Banana Rocky Road Clusters, 661
Grasshopper Dessert, 607
Marshmallow Crispy Bars, 259
Marshmallow Nut Cocoa Fudge, 642
Marshmallow Sandwich Cookies, 155
Milk Chocolate Fudge, 663
Mini Kisses Pumpkin Mousse Cups, 563
Mississippi Mud Brownies, 396
Monkey Bars, 316
Nutty Nougat Caramel Bites, 652
Peanut Butter Cereal Bars, 301
Peanut Butter Cremes, 273
Peanut Butter S'Mores, 297
Peppermint Rice Cloud, 545

**Marshmallow** *(continued)*
Rocky Road Bars, 270
Rocky Road Clusters, 669
Rocky Road Tasty Team Treats, 376
Semi-Sweet Chocolate Fudge, 645
S'More Cookie Bars, 361
S'More Pie, 505
Walnut-Granola Clusters, 306
Mexican Sugar Cookies (Polvorones), 129
Michigan Blueberry Pie, 490
Microwave Double Peanut Bars, 317
Milk Chocolate Almond Brickle, 680
Milk Chocolate Fudge, 663
Mini Cheesecakes, 470
MiniChip Glaze, 410
Mini Chip Slice and Bake Cookies, 120
Mini Chip Snowball Cookies, 154
Mini Chocolate Pies, 498
"Mini" Fruitcakes, 481
Mini Kisses Blondies, 384
Mini Kisses Pumpkin Mousse Cups, 563
Mini Lemon Sandwich Cookies, 91
Mini Morsel Meringue Cookies, 41
Mini Pizza Cookies, 286
**Mint**
Bittersweet Chocolate Mints, 649
Brownie Mint Sundae Squares, 409
Chocolate Mint Ravioli Cookies, 89
Chocolate Mint Sandwiches, 110
Chocolate Peppermint Wafers, 658
Cocoa Mint Sherbet, 545
Creamy Mint Filling, 110
Grasshopper Dessert, 607
Green's Mint Meringue Trees, 240
Hershey's Mint Chocolate Cookies, 23
Holiday Peppermint Cookies, 221

**Mint** *(continued)*
Irish Chocolate Mint Dessert, 588
Mint Chocolate Banana Bars, 378
Mint Chocolate Pinwheels, 100
Mint in the Mix Brownies, 392
Mocha Mint Crisps, 164
Mocha Mint Sugar, 164
Peppermint Ice Cream Pie, 507
Peppermint Patties, 639
Peppermint Rice Cloud, 545
Scrumptious Minted Brownies, 422
Mississippi Mud Bars, 355
Mississippi Mud Brownies, 396
Mississippi Mud Pie, 506
Miss Kathleen's Texas Sheet Cake, 468
Mixed Berry Pie, 525
Mixed Berry Tart with Ginger-Raspberry Glaze, 501
Mocha Decadence Pie, 517
Mocha Fudge Brownies, 424
Mocha Marble Cheesecake, 463
Mocha Melt Cookies, 38
Mocha Meringue Pudding, 615
Mocha Mint Crisps, 164
Mocha Mint Sugar, 164
Mocha Mousse, 578
Mocha Pecan Pinwheels, 106
Mocha Truffle Pie, 492
Mocha Truffles, 660
Molasses Oatmeal Cookies, 130
Molasses Spice Cookies, 137
Molten Mocha Cakes, 439
Monkey Bars, 316
Moons and Stars, 260
**Mousse**
Amy's Lemonade Mousse, 541
Chocolate Truffle Mousse, 571
Fruit Mousse, 536
Heavenly Chocolate Mousse Pie, 527
Mini Kisses Pumpkin Mousse Cups, 563
Mocha Mousse, 578
Orange Mousse with Strawberry Sauce, 540

**Mousse** *(continued)*
Peanut Butter and Chocolate Mousse Pie, 518
Quick Chocolate Mousse, 576
Sweetheart Chocolate Mousse, 552
Mrs. J's Chip Cookies, 162

**N**
Nathaniel's Jumble, 310
Neopolitan Chip Bomb, 558
Nestlé® Toll House® Chocolate Chip Pie, 522
No-Bake Banana Peanut Butter Fudge Bars, 309
No-Bake Butterscotch Haystacks, 319
No-Bake Cherry Crisps, 309
No-Bake Chocolate Caramel Bars, 323
No-Bake Chocolate Oat Bars, 316
No-Bake Chocolate Peanut Butter Bars, 324
No-Bake Fudgy Brownies, 313
No-Bake Gingersnap Balls, 300
No Bake Peanut Butter Pie, 513
No-Bake Peanutty Chocolate Drops, 307
No-Bake Pineapple Marmalade Squares, 304
Nuggets o' Gold Brownies, 403
Nut Filling, 365
**Nuts** *(see also individual listings)*
Baker's® One Bowl Chocolate Fudge, 650
Championship Chocolate Chip Bars, 329
Chocolate Chip Cookie Brittle, 640
Chocolate Nut Bars, 337
Chocolate Sheet Cake, 444
Chunky Milk Chocolate Chip Cookies, 6
Colorful Caramel Apples, 603
Creamy Filled Brownies, 410
Crunchy Chocolate Chip Cookies, 55
"Cupcake" Fruitcakes, 480
Double Chocolate Chewies, 367
Grandma's Favorite Molasses Fruitcake, 480
Jumbo 3-Chip Cookies, 282

Nuts *(continued)*
Layered Chocolate Cheese Bars, 374
Marshmallow Nut Cocoa Fudge, 642
"Mini" Fruitcakes, 481
Miss Kathleen's Texas Sheet Cake, 468
Nestlé® Toll House® Chocolate Chip Pie, 522
Pistachio and White Chocolate Cookies, 53
Pistachio Chip Cookies, 39
Pumpkin Cheesecake Bars, 214
Quick No-Bake Brownies, 419
Rocky Road Clusters, 669
Rum Fruitcake Cookies, 239
Santa's Thumbprints, 228
Sour Cream Brownies, 399
Nutty Chocolate Chunk Bars, 354
Nutty Footballs, 285
Nutty Nougat Caramel Bites, 652
Nutty Rich Cocoa Fudge, 642

**O**
Oat & Dried Fruit Balls, 310
Oatmeal Apple Cookies, 256
Oatmeal Carmelita Bars, 276
Oatmeal Chocolate Chip Cake, 460
Oatmeal Hermits, 43
Oatmeal Macaroons, 17
Oatmeal Raisin Cookies, 51
Oatmeal Scotchies, 47
Oatmeal Toffee Lizzies, 136
**Oats**
Absolutely Wonderful Pecan Bars, 339
Anna's Icing Oatmeal Sandwich Cookies, 268
Apple Crumb Squares, 348
Applesauce Raisin Chews, 33
Banana Jumbles, 8
Banana Oatmeal Cookies with Banana Frosting, 27
Chewy Chocolate No-Bakes, 318
Chewy Oatmeal Trail Mix Cookies, 35
Chewy Red Raspberry Bars, 354
Chocolate Chip Almond Oatmeal Cookies, 40

Oats *(continued)*
Chocolate Oat Chewies, 147
Cowboy Cookies, 14
Dandy Candy Oatmeal Cookies, 293
Double Decadence Chocolate Chip Brownies, 390
Fudgey Cocoa No-Bake Treats, 302
Fudgy Banana Oat Cake, 476
Fudgy Oatmeal Butterscotch Cookies, 39
Fudgy Peanut Butter Jiffy Cookies, 311
Ginger Snap Oats, 57
Granola Bars, 348
Happy Face Oatmeal Monsters, 291
Heavenly Oatmeal Hearts, 176
Jam-Up Oatmeal Cookies, 75
Jeremy's Famous Turtles, 142
Kentucky Oatmeal-Jam Cookies, 42
Lemon Yogurt Cookies, 152
Mint Chocolate Pinwheels, 100
Molasses Oatmeal Cookies, 130
Monkey Bars, 316
No-Bake Banana Peanut Butter Fudge Bars, 309
No-Bake Chocolate Oat Bars, 316
No-Bake Peanutty Chocolate Drops, 307
Nutty Chocolate Chunk Bars, 354
Oat & Dried Fruit Balls, 310
Oatmeal Apple Cookies, 256
Oatmeal Carmelita Bars, 276
Oatmeal Chocolate Chip Cake, 460
Oatmeal Hermits, 43
Oatmeal Macaroons, 17
Oatmeal Raisin Cookies, 51
Oatmeal Scotchies, 47
Oatmeal Toffee Lizzies, 136
Old-Fashioned Caramel Pie, 493
Old-Fashioned Harvest Cookies, 46
Peachy Oatmeal Bars, 350

Oats *(continued)*
Peanut Butter 'n' Fudge Filled Bars, 370
Peanut Butter Bears, 279
Peanut Butter Cereal Bars, 301
Peanut Butter Chocolate No-Bake Bars, 314
Peanut Butter Oatmeal Treats, 20
Peanut Chip Cookies, 60
Peppermint Ice Cream Pie, 507
Pineapple Oatmeal Crunchies, 31
Plum Oat Squares, 349
Power Bars, 341
Quaker's Best Oatmeal Pie, 500
Raisin Spice Drops, 54
Ranger Cookies, 59
Razzle-Dazzle Apple Streusel Bars, 358
Santa's Thumbprints, 228
Snow-Covered Almond Crescents, 153
Spicy Oatmeal Raisin Cookies, 61
3-Minute No-Bake Cookies, 315
Tropical Snack Cake, 455
Walnut-Granola Clusters, 306
White Chip Apricot Oatmeal Cookies, 170
White Chocolate Chunk Brownie Drops, 12
Yummy Oatmeal Apple Cookie Squares, 377
Old World Pfeffernüsse Cookies, 231
Old-Fashioned Caramel Pie, 493
Old-Fashioned Harvest Cookies, 46
Old-Fashioned Molasses Cookies, 65
**Orange**
Ambrosia, 555
Candied Orange Peel, 641
Creamy Strawberry-Orange Pops, 576
"Cupcake" Fruitcakes, 480
Double Chocolate Orange Nut Fudge, 650
Fabulous Fondue, 627

**Orange** (*continued*)
Fresh Orange Cookies, 24
Grandma's Favorite Molasses Fruitcake, 480
"Mini" Fruitcakes, 481
"Orange and Spice Make Everything Nice" Cookies, 43
Orange Cappuccino Brownies, 411
Orange-Cardamom Thins, 98
Orange Creams, 668
Orange Glaze, 24
Orange Marmalade Cookies, 11
Orange Mousse Cake, 483
Orange Mousse with Strawberry Sauce, 540
Pumpkin Cake with Orange Glaze, 452
Walnut-Orange Chocolate Chippers, 19
Oreo® Cookie Bread Pudding, 598
Oreo® Shazam Bars, 326
Oreo® White Chocolate Mousse Cake, 484
Ornament Brownies, 209
Outrageous Cookie Bars, 288

**P**
Party Peanut Butter Cookies, 102
Passionate Sorbet, 586
Patriotic Ice Cream Sandwiches, 181
P.B. and Jelly Peanut Log, 118
P.B. Graham Snackers, 302
P.B. Swirls, 107
**Peach**
All-American Pineapple & Fruit Trifle, 542
Coconut Peach Crunch Pie, 500
Creamy Peach-Raspberry Melba, 560
Easy Peach Cobbler, 617
Fruit Dessert Pizza, 584
High Country Peach Pie, 532
Mango-Peach Frozen Yogurt, 557
Mixed Berry Tart with Ginger-Raspberry Glaze, 501
Peaches & Cream Gingersnap Cups, 565

**Peach** (*continued*)
Peach Melba Freeze, 577
Peach Sorbet, 538
Peach Tapioca, 553
Peachy Blueberry Pie, 495
Peachy Oatmeal Bars, 350
Peach Yogurt Pie with Raspberry Sauce, 504
Warm Fresh Fruit Sauté, 611
Peachy Blueberry Pie, 495
Peachy Oatmeal Bars, 350
Peanut Blossom Cookies, 139
**Peanut Butter**
Chocolate and Peanut Butter Hearts, 178
Chocolate & Peanut Butter Tweed Cookies, 117
Chocolate-Peanut Butter Checkerboards, 96
Chocolate Peanut Butter Cookies, 272
Chocolate Peanut Butter Fudge, 655
Chocolate Peanut Butter Parfaits, 537
Choco-Peanut Pinwheels, 662
Chunky Peanut Butter Cookies, 41
Classic Peanut Butter Cookies, 160
Crispy's Irresistible Peanut Butter Marbles, 257
Dandy Candy Oatmeal Cookies, 293
Double Chocolate Peanut Butter Thumbprint Cookies, 158
Double Peanut Butter Cookies, 144
Emily's Dream Bars, 346
Festive Black or White Peanut Clusters, 660
Flourless Peanut Butter Cookies, 131
Frozen Peanut Butter-Banana Dessert, 575
Fudgy Peanut Butter Jiffy Cookies, 311
Giant Peanut Butter Cup Cookies, 37
Golden Peanut Butter Bars, 368

**Peanut Butter** (*continued*)
Heath Bits Peanut Butter Cookies, 52
Hershey's Buckeyes, 666
Irresistible Peanut Butter Chip Brownies, 425
Irresistible Peanut Butter Jack O'Lanterns, 194
Kids' Favorite Jumbo Chippers, 266
Lone Star Peanut Butter Cutouts, 74
Marbled Peanut Butter Brownies, 393, 426
Marshmallow Crispy Bars, 259
Microwave Double Peanut Bars, 317
Nathaniel's Jumble, 310
No-Bake Banana Peanut Butter Fudge Bars, 309
No-Bake Cherry Crisps, 309
No-Bake Chocolate Peanut Butter Bars, 324
No Bake Peanut Butter Pie, 513
Nutty Chocolate Chunk Bars, 354
Party Peanut Butter Cookies, 102
P.B. and Jelly Peanut Log, 118
P.B. Graham Snackers, 302
P.B. Swirls, 107
Peanut Blossom Cookies, 139
Peanut Butter and Chocolate Bars, 367
Peanut Butter & Chocolate Dipped Strawberries, 595
Peanut Butter and Chocolate Mousse Pie, 518
Peanut Butter and Chocolate Spirals, 99
Peanut Butter 'n' Fudge Filled Bars, 370
Peanut Butter & Jelly Kolacky, 72
Peanut Butter and Jelly Sandwich Cookies, 258
Peanut Butter Bears, 279
Peanut Butter Blocks, 680
Peanut Butter Bon Bons, 677
Peanut Butter Brickle Cookies, 162

**Peanut Butter** (continued)
Peanut Butter Caramel Macadamia Bars, 342
Peanut Butter Cereal Bars, 301
Peanut Butter Cheesecake, 467
Peanut Butter Chip Triangles, 338
Peanut Butter Chocolate Chip Cheesecake, 478
Peanut Butter Chocolate Chip Cookies, 169
Peanut Butter Chocolate No-Bake Bars, 314
Peanut Butter Cremes, 273
Peanut Butter Critter Cookies, 281
Peanut Butter Crunch Candy, 638
Peanut Butter Cup Bars, 345
Peanut Butter Cup Cookie Ice Cream Pie, 496
Peanut Butter Cups, 668
Peanut Butter Cut-Out Cookies, 86
Peanut Butter-Hop-Scotch Treats, 321
Peanut Butter Layered Brownies, 394
Peanut Butter Oatmeal Treats, 20
Peanut Butter Power Bars, 305
Peanut Butter Pudding Cake, 449
Peanut Butter Secrets, 263
Peanut Butter Shortbreads, 332
Peanut Butter S'Mores, 297
Peanut Butter Thumbprints, 149
Peanut Buttery Frosting, 295
Peanut Chip Cookies, 60
Peanut Maple Triangle Puffs, 597
Peanutty Chocolate Fudge, 663
Peter Pan's Cloud Dessert, 559
Quick Peanut Butter Chocolate Chip Cookies, 275
Reese's® Chewy Chocolate Cookies, 54
Reese's® Chocolate Peanut Butter Cheesecake, 446
Reese's® Nut Brittle Cookie Bars, 365

**Peanut Butter** (continued)
Rocky Road Peanut Butter Bars, 300
Scotcheroos, 312
Simpler Than Sin Peanut Chocolate Cookies, 141
Tinker Bell Peanut Butter Pie, 515
Two Great Tastes Pudding Parfaits, 548
Winter Wonderland Snowmen Brownies, 218
Peanut Buttery Frosting, 295
Peanut Chip Cookies, 60
Peanut Maple Triangle Puffs, 597
**Peanuts**, 294
Banana Peanut Jumbles, 17
Bananaramas, 280
Caramel Marshmallow Bars, 287
Chewy Choco-Peanut Pudgies, 284
Chocolate Peanut Brownie Bars, 389
Emily's Dream Bars, 346
Fast and Easy Microwave Peanut Brittle, 665
Fudgy Banana Rocky Road Clusters, 661
Golden Peanut Butter Bars, 368
Granola Bars, 348
Heavenly Oatmeal Hearts, 176
Microwave Double Peanut Bars, 317
No-Bake Peanutty Chocolate Drops, 307
Nutty Chocolate Chunk Bars, 354
Nutty Nougat Caramel Bites, 652
Peanut Butter Blocks, 680
Peanut Butter Pudding Cake, 449
Peanuts, 294
Southern Peanut Pie, 503
Texas Peanuts 'n' Caramel Cake, 482
Peanutty Chocolate Fudge, 663
Pebbles and Stones Chocolate Cake, 437

**Pecans**
Absolutely Wonderful Pecan Bars, 339
Banana Chippers, 233
Bourbon Pecan Pie, 523
Butter Pecan Pie, 509
Butterscotch Pan Cookies, 350
Carrot Cake, 457
Choco-Coco Pecan Crisps, 113
Chocolate Bunny Cookies, 189
Chocolate Bursts, 50
Chocolate Caramel Drops, 672
Chocolate Fudge Pecan Bars, 343
Chocolate Ice Cream Cups, 622
Chocolate-Nut Cookies, 62
Chocolate Pecan Pie, 491
Coconut and Pecan Filling, 157
English Thumbprint Cookies, 135
Fruit & Pecan Brownies, 422
Fudge Cookies, 58
Fudge Rum Balls, 664
Jam-Up Oatmeal Cookies, 75
Jeremy's Famous Turtles, 142
Layers of Love Chocolate Brownies, 414
Lemon Pecan Cookies, 29
Molasses Oatmeal Cookies, 130
Pecan Rolls, 674
Rocky Road Tasty Team Treats, 376
Super-Duper Chocolate Pecan Cookies, 143
Sweet 'n' Spicy Pecan Pie, 502
Truffles, 638
Upside-Down German Chocolate Cake, 450
Vanilla Butter Crescents, 126
Peek-A-Boo Apricot Cookies, 77
Peppermint Ice Cream Pie, 507
Peppermint Patties, 639
Peppermint Rice Cloud, 545
Peppersass Cookies, 106
Peppery Poundcake, 459
"Perfectly Chocolate" Chocolate Chip Cookies, 9
Peter Pan's Cloud Dessert, 559
Philadelphia® Snowmen Cookies, 208
Philadelphia® Sugar Cookies, 64
Philadelphia® 3-Step® Chocolate Chip Cheesecake, 478

Picture Perfect Creamy Banana Pie, 520
**Pineapple**
All-American Pineapple & Fruit Trifle, 542
Ambrosia, 555
Banana Split Dessert Pizza, 612
Fruit Dessert Pizza, 584
Fruity Jell-O® Cake, 464
Gingerbread Upside-Down Cake, 447
No-Bake Pineapple Marmalade Squares, 304
Pineapple Carrot Cookies, 22
Pineapple Oatmeal Crunchies, 31
Speedy Pineapple-Lime Sorbet, 573
Tropical Snack Cake, 455
Pinwheel Cookies, 108
Pistachio and White Chocolate Cookies, 53
Pistachio Chip Cookies, 39
Plantation Gingerbread, 630
Plum Oat Squares, 349
Powdered Sugar Cookies, 30
Power Bars, 341
Premier Cheesecake Cranberry Bars, 206
Pudding in a Cloud Dessert, 570
**Pumpkin**
Butterscotch Pumpkin Cake, 441
Frost-on-the-Pumpkin Cookies, 193
Gingered Pumpkin Custard, 601
Honey Pumpkin Pie, 499
Jack-O-Lantern Bars, 196
Libby's® Famous Pumpkin Pie, 488
Macadamia Nut White Chip Pumpkin Cookies, 226
Mini Kisses Pumpkin Mousse Cups, 563
Pumpkin Cake with Orange Glaze, 452
Pumpkin Cheesecake, 466
Pumpkin Cheesecake Bars, 214
Pumpkin Spiced and Iced Cookies, 236

**Pumpkin** *(continued)*
Pumpkin White Chocolate Drops, 241
Walnut Crunch Pumpkin Pie, 534

**Q**
Quaker's Best Oatmeal Pie, 500
Quick Chocolate Mousse, 576
Quick Creamy Chocolate Pudding, 574
Quick Holiday Raspberry Fudge, 671
Quick No-Bake Brownies, 419
Quick Peanut Butter Chocolate Chip Cookies, 275
Quick Tiramisu, 585

**R**
Rainbow Sugar Doodles, 278
**Raisins**
Applesauce Raisin Chews, 33
Chewy Chocolate No-Bakes, 318
Chunky Milk Chocolate Chip Cookies, 6
Cranberry Brown Sugar Cookies, 244
"Cupcake" Fruitcakes, 480
Ginger Snap Oats, 57
Grandma's Favorite Molasses Fruitcake, 480
Granola Bars, 348
"Mini" Fruitcakes, 481
Oatmeal Hermits, 43
Oatmeal Raisin Cookies, 51
Pineapple Carrot Cookies, 22
Raisin Spice Drops, 54
Rum Fruitcake Cookies, 239
Spicy Applesauce Cake, 464
Spicy Oatmeal Raisin Cookies, 61
Ranger Cookies, 59
**Raspberry**
All-American Pineapple & Fruit Trifle, 542
Brownie Berry Parfaits, 557
Brownie Raspberry Bars, 387
Buttery Black Raspberry Bars, 327
Chewy Red Raspberry Bars, 354

**Raspberry** *(continued)*
Chocolate Hazelnut Terrine with Raspberry Sauce, 554
Chocolate-Raspberry Cupcakes, 594
Chocolate Raspberry Fudge, 648
Chocolate-Raspberry Kolacky, 234
Chocolate-Raspberry Kolacky Cups, 235
Chocolate Raspberry Thumbprints, 249
Cran-Raspberry Hazelnut Trifle, 550
Creamy Peach-Raspberry Melba, 560
Danish Raspberry Cookies, 211
Holiday Red Raspberry Chocolate Bars, 250
Mixed Berry Tart with Ginger-Raspberry Glaze, 501
Peach Melba Freeze, 577
Peach Yogurt Pie with Raspberry Sauce, 504
Quick Holiday Raspberry Fudge, 671
Raspberry & White Chip Nut Bars, 366
Raspberry Crisp Bars, 335
Raspberry Swirl Cheesecakes, 433
Smucker's® English Berry Pudding, 551
Trifle Spectacular, 624
Razzle-Dazzle Apple Streusel Bars, 358
Red, White & Blueberry Cream Pie, 530
Red's Ultimate "M&M's" Cookies, 60
Reese's® Chewy Chocolate Cookies, 54
Reese's® Chocolate Peanut Butter Cheesecake, 446
Reese's® Nut Brittle Cookie Bars, 365
**Refrigerator Cookies** *(see also pages 95–122)*
Crispy's Irresistible Peanut Butter Marbles, 257
Fruitcake Slices, 215

**Refrigerator Cookies** *(continued)*
  Holiday Peppermint Cookies, 221
  Peanut Butter and Jelly Sandwich Cookies, 258
  St. Pat's Pinwheels, 182
  Three-in-One Chocolate Chip Cookies, 292
Rich Cocoa Fudge, 642
Ricotta Cheese Brownies, 395
Ritzy Banana Cream Pie, 510
Rocky Road Bars, 270
Rocky Road Brownies, 401
Rocky Road Clusters, 669
Rocky Road Peanut Butter Bars, 300
Rocky Road Tasty Team Treats, 376
Royal Icing, 186
Rum Fruitcake Cookies, 239
Rustic Apple Croustade, 489

**S**
St. Pat's Pinwheels, 182
**Sandwich Cookies**
  Anna's Icing Oatmeal Sandwich Cookies, 268
  Black and White Sandwiches, 79
  Cardamom-Chocolate Sandwiches, 121
  Chocolate Halloween Ice Cream Cookie Sandwiches, 201
  Chocolate Mint Sandwiches, 110
  Chocolate Sandwich Cookies, 289
  Christmas Tree Ice Cream Sandwiches, 181
  Fudgey German Sandwich Cookies, 157
  Ice Cream Cookie Sandwich, 586
  Linzer Sandwich Cookies, 207
  "M&M'S" Jam Sandwiches, 80
  Marshmallow Sandwich Cookies, 155
  Mini Lemon Sandwich Cookies, 91
  Patriotic Ice Cream Sandwiches, 181

**Sandwich Cookies** *(continued)*
  Peanut Butter and Jelly Sandwich Cookies, 258
  Peanut Butter S'Mores, 297
  Pumpkin Ice Cream Sandwiches, 181
  Shamrock Ice Cream Sandwiches, 180
  Smushy Cookies, 269
  Valentine Ice Cream Sandwiches, 181
Santa's Chocolate Cookies, 251
Santa's Thumbprints, 228
Scotcheroos, 312
Scrumptious Fruit and Nut Cookies, 45
Scrumptious Minted Brownies, 422
Semi-Sweet Chocolate Fudge, 645
Sensational Peppermint Pattie Brownies, 408
Shamrock Chocolate Cookies, 183
Shamrock Glaze, 183
Shamrock Ice Cream Sandwiches, 180
**Shaped Cookies** *(see also pages 123–170)*
  Banana Chippers, 233
  Banana Split Cups, 262
  Basic Banana Holiday Cookies, 232
  Berlinerkranser (Little Wreaths), 224
  Candy Cane Cookies, 220
  Chewy Choco-Peanut Pudgies, 284
  Chocolate Banana Stars, 232
  Chocolate Bunny Cookies, 189
  Chocolate Crackletops, 298
  Chocolate Halloween Ice Cream Cookie Sandwiches, 201
  Chocolate Raspberry Thumbprints, 249
  Chocolate Snowball Cookies, 254
  Chocolate Spritz, 230
  Christmas Spritz Cookies, 217
  Cocoa Sugar Doodles, 278
  Colorful Cookie Buttons, 295
  Cookie Cups, 271

**Shaped Cookies** *(continued)*
  Crayon Cookies, 277
  Dandy Candy Oatmeal Cookies, 293
  Danish Raspberry Cookies, 211
  Edible Easter Baskets, 184
  Fluffy Cottontails, 185
  Ghostly Delights, 195
  Giant Cookie Cups, 271
  Green's Mint Meringue Trees, 240
  Heavenly Oatmeal Hearts, 176
  Holiday Almond Wreaths, 240
  Holiday Cookies on a Stick, 212
  Holiday Hideaways, 248
  Icicle Ornaments, 213
  Irresistible Peanut Butter Jack O'Lanterns, 194
  Jolly Snowman Cookies, 222
  Mini Pizza Cookies, 286
  No-Bake Cherry Crisps, 309
  No-Bake Gingersnap Balls, 300
  Oat & Dried Fruit Balls, 310
  Old World Pfeffernüsse Cookies, 231
  P.B. Graham Snackers, 302
  Peanut Butter Bears, 279
  Peanut Butter Secrets, 263
  Peanut Butter S'Mores, 297
  Peanuts, 294
  Philadelphia® Snowmen Cookies, 208
  Rainbow Sugar Doodles, 278
  Santa's Chocolate Cookies, 251
  Santa's Thumbprints, 228
  Smucker's® Spider Web Tartlets, 198
  Snowmen, 238
  Springtime Nests, 187
  Sugar Doodles, 278
  Sweet Spiders, 200
  Walnut-Granola Clusters, 306
  Worm Cookies, 288
  Yummy Mummy Cookies, 202
  Zana Kringles, 233
Shortbread Cookies, 140
Silky Cocoa Cream Pie, 511
Simpler Than Sin Peanut Chocolate Cookies, 141
Skeleton Cookies, 197
S'More Cookie Bars, 361
S'More Pie, 505

Smucker's® Double Apple Turnovers, 625
Smucker's® English Berry Pudding, 551
Smucker's® Spider Web Tartlets, 198
Smushy Cookies, 269
Snow-Covered Almond Crescents, 153
Snowmen, 238
Soft Apple Cider Cookies, 18
Soft Molasses Spice Cookies, 223
Soft Spicy Molasses Cookies, 163
Sour Cream Brownies, 399
Sour Cream Pound Cake, 436
Southern Belle White Chocolate Cookies, 26
Southern Jam Cake, 443
Southern Peanut Pie, 503
Special Treat No-Bake Squares, 322
Speedy Pineapple-Lime Sorbet, 573
Spiced Cream, 533
Spiced Date Bars, 357
Spiced Wafers, 105
Spicy Applesauce Cake, 464
Spicy Ginger Molasses Cookies, 34
Spicy Lemon Crescents, 144
Spicy Oatmeal Raisin Cookies, 61
Spring Macaroon Bars, 351
Springtime Nests, 187
Star Christmas Tree Cookies, 242
Strawberries with Honeyed Yogurt Sauce, 616
**Strawberry**
All-American Pineapple & Fruit Trifle, 542
All-American Trifle, 580
Angel Strawberry Bavarian, 582
Brownie Ice Cream Pie, 494
Chocolate Truffle Cake with Strawberry Sauce, 472
Creamy Strawberry-Orange Pops, 576
Englishman's Trifle, 538
Fruity Jell-O® Cake, 464
Orange Mousse with Strawberry Sauce, 540
Peanut Butter & Chocolate Dipped Strawberries, 595

**Strawberry** *(continued)*
Smucker's® English Berry Pudding, 551
Strawberries with Honeyed Yogurt Sauce, 616
Strawberry-Banana Granité, 578
Strawberry Bon Bons, 670
Strawberry Cheesecake Squares, 352
Strawberry Chocolate Chip Shortcake, 458
Strawberry Hearts, 179
Strawberry Honey Parfaits, 623
Strawberry Shortcake, 609
Trifle Spectacular, 624
Vanilla-Strawberry Cupcakes, 614
White & Chocolate Covered Strawberries, 618
Sugar & Spice Jack-O'-Lantern Cookies, 199
Sugar Doodles, 278
Super-Duper Chocolate Pecan Cookies, 143
Supreme Chocolate Saucepan Brownies, 388
Sweet 'n' Spicy Pecan Pie, 502
Sweet Potato Pies, 516
Sweetheart Chocolate Mousse, 552
Sweetheart Layer Bars, 177
Sweet Spiders, 200
Swirl of Chocolate Cheesecake Triangles, 373
Swiss Chocolate Crispies, 152

**T**
Texas Peanuts 'n' Caramel Cake, 482
Three Great Tastes Blond Brownies, 402
Three-in-One Chocolate Chip Cookies, 292
3-Minute No-Bake Cookies, 315
Tiger Stripes, 676
Tinker Bell Peanut Butter Pie, 515
Toasted Almond Bark, 679
Toffee Bars, 333
Toffee Brownie Bars, 386
Toffee Diamonds, 654

Toffee Spattered Sugar Stars, 88
Traditional Cherry Pie, 493
Traditional Rice Pudding, 604
Traditional Ricotta Cheesecake, 448
Trifle Spectacular, 624
Triple Chocolate Brownies, 421
Triple Chocolate Cookies, 25
Triple Chocolate Squares, 681
Triple Layer Chocolate Bars, 264
Tropical Gardens Cookies, 150
Tropical Snack Cake, 455
Truffles, 638
Truffle Treats, 673
Tuxedo Cheesecake, 456
Two Great Tastes Pudding Parfaits, 548

**U**
Ukrainian Rolled Cookies, 90
Ultimate Sugar Cookies, 92
Uncle Sam's Hat, 192
Upside-Down German Chocolate Cake, 450

**V**
Valentine Ice Cream Sandwiches, 181
Valentine's Day Cookies Cards, 172
Valentine Stained Glass Hearts, 174
Vanilla Butter Crescents, 126
Vanilla Flan, 546
Vanilla Frosting, 85
Vanilla Glaze, 236, 435, 474
Vanilla-Strawberry Cupcakes, 614
Velvet Chocolate Cheesecake, 442
Velvety Chocolate Cake, 481
Viennese Hazelnut Butter Thins, 116

**W**
**Walnuts**
Apple and Walnut Strudel, 599
Apple-Walnut "Pizza Pie," 634
Buttery Black Raspberry Bars, 327

**Walnuts** *(continued)*
Chocolate Caramel Nut Bars, 347
Chocolate Chip Nougat, 644
Chocolate Chip Walnut Pie, 533
Chocolate Walnut Truffles, 664
Christmas Spirits, 235
Cinnamon Nut Chocolate Spirals, 119
Confetti Chocolate Chip Cookies, 296
Double Chocolate Orange Nut Fudge, 650
Honey Brownies, 423
Maple Walnut Bars, 356
Maple Walnut Cookies, 10
Maple Walnut Pound Cake, 440
Molasses Spice Cookies, 137
Mrs. J's Chip Cookies, 162
Outrageous Cookie Bars, 288
Pineapple Carrot Cookies, 22
Powdered Sugar Cookies, 30
Rocky Road Bars, 270
Spicy Applesauce Cake, 464
Toffee Diamonds, 654
Walnut Apple Dumpling Bars, 379
Walnut Cherry Fudge Logs, 643
Walnut Crunch Pumpkin Pie, 534
Walnut-Granola Clusters, 306
Walnut Minichips Biscotti, 128
Walnut-Orange Chocolate Chippers, 19
Zesty Fresh Lemon Bars, 381
Warm Fresh Fruit Sauté, 611
West Haven Date Bars, 331
White & Chocolate Covered Strawberries, 618
White Chip Apricot Oatmeal Cookies, 170
White Chip Coating, 678
White Chip Island Blondies, 420
White Chip Lemon Bars, 359
**White Chocolate**
Black & White Bombe, 591
Black and White Chocolate Chunk Cookies, 28

**White Chocolate** *(continued)*
Black and White Cutouts, 78
Black and White Sandwiches, 79
Candy Crunch, 657
Cherry Cashew Cookies, 56
Chewy Macadamia Nut Blondies, 407
Chocolate Cookie Pops, 274
Chocolate Peppermint Wafers, 658
Chocolate Pudding Parfaits, 569
Colorful Caramel Apples, 603
Danish Raspberry Cookies, 211
Delicate White Chocolate Cake, 479
Double Chocolate Orange Nut Fudge, 650
Double-Dipped Hazelnut Crisps, 76
Fabulous Blonde Brownies, 418
Festive Fruited White Chip Blondies, 430
Heavenly Oatmeal Hearts, 176
Holiday Chocolate Shortbread Cookies, 247
Holiday Hideaways, 248
Icicle Ornaments, 213
Jumbo 3-Chip Cookies, 282
Macadamia Nut White Chip Pumpkin Cookies, 226
Mississippi Mud Bars, 355
Molasses Spice Cookies, 137
Oreo® Shazam Bars, 326
Oreo® White Chocolate Mousse Cake, 484
Pistachio and White Chocolate Cookies, 53
Premier Cheesecake Cranberry Bars, 206
Pumpkin White Chocolate Drops, 241
Raspberry & White Chip Nut Bars, 366
Southern Belle White Chocolate Cookies, 26
Tiger Stripes, 676
Toasted Almond Bark, 679
Triple Chocolate Squares, 681

**Walnuts** *(continued)*
Tuxedo Cheesecake, 456
White & Chocolate Covered Strawberries, 618
White Chip Apricot Oatmeal Cookies, 170
White Chip Coating, 678
White Chip Island Blondies, 420
White Chip Lemon Bars, 359
White Chocolate Bread Pudding, 606
White Chocolate Brownies, 427
White Chocolate Cheesecake Squares, 380
White Chocolate Chunk Brownie Drops, 12
White Chocolate Chunk Cookies, 165
White Chocolate Coconut Cream Pie, 526
White Chocolate Cranberry Cookie Bars, 230
Yummy Mummy Cookies, 202
Zesty Lemon Pound Cake, 462
White Icing, 222
Winter Wonderland Snowmen Brownies, 218
Worm Cookies, 288

**Y**
Yuletide Linzer Bars, 228
Yummy Mummy Cookies, 202
Yummy Oatmeal Apple Cookie Squares, 377

**Z**
Zana Kringles, 233
Zesty Fresh Lemon Bars, 381
Zesty Lemon Pound Cake, 462

# Metric Conversion Chart

## VOLUME MEASUREMENTS (dry)

1/8 teaspoon = 0.5 mL
1/4 teaspoon = 1 mL
1/2 teaspoon = 2 mL
3/4 teaspoon = 4 mL
1 teaspoon = 5 mL
1 tablespoon = 15 mL
2 tablespoons = 30 mL
1/4 cup = 60 mL
1/3 cup = 75 mL
1/2 cup = 125 mL
2/3 cup = 150 mL
3/4 cup = 175 mL
1 cup = 250 mL
2 cups = 1 pint = 500 mL
3 cups = 750 mL
4 cups = 1 quart = 1 L

## VOLUME MEASUREMENTS (fluid)

1 fluid ounce (2 tablespoons) = 30 mL
4 fluid ounces (1/2 cup) = 125 mL
8 fluid ounces (1 cup) = 250 mL
12 fluid ounces (1 1/2 cups) = 375 mL
16 fluid ounces (2 cups) = 500 mL

## WEIGHTS (mass)

1/2 ounce = 15 g
1 ounce = 30 g
3 ounces = 90 g
4 ounces = 120 g
8 ounces = 225 g
10 ounces = 285 g
12 ounces = 360 g
16 ounces = 1 pound = 450 g

## DIMENSIONS

1/16 inch = 2 mm
1/8 inch = 3 mm
1/4 inch = 6 mm
1/2 inch = 1.5 cm
3/4 inch = 2 cm
1 inch = 2.5 cm

## OVEN TEMPERATURES

250°F = 120°C
275°F = 140°C
300°F = 150°C
325°F = 160°C
350°F = 180°C
375°F = 190°C
400°F = 200°C
425°F = 220°C
450°F = 230°C

## BAKING PAN SIZES

| Utensil | Size in Inches/Quarts | Metric Volume | Size in Centimeters |
|---|---|---|---|
| Baking or Cake Pan (square or rectangular) | 8×8×2 | 2 L | 20×20×5 |
| | 9×9×2 | 2.5 L | 23×23×5 |
| | 12×8×2 | 3 L | 30×20×5 |
| | 13×9×2 | 3.5 L | 33×23×5 |
| Loaf Pan | 8×4×3 | 1.5 L | 20×10×7 |
| | 9×5×3 | 2 L | 23×13×7 |
| Round Layer Cake Pan | 8×1½ | 1.2 L | 20×4 |
| | 9×1½ | 1.5 L | 23×4 |
| Pie Plate | 8×1¼ | 750 mL | 20×3 |
| | 9×1¼ | 1 L | 23×3 |
| Baking Dish or Casserole | 1 quart | 1 L | — |
| | 1½ quart | 1.5 L | — |
| | 2 quart | 2 L | — |